T0142862

Lecture Notes in Computer Science 14030

The series Lecture Notes in Computer Science (LNCS), including its subseries Lecture Notes in Artificial Intelligence (LNAI) and Lecture Notes in Bioinformatics (LNBI), has established itself as a medium for the publication of new developments in computer science and information technology research, teaching, and education.

LNCS enjoys close cooperation with the computer science R & D community, the series counts many renowned academics among its volume editors and paper authors, and collaborates with prestigious societies. Its mission is to serve this international community by providing an invaluable service, mainly focused on the publication of conference and workshop proceedings and postproceedings. LNCS commenced publication in 1973.

Aaron Marcus · Elizabeth Rosenzweig ·
Marcelo M. Soares
Editors

Design, User Experience, and Usability

12th International Conference, DUXU 2023
Held as Part of the 25th HCI International Conference, HCII 2023
Copenhagen, Denmark, July 23–28, 2023
Proceedings, Part I

 Springer

Editors
Aaron Marcus
Aaron Marcus and Associates
Berkeley, CA, USA

Elizabeth Rosenzweig
World Usability Day and Bubble Mountain
Consulting
Newton Center, MA, USA

Marcelo M. Soares
Southern University of Science
and Technology – SUSTech
Shenzhen, China

ISSN 0302-9743   ISSN 1611-3349 (electronic)
Lecture Notes in Computer Science
ISBN 978-3-031-35698-8   ISBN 978-3-031-35699-5 (eBook)
https://doi.org/10.1007/978-3-031-35699-5

This Springer imprint is published by the registered company Springer Nature Switzerland AG
The registered company address is: Gewerbestrasse 11, 6330 Cham, Switzerland

Foreword

Human-computer interaction (HCI) is acquiring an ever-increasing scientific and industrial importance, as well as having more impact on people's everyday lives, as an ever-growing number of human activities are progressively moving from the physical to the digital world. This process, which has been ongoing for some time now, was further accelerated during the acute period of the COVID-19 pandemic. The HCI International (HCII) conference series, held annually, aims to respond to the compelling need to advance the exchange of knowledge and research and development efforts on the human aspects of design and use of computing systems.

The 25th International Conference on Human-Computer Interaction, HCI International 2023 (HCII 2023), was held in the emerging post-pandemic era as a 'hybrid' event at the AC Bella Sky Hotel and Bella Center, Copenhagen, Denmark, during July 23–28, 2023. It incorporated the 21 thematic areas and affiliated conferences listed below.

A total of 7472 individuals from academia, research institutes, industry, and government agencies from 85 countries submitted contributions, and 1578 papers and 396 posters were included in the volumes of the proceedings that were published just before the start of the conference, these are listed below. The contributions thoroughly cover the entire field of human-computer interaction, addressing major advances in knowledge and effective use of computers in a variety of application areas. These papers provide academics, researchers, engineers, scientists, practitioners and students with state-of-the-art information on the most recent advances in HCI.

The HCI International (HCII) conference also offers the option of presenting 'Late Breaking Work', and this applies both for papers and posters, with corresponding volumes of proceedings that will be published after the conference. Full papers will be included in the 'HCII 2023 - Late Breaking Work - Papers' volumes of the proceedings to be published in the Springer LNCS series, while 'Poster Extended Abstracts' will be included as short research papers in the 'HCII 2023 - Late Breaking Work - Posters' volumes to be published in the Springer CCIS series.

I would like to thank the Program Board Chairs and the members of the Program Boards of all thematic areas and affiliated conferences for their contribution towards the high scientific quality and overall success of the HCI International 2023 conference. Their manifold support in terms of paper reviewing (single-blind review process, with a minimum of two reviews per submission), session organization and their willingness to act as goodwill ambassadors for the conference is most highly appreciated.

This conference would not have been possible without the continuous and unwavering support and advice of Gavriel Salvendy, founder, General Chair Emeritus, and Scientific Advisor. For his outstanding efforts, I would like to express my sincere appreciation to Abbas Moallem, Communications Chair and Editor of HCI International News.

July 2023   Constantine Stephanidis

HCI International 2023 Thematic Areas and Affiliated Conferences

Thematic Areas

- HCI: Human-Computer Interaction
- HIMI: Human Interface and the Management of Information

Affiliated Conferences

- EPCE: 20th International Conference on Engineering Psychology and Cognitive Ergonomics
- AC: 17th International Conference on Augmented Cognition
- UAHCI: 17th International Conference on Universal Access in Human-Computer Interaction
- CCD: 15th International Conference on Cross-Cultural Design
- SCSM: 15th International Conference on Social Computing and Social Media
- VAMR: 15th International Conference on Virtual, Augmented and Mixed Reality
- DHM: 14th International Conference on Digital Human Modeling and Applications in Health, Safety, Ergonomics and Risk Management
- DUXU: 12th International Conference on Design, User Experience and Usability
- C&C: 11th International Conference on Culture and Computing
- DAPI: 11th International Conference on Distributed, Ambient and Pervasive Interactions
- HCIBGO: 10th International Conference on HCI in Business, Government and Organizations
- LCT: 10th International Conference on Learning and Collaboration Technologies
- ITAP: 9th International Conference on Human Aspects of IT for the Aged Population
- AIS: 5th International Conference on Adaptive Instructional Systems
- HCI-CPT: 5th International Conference on HCI for Cybersecurity, Privacy and Trust
- HCI-Games: 5th International Conference on HCI in Games
- MobiTAS: 5th International Conference on HCI in Mobility, Transport and Automotive Systems
- AI-HCI: 4th International Conference on Artificial Intelligence in HCI
- MOBILE: 4th International Conference on Design, Operation and Evaluation of Mobile Communications

List of Conference Proceedings Volumes Appearing Before the Conference

47. CCIS 1836, HCI International 2023 Posters - Part V, edited by Constantine Stephanidis, Margherita Antona, Stavroula Ntoa and Gavriel Salvendy

https://2023.hci.international/proceedings

Preface

User experience (UX) refers to a person's thoughts, feelings, and behavior when using interactive systems. UX design becomes fundamentally important for new and emerging mobile, ubiquitous, and omnipresent computer-based contexts. The scope of design, user experience, and usability (DUXU) extends to all aspects of the user's interaction with a product or service, how it is perceived, learned, and used. DUXU also addresses design knowledge, methods, and practices, with a focus on deeply human-centered processes. Usability, usefulness, and appeal are fundamental requirements for effective user-experience design.

The 12th Design, User Experience, and Usability Conference (DUXU 2023), an affiliated conference of the HCI International conference, encouraged papers from professionals, academics, and researchers that report results and cover a broad range of research and development activities on a variety of related topics. Professionals include designers, software engineers, scientists, marketers, business leaders, and practitioners in fields such as AI, architecture, financial and wealth management, game design, graphic design, finance, healthcare, industrial design, mobile, psychology, travel, and vehicles.

This year's submissions covered a wide range of content across the spectrum of design, user-experience, and usability. The latest trends and technologies are represented, as well as contributions from professionals, academics, and researchers across the globe. The breadth of their work is indicated in the following topics covered in the proceedings.

Five volumes of the HCII 2023 proceedings are dedicated to this year's edition of the DUXU Conference:

- Part I addresses topics related to design methods, tools and practices, as well as emotional and persuasive design.
- Part II addresses topics related to design case studies, as well as creativity and design education.
- Part III addresses topics related to evaluation methods and techniques, as well as usability, user experience, and technology acceptance studies.
- Part IV addresses topics related to designing learning experiences, as well as design and user experience of chatbots, conversational agents, and robots.
- Part V addresses topics related to DUXU for cultural heritage, as well as DUXU for health and wellbeing.

The papers in these volumes were included for publication after a minimum of two single–blind reviews from the members of the DUXU Program Board or, in some cases, from Preface members of the Program Boards of other affiliated conferences. We would like to thank all of them for their invaluable contribution, support, and efforts.

July 2023

Aaron Marcus
Elizabeth Rosenzweig
Marcelo M. Soares

12th International Conference on Design, User Experience and Usability (DUXU 2023)

The full list with the Program Board Chairs and the members of the Program Boards of all thematic areas and affiliated conferences of HCII2023 is available online at:

http://www.hci.international/board-members-2023.php

HCI International 2024 Conference

The 26th International Conference on Human-Computer Interaction, HCI International 2024, will be held jointly with the affiliated conferences at the Washington Hilton Hotel, Washington, DC, USA, June 29 – July 4, 2024. It will cover a broad spectrum of themes related to Human-Computer Interaction, including theoretical issues, methods, tools, processes, and case studies in HCI design, as well as novel interaction techniques, interfaces, and applications. The proceedings will be published by Springer. More information will be made available on the conference website: http://2024.hci.international/.

General Chair
Prof. Constantine Stephanidis
University of Crete and ICS-FORTH
Heraklion, Crete, Greece
Email: general_chair@hcii2024.org

https://2024.hci.international/

Contents – Part I

Design Methods, Tools and Practices

Desirability of Imagined Futures: Human-Centered Design and Analysis

Sisira Adikari[1]([✉]) [iD], Hamed Sarbazhosseini[1] [iD], and Oranuch Sawetrattanasatian[2] [iD]

[1] University of Canberra, Bruce ACT 2617, Canberra, Australia
sisira.adikari@canberra.edu.au
[2] Chulalongkorn University, Bangkok, Thailand

Abstract. The future is known to be uncertain. Uncertainty is an inherent aspect of the future and impacts future predictions. Designers often require analyzing current situations to identify complexities, deficiencies, pain points etc., to gain empathy and insights as the basis for preferred Human-Centered Design (HCD) solutions. When creating preferred HCD design solutions for the near future or long-term future, designers face the unforeseen and unprecedented constraints of the future, which require careful analysis from the future perspective. Designing human-centered focused, futuristic systems is challenging. There is no abundant published literature to support specific and effective human-centered focused futuristic systems design. Generally, designers follow one or many HCD methods they frequently use for futuristic design without significantly considering futuristic aspects. This paper discusses current futuristic models and presents a human-centered design and analysis approach to design effective and desirable futuristic systems.

Keyword: Human-centered design · Design thinking · Futuristic design

1 Introduction

The main focus of Human-Centered Design (HCD) is to place all concerned stakeholders, including end-users, at the centre of the design process for interactive systems design and development. As Benyon [1, p.22] identified, designing for user experience (UX) needs to be human-centred. The human-centered mind shift is characterized by a central focus on empathy for all user types, who are the main concern of the design [2]. Empathy is the affective reflection of others' perspectives by placing oneself into someone else's position and adopting their perspective for a specific situation [3]. On the other hand, desirability is a critical aspect of UX that gauges how much users want in an artifact (product, system, or service) in terms of their interaction. Desirability is the pleasure and happiness in using a product based on the emotional response to an interaction that comes from multiple factors, such as the look and feel of the product and the marketing messages that make sense to the product users [4, p.23]. When an artifact is desirable, users are attracted to it, and it keeps them engaged, compelling and exploring to discover its usefulness and features [5].

A. Marcus et al. (Eds.): HCII 2023, LNCS 14030, pp. 3–15, 2023.
https://doi.org/10.1007/978-3-031-35699-5_1

Accordingly, desirability is an important factor that needs to be considered in HCD and designing for UX. The orientation of HCD is to understand the present (problem space) for creating the future (generating possible solutions) based on empathic design [6]. In HCD, designers often require analyzing current situations to identify complexities, deficiencies, pain points etc., to gain empathy and insights as the basis for desirable design solutions. When creating preferred HCD solutions for the near future or long-term future, designers face the unforeseen and unprecedented challenges, issues, and constraints of the future, which require careful analysis from the future perspective. Designing human-centered focused, futuristic systems is challenging. There is no abundant published literature to support specific and effective human-centered focused futuristic systems design. In such situations, generally, designers follow one or many HCD methods they frequently use or are familiar with for their futuristic design assignments. Such HCD methods may not necessarily and sufficiently consist of futuristic design aspects, principles, and guidelines that can be applied in generating design solutions.

This paper aims to review current futuristic models published in the literature and present an HCD analysis approach to design effective and desirable futuristic systems.

The paper's overall structure is organized as follows: Sect. 2 reviews the relevant futuristic design and approaches; Sect. 3 discusses human-centred design methods. Section 4 details the methodology for developing the proposed human-centred futuristic design and analysis framework. Sample guidance for the design and impact analysis of the HCD futuristic system is presented in Sect. 5. Lastly, the paper concludes by summarizing key arguments and an outlook to further HCD futuristic studies.

2   Futuristic Design and Approaches

The future is known to be uncertain [7, p.115] and constantly changing. The uncertainty of the future creates challenges in predicting anticipated outcomes for a future scenario. However, it is a mere fact that people give direction to their decisions and actions in the present and attempt to make the future real and relevant [8]. Designing futures (also known as futuristic design) involves envisioning futures and designing artifacts that meet user and stakeholder needs to serve organizational requirements. The futuristic design is a concept that has been used to specify the design of artifacts that make prominent reference to a vision of the future [9, p.183]. The futuristic design aims to learn about the future and its uncertainty with vision and create preferred futures effectively [10]. For organizational sustainability, public and private enterprises are often required to plan future products and services but need help anticipating the long-term effects of current decisions. Many authors have discussed specific approaches, methods, and tools to create the 'futures' more effectively in the literature. This section briefly details the review of futuristic design approaches, methods, and tools to inform and identify the commonality and differences among these with the aim of discovering a generic futuristic design approach for our discussion.

2.1 Futuristic Methods and Tools

Van der Duin [8] reported a comprehensive set of methods and tools that can be used for foresight analysis in organizations, namely, 1) Scenarios, 2) Delphi method, 3) Trend analysis, 4) Technology forecasting, 5) Technology assessment, 6) Backcasting, and 7) Roadmapping. In their discussion, they point out that the future can be approached in three different ways based on time preferences past, present, and future:

- Predictive approach - inclines on historical data and patterns onto the future.
- Explorative approach - focuses more on what could happen in the future, which is not a continuation of the past.
- Normative approach – Disregards present state of affairs and sees the future, above all, as a possibility to fix things.

A summary of their foresight methods on the continuum is shown in Fig. 1.

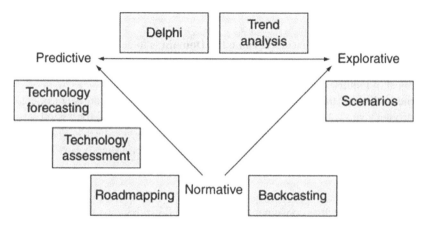

Fig. 1. Foresight methods and tools on the continuum presented by Van der Duin [8, p.6]

The author [8] has clearly mentioned that the criteria for the application of foresight methods vary on the basis of the type of method, and the best method needs to be chosen depending on the situation, the goals, and the application of the study of the future, the available data, the type of organization and sector, the specific questions that need to be answered, etc.

2.2 Strategic Foresight

Strategic Foresight [11] is a futuristic framework that can be applied to anticipate the future, innovate new products or services, determine the impact of choices and to best serve societal needs with appropriate futuristic service delivery. The strategic foresight framework consists of six main steps: Frame the domain; Scan for trends; Forecast scenarios; Envision the future; Backcast; and Implement.

Table 1 shows the six main steps of the framework and the key focus of each step in the form of a user-focused question.

Table 1. Six main steps of the Strategic Foresight framework

Step #	Description	Focused Question
Step one	Frame the domain	What is the domain you will explore?
Step two	Scan forces and trends	Whom will you invite to help you scan include?
Step three	Forecast scenarios	What are the plausible futures for your domain?
Step four	Envision the future	What does success look like for your domain?
Step five	Backcast	What milestones must you complete to ensure success in your domain?
Step six	Implement	What must you start now, to secure your domain's future

The key focus of the first step **Frame the Domain** is to define the future that needs to be explored with careful consideration and analysis in two areas:

- Subject of inquiry - to specify the areas to be explored, and
- Time horizon of the futuristic study – five years of time horizon is considered too short; ten years is better, and twenty years is considered as ideal for a good strategic futuristic study.

The second step **Scan Forces and Trends** is concerned with identifying all trends that impact the domain in the foreseeable future based on credible evidence and facts based on five categories:

- Social trends – such as consumer behaviors' and lifestyles
- Technology trends – such as innovation or advances in communication and the life cycle of products.
- Economic trends – such as interest rates and inflation
- Environmental trends – such as ecosystem factors and environmental regulations.
- Political trends – such as political stability, tax policies and trade unions.

Subsequently, the identified domain's trends are validated and sorted according to their impact on the domain (low to high) and their certainty (from uncertain to completely certain). The *high-impact* and *completely certain* trends are the focus for further analysis in the next step.

Forecast Scenarios is the third step which aims at developing multiple scenarios for the validated *high-impact* and *completely certain* trends (sourced from step two) relevant to the future of the project domain. The purpose of such scenarios is to identify the spectrum of possible futures the project domain could face and required to meet three critical criteria:

- Plausible – scenarios that are likely to happen

- Relevant – scenarios are connected to the aspects of the project/organization
- Challenging – scenarios test the project domain/organization and demands beyond the status quo of the project domain/organization.

In Strategic Foresight, a variation of the Cone of Plausibility [12] has been used to emphasize that developed scenarios are required to fall within upper and lower limits of plausibility, as shown in Fig. 2.

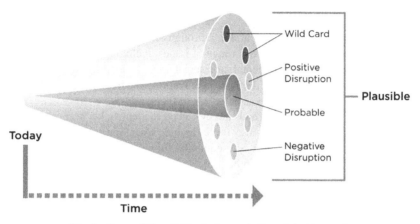

Fig. 2. Cone of Plausibility in Strategic Foresight [11, p.14]

Wild cards [13] refer to perceived low-probability and potentially high-impact events. Positive/negative disruptions [14] are plausible disruptions that could happen and impact positively/negatively on the project/organization. Once the scenarios are completed, further analyses are undertaken to highlight what issues and factors show up, which of these can be controlled or influenced by the project/organization, and which of these mitigate risk or gain an advantage in some way. Such issues or factors are the transformational factors of the project domain/organization.

The fourth step, **Envision the Future** looks at developing one vision for each transformational factor identified in step three. The foundation for such visions is based on the answers to the question, 'What would outrageous success for the given transformational factor look like in the given future (year)?'.

During the fifth step, **Backcast**, the vision statement of each transformational factor is analyzed backward from the future to the present to identify the milestones required to complete achieving each vision. The purpose of backcasting [15] is to connect the specified future to the present to better understand future possibilities for each identified transformational factor.

The final step, **Implement** is concerned with realizing the envisioned transformative factors to achieve anticipated goals and envisioned futures. This step involves identifying objectives, strategies, and tactics, producing periodic reporting, and placing ongoing monitoring tools to scan the environment for changes that are likely to impact your visions of transformative factors relevant to the desired futures.

2.3 Aspirational Futures

Aspirational Futures [10] is a futuristic design approach that specifically strives for biases, and projects participants' fears and aspirations related to the future in design analysis [16]. Aspirational futures involves understanding likely and alternative futures) and creating the preferred future for the organization and consists of three interrelated phases, namely: 1). Environmental assessment and scenario development, 2). Visioning to clarify aspirations and identity, and 3). Strategic analysis.

The first phase, the **Environmental Assessment and Scenario Development phase** consists of a number of processes [10]:

- *Scanning for Trends* – involves searching through different sources of information in the environment relevant to a broad range of issues, including global, political, economic, technological, environmental, and social areas, to identify trends and emerging developments in the project domain/organization. The trends that could affect the project domain/organization are selected for further analysis.
- *Identify Key Forces* – selected trends are evaluated to identify key forces shaping the future and relevant to each trend. Key forces include what factors and drivers are most important for shaping the future. Subsequently, forecasts are developed, and, using forecasts, identified key forces can be projected into the future.
- *Scenarios* development - The key forces, forecasts, factors, and drivers are used as the basis for scenario development. Multiple scenarios are developed to imagine and examine alternative views of the future with a broad range of possibilities:
- Best guess scenario, which is developed based on the best available intelligence and key assumptions.
- A scenario based on the concept of what could go wrong in the future and covers relevant factors and implications.
- Visionary scenarios which are based on visionary strategies and the path to relevant visionary outcomes.
- A scenario that considers an alternative path to similar visionary outcomes.

The second phase, the **Visioning and Audacious Goals phase**, aims to develop a shared vision of the preferred future based on the aspirations of the organization and the organizational community and consists of a number of processes [10]:

- Develop *Vision* - Vision descriptions are developed for preferred futures based on the opportunities and threats of the external environment summarized in scenarios.
- Develop *Values* – Values are developed as guiding principles that underpin the vision and mission of preferred futures.
- Develop *Mission* – A mission statement is developed to outline the efforts to achieve respective visions.
- Develop *Goals* – In order to realize the vision and the mission, achievable goals are established and well defined with measures to assess the success, who does what and by when.

The third phase, the **Strategic Analysis phase** [10], is concerned with developing strategies and action plans for achieving the vision. In this phase, scenarios and relevant goals are analyzed to develop *Revised & New Strategies* and then to establish a *Prioritized Action plan.*

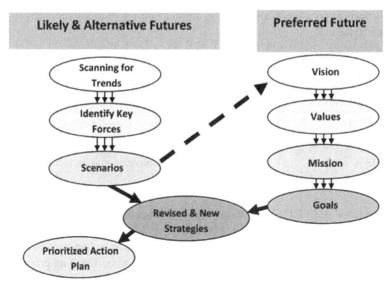

Fig. 3. Aspirational futures process [10 p.86]

Figure 3 shows a summarized view of the Aspirational futures process covering all three phases. As stated by the author [10], the process can be deployed as a full cycle or in part according to the settings of the project/organization.

Each of the above three futures design approaches shares common characteristics, such as:

- Trend analysis - Scanning various issues, including global, political, economic, technological, environmental and social trends.
- Scenario development - Creating a set of scenarios covering current and futures trends and drivers of change in support of investigating the futures and future possibilities.
- Envisioning futures – Use of scenarios to envision how the futures and related contexts, activities and the right mix of technologies (hardware and software) could function to achieve the futuristic system's purpose and deliver a good UX.
- Implementation plan - Setting up action plans and strategies to realize the vision and achieve set futures' goals.

3 Human-Centered Design Methods

HCD methods and approaches aim to ensure human-centredness in artifacts. There are many HCD approaches reported in the literature by many authors [17, 18]. These HCD approaches involve many HCD methods, such as contextual enquiry, task analysis, iterative design, prototyping, testing etc. [19]. As Benyon [1, p.43] reported, PACT analysis has been recognized as an approach and framework for UX design and envisioning future situations. A PACT analysis framework can also be used for analyzing impacts in designs.

Importantly, Design Thinking is widely used in HCD projects [20]. Micheli et al. [21] identified the three most influential applied design thinking models in a recent research study. These three proponents and the main stages of design thinking for each proponent are shown in Table 2.

Table 2. Most influential applied models of Design Thinking [21 p.131]

Proponent	Main Stages of Design Thinking
IDEO	Inspiration, ideation, implementation
Stanford Design School	Empathy, define, ideate, prototype and test
IBM	Understand, explore, prototype, and evaluate

All three models in Table 2 demonstrate an extent of commonality; they undertake an initial exploration to understand the problem space, followed by moving onto an ideation stage to generate possible alternatives and concluding with an implementation and testing phase based on prototyping and iteration. Notably, the Design Thinking process model by Stanford Design School [24] shows a distinct stage, empathy, to highlight the strong initial human-centredness during the initial exploration.

4   Methodology

This paper aims to present a human-centered design and analysis approach to designing effective and desirable futuristic systems. Our proposed theoretical framework for the futuristic human-centered design consists of the following components:

1. Futures Modelling
   Based on the Aspirational futures process shown in Fig. 3.
2. Human-Centered Modelling.
   Based on the Design Thinking process model by the Institute of Design at Stanford [24].
3. Requirements Analysis
   Discovering requirements based on modelling the current situation, possible futures, and human-centered modelling.
4. Impact Analysis
   Analyzing the impacts of the design solutions using the PACT framework from the perspectives of People, Activities, Contexts, and Technologies.
5. Design Analysis
   Designing solutions for desirable futuristic systems based on the requirements generated in step 3, along with outcomes from the Impact Analysis. Part of the design analysis includes providing an assessment of the desirability of the futuristic design solutions based on the desirability in UX analysis [25].

The relationships among these five components have been schematically diagrammed and shown in Fig. 4 to form the proposed human-centered futuristic design and analysis framework.

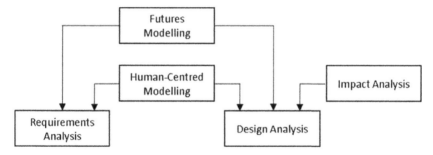

Fig. 4. Schematic diagram of the human-centered futuristic design and analysis framework

Based on the appropriate futures modelling and human-centered modelling, the proposed research framework includes the capability to provide the following outcomes:

- Analysis of the current situation from the perspectives of human-centered modelling and futuristic modelling
- Discovering all types of requirements
- Providing desirable futuristic design solutions and impact assessments of the overall design
- Providing an assessment of the desirability of the futuristic design solutions.

5   Sample Guidance for Design and Impact Analysis of a Human-Centered Futuristic Smart Home System

Current Situation: IoT devices help homeowners to manage their homes and surroundings with greater flexibility. However, these devices also expose smart homes to unwanted threats as well. There are several challenges for IoT-based smart homes, such as:

1. Confidentiality of data communication with other devices
2. Authentication and integrity of connections from other entities
3. Access control issues

The Sample Challenge: How might we provide a well-secured futuristic design solution for smart homes?

5.1   Futures Modelling - Environmental Assessment and Scenario Development

Scanning for trends points out that a variety of smart products and technologies are on the rise and make up the connected home [22] and face a variety of challenges, such as internet hacking, system security and privacy issues [23]. *Key forces* include the factors relevant to privacy and security, which are important for shaping the future of smart homes. Based on the analysis of key forces, an example of one *forecast* is that future smart home products and services will be based on ambient sensors. As per the guidelines of Aspirational Futures, several scenarios can be developed. An example scenario based on the concept of what could go wrong in the future can cover serious disruption to data communication because of natural disasters. And covers relevant factors and implications.

5.2 Futures Modelling - Visioning and Audacious Goals Phase

An example *Vision*: To provide a well-secured futuristic design solution for smart homes with technologically advanced mechanisms for confidentiality, authentication, and access control. One sample *Mission* statement: We deliver 24/7 advanced smart home security technology which is demystified and ready for use. Sample *Values* are: 1). Reduction of environmental impact, 2). Reduction of maintenance costs, 3). Enhance the quality of life of smart home users. Possible sample *Goals* are: 10 Provide enhanced security, 2). Provide energy efficiency, 3). Provide highly responsive and flexible service.

5.3 Futures Modelling – Strategic Analysis

One example of the New Strategies and Action Plans to achieve the vision would be the Identification of relevant advanced technology for enhanced confidentiality, authentication, and access control (new strategy) and Securing funding to achieve such technology (action plan).

5.4 Human-Centered Modelling

Human-Centered Modelling is based on the d.School design thinking process model consists of five phases; Empathize, Define, Ideate, Prototype and Test.

Empathize aims at gaining key users' and stakeholders' insights such as what users need now and future, issues, challenges, pain points, frustrations, trust, and confidentiality issues, fears etc. During the *Define* phase, designers organize the information gathered during the Empathize phase as user requirements to be further explored. In the *Ideate* phase, designers generate more ideas from different perspectives to the user requirements discovered during the Define phase. The best ideas that show business value are chosen for further analysis. The *Prototype* phase allows designers to identify the best possible solution for each of the problems identified during the first three stages. The last phase *Test* aims to assess the solutions identified in the Prototype stage.

5.5 Requirements Analysis

Requirements Analysis is based on the outcomes generated from futures modelling and human-centered modelling, along with the analysis of the current situation. Ideally, the output from requirements analysis can be of two categories: Stakeholder requirements (including user requirements) and Business requirements.

Sample *Business Requirements* are: System reconfigurability according to user needs; Enhanced security, privacy, and access control etc. Sample *Stakeholder Requirements* are: Enhanced user experience (easy to use, operate with greater satisfaction); Meeting accessibility needs of the impaired user types etc.

5.6 Impact Analysis

Impact Analysis aims at analyzing the impacts (positive and negative consequences) of the design solutions using the PACT framework from the perspectives of four attributes: People, Activities, Contexts, and Technologies. Some sample impacts for each category:

People – 1). Physical Differences (devices should be accessible for physically impaired users), 2). Psychological Differences (the use of standard symbols to show system functionality so that all users understand the system easily) etc.

Activities – 1). Complexity (simplified user actions to avoid frustration), 2.) Safety-critical (enhanced privacy, security, and data protection schemes).

Contexts – 1). Physical environment (devices in the system can be operated from anywhere using the Internet), 2). Organizational context (customer support to the user in the event of a system failure).

Technology – 1). Input (users can key in/ transfer data safely for intended operations), 2). Output (Availability of all three perceptual capabilities of sight, touch and sound to support all users) etc.

5.7 Design Analysis

Design Analysis is based on the outcomes generated from futures modelling, human-centered modelling, and impact analysis. Design analysis aims at designing solutions for desirable futuristic systems based on the findings of the design analysis.

Some sample inclusions to a generic smart home solution are: 1). Voice-activated home assistants, 2). Smart retina scan/facial recognition locking devices, 3.) Smart air purifiers, 4.) Enhanced privacy, security, and access control solutions etc.

The design analysis also includes an assessment of the desirability of the futuristic design solutions based on the desirability in UX analysis. Sample desirability assessment components are: 1). Easy to use,2). Meaningful, 3.). Organized, 4). Satisfying, 5). Usable, 6). Useful etc.

6 Conclusions

This paper highlights an issue not previously addressed sufficiently in human-centered focused futuristic systems design. The lack of abundant published literature in this area compels designers to follow one or many HCD methods they frequently use or are familiar with for their futuristic design assignments. Such HCD methods may not sufficiently consist of futuristic design knowledge, principles, and guidelines that can be applied to generate good design solutions.

Our paper presents a comprehensive review and analysis of futuristic design methods published in the literature and identifies common characteristics in them. In our discussion, we emphasized the concept of desirability as one of the important and compelling factor in the system acceptance by users. Following a discussion on human-centered design methods, we present a human-centered futuristic design and analysis framework consisting of futures modelling, human-centered modelling, requirements analysis, impact analysis and design analysis as the basis for human-centered futuristic design and analysis. We also present sample guidance for the design and impact analysis of a human-centered futuristic smart home system.

The significance of our proposed framework is that it clearly shows all important modelling and analysis for creating desirable futuristic design and analysis. We anticipate that our framework benefits designers with clear direction and guidance for designing and analyzing HCD-led futuristic systems design.

References

1. Benyon, D.: Designing user experience: a guide to HCI, UX and interaction design. Pearson (2019)
2. Goldman, S., et al.: Assessing d. learning: capturing the journey of becoming a design thinker. In: Plattner, H., Meinel, C., Leifer, L. (eds.) Design Thinking Research: Measuring Performance in Context, pp. 13–33. Springer (2012). https://doi.org/10.1007/978-3-642-31991-4_2
3. Köppen, E., Meinel, C.: Empathy via design thinking: creation of sense and knowledge. In: Plattner, H., Meinel, C., Leifer, L. (eds.) Design Thinking Research. UI, pp. 15–28. Springer, Cham (2015). https://doi.org/10.1007/978-3-319-06823-7_2
4. Goodman, E., Kuniavsky, M.: Observing the user experience: a practitioner's guide to user research. Elsevier (2012)
5. Interaction Design Organization, https://www.interaction-design.org/literature/topics/desirability
6. Steen, M.: Human-Centered Design and its inherent ethical qualities. In: Diane, P.M., Neelke, D. (eds.) The Routledge Handbook of the Philosophy of Engineering, pp. 328–341. Routledge (2020)
7. Van Asselt, M.: Foresight in Action: Developing Policy-Oriented Scenarios. Routledge (2012)
8. Van der Duin, P.: Introduction. In: Van der Duin, P. (ed.) Foresight in Organizations: Methods and Tools, pp. 1-10. Routledge (2016)
9. Erlhoff, M., Marshall, T.: Design Dictionary: Perspectives on Design Terminology. Walter de Gruyter (2007)
10. Bezold, C.: Aspirational futures. J. Futures Stud. **13**, 81–90 (2009)
11. https://higherlogicdownload.s3.amazonaws.com/AGRIP/613d38fc-c2ec-4e1a-b31f-03fa70 6321aa/UploadedImages/documents/AGRiP_Workbook_FramingTheFuture_FINAL.pdf
12. Taylor, C.W.: Creating Strategic Visions. Strategic Studies Institute, U.S. Army War College, Carlisle (1990)
13. Rockfellow, J.D.: Wild cards: preparing for 'the big one.' The Futurist **28**, 14 (1994)
14. Holland, B.J.: Strategic foresight tools for planning and policy. Encyclopedia of Organizational Knowledge, Administration, and Technology, 775–797 (2021)
15. Robinson, J.B.: Futures under glass: a recipe for people who hate to predict. Futures **22**, 820–842 (1990)
16. Futuribles International, https://www.futuribles.com/aspirational-futures-2/
17. Gall, T., Vallet, F., Douzou, S., Yannou, B.: Re-defining the system boundaries of human-centered design. Proc. Des. Soc. **1**, 2521–2530 (2021)
18. Steen, M.: Tensions in human-centered design. CoDesign **7**, 45–60 (2011)
19. Babione, J.N., et al.: Human-centered design processes for clinical decision support: a pulmonary embolism case study. Int. J. Med. Informatics **142**, 104196 (2020)
20. Dittenberger, S.: Putting theory to practice: reflections on the integration of product de-sign aspects in AAL projects. In: DS 92: Proceedings of the DESIGN 2018-15th International Design Conference, pp. 567–578 (2018)

21. Micheli, P., Wilner, S.J.S., Bhatti, S.H., Mura, M., Beverland, M.B.: Doing design thinking: conceptual review, synthesis, and research agenda. J. Prod. Innov. Manage. **36**, 124–148 (2019)
22. Nižetić, S., Šolić, P., González-De, D.L., Patrono, L.: Internet of Things (IoT): opportunities, issues and challenges towards a smart and sustainable future. J. Clean. Prod. **274**, 122877 (2020)
23. El-Azab, R.: Smart homes: potentials and challenges. Clean Energy **5**, 302–315 (2021)
24. d.School, https://web.stanford.edu/~mshanks/MichaelShanks/files/509554.pdf
25. Adikari, S., McDonald, C., Campbell, J.: Quantitative analysis of desirability in user experience. arXiv preprint arXiv:1606.03544 (2016)

How Can BOLE Identify, Cultivate, and Judge User Experience (UX) Talents? Inspiring and Designing the Playful Experience of Tomorrow

Mei Ai[1], Qiwen Cai[1], Yun Fan[1], Bowen Li[1], Ruonan Huang[1], Shuya Liu[1], Yuxin Ran[1], Ruikang Wang[1], Yanna Wang[1], Kaihe Zhang[1], Amanda Liu[2], Zheng Zou[3], Larry Leifer[4], Taiyu Huang[5], Mengzhen Xiao[5], Zhaohui Zhu[5(✉)], and Wei Liu[1(✉)]

[1] Faculty of Psychology, Beijing Normal University, Beijing 100875, China
wei.liu@bnu.edu.cn
[2] Department of Psychology and Neuroscience, Duke University, Durham, NC 27708, USA
[3] Stanford Center at Peking University, Stanford University, Beijing 100871, China
[4] Center for Design Research, Stanford University, Stanford, CA 94305, USA
[5] Department of China Digital Technology, The LEGO Group, Shanghai 200031, China
wei.liu@bnu.edu.cn

Abstract. In the digital era, what the toy industry wants to do is not only the toy part but to attract more users. Several studies have addressed that traditional industrial design can no longer fully meet users' needs. Reflecting on the literature and user studies, we describe project-based learning (PBL) practice and four sets of novel contexts, personas, and design directions to support future user interactions. The results demonstrate how to operationalize the playful experience in a human-centered design (HCD) process. This study would interest applied researchers and educators in teaching students with transdisciplinary backgrounds.

Keywords: User eXperience · Human-Centered Design · Digital Play · LEGO Toys · Generation Z · User Research · Interaction Design

1 Introduction

Along with the rapid development of China's designer toy market, building blocks as both entertainment and educational products have returned to the people's view [1]. Among them, The LEGO Group is the undisputed industry leader. Since entering the Chinese market in 2012, the company has seen the massive potential of the Chinese market and ranked China as the fifth largest independent region in the world in 2016. Its current marketing strategy in China is more inclined to open offline stores, which have covered more than 100 cities [2]. As opposed to the offline business, its online play experience is currently relatively single, with mobile applications and mini programs mainly undertaking online mall features.

A. Marcus et al. (Eds.): HCII 2023, LNCS 14030, pp. 16–26, 2023.
https://doi.org/10.1007/978-3-031-35699-5_2

With the advent of the era of digital life, people's access to information channels also shows a trend of diversification [3]. Xiaohongshu, Weibo, and other media give consumers more diversified reasons to buy. At the same time, online games have had a significant impact on the traditional toy industry [4]. The combination of online and offline play is sweeping the industry. The success of blind boxes and garage kits (i.e., PVC figures in China and Japan) reflects this trend, and the toy market shows a trend of diversification in demand. Users are increasingly pursuing products to form emotional ties with themselves, eager to establish their attitudes or attributes through the purchase and use of products [5, 6].

Young people are gradually increasing their consumption ability and have some labels on them, such as paying attention to hot spots, being eager to express themselves, and focusing on enjoyment. Interest-oriented consumption habits, the designer toy market, and the booming of the Internet celebrity economy prove this [7]. Companies are bringing a more innovative interactive experience for children and parents, creating a more harmonious parent-child relationship, and making toys an educational label in traditional culture and a tool [8]. The LEGO Group needs to maintain its conventional advantages while considering new user needs and creating a more distinctive online and offline digital playful experience.

Since the summer of 2019, a collaborative project between Beijing Normal University and the LEGO Group took place to co-create the playful experience and digital applications, e.g., functionality definitions, visionary scenarios, and concept designs. The research team consisted of various stakeholders, including project managers, designers, developers, teachers, and students. We adopted a human-centered design (HCD) process [9, 10] for designing and developing user experience (UX) scenarios and applications [11]. Therefore, additional scenarios can be easily added in the future. This HCD process requires close and timely collaboration with experts in the fields of human-computer interaction (HCI), engineering psychology, industrial design, sociology, and cultural anthropology. The key aspects are expressiveness of products, usability, aesthetics, meanings of product forms, and design in a socio-cultural context [12]. BOLE was a horse tamer and a famous judge of horses in Spring and Autumn period in China. He was the legendary inventor of equine physiognomy, i.e., judging a horse's qualities from appearance. In Modern Standard Chinese, BOLE figuratively means 'good judge of (especially hidden) talent'. In this research, we used this name to represent this collaborative project and hope to identify, cultivate, and judge UX talents.

2   Methodology

In the fall semester of 2022, 20 graduate students of Master of Applied Psychology (MAP) worked in four teams on two design briefs. Regular workshops, review sessions, and company visits took place, ensuring that the results provide the research team with key design and growth opportunities. To achieve this overarching goal, we sought to answer the following research questions.

1. What are the trends and user interactions of future playful experience?
2. What are the characteristics of the target user groups?
3. What are the typical user scenarios and journeys?
4. What are the new design concepts to enable the playful experience?

2.1 The Fourth Classroom

Intending to cultivate UX talents with applied and innovative abilities to meet the demands of the development of contemporary society, the essential mission of higher education teaching is to meet the urgent needs of talents in the community and to make the utmost of the advantages of scientific research in universities, to lead the development of a career in the future and provide the preliminary training of entering society for students. The concept of the Fourth Classroom [13] links universities and the society. It introduces the actual and complicated social professions in higher education teaching. In this way, students are deeply immersed in the role of pre-profession, and with the guidance from teachers, they can realize their role adaptation and shift from a college student to a professional. The Fourth Classroom has four characteristics: 1) the circulation mode of research-production-learning, 2) the interdisciplinary scientific research advantages, 3) the results-oriented mass innovation and entrepreneurship education, 4) the pluralistic and open fields and time. In recent years, several institutions world-wide are committed to cultivate both innovative research talents and entrepreneurial talents to build a world-class curriculum and pedagogy.

2.2 Design Thinking

Design thinking as a HCD innovation approach has become more and more widespread during the past years. An increasing number of people and institutions have experienced its innovative power [14]. In the past, teaching and learning engineering's primary concern has been with feasibility. As educators are asked to be more innovative in today's commercial and industrial environment, it becomes critical to weigh in on design thinking, transdisciplinary domains, and a global context as well. Pleasurable UX of product service system (PSS) is obviously becoming more valued and requires us to focus much more strongly on human values in addition to technical requirements [15]. The huge demand for transdisciplinary teaching and learning, and the rapid development of information technology have laid a solid foundation for innovations in multiple domains, e.g., education, healthcare, and personal mobility.

2.3 The Corporate Partner

The LEGO Group has been sparking children's imagination and inspiring the builders of tomorrow since 1932 [16]. With the Department of China Digital Technology (CDT) being a critical group setup for building core capabilities for the accelerating digital transformation landscape. The team of designers and developers work together to share expertise to create an environment where creativity, imagination, and tech thrive. They also have a strong appetite for continual learning, which often manifests in their community contributions. CDT is continually looking for innovative products that pushes boundaries, much like the ways we are aiming to creating a world for our children that bridges the gap between responsibilities and creative playfulness. They met with the student teams biweekly to provide feedback and critiques, with a wealth of knowledge and professional experience.

2.4 Transdisciplinary Student Teams

All students had core competencies in their respective fields, and some had prior project-based learning (PBL) [17] experience in academia or industry. Unlike many other academic psychology projects, students must design digital user interface (UI) with usability, desirability, and learnability. They had different professional backgrounds and study/work experiences, which gave the team formed with incomparable advantages, as reflected in the following:

- Diverse disciplines. In addition to psychology, there were students from industrial design, computer science, business administration, finance, and other majors. The collision of diversified disciplines meant diversified perspectives, viewpoints, and modes of thinking in problem discovery and problem-solving, which brought an additive effect of $1 + 1 > 2$. Students radiated and dispersed from multiple directions and levels through user research, theories, methods, and tools, combined with practice, eventually forming a complete solution.
- Core competencies complemented each other. The group members had multiple areas of expertise, such as data analysis, user interviews, design innovation, prototype building, etc., as well as their outstanding abilities and qualities, such as market insight, coordination, execution, communication and collaboration skills, etc. In practice, students took on different responsibilities in group discussions, presentations, and prototyping. Each student's ability and quality improved comprehensively through collaboration and communication.

2.5 The Design Brief Assignments

To promote PBL, there were two design briefs assigned by the corporate collaborator. Figure 1 shows the assignment focus. Practical product design pipeline should be considered, including user interviews, personas, design ideation, prototyping, and mockups.

1. Play for Generation Z [18]. Two student teams should explore the playfulness and innovative possibilities of LEGO Toys. They should consider and expand on the value of "play" for the Generation Z demographic by means of a digital solution.
2. Family Engagement. Two student teams should explore the social and connectedness aspects [19] of engaging with LEGO Toys. They should consider and design on the value of 'play' for the family demographic by means of a digital solution.

3 Results

Table 1 lists the mapping of the personas (i.e., target user groups) [20], contexts of use [21], and the key jobs-to-be-done (JTBD) [22] applied. Below, research scopes, personas, and JTBDs are presented for all results.

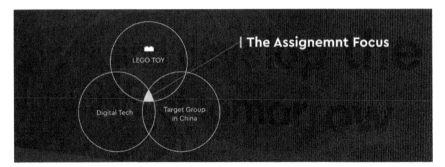

Fig. 1. The design brief assignment focus.

Table 1. Mapping of the teams, personas, and JTBDs of the results.

Team	Persona	JTBD
1	Product manager, 22	Make the toys as ornaments and helpful items
2	Online streamer, 25	Keep toys up-to-date
3	Accountant, 36	Have private time and don't have to be around kids all day
4	Engineer, 36	Play with fluidity and full engagement in pleasure

3.1 Team 1: Play for Generation Z

Office workers believe that LEGO Toys are single-functional and must merge better into their daily lives. Currently, they put them on their desks as ornaments, but after the novelty wears off, they are set aside and unattended. To solve this problem, this team designed several toy-shaped office supplies, such as cell phone holders, tea trays, cups, and vases, for the office workers to create with a patchwork approach. In this way, the toys are lovely ornaments in the office and helpful office supplies. This design increases the toy's functionality and integrates it into their daily work and lives. See Fig. 2 for an impression.

Jing, 22-year-old, is a product manager at an Internet company. She loves hiking, traveling, and making toys. She is new to the workplace and under a lot of pressure and wants her office environment to have a sense of space and companionship. She often says: I want to dress up my desk beautifully and delicately, and I hope all the office supplies are interesting and cute.

Among the JTBDs below, functional diversity was the focus. (1) Functional diversity: Make the toys as ornaments and helpful items. (2) Aesthetically pleasing: Design the shape cute for healing the soul. (3) The convenience of use: Play online and offline at any time. (4) Emotional experience: Keep the toys engaging and the play process focused enough to avoid interruptions or cognitive dissonance. (5) Socialization: Enable the toys to become a way to socialize.

Fig. 2. The user scenario.

3.2 Team 2: Play for Generation Z

Some loyal users want to create personalized models and share their ideas and achievements with others. This team designed a mobile application to help users produce and realize their ideas with online social and sharing functions. Users can use their devices to scan and transform real or imaginary objects into digital models. After building, they can share their creations and collect them in virtual showrooms. This design meets users' creative needs and enhances the playful experience and sense of accomplishment. See Fig. 3 for an impression.

Cong, 25-year-old, is an online streamer. He likes to buy and build toys. He often watches veteran players online and learns about modeling independently. He aspires to make personalized models and hopes to quickly create his own LEGO Toys kingdom and let many people see his achievement.

Among the JTBDs below, innovating play mode was the focus. (1) Innovating play mode: Keep toys up-to-date. (2) Promoting socialization: quickly and easily send information about players to people who might be interested. (3) Reducing cost: Reduce players' time and economic costs to buy and build. (4) Reflecting value: Let players highlight their interests and strengthen their traits. (5) Enjoying the process: Allow players to enjoy playing at home without burden.

3.3 Team 3: Family Engagement

Some mothers have demands for expressing themselves in the hectic pace of work and life in first-tier cities. Still, their busy schedules make them encounter the problem of lack of time for themselves and single forms of companionship when they are with their children. To solve this problem, this team has designed a small program that allows mothers and children to be more intimate and receive detailed guidance. While freeing up the mother's time, the online and offline play makes the mother's companionship more efficient. See Fig. 4 for an impression.

Di, 36-year-old, is an accountant living in a first-tier city, and a mother of an eight-year-old. She loves life and has many hobbies, such as outings and flower arranging. But her busy schedule often makes her feel lost in herself. She is eager to find some common

Fig. 3. The user scenario.

interests with her children and to release some stress in the company of her parents and children. She often says, "We are mother and son, but we are also two separate individuals."

Among the JTBDs below, making personal life more manageable was the focus. (1) Making personal life more manageable: Have private time and don't have to be around kids all day. (2) Making raising children easier: Help raise their children and make the toys more fun and meaningful to grow with their children. (3) Highlighting LEGO Toys' unique functions and value: Update the design of products to inspire moms to buy them. (4) Lowering the threshold of owning toys: Reduce the purchase cost and the energy of putting them together and facilitate the arrangement of children's playtime.

Fig. 4. The user scenario.

3.4   Team 4: Family Engagement

Parents of urban working families often lack time and energy to spend with their children due to their busy or strenuous schedules. They usually need to find engaging events to play with their children, but they also need to maintain good interaction. The design of this team incorporated AR puzzle guidelines, community DIY story creation, game-breaking, and cooperative assembly. The design stimulated the competitive and curious minds of both parents and children. Through collaborative games developed by the wider community, the parents and children can enjoy the toys together while reusing LEGO parts and increasing interaction. See Fig. 5 for an impression.

Min, 36-year-old, is a software engineer. He is trying to learn professional skills and earn money while focusing on his children's development. He wants to facilitate his children's growth and development in his limited time and enhance the parent-child relationship. He often says, "I want to spend time with my children, but I'm too busy at work, and I don't have much time."

Among the JTBDs below, enjoyment was the focus. (1) Enjoyment: Play with fluidity, sound guidance, and full engagement in pleasure at all times. (2) Re-energizing: Gain new energy to continue playing after playing. (3) Simultaneous Interaction: Enjoy playing with the same toys for both the parents and the children. (4) Effective Communication: Interact and collaborate effectively.

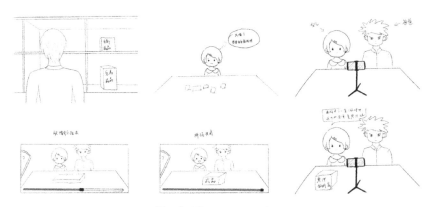

Fig. 5. The user scenario.

4   Discussion and Reflection

4.1   The Fourth Classroom

The introduction of the Fourth Classroom allowed the "application of learning" to be implemented in the students' teaching practice. The teacher's guidance, students' communication, and reviews from designers and developers from CDT gradually improved the results. They discussed and defined target users, contexts, JTBD, specific design briefs, and UI design details through online and offline meetings. For example, after the third-round review, they suggested digging deeper into the psychological mechanism and clarifying the competing products.

Another unique feature of the Fourth Classroom was that the students took full ownership of the discussion with the corporate partner. Where the experts' suggestions were unreasonable, the students could follow the team's planning according to the situation. For example, after the first-round review, they wanted to define the target users as non-toy fan groups. Still, after data analysis, the students finally determined the target user group as those who have been exposed to LEGO Toys and have some interest in them. They hoped to create, consolidate and develop a domestic "LEGO circle" by enhancing the playful experience.

The student's role is no longer homogeneous through the connection between the university and the corporate partner. Their thinking is upgraded from "a product" to "a playful way applicable to the target users."

4.2   Transdisciplinary Learning

Students from different professional backgrounds worked in teams to divide and collaborate on this project. The students complemented each other's strengths, generated different ideas, and made constructive suggestions for deletions and additions based on their understanding of each other's viewpoints. Students gave full play to their strengths. Some were responsible for literature searches, some for sorting out logic, some for drawing high-fidelity user interfaces, and some for shooting and editing videos. They had different interests, some were fans of LEGO Toys, and some had never played with them, facilitating targeted suggestions from different perspectives.

The students had teething problems in the early stages of the collaboration. For example, some already have rich work experience and tend to rush to summarize conclusions at the early stage of discussion. After the teacher's guidance and other students' communication, they could adjust in time and finish the work according to the requirements.

The collaboration encountered the situation of divergent opinions, and the students each had their own set of complete logic, and it was challenging to convince each other. For example, when discussing interactive gameplay, some students thought they should provide only a few instructions but let the users explore and discover the fun. Some students believed that the user should be treated as a novice user who had never been exposed to this gameplay and provided a detailed tutorial. If the two sides keep arguing, the research progress would be hindered. In the end, the students followed HCD principles, left the decision to the users, and asked students to test and evaluate the new designs.

4.3   What if We Start All Over

Students familiarized themselves with the complete UX process and honed their skills in communicating with the corporate partner.

- Take time to get things done. Although the teacher repeatedly emphasized the need to follow the UX process strictly, students were prone to jumping into their thinking and taking some expectations for granted in the actual operation process. Rushing to get results would lead to poor research work in the early stage, a flawed derivation process, and a mismatch of logic. Thus, students need to rework and waste time.

- Learn to "grasp the big and put the small." Diverse disciplines collided to bring multiple perspectives and multi-dimensional views. Students have produced many excellent ideas, which should be selected and prioritized well for the final presentation. Otherwise, the focus would be too scattered.
- Mastering presentation skills. Presentation skills are as essential as the ability to write a proposal, and the lack of either would significantly reduce the effectiveness of the final presentation. Good ideas should be visualized through drawings, videos, and other forms of expression. The text should be as concise as possible so that the audience do not take up too much cognitive resources. The rhythm of the language in the presentation process is crucial. In addition to the logical connection of the context to give the audience an overall sense of fluency, it is also necessary to provide the audience with tips by slowing down the speed of speech and raising voices when showing important information, leading to "twice as much can be accomplished with half the effort."

Acknowledgment. We would like to thank the students at UX Program of MAP at Faculty of Psychology at Beijing Normal University and the researchers at Department of China Digital Technology at the LEGO Group.

References

1. Wang, T.: Analysis on the design of children's puzzle toys. In: International Conference on Management Science, Education Technology, Arts, Social Science and Economics, pp. 302–306 (2016)
2. Törmer, R.L., Henningsson, S.: Platformization and internationalization in the LEGO Group (2020)
3. Baciu, D.C.: Creativity and diversification: what digital systems teach. Thinking Skills and Creativity **41**, 100885 (2021)
4. Cassell, J., Jenkins, H.: From Barbie® to Mortal Kombat: Gender and computer games. MIT Press (2000)
5. Desmet, P., Xue, H., Xin, X., Liu, W.: Emotion deep dive for designers: seven propositions that operationalize emotions in design innovation. In: Proceedings of the International Conference on Applied Human Factors and Ergonomics, pp. 24–28 (2022)
6. Zhang, F., Sun, S., Liu, C., Chang, V.: Consumer innovativeness, product innovation and smart toys. Electron. Commer. Res. Appl. **41**, 100974 (2020)
7. Geng, R., Wang, S., Chen, X., Song, D., Yu, J.: Content marketing in e-commerce platforms in the internet celebrity economy. Ind. Manag. Data Syst. **120**(3), 464–485 (2020)
8. Karnilowicz, H.R., Waters, S.F., Mendes, W.B.: Not in front of the kids: effects of parental suppression on socialization behaviors during cooperative parent–child interactions. Emotion **19**(7), 1183 (2019)
9. Norman, D.: The design of everyday things: Revised and expanded edition. Basic books (2013)
10. Desmet, P., Fokkinga, S.: Beyond Maslow's pyramid: introducing a typology of thirteen fundamental needs for human-centered design. Multimodal Technologies and Interaction **4**(3), 38 (2020)

11. Liu, W., Lee, K.P., Gray, C.M., Toombs, A.L., Chen, K.H., Leifer, L.: Transdisciplinary teaching and learning in UX design: a program review and AR case studies. Appl. Sci. **11**(22), 10648 (2021)

12. Gray, C.M.: Languaging design methods. Des. Stud. **78**, 101076 (2022)

13. Liu, C., et al.: From theory to practice: on the connotation and characteristics of 'the Fourth Classroom.' Res. Teach. **41**(6), 1–6 (2018)

14. Liu, W., Byler, E., Leifer, L.: Engineering design entrepreneurship and innovation: transdisciplinary teaching and learning in a global context. In: Marcus, A., Rosenzweig, E. (eds.) HCII 2020. LNCS, vol. 12202, pp. 451–460. Springer, Cham (2020). https://doi.org/10.1007/978-3-030-49757-6_33

15. Ohashi, T., Auernhammer, J., Liu, W., Pan, W., Leifer, L.: NeuroDesignScience: systematic literature review of current research on design using neuroscience techniques. In: Design Computing and Cognition'20, pp. 575–592 (2022). https://doi.org/10.1007/978-3-030-90625-2_34

16. Kerr, C., Phaal, R., Thams, K.: Customising and deploying roadmapping in an organisational setting: the LEGO group experience. J. Eng. Tech. Manage. **52**, 48–60 (2019)

17. Kokotsaki, D., Menzies, V., Wiggins, A.: Project-based learning: a review of the literature. Improv. Sch. **19**(3), 267–277 (2016)

18. Zhu, Di., Wang, R., Zhang, Z., Wang, D., Meng, X., Liu, W.: Exploring and reflecting on generation Z interaction qualities and selfie scenario designs. In: Markopoulos, E., Goonetilleke, R.S., Ho, A.G., Luximon, Y. (eds.) AHFE 2021. LNNS, vol. 276, pp. 352–357. Springer, Cham (2021). https://doi.org/10.1007/978-3-030-80094-9_42

19. Zhu, D., Chen, Y., Li, L., Dunsmore, J.C.: Family functioning, emotion socialization, and children's social competence: gender-specific effects in Chinese families. Journal of Child and Family Studies, 1–15 (2022)

20. Ferreira, B., Silva, W., Oliveira, E., Conte, T.: Designing personas with empathy map. In: SEKE, vol. 152 (2015)

21. Visser, F.S., Stappers, P.J., Van der Lugt, R., Sanders, E.B.: Contextmapping: experiences from practice. CoDesign **1**(2), 119–149 (2005)

22. Lucassen, G., van de Keuken, M., Dalpiaz, F., Brinkkemper, S., Sloof, G.W., Schlingmann, J.: Jobs-to-be-done oriented requirements engineering: a method for defining job stories. In: Kamsties, E., Horkoff, J., Dalpiaz, F. (eds.) REFSQ 2018. LNCS, vol. 10753, pp. 227–243. Springer, Cham (2018). https://doi.org/10.1007/978-3-319-77243-1_14

Defining the Problem's Solution to Lead to the Ideation Phase
- A Case Study on the Use of "How Might We..."

Yuki Asano[✉]

Shibaura Institute of Technology, 3-7-5 Toyosu, Koto-Ku, Tokyo, Japan
yuuki.aoki.zzz@gmail.com

Abstract. Year by year, increasing attention is being paid to design thinking, and various schools are now teaching it. There are five stagwees in design thinking: empathy, definition, ideation, prototypes, and testing. This paper focuses on the definition stage before addressing the ideation stage. Within the definition stage of design thinking, the problem or issue is identified and the point of view is defined accordingly. One develops solutions from the defined point of view, and then narrows that down and defines the issues to be addressed. In the problem definition stage, it is important to decide what kind of solution to arrive at from a particular point of view; depending on how that point of view is defined, the same perspective can become a completely different idea. IDEO utilizes the "How might we…" template for organizing the solution to a problem, an approach that has been widely used. In addition, d.school is developing "How might we…" to organize the issues to be solved by breaking them down into 10 different items. Therefore, this paper discusses the stumbling blocks that subjects encounter pertaining to the development and organization of issues in the definition phase of a problem's solution and their impact on the idea generation phase, utilizing 10 different items of "How might we…" as examples. This paper analyzes the results of a survey of 117 participants. The discussion is based on the results of the analysis, the current trends, and future prospects for the utilization of the "How might we…" template.

Keywords: Design thinking philosophy and patterns · Service Design · Ideation · Workshop · Point of view

1 Introduction

1.1 About "Design"

The word "design" has come to be used not only in the sense of design, but also in the broader sense of design. Today, there are many educational institutions that deal with design thinking, including business schools [1, 2]. The environments in which it is practiced vary, and it is not limited to designers, but is now being used in a wide range of genres [3]. In Japan, the government has also begun to make use of design, including the Japan Patent Office's Design Management Declaration [4, 5]. Today, the term "design" is used in a variety of cases, making it very difficult to describe it in a single word. Further, interest in design in a broad sense, including design thinking, is growing [6].

A. Marcus et al. (Eds.): HCII 2023, LNCS 14030, pp. 27–37, 2023.
https://doi.org/10.1007/978-3-031-35699-5_3

1.2 About Design Thinking

Design Thinking. When it comes to what design thinking is, given the current state of the design industry, there is no single clear definition. The term "design thinking" itself is an old term [7]. In Dunnen's Design Thinking in Practice, in presenting examples of implementing design thinking in organizations, he notes that "design thinking is often seen as a recent fad, but as a term it has been used for decades," and that "design thinking is not an ad hoc solution either. It takes years to successfully embed design thinking in an organization" [8]. In addition, the consulting firm IDEO's work on design thinking is being fostered on a daily basis, and the firm is entering a stage where it is practicing and reflecting on its practice and applying it to its next opportunity [9]. On the other hand, the acquisition of design thinking is addressed by many educational institutions, one of the most famous of which is Stanford University's d.school [10]. There are many methods for implementing design thinking as a business, and there are many lectures and frameworks for practice [11].

Five Stages of Design Thinking. There are five stages in design thinking: empathy, definition, idea, prototype, and testing. In this study, I focused on the second stage, the stage before defining the idea and after defining the point of view (see Fig. 1). Within the definition phase of design thinking, problems and issues are found and used to define the focal points. From this defined focus, solutions are developed, and the issues to be addressed are narrowed down and defined. In the problem definition stage, it is important to determine what kind of solution is to be landed on from the focal point, and depending on how this is defined, the same focal point can lead to completely different ideas.

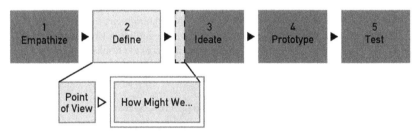

Fig. 1. Positioning within the five stages of design thinking.

1.3 Define

About Ideas. In this study, an idea was defined as a concrete proposal based on an original point of view on a pre-defined topic. In terms of the five stages of design thinking, this is the content to be considered in the third stage, ideate. It is said that an idea is nothing more than a new combination of existing elements [12]. However, many people find it difficult to come up with ideas, and many studies have been conducted on methods to support idea generation [13].

Importance of the Define Phase. How the definition phase is converged will determine what is considered in the subsequent stages of examining ideas. How to define the definition stage is one of the major concerns of the design industry. The importance of the definitional stage has been studied and advocated in various ways, not just in design thinking. For example, the importance of "problem setting" is discussed in reflective practice [14]. Anzai (2020) also described questions as "a medium through which people weave perceptions and relationships through creative dialogue" [15]. How to formulate questions is studied through various approaches, but how to set the point of view is exactly the same as how to formulate questions, and it involves placing one's perspective. How you formulate the question will determine where you place your perspective, which in turn will change what you consider in the next stage of ideation.

Definition of the Term. The process of defining is not just about where to place the perspective as the point of view. It is necessary to define where to focus and then what to refer to. If this stage is vague, it is difficult to develop into an idea. In "The Design Thinking Playbook," it is stated that one of the key points in finding the proper focus is to find a 360° viewpoint [16].

2   How Might We…

About "How Might We…". "How Might We…" is a concept that is used in discussions at d.school and throughout the design thinking process. It helps you to connect your point of view to an idea. Many people may find it difficult to just come up with ideas in the dark when thinking about how to solve a problem they have identified. In this case, "How Might We…" can be a great help [17]. When it comes to the question "How Might We…," according to Wu (2019), "Having this clear will serve as a destination for the team to aim for so that we don't lose direction in the ideation process or lose sight of what we are solving for in the first place." He mentioned the d.school and that "How Might We…" advises 10 different approaches (see Table 1). Although the items may not necessarily be 10 different types depending on the reference, this study experimented with the 10 different approaches discussed by Wu (2019) [18].

Purpose of This Study. In this study, "How Might We…" was distributed to individuals as a framework and used as a template for individual work (homework) on the points of view that each individual focused on. The purpose of this study was to investigate the feeling of using "How Might We…" as a template for individual use, and to analyze the degree of utilization of its contents. In general, "How Might We…" is used in a discussion format, with multiple people digging deeper into the points of view and breaking them down. However, there are situations in design work in which the point of view has to be connected to an idea by an individual. For example, when multiple points of view are simultaneously being developed for a single project, the amount of time and the number of people that can be spent on a single point of view are limited. Also, when students are trained to think of ideas, there is great value in receiving stimulation from other people's viewpoints through discussion, but there must also be a learning experience in developing individual thinking skills by oneself. Thus, breaking down and organizing viewpoints on an individual basis without discussion is necessary, but has not been studied. This study analyzed the use of templates by individuals based on the content of the exercise lectures conducted in this study. Based on the results of this analysis, we will discuss the future prospects of the template (see Fig. 2).

Table 1. Wu (2019) advocates 10 different approaches to "How Might We…"

1: Develop good points
2: Eliminate the bad parts
3: Turn it upside down
4: Reexamine the premise
5: Change the adjectives
6: Use other resources
7: Associate with needs and context
8: Apply the focus to the topic
9: Change the status quo
10: Decompose the focus

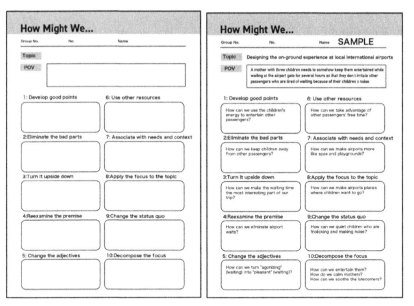

Fig. 2. A sample of the template used for the experiment and the Wu (2019) reference case filled out.

Experimental Details. The experiment was conducted on 117 s-year students from the Department of Design Science, Faculty of Creative Engineering, Chiba Institute of Technology. During three days of lectures on creative design and exercises, the students examined and presented their ideas in a workshop format (see Fig. 3). The theme was "Thinking about the new value of real stores." In today's world of online mail-order sales and take-out food, the value of daring to use a real store is being questioned. In Japan, stores that remain vacant amid the declining birthrate and aging population are becoming a social problem. It is an important social issue, as the Small and Medium Enterprise Agency has introduced initiatives related to the revitalization of shopping arcades with many vacant stores [19].

The flow of the experiment was based on the sharing of actual experiences through group work (see Fig. 4) and a deep investigation of the problem, followed by individual determination of the point of view and organization of the problem to be solved using the "How Might We…" template. On the final day, each participant created a proposal on a sheet of A4 paper and presented it (see Fig. 5).

Fig. 3. The venue on the day of the experiment.

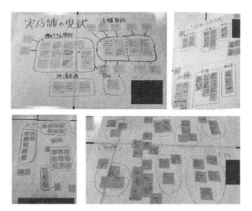

Fig. 4. The venue on the day of the experiment.

Fig. 5. The venue on the day of the experiment.

3   Results

Results. A participant questionnaire was administered during the experiment to investigate the use of the template. The resulting observations are summarized below. Each question was based on the subjective evaluation of each subject rather than an objective assessment.

Whether Participants Felt that the Quality of the Assignment Was Improved Through How Might We…. Approximately 95% of the participants tended to experience an improvement in the quality of their assignments.

In reviewing the free comments, the most common positive comments were "I could see where I was going by breaking down the ideas," "It gave me hints," "It helped me make sense," "I could dig deeper," and "I could think in a variety of ways. Comments that the participants were able to think about the point of view from a different direction from their initial one stood out, and this result shows the value of the work (Fig. 6 and Table 2).

Table 2. Do you think the quality of the problem has improved through the work of How Might We…?

Do you think the quality of the problem has improved through the work of How Might We…?		
1: Decreased very much	0	0%
2: Decreased	1	1%
3: Slightly decreased	4	3%
4: Slightly improved	59	50%
5: Improved	45	38%
6: Very much improved	8	7%
	117	100%

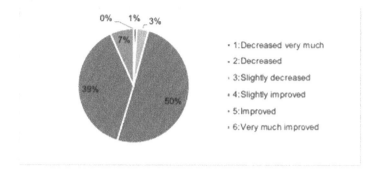

Fig. 6. Percentage of subjects who saw improved quality or not.

Whether or not Participants Felt that Doing How Might We Changed Their Ideas. Again, a high percentage of participants (approximately 85%) felt that there was some change in their ideas (Fig. 7 and Table 3).

Table 3. Did your ideas change through the How Might We… work?

Did your ideas change through the How Might We… Work?		
1: There was no change at all	5	4%
2: No change	3	3%
3: Slightly unchanged	12	10%
4: Slightly changed	59	50%
5: There was a change	30	26%
6: Very much changed	8	7%
Total	117	100%

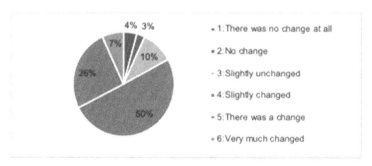

Fig. 7. Percentage of respondents who felt that their ideas changed.

Whether the Item Could Be Utilized or not. The survey asked respondents to indicate which items they felt they were able to utilize in the "How Might We…" section. In this survey, there was considerable variation in the items that each respondent felt they were able to utilize. An analysis of variance showed that the P-value was smaller than the rejection range, and the comparison of the variance ratio (F value) to the boundary value also confirmed that the variance ratio (F value) was small. Thus, it was confirmed that there was a difference in the results for each item.

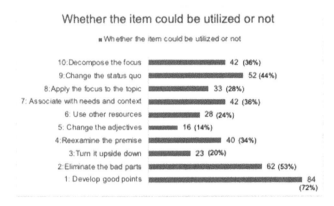

Fig. 8. Percentage of respondents who felt that their ideas had changed.

In particular, items 1, 2, and 9 were utilized by more than 40% of the respondents. Conversely, the items with low utilization (less than 20%) were 3 and 5 (see Fig. 8 and Table 4).

Table 4. Analysis of variance on which items in the How Might We… section that respondents felt they were able to utilize.

Group	Sample size	Total	Average	Variance
1: Develop good points	117	84	0.72	0.20
2:Eliminate the bad parts	117	62	0.53	0.25
3:Turn it upside down	117	23	0.20	0.16
4:Reexamine the premise	117	40	0.34	0.23
5: Change the adjectives	117	16	0.14	0.12
6: Use other resources	117	28	0.24	0.18
7: Associate with needs and context	117	42	0.36	0.23
8:Apply the focus to the topic	117	33	0.28	0.20
9:Change the status quo	117	52	0.44	0.25
10:Decompose the focus	117	42	0.36	0.23

Analysis of Variance Table

Variance Factors	Change	Degree of freedom	Variance	Observer Variance Ratio	P-value	F-boundary value
Between Groups	30.61196581	9	3.401329535	16.49615653	9.73714E-26	1.887936146
Within Group	239.1794872	1160	0.206189213			
Total	269.791453	1169				

Ease of Filling Out the Form. Ease of filling out the questionnaire was also investigated in the same way. An analysis of variance was conducted, and it was confirmed that the P value was smaller than the rejection range, and the variance ratio (F value) was also smaller than the F boundary value. Thus, as a result, we were able to confirm that there were differences in the results for each item.

In terms of the free response section, comments such as "good points are easy to think about," "easy to associate," and "easy to write" stood out with regard to item 1. On the other hand, we also received some comments that "the good points could not be fully developed.

As for item 2, comments such as "it was easy to think from experience," "it was easy to find the bad points," and "it was easy to understand" stood out.

As for item 9, many commented that "it was easy to think about because it was experience based" and "it was easy to find new discoveries by questioning the current situation," while others commented that it was similar to item 2 and that it was difficult to understand.

In addition, item 5, which had a particularly low level of utilization, was not used in some cases because no adjectives appeared in each subject's point of view, and many subjects felt that it was difficult to utilize.

When we checked the other free-answer items, we found that some items were difficult to handle due to their compatibility with the respondent's point of view (Fig. 9 and Table 5).

Fig. 9. Item-by-item results for ease of entry.

Table 5. Analysis of variance results for ease of completion

Group	Sample size	Total	Average	Variance
1: Develop good points	117	552	4.72	1.39
2:Eliminate the bad parts	117	565	4.83	1.04
3:Turn it upside down	117	368	3.15	1.76
4:Reexamine the premise	117	415	3.55	1.35
5: Change the adjectives	117	334	2.85	2.28
6: Use other resources	117	371	3.17	1.69
7: Associate with needs and context	117	385	3.29	1.78
8:Apply the focus to the topic	117	345	2.95	1.84
9:Change the status quo	117	446	3.81	1.74
10:Decompose the focus	117	414	3.54	1.85

Analysis of Variance Table

Variance Factors	Change	Degree of freedom	Variance	Observer Variance Ratio	P-value	F-boundary value
Between Groups	500.29487	9	55.58831909	33.20999175	2.92E-52	1.88793615
Within Group	1941.65812	1160	1.673843207			
Total	2441.95299	1169				

4   Considerations and Future Prospects

This research study summarized content dealing with one theme as an example of the use of a template. Depending on the contents of the theme, there may be differences in which items are easy to fill out.

Since the templates were written as individual homework this time, there was no way to follow up on cases where the items themselves were difficult to understand. This is another issue that needs to be addressed when conducting individual work in the future. If there is to be a follow-up, one solution may be to prepare multiple example entries.

There is still room for more work to be done to deepen the individual discussion. For example, the wording and content of the "How Might We…" itself could be revised. Also, although the content of the template created this time consisted of 10 items in parallel, it may be possible to reorganize the relationship between these items and insert them into the template. The idea is to place items 1, 2, and 9 in a central position, since they had a high degree of utilization. In addition, if items with strong relationships can be considered, it may be helpful to follow up on the entries by including the relationships and illustrating them on the template.

Since this study confirmed the effectiveness of the template for use in individual work, we would like to further consider making it easier to use in the future.

References

1. IIT Institute of Design, https://id.iit.edu/design-camp/MITidm/. last accessed 2023/02/05
2. i.school, https://ischool.or.jp/, last accessed 2023/02/05
3. Ministry of Economy, Trade and Industry, Japan Patent Office, https://www.meti.go.jp/rep
   ort/whitepaper/data/pdf/20180523001_01.pdf. last accessed 2023/02/05
4. Jumpei, I., Makito, O.: The understanding and acceptance of design thinking among local
   government officers. Bulletin of JSSD **68**(2), 19–28 (2021)
5. Rui, M.: A study of the concept of design in design-driven management. Japan Marketing
   Journal **42**(1), 81–89 (2022)
6. Hitotsubashi University Institute of Innovation Research.: Hitotsubashi Business Review 2022
   Win, 1st edn., vol. 70, no. 3, pp. 52–56. Toyokeizai, Japan (2022)
7. Toshiaki, T.: Design thinking. J. Japan Soc. Fuzzy Theor. Intell. Informat. **32**(5), 155 (2020)
8. Dunne, D.: Design thinking at work: how innovative organizations are embracing design
   (=2019, Translated by Kazuo, K., Ippei, M., Kagetaka, N., Masato, S., Takeshi, O., Osamu,
   S.K., p. 155), 1st edn. University of Toronto Press, Canada (2018)
9. Harvard Business Review.: HBR'S 10 must reads on design thinking (=2020, Translated by
   DIAMOND Harvard Business Review Editorial Department, p. 26), 1st edn. Harvard Business
   School Publishing Corporation (2020)
10. Stanford University d.school, https://dschool.stanford.edu/. last accessed 2023/02/05
11. Nayuta, O.: Korekara no design shikou, 1st edn. MdN Corporation, Tokyo (2021)
12. James, Y.: A technique for producing ideas (=1988, Translated by Shigeo, I., pp. 32–42).
    McGraw Hill, Columbus (1965)
13. Foster, J.: How to get ideas (=2003, Translated by Aoshima, Y. IDEA no Hint, pp. 44–48),
    c/o Linda Michaels Ltd., International Literary Agents, New York (1996)
14. Donald, A.S.: The Reflective Practitioner: How Professionals Think in Action (=2007, Trans-
    lated by Shoichi, Y., Kenji, M. Shosatsuteki jissen toha nanika, p. 40). Basic Books, Ink.,
    United States (1983)
15. Anzai, Y., Takayuki, S.: Toi no design Souzoutekitaiwa no facilitation, 4th edn. Gakugei
    Shuppansha, Kyoto (2020)
16. Lewrick, M., Link, P., Leifer, L.: The design thinking playbook (=2019, Translated by Miki,
    I. Design Thinking Play Book, p. 89.). John Wiley & Sons, Inc. through Tuttle-Mori Agency,
    Inc., Tokyo (2018)
17. Design Thinking Bootleg, https://dschool.stanford.edu/resources/design-thinking-bootleg.
    last accessed 2023/02/05
18. Wu, J., Misaki, D.: Jissen Stanford Shiki Design Shikou, 1st edn. Impress Corporation, Tokyo
    (2019)
19. Chusho Meti, https://www.chusho.meti.go.jp/pamflet/hakusyo/2022/shokibo/b2_2_2.html.
    last accessed 2023/02/05

Prioritization Matrix to Highlight Business Opportunities

Adriano Bernardo Renzi[1] and Luiz Agner[2][✉]

[1] Design and Research Department, MobileLive Inc, Toronto, Canada
adrianorenzi@gmail.com
[2] Design Department, Instituto Brasileiro de Geografia e Estatística, Rio de Janeiro, Brazil
luizagner@gmail.com

Abstract. Lilia Schwarcz, relates the Covid-19 pandemic event to the end of the 20th century, as the 1st World War marked the beginning of it. The 1900s was "the century of technology, with fast-growing technology development, and the pandemic event was coming to present technology's limitation" (Schwarcz 2020 and 2020). Countries around the world adopted different strategies to minimize the impact on their health system, population, and economy. Companies started adapting business strategies, in an attempt to keep the flow of projects and contracts. These changes affected not only management, projects, and how people work together, but also design and research methods. This paper presents the prioritization matrix method adaptation to remote research scenarios, using a real case to follow through the whole research process, mixing remote unstructured interviews, and an online working board. The adaptation has much of its structure from the adaptation of card sorting for remote scenarios, leading to meaningful insights and results for thinking. The description of the whole process presented here encompasses three phases: preceding interview, matrix workshop, and analysis. Due to non-disclosure contracts with the companies involved, this paper will focus mainly on the research structure and process, without presenting sensitive data connected to specific features.

Keywords: User Experience · Prioritization Matrix · Human-Computer Interaction

1 Introduction: World Change and Work Adaptation

On December 31st of 2019, the WHO office in China was informed of new pneumonia cases in Wuhan. Although immediate quarantine isolation started, 44 patients were registered with similar symptoms and 9 days later the first death was registered (WHO 2020). On February 11th, WHO designated the sickness as Covid-19 and its virus as SARS-CoV-2. Two weeks before, Italy registered its fourth death derived from it (Gan et al. 2020 and Li and Hui 2020). On March 21st, Europe was the new epicenter of the pandemic with 4,825 deaths and 53,578 registered cases in Italy. In less than 2 weeks – March 31st, the number of dead in the USA had surpassed the numbers in China (WHO 2020 and Aljazeera 2020).

© The Author(s), under exclusive license to Springer Nature Switzerland AG 2023
A. Marcus et al. (Eds.): HCII 2023, LNCS 14030, pp. 38–50, 2023.
https://doi.org/10.1007/978-3-031-35699-5_4

Lilia Schwarcz, Ph.D. in social anthropology at Universidade de São Paulo, relates the Covid-19 pandemic event to the end of the 20th century, as much as the 1st World War marked the beginning of it. The 1900s was "the century of technology, with fast-growing technology development, and the pandemic event was coming to present technology's limitation" (Schwarcz 2020 and 2020). A series of interviews conducted during the apex of people under quarantine in 2020, with participants from Z, Y, X, and baby boomer generations, presented a glimpse of how technology and social interactions have been affected by isolation (Renzi *et al.* 2020).

Countries around the world adopted different strategies to minimize the impact on their health system, population, and economy. Companies started adapting business strategies, systems, and office *modus operandi,* in an attempt to keep the flow of projects and contracts. The working stations and in-person offices were substituted by home office and remote meetings. These changes affected not only management, projects, and how people work together, but also design and research methods, leading to new research strategies, new script structures, new online tools, and new ways to reach out to users.

Guimarães et al. (2020) write briefly about the process behind design development in the digital industry, where each phase of a project is presented to stakeholders for closer integration of the "Triad relation" (design team – agency – client) to make sure that taken steps are validated by all actors involved – different from academic research. In order to compensate for the number of phases, the authors show to have adopted the agile process to fasten the methods and attend market timing expectations.

Mckinsey released a report (2020) regarding remote working and how each line of work showed more and less adaptation to the new scenario. The report presents the remote work potential by 2 metrics: the maximum potential, including all activities that theoretically can be performed remotely, and a lower bound for the effective potential for remote work, which excludes activities that have a clear benefit from being done in person. As shown by the Mckinsey report, the 5 major areas for faster adaptation are connected to (1) updating knowledge and learning, (2) interacting with computers, (3) thinking creatively, (4) communicating with and guiding colleagues or clients, (5) processing, analyzing and interpreting information. All 5 areas are directly connected to digital products, interaction design, and research, leading this discussion towards digital products and companies that offer services and consulting in the digital area.

In May 2021, with people already more experienced in working remotely, a Mckinsey consumer survey (Alexander et al. 2021) showed 41% of employees saying they were more productive working remotely than in the office. Their confidence in their productivity has grown, and the number of people agreeing with this statement increased by 45% from April to May. By November, across all sectors, the expectation of hybrid and full remote work increased, totaling 63%, suggesting executives would anticipate operating their business with a hybrid model of some sort.

Throughout the pandemic, I have worked on projects for different companies around the world and each company showed different solutions to the new challenges ahead. From these experiences, some factors showed to influence their adaptation to the new era: (1) the company's size, (2) the technology available, and (3) the company's culture.

1. Company's size – bigger companies with more employees had a bigger challenge to sync systems and home offices to a lot more people than smaller Companies.

2. Technology available – not every company had appropriate technology for meetings, chats, calls, and ideation practices remotely. Many companies had to adopt new tools, acquire new licenses, and provide training. Software with geographical licenses and difficulty to work cooperatively had to be discarded.
3. Company's culture – companies that already had employees working from different countries were able to adapt faster to the new scenario, as culturally they were more tuned with cooperative tools, asynchronous collaboration work, fewer meetings, and goal-achieving work hours.

The research presented in this paper was conducted at MobileLIVE, which has employees located in different timezones (Toronto, Montréal, Vancouver, Richmond, and Edmonton in Canada and Islamabad, Sahiwal, and Lahore in Pakistan) totaling a difference of 12h between Vancouver and Islamabad, suggesting a remote culture easily adapted to pandemic new requirements.

As a consulting company, the design and IT teams are distributed throughout various clients, and therefore, integrated into clients' teams, synced with their particular systems and available technologies. Its technological background also suggests that items (1) syncing systems, and (2) technology have been well adapted to pandemic times. The triad relation (Guimarães et al. 2020) occurs in closer ground, conceptually speaking, although physically far from each other.

Having a company well adapted to the 3 factors that influence the working flow, this paper focuses primarily on the prioritization matrix method adaptation to remote research scenarios, using a recent real case, to better follow through the whole research process: a mix of remote unstructured interviews, and online cooperative working board. The process has much of its structure from the adaptation of card sorting for remote scenarios, leading to meaningful insights and results for future pondering.

2 Prioritization Matrix

The objective of the prioritization matrix is to compare alternatives within specific scenarios and map the most important alternatives from the perspective of users. It can help make decisions by narrowing options down by systematically comparing choices through the selection, weighing their values through the application of criteria.

According to Gibbons (2018), the term "prioritization matrix" is used in the design thinking community to refer to a variety of prioritization techniques and representations that, technically, do not all qualify as matrices in the mathematical sense. The author (*ibidem*), from the NN group, adds notes from a historical perspective, where time-management matrices are based on the Eisenhower Method (attributed to Dwight D. Eisenhower – an American army general during World War II): "I have two kinds of problems, the urgent and the important. The urgent are not important, and the important are never urgent." Using this method, activities are to be allotted in one of four quadrants: important/urgent, important/not urgent, unimportant/urgent, and unimportant/not urgent (Homére *et al.* 2019).

Two decades after Eisenhower's matrix, Thomas L. Saaty (1987) developed the Analytic Hierarchy Process. From his theory, the methodology is for relative measurement, used to derive ratio scales from both discrete and continuous paired comparisons – from the most basic to the most complex problems can be presented as a hierarchy with the same basic structure. It could be an object, a feeling, an idea, or another entity. Nevertheless, the research must include only other similar entities and relate to them by making comparisons, in such a way that the resulting decision is less influenced by personal judgment and as objective as possible.

Cossenza (1996) presents a version of the priority matrix, part of his conclave techniques guidebook, is to be used in situations where people face many alternatives and have to organize them according to their importance. Opposed to Saaty's theory, the Cossenza priority matrix expects personal judgment from participants and inputs based on their own user experiences and expectations. The method is direct, and analyzes alternatives systematically, considering the criteria set that should guide the decisions.

The author divides the method into 2 sequential phases: criteria x criteria and alternative x alternative. In the criteria x criteria phase, the researcher selects all options (ideas, features, location, object, etc.) to be compared and distributes them on the top row and mirrors them through the left column of the matrix (Fig. 1). Each participant will compare the criteria with each other, and attribute values in the matrix boxes according to their comparative importance:

- Much more important than = 10 pts
- More important than = 5 pts
- Equally important = 0 pts
- Less important than = 0.5 pts
- Much less important than = 0.1 pts

The summations of points for each criterion are included in the far right column and the final value will determine which criteria are most important for users.

	Item A	Item B	Item C	Σ
Item A	X	1	0.1	1.1
Item B	1	X	0.5	1.5
Item C	10	5	X	15

Fig. 1. Example of prioritization matrix criteria x criteria by Cossenza (1996)

For the second phase, alternatives for each criterion (items A, B, and C) are compared with each other to map what is the best alternative related to the Criteria studied. In the presented example Item C was considered the most important criterion, therefore the second phase takes item C and compares alternatives that offer Item C.

The item C for purchase can be found in stores K, Y, and Z. Which store is the best place to buy item C (Fig. 2)? From the presented simulation, store K seems to be the best choice to purchase item C.

	Store K	Store Y	Store Z	Σ
Store K	X	5	1	6
Store Y	0.2	X	5	5.2
Store Z	1	0.2	X	1.2

Fig. 2. Example of prioritization matrix alternative x alternative by Cossenza (1996)

Renzi and Freitas (2008) utilized this method to compare factors (book preview, writer's information, recommendation, readers' reviews, price, and Synopsys) considered by readers when purchasing books and which online bookstores in Brazil were considered to offer best service regarding the voted most important factor. The application of the method was through an online questionnaire and 70 people participated. The results evinced at the time that Travessa bookstore was the best place to go considering the factors Synopsys, price, and recommendation.

Cossenza's priority matrix is very objective and effective to highlight the users' preferences, but it lacks the possibility of understanding users' journeys that lead to decisions. For the project at hand, presented in this paper, the prioritization matrix is based on the Eisenhower Method, properly adapted to our needs.

2.1 Adapting Prioritization Matrix for Remote Research

The main objective of this research was to understand users' preferences regarding information and features when interacting with a telecommunication provider website. The prioritization matrix method was adapted for remote scenarios, following similar steps of previous research described in the "Cardsorting for the new remote era". The adaptation would allow the research team to get a deeper understanding of users' journeys and relate to their decisions.

The matrix board was built in Mural.co, an online tool that provides boards for remote collaboration, with 2 main axes that would range from less important to more important (X) and less frequent to more frequent (Y). Changing the urgency axis from Eisenhower's matrix, to the frequency axis is important to measure the relationship between importance and frequency, as some features on the website can be very important, but not necessarily of frequent usage. For this research, the use of urgency as one of the axes would bring no relevant data.

The importance range was laid as the horizontal axis (X) and the frequency range was presented as the vertical axis (Y) – Fig. 3, separating the board into 4 quadrants: most important and more frequent, less important and more frequent, more important and less frequent, and less important and less frequent. Stickers with the names of features and tasks from the homepage were distributed on the right side (following Renzi 2022 directives), so that users would have their visual reading from left to right and see the full board first. The whole proceeding was presented to participants (1st the board with axes, 2nd the stickers, 3rd the suggestion stickers) before granting access to the board as visitors.

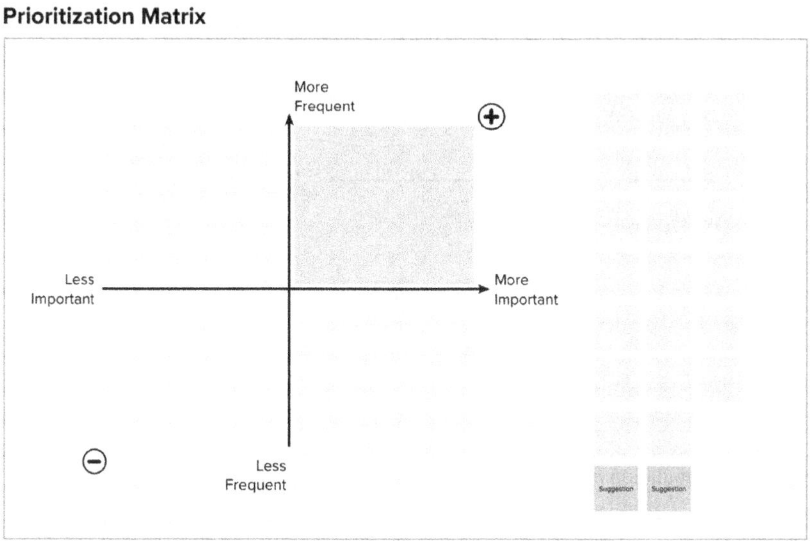

Prioritization Matrix

Fig. 3. Initial arrangement of the Prioritization Matrix board in Mural.co

Aside from the 20 yellow stickers, there were 2 pink stickers for participants to add suggestions based on their personal experiences and needs. After the full explanation, participants were invited to enter the board and freely arrange the stickers over the prioritization matrix board.

Participants were interviewed prior to the board interaction, in order to map their experience, and mental model regarding telecommunication services and prepare them for the prioritization matrix. This prior information would help the researcher to connect their sticker placement with their story, and make precise further questions related to their choices. Based on the prior interview, each session starts the matrix session pointing first to the most obvious feature stickers of placement, due to their back story – following directives presented at the card sorting experiment (Fig. 4).

After all stickers were positioned throughout the board for each interview session, the researcher conducted the participants through all chosen positions and made comparative questions to confirm the positioning and amplify the discussion, with questions that would relate to answers from the interview at the beginning of the session. The 2 suggestion stickers were introduced at the end of the session when all participants already confirmed their choices and could add anything they were missing from the presented set. The pink stickers were then allocated on the board in a position of importance/frequency, in comparison to all 20 yellow stickers.

Prioritization Matrix

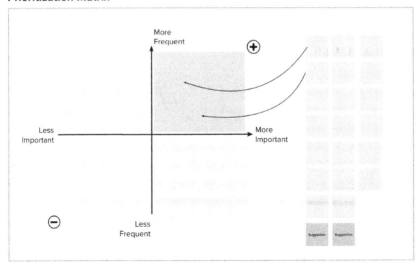

Fig. 4. Simulation of user interaction to allocate stickers within the 4 quadrants

2.2 Recruiting

The recruitment of 20 participants for this research was done through Usertesting.com for 60 min individual sessions. Screening questions were used for the recruiting process in order to select digitally enabled people from all genders, residing in Canada, with ages between 18 and 65, English speakers, annual income between 22 k and 175 k, responsible financially for their telecom services and who would go to their telecom provider's website for paying bills and solving issues. The 20 interview slots, distributed throughout 2 weeks, were fulfilled within minutes of the invitation release on the system.

Although Usertesting provides a prioritization matrix tool, it was considered not appropriate for this research. Therefore, the recruiting, scheduling, video calls, and recording were done through the Usertesting system, but participants were invited to join the researcher at Mural.co for the matrix interaction while sharing their screens.

3 Results

The 20 boards showed visual patterns that can be easily resumed in one final board (Fig. 5). It is possible to see 4 major areas of confluences that can be classified as:

1. top importance and frequency features,
2. major importance/frequency features,
3. minor importance/frequency features,
4. least importance/frequency features.

The details of each sticker are hidden due to non-disclosure contracts.

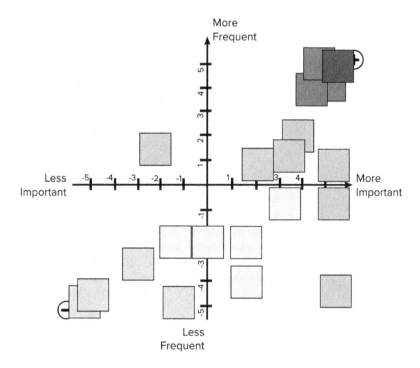

Fig. 5. Distribution of stickers throughout the board and identification of areas of importance.

According to users, 4 features are considered of (1) extreme importance and frequency when interacting with telecom providers' websites. They are very close to each other and are actions connected to each other.

In the (2) major importance/frequency features area, it is noticeable that these 5 features show high importance (some equally important to the first group), but are used on specific situations that would classify the actions with less frequency of use.

The spread area occupied by the 5 minor importance/frequency features is very central, with medium importance and even less frequency. These are features that users see as out of their primary range of interest and use rarely. It is interesting to notice that the 2 suggestion pink stickers fluctuate in this area of medium importance, as the suggested features are considered by participants to be not urgent, nor deal-breakers, but it would be good to have.

The last group (4), encompassing the 4 least importance/frequency features are the features considered by users to be never considered or only attained in very specific situations.

The graphic of Fig. 5 was reorganized as a heat map (Fig. 6) to better classify the different areas and discuss with stakeholders appropriate actions for each area of importance:

Fig. 6. Reorganization of items in a heat map

4   Conclusion and Discussion

Following the directives used in the card sorting experiment to adapt the prioritization matrix for remote scenarios proved to be very successful. Including an interview at the start point of each session showed also to be very fruitful and a means to gather basic data to be used for leveraging the discussion with participants during the matrix interaction. The working together feeling helped to deepen the investigation and understand the story behind each positioning of the stickers. Even remotely, the method presented results of easy to map behavior patterns by visual analysis of the boards and participants' stories behind decisions. During the interviews, it became obvious that it is better when participants have their camera on, for better analysis of body behavior while speaking and interacting with the matrix board.

Analyzing each section of importance/frequency separately, makes it easier to map issues and build business strategies for a better user journey and service design.

The 4 most important/frequent features (hot spot area) chosen by the participants are the features that users need to have at hand and can't avoid using. The features are connected to each other and related to tasks to be done on a regular basis. It can directly affect users negatively, if not properly done. The best strategy regarding this "hot spot" section, since they are related to unavoidable tasks, is to build experiences with better usability and better user-centered interaction. These are the features where the design team has to make icons, buttons, and interactions easy to understand, with actions obvious to perform and, if possible, reduce the steps to completion. As users have no way to avoid these tasks, it becomes important to make them easy to use and avoid frustration from users.

The group of 5 major important/frequent features is connected to actions of users' personal interest. These are features that users need, moved by specific challenges they are facing and from intrinsic personal interest – not regular mandatory actions. The major important/frequent feature area is the section to show service reliability and expand the business. The 3 main grounds of actions go beyond usability: (1) project managers, together with designers, should focus on service design strategies, (2) proper information architecture for communicating relevant decision making information, and (3) artificial Intelligence for personalization, in order to help and support customers in their actions and personalize service offers.

From the results gathered in this research, 2 main ways of service personalization could increase customer adherence and business expansion. Considering that recommender systems (or recommendation engines) – programs that belong to the category of information filtering system – seek to predict which classification a user will give to an item of information, based on calculations and statistical inferences (algorithms designed to suggest items relevant to the user), the system can present personalized information, deals, shortcuts and new products based on 2 sets of collected information: Collaborative filtering and Content-based filtering.

Collaborative Filtering—Collaborative methods are based only on past interactions recorded among users and items to produce new recommendations. The more the users interact with the items, the more accurate the recommendations become (Rocca, 2019).

Data collected to model user behavior can be either explicit or implicit. Explicit forms of data collection include: search terms, asking a user to sort items or creating a wish list. Implicit forms of data collection include: observing browsing times, registering purchased products, viewing product lists, or analyzing the social network. With a broad set of tracked user data, it is possible to identify clusters representing user communities with very similar tastes to observe their collective behavior (Kathayat *apud* Agner et al., 2020).

Content-Based Filtering—According to Rocca (2019), while collaborative methods depend only on item-user interactions, content-based approaches need additional information about users and items. They need a description of each item as well as a profile of user preferences. In this case, keywords are entered to describe the items and a user profile created.

Hybrid Recommendation Systems—Pandey (2020) points out that both collaborative and content-based approaches have strengths and weaknesses. Therefore, most of the recommendation systems take a hybrid approach, merging collaborative filtering solutions with content-based approach methods, as well as other approaches.

For this particular research, Content-based filtering can be associated to customer collected data gender-age-income-location classification related to purchase behavior. Collaborative filtering can be based on customers' interaction history that should include interactions with actors and physical stores in a cross-channel journey (Renzi 2017, 2018).

According to Pandey (2020), recommendation systems aim to solve two types of problems: prediction (data used to predict the evaluation a user will give to an item he has not interacted with) and ranking (defining a finite list of items to be presented to the system's user), confirming Rocca's recent studies (2019), where recommendation systems can play a central role in our lives.

From e-commerce (suggesting to buyers articles that might interest them) to digital marketing (suggesting to users the right ad that can generate the highest click- through rate), recommendation systems have now become inevitable in online journeys. They are increasingly employed in commercial services that people use on a day to day basis, especially telecommunication and digital media.

The group of 7 minor important/frequent features calls attention for integrating all suggestions for new features during the research. The 5 already existing features allocated here are features with minor importance, considering the whole scenario organized by the participants. These 5 are not business opportunities, nor considered essential actions, but users still expect these task flows to be supported by good usability.

For this group, the business opportunities reside in the participants' suggestions, as they are things that users would like to have access to, but have not seen in this line of business so far. It is interesting to note that the suggestions are all based on personal experiences prior to interacting with the provider itself and from services not related directly to telecommunication, confirming previous research results (Renzi 2016, Sande et al. 2017, Renzi 2017) where users' experience journey starts outside a company's product/system and it is important to understand the triggers that could bring these users to reach out the system/service.

The least important area of features (4) are the ones users don't pay attention to and are out of their particular interests. Nevertheless, these are connected to very specific situations and customers expect support from the provider. There is also an area for improvement, as this section is connected to service reliability, a factor very important to users.

Although some details can't be shared, due to non-disclosure contracts, the method clearly helps identify the areas of interest from customers' perspective and map opportunities for service improvement and business opportunities – easily adapted to various industry areas.

The 3 main elements for adaptation towards the new remote/hybrid era have proven to be effective in this research. The well-synced systems between MobileLIVE and the client, the technology availability for remote working, and the company's culture did lead to a smooth triad relationship (guimarães et al. 2020), making it easy to conduct the research itself, as well as sharing results and discussing future actions with all stakeholders involved in the project. We expect to experiment in the future with other complex methods and see if these experiences with adaptation to remote environments can result in further discussions regarding methodologies.

References

Agner, L., Necyk, B., Renzi, A.: Recommendation systems and machine learning: mapping the user experience. In: Marcus, A., Rosenzweig, E. (eds.) HCII 2020. LNCS, vol. 12201, pp. 3–17. Springer, Cham (2020). https://doi.org/10.1007/978-3-030-49760-6_1

Alexander, A., De Smet, A., Langstaff, M., Ravid, D.: What employees are saying about the future of remote work, April 2021. <https://www.mckinsey.com/capabilities/people-and-org anizational-performance/our-insights/what-employees-are-saying-about-the-future-of-rem ote-work>

Cossenza, O.N. Manual de técnicas de conclaves. - 2 edição – Rio de Janeiro. 173. - (IPR. Publ. 656) (1996)

Gan, N., Xiong, Y., Mackintosh, E.: China confirms new coronavirus can spread between humans. In: CNN, January 23rd, 2020. https://edition.cnn.com/2020/01/19/asia/china-corona virus-spike-intl-hnk/index.html

Gibbons, S.: Using Prioritization Matrices to Inform UX Decisions. NN Group, May 27, 2018. <https://www.nngroup.com/articles/prioritization-matrices/>

Guimarães, M.A., Zisman, R.P., Renzi, A.B.: Pharmaceutical online store project: usability, affor-dances and expectations. In: Nunes, I.L. (ed.) AHFE 2019. AISC, vol. 959, pp. 523–534. Springer, Cham (2020). https://doi.org/10.1007/978-3-030-20040-4_47

Homère, A.N.M., Tchindjang, M., Mfondoum, V., Makouet, I.: Eisenhower matrix * Saaty AHP = Strong actions prioritization? Theoretical literature and lessons drawn from empir-ical evidences. In: IAETSD Journal for Advanced Research in Applied Sciences **6**(2), 13-27 (2019)

Li, J., Hui, M.: China has locked down Wuhan, the epicenter of the coronavirus outbreak. In: Quartz, January 30th, 2020. https://qz.com/1789856/wuhan-quarantined-as-china-fights-cor onavirus-outbreak

Lund, S., Madgavkar, A., Manyika, J., Smit, S.: Mckinsey Global Institute. What is next for remote work: an analysis of 2,000 tasks, 800 jobs, and nine countries, November 2020. <https://www.mckinsey.com/featured-insights/future-of-work/whats-next-for-remote-work-an-analysis-of-2000-tasks-800-jobs-and-nine-countries>

Pandey, P.: The Remarkable world of Recommender Systems. https://towardsdatascience.com/the-remarkable-world-of-recommender-systems-bff4b9cbe6a7. last accessed 2020/01/28

Renzi, A.B., Freitas, S.: Aplicação de Matriz de Prioridade na verificação de preferências de leitores na compra de livros em livrarias online. Interaction South America (2008)

Renzi, A.B.: Experiência do ususário: a jornada de Designers nos processos de gestão de suas empresas de pequeno porte utilizando sistema fantasiado em ecossistema de interação cross-channel. Tese de doutorado, p. 239. Escola Superior de Desenho Industrial, Rio de Janeiro, Brazil (2016)

Renzi, A.B.: Experiência do usuário: construção da jornada pervasiva em um ecossistema. In: Proceedings SPGD2017, vol. 1. Rio de Janeiro (2017)

Renzi, A.B.: UX Heuristics for cross-channel interactive scenarios. In: Marcus, A., Wang, W. (eds.) DUXU 2017. LNCS, vol. 10288, pp. 481–491. Springer, Cham (2017). https://doi.org/10.1007/978-3-319-58634-2_35

Rocca, B.: Introduction to recommender systems. https://towardsdatascience.com/introduction-to-recommender-systems-6c66cf15ada1/22. last accessed 2019/12/19

Saaty, R.W.: The analytic hierarchy process-what it is and how it is used. Math Modelling **9**(3–5), 161–176 (1987)

Sande, A., Renzi, A.B., Schnaider, S.: Experience, usability and sense of things. In: Marcus, A., Wang, W. (eds.) DUXU 2017. LNCS, vol. 10289, pp. 77–86. Springer, Cham (2017). https://doi.org/10.1007/978-3-319-58637-3_6

Schwarcz, L.: Pandemia marca o final do século 20. In: https://www.hypeness.com.br/2020/04/lilia-schwarcz-sobre-coronavirus-pandemia-marca-o-final-do-seculo-20

Schwarcz, L., Século XX só acaba com o fim da pandemia. In: https://www.otempo.com.br/o-tempo-contagem/seculo-xx-so-acaba-com-o-fim-da-pandemia-diz-historiadora-1.2335100

WHO declares coronavirus global emergency as death toll rises. In: Aljazeera, January 30th, 2020. https://www.aljazeera.com/news/2020/01/declares-coronavirus-global-emergency-death-toll-rises-200130231243350.html

A Case Study in Organizational Adoption of User Personas: Assessing Perceptions, Awareness, and Hesitation to Adopt

Rachael Boyle[1]([✉]) [iD], Ruslana Pledger[2] [iD], Hans-Frederick Brown[1] [iD], and Rachel Vanderbilt[1] [iD]

[1] LiveRamp, San Francisco, CA, USA
{rachael.boyle,hansfrederick.brown}@liveramp.com
[2] LiveRamp, Issaquah, WA, USA
lana.pledger@liveramp.com

Abstract. In a prior study, our team created research-based personas through an iterative, mixed-methods approach; however, as a B2B SaaS (business-to-business, software as a service) company, we faced unique challenges not only when generating those personas but evangelizing them throughout our organization. In examining the existing literature on persona building, we notice a distinct gap in reflecting on the organizational buy-in of these personas after their development. Much of the research in this area emphasizes the "how" of persona building, without exploring their ultimate impact, utility, and effectiveness in an actual organization. Therefore, the current study will explore the aftermath of persona generation, assessing adoption within our organization. To this end, we implemented a survey to assess employee perceptions of our user personas a year after their development, both within and outside of the product team. Measures within the survey assessed persona perceptions [10], awareness, and perceived utility. Additional open ended questions asked employees about any hesitations they have regarding our user personas that might lead them to not adopt them, opportunities for educating the broader organization on the existence of and utility of these personas, and how employees are using personas to influence decisions and communicate today. Analysis of these open ended questions helped define future directions for our personas, and additional education to facilitate organizational adoption of personas and effective communication about our users.

Keywords: Persona Generation · Persona Impact · Organizational Adoption

1 Introduction

1.1 Generating B2B SaaS Personas

One way that organizations can better serve their customers is through engaging in user-centered design practices. Creating research-based user personas is one way organizations can accomplish this [4, 5]. User personas are profiles of typical users of a

A. Marcus et al. (Eds.): HCII 2023, LNCS 14030, pp. 51–65, 2023.
https://doi.org/10.1007/978-3-031-35699-5_5

product and/or service, delineated through certain characteristics (e.g., typical behaviors, job titles, work responsibilities). By creating these personas, user experience (UX) and product design teams are able to refer to profiles of actual user based behaviors to generate new products or features that meet their needs. In addition, designers and product managers are able to more effectively communicate their designs and recommendations to the broader organization through referencing these persona groups [3].

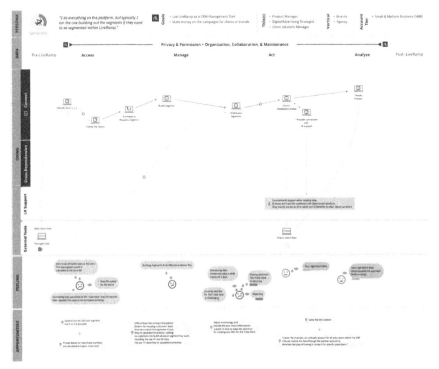

Fig. 1. The above image is an excerpt from our persona packet we disseminated across our organization. This excerpt is a user journey map; each persona has a map that details their progression through our product, their pain points and feelings during this progression, and the services they touch along the way (i.e. documentation, customer support, analytics tools).

As researchers at a small, B2B SaaS (business-to-business, software as a service) company with complex products and disjointed user journeys across these products, we saw an urgent need to more deeply understand our users for the same communication and ideation purposes. However, as we generated personas, we faced unexpected challenges prior research could not guide us on due to our existence as a B2B SaaS company and the nascency of both UX and persona generation in this context [11]. These challenges partially stemmed from having a smaller user base (less than 10,000 total monthly active users) and limitations of our data capture process (e.g., data aggregation at the hour level). Through a novel, mixed-methods approach, our researchers identified behavioral clusters through quantitative modeling, surveys, and qualitative interviews in an iterative process [1]. This resulted in the creation of six persona groups for two of our products.

Fig. 2. The above images are excerpts from our persona packet we disseminated across our organization. Each persona has a persona card (the first image) which details the most pertinent information about the persona such as a description, goals/responsibilities, and pain points. The second image holds additional information about the persona from the product analytics data and survey in case members of our organization wanted to dive deeper.

We have since created personas for three other of our core products using a similar method with the goal of enabling the entire product organization to more effectively make and communicate decisions.

Personas need to be evangelized within an organization in order for the impact of personas to be realized within that organization [6]. For this kind of "organizational integration," a variety of methods can be implemented [5] such as posters, flyers, giveaways, and email communication [6]. To facilitate the adoption of our data-driven personas across the organization, the research team disseminated persona packets (see Figs. 1 and 2) and held public sessions where they explained the process of generating the new personas, overviewed the persona groups, made room for questions, and provided additional resources for members to reference. A guide for user persona usage was posted in our internal communication tool, Slack, across channels for product and design teams as well as on our internal knowledge base for posterity. This guide explained what personas are, how to use them, and when they are most useful in the design and product development process.

1.2 Assessing Organizational Adoption of Personas

An unexpected challenge in garnering buy-in of this research was other teams had also created personas. The sales organization had profiled potential buyers, referring to them as 'buyer personas'. This created some internal confusion around which personas were generated from user behaviors and which were meant to identify sales opportunities. This unintentionally created hesitancy for product team members around implementing the new persona language. There was also some reluctance on the part of the sales organization to adopt the behavioral personas because they did not aid in generating sales, however, the product organization relies on the sales team to identify current users within the platform to garner feedback for use in prioritizing feature development and identifying potential user needs.

In examining the existing literature on persona building, we notice a distinct gap in reflecting on the organizational buy-in of these personas after their development. Much of the research in this area emphasizes the "how" of persona building, without exploring their ultimate impact, utility, and effectiveness in an actual organization. Therefore, in this study we explored the aftermath of persona generation, assessing adoption within our organization. To this end, we implemented a survey to assess employee perceptions of our user personas a year after their development, both within and outside of the product team.

Measures within the survey assessed persona perceptions [10], awareness, and perceived utility. Persona perceptions include clarity, completeness, consistency, credibility, empathy, likability, and willingness to use. Awareness measures assess the extent to which employees are informed about the existence and purpose of personas specific to users of our platforms, as well as where they would expect to find persona-relevant information. Perceived utility assesses whether, and for what purposes, employees find personas useful to doing their job [3].

Additional interviews were conducted to ask employees open-ended questions about any hesitations they have regarding our user personas that might lead them to not adopt them, opportunities for educating the broader organization on the existence of and utility of these personas, and how employees are using personas to influence decisions and communicate today. The results of this study have helped define future directions for our personas and educational resources to facilitate organizational adoption of personas and effective communication about our users.

We believe this study is of significance to the broader UX community, and specifically the B2B SaaS UX research community, because it can help define future directions for their personas too. Objective assessments of and reflections on the effectiveness of personas post creation within a mid-sized business are rare in existing literature. But we believe this work is important due to the time and resources involved in persona generation in the first place, a high cost that typically excludes other companies like ours from taking on the initiative [8]. With this case study, we build upon our prior persona generation research and dig into the return on investment of these projects. We hope the insights we uncover will help others make informed decisions in their pursuit of persona generation, unlock the full value of the personas they will generate or have already generated, illuminate the factors that influence persona adoption, and be a launchpad for future research in this space.

2 Literature Review

Salminen breaks down the typical lifecycle of a persona project into the following three categories: creation of personas, evaluation of personas, and use of personas [8]. While Salminen uses these loose categories as a way to bucket research issues faced in each phase, we posit that this serves as useful scaffolding to look at existing persona literature as well.

2.1 Persona Creation

In terms of creation, the persona generation process and the methods used to do so have been greatly examined in the field. Some work focuses on qualitative methods, quantitative methods, or mixed methods. While personas may have started as a one method (and often qualitative) approach, more and more emphasis has been placed on making these personas data-driven by leveraging quantitative methods and online analytics [5, 9]. In this way, personas can become more credible and objective rather than subjective [5]. The value in objectivity comes from the usability and usefulness of the personas for their target audience, with much of the practical research and case studies targeting product and design teams as the users of personas. How personas are generated can influence their success in terms of use and adoption. Literature in this bucket does not investigate the use of personas directly, but highlights its importance as a way of influencing the approach to persona creation.

2.2 Persona Evaluation

In terms of evaluation, the benefits and criticisms of personas as a design technique has been greatly explored within the literature as well [2, 8, 9]. Salminen places the main benefits of their use into four categories, separated by impact (communication, psychology, transformation, and focus), and the main criticisms into three categories, bucketed by persona generation stage (creation, evaluation, use) [8]. The listed threats to the use of personas hit on both organizational issues (e.g., internal politics, preconceptions) and validation issues (e.g., lack of trust in personas due to data sources).

However, many of the examples of these threats come from decades old research, prior to the onset of online analytics and data-driven personas. They highlight the situation where "personas are fully developed but then left without meaningful use," but do not dive into the factors that may have led to this situation [8]. Overall, this work highlights the lack of consensus on the effectiveness of personas, the need for more rigorous evaluation of their usefulness, and a call for more research on digital data-driven personas.

2.3 Persona Use

In terms of use, there seems to be a much smaller repository of research. However, research in this area is important because understanding the use and impact of personas can help lead to greater chances of organizational acceptance and adoption. To that end, the Persona Perception Scale (PPS) was created as a useful toolkit to assess "persona users' (e.g., designers, marketers, software developers) perceived credibility of the persona and their willingness to use it" [10].

Tomasz Miaskiewicz and Coryndon Luxmoore touch on the use of personas in their case study on persona creation and organizational adoption within a B2B SaaS company [5]. The authors found that using data-driven personas can facilitate organizational adoption of user-centered design by providing a clear understanding of user needs and goals. While this source provides valuable guidance on how to embed and integrate personas in an organizational setting, it doesn't investigate the utility and value of those personas in the first place. This is important since, like our and many others' generated personas, their work was produced as a snapshot in time (e.g., may lose fidelity over time) and is not leveraged much by other teams (e.g., indicates information may be missing).

Additionally, just because personas have been integrated into existing product design processes does not mean they are used and/or useful. In fact, it is a major assumption within persona literature that UX professionals will readily and consistently use personas. One study showed that practitioners "used personas almost exclusively for communication, but not for design" and found them to be "abstract, impersonal, misleading and distracting" [3].

2.4 Summary

Overall, research that investigates adoption of personas and the factors that influence its adoption is slim. Those that do exist seem to focus on personas as a conceptual method (in the evaluation bucket) rather than personas as a tangible output within an organization (in the use bucket). Additionally, existing literature on persona effectiveness largely focuses on personas generated from qualitative methods rather than those created from or in conjunction with online analytics. Due to this, there is limited research into the adoption and use of data-driven personas, the ways to improve existing personas given barriers to use or criticisms, or the factors that influence the use of these personas in an industry setting. In our case study, we leverage a combination of tools and measures prior researchers have outlined and apply it to assess a specific instance of data-driven personas that were created using an iterative mixed-method approach.

3   Methodology

3.1   Survey

Research Design and Approach. We constructed our survey to assess the amalgamation of measures we found in existing literature. The measures of perception, awareness, and utility would then help us understand the status for organizational adoption of our personas and give us insight into where we could improve.

Persona *perceptions* [10] include clarity (e.g., "the information in the persona profile is easy to understand"), completeness (e.g., "the persona profile is detailed enough to make decisions about the customers it describes"), consistency (e.g., "the quotes of the persona match other information shown in the persona profile"), credibility (e.g., "this persona seems like a real person"), empathy (e.g., "I feel strong ties to this persona"), likability (e.g., "this persona is interesting"), similarity (e.g., "this persona feels similar to me"), and willingness to use (e.g., "this persona would improve my ability to make decisions about the customers it describes"). *Awareness* measures assess the extent to which employees are informed about the existence and purpose of personas specific to users of our platforms.

Perceived *utility* assesses whether, and for what purposes, employees find personas useful to doing their job [3]. Persona utilities include internal training (e.g., the persona is used to inform the onboarding program), design (e.g., the persona is leveraged to validate and influence design work), communication (e.g., the persona is used to communicate user needs and goals to stakeholders); role playing (e.g., "the persona is 'put on' by the designers and the designers make decisions while 'wearing' that persona") [2, 3], clarification (e.g., "the persona is used to clarify a position and to make certain that an action assumed by the designer is the correct one"), focusing (e.g., "the persona is used to eliminate other issues and to focus the designers on the needs of a particular end user as established through the persona"), meeting maintenance (e.g., "the persona is used to move a meeting along or to correct a colleague who has used the wrong persona"), empathy (e.g., "the persona is used to engender empathy and to make the end user personable and relatable"), and approximation (e.g., "the persona is used as an approximation of the end user").

We consolidated and tailored the above measures for survey deployment in our unique B2B SaaS context. Thus, we removed some perception constructs (e.g., likability and similarity) that did not apply to this setting and utility constructs (e.g., approximation) that were redundant in conjunction with other measures, as well as reframed or added other utility constructs (e.g., stakeholder alignment, testing/validation) to better address our setting.

Our survey had a total of 38 questions with four separate sections for background information and each measure group: background (2 questions), awareness (2 questions), utility (9 questions), and perception (24 questions).

Data Collection and Analysis. We constructed the survey in Qualtrics and disseminated the link internally via relevant Slack channels and email groups for product and design. We had a total of 60 respondents, which is 40% of the total 150 members of our global product team which includes professionals from a variety of career tracks (e.g., design and research, technical documentation, product management, product marketing, technical program management).

3.2 Interview

Research Design and Approach. To understand the "why" behind the results of our survey and capture open-ended responses, we conducted semi-structured interviews with members of our organization. The goal with this research method was to understand any hesitations members of our organization have regarding our user personas that might lead them to not adopt them, opportunities for educating the broader organization on the existence of and utility of these personas, and how employees are using personas to influence decisions and communicate today. The interview script consisted of 13 questions with four sections: background (2 questions), awareness/use (5 questions), barriers (5 questions), and ideas for improvements (1 question).

Data Collection and Analysis. We conducted 1:1 thirty minute interviews remotely over Zoom. 16 total interviews were executed, spanning several groups (5 designers, 5 product managers, 1 engineer, 2 product marketing managers, 1 sales) and various levels of our hierarchy (2 leadership team members, 4 managers, 10 individual contributors). Each session was recorded and later transcribed, tagged, and annotated by our researchers in a process known as interview "coding" [7]. The insights from this coding process was then bucketed into broader qualitative themes and synthesized in this report.

4   Results

4.1   Quantitative

We shared our survey with product (e.g., product managers, product marketing managers, technical program managers, designers, tech writers), engineering, and customer support. These individuals are not just split by job function but also by product hierarchy/specialization, which we denote as pillars (e.g., manage, analyze, activate, access). The distribution of responses across pillars and role generally followed the distribution of team members across pillars and roles as well. The notable exceptions to this are engineering and customer support, who fall a bit outside our target audience for personas. Hence, we did not communicate the survey repeatedly to those groups as we did with product managers and designers.

In terms of role breakdown, the highest responses were from the two main audiences we had in mind for our personas: product managers (22 responses out of 25 total product managers) and designers (12 responses out of 14 total designers). This high response rate among our target groups decreases the possibility of sampling bias and lends further credibility to the results.

Organizational Awareness. Results (see Fig. 3) showed that a substantial majority of survey respondents are aware of our personas (49% somewhat agree, 38% strongly

Q6 - I am aware of LiveRamp Personas (i.e. I know where to find them, I have seen them or heard of them, I have used them)

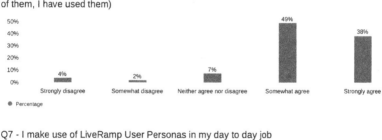

Q7 - I make use of LiveRamp User Personas in my day to day job

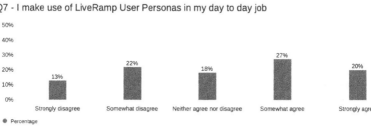

Fig. 3. The above figure shows the results of the awareness measures, specifically the percentage of our survey respondents who are aware of our personas vs. those who use them daily.

agree) but the use of our personas in their day to day job is relatively split (13% strongly disagree, 22% somewhat disagree, 18% neither agree nor disagree, 27% somewhat agree, 20% strongly agree), as shown in Fig. 3. We saw a 40% decrease from awareness (87% strongly and somewhat agree) to use (47% strongly and somewhat agree). Overall, these results indicate that we have done a successful job communicating and bringing awareness to our personas with our target audience. However, it also shows we are significantly less successful in terms of the actual use of those personas by our target audiences. This indicates that there is something suboptimal with the current state of our personas, meaning something may either be missing, conflicting, or ineffective.

Organizational Utility. Our personas are most utilized in the following contexts (meaning majority of respondents selected that they always, most of the time, or half the time use personas for this use case): role playing, focusing, stakeholder alignment. Our personas are least utilized in the following contexts (meaning majority of respondents selected that they sometimes or never use personas for this use case): communication, testing and validation, internal training. These areas show opportunities for personas to make a bigger impact. For instance, incorporating our personas into internal training would help all members of the product team understand our users better. This is especially important given the complexity of our products, the long "ramp-up" time it takes for new hires to understand our products and thus our users, and how siloed our products and teams can be. The low utility ratings for these areas indicates some barriers to use, such as a lack of education on how to leverage personas in the first place.

Persona use was split in the following contexts (meaning a relatively equal number of respondents selected that they always, most of the time, half the time use personas vs. sometimes, never use personas): empathy, clarification, design. These utility contexts are some of the most fundamental, incredibly important for our team considering the original goals of the project. Thus, we would expect these areas, specifically empathy and design, to be some of our highest used persona utility measures. For instance, our primary target audience for personas is the design team, whom we have done the most persona integration work with and have been early evangelizers of our work. However, only 66% of designers filling out the survey use personas in their design work. This either indicates that there are barriers to using our personas and/or a lack of persona integration into the design process.

Organizational Perception. We got a high number (40%–52%) of 'strongly agree' responses for the following statements: the information in the persona profile is easy to understand, the personas are interesting, the personas are data-driven. These indicate the perception areas we are doing right and the strengths of our personas in their current state, most notably interpretability and credibility. The latter is likely influenced by the data-driven persona generation process we used and the public sessions we hosted.

We got a high number of 'somewhat agree' (45%–58%) to the following statements: persona cards are detailed enough to make decisions, I understand the people the personas describe, the persona cards enable me to imagine a day in the life of the persona, the personas are credible. These indicate areas we are doing well in but could still improve, most notably around decision-making details and imagining the person the persona represents. We got a high number of neutral or negative responses (neither agree or disagree, somewhat disagree, strongly disagree; 40%–50%) to the following statements: the personas seem like real people, I feel like I've met customers like these personas, the persona cards are not missing vital information. This shows the weaknesses with our current personas and represents key issues our team needs to address in order to improve adoption.

Overall, these results seem to indicate that while our personas are perceived as credible and data-driven, it is hard for our target audience to imagine them as real people and link them back to the customers they have interacted with already. We likely over-indexed on surfacing and explaining the underlying data statistics of the personas from the cluster analysis we performed. This could have made it harder for our target audience to empathize with our personas (a utility measure listed above), see them as real people and familiar user groups, and ultimately use the personas in existing product development workflows.

4.2 Qualitative

Persona Success Stories. We found concrete examples of success stories through anecdotal evidence of past research we consulted on within our organization, such as: one team using our personas to build journey maps for their product's user experience (see Fig. 4); another team using personas to focus their research and their recruitment process; two teams using our personas to inform their research study, a Jobs To Be Done (JTBD) survey; and another team using personas to focus their narrative in a product requirements documentation (PRD).

Additionally, our interviews showed success stories for persona use, with evidence of the following utility and perception measures given these example quotes:

- *Focus* (e.g., accelerating project development): "One example is where personas accelerated a project, in this case, the data hub team wanted more info from an API user, but also the timeline was really short. Having API personas allowed me to accelerate, get traction building this journey map and thinking about the API implementer."
- *Empathy* (e.g., importance of understanding user needs): "Personas are indispensable in my opinion for product management and good discovery. You can't build something without thinking about who it's for or who is going to derive the most value from the thing you're creating."
- *Communication* (e.g., using personas in PRDs and planning): "I think it's really instrumental in helping me understand why these customers are utilizing LiveRamp and how the features that we're trying to build and support, impact the customers based on what they're using LiveRamp for."
- *Internal Training* (e.g., personas as a useful tool in onboarding and understanding user interactions): "When I started, one of the first things I did is I asked about who are the users that are most frequently accessing LiveRamp, applications, software, what have you. And I was pointed to the Connect User Personas document"
- *Role Playing*: "We used personas during role play to create a NorthStar vision of our product."

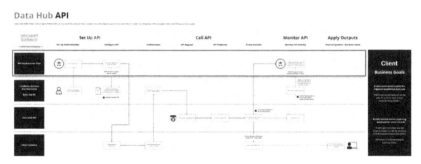

Fig. 4. The above figure shows an example of how our personas were leveraged by other teams in our organization, specifically by a product team for building journey maps of their product's user experience. They used the API implementer we created (outlined in red) for envisioning the user experience of their product's new API. (Color figure online)

Barriers to Use. Through our interviews, we uncovered feedback on why members of our organization do not use our personas. We transcribed the interview recordings, annotated the transcriptions with our insights, and grouped these into the following themes: representation, similarity, ways of working, training and education, and lack of collaboration.

Representation. Some interview participants felt a lack of alignment between our personas and the user groups they've experienced first hand or expected given prior internal user segmentation. Some notable examples were less technically savvy users, internal users, users who use a service we provide that is not tied to a UI, and users from brand clients vs. users from publisher clients. This distinction between client types has been the historical way we differentiated our users within and across our company. Without these users or distinctions highlighted, our target audience felt (1) unsure about which ones applied to their work, (2) important elements were not represented, and/or (3) some personas were even missing ("in our team we are not using [many] LiveRamp defined user personas because there is none that corresponds to our users").

Similarity. Some participants highlighted that distinguishing between personas was a challenge, feeling like many were similar to each other. This similarity led to confusion and thus a lack of adoption. One user said: "I would say [one thing that] was a bit challenging was some of the personas were like really, really close, right? Like, I think like some were like, they're just like shades different than each other."

Ways of Working. Another aspect that poses a barrier to using and deriving value from personas is how members of our organization approach the product development life cycle (PDLC) for their various projects. Some highlighted that traditional methods of discovery and ideation are often skimmed over, thus making it harder to use personas in certain contexts. This is particularly prevalent when product managers and designers are doing work that contributes to another team's initiative. In these cases, it's very clear cut what needs to be done and everything is already dictated to them, leaving little room to leverage personas if the other team did not do so.

Training and Education. Our interview participants emphasize a lack of training and education on how to use personas. Their limited understanding of the personas present a barrier for adoption.

Lack of Collaboration. Our organization has a variety of personas, such as those created by the sales team (e.g., buyer personas), those created by product marketing, and those created by us (e.g., user personas). This was highlighted as a source of misalignment and confusion. Users felt that while having so many sets of personas is confusing, those crafted by different teams (e.g., sales, product marketing, UX research) have different goals and audiences. Thus, all are needed but better alignment and consolidation would decrease the cognitive load required to use them.

Ways to Improve and Increase Adoption. Users had many ideas on how we could improve our personas and increase adoption, such as:

- Attaching brand names to personas: "I think it would help to attach some brand names to the personas, since that helps make them more real. ie: examples of who is acting like that persona"

- Understanding the impact particular personas have on decisions: "It would also be interesting for me to know how much that persona influences data choices and budget decisions, on a scale relative to the others."
- Incorporating personas into project management tools: "Maybe we can put in which personas are involved for each product improvement/update in the Jira tickets. As a writer, this would really help us understand quicker who the improvements are for and make the user story much easier to understand."
- Making persona use mandatory: "Maybe it should be a prerequisite for any project. Like, make it mandatory for any type of presentation?"
- Enhancing personas with additional materials: "I think our Personas are very strong but combining them with other types of materials such as video recordings is helpful. There were user videos I watched during my onboarding that were invaluable to me."
- Incorporating personas in the discovery and planning process: "Maybe… every UX discovery ticket should have an initial paragraph talking about the personas…to make sure that we keep them on top of our minds."
- Sharing examples of how personas have been used in the past: "I would just love to see like someone presenting a project that they worked on, and at some point they use personas somehow in their process… maybe it's when we are defining the strategy and the roadmap and planning our next quarter work, we went to the goals and pain points of our personas."

5 Recommendations

The key takeaways from our survey and interview show that we need to address the barriers to using our personas and make our personas more usable for our organization by:

- making our personas feel more like real customers by tying them to relevant and up-to-date user stories
- identifying areas of alignment and areas of conflict given our target audience's (e.g., product manager, designers) contextual knowledge
- identifying collaboration areas and relationships between personas
- explicitly mapping personas to product areas and teams for clarity
- renaming confusing/unclear personas and consolidating redundant personas
- highlighting specific and granular features/products that are leveraged by these personas more clearly
- including new features that have been created since the persona study was conducted
- running TEDTalks and workshops on personas to educate the broader organization on who they represent and how to use them

Pruitt and Adlin state that evangelizing personas is key to realizing the impact of those personas for your organization. From the results of our study, we expand on this statement and claim that assessing the awareness, perceptions, utility, and barriers to use after you generate these personas and addressing the insights from such an assessment is pivotal to fostering adoption and unlocking the full potential personas. We recommend those with existing personas to leverage our findings and/or perform a similar level of assessment along these measures, especially if they are unsure about the current impact and use of their personas. This way, fellow researchers can still leverage the results of their large-scale empirical study on personas while making it more applicable for and usable by its intended audience.

In our experience, generating personas was time and resource intensive. Not many organizations have the means to do so. For those that do, extracting value from the personas and ensuring return on investment is key. We recommend follow up research to assess the adoption of automatically generated personas. These types of personas are generally viewed as the future of the field since it adapts as the product changes and is data-driven [5, 8]. However, our insights showed that while many believed our personas were data driven and credible, that didn't translate to actual day-to-day use. Since actual use of personas is the ultimate measure of its own success, it seems important to replicate this type of assessment across various contexts (e.g., academia, business-to-consumer), generation methods (e.g., purely qualitative, purely quantitative, automatic), and persona representations. This way, the broader human computer interaction and user experience field can determine the best way to approach user-centered design and persona generation in the future.

6   Conclusion

In conclusion, we constructed a survey to assess persona perceptions, awareness, and utility as well as utilized interviews with key stakeholders from our organization to understand barriers to use and ideas for improvements. Our findings show that just evangelizing personas across your organization and increasing awareness for the generated personas is not enough. Embedding personas into existing product development processes, keeping them up-to-date (if developed from a static snapshot in time), providing continual training resources, mapping personas to specific teams within the organization, creating alignment and/or consolidating with other existing personas in the organization, and making the personas feel like real people (instead of a collection of data points) are some of the ways to unlock the value of previously created personas and increase adoption.

References

1. Boyle, R.E., Pledger, R., Brown, H.F.: Iterative mixed method approach to B2B SaaS user personas. Proc. ACM Hum. Comput. Interact. **6**, 1–44 (2022). https://doi.org/10.1145/353 4523
2. Friess, E.: Personas and decision making in the design process: an ethnographic case study. In: Proceedings of the SIGCHI Conference on Human Factors in Computing Systems (CHI '12), pp. 1209–1218 (2012). https://doi.org/10.1145/2207676.2208572
3. Matthews, T., Judge, T., Whittaker, S.: How do designers and user experience professionals actually perceive and use personas? In: Proceedings of the SIGCHI Conference on Human Factors in Computing Systems, pp. 1219–1228 (2012).https://doi.org/10.1145/2207676.220 8573
4. Miaskiewicz, T., Kozar, K.A.: Personas and user-centered design: how can personas benefit product design processes? Des. Stud. **32**, 417–430 (2011). https://doi.org/10.1016/j.destud. 2011.03.003

5. Miaskiewicz, T., Luxmoore, C.: The use of data-driven personas to facilitate organizational adoption–a case study. Des. J. **20**, 357–374 (2017). https://doi.org/10.1080/14606925.2017.1301160

6. Pruitt, J., Adlin, T.: The Persona Lifecycle: Keeping People in Mind Throughout Product Design. Morgan Kaufmann, San Francisco (2006)

7. Weiss, R.S.: Learning from strangers: the art and method of qualitative interview studies. Simon and Schuster (1995)

8. Salminen, J., Jansen, B.J., An, J., Kwak, H., Jung, S.-G.: Are personas done? Evaluating their usefulness in the age of digital analytics. Persona Studies **4**(2), 47–65 (2018). https://doi.org/10.21153/psj2018vol4no2art737

9. Salminen, J., Guan, K., Jung, S.-G., Chowdhury, S.A., Jansen, B.J.: A literature review of quantitative persona creation. In: Proceedings of the 2020 CHI Conference on Human Factors in Computing Systems (CHI '20), pp. 1–14 (2020). https://doi.org/10.1145/3313831.3376502

10. Salminen, J., Santos, J.M., Kwak, H., An, J., Jung, S.G., Jansen, B.J.: Persona perception scale: development and exploratory validation of an instrument for evaluating individuals' perceptions of personas. Int. J. Hum Comput Stud. **141**, 102437 (2020). https://doi.org/10.1016/j.ijhcs.2020.102437

11. Roto, V., Kaasinen, E., Nuutinen, M., Seppänen, M.: UX expeditions in business-to-business heavy industry: lessons learned. In: Proceedings of the 2016 CHI Conference Extended Abstracts on Human Factors in Computing Systems, pp. 833–839 ((2016))

Reflecting on Collaboration in Participatory Design Facilitation

Klaudia Çarçani(✉) and Susanne Stigberg

Department of Computer Science and Communication, Østfold University College,
Halden, Norway
{klaudia.carcani,susannks}@hiof.no

Abstract. While democratic practices, balancing powers, mutual learning and tools and techniques are the principles of Participatory Design (PD), they are all influenced by the practice of PD "facilitation" and the role of the facilitator(s). Facilitation in PD has been usually studied as a single entity with a facilitator that faces dilemmas in her/his role in relation to PD participants and her/his own motives and values. In this paper, we contribute to PD facilitation practice literature by studying facilitation as collaboration work compounded by many entities. We conducted a reflective analysis of the facilitation practices in two PD projects that we have managed. We found that PD projects have a multitude of facilitators. These facilitators belong to four categories: user experts, domain experts, PD experts and assistant facilitators. In time and in different PD activities facilitators may join or leave the project and also shift between categories while their expertise expands. We define this as "the network of facilitators" and discuss how such a perspective can help to improve the facilitation practice in PD.

Keywords: participatory design · facilitation · reflective practice · network of facilitators

1 Introduction

Participatory Design (PD) is a design discipline that builds on the principles of democratic and power balanced participation of stakeholders in the design process of technologies that will influence them and, as such, relies on facilitation to enable the interaction of people for and with which the design should happen [15]. In PD, we understand facilitation as a process of enabling a group of people to discuss, critique, and ideate visions about future lives with designers. Facilitated activities need to ensure the core principles of PD are applied in the co-design practice and that users participate equally in decision decision-making and the result [8]. Dahl and Sharma [4] state that "a person that facilitates such activities is typically referred to as the "facilitator," and they discuss six facets of a facilitator role: trust builder, enabler, inquirer, direction setter, value provider, and users' advocate. Participatory design facilitators significantly impact participatory activities, processes, and outcomes. While the position of the facilitator in a PD session is critical for PD, there is a continuous discussion on the implications that facilitators can have in a PD project as Dahl and Svanæs [5] state "what, whose and how perspectives and values become embedded in the results from participatory design activities". Light and Akama [11] call for a reorientation of PD research to acknowledge "the act of designing with groups of people involving embodied knowing - at once affective, experiential, phenomenological and significantly marked by slight shifts in context". Here, we will discuss how we understand facilitation in a PD project as a collaboration of facilitators shifting over time. We present two PD projects that we have facilitated as PD experts, discuss our reflective practice, and analyze collaboration in these two PD projects.

1.1 Facilitation in Participatory Design

Facilitation means "make easy, render less difficult," etymologically deriving from French, stemming from Latin facilis "easy to do," and facere "to do". Zimmerman and Evans [17] state that facilitation is one of the most misunderstood words upon which various definitions exist. In this paper, we discuss facilitation as a collaborative practice in Participatory Design. Participatory Design as a design discipline builds on the principles of democratic and power balanced participation of stakeholders in the design process of technologies that will influence them and, as such, relies on facilitation to enable the interaction of people for and with which the design should happen. Harvey et al. [9] have described facilitation as a dichotomic role, moving from doing tasks for others to enabling others. Facilitators in PD workshops by principle enable others. However, they achieve enabling by doing tasks that promote critical and creative thinking. Sibbet [14] defined facilitation as "the art of moving people through processes to agree-upon objectives in a manner that encourages participation, ownership and creativity from all". It is the art of facilitating PD projects that we reflect upon in this paper. We refer to a PD project as a project that applies an overall PD approach in achieving the result of designing a new technology or service for and with [1]. A PD project may be compounded by several activities that could be workshops or other design-led activities. We will refer to these as PD sessions. PD sessions stand under the umbrella of a PD project.

2 Method

Reflective practice is 'learning through and from experience towards gaining new insights of self and practice' [7]. Dewey [6] was among the first to identify reflection as a specialized form of thinking. He considered reflection to stem from doubt, hesitation, or perplexity related to a directly experienced situation and stresses how we learn from 'doing', i.e. practice. Schön [12, 13], in his explorations of a designer's practice and how designers think in practice, defined reflection as a method to move from one design cycle to another until one reaches a final product. Schön proposes two types of reflection that contribute to the advancement of design work: reflection-in-action referring to the act of thinking and doing while in action, and reflection-on-action referring to the analysis of a design move after the process has happened. We have applied Schön's notion of reflection-on-action to reflect on facilitation in two PD projects where we have been lead researchers, and we have collaborated with other stakeholders to maintain a PD approach to enable people's participation throughout the project. We did our reflective analysis in three steps. The first step was conducted as the projects unfolded, including documentation of reflections-on-action and reflection-in-action for each of the PD sessions (e.g. [3]). We used these findings to focus on those reflections that referred to facilitation or facilitators. We grouped our findings into major themes. Once we defined a theme with little discourse in the PD community, we focused on the theme and did another cycle of analysis in each of the two projects to explore different facets of the theme. We have chosen a storytelling approach to share our findings by exemplifying findings with vignettes from our PD projects. We were inspired by the concept of method stories [10], where Lee calls on the design field to "reflect and re-specify its research direction for design methods, especially for empathic design methods, that is, not by developing new tools or pinning-down practices into recipes, but rather towards empowering designers to be more sensitive and comfortable with the design-led, local approaches that are essential to empathic design methods".

3   Two Cases of Participatory Design Projects

3.1   Project Rehab: Designing a Cooperative Rehabilitation for People with Mild Acquired Cognitive Impairments (MACI)

This was a four-year project between our University and a Rehabilitation Hospital in Norway (RH). The aim of the project was to design a tool that could be used by patients with MACI and their healthcare practitioners during the rehabilitation journey. MACI people had developed cognitive challenges after an acquired brain injury caused by traumatic or non-traumatic reasons. They were in need and could strongly benefit from rehabilitation and that is why they were invited to attend a rehabilitation program at RH. As part of the project, several workshops were organized with a) patients alone (3 workshops), b) healthcare practitioners (2 workshops) and c) the two user groups at once (2 workshops). The aim of the workshops was to understand current practices of rehabilitation and to facilitate patients and healthcare practitioners to express needs and wishes they had for a collaborative tool that would empower patients to take control of their rehabilitation by becoming the ones steering their rehabilitation process with the continuous support of healthcare practitioners. Different methods, techniques and tools were applied in the workshops. A detailed description of the workshops is provided in [3]. At the ideation stage of the project, two researchers from our university, a medical doctor and the head of the cognitive unit at RH were involved. Based on RH's values and the research experience of RH, they decided that the best approach for the project would be applying Participatory Design. The junior researcher was responsible for planning and handling all the PD sessions developed as part of the project. The senior researcher was continuously involved in discussion, ideation and planning through critical brainstorming sessions. At RH, a working group (steering committee) was assigned to work on the planning of activities in a way to represent the voice of patients and clinicians from the start. A healthcare practitioner member of the steering committee with a profession as an occupational therapist with deep knowledge of patient needs, processes at the hospital and the necessity of the tool to be designed started immediately collaborating with the PD researcher planning the PD sessions. The rest of the steering committee was consulted for decision-making. The healthcare practitioner became the point of contact with the work group at RH. She supported the setting up of the venue and, together with other members of the steering committee, invited participants to the workshops. During the patient workshops, a patient language and communication therapist was invited to support patients' understanding of the activities and guarantee patients' well-being. We call this role "the knowledgeable third party" [2]. The PD researcher and the knowledgeable third-party facilitated the three PD sessions with the patients. On the other hand, the two workshops with the healthcare practitioners were facilitated by the PD researcher and the healthcare practitioner, who had contributed to the planning and preparing everything for the workshops. In the last two patient-healthcare practitioners PD sessions, the healthcare practitioner and the PD researcher were planning the workshops. Another person from the work group facilitated the distribution and review of invitations to the workshops (Fig. 1).

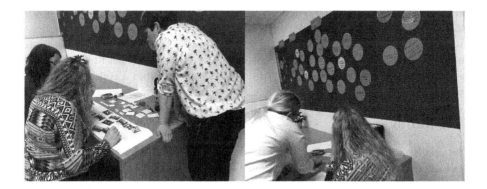

Fig. 1. Two facilitators involved in the workshop interacting with the same group

The PD researcher and healthcare practitioner facilitated together the PD sessions by distributing tasks and having the responsibility to be available around the room for each of the participants. Meanwhile, a researcher colleague from the university came to facilitate logistics, distribution of tools and make sure that all recorders and cameras were working as they should. The senior researcher, the medical doctor at the hospital and the head of the cognitive unit at RH were involved in discussing the PD sessions and outcomes after each workshop as reflective practice.

3.2 Project SmartWater: Enabling Citizens' Involvement in Envisioning the Function of New Smart Water Meters Implemented in Their Municipality

The project is ongoing and part of the smart city initiative, a collaborative effort of the municipality, university, National Energy Institute, and local businesses and innovation organizations. To secure the goal of a zero-emission society, adapt to climate change, safeguard democracy, create new jobs and safeguard an aging population, the digitization of society will be one of several important instruments. The SmartWater project focuses on giving citizens a voice when it comes to the introduction of new water meters in municipality households. So far, water has been a shared resource for all citizens. Digital water meters open opportunities to make consumption visible and create new services and products. This visibility can have both positive and negative aspects, which are addressed in the project. So far, we have implemented the first workshop using design fiction to explore three relevant themes: environment, security, and privacy (see Fig. 2). The project is led by the project owner from the municipality (PO), the project coordinator at a local innovation organization (PC) and 3 PD researchers from the university (PDR). There have been several meetings to agree on common objectives, create a common understanding of participatory design and plan the facilitation of the first workshop. The PDRs facilitated the PD activities during the workshop. The PO was responsible for inviting citizens. The PC organized the infrastructure, such as location, equipment, and catering for the workshop. She documented the overall process as well as the communication between facilitators. After the workshop, the PC took care of an evaluation and documentation of the workshop results. The outcome of the first workshop was disseminated both for research and industry and created a common case for further PD activities in the project.

4   Findings

The practice of facilitation in PD is often discussed in a singular form, though in most cases, it is not a one-man show. From the analysis of our cases, we understand facilitation as collaboration work, compounded by a network of facilitators. The practice of facilitation often involves different facilitators that contribute to the planning, ideation, operationalization, arrangement and evaluation of a PD session, even if not all are actually facilitating a PD session.

4.1   Categories of Facilitators

Based on the analysis of the PD process and facilitators that contributed to the Rehab and SmartWater projects, we found the following categories of facilitators:

Fig. 2. Citizens discussing design fiction scenarios.

Domain Experts are people that have knowledge of the overall context of the project, insights on user(s) groups and the context in which the design should take place. They are valuable in ideating and planning PD sessions. We see domain experts in both projects. In the Rehab project, the steering committee at RH represents this category. In the SmartWater project, both the PO and PC helped organize the PD workshop. Domain experts may or may not be present during each PD session, but they pre-facilitate these activities to go smoothly and as planned. Considering their domain knowledge, these facilitators play a vital role also in PD session facilitation of activities. Such an example is the healthcare practitioner in the rehab project, who started with no background in participatory design, but, through collaboration with the PD researcher, was able to facilitate a PD session together with the PD researcher in the later project. Domain experts are also the medical doctor and the head of the cognitive unit, who participated in the ideation and evaluation of the workshops and their outcomes. The motivation of domain experts is to situate the PD project in the domain, assure that domain values and perspectives are represented and brought out for discussion and make the results valuable for the domain.

Users Experts participate in PD sessions as users' advocates but do not act as users' proxies. Instead, they participate in the session to make sure that users have the support needed to express themselves better. These facilitators may be from different disciplines depending on the people involved in the session. User experts play an especially important role in projects with vulnerable groups. The example of the knowledgeable third party in the Rehab project belongs to this category. The involvement of user experts is motivated by the necessity to guarantee that the users are able to represent their ideas and influence decision-making throughout the PD sessions. This category can be involved in facilitating the planning of the right techniques and tools for the right user group as well as be present during PD sessions.

Participatory Design Experts contribute to keep aligned and facilitate the PD approach of the project. The PD researchers are considered the participatory design experts in both projects. In both projects, there were multiple PD researchers involved in the discussion, ideation and planning of PD sessions. In the Rehab project, only one PD researcher facilitated the PD session, whereas, in the SmartWater workshop, all three PD researchers collaborated in the workshop facilitation. Participatory design experts are motivated by their research interest in understanding and developing PD practices in general or in the specific context of the project. The aim of the researcher in the rehab project was to develop PD methods that balance powers in a PD session between MACI and their healthcare practitioners. In the smart water meter project, the research objective is to explore methods that support citizen engagement in innovation projects in local communities.

Assistant Facilitators support with the infrastructure of logistics of the PD sessions. In the rehab project, this was a fellow research colleague. In the Smart-Water project, the PC helped to secure the location, material and equipment. They do not have a central role in the project but are available to provide administrative support. This can be professional companies or just a colleague that has the possibility to help in a specific situation.

4.2   A Network of PD Facilitators

Our reflections-on-action of the two projects show that the facilitation of a PD project involves several facilitators who contribute in different ways and whose motivations vary. We do not claim that these categories of facilitators are complete. Instead, we want to highlight that the facets described by Dahl and Sharma [4] can be embodied by different facilitators in PD projects. Hence, a PD project involves what we will define as "the network of facilitators" in PD practice.

In Fig. 3, we present a chronological diagram of the Rehab project activities and the respective facilitators that have been involved in each of the activities. As described above, the project consisted of three types of workshops - patients workshops, healthcare practitioners workshops and patients and healthcare practitioners workshops. Each of these PD activities in the diagram has been divided into three phases that have been relevant in ensuring the PD approach - preparation, PD session, and reflection on action on the work of the facilitator and the PD experience.

Each of the gray boxes shows which facilitators were involved in that specific activity. The project was initiated in 2017 and in the ideation phase, both researchers were involved together with the lead medical doctor from RH and the head of the cognitive unit. RH interest in participatory approaches and the

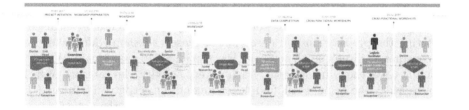

Fig. 3. Network of facilitators visualized in relation to project timelines and activities for project Rehab

aim of empowering patients in their rehabilitation process was in line with two PD researchers' interest in the politics of design and the use of technology in empowering marginalized user groups. While the direction of the project was set, in the second phase of the preparation of the patient workshops, the senior PD researcher and the medical doctor moved more to the background. Meanwhile, new facilitators joined the team - such as the domain experts steering committee and the occupational therapist, or took more responsibilities - such as the junior PD researcher and the head of the cognitive unit. The domain experts committee, the head of the cognitive unit and the occupational therapist had a crucial role in the planning. However, they were not the ones visible during the PD sessions organized with the patients. In that activity, the knowledgeable third party joined the facilitators' team together with the junior PD researcher. For the patients, these two facilitators were the ones that handled the participating activities. The choice to have only two facilitators was to not overwhelm the patient participants during these sessions and also not have any healthcare practitioner figure that would influence the patients' engagement in the session. In the next activity of reflections on action, the occupational therapist, the head of the cognitive unit, the domain experts committee and the senior researchers reentered to the facilitators' network. The PD sessions with healthcare practitioners were facilitated by the occupational therapist and the junior PD researcher, each leading a session of their own. Both had been working closely together during the preparation. This contributed to mutual learning and eventually prepared the occupational therapist to have a lead facilitator role in the PD sessions. Meanwhile, during the healthcare practitioners' workshops, the head of the cognitive unit had returned to his RH role and blended with the co-workers as a participant in the workshop. Meanwhile, there was no need for a knowledgeable third party in this specific activity, so the facilitator left the network. The timeline in Fig. 3 provides a perspective on the time that it took among activities. PD projects usually cover long timelines. During this time, the status of engaged facilitators might change. The occupational therapist that had a crucial role in the facilitation of the project during patients' and healthcare practitioners' workshops moved to another role within the hospital during the reflection on action of the healthcare practitioners' workshops. Some co-reflection took place after the workshops, but she was not involved in the in-depth analysis. A year after while we had new plans for the cross-functional workshops, she was reassigned to work on the project and eventually engaged in facilitating the preparation and execution of those workshops. Meanwhile, the only constant facilitator in all activities was the junior PD researcher. While the junior PD researcher's involvement was in every activity, the category of facilitation to which she belonged shifted depending on the activity and in time. For example, while having the role of the only lead facilitator in the patients' workshop, it shared the lead facilitation in the other two sets of workshops, healthcare practitioners and the cross-functional workshops. Moreover, while the junior PD researcher started the project belonging to the PD experts category, in time also started moving toward the user expert category and the domain expert category as her knowledge about the patients and the rehabilitation process broadened. On the other hand, the occupational therapist that started the project belonging to the domain experts and user experts category of facilitation toward the end of the project also moved to the participatory design experts category. The process of mutual learning in time contributed to such shifts in facilitation roles.

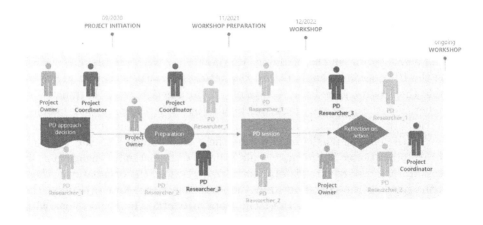

Fig. 4. Network of facilitators visualized in relation to project timelines and activities for project SmartWater

In Fig. 4, we visualize the network of facilitators in the SmartWater project. Similarly, as above, a multitude of facilitators was involved. The facilitators' roles and involvement changed over time. For example, the PD researcher_3 was not part of the network of facilitators during the workshop despite it contributed to the preparation and setting up of the room. The presence was influenced by health issues. For the participants in the workshop, PD researcher_3 was invisible in the process as there were no direct interactions. In the reflective analysis of the facilitators' experience during the workshop, we found that the two PD experts experienced a feeling of confidence and trust in each other as they had the opportunity to add on each other and make joint decisions. After the workshop, the reflection on action were debated between five stakeholders with different perspectives and motivations. Such reflections contributed to rich discussions, mutual learning between facilitators, and uncovering a variety of themes of the facilitation process and results.

Gleaned from the above analysis, we conclude that the network of facilitators is characterized by the following:

- a multitude of facilitators
- the facilitators' involvement in a PD project variate in time and based on the activity
- facilitators might change category (as described in the previous subsection) in time and per PD activity
- facilitators may have a visible role in facilitating PD sessions or provide support in the background to assure the implementation of a PD session and overview the process of the PD project. We will define the latest as "invisible facilitators" (the concept of invisible facilitators was inspired by Anselm Strauss, invisible work [16]).

4.3   Tensions in the Network of PD Facilitators

In both projects, the different facilitators who contribute with different roles are crucial for the well-organization of the PD sessions. However, common in collaborative work, tensions arose in both projects. Looking at the network of facilitators in our PD projects, tensions originate from differences in motivation, values and perspectives. Such tensions were addressed with techniques of mutual learning and negotiation as part of our reflective practices. Highlighting and consciously making choices to address tensions is decisive to the principle of power balance and democratic design practices in PD. The involvement of domain experts as facilitators is relevant to the project context but needs to be balanced to not impose pre-defined ideas for PD session outcomes. PD expert facilitators contribute to safeguarding PD principles such as power balance and democratic design decisions by applying the PD mindset as well as PD tools and techniques. PD tools need to be discussed among the facilitators, especially user experts facilitators who should ensure that no unsuitable PD activities are planned for certain participants which could undermine the democratic process. In the Rehab project, the network of facilitators contributed to discussing PD activities to avoid elements that may affect MACI patients' ability to co-design on equal terms as their healthcare practitioners. Occasionally, PD researchers took the role of user's advocate as well, to assure that the values of all groups were considered equally. In the SmartWater project, the PD researchers and the PO had initially different views on the deliverables of the PD sessions even though there was a formal agreement on the objectives of the project. Through several meetings, all facilitators negotiated common goals that would provide valuable knowledge for both the municipality and the researchers.

5   Conclusion

In this position paper, we reflect on PD project facilitation as collaboration, presenting four types of facilitators (domain experts, users experts, participatory design experts and assistant facilitators) taking on different facets as presented by Dahl and Sharma [4] (trust builder, enabler, inquirer, direction setter, value provider, as well as user's advocate). It is crucial that Participatory design experts ensure that PD principles are upheld and take on a leading role in all six facets. However, we observed that other facilitators also contribute to each facet. User experts play a vital role in projects involving vulnerable groups and support participatory design experts in building trust, enabling participants, and adding value through their knowledge of the user group. They support to design activities for inquiring into users' needs and can situate user needs. Domain experts can situate the PD project in the domain and assure that domain values and perspectives are represented and brought out for discussion to make the results valuable for the project and contribute to setting directions.

We see both opportunities and challenges with these collaborations. On one hand, it can improve the facilitation and outcomes of PD projects by involving facilitators with different knowledge and expertise. On the other hand, we experienced tensions in the network of facilitators that needed to be negotiated to ensure the continuation of the PD project. While this paper initiates the discussion on facilitation as collaboration work among a network of facilitators, we are aware that more research in different PD settings and different PD projects is needed. We want to invite other researchers to look into more themes of PD facilitation as a network of facilitators with the aim to contribute to facilitation practices that enable PD principles.

Acknowledgement. We would like to give special thanks to the participants and partners of the included projects. Acknowledgments also go to Joakim Karlsen, the lead researcher in the SmartWater project. The presented PD projects are covered by the Norwegian Personal Data Act (Sect. 31) and approved by the Norwegian Centre for Research Data (NSD).

References

1. Bratteteig, T.: Design for, med og av brukere: å inkludere brukere i design av informasjonssystemer. Universitetsforlaget (2021)
2. Carçani, K., Holone, H.: A participatory design "Method Story": the case of patients living with mild acquired cognitive impairments. In: ACHI 2019, The Twelfth International Conference on Advances in Computer-Human Interactions, pp. 210–217 (2019)
3. Carçani, K., Holone, H.: Guidelines for participatory design with people living with mild acquired cognitive impairments. Int. J. Adv. Intell. Syst. **13**(1&2), 59–84 (2020)

4. Dahl, Y., Sharma, K.: Six facets of facilitation: participatory design facilitators' perspectives on their role and its realization. In: Proceedings of the 2022 CHI Conference on Human Factors in Computing Systems. CHI 22, New York, NY, USA, pp. 1–14. Association for Computing Machinery, April 2022. https://doi.org/10.1145/3491102.3502013

5. Dahl, Y., Svanæs, D.: Facilitating democracy: concerns from participatory design with asymmetric stakeholder relations in health care. In: Proceedings of the 2020 CHI Conference on Human Factors in Computing Systems. CHI 2020, pp. 1–13, New York, NY, USA. Association for Computing Machinery, April 2020. https://doi.org/10.1145/3313831.3376805

6. Dewey, J.: How We Think: A Restatement of the Relation of Reflective Thinking to the Educative Process. D.C. Heath (1933)

7. Finlay, L.: Reflecting on 'Reflective practice'. publisher: Practice-based Professional Learning Paper 52, The Open University (2008)

8. Greenbaum, J., Kensing, F.: Heritage: Having a Say, pp. 41–56. Routledge (2012)

9. Harvey, G., et al.: Getting evidence into practice: the role and function of facilitation. J. Adv. Nurs. **37**(6), 577–588 (2002). https://doi.org/10.1046/j.1365-2648.2002.02126.x

10. Lee, J.J.: The true benefits of designing design methods. Art. J. Des. Pract. **3**(2), 5.1–5.12 (2014). https://doi.org/10.14434/artifact.v3i2.3951/art.3.2.5.1_1

11. Light, A., Akama, Y.: The human touch: participatory practice and the role of facilitation in designing with communities. In: Proceedings of the 12th Participatory Design Conference: Research Papers - Volume 1. PDC 2012, New York, NY, USA, pp. 61–70. Association for Computing Machinery, August 2012. https://doi.org/10.1145/2347635.2347645

12. Schön, D.A.: The Reflective Practitioner: How Professionals Think in Action. Routledge, London (2017). https://doi.org/10.4324/9781315237473

13. Schön, D.A., Wiggins, G.: Kinds of seeing in designing. Creat. Innovat. Manage. **1**(2), 68–74 (1992). https://doi.org/10.1111/j.1467-8691.1992.tb00031.x

14. Sibbet, D.: Principles of Facilitation: The Purpose and Potential of Leading Group Process by David Sibbet. The Grove Consultants International, February 2002

15. Simonsen, J., Robertson, T.: Participatory Design: An Introduction, pp. 21–38. Routledge (2012)

16. Strauss, A.: Work and the division of labor. Sociol. Quart. **26**(1), 1–19 (1985). https://www.jstor.org/stable/4106172

17. Zimmerman, A.L., Evans, C.J.: Facilitation?: From Discussion to Decision. Nichols Pub Co, East Brunswick (1992)

Analysis of User Participatory Design and Gamification in Modern Media

Xiandong Cheng[1]([✉]), Hao He[2], and Yushan Jiang[1]

[1] Beijing City University, Hai Dian District, No. 269 Bei Si Huan Zhong Lu, Beijing, China
`doudesign@126.com`
[2] Central Academy of Fine Arts, No. 8 Hua Jia Di Nan Street, Chao Yang District, Beijing, China

Abstract. The rapid advancement in digital technology has greatly transformed the modern media industry. In this era of multimedia convergence, the media industry is experiencing a significant revolution, with changes in the channels and forms of mass participation. Currently, short videos on the internet have become the main form of media. The emergence and growth of short videos in recent years have led to the establishment of many short video platforms both domestically and internationally. Lightweight and easily accessible short videos now occupy a significant portion of our leisure time and have become the preferred method for obtaining information. Additionally, participatory design and gamification communication play an increasingly significant role in people's lives and cognitive processes. Each generation of new media thrives on technology, and short videos are no exception. The widespread use of mobile devices and the maturity of 5G technology have greatly impacted the media landscape, solidifying short video platforms as a dominant form of contemporary media and shaping the lifestyles of younger generations. This paper aims to analyze the randomly recommended content on short video platforms, interpret the content production, design, communication method, interaction form, audience psychology, and industry influence, and present the research outcomes in the form of information visualization. The analysis reveals the clear advantages of short videos, such as the ability to access information anytime and anywhere with ease. The openness of short video platforms provides a relatively equal platform for everyone to gain attention, but it also brings fragmented thinking patterns, closed cognitive states, and impulsive emotions. Ultimately, the paper interprets the medium of short videos from the perspectives of participatory design and gamification communication to help individuals better understand and reflect on their use.

Keywords: Short Videos · Participatory Design · Gamification Communication

1 Introduction

The application of science and technology in the media field has revolutionized traditional forms of media such as radio, television, and newspapers. The widespread use of mobile internet applications and electronic display screens has made digital media a dominant means of communication. This new type of media is characterized by its reliance on computer networks, use of digital multimedia technology and modern communication technology, and presentation of digital and multimedia information. The internet, as a new form of media, offers unique experiences and opportunities with its powerful functions and diverse forms. This paper explores the medium of short video through the lenses of participatory design and gamification communication to enhance understanding and deeper reflection.

1.1 Significant Features of Modern Media

The growth and integration of the internet have deepened people's understanding of network media. The progress of information technology has driven the advancement of network media technology, making it a multi-level, multi-faceted, and comprehensive means of information communication. This includes various forms of media such as text, sound, graphics, images, animation, and more.

Key Characteristics of Modern Media:

- Diversity: Modern media encompasses both traditional forms (such as newspapers and television) and new forms (such as the internet and social media).
- Interconnectivity: Modern media forms are interconnected and can interact and communicate across different platforms.
- Globalization: Contemporary media has the potential to transcend national borders and reach global audiences.
- Instantaneity: Modern media usually reports and disseminates information in real-time.
- Digitization: Many modern media are digitized and can be stored and accessed online.

Short videos have gained widespread popularity in modern society due to their fast speed of dissemination, broad coverage, rich content, high interactivity, and large information volume. From a mass communication perspective, short videos serve as both a tool for information exchange and an important means for people to understand and transform the world. The impact of short videos is a new phenomenon in the dissemination process, shaped by the characteristics of network communication. Its sensory appeal caters to the diverse needs of audiences, leading to a diversified reception of information. The internet has changed the way people access information, and short videos continue to influence people's lifestyles and work habits.

1.2 User Participatory in Design

User Participation in Design refers to a design approach where users are actively involved in the design of products, services, or systems. This approach emphasizes collaboration between designers and users, giving users a voice in the design process and allowing them to shape and co-create the final solution. The objective of User Participation in Design is to ensure that the final product is centered around the user and addresses their needs and desires.

This approach involves understanding user behavior, gathering feedback, and incorporating user insights to create solutions that enhance user experience. User Participation in Design emphasizes collaboration, making the design process a shared experience between designers and users. By taking user perspectives into consideration, this approach results in solutions tailored to the specific needs of users and a more user-friendly experience.

1.3 Gamification Communication

Gamification in communication refers to the use of game elements and mechanics, such as points, leaderboards, rewards, and challenges, to engage and motivate individuals to participate in a specific behavior or activity. It is often used in marketing, advertising, and other forms of communication to increase brand awareness, improve customer engagement, and drive behavior change. The aim of gamification in communication is to make the experience more enjoyable and entertaining for the target audience, while also achieving the desired outcome.

2 The Transformation of Modern Media by the Internet

Modern media encompasses both traditional and emerging forms of media used in contemporary society. While traditional media refers to well-established mediums in human history, emerging media is a new form of media that has emerged and developed with the advent of information technology. The internet, known as the "fourth media," has played a major role in transforming modern media by giving rise to new media and transforming old media.

The omnipresence and dynamic nature of information technology have drastically changed the media landscape, with the internet leading the way as the driving force behind new media. This has led to a surge in news websites and mobile communication, resulting in new achievements and changes in the media industry. The continuous development of new media, represented by the internet and social media, is changing the behavior of audiences in their daily lives, work, and learning.

The modern media landscape encompasses a wide range of information carriers, including books, magazines, newspapers, advertisements, posters, broadcast, film and television, communication, computers, and the internet. These carriers range from 2D to 3D, from static to dynamic, forming a complete multimedia system that seamlessly integrates visual and auditory elements.

In conclusion, the rise of the internet and new media is driving the development and change of modern media, leading to the decline of traditional media and the rise of emerging media. The modern media landscape is a diverse and dynamic system that seamlessly integrates different forms of media to provide a comprehensive multimedia experience.

2.1 The Evolution of Media: From Print to Electronic to Digital

From Print to Radio and TV

The media has undergone significant transformations, evolving from print newspapers to radio and TV. In the early 20th century, newspapers dominated as the primary source of information, including local and national news, entertainment, and advertising. However, with the development and widespread adoption of radio, it emerged as an alternative source of information and entertainment. The 1950s marked the rise of TV as the dominant form of mass media, offering a visually immersive experience. With advancements in technology, TV signals could be transmitted over long distances, leading to a global impact on society.

From TV to Internet

The 1990s saw the widespread adoption of personal computers and the World Wide Web, leading to a transition from TV to the internet. This shift moved from a broadcast-based information model to a decentralized, interactive one, allowing for access and contribution to a wealth of content. Social media, video sharing platforms, and online news sources have revolutionized the media industry, creating new forms of interaction and collaboration between content creators and consumers. The rise of the internet has enabled people to access and consume media at any time, blurring the traditional division between TV and the internet.

From Internet to Mobile

The move from desktop Internet to mobile was driven by the rise of mobile devices, such as smartphones and tablets, as well as the advancement of wireless networks and mobile broadband technology. This change made accessing the Internet more convenient and accessible, as users could now connect from anywhere, anytime. The increase in popularity of mobile devices and mobile internet also led to the creation of new forms of media and communication, including social media, mobile gaming, and mobile commerce.

The Rise of Short Videos in Media

The transformation of media has led to the emergence of short videos. High-quality cameras on smartphones and widespread internet access have allowed for the creation and sharing of short-form video content. Social media platforms such as TikTok, Instagram, and Snapchat have made short videos popular, changing the way media is consumed. These platforms offer easily accessible and shareable content on multiple devices, leading to changes in content creation and consumption, and the advertising and entertainment industries.

Short videos have disrupted the traditional media model by challenging its distribution and monetization. This has resulted in new players, like social media platforms, entering the industry. Short videos also require a different style of storytelling and a focus on visual appeal, changing the media production process.

Short videos offer new opportunities for creative expression and have democratized media production. They empower individuals to create and share their own content, increasing the diversity of voices and perspectives in media.

2.2   The Impact of Short Videos on Today's Society

Industry Perspective

From an industry perspective, the surge of short videos has had a profound impact on the media industry. The convenience and cost-effectiveness of creating, sharing, and distributing short videos through social media platforms have disrupted traditional media models and presented businesses with a new avenue to reach their target audience.

With the widespread use of mobile internet, short videos have become a favored means of consuming and advertising content. As a result, many traditional media companies have had to adjust their strategies and integrate short videos into their marketing strategies. This shift has also created new job opportunities and revenue streams in the media industry, including content creation, production, and distribution.

Short videos have become the most sought-after form of information dissemination. They offer a new level of accessibility, speed, and interactivity in the way people consume information. Thanks to advancements in internet technology, anyone can now participate in creating and sharing short videos. This new form of information dissemination not only transforms the traditional methods of obtaining information but also influences the way people perceive and accept information. This new form of information consumption has become a ubiquitous lifestyle that has a far-reaching impact on society.

User Perspective

From the perspective of users, short videos have exerted a considerable influence on the way people engage with and consume media. The advent of platforms such as Tik-Tok and Instagram Reels has ushered in a new era of content consumption that prioritizes conciseness, creativity, and interaction. The ease of creating short videos and the ability to share and discover content through social media networks has made short videos a favored means of self-expression and communication for individuals.

In addition, short videos have reshaped the advertising and marketing industry, as brands now utilize them as an effective tool to reach and connect with their target audience. The proliferation of short videos in people's lives has made them the mainstream form of information consumption for the younger generation. This evolution underscores the changing nature of society and the way it consumes information. Additionally, short videos allow individuals to access new knowledge and information anytime and anywhere, altering the methods of production and communication in society. It's worth mentioning, however, that some short videos may also impact people's values and beliefs (Fig. 1).

Production Perspective

The growth of short videos has resulted in a significant increase in video production, with individuals and companies readily producing and distributing their content through social media and online platforms. This provides new opportunities for content creators and businesses, but also poses challenges such as competition in a crowded market and the potential for the spread of false information. Additionally, the widespread adoption of short videos has changed people's media consumption habits, resulting in a preference for visually appealing, brief content.

The advent of short videos has impacted both the production process and content of videos. As short videos are typically easier and quicker to produce and share, they have

User Scale and its Forecast of China Micro-Video Industry from 2017 to 2021

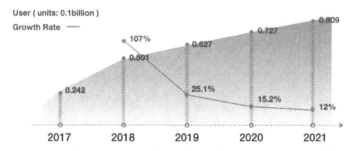

Fig. 1. User Scale and its Forecast of China Micro-Video Industry from 2017 to 2021[1]. Data From: data.iimedia.cn. Chart Design by Xiandong Cheng.

democratized the video production process, enabling a wider range of individuals and organizations to create and publish videos. Furthermore, the popularity of short videos has also led to a diversification of content, offering a wider range of options to cater to the interests of diverse audiences.

In contrast to traditional video production, which follows a script-filming-post-production-publishing process, short videos can be created and published without a script and can be recorded directly by the user. They can also be produced through live streaming interactions with the audience, where users can participate in co-screen interactions, comments, retweets, likes, and more. Additionally, short videos can be edited with special effects during filming or undergo advanced modifications before being published.

Platform Perspective

From a platform perspective, the surge in popularity of short videos has brought about numerous changes and impacts. These videos have increased user engagement and interactivity, leading to enhanced user stickiness and activity on the platform. Additionally, they have enriched the platform's content forms and user experiences. Short videos also present new advertising and commercial opportunities, thereby increasing the platform's revenue and profitability. However, they also pose challenges such as content review and management and copyright protection.

In conclusion, short videos are a crucial driving force for the growth of network platforms and an integral part of the current media landscape. It is imperative for platform algorithms to be mindful of their influence on video traffic and distribution. The algorithms used by online platforms can significantly impact the viewership of videos, and it is crucial for content creators to be aware of these changes and adapt their strategies accordingly. Platform algorithms are designed to recommend and surface content that is relevant and engaging to users, and regular updates to these algorithms are necessary to better serve users' needs (Fig. 2).

---

[1] According to data from iiMedia Research, the number of Chinese short-video users has significantly increased in the past five years, surpassing 0.7 billion users in 2020 and expected to grow to 0.809 billion users in 2021. From: Data.iimedia.cn.

Market Scale and its Forecast of China Micro-Video Industry from 2017 to 2021

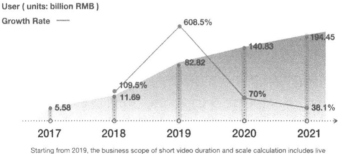

Fig. 2. Market Scale and its Forecast of China Micro-Video Industry from 2017 to 2021[2].Data From:data.iimedia.cn. Chart Design by Xiandong Cheng.

3   Project Research Analysis

The popularity of short video platforms, such as TikTok, Instagram Reels, and Snapchat, has seen a significant increase in recent years, especially among younger generations. These platforms are known for their short-form video content, typically 30 s or less in length, which provide users with a creative outlet to express themselves, share their daily lives, and connect with others through brief video clips. A research study in this field could examine user behavior, content creation and sharing trends, popular content patterns, and the societal and communicative impact of these short video platforms (Fig. 3).

According to the data analyzed by iiMedia Research, the micro-video market in China is expected to reach 140.83 billion yuan in 2020. The results of the survey on the most frequently used micro-video applications by the participants indicate that TikTok was the clear leader, with usage reported by 45.2% of the respondents, while Kwai came in second place with 17.9% usage.

The analysis of 100 Tik-Tok videos is intended to shed light on the current state of information dissemination via short video transmission. (Fig. 4) The essay will delve into various aspects of the videos, such as content, production, duration, presentation forms, gender, and influence. Information visualization will be employed to categorize and synthesize the findings, giving a comprehensive overview of the characteristics of modern information dissemination. Information visualization involves presenting data and information graphically, making it easier for individuals to comprehend and interpret complex information swiftly.

---

[2] In recent years, micro-video platforms have been consistently exploring business models. On the one hand, they have become innovative new media marketing platforms. On the other hand, they have ushered in a new growth point combined with live-streaming e-commerce. As the data of iiMedia Research showed, China's micro-video market will reach 140.83 billion yuan in 2020. From: Data.iimedia.cn.

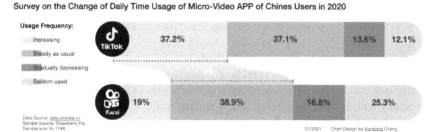

Survey on the Change of Daily Time Usage of Micro-Video APP of Chines Users in 2020

Fig. 3. Survey on the Change of Daily Time Usage of Micro-Video APP of Chines Users in 2020[3].Data From: data.iimedia.cn. Chart Design by Xiandong Cheng.

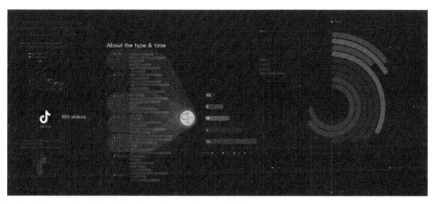

Fig. 4. Information Visualization. Short Video Platform Research.P1. Design by Yushan Jiang and Xiandong Cheng.2021

3.1 Factors Influencing Short Videos

The length of a short video is typically determined by a combination of several factors, including the platform's specific guidelines, the type of content being produced, and the goals of the content creator. Some platforms have specific time limits for short videos, such as 15 s or 60 s. Additionally, the type of content, such as a quick update, tutorial, or story, can also dictate the length of the video. The content creator's goals, such as providing information or entertainment, can also play a role in determining the length

---

[3] According to data from iiMedia Research, 37.2% of users are using Tik Tok more and more each day, while 37.1% and 38.9% of users use Tik Tok and Kwai about the same as usual. The iiMedia's analysts believe that short video apps have been gradually strengthening their maintenance of user stickiness and increasing their social attributes in recent years, therefore, users tend to increase their use of short video applications, and Tik Tok has increased users' satisfaction with the content and recognition of the platform, which drives users to increase their use time. From: data.iimedia.cn.

of the video. Factors such as audience attention span and the need for a longer or shorter video to effectively communicate the message can also impact the length.

The Impact of Content Factors on Short Videos

The typical length of short videos is relatively short, usually falling between 15 s and 3 min. This is due to the need to capture and sustain the viewer's attention, as viewers are not typically willing to invest a lot of time watching a single short video. However, the length of some short videos may exceed this range, depending on the content's position and the production objectives of the video.

Content factors have a significant impact on the length of short videos. The type of information being presented, the target audience, and the intended purpose of the video all contribute to determining the appropriate length. For example, educational videos may need to be longer to effectively communicate the information, while entertainment videos may be shorter to maintain the audience's interest. Advertisements, on the other hand, may be shorter and more focused on delivering a quick, memorable message, while tutorials may be longer to provide step-by-step instructions.

Statistics from a random sampling of short videos show that videos ranging from 15 to 30 s accounted for over 50%, while videos from 30 to 45 s accounted for about 22%, from 45 to 60 s accounted for about 16%, from 60 to 90 s accounted for about 7%, and videos over 90 s accounted for about 7%. This ratio is not solely the result of content factors. Most content is designed based on user demand, and user demand determines the content. This objectively reflects people's psychology today, as most people no longer have the patience to watch longer video content and need to access information in the shortest amount of time possible. Short and concise content is becoming increasingly popular as people have limited time and attention span. Quick and to-the-point video content is more likely to be watched and remembered. Furthermore, internet algorithms and commercial factors also play a role in determining the length of short videos, influencing what is considered engaging and profitable and driving the creation and promotion of content that meets these criteria.

The Impact of User Demand on Short Videos

The impact of user demand on short videos refers to the extent to which users' preferences and behaviors can influence the content and duration of these videos. For instance, if a significant number of users express a strong interest in watching videos on a particular topic, such as beauty or cooking, platforms and content creators may respond by producing more videos on that subject to satisfy this demand. Additionally, this user demand can also affect the format and duration of videos, as users may prefer shorter, more digestible content instead of longer, detailed pieces.

User needs drive the length of short videos. User needs play a crucial role in determining the length of short videos. As people's attention span shortens and they demand quick access to information, the popularity of short, concise videos has increased. To meet the needs of their audience and maintain their attention, content creators are increasingly focusing on producing videos that are short and straightforward. This trend has also been influenced by the rise of social media, where short videos are easier to share and engage with.

The content of the videos should aim to be inclusive and serve all people, but the gender perspective in today's short videos on the internet is evident. Some producers create short videos with controversial sexual content to appeal to their audience in exchange for more attention and traffic. This reflects the current state of short videos on the internet, where the content is often designed to attract attention and generate traffic, often by appealing to specific gender interests or using controversial themes.

The Impact of Business Factors on Short Videos

The impact of business factors on short videos refers to how business considerations, such as generating revenue and attracting users, can influence the content and format of these videos. This can include the incorporation of advertisements and promotions for products, the use of controversial themes and sensationalism to grab attention, and the targeting of specific demographics based on their interests and preferences. These factors can shape the overall content and quality of short videos, potentially leading to a narrow focus on profit over creating meaningful and educational content.

Business factors such as advertising and monetization also have a significant impact on short video content. Many short videos are created with the primary goal of generating revenue through advertising or other monetization methods, such as sponsored content. As a result, the content may be tailored to attract more views or clicks, leading to increased revenue. This can also influence the length of the video and the type of content that is produced.

Many live streams are for the purpose of selling, rather than sharing and communicating. There are also many videos that are longer than 1 min and have product or advertisement elements embedded in the story script. This underscores the influence of business factors in shaping the content of short videos. Companies and businesses use these videos as a marketing tool to promote their products and services, often using creative storytelling and engaging visuals to appeal to their audience. This can impact the quality and nature of the content that is produced, as commercial considerations take precedence over other factors. This has led to a situation where the platform has become a place where merchants can promote their products, but it can also be challenging for users to determine the quality of the products being offered.

The Impact of Data Algorithms on Short Videos

The impact of data algorithms refers to how algorithms used by short video platforms can influence the content and recommendations that users see. These algorithms are based on user behavior data such as viewing history, search terms, and likes, and they can shape users' viewing experiences by presenting them with content that is more likely to keep them engaged and spending more time on the platform. This can lead to users being exposed to a narrow range of content and opinions, and potentially missing out on diverse perspectives and ideas (Fig. 5).

Algorithms can also perpetuate harmful biases and perpetuate discrimination, particularly in terms of gender and ethnicity. If the training data used to develop the algorithms reflects these biases, they may be amplified and reinforced through the recommendations they generate, leading to a homogenized and biased view of the world. The impact of data algorithms on short video platforms is an area of ongoing concern and research,

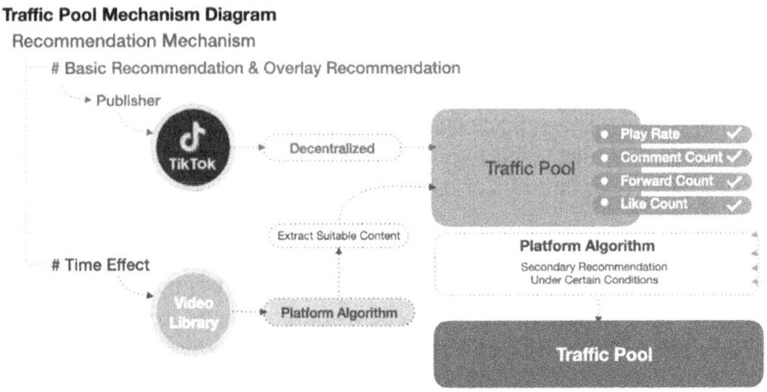

Fig. 5. Traffic Pool Mechanism Diagram.

and efforts are being made to ensure that these algorithms are transparent, fair, and free from bias.

3.2 Short Video and User-Participatory Design

The design of short videos, which incorporates a user-centered approach, means that users play both the role of producers and consumers of short video content. This is achieved by offering users tools to create and share their content on an open platform and by engaging them in content evaluation and generation through likes, comments, and other methods.

This user-centered design approach can enhance user engagement, encourage content diversity, and drive improvements in content quality through user interaction and evaluation. However, it's also crucial to address issues related to the review and management of user-generated content to ensure legality and safety.

3.3 Short Video and Gamification

Gamification in short videos refers to designing the content and features of short video platforms in a game-like experience, to attract and increase user engagement. This gamification design typically includes elements such as points systems, leaderboards, rewards mechanisms, and more, allowing users to earn rewards through activities such as creating, sharing, and commenting on content. The gamification approach encourages users to produce more content and increases platform activity through user competition and interaction.

Gamification design in short videos not only increases user engagement, but also enhances content diversity and quality, increases user loyalty and retention, and boosts the commercial value of the platform.

Excessive gamification can also impact the content and habits of short video users. The consequences of excessive gamification in short videos can Include:

- Addiction: Gamification can be highly engaging, but it can also lead to addiction, causing users to spend excessive amounts of time on the platform.

- Decreased content quality: The focus on earning rewards can lead to users creating low-quality content just to receive points, instead of putting effort into creating meaningful and entertaining content.
- Decreased diversity: Gamification may encourage users to create content that is popular or favored by the system, leading to a decrease in the diversity of content on the platform.
- Pressure to conform: Gamification can create pressure for users to conform to certain standards, leading to a homogenization of content.
- Decreased user privacy: Some gamification designs may require users to share personal information to take part, which can lead to a reduction in privacy for users.
- Legal and ethical concerns: Gamification designs can raise legal and ethical concerns, particularly if rewards are tied to personal data or if the platform is collecting and using user data in an unethical manner.

Therefore, it's important to carefully consider the balance between gamification and other factors, such as user experience, privacy, and ethics, to ensure that the gamification design does not have negative impacts on users and the platform.

4 Discussion

4.1 Content and Benefits

Induced by economic benefit, the Internet video platform early began to use the algorithm to push some extreme content to the user to provoke the user's attention. Because they find that controversial content is more likely to arouse people's discussion. This content results in higher data metrics, such as posts, comments, likes, and ad clicks.

The more controversial the content is, the more lucrative it becomes. The primary role of contemporary media is to generate controversial or sensational topics. When individuals are immersed in this kind of online media environment for an extended period, their attitudes and actions may become increasingly extreme, rigid, and confined, ultimately leading to societal division and fragmentation.

It is true that the use of algorithms to push controversial or extreme content can have negative consequences. The prioritization of this type of content by algorithms can result in the amplification of divisive and polarizing topics, leading to a further fragmentation of society. Additionally, exposure to a constant stream of extreme or sensational content can also impact a user's thoughts and behaviors, leading to a narrow-minded and potentially harmful perspective. It's important for platform operators and content creators to consider the potential impacts of their actions and to strive for promoting a more balanced and diverse media landscape.

4.2 Do Algorithms Have Values?

It certainly does. Algorithms themselves do not have values or beliefs as they are simply a set of instructions designed to carry out a specific task. However, the values and beliefs of the people who create and design algorithms can influence the outcome of the algorithm.

For example, if the creators of an algorithm have a certain bias or value system, they may design the algorithm in a way that reflects those biases.

The self-media era has made information generation, dissemination, and access easier. However, the information people receive is becoming increasingly limited, which is not due to how individuals obtain information but rather the algorithms used by platforms. The algorithms reflect the values of the platforms, and from a capitalist perspective, the values of the algorithms prioritize "Traffic First" and profit above all else. Futurist Marc Goodman stated that "If you control the code, you control the world," which may seem like an exaggeration but is also a reflection of the reality of the influence of algorithms in shaping our world.

There is a tension between the priorities of "Traffic First" and "Content First." Entertaining and popular content is more likely to go viral. It's important to keep in mind the influence of platform algorithms and the values they embody in shaping the information we receive. The current system prioritizes popular and entertaining content over thought-provoking and insightful content, which may get lost in the vast sea of information without intentional searches.

Algorithms play a dual role in shaping content on digital platforms - not only do they dictate the substance of the content, but they also influence the direction of content production. If a platform's algorithm prioritizes "Traffic," it will have a gradual impact on the motivation of the platform's content producers when creating content. The algorithms employed by platforms can greatly impact the way content is produced by creators. When a platform prioritizes traffic, for example, content creators may be inclined to choose topics and styles that are more likely to generate clicks, even if these don't align with their personal interests or goals. This can lead to a homogenization of content, reducing diversity on the platform.

Algorithms play a significant role in shaping the content and direction of production on digital platforms. If a platform's algorithm is "Traffic First", it will gradually affect the platform's content producers' motivation when creating content. It can have a noticeable impact on the motivations of content creators, particularly those creating short videos. Short video creators will always conjecture the psychological needs of users and consider the amount of traffic. The evaluation of the quality and value of the content itself is turned to the evaluation of the traffic.

Such an algorithm will only encourage producers to create more sensational or entertaining content and discourage them from producing insightful content because there is no traffic or revenue in doing so. For example, on a short video platform, online celebrities hold the traffic by using controversial, vulgar, or unrestrained content to attract attention and generate income. Many people are competing to become online celebrities.

This has already happened when Neil Postman[4] wrote Amusing Ourselves to Death (1985).When television replaced newspapers as the mainstream of communication, at least there was still some room for insightful content. Now, the attention of the public has been completely exhausted, but insightful content is increasingly of no interest to anyone. People do not even have the patience to finish an article of more than 500 words.

---

[4] Neil Postman (March 8, 1931 – October 5, 2003) was an American author, educator, media theorist and cultural critic.

4.3 Excessive Entertainment

Excessive entertainment refers to a situation where entertainment content dominates over more serious or informative content in media. This can lead to a reduction in the diversity of information and ideas that are being presented to the public and can have a negative impact on society by reducing the public's exposure to important issues and ideas. The trend towards excessive entertainment in the media is often driven by the pursuit of profit, as entertainment content is typically more popular and generates more revenue than serious or informative content. However, it can also be influenced by political or ideological factors, as governments or other powerful actors may seek to limit the exposure of the public to certain ideas or information.

China's investigation journalists have almost disappeared, and many mainstream media are busy making fast, funny, warm, positive short video which can satisfy the algorithms. The media landscape in China has been undergoing significant changes in recent years, with many mainstream media outlets focusing more on creating short videos that are designed to be popular on social media platforms. This trend is partly driven by the increasing importance of online platforms in disseminating news and information. As a result, investigative journalism has become more difficult in China.

When people receive fragmented videos and shallow articles every day for a long time, they will gradually lose their ability to think deeply and focus. There is a concept in communication science called Pseudo- Environment. It means that the media is somehow a simulation of the environment.

4.4 Data-Driven Artistic Creation

Data-driven artistic creation refers to the process of using data and technology as the primary source of inspiration and guidance in creating art. This type of creation typically involves collecting and analyzing large amounts of data and using algorithms, machine learning, and other computational techniques to generate creative outputs. The goal of data-driven artistic creation is to create art that is informed by data, patterns, and insights, and that incorporates elements of surprise and unpredictability. The impact of data-driven artistic creation can include a greater level of accuracy, objectivity, and efficiency in the creative process, as well as new and unique forms of expression that can challenge traditional notions of art (Figs. 6 and 7).

The widespread use of short videos and the popularity of social media platforms has had a significant impact on the music industry. The trend of using music in short videos has created new demand for music that is well-suited to the format, such as upbeat, energetic tracks that can be used to accompany 15–30 s clips. This has led to increased exposure and popularity for certain types of music and has created new opportunities for musicians and music creators. At the same time, the use of music in short videos also raises important legal and ethical questions about the use of copyrighted material in digital content.

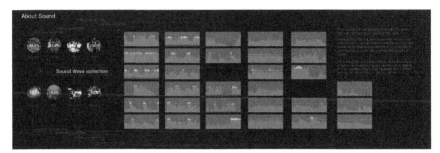

Fig. 6. Information Visualization. Short Video Platform Research. P6. About Sound. Design by Yushan Jiang and Xiandong Cheng. 2021

Fig. 7. Information Visualization. Short Video Platform Research. P6. About Sound. Design by Yushan Jiang and Xiandong Cheng. 2021

5   Conclusion

The popularity of short videos, represented by Tik-Tok, has skyrocketed in China, becoming the main source of information dissemination. Tik-Tok's daily active user target for 2021 was a staggering 680 million. With the rise of self-media, generating, disseminating, and accessing information has become increasingly effortless.

Gamification and user participatory design are two crucial trends in modern media communication that are revolutionizing the way people engage with media. These elements provide a more captivating and interactive experience for audiences, empowering them to play a more active role in the creation and consumption of media content. As a result, gamification and user participatory design are expected to continue to grow in significance in the future of media communication.

Algorithmic recommendations have permeated our daily lives, from e-commerce to takeout and from video sites to social platforms. News aggregation platforms driven by strong algorithms have surpassed traditional news platforms, and more and more people are relying on social media and short video apps for their information. Traffic is the most critical metric for these platforms.

In recent years, the popularity of algorithm-driven news aggregation platforms has increased as people are turning to social media and short video apps for their information. However, these platforms prioritize traffic, and their algorithms often prioritize sensational or controversial content, leading to a distorted representation of the news. This has had a significant impact on the media landscape and raised concerns about the reliability and accuracy of information being shared through these channels. It underlines the significance of media literacy and critical thinking skills, enabling users to evaluate the information they receive and make informed decisions.

Modern media has become faster and more convenient, and the era of self-media has also made the information content more democratic, more attention to people's lives. They are advantages. People have more self-control, but the interests of the platform behind the algorithm is why people gradually lose selectivity and creativity, which is undoubtedly. People cannot reject the algorithm; the key is how to make the algorithm more social valuable. We should domesticate the algorithms instead of being controlled by the algorithms.

It is important for social media platforms to carefully consider the content that they promote to users and to take steps to mitigate the potential harm that may result from the exposure to certain types of content. This may include implementing policies and systems to remove harmful content, providing information and resources to help users make informed decisions, and promoting positive and healthy content. By taking these steps, social media platforms can help to promote the well-being of their users and to create a safer and more positive online environment.

References

1. Analysis of China's Short Video Head Platform Development, EB/OL. www.data.iimedia.cn
2. A vision of crimes in the future, EB/OL. www.ted.com

Local Communities and Their Visitors: An Interaction Design Approach

Filipe Cruz[1]([⊠]) [iD] and Marco Neves[1,2] [iD]

[1] CIAUD, Research Centre for Architecture, Urbanism and Design, Lisbon School of Architecture, Universidade de Lisboa, Lisbon, Portugal
filipedacruz@gmail.com, mneves@fa.ulisboa.pt
[2] ITI/LARSyS, University of Lisbon, Lisbon, Portugal

Abstract. Digital age has changed the way we interact with space, allowing us to explore places all over the world without leaving home and to communicate with people instantly, regardless of distance. However, a lack of physical contact or experience of place can significantly contribute to the loss of local identity within a community and the absence of visitors. Interaction design can act significantly to promote localities, by enhancing interactions between human beings and environments (digital and non-digital). This paper aims to present opportunities for interaction design intervene in the context of a locality, by discussing how different design methods can be applied. Structured as a literature review, it revisits the main schools of thought and the scope of three different methods: persuasive techniques, design thinking and tangible interaction. It also proposes collaborative networks and connectivity as a possible focus of intervention, as the case study Route EN/N2 in Portugal suggests. We questioned whether a process that prioritizes comfort and human desires is the right practice when interaction design intervenes in territories. We also considered context mapping, facilitation techniques, and consequence anticipation, achievable through a humanity-centered design approach, as the most appropriate practices for achieving measures with greater long-term impact. This approach looks at humans not as individuals, but as part of a complex society with deep-rooted systems and issues of sustainability, inclusion, accessibility, and representation. Our goal is to promote understanding of interaction design as a behavior facilitator, able to generate new experiences for its participants and attract others, making a territory more understandable, attractive and memorable. Opening space for new interactive models, this paper analyzes the importance of creating new relationships and collaborations as a method of decoding and understanding a local community.

Keywords: interaction design · design methods · design for territories · humanity-centered design

1 Introduction

Territory is the space established by man from the moment he is placed in it. The sum of behavior, knowledge, and know-how acquired by a continuous process of assimilation and acculturation determines the local identity of a community [1]. However, the

A. Marcus et al. (Eds.): HCII 2023, LNCS 14030, pp. 94–109, 2023.
https://doi.org/10.1007/978-3-031-35699-5_8

traits that make up local identity – understanding of singularities and coordination of narratives stemming from local history and community memories - tend to dissipate with the industrialization of modern societies. Evolution of information and communication technologies, through the increasing accessibility of digital communication, have dramatically affected communities, interpersonal relationships, and cultures [2]. There is a tendency for the sociocultural bonds and values of traditional society to be lost as these emerging technologies take over social interaction. Causing local communities to become even more isolated in the absence of those who visit them. Because there is no direct interaction with the community, tourists who seeks authenticity (who wants to be part of that territory, even if only briefly), end up feeling frustrated and do not return.

Interaction design uses digital technologies to create, shape and implement digital artifacts to solve complex problems (structural, functional, ethical and aesthetic) to further improve human well-being [3, 4]. By intervening in territories, interaction design streamlines the process of communication and interaction between people, contributing to physical, social, sensory and memory factors – the local identity – persisting in the community and can be experienced by those who visit it. Since its multidisciplinary roots (industrial design and graphic design, human factors and human-computer interaction) are associated with behavior, in a dialogue between people, machines and systems [3, 5].

In this sense, several authors [4–8] suggest that interaction design can follow three major schools of thought:

1. **Technology-centered design.** Emphasizes the possibilities of technology instead of user experience. Developed by engineers and programmers, and then molded into useful and functional products by interaction designers it is often used in areas such as web design, application design and game design. The kialo Edu platform [9] is an example of this. This tool, developed specifically for use in a classroom context, aims to promote debate between students, allowing them to put their knowledge into practice, develop their own views on class content and consolidate what they have learned. Discussions are presented graphically in the form of an interactive tree. At the top of the discussion is the thesis, which is then broken down into arguments for and against. This in turn gives rise to new arguments in favor of or challenging the previous idea. In this way, this collaborative platform encourages students to work together to find the best way to express each idea.
2. **Behavioural design.** Studies how people interact with technology and how technology can be designed to intentionally and systematically influence human behavior. There are a variety of techniques, the most common include: rewards and incentives; social norms; gamification; personalization; behavioral tracking; progress reporting; reminders and notifications; and more. Several hotel companies (such as Accor Hotels, Barceló Hotel Group, Iberostar Hotels & Resorts, etc.) use the gamification technique for their loyalty programs by awarding different cards and points for completing tasks (amounts of nights spent or services) that members/users can exchange for discounts, upgrades or experiences on future visits.
3. **Social Interaction Design.** Its preamble is inherently social, it is the process of facilitating or instigating interactions/connections between humans through products and services. Technology is almost irrelevant in this approach – any object or device can

create a connection between people. What is essential is that tools allow for flexible communication across multiple contexts. EatWith [10] illustrates this point. This social platform is primarily focused on sharing personal experiences. Very similar to the Airbnb Ecosystem, guests (the guests) looking to taste a bit of local life select, through the website, the dining experience they would like to have by requesting a "meeting" with the host, who in turn accepts or refuses the request based on a guest profile assessment. EatWith aims to transform the way we eat, meet and interact. Using new technology to socialize the old-fashioned way.

This is where the scope and applicability of interaction design is understood. The field of action is vast and multidisciplinary, but with a single objective: to make the product or service more efficient, effective, engaging and easy to learn, so that user experience is as positive as possible [6].

2   Design Methods for Territories

One of the main concerns is how interaction design can be conducted in territories intervention. What methods, techniques and procedures of interaction design are best suited to designing successful products or services? The character, convictions and vision of the work and users of a project usually help the designer to determine the most pertinent methods, however we suggest three procedures that we consider to be the most relevant, because they direct the focus towards solutions that meet users' needs when they relate to the design process and physically interact with a final product. We will analyze in detail each of these methods: persuasive techniques, design thinking, and tangible interaction.

Fogg [11] considers that the concept of persuasion implies a voluntary change in behavior, without the use of coercion or deception. And that the art of persuading is not as simple as it seems, that sometimes designers fail because they do not understand the factors that lead to a change in human behavior. That said, he developed the Fogg Behavior Model (FBM) in order to empower designers to better understand the factors underlying behavior change in order to create more efficient and effective design solutions. The model describes human behavior as the result of three main elements – motivation, ability, and trigger [12] – that is, for a behavior to occur, a person must have sufficient motivation and dexterity, and an effective trigger, the absence of one of these elements can determine non-existence of the behavior. According to this point of view, design of an interactive product or service must understand the extrinsic motivation (such as money, rewards or public praise) and intrinsic motivation (such as hope and sense of accomplishment) of the user; it should enhance skill by simplifying the process so that actions are as easy as possible and conforms to the user's mental models; and have triggers that assist users in completing a task (facilitator triggers), that call for action (signal triggers), and that provide quick boosts to a user's motivation (spark triggers).

From this context, six guidelines for persuasive design are established: (i) visual influence (colors, images, contrast, and repetition); reciprocity (returning favors); authority (credible sources or experts); social proof (influential conformity); scarcity (limiting the offer); and consultation (giving advice to improve) [13–15].

An important characteristic of the persuasive design approach is that it does not require the user to be given a great deal of information in order to be convinced. To achieve this goal, tasks and support elements must be designed in a way that increases the likelihood of seeing desired behavior from the user. For instance, athletic training can be encouraged simply by assigning virtual achievement badges, in which several specific actions are triggered that reflect the increased user's motivation to exercise in order to achieve a goal or goals. Such is the case with Apple's Fitness app [16], an interactive software that records movements throughout the day. The user sets the workout metrics according to his or her abilities, monitoring his or her performance through the notifications sent by the app or by checking the performance bars graphically represented by three circles: the red one translates the distance traveled, the green one indicates the time exercised, and the blue one indicates the time spent standing. As soon as the goals are reached, the app awards various prizes represented by badges that the user can collect or share on social media accounts. And so that motivation does not disappear, this app allows you to challenge friends to healthy competition.

Given this example, it is possible to see the importance of persuasive techniques for interaction design, as they allow the development of mechanisms based on various themes (health, gastronomy, sports, etc.) in favor of promoting a locality through interactions with the visitor and the community.

Another method that helps design better products, services, spaces and experiences, while making them more accessible and useful for their users, is design thinking. Optimal solutions that meet users' needs can only be created by keeping the focus on them and listening to them. Introduced by design companies like IDEO and university courses by the Hasso Plattner Institute of Design at Stanford (D-School), this approach seeks innovative opportunities by combining what is desirable from a human perspective with possible and economically feasible technologies. Turning ideas into tangible, testable products or processes as quickly as possible. This human-centered toolkit for problem-solving innovation aims to help people and organizations become more innovative and more creative [8, 17–19].

It should be noted that human-centered design (HDC) is not the same as design thinking, but is an important part of the design thinking process. In that it is a problem-solving process that puts user experience at the center of the design process, listening to their wants, creating innovative solutions to meet those needs, and providing financially sustainable outcomes [8, 20]. Design thinking is a more holistic approach to problem solving that emphasizes creative exploration of solutions. It involves understanding the challenges, researching their context, devising solutions, and testing and refining them.

To make design thinking more easily understandable and applicable, many models have been created over the years. Because it is a multidisciplinary method, the graphical synthesis of process dynamics and phases allows for much more fluid and effective creative action. Let's take a look at IDEO's and D-School's models.

According to IDEO, the process takes place in three moments or phases, which diverge and converge sometimes, and with each new cycle they get closer and closer to a solution ready for the market (see Fig. 1). Inspiration is when the team analyzes the current situation, constraints and opportunities that motivate the search for solutions. The second moment is ideation, through the process of generating, developing and testing ideas that can lead to solutions. This phase will become tangible by building prototypes that bring us closer to final results that will be shared with users. Finally, there is implementation, the moment when a clear vision of the solution is achieved and a path is laid out to be implemented in the market [21, 22]. The process is extremely iterative, so designers can quickly identify and solve problems, reducing the chance of errors or omissions, while creating more intuitive user experiences tailored to the user's needs, and making the design process more efficient and consistent over time.

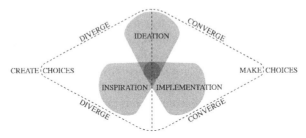

Fig. 1. The three core activities of design thinking during divergent and convergent phases. Redesigned from two IDEO's models (authors, 2023).

It is an easy model to memorize, but not very detailed. Perhaps because of this, D-School [18, 23] felt the need to schematize the process in five steps:

1. **Empathize.** Understand the problem, people, and context through research and observation;
2. **Define.** Identify central problems and develop a point of view;
3. **Ideate.** Develop innovative solutions to a problem;
4. **Prototyping.** Create low-fidelity tangible representations to explore ideas;
5. **Test.** Iterate the solutions with users and stakeholders.

In this model, the information is more detailed, exemplifying more clearly that the phases of a design process are not always carried out sequentially and that projects can return to previous phases. Still, there is no single, unifying and common model of design thinking, and which model is used will depend on the designer's own preferences and experience. Several factors must be taken into account when choosing the right process model, such as characteristics of the innovation task, context, composition and activity of the team, and the amount of time allocated to a procedure [24, 25].

Considering these criteria and the design framework, as an essential process in interaction design, these authors [17, 26] suggest adding two more steps to make the process as complete as possible:

1. **Implement.** Choose the solution that gathers the most consensus and launch it;
2. **Evaluate/learn.** Measure the success of the solution and improve the prototype for the benefit of the customer.

By following these steps, interaction designers ensure that their solutions provide a better user experience because they are the result of conducting research with users (what they really need rather than what they want), understanding their behavior, and designing solutions that fit their goals and motivations [3, 27].

Another relevant fact is that with intervention in territories, interaction design helps to innovate (creating new products, services or experiences) and to improve existing products or services, combining the intangible and tangible means existing in the community with the creation of pleasant experiences that exceed visitors' expectations [28–31]. In this way, we introduce the last method we would like to analyze, tangible interaction.

Tangible interaction or tangible user interface (TUI) is increasingly being used in interaction design, and is a key component of the design process, as well as the design of user experience. It consists in giving physical form to digital information, making data directly manipulable and perceptible, seeking the perfect intersection between physical objects and virtual data. It is simultaneously an interface, an interaction object (e.g., keyboard or mouse) and an interaction instrument (e.g., cursor or scrollbar) [32–34].

The TUI designation appeared in 1993, in a special issue of Communications of the ACM (Association for Computing Machinery) entitled *Back to the Real World*, in which Wellner et al. [35] stated that computers and virtual reality took users away from their natural environment and for that reason, instead of forcing users into the virtual world, the real world should be augmented and enriched with digital functionality, incorporating digital interfaces in human environments and activities. Thus, allowing a fluid transition between what is digital and what is real. In the first 10 years, tangible interaction has focused essentially on the creation of systems that explored existing technical possibilities [36], the concept has matured into a research area, mainly through the contributions of Hiroshi Ishii[1] and his Tangible Media Group, as well as by the dissemination of the word 'tangible' by other research groups, in article entries, workshops and conference titles around the world.

Tangible interaction breaks away from traditional computational interaction (graphical user interface), where interaction is done through WIMP (Windows, Icons, Menus and Pointers) style, to act and touch the interface itself. Instantly appealing to a wide range of users using the simplest and most creative body movements of hands with social and environmental skills with the real world [38]. Such is the case with Sonic Bench and TouchMe, both from Playtronica [39]. These physical artifacts of tangible interaction challenge users, through touch, to explore how the real and the artificial can coexist in harmony, creating unique and meaningful experiences through technology and sound. Developed by a studio focused on tangible sound experiences, these artifacts transform the human touch into a musical instrument, where the sound changes as the touch area and intensity increases.

Tangible Interaction, according these authors [33, 40–42], encompasses user interfaces and approaches to interaction: (i) with tangible objects through direct haptic manipulation which allows for sensory and playful pleasure; (ii) with physical representations of digital data through use of physical storage media or printed documents (e.g., compact discs, hard drives, USB drives, and photographs); (iii) with the human body as an

---

[1] In 1997, Ishii and his group published *Tangible Bits: Beyond Pixels*, a more comprehensive vision focused on using the physical world as a canvas and a means of manipulation. An interface capable of connecting data to physical artifacts and architectural surfaces, making bits tangible, and allowing for the creation of new and improved objects. Based on this work, a tangible user interface emerged – a new interface and new forms of interaction with the user interface. [37].

interaction device, through reflexive and critical exploration of the body's own movements as they are captured by 3D sensors; and (iv) with people, physical objects, and environments through physical movements, gestures, and other inputs (e.g., augmented reality, virtual reality, interactive displays, and gesture-based systems).

This categorization allows for the analysis and conceptual orientation of products or systems through different perspectives and methods. This is because objects carry multiple levels of meaning: as distinct entities, as elements in system practice, and as signifiers of social significance [42].

Another significant factor is social behavior. Collaborative activity provides a useful basis for tangible interaction design. To engage in meaningful conversations, establish and maintain relationships, and build trust, people need to communicate effectively both verbally and non-verbally, share physical objects, and work cooperatively with others in order to achieve a common goal [33, 38, 43–45]. Take the example of LeakyPhones [46], a pair of headphones that promote interaction through music sharing by allowing the user to hear other people's music as soon as they look at it.

Combining the three methods analyzed above (persuasive design, design thinking and tangible interaction), designers can design and intervene in territories through interaction; i.e., they can create unique and immersive experiences, adapted to the specific needs of the space, which encourages users to explore and interact with territories. We can use persuasive design to create visual cues that guide users through the space and encourage them to explore; design thinking to identify user needs and design solutions tailored to the context of the space; and tangible interaction to build physical objects that allow users to interact and control digital elements within the physical environment. These approaches result in both intrinsic interactive experiences, in a person's momentary feelings about the quality of a product, and the complex interactions between cognitive, motivational, and behavioral factors; and extrinsic, in the individual's experience of the socioeconomic and technological context in which the interaction occurs [47, 48]. These are not the only procedures available, but they certainly help as a starting point to such an intriguing and challenging goal as the promotion of a territory through connections between local communities and visitors.

3   Collaborative Networks and Connectivity

One of the strategies used to connect people is to bring them together through a network. A network is an organizational web formed by several actors where diverse resources, actions, visions, and lessons are articulated in a cooperative manner. Collaboration is a form of collective work. The term is commonly used when individuals or organizations collaborate to achieve a common goal [49]. Partnerships and alliances are other terms used to describe collaboration between organizations that maintain their independence, integrity, and diversity. The process of collaboration involves sharing resources, know-how, and information to mimic a single organization. Collaboration constructively explores differences and finds solutions that go beyond the limited perspective that each participant has on a problem. Collaborative networks offer significant advantages to local communities that lack specific skills or resources within a locality. Through synergy and mutual learning, they achieve complementary skills that allow them easier access to new markets, such as tourism [50].

To implement a responsible, collaborative network and connectivity that improves sustainability and creates meaningful connections between travelers and locals, it is essential to have a clear and widely shared vision of what it proposes to do; membership should be voluntary, based on individual or organizational commitment; there should be agreement on a process to coordinate activities, facilitate conversations, and communicate information among members; have a set of operating principles that guide the behavior of network members and an effective governance structure that provides leadership and guidance; its members must have a clear understanding of the benefits they will receive from their participation, as well as access to the resources they need to achieve the network's goals [51–53].

By equipping localities with collaborative network and connectivity that involve society in a logic of co-creation of interaction projects for tourism development (in initiatives of welcoming and well-being to the visitor) it is a plausible method for the promotion and sustainable development of local communities in such a globalized and competitive economy. Community involvement not only plays a key role in understanding the uniqueness of each place and coordinating the narratives from local history and community memories, but also encourages the sharing of values and ambitions, facilitates dialogue between the different actors and helps to promote a greater sense of community and empowerment that will prevail temporarily.

Let us take the case study *Route of the National Road 2* in Portugal (EN/N2). The only one of its kind in Europe, National Road 2 is the third longest route in the world, after Route 66 in U.S. and Ruta 40 in Argentina. The road connects Chaves to Faro, along more than 739 km, crossing thirty-five municipalities spread over eleven districts. In 2016, the Association of Municipalities of the Route of National Road 2 (AMREN2) was formed, with the aim of developing tourism and economic and cultural promotion of the territories crossed by the mythical road. This inter-municipal collaboration project was developed by the Lusófona University, through the creative and technological incubator PLAY (Projects Lab Alliance for You) and CICANT (Centre for Research in Applied Communication, Culture and New Technologies) and is based on three fundamental axes:

- **Signage.** Placement of signs with information of each municipality along the road and installation of indicative information of the N2 in the localities (see Fig. 2).
- **Content.** Design of the website[2] and the mobile application that gives information to the traveler about the place where he is, such as what to visit, where to eat or where to sleep; and the creation of the passport Route of the National Road 2, where the visitor registers his trip through a collection of stamps (see Fig. 2).
- **Capacity building of the partners that join the Route.** Creation of a network of agents that become a kind of tourist guide in each territory, who know the history of each locality and the stories of the EN2.

---

[2] https://www.rotan2.pt.

Fig. 2. Signposting of Route EN/N2, passport and stamp, and the tourist office in Sertã (authors, 2023).

In view of this, to prove the effectiveness and viability of the project, the Municipality of Chaves - the first municipality (km zero) - prepared in 2020, the report *Presentation of the Statistical Results of the Tourism Office of Chaves of 2019* [54], with the objective of understanding, in addition to other factors, the impact of the EN2 Route on the municipality and the possibility of receiving more tourists if the Route continues to be disseminated through various means. It found that during 2019, 20.351 tourists (87%)[3] visited the city of Chaves motivated by culture (tangible/intangible). The cultural product that obtained greater prominence in the choice of visitors was the Tourism Office, which focused, mostly, on the historical heritage of the region and its cultural heritage. Immediately after, Route of the National Road N2 was the product that obtained greater adhesion, with a total of 2337 visitors (10%)[4] who came to Chaves mainly to perform this route. Considered as a "novelty" tourism product, Route on National Road 2 attracted many visitors to the city of Chaves to perform the route, in order to discover and experience the essence of Portugal. In a survey prepared by employees of Chaves Tourism Office, based on all those who traveled and completed the route, the final balance was positive. In 2019, a total of 1928 passports were made available at the Tourism Post, with 49.8% of the total being concentrated in the months of July, August and September. Those who obtain passports on Route EN2 are mostly Portuguese, however there is some adhesion to foreign tourists, especially in the months of July and August. As a result, the Municipality of Chaves verified that the N2 National Road Route has contributed, in a considerable way, to the increase of visitors to the Tourist Office and, naturally, to the city of Chaves. Given that the number of visitors to the Tourist Office in the year 2019 evolved 68.44% compared to the year 2018.

The result has been so positive that similar initiatives have been replicated by other entities or organizations, such as the Intermunicipal Project Valorização dos Caminhos

---

[3] The percentage of tourists in the city that year, compared to the total number of tourists.

[4] The percentage of tourists in the city that year, compared to the total number of tourists.

de Santiago - Caminho Português da Costa [55] or the Passaporte Douro of the Douro Intermunicipal Community (CIM Douro) [56].

Collaborative network and connectivity between municipalities allowed them to work collectively and better respond to emerging business opportunities, creating a project likely to increase internal value for the municipalities (greater economic resource) and provide better external value to the end customer (visitor satisfaction). Design practices developed for Route of the National Road 2 took a more active role, producing new practices for how to experience places, contributing as a lever for sustainable development of the various municipalities, enabling the three dimensions of sustainable development (economic, social and environmental), thus reversing the devaluation of the interior and mitigating regional asymmetries in Portugal. A solution based on understanding the desires and constraints of communities by putting their needs at the center of the design process, reaping the benefits that a network of collaboration and connectivity can provide.

4   Human-centered Design to Humanity-Centered Design

Know your user is probably the main rule for those engaged in user interface design (UI Design) and human-computer interaction (HCI). Ignoring users for whom the design is intended has contributed to the increasing proliferation of 'bad designs' in the world [57]. If usability focuses on the study of human interaction with any artifact, human-centered design (HCD) is the approach that makes it possible to build products or systems that meet people's needs [58]. HCD derives from HCI, not as a subset of usability, but as a design practice that puts people at the center of the development process, integrating the entire user experience with the product or system, both physical and emotional reactions [59, 60]. That it does not end with ergonomic, psychological, sociological, and anthropological studies of what fits the human body and mind, but rather with an ongoing process of what can be done to support and enhance human dignity in various social, economic, political, and cultural contexts [61].

The HCD process is guided, according to Norman and Spencer [62], by four basic principles: (i) understand and solve the main problems, not the symptoms; (ii) focus on people as opposed to technology, ensuring that the result is appropriate to their needs; (iii) use an approach that focuses the design on the whole activity and not just on isolated components; and (iv) start the process with simple prototypes, and then test, refine and improve, through successive iterations.

But this constant demand for new solutions focused on human satisfaction, pleasure and well-being, which uses ergonomic factors, usability knowledge and persuasive techniques in the creation of usable and useful interactive systems, leads us to question whether HCD is the best practice to adopt when interaction design intervenes in territories. Since, the creation of products or services for instant consumption, in the name of immediate reward (convenience, usability or cost), has led interaction designers to opt for short-term solutions without analyzing future impact of these measures. Wakkary [61] states that HCD, in an ecological sense, has contributed in a way to the very reality of climate change and the ongoing extinction of other species and natural resources by exploiting, extracting, and reducing their relationship to human use. It is critical to integrate systemic thinking that takes into account the underlying connections, interactions, and structures of dynamic systems over time, and to understand the underlying processes that drive these systems. As a result, interaction designers can anticipate and mitigate the long-term negative consequences of well-intentioned solutions. Designing products or systems with minimal negative impact and equity, and building on technological advances without destabilizing the moral and ethical foundations of society and the world around us. That allows free will, preserves and promotes justice, equality and community, and that, for example, fosters face-to-face interaction in a less competitive and addictive environment like the digital world.

The solution may lie in a different approach that looks at the needs of people not as individuals, but as part of a complex society with deep-rooted systems and problems, such as sustainability, inclusion, accessibility and representation. Humanity-centered design (HYCD) broadens the spectrum of action, establishing in a more conscious way the rights of all humanity and the natural ecosystem [63, 64]. According to the authors [65, 66], HYCD accepts as a basic framework the principles of HCD, but adjusts them to be more explicit, involving all living things and the physical environment, and looking at long-term impact, namely: (i) humanity as the totality of human beings. Designers should be enablers, facilitators and a resource, designing products or services with and for community members. And (ii) humanity as a complement to the man-machine dualism. Products or services should preserve the human side of the interaction between humans and machines, relieving the knowledge burden, giving people the opportunity to focus on what is essential, contributing to a more humane and just future for humanity.

Given this context, to act significantly in promoting localities, interaction design must preserve more humanity-centered practices, such as:

- **Context Mapping**. Clarifies the context in which the product or service is used, mapping social, cultural and emotional issues, as well as aspects of user-product or service interaction that the community needs [67].
- **Facilitation Techniques**. Allows the mutual construction of knowledge and power for the benefit and enrichment of all actors involved, through reciprocal strategies of cooperation in development. Facilitators build a shared space for inclusive and creative participation, and a set of activities for participants to contribute to a common goal [68].
- **Consequence Anticipation**. Assesses and predicts the possible outcomes of different solutions to a problem, for people, society and the environment [69].

Such considerations point to a change in the way interaction design should act when its object is territories. These include neglecting strategies and practices of design for mass markets and directing the focus to differences and not similarities to a local community identity, interpreting them as differentiating and competitive factors, but without interfering with their real meaning. As well as, by building a participative context, with ecological awareness and social and environmental responsibility, supported by multidisciplinary processes and by the commitment and direct contact of the designer with the community, in order to eliminate abstraction and generic ideas through valuable design activities such as workshops, consultations, interviews, co-creation, etc. A sustainable and inspiring model, open to knowledge sharing and unity, demand-driven rather than supply-driven, and which, due to its characteristics, must be adapted and customized to local resources and skill sets and the needs of the local population.

5 Conclusion

This paper aims to demonstrate the impact that interaction processes and projects can have in territories. Also, discuss the application of different design methods when the focus is on interaction design, as facilitator of behaviors, generator of experiences between visitors and local communities, and promoter of the territory (making it more understandable, attractive and memorable).

In order to achieve this goal, we conducted a preliminary study on currents of thought in interaction design, in order to understand the scope and applicability of this discipline, which excels in defining the form and behavior of interactive products, services and systems that are used to create and maintain interaction design. We identified three approaches as being the most relevant in guiding interactive solutions to user needs and the promotion of a locality: (i) persuasive techniques to create more effective, fun and engaging interactions; (ii) design thinking to understand users, challenge assumptions, redefine problems and create innovative solutions; and (iii) interactive tangibility to give physical form to digital information, allowing users to act and touch the interface itself.

We proposed the creation of collaborative networks and connectivity as a new interactive model, as a method of intervention and for understanding local identity and interconnectedness in the context of the global economy. Demonstrating the case study Route of the National Road 2 as an example capable of increasing the internal value for municipalities (contributing as a lever to the sustainable development of the various municipalities, enabling the three dimensions of sustainable development: economic, social and environmental) and providing better external value to the final customer (visitor satisfaction).

Finally, we analyzed the human-centered design approach and concluded that principles that only prioritize human comfort and satisfaction were not the most appropriate methodology if one wanted a more systemic view that takes into account connections, interactions and underlying structures of dynamic systems of territories in the long term. In this sense, the focus converged on humanity-centered design, in the way it looks at humans not as individuals, but as part of a complex society, and in the way it operates using interactive strategies that are responsible (both socially and environmentally) to promote a locality. Described methods analyze contexts in which a product or system is placed, drive participation of all involved, and predict possible consequences for people, societies, and the environment.

The research and reasoning presented here need not be considered conclusive. However, the methods analyzed and the questions raised can be a practical tool for interaction designers and a starting point for future research in this area of design. We hope to provide a working basis for design professionals and researchers, increasing their potential to create more appealing and dynamic interactive solutions within the scope of design for territories and/or allowing them to further develop a theoretical basis of their work.

Acknowledgements. This work is financed by national funds through FCT - Fundação para a Ciência e a Tecnologia, I.P., under the Strategic Project with the references UIDB/04008/2020 and UIDP/04008/2020.

References

1. Lupo, E.: Il Design per i Beni Culturali. Pratiche e Processi Innovativi di Valorizzazione. Franco Angeli (2009)
2. Mamaghani, N.K., Asadollahi, A.P., Mortezaei, S.-R.: Designing for improving social relationship with interaction design approach. Procedia. Soc. Behav. Sci. **201**, 377–385 (2015). https://doi.org/10.1016/j.sbspro.2015.08.190
3. Kolko, J.: Thoughts on Interaction Design. Morgan Kaufmann, MA, USA (2010)
4. Sharp, H., Rogers, Y., Preece, J.J.: Interaction Design: Beyond Human-Computer Interaction, 5th edn. Wiley, New York, USA (2019)
5. Saffer, D.: Designing for Interaction: Creating Innovative Applications and Devices, 2nd edn. New Riders, California, USA (2010)
6. Moggridge, B.: Designing Interactions. MIT Press, Cambridge, Massachusetts (2007)
7. Zimmerman, J., Forlizzi, J., Evenson, S.: Research through design as a method for interaction design research in HCI. In: Proceedings of the SIGCHI Conference on Human Factors in Computing Systems, pp 493–502. Association for Computing Machinery, New York, NY, USA (2007)
8. Norman, D.A.: The Design of Everyday Things: Revised and, Expanded Basic Books, New York (2013)
9. Kialo Homepage. https://www.kialo-edu.com. Accessed 4 Feb 2023
10. Eatwith Homepage. https://www.eatwith.com Accessed 4 Feb 2023
11. Fogg, B.J.: Persuasive Technology: Using Computers to Change What We Think and Do. Morgan Kaufmann Publishers, California, USA (2003)
12. Fogg, B.: A Behavior model for persuasive design. In: Proceedings of the 4th International Conference on Persuasive Technology. Association for Computing Machinery, New York, NY, USA (2009)
13. Anderson, S.P.: Seductive Interaction Design: Creating Playful Fun and Effective User Experiences. New Riders, Berkeley, CA (2011)
14. Nodder, C.: Evil by Design: Interaction Design to Lead Us into Temptation. Wiley, Indianapolis, Indiana (2013)
15. Yocco, V.: Design for the Mind: Seven Psychological Principles of Persuasive Design. Manning Publications, New York, USA (2016)
16. Williams, J.: Empowering People to Live a Healthier Day: Innovation Using Apple Technology to Support Personal Health, Research, and Care. https://www.apple.com/newsroom/pdfs/Health-Report-July-2022.pdf. Accessed 4 Feb 2023
17. Lockwood, T.: Design Thinking: Integrating Innovation Customer Experience and Brand Value. Allworth Press, New York (2009)
18. Brown, T.: Change by Design, Revised and Updated: How Design Thinking Transforms Organizations and Inspires Innovation. HarperCollins Publishers, New York, USA (2019)
19. Curedale, R.: Design Thinking Process & Method, 5th edn. Design Community College, Topanga, CA (2019)
20. Boy, G.A.: Orchestrating Human-Centered Design. Springer, Florida, USA (2013)
21. Meinel, C., von Thienen, J.: Design thinking. Informatik-Spektrum **39**(4), 310–314 (2016). https://doi.org/10.1007/s00287-016-0977-2

22. IDEO.org.: The Field Guide to Human-Centered Design. Design Kit, San Francisco, CA (2015)

23. Plattner, H.: An Introduction to Design Thinking: Process Guide (2010). https://web.stanford.edu/~mshanks/MichaelShanks/files/509554.pdf. Accessed 4 Feb 2023

24. Tschimmel, K.: Design thinking as an effective toolkit for innovation. In: Proceedings of the XXIII ISPIM Conference: Action for Innovation: Innovating from Experience (2012)

25. Mootee, I.: Design Thinking for Strategic Innovation: What They Can't Teach You at Business or Design School. Wiley, Hoboken, New Jersey (2013)

26. Cross, N.: Design Thinking: Understanding How Designers Think and Work. Berg, London (2011)

27. Krug, S.: Don't Make Me Think, Revisited: A Common Sense Approach to Web Usability, 3th edn. New Riders Peachpit Pearson Education, San Francisco, California (2014)

28. Li, Y., Kothiyal, A., Weber, T., et al.: Designing Tangible as an Orchestration Tool for Collaborative Activities. Multimodal Technol. Interact. **6** (2022). https://doi.org/10.3390/mti6050030

29. Stickdorn, M., Schneider, J.: This is Service Design Thinking: Basics, Tools Cases. BIS Publishers, Netherlands (2011)

30. Parente, M., Lupo, E., Sedini, C.: Tangibile/Intangibile. Dialoghi sul Design per i Territori 02. D4T Design for Territories - Dipartimento di Design, Politecnico di Milano, Milano (2017)

31. Hansen, L.K., Rico, J., Jacucci, G., et al.: Performative interaction in public space. In: CHI 2011 Extended Abstracts on Human Factors in Computing Systems, pp. 49–52. Association for Computing Machinery, New York, NY, USA (2011)

32. Beaudouin-Lafon, M.: Instrumental interaction: an interaction model for designing post-WIMP user interfaces. In: Proceedings of the SIGCHI Conference on Human Factors in Computing Systems, pp 446–453. Association for Computing Machinery, New York, NY, USA (2000)

33. Hornecker, E., Buur, J.: Getting a grip on tangible interaction: a framework on physical space and social interaction. In: Proceedings of the SIGCHI Conference on Human Factors in Computing Systems, pp 437–446. Association for Computing Machinery, New York, NY, USA (2006)

34. Ishii, H.: The tangible user interface and its evolution. Commun. ACM **51**, 32–36 (2008). https://doi.org/10.1145/1349026.1349034

35. Wellner, P.D., Mackay, W.E., Gold, R.: Back to the real world. Commun. ACM **36**, 24–26 (1993)

36. Shaer, O., Hornecker, E.: Tangible user interfaces: past, present, and future directions. Found. Trends Hum. Comput. Interact. **3**, 1–137 (2009). https://doi.org/10.1561/1100000026

37. Ishii, H.: Tangible bits: beyond pixels. In: Proceedings of the 2nd International Conference on Tangible and Embedded Interaction, pp xv–xxv. Association for Computing Machinery, New York, NY, USA (2008)

38. Jacob, R.J.K., Girouard, A., Hirshfield, L.M., et al.: Reality-based interaction: a framework for post-WIMP interfaces. In: Proceedings of the SIGCHI Conference on Human Factors in Computing Systems, pp 201–210. Association for Computing Machinery, New York, NY, USA (2008)

39. Playtronica Homepage. https://playtronica.com. Accessed 5 Feb 2023

40. Ullmer, B., Ishii, H.: Emerging frameworks for tangible user interfaces. IBM Syst. J. **39**, 915–931 (2000). https://doi.org/10.1147/sj.393.0915

41. Buur, J., Jensen, M.V., Djajadiningrat, T.: Hands-only scenarios and video action walls: novel methods for tangible user interaction design. In: Proceedings of the 5th Conference on Designing Interactive Systems: Processes, Practices, Methods, and Techniques, pp 185–192. Association for Computing Machinery, New York, NY (2004)

42. Dourish, P.: Where the Action Is: The Foundations of Embodied Interaction. The MIT Press (2014)
43. Gaver, W.W.: Situating action II: affordances for interaction: the social is material for design. Ecol. Psychol. **8**, 111–129 (1996). https://doi.org/10.1207/s15326969eco0802_2
44. Battarbee, K., Koskinen, I.: Co-experience: user experience as interaction. CoDesign **1**, 5–18 (2005). https://doi.org/10.1080/15710880412331289917
45. Hornecker, E.: The role of physicality in tangible and embodied interactions. Interactions **18**, 19–23 (2011). https://doi.org/10.1145/1925820.1925826
46. MIT Media Lab Homepage. https://www.media.mit.edu/projects/leakyphones/overview. Accessed 5 Feb 2023
47. Hassenzahl, M., Tractinsky, N.: User experience - a research agenda. Behav. Inform. Technol. **25**, 91–97 (2006). https://doi.org/10.1080/01449290500330331
48. Hassenzahl, M.: User Experience (UX): towards an experiential perspective on product quality. In: Proceedings of the 20th Conference on l'Interaction Homme-Machine, pp 11–15. Association for Computing Machinery, New York, NY, USA (2008)
49. Huxham, C.: Creating Collaborative Advantage. SAGE Publications, London (1996)
50. Child, J., Faulkner, D., Tallman, S.: Cooperative Strategy: Managing Alliances, Networks, and Joint Ventures. Oxford University Press, New York (2005)
51. Balestrin, A., Verschoore, J.: Redes de Cooperação Empresarial: Estratégias de Gestão na Nova Economia. Bookman (2008)
52. Plastrik, P., Taylor, M., Cleveland, J.: Connecting to Change the World: Harnessing the Power of Networks for Social Impact. Island Press, Washington, DC (2014)
53. De Noni, I., Orsi, L., Belussi, F.: The role of collaborative networks in supporting the innovation performances of lagging-behind European regions. Res. Policy **47**, 1–13 (2018). https://doi.org/10.1016/j.respol.2017.09.006
54. CMC (Câmara Municipal de Chaves): Apresentação de Resultados Estatísticos do Posto de Turismo de Chaves 2019. Chaves, Portugal (2020)
55. Caminho Português da Costa Homepage. http://www.caminhoportuguesdacosta.com/pt. Accessed 5 Feb 2023
56. CIM Douro Homepage. https://cimdouro.pt/2022/04/07/passaporte-douro-2/. Accessed 5 Feb 2023
57. Norman, D.A.: Human-centered design considered harmful. Interactions **12**, 14–19 (2005). https://doi.org/10.1145/1070960.1070976
58. Lowdermilk, T.: User-Centered Design: A Developer's Guide to Building User-Friendly Applications. O'Reilly Media, California, USA (2013)
59. Boy, G.A.: The Handbook of Human-Machine Interaction. A Human-Centered Design Approach. Ashgate, England (2011)
60. Wakkary, R.: Things We Could Design: For More Than Human-Centered Worlds. The MIT Press, London, England (2021)
61. Buchanan, R.: Human dignity and human rights: thoughts on the principles of human-centered design. Des. Issues **17**, 35–39 (2001). https://doi.org/10.1162/074793601750357178
62. Norman, D., Spencer, E.: Community-Based, Human-Centered Design (2019). https://jnd.org/community-based-human-centered-design/. Accessed 4 Dec 2022
63. Brush, J.: How Design Contributes to Toxic Individualism, and What Can Be Done About It. In: UX Collective (2023). https://uxdesign.cc/how-design-contributes-to-toxic-individualism-and-what-can-be-done-about-it-4933b47b15cc. Accessed 6 Feb 2023
64. Interaction Design Foundation.: What Is Humanity-Centered Design (2022). https://www.interaction-design.org/literature/topics/humanity-centered-design. Accessed 6 Feb 2013
65. Donelli, F.: It's time for a Humanity-Centered Design. A new approach to create technology for our society. In: Medium: Write. Connect. Earn (2016). https://medium.com/@fdonelli/its-time-for-a-humanity-centered-design-59f9fa551d8e. Accessed 6 Feb 2023

66. Norman, D.A.: Humanity-Centered versus Human-Centered Design (2022). https://jnd.org/humanity-centered-versus-human-centered-design/. Accessed 2 Feb 2023
67. Visser, F.S., Stappers, P.J., van der Lugt, R., Sanders, E.B-N.: Contextmapping: experiences from practice. CoDesign **1**, 119–149 (2005). https://doi.org/10.1080/15710880500135987
68. Seeber, I., de Vreede, G.-J., Maier, R., Weber, B.: Beyond brainstorming: exploring convergence in teams. J. Manag. Inf. Syst. **34**, 939–969 (2017). https://doi.org/10.1080/07421222.2017.1393303
69. Zamenopoulos, T., Alexiou, K.: Towards an anticipatory view of design. Des. Stud. **28**, 411–436 (2007). https://doi.org/10.1016/j.destud.2007.04.001

Resources and Skills for Information Design Practice

Cristina Pires dos Santos[1,2]($\boxtimes$) ⓘ, Marco Neves[1,3] ⓘ, and Carolina Bozzi[1] ⓘ

[1] CIAUD, Research Centre for Architecture, Urbanism and Design, Lisbon School of Architecture, Universidade de Lisboa, Rua Sá Nogueira, Polo Universitário do Alto da Ajuda, 1349-063 Lisbon, Portugal
cristina.santos@ipbeja.pt, mneves@fa.ulisboa.pt, carolinamarianna@campus.ul.pt

[2] Polytechnic Institute of Beja, Escola Superior de Educação de Beja, Rua Pedro Soares, 7800-295 Beja, Portugal

[3] ITI/LARSyS, University of Lisbon, Lisbon, Portugal

Abstract. Information Design (ID) is increasingly asserting itself as a fundamental subject as it plays a vital role of making complex information easy to understand and use. In the modern world, there is a need for ID, in the way that data is organized, written, and presented so that we can all understand it. When things get too complex, when an environment defies common sense, when technical requirements are allowed to prevail over human considerations, then someone must intervene – and this is where the information designer comes in. As such, this professional presents specificities that are important to emphasize. This article intends to reflect on some important issues for the definition of ID, such as: a) to justify its interdisciplinarity, and b) to clarify two fundamental axes for its practice (Infographics and DataViz) which have distinct features and contexts. Through a comprehensive literature review, we compile reflections from several scholars and professionals in this field of study, contributing to the affirmation of ID today, focusing on exclusive specificities that need to be highlighted. Information designers can have very different backgrounds and are often part of interdisciplinary teams that allow greater control and validation of the information presented. The eternal confrontation between form and function is once again in evidence in ID through two distinctive aspects of its practice, which demand professionals with different profiles. The differentiating characterization that exists allows a more specific knowledge of what ID is, aiming at a more informed practice and better preparation for the training of professionals.

Keywords: Information Design · Infographics · DataViz · Interdisciplinary · Wayfinding Systems

1 Information Design Interdisciplinarity

Krum [1] states that people are constantly looking for information and that this is our main enemy in the current context - we are confronted with too much information because we are looking for it. We want to be better informed so we can make better decisions. The same author says that the big challenge is to "filter" the information "rubbish", focus on what is relevant, and memorise the important things. Information overload is reported by several authors, Spiekermann [2], for example, reports that we are constantly flooded by messages, all trying to make us look, listen, and react. Some of these messages, however, are more important than others - but often the information we need is not provided in a way we can easily understand. In the modern world, there is clearly a need for information design (ID) in the way data is organised, written, and presented so that we can all understand it. Baer and Vacarra [3] highlight the same idea, saying that we are currently overloaded with too much information and often encounter navigational problems that make us feel lost. This overload of information is also underlined by Hansen [4] who states: "A multitude of environmental events perceived as chaos, heard as noise, and read as information overload are continuously present to us, clamouring for our attention" (p. 198). ID, therefore, becomes a fundamental area of knowledge to make information more efficient in how it reaches people, involving various factors and skills that must be looked at with some attention.

Bonsiepe [5] mentions that the growth of information volume has caused the traditional vision of the graphic designer to be revised. In addition to visualizing concepts, the designer organizes information to reduce cognitive entropy. The information designer structures and organises information and provides guidance so that users find their way through the current'information maze'. He reinforces that this change assumes cognitive and organisational skills, which are sometimes neglected in design training. This opinion is shared by Sless [6], who reinforces the idea, saying that there is a significant difference in objectives between ID and traditional graphic design, and Horn [7] states that the values that distinguish ID from other types of design are efficiency and effectiveness in achieving the communicative purpose.

Jan Schwochow[1] in an interview he gave to Cairo [8], highlights the importance of a multidisciplinary team in an ID project, made up of elements with varied skills, to respond to the several challenges imposed on its practice. This interdisciplinarity of ID emphasized by Schwochow is underlined by numerous authors and professionals in the field. Holmes [9] reinforces this necessary interdisciplinarity when talking about the enormous portfolio of infographics for National Geographic in recent decades. He claims that infographics are the result of editing work between writers, editors, and scientists, whose work is explained in the journal in an easier-to-understand way. According to Holmes, if there is too much data, readers get confused. However, he reinforces that editing is not the same as simplifying – a dangerous word that can mean'stupefy', so what National Geographic does, and does so well, is clarify data, facts, and concepts [9].

Frascara [10] states that ID is not defined by what is done, but, by the way, it is done and that it responds to people's needs, regarding the understanding and use of products, services and facilities, based on interdisciplinary knowledge, founded on ergonomics, linguistics, psychology, sociology, anthropology, graphic design, and informatics - among other fields. He reinforces the idea, quoting the International Institute

---

[1] Creative Director at *Golden Section Graphics Agency.* Works available in Golden Section Graphics News, in http://goldensectiongraphics.blogspot.com/ >, last accessed 2023/02/04.

for Information Design (IIID) saying that *"good information design"* makes information accessible (easily available), appropriate (to its contents and users), attractive (inviting), concise (clear and straightforward), relevant (interconnected to the user's purpose), timely (available when the user needs it), understandable (without doubts or ambiguities), appreciated (for its usefulness) and usable. He says, however, that interdisciplinarity was neither invented by ID nor is it exclusive to it. Even before, advertising agencies or organisations such as the International Standards Organization (ISO) brought together designers, psychologists, sociologists, and anthropologists to ensure that design decisions were made considering users' skills and profiles. He eventually categorically states that any piece of ID requires an interdisciplinary team and that *"every design problem is interdisciplinary"* [10].

Pettersson [11] states that ID has its origin and roots in graphic design, education and teaching, architecture and engineering, construction, and production. In these broad areas, people have recognised the need for clarity, distinctive presentation, trust, and interpretation of verbal as well as visual messages. Walker and Barratt [12] corroborate this idea and consider that the information designer draws on specialist knowledge and skills in several key areas and therefore has a vital role in turning complex information into easy-to-understand and use information. Schuller [13] even says that ID evolved from an interdisciplinary attitude and that people, who have had a lasting influence in the field, come from different subjects and use these other approaches and thinking methods as inspiration. In addition to innovative graphic representations, they invented, above all, new methods of order, navigation, and interaction, establishing essential standards for the interpretation of complex sets of facts and providing new aids to guide our daily lives. Schuller [13] also states that ID requires an interdisciplinary approach to communication, combining the skills of graphic design, 3D design, digital arts, cognitive science, computer theory, and cultural sciences, to develop common strategic solutions combined with other disciplines.

Baer and Vacarra [3] reinforce that human beings have a multitude of ways of absorbing and understanding information and for that reason, they must use numerous tactics and methods to make information meaningful. This is where the interdisciplinary nature of ID comes in; writing, editing, graphics, and illustrations all have a place in the practice of ID. Researching or testing the ideas on the potential target audience is proven equally important so that we can be sure that the right choices are made and not just guessing.

Besides the interdisciplinary nature of the skills involved in the practice of ID, the relationship with other fields of knowledge is also justified through its applicability in the communication of visual information more clearly. Hannah Fairfield[2], who also gave an interview to Alberto Cairo [8], highlights the intersection of ID with other fields of knowledge and exemplifies this idea through the infographic "Short guys can dunk"[3] (an example of an intersection between the fields of sports and physics). Another aspect to highlight in this example is the sequential way in which information is sometimes presented, helping us to understand several phases or a certain movement that is important for the message that is transmitted. Through a flip-book-like sequence, it is shown that

---

[2] Senior Graphic Editor at The New York Times.

[3] Available at: https://pin.it/2X3gfqU/ >, last accessed 2023/02/04.

shorter men are also able to 'dunk' in basketball, if they use the correct technique, through muscle strength and technique that is explained in the infographic.

2 Several Paths of Information Design: Infographics vs DataViz?

This interdisciplinary diversity in professionals associated with ID has also provoked a lot of discussions about the best way to present visual information. Cairo [8] says that some professionals and academics have made a clear distinction between the two most referenced forms of information presented in the ID practice (infographics and DataViz). They support the idea that infographics present information using statistical graphs, maps, and diagrams, while DataViz offers visual tools that the public can use to explore and analyse data sets. Cairo [8] reinforces that while infographics tell stories conceived by communicators, DataViz helps readers discover stories for themselves. Krum [1] states that until recently, the common definition of infographics was simply "a visual representation of data", however, the author argues that the definition is outdated and is more appropriate to define DataViz. Infographics originally derived from the term "information graphics" and was a term used to define the production of graphics for newspapers and magazines. Today, the use of the word "infographics" has evolved to include a new definition that means a more comprehensive graphic design that combines data visualisations, illustrations, text, and images in a format that tells a complete story. In this way, data visualisations alone, are no longer considered complete infographics but are a powerful tool that designers often use to help tell their stories visually. Gadney [14] says that modern ID is divided into two main fields, defined by the amount of editing of meaning in each. DataViz allows more interaction and infographics are more edited. DataViz is generally interactive and allows experienced users to find meaning in complex data fields. In DataViz, the meaning is there, and the user must find it. Infographics maximise their message by providing engaging forms suited to the audience, which is ideal when communicating to a wider, mass audience. We are used to seeing infographics in newspapers and formats such as 'tower graphics' or 'tall infographics'[4], formats that are increasingly popular among marketing companies that want to go further in communication. According to Gadney [14], there is always the risk that communicating through simplicity may be considered trivial but just as DataViz needs to moderate its wit to reach its audience, infographics need to balance engaging visual quality with a solution to information that respects its audience. Cairo [8] refers to the two distinct points of view and in his interview with Moritz Stefaner[5], mentions that more traditional information designers claim that most DataViz does not tell a story and further argues that contemporary viewers basically throw users into an 'ocean of data' and let them drift without any guidance. Moritz Stefaner agrees with this idea, but says, that it is a positive one - the most fascinating thing about the rise of DataViz is that anyone can explore all this amount of information without anyone telling them what the key

---

[4] Formats that are widely used in blogs and websites and are characterised by having a vertical and long format in order to adapt to screen navigation with vertical scrolling of the information.

[5] One of the most prestigious information designers, working mainly on DataViz. Many of his works can be seen on the website *Truth & Beauty - Data visualization by Moritz Stefaner*. Available at: http://truth-and-beauty.net/ >, last accessed 2023/02/04.

is to understand. He reiterates that in his work, he does not try to tell one story, but rather, thousands of stories, all of which cannot be presented simultaneously or with the same priority, but can all be present, hidden in the raw data, waiting to be discovered through the interface of the applications. Stefaner considers this to be the key to the difference between the DataViz genre compared to more traditional infographics. Cairo [8] also interviewed Geoff McGhee[6], who states that DataViz and its application to various areas of knowledge have grown considerably in recent years, coupled with the development of the internet and access to it through mobile devices, as well as, new programming languages and software that can present, in an accessible way, vast and complex groups of information. McGhee mentions, among others, the project "The Growth of Newspapers Across US: 1690–2011"[7]. A project that affirmed some of the advantages of interactive data visualisation, such as one could select what they were interested in knowing; one could select the decade or the language of the publication, and check how many newspapers there would be in each US state, for example. McGhee says that algorithmic data visualisation often uses a programming language to animate graphs from a given base of information - it is a strong analytical tool and can be very useful in helping many professionals of different fields.

2.1 Form or Function in ID?

Gadney [14] notes that the current debate is between the engaging David McCandless[8] and the analytical Stephen Few[9], they are debating the same issues as 30 years ago, between the academic Edward Tufte[10] and the populist Nigel Holmes[11]. The author believes that both are talented and insightful in this area and their differences should only be seen as a warning, telling the industry that there are issues that must be discussed. He reinforces that these conflicts are essential to the designer's condition because there will always be a healthy dilemma between form and function. Holmes [9] states that the result of data visualisations is often beautiful but appears out of place in a magazine like National Geographic, for example. He explains that the magazine has always tried to

---

[6] A researcher at the Bill Lane Center at the Stanford University Research Institute in the US whose work focuses primarily on interactive, multimedia data visualisation [8].

[7] The project is no longer available online, but the demo of the interaction can be found at: https://www.youtube.com/watch?v=28TG2QJYSGc&t=12s/ >, last accessed 2023/02/04.

[8] David McCandless, visual data writer and journalist, designer, runs the blog InformationIsBeautiful.net. He published the books "Information is Beautiful", 2009 and "Knowledge is Beautiful", 2014. Both use data visualisation and information design to tell new kinds of stories.

[9] Stephen Few has worked for over 30 years as an IT innovator, consultant, and educator. He was a director of his own consultancy Perceptual Edge from 2003 to 2020, where he focused on data visualisation to analyse and communicate quantitative business information. Stephen is recognized as a world leader in the field of data visualization, and he teaches regularly at conferences.

[10] Edward Tufte is Emeritus Professor of Statistics, Graphic Design and Political Economy at Yale University and a leading expert on infographics. He is the author of several reference books in the field of ID.

[11] Holmes is a British graphic designer, author, and theorist whose work focuses largely on information graphics and information design.

bridge the gap between what scientists do and what the universal reader can understand. The problem is that a DataViz is created by a computer from scientific data discoveries, which often exist in large quantities (hence the name big data). The idea of editing that data is nonsense, which is only now beginning to be accepted (somewhat unwillingly) in scientific and academic circles. However, editing is what has made National Geographic so relevant and understandable to so many readers. Cairo [8] says that what distinguishes infographics from the arts is that it is designed to help us complete certain intellectual tasks. They are more than a way for the artist to express his or her inner world and feelings, an infographic or visualization aspires to objectivity, precision, and functionality, as well as beauty. He justifies it with the following phrase, "the function constrains the form". He explains further, in detail [8]: "The form should be constrained by the functions of your presentation. There may be more than one form a data set can adopt so that readers can perform operations with it and extract meanings, but the data cannot adopt any form. Choosing visual shapes to encode information should not be based on aesthetics and personal tastes alone" (p. 36).

The same author reinforces, that it is important to remember, that it does not matter how creative and innovative we should be in our graphics and visualizations but to ask ourselves what users are likely to do with them. Cairo [8] again refers to Moritz Stefaner, who defines himself as a "Truth and Beauty Operator". For Stefaner, truth and beauty always carry equal weights; he does not want to choose or exchange truth for beauty or vice versa, he works with both. What he evaluates in his work is whether he is "helping to find the truth" and if he is "doing it elegantly". He considers that in an information visualisation project, if one exists without the other, then the project is not complete and refers to Buckminster Fuller[12], who said that he did not think about beauty when he started a design, engineering, or architectural project. He was only concerned with function; he wanted to find the best way to invent a product. However, in the end, if the solution he found was not beautiful, he knew something was wrong. For Buckminster Fuller, somehow, beauty was an indication of functionality and truth. For Stefa-ner, good design is closely linked to the content it presents and consists in thinking about what to show, what to leave out, what to emphasize, how to structure the information, to define the rhythm, the visual flow one wants the story to contain – "I would say that structure dictates pretty much what comes out visually" (p. 317) [8].

When we talk about this sometimes controversial issue (form or function), having as context the practice in ID, it is inevitable not to talk about the debate that existed between Edward Tufte and Nigel Holmes, reflecting some discussion that also exists about which is the best specialization for the practice of ID (engineers or designers). Cairo [8] states that there has always been a fundamental clash between infographics and DataViz, between those who prefer a rational and scientific approach to the practice of ID, emphasizing functionality, and those who consider themselves 'artists', emphasizing emotion and aesthetics. For the author, this division is related to the more technical

---

[12] Buckminster Fuller (1895–1983) was a 20th century inventor and visionary who did not limit himself to a single field of study but worked as a "comprehensive scientist in anticipatory design! to solve global problems. Fuller's ideas and work continue to influence new generations of designers, architects, scientists, and artists working to create a sustainable planet. Information available at: https://www.bfi.org >, last accessed 2023/02/06.

training for those who advocate greater functionality (in statistics, cartography, computer science, and engineering) and those who advocate aesthetics (in graphic design, art, and journalism). This 'war' was formally declared between these two parties by Edward Tufte in 1990, when he criticised an infographic chain in the USA between the late 1980s and early 1990s, thanks to the success of the visual style of USA Today and Time Magazine, where illustrated graphs and maps became very popular. Tufte used the term 'chartjunk', to define pictograms and illustrations in charts and maps and chose a graphic from Time, created by Nigel Holmes, the magazine's graphic director at the time[13]. Holmes acknowledged that this was not his most inspiring work but accused Tufte of choosing only one graphic among hundreds to justify his idea.

Cairo [8] contests the extreme functionalism of Tufte and even says, that the assumption that Tufte makes is doubtful and presents some studies that contradict his theory. In 2007, a study at Ben-Gurion University (Israel) showed 87 students a traditional bar chart and a similar chart with only lines. The 'minimalist' version was rejected by most participants, perhaps because the bar chart is a more common graphical form. However, when the researchers tested whether readers interpreted the minimalist graph better and faster than the more elaborate one, they found no significant differences. In this case, radically reducing the bar chart to its main components was not a matter of functionality but of visual style. In another study, also mentioned by Cairo [8], from the University of Saskatchewan (Canada), conducted by Scott Bateman and his colleagues, 20 students analysed four old Nigel Holmes graphs and their corresponding minimalist versions designed by other researchers. One of the graphs was the one that Tufte criticised[14]. The study was divided into 3 phases. First, the researchers used eye-tracking to record the movement of the eyes whenever each participant read the graphs under analysis; second, each participant answered a questionnaire about the contents of the graphs. Like the previous study, the researchers found no significant differences in effectiveness between the more decorative and the minimalist graphics. The components of each set of graphics communicated the message equally well. The most interesting part of the study was the third phase, in which the researchers tested the level of short-term and long-term recall for each graphic. In conclusion, the participants were better able to remember the topics and contents of Nigel Holmes's graphs. This study is also referred to in the book Infographics - The Power of Visual Storytelling [15]. The authors describe this study and pose the question: what visual elements should be used to ensure that individuals store their understanding in their long-term memory? Bateman and his colleagues involved in the study offered three possible explanations for the results of their experiments: 1. Additional images allowed people to encode information more deeply, as there were more visual items to recall and use memory available; 2. The variety of styles of Holmes's graphs gave it a unique advantage in being memorable, compared to the style of minimalist graphics, in which all had similar visual elements; 3. User preference highlighted a hidden factor: participants' emotional responses to the graphs, combined with the images used, helped solidify the image in their memories.

---

[13] Image available at: https://images.app.goo.gl/Ysn96V8xNVMFiaXM8/ >, last accessed 2023/02/04.

[14] Image available at: https://images.app.goo.gl/92PtG4oHLjaFndEV9/ >, last accessed 2023/02/04.

Lankow, Ritchie, and Crooks conclude that graphics that contain a more refined visual component behind the information presented may be superior not only in terms of attractiveness but also, in having the power to ensure that readers perceive and retain the message and state: "appealing to someone not only aesthetically but also emotionally prompts a deeper connection with the information, which makes them more likely to remember it" (p. 52).

These authors also highlight the opposing views (between Tufte and Holmes) and express that both views are right because the main point is the objective. Both may represent the same data set for different reasons. Tufte wishes to present the information as neutrally as possible, to encourage his audience to analyse it without any bias. On the other hand, Holmes's job is to edit the message to appeal to the viewer, while communicating the information he wants readers to absorb. They characterise Tufte's communication as explorative, that is, it encourages the reader to explore and extract their ideas. In turn, Holmes's communication is narrative and prescribes the intended conclusions to the viewer. The difference is inherent to their areas of work, as the objectives of science and research are very different from those of the publishing world, i.e., "there's no need to establish a universal approach to govern all objectives, rather, different individuals and industries should develop best practices unique to each application's specific goal" (p. 37).

Cairo [8] points out, however, that thinking that these two studies are conclusive may be a mistake (these studies have been criticized by several scholars in the field). He believes there are convincing reasons to doubt that reducing graphics to their basic structure will facilitate understanding and memorability. He claims that it depends on the nature, knowledge, tastes, and expectations of the target audience. For Lankow et al. [15], although the conclusion is obvious, i.e., a more visually dynamic and stimulating representation is preferable to a more basic and flat representation - it is important to consider it in an approach to design. It is not enough to make the content visual; it must be made visually interesting. You can use representative iconography, illustrative metaphors, or use decorative framing mechanisms that are relevant - all influential tools to communicate the message. However, we must always remember the purpose, as the appropriateness of decorative and illustrative elements varies according to application and use. If used incorrectly, decorative elements have the power to distract the reader from the information, which diminishes the overall value of the graphic. Mastering this practice and finding the balance between attraction and clarity can be a subtle process. Norman [16] states that beautiful things are more functional, and beauty is as much in the eye of the designer as it is in the eye of the beholder. Feeling good about an artifact makes us better at using it to accomplish a goal. Cairo [8] also refers to Holmes, as being always an advocate of humanising graphic information and using humour to instil affection in readers for numbers and graphics. Cairo refers to the book Designer's Guide to Creating Charts and Diagrams, from 1984, where Holmes wrote what seems to be a direct reference to Tufte's Visual Display of Quantitative Information, published the year before: "(…)" (…) as long as the artist understands that the primary function is to convey statistics and respects that duty, then you can have fun (or be serious) with the image; that is, the form in which those statistics appear" (p. 68). Holmes also praises the power of humour" (p. 69): "Humour is a great weapon in your visual arsenal. As long as it is not malicious, making people laugh with you will usually help them remember your image and therefore the point of the chart ". Cairo [8] states that many of Holmes's examples included in his book are problematic from a structural point of view, as they integrate lines and bars with illustrations, leading to misleading distortions. However, they use humour and are memorable. Cairo points out that many of the graphics might not be published today, but we must be aware that Holmes's book was published 30 years ago and is a product of his time.

3   The Multidimensionality of Information Design

ID can take on very different expressions in terms of application and we have already mentioned the case of infographics and DataViz. According to Coates and Ellison [17], there are three possible contextual categories (print, interactive - including screen-based design - and environmental). There are other more particular categorizations, advocated by other authors [1, 15], but we will focus on this approach advocated by Coates and Ellison for covering, in a clear way, the three main axes of ID (Infographics, DataViz, and the Wayfinding systems). These categorizations help reinforce the complexity of skills and the different profiles that an information designer may have. The authors consider that these three categories also overlap, since various types of information often appear in one or more categories and, depending on the project, information may have to be conveyed across various platforms and through various media, and in this case, provide various ways of presenting data through many different materials.

3.1   Print-Based Information Design

Printed information relies on a single image or sequence of images to convey complex sets of data and may use diagrams or graphs, but also photography, illustration, and text to communicate, for example, a newspaper or magazine article. According to Coates and Ellison [17], printed infographic, "is static and the reader is passive in the transmission of the material. The user does not interact with it in any way other than to decode the visual data presented to gain the facts or figures more quickly than by reading long passages of explanatory text" (p. 21).

The same authors state that this type of infographic presents all the information together and, in this way, the complexity of the data must be considered - the target audience may have difficulty if too much information is presented in a single piece. Navigating the information is necessary: unlike interactive ID, in this case, the user cannot isolate sets of data. This may mean that some sort of 'key' (e.g.: colour coding or symbolic pictograms) is needed to decipher the material. The two images shown in Fig. 1 exemplify two infographics in this category and use different visual representations - illustration and three-dimensional representation. In the examples shown, we can also observe the use of additional visualisation systems such as maps, graphs, or diagrams, but it is also common to use pictograms or tables to help communicate the content of the informative message.

Fig. 1. (left) "Bonelli's eagle (Aquila fasciata)" infographics, Cristina Pires dos Santos (infographics), Diana Costa (main illustration), 2019. (right) "Castelo de Aljezur" infographic, Leonor Nobre (infographics and 3D model) with the guidance of Cristina Pires dos Santos, 2018.

3.2 Interactive Information Design

Interactive ID requires a very different approach from print-based DI as the user is no longer passive. In this case, the user is active in making decisions and those choices need to be considered and presented and the user needs to be involved or immersed in the information. Coates and Ellison [17] state that this procedure involves filtering data to show particular facts, figures, or statistics. The user selects the criteria by which the data or information is measured or compared, and the navigation of this information is very important because the available options have to be clear and should lead to some meaningful resolution.

The same authors underline that the designer can also apply sound and animated images as part of the experience, justifying the existence of various ways of visualising data; we are also familiar with various graphic representations such as graphs, diagrams, tables, maps and pictograms, and many software tools. One of the many examples of DataViz available online is *No Ceilings: The Full Participation Project* [18], created by Ben Fry and Fathom his ID studio. This is an example of a data-driven platform that explores 20 years of progress and setbacks towards women's equality (health, education, economic participation, and social inclusion) based on almost one million data-generating interactive visualisations, exploratory maps, videos, articles, and shareable images. Another example of reference is the *OECD* project *Better Life Index* [19], authored by Moritz Stefaner, which allows the user to visualise and compare some key factors such as education, housing, and environment, factors that contribute to the well-being of the OECD[15] countries or the project *An Interactive Visualisation of NYC Street Trees* [20], authored by Cloudred, which allows us to analyse the types of trees present in the various districts of New York, where they are located and what their representation is. We can select by tree species (each species is associated with a different colour) and automatically observe the number and percentage of that species in each borough of New York and even make a comparative analysis between tree species.

---

[15] Organisation for Economic Co-operation and Development.

3.3   Environmental Information Design

When we talk about environmental ID, most people think of signage, although wayfinding systems, exhibition design, and large-scale installations can also be included in this category. According to Coates and Ellison [17], the function of wayfinding is to inform an audience of where they need to go, how to find it, and what to do once they have arrived. To achieve these goals, the designer must be aware of the physical limitations of an environment and the users' needs. They must make informed choices based on how real people use the area, and for that, they have to analyse the space very well.

The designer may have to think about whether it is possible to use multiple platforms to communicate, choosing print and interactive elements - the wayfinding project *Walk New York* [21], a pedestrian wayfinding plan for New York City, developed by the ID studio, Two Twelve, in 2011, had to take into consideration different users and different places and, consequently, different needs. This example demonstrates the strategy for implementing a system that uses a wide variety of platforms to provide effective information to residents, travellers, and visitors.

In the case of exhibition design, the challenge is how to communicate important facts or data to a wide audience in a specific place. The material displayed will need to be on a larger scale, but it is not just that, the designer needs to think about the distance from which a project is viewed, where it is positioned and even the lighting conditions of the physical environment to ensure it is legible [17]. A good example is the museography project for the 2017 *Mohammed VI Museum of the Moroccan Civilisation of Water* in Marrakech, Morocco [22], by the company MUSE. Its theme revolves around the supply of water to the centre of society, disseminating information, raising awareness, and creating awareness of the challenges that sustainable development poses, requiring a new strategic vision for water. The whole project highlights the Moroccan Water School's heritage, unique in the world, and its wealth of knowledge, based on traditional practices, which should be preserved and shown, and contribute to setting an example to be followed as a model of sustainable and effective management of water resources [23].

In the case of a wayfinding system, Coates and Ellison [17] make a parallel between the learning process of the brain and a wayfinding system. They claim that we know places through a series of steps, first by learning points, then routes, and finally the whole area. For this reason, we need a system that helps people build this knowledge quickly and safely because our brain is like a muscle; the more we exercise certain parts, the more developed they become, the hippocampus is the area of the brain associated with the mind mapping. One of the most important wayfinding projects in the world is the *Legible London* project, a wayfinding system to help people walk in the city of London, which argues that walking is the best way to discover the city; the first prototype of the project was installed in the Bond Street area in November 2007 [24]. In this project, we can see these strategies applied to help people to orientate themselves in a certain place, even if that place is highly complex as is the case of central London [25][16].

---

[16] In the available reference, you can see images and explanatory videos about the *Legible London* project to better understand the concept of knowledge construction (in this case, the acquisition of orientation in a certain space), through several stages.

4 Final Thoughts

The information designer has the communication of information as his/her main task and this implies responsibility so that the content is both accurate and impartial in its presentation; he/she should be very rigorous in the search for and dissemination of information, trying to present it in a visually effective way and always bearing in mind the target audience. They should also practice methodological procedures that contribute to clear and trustworthy communication of data. The information designer can have very different backgrounds and are often part of interdisciplinary teams that allow greater control and validation of the information presented. The ID can have very different practices and contexts (three different, but intersecting categorizations were mentioned in this article - print-based ID, interactive ID, and environmental ID), justifying the various competencies that the area requires, as well as their intervention in other differentiated areas.

The eternal confrontation between form and function is once again in evidence in ID through two distinctive aspects of its practice (Infographics and DataViz), which demand professionals with different profiles. It can be concluded that both expressions are valid, as they have very different ends, which increasingly underpins their autonomy, without needing to be discordant. This article proposed a theoretical reflection on all these issues, confirming that ID is an area of knowledge with its specificities when compared to traditional graphic design, justifying its necessary interdisciplinarity both in project teams and in the profile of ID professionals. In addition, and to reinforce this issue, we also tried to clarify the various practices of ID, providing concrete examples that help to better understand this multidimensionality associated with ID, aiming at a more informed practice and better preparation for the training of professionals in this field of knowledge.

Acknowledgements. This work is financed by national funds through FCT - Fundação para a Ciência e a Tecnologia, I.P., under the Strategic Project with the references UIDB/04008/2020 and UIDP/04008/2020.

References

1. Krum, R.: Cool Infographics: Effective Communication with Data Visualization and Design. Wiley, Hoboken (2014)
2. Spiekermann, E.: Information Design. Aiga (2002). http://www.aiga.org/content.cfm/inform ation-design_1. Accessed 1 Aug 2009
3. Baer, K., Vacarra, J.: Information Design Workbook: Graphic Approaches, Solutions, and Inspiration + 30 Case Studies. Rockport Publishers, Beverly (2008)
4. Hansen, Y.M.: Visualization for thinking, planning, and problem solving. In: Jacobson, R. (ed.) Information Design, pp. 193–220. The MIT Press, Massachusetts (2000)
5. Bonsiepe, G.: Cool Interface - An Approach to Design. Jan Van Eyck Akademie, Netherlands (1999)
6. Sless, D.: What is information design. In: Proceedings of the Designing Information for People Symposium, pp. 1–16 (1992). https://www.academia.edu/449792/What_is_Informa tion_Design. Accessed 5 Feb 2023

7. Horn, R.E.: Information design: emergence of a new profession. In: Jacobson, R. (ed.) Information Design, pp. 15–33. The MIT Press, Massachusetts (2000)
8. Cairo, A.: The Functional Art – An Introduction to Information Graphics and Visualization. New Riders – Voices that Matter, San Francisco (2013)
9. Holmes, N.: Precisão Fantástica: Aperfeiçoando a Arte da Informação [Fantastic Forecasting: Perfecting the Art of Information]. In: Wiedemann, J. (ed.) National Geographic Infographics, pp. 31–35. Taschen, Koln (2016)
10. Frascara, J.: What is information design?. In: Frascara, J. (ed.) Information Design as Principled Action. Making Information Accessible, Relevant, Understandable and Usable, pp. 5–55. Common Ground Publishing, Illinois (2015)
11. Pettersson, R.: Basic ID-concepts, Concepts & Terms, 4th edn. International Institute for Information Design (IIID), Austria (2012). https://www.iiid.net/PublicLibrary/Pettersson-Rune-ID-It-Depends.pdf. Accessed 6 Feb 2023
12. Walker, S., Barratt, M.: Information Design: The Essentials of Information Design. Design Council (2007). http://webarchive.nationalarchives.gov.uk/20080728102550/http://www.des igncouncil.org.uk/en/About-Design/Design-Disciplines/Information-Design-by-Sue-Wal ker-and-Mark-Barratt/. Accessed 6 Feb 2023
13. Schuller, G.: Information Design = Complexity + Interdisciplinarity + Experiment. Aiga (2007). http://www.aiga.org/content.cfm/complexity-plus-interdisciplinarity-plus-exp eriment. Accessed 29 Dec 2017
14. Gadney, M.: You are here. Eye **82** (21), 38–39 (2017). https://www.eyemagazine.com/fea ture/article/you-are-here. Accessed 6 Feb 2023
15. Lankow, J., Ritchie, J., Crooks, R.: Infographics. The Power of Visual Storytelling. Wiley, Hoboken (2012)
16. Norman, D.A.: Emotional Design – Why We Love (Or Hate) Everyday Things. Basic Books, New York (2004)
17. Coates, K., Ellison, A.: An Introduction to Information Design. Laurence King Publishing, London (2014)
18. No Ceilings: The Full Participation Project. http://www.noceilings.org. Accessed 6 Feb 2023
19. OECD Better Life Index. http://www.oecdbetterlifeindex.org/pt. Accessed 6 Feb 2023
20. An Interactive Visualization of NYC Street Trees. https://www.cloudred.com/labprojects/nyc trees/. Accessed 6 Feb 2023
21. I Walk NY – Transportation – Two Twelve. http://www.twotwelve.com/transportation/i-walk-ny.html. Accessed 6 Feb 2023
22. Musée Mohammed VI Pour La Civilization de L'Eau au Maroc. https://www.youtube.com/watch?v=lQ_emzVceWc. Accessed 6 Feb 2023
23. MUSE | Museums & Expos. http://www.museintl.co.uk. Accessed 6 Feb 2023
24. Santos, C.: O Design de Comunicação na Área do Turismo Cultural. A Importância da Infografia em Suportes Comunicacionais de Divulgação e Informação, Aplicados a Percursos Temáticos na Cidade de Almada [The Communication Design in the Area of Cultural Tourism. The Importance of Infographics in Communicational Media of Dissemination and Information, Applied to Thematic Routes in the City of Almada]. Master's thesis unpublished, Faculty of Architecture - University of Lisbon, Portugal (2010)
25. Applied | Legible London. https://www.appliedinformation.group/projects/legible-london. Accessed 6 Feb 2023

The Application of Digital Media Technology in Display Design

YiJia Gao[1(✉)] and YunQiao Su[2]

[1] School of Art and Design, Jiangxi Institute of Fashion Technology, Nanchang 330000, Jiangxi, China
630492407@qq.com
[2] Shandong College of Arts and Design, No. 1255, College Road, Changqing District, Jinan, China

Abstract. With the development of society and the progress of technology, digital media technology is applied to various fields, and began to popularize and spread in life. Artists are applying digital media technology to their creations. Especially in display design, new media technology is more prominent. The present display design can no longer see the shadow of traditional culture, more is the use of high-tech technology, digital media and display design better combination. The application of digital media technology in display design has greatly changed the language and design method in display design. It has greatly improved the display effect in the traditional sense.

Exhibition design can be said to be the best combination of art and science and technology, the combination of the two together, the collision of a new spark. At present, display design faces the public and undertakes the important task of transferring culture. It is also an important way for people to update their knowledge, broaden their horizons and improve their spiritual quality. This paper hopes to make a thorough study on the integration of digital media technology and display design, so as to summarize the correct design method. Specifically, the core is to show the theme, the support is digital technology, the support is digital culture, and the precursor is art and design. This paper starts with the specific application of digital media technology, summarizes the problems existing in the practical application, and sorts out the correct and reasonable creative methods of digital media display. This paper mainly discusses the main technical means of digital media technology in modern exhibition and exhibition, and predicts the development trend of exhibition design.

Keywords: digital media · Display design · Virtual reality · VR technology

1 Introduction

In the age of artificial intelligence, digital media technology has penetrated into every field of life. Especially in the field of exhibition design, the application of new technology and new methods is always the focus of attention. Through the active exploration of the application and development of digital technology in display design, the paper seeks for the future of display design.

2 Digital Media Technology and Display Design

Digital media art originated in the 1960s. In April 1965, Michael. Dr. Noel, a famous digital artist and engineer, has conducted 50 years of research on computer graphics and images, and held the Computer Art Exhibition in New York, the earliest digital media art exhibition in the world. Although it was only simple animation and graphics at that time, it marked the formal introduction of digital media technology into the field of display design. It has a profound influence on the development of display design. The 1970 World Expo in Osaka, Japan was a landmark event that combined technology, media, art, and large-scale public events. In 1973, the first SIGGRAPH exhibition was held, which showcased various techniques and achievements in computer graphics, such as virtual water cups and Beetle models. CG art also began to be used in display design. The Urban Future Pavilion of Expo 2010 Shanghai uses many advanced digital technologies to greatly enrich and enhance the content and effect of the exhibition. Nowadays, exhibitions and works of art using digital media are emerging in an endless stream. It opens up a colorful world for the viewer. For example, the digital media exhibition "What China Is Like" – the cultural relics interactive exhibition "Time Capsule, Exploring the Source Civilization", launched on August 20, 2022, caused a social sensation. The digital media exhibition takes cultural relics as the main body, expands the online exhibition space of cultural relics through digital technology, and innovates the educational forms of cultural relics through interactive means of edutainment. To enhance the audience, especially young people's attention to cultural relics and love (Fig. 1).

Fig. 1. "Why China" digital media exhibition – "Time Capsule, Exploring the Source of Civilization" cultural relics interactive exhibition

3 Digital Media Technology is Demonstrating the Performance of Design

Digital media technology is evolving rapidly, updating and iterating rapidly, and integrating with display design in a variety of ways. Here are a few popular forms of technological expression.

3.1 Giant Screen Projection

In order to improve the display effect, let the audience better understand the required display content, using dynamic audio to display static graphics in the design of the technical means. It includes animation, video and film. It can not only be more vivid in front of the audience, through the animation to enhance the display process, even if the display space is small, but also can provide the audience with a good feeling, the last century dynamic video and audio is the display of the carrier, they need to have an independent space, but also can form a certain wall enclosed space, has a strong visual impact. In two-dimensional display, large screen and ring screen are the most common forms of display. The display effect of images is usually achieved through the segmentation of images, which can be divided into a single or special screen form, giving people a sense of immersive interaction. Through the combination of unique sound, image, color and light projection technology, the rich information is combined together, which is deeply loved by the audience (Fig. 2).

Fig. 2. Suzhou large projection fusion giant screen

3.2 Multimedia Display Technology

The development of multimedia technology in the information age is fast. The unique images and sound effects of audio-visual equipment can vividly show the activities and impress visitors. Multimedia interactive technology not only enables visitors to fully understand the information of products, but also enables them to experience the sudden changes brought by the display space. For example, the technology used in the space displayed in Shanghai World Expo is hologram and air projection system, accounting for more than 60%, which is the most friendly way of display in the world. The space display mainly includes the following application forms, such as the virtual architecture of the scene, the interactive application of interactive technology, virtual network display space and so on. There may be more new technologies in the future, such as computer break-through technology, the era of network communication technology, intelligent monitoring technology, efficient and convenient graphics and image display technology. And with the application of advanced multimedia technology, more diversified exhibition space will be provided to visitors in the future (Fig. 3).

Fig. 3. Digital sand table

3.3 Holography

4D technology and holographic technology are the most prominent digital media technologies in exhibition space. The influence of the latter on exhibition space is mainly reflected in the following points: using limited space to create infinite space, and creating virtual space through physical space. Holographic technology is mainly derived from laser technology after World War II. The principle of this technology is to divide the laser beam into two beams, respectively shining on the photographed object and the projected film, record the halogen light under the special film object, and map it into a stereo image. If the viewpoint is moved properly, the side of the object can be seen. At present, the development of holographic technology not only extends to super height and high score, but also extends to the technical processing of mixing, bending, connecting and computer images. The application of holographic technology in display design provides a new language and development possibility, which can achieve the purpose of breaking the physical space restrictions, showing better effects and carrying more information (Fig. 4).

Fig. 4. Hologram technology

3.4 Virtual Reality Technology

The "Ultimate display" proposed by Sutherland in his paper is the origin of the earliest "virtual reality". He believes that the computer is the entrance to the virtual world and can have some interaction with people. In the 1980s, American Jararenla Neal defined the meaning of virtual reality. Virtual reality technology is an interactive virtual environment integrating the senses of sight, hearing and touch through the integration of information image technology, electronic induction setting, artificial intelligence and sensory tracking technology. Users can interact with computers and experience the real world through devices such as data helmet displays, clothes and gloves.

Experience this virtual scene in a virtual museum. People can not only see it, but experience it for themselves, modify what they don't quite like, or reset what they want from the past, present and future. For example, in the virtual dinosaur museum, we can see the terrain, the landforms, see dinosaurs and other animals and plants, and hear their calls. Click on the virtual environment of dinosaurs, you can further understand and learn their features and living characteristics. It can also redistribute the effects in the virtual environment. It can let the players take all the corresponding things according to their own wishes. At the same time, it can also simulate the climate at that time and adjust it to a certain extent. Another example is the multimedia projection imaging technology of Shanghai World Expo, which shows the modern scene of Shanghai under construction outside through the Windows of the "Stone Gate" building, so that visitors can inadvertently walk into the "New Shanghai" exhibition area.

Virtual reality technology has become a new force in the display and sale of cars. For example, the virtual reality car selection service jointly launched by Audi and Oculus allows consumers to experience various driving states of vehicles immersive through virtual reality technology, and can quickly switch interior style and model for comparison. Customers can browse a wide range of car models at any car seller Oculus. Oculus gives customers a more realistic experience, and the Oculus Rift headset provides a clearer understanding of the actual condition of the car's interior and exterior. The display is excellent (Fig. 5).

Fig. 5. Audi virtual test drive game

In addition, the virtual exhibition hall also opens a new era of auto exhibition. The virtual exhibition hall can stand on its own, without relying on reality. After the designer has completed the virtual scene according to the exhibition party's request, the exhibition can put it on the mobile app market or the computer app market (Figs. 6 and 7).

There are also cases of virtual technology and e-commerce platforms. Alibaba is also at the forefront in this respect. Seizing the technological trend, Alibaba took the lead in putting forward the concept of Buy + VR shopping in China, "registering" shoppers' body images and making them the protagonists in the virtual world. Then the VR experience device will introduce the shopper to the virtual mall, the specialty store, and these virtual scenes are very realistic, but the most amazing part is that the shopper can try out in this environment, so as to achieve the physical shopping experience. Helping people buy the world's wealth of products from the comfort of their homes (Figs. 8-1, 8-2).

Fig. 6. Real Exhibition Hall

Fig. 7. Virtual Exhibition Hall

In terms of exhibition, virtual reality technology will be used as part of the exhibition, allowing visitors to experience the novelty of the virtual world. For example, the

Fig. 8-1. Virtual dressing

Fig. 8-2. Virtual dressing

"Immortal Van Gogh" Sensitive Art Exhibition was launched in the Art Castle of Shanghai Xintiandi. The biggest feature of the exhibition is the use of dynamic technology to make Van Gogh's oil paintings "move". Through the technology created by the copyright owner of the exhibition, many Van Gogh paintings were added to the exhibition with animation effect, allowing the audience to enter the world of Van Gogh (Figs. 9-1, 9-2).

Fig. 9-1. "The Immortal Van Gogh" sensory art Exhibition

Fig. 9-1. "The Immortal Van Gogh" sensory art Exhibition

In the exhibition, more than 120 of Van Gogh's works are made into a dynamic holographic film through technical processing. Viewers can eat potatoes with a simple and honest farmer's family, enjoy the night view of street corners in a cafe at night, and pick fruits together in a red vineyard… Let people enter the world of painting.

4 The Development Trend of Display Design Under the Background of Digital Media Technology

Digital media technology has brought new changes to display design. Whether it's a change in fashion design, a change in structural technology, or even a change in social thought, the changes are huge. Display design has unique advantages in disseminating information, which needs to be made public through display. Digital media technology creates new experiences and new possibilities for display design. The rapid development of science and technology has promoted the progress of technology, and the exhibition mode has gradually changed from the silent, static, unimedia and passive in the past to the sound, dynamic, multi-media and active, bringing visitors a full range of sensory experience such as vision, touch and hearing, and the viewer's own activities have also become part of the exhibition.

The 21st century is an era of information technology. From connotation to extension, exhibition design is no longer limited to the scope defined by the design discipline. Driven by the new technical concept and the wave of technological innovation, spatial exhibition design has become a cultural activity that integrates high-density information integration with cutting-edge technology. Exhibition design, as a design discipline integrating various art forms, has also followed the pace of The Times and embarked on the road of technological development. The emergence of new digital media technology has changed modern display design to some extent, and gradually developed it into a core technology. The reason why it emerged and developed is mainly because it fully connects culture, economy, technology and other fields. It is an inevitable trend of historical development, with a strong sense of The Times. It enriches the content and form of display design, improves the ways and methods of display design, and establishes a more complex information system for improving the quality of display design. Both traditional display design and new digital media technology, in essence, are designed to deal with the relationship between display space, content and visitors, and the better the display effect, the more effective the display communication. With the progress of The Times and the change of technology, display design has an increasing demand for multimedia, while digital media display technology keeps up with the pace of The Times in the aspects of "field", "object", "person" and "experience", showing a specific development trend, and will surely create more updated application scenarios in the future.

5 Conclusion

Digital media art has the characteristics of comprehensiveness and diversification. Through the elaboration of display design and digital media technology, the paper summarizes the specific impact of digital media technology on display design. See the future display design development of new changes and new trends. Digital media technology provides a more intuitive and scientific display form for the field of display design. The future society is bound to be the carrier of science and technology, and display design will continue to move forward in this direction. The integration of digital media technology and display design will become closer and closer, and it will also play a bigger and stronger role in display design.

References

1. Li, S.: Art History of Digital Media. Tsinghua University Press, Beijing (2008)
2. Chen, L.: History of New Media Art. Tsinghua University Press, Beijing (2007)
3. Tong, F.: New Media Art. Southeast University Press, Nanjing (2006)
4. Wang, D.: Digital media and Art Development. Sichuan Publishing Group Bashu Press, Chengdu (2007)
5. Ren, Z.: Exhibition Design Concept and Application. China Water Resources and Hydropower Press, Beijing (2008)
6. Chen, M.: Principle of Art Communication. Shanghai Jiao Tong University Press, Shanghai (2009)
7. Zeng, Y.: Art and Communication. Tsinghua University Press, Beijing (2007)
8. Ye, P.: The Art of Display. China Architecture and Building Press, Beijing (2010)
9. Wang, H.: Exhibition Art. People's Publishing House, Beijing (2008)
10. Jie, F.: Exhibition Design. Shanghai Pictorial Publishing House, Shanghai (2007)
11. Fang, X., Yang, X., Cai, X., Gui, Y.: Digital Art Design. Wuhan University of Technology Press, Wuhan (2004)
12. Zhong, S.: Interpretation of Communication Methods – Theory and Research of Contemporary Exhibition Design. Hunan Art Production Society, Changsha (2003)
13. Chalume, J.-L., Liu, F.: Translated by Lv Qibeng. Interpretation of Art. Culture and Art Press, Beijing (2005)
14. [De] Benjamin, W., Hu, U.: Technical Reproduction of the Contemporary Generation of Technical Works. Zhejiang Literature and Art Publishing Society, Hangzhou (2005)
15. Liu, S.: Research on the Principle of Visual Composition in Exhibition Space. Jiangnan University, Wuxi (2008)
16. It's a big deal. Art Design of Exhibition. Jilin: Jilin University (2009)
17. Lu, J.: Research on Art Design of Exhibition Space. Wuhan University of Technology, Wuhan (2002)
18. Liu, S.: Research on the Principle of Visual Composition in Exhibition Space. Jiangnan University (2008)
19. Rush, M.: Yu Qing translated. New Media Art. People's Fine Arts Publishing House, Shanghai (2015)
20. Ma, L.: Philosophy of Digital Art. China Social Sciences Press, Beijing (2012)
21. Lu, X., Liao, X.: Introduction to Digital Media Art. Higher Education Press, Beijing (2014)
22. Huang, J.: Spatial Display Design. Peking University Press, Beijing (2007)
23. Huang, J.: Guangxi Fine Arts Publishing House, Nanning (2003)
24. Jiang, S., Mo, J.: Exhibition Design. Central South University Press, Changsha (2004)
25. Li, Y., Song, C.: Exhibition Design. Huazhong University of Science and Technology Press, Wuchang (2007)
26. Jiang, Y.: Today's Pioneer. Tianjin Academy of Social Sciences Press, Tianjin (2001)
27. Negroponte: Digital Survival. Hainan Publishing House, Haikou (1996)

The Awareness and Practices of Web Developers Toward Sustainable Web Design

Ola Hulleberg⬤, Henrik Landgraff Granum⬤, Sivert Gullberg Hansen⬤,
Magnus Moen⬤, Carlos Vicient Monllaó⁽⬛⁾, and Yavuz Inal⬤

Department of Design, Norwegian University of Science and Technology, Trondheim, Norway
`carlos.vicient@ntnu.no`

Abstract. Sustainable design should be one of the main objectives of digital systems and services to use the resources efficiently. Designing low-carbon websites through careful implementation of images, fonts, videos, and colour is useful to minimise environmental impact. Yet, low awareness and practices of web developers are the main challenges in developing sustainable digital systems and services. This study explores how web developers view and practise sustainable web design. We collected data from 77 developers in Norway using an online survey. Our results show that, generally, web developers are aware of the web's impact on the climate, however they do not use the correct practices such as image file format, font subsetting, video codec, dark mode energy, and compression of audio/software to reduce this impact. We discuss the practical implications of the study results and provide preliminary recommendations for addressing the need for delivering sustainable web design.

Keywords: Sustainable Web · Sustainability · Web Developers · Web Design · Awareness · Practices · Internet · Climate · Carbon Footprint

1 Introduction

The Internet offers a wide variety of ever-growing application areas. All these services provided through the Internet have a considerable environmental impact. The infrastructure required to support the Internet, including data centres, servers, and routers, has a significant energy consumption [29]. This, combined with activities like using search engines, online gaming and video streaming, results in a notable production of CO2 emissions [12]. Data from 2018 suggests that if the Internet were a country, it would be ranked as the sixth most polluting country in the world [11]. Current development trends predict that by 2025, the Internet will be ranked as the fourth most polluting country, according to a report by Mozilla [30].

Today, there are approximately 2 billion websites worldwide [21]. As the number of internet users and websites continues to grow, it is expected to impact global electricity usage significantly. Electricity usage from communication technologies is projected to increase from 4% in 2020 to 14% by 2040 [5]. This increasing environmental impact

© The Author(s), under exclusive license to Springer Nature Switzerland AG 2023
A. Marcus et al. (Eds.): HCII 2023, LNCS 14030, pp. 134–145, 2023.
https://doi.org/10.1007/978-3-031-35699-5_11

highlights the importance of making the Internet greener and more sustainable in the future.

Sustainable web design is defined as "an approach to designing web services that prioritizes the health of our home planet. At its core is a focus on reducing carbon emissions and energy consumption" [11, p. 5]. Raising awareness among developers about the importance of sustainability is crucial because they are responsible for creating and maintaining websites and web applications. By being aware of the environmental impact of their work and taking steps to make their solutions more sustainable, developers would help reduce the growth of the Internet's overall environmental footprint.

All measures that involve minimising the page weight are essential for sustainable web design, since a larger page weight equals higher energy usage and CO_2 emissions. Designing low-carbon websites through careful implementation of images, fonts, videos, and colour is, therefore, useful to minimise the total page weight. Using darker colours over brighter ones, and the built-in system fonts on the user's devices over external fonts are just some of the methods to decrease energy usage. In addition, reusable code and modularity contribute to more efficiency.

Image and video files are the main contributors to the amount of data transfer, with images being the single largest source of carbon emissions on the average website [11]. To reduce energy consumption, it is crucial to evaluate the necessity of each resource, whether it be an image, video, or external font, as they all consume bandwidth and electricity [11]. Even if the most sustainable solution would be not to utilise any external files, sustainable web design should not be a limiting factor. Sustainable web design should rather be a design principle guiding developers towards the most sustainable version of their creations. Measuring sustainability based on file formats and file sizes allows us to understand the environmental impact of the technology we use and guide us towards the most sustainable formats. File sizes of different formats determine the amount of storage and bandwidth required, which might significantly impact the overall environmental footprint of websites.

Web developers are not required to follow standards and guidelines that help them develop a sustainable design. However, in the context of web accessibility, it is legally obliged for public and private organisations to follow the Web Content Accessibility Guidelines (WCAG) in many countries including Norway [27, 36]. Previous research has consistently shown that developers have different levels of awareness, understanding, and interpretation of accessibility requirements not only in Norway, but also in many other countries [14, 18, 26]. Moreover, developers' adherence to accessibility guidelines is relatively low due to the lack of awareness [3, 17, 20]. This results in partially or entirely inaccessible websites to people with a disability and the elderly [2, 17, 19, 22, 24, 25, 31].

In contrast, the field of sustainable web design lacks well-established guidelines and standards for developers to implement sustainability practices when developing web solutions. Few attempts to provide recommendations to guide developers towards a more sustainable design approach have been made by authors such as Greenwood [11] and Frick [10]. Scant attention has been paid to how web developers view and practise sustainability in their web projects, despite the growing importance of sustainable web design in recent years. To this end, we aim to understand the practices and awareness of web developers regarding sustainable web design.

2   Methods

We developed and administered an online survey over a period of three weeks between November and December 2022. Data was collected from web developers working in Norway. The survey was in Norwegian and distributed through the personal contacts of researchers. The data analysis was conducted as a descriptive statistical analysis and plotted with Matplotlib [15].

2.1   Participants

With a total of 77 complete survey responses, most survey participants were web professionals working for a company in Norway. We also distributed the survey to web development students (as prospective web developers) at the Norwegian University of Science and Technology via a private online forum. The age distribution of the participants ranged between 18–24 years (15.6%, n = 12), 25–34 years (50.6%, n = 39), 35–44 years (26%, n = 20), and above 45 years (7.8%, n = 6).

2.2   Questionnaire

We created a survey that included 33 questions related to various aspects of sustainable design. The questionnaire was divided into three sections. The demographics section aimed to gather information about the participants, including their job titles, work experience, education, and company size. The practices section aimed to gather information about the techniques and methods related to sustainable web design that the participants use in their work. These questions were developed based on the sustainable web design practices suggested by Greenwood [11] and Frick [10]. The final section on awareness aimed to measure the participants' knowledge and understanding of sustainable web design and its importance.

2.3   Comparing Efficiency of Media Files

We ran comparisons on a rasterised- and a vectorised image, to understand what file format would likely be more sustainable. It can be assumed that logos are often vectorised, while regular photos are rasterised. To convert between the different image formats, we set up a script to run the file through ImageMagick [16], an open-source command-line software to display, edit and convert image files. The vector image was exported using default settings with Adobe Illustrator [1]. The original file size for the rasterised image was 24,704 KB (.ARW - a raw image format by Sony), and the original file size for the vectorised image was 13.7 KB (.SVG). In order to juxtapose the different format comparisons, we had to scale the sizes to a similar scale (0–100 K), with the maximum scale value corresponding to the largest file size from each image comparison. That allowed us to put both comparisons on the same graph, regardless of size differences.

To measure the difference between the final file size of each video codec, we used FFmpeg [8] as our transcoder. FFmpeg is a set of tools used to manipulate and edit various forms of multimedia content, including video, audio, and subtitles. When transcoding the video files, we used fast presets ("8" for AV1 and "fast" for H264/H265) and the highest possible CRF value ("63" for AV1 and "51" for H264/H265). The video files were transcoded into MP4 containers. The reason for using MP4 as a baseline for the image format comparison was based on MP4 being the most popular format from the questionnaire. MP4 is an efficient format that also offers improved accessibility with features like audio description tracks and captioning Greenwood [11].

3   Results

Here, we present the results beginning with the demographics. This is followed by our findings related to practices and awareness of web developers regarding sustainable web design.

3.1   Demographics

More than half of the participants were full-stack developers (55.8%, n = 43), followed by front-end developers (15.6%, n = 12), designers (9.1%, n = 7), students (7.8%, n = 6), managers (5.2%, n = 4), back-end developers (3.9%, n = 3), and computer engineers (2.6%, n = 2). Concerning education attainment, 38 participants (49.4%) had a master's degree, 23 (29.9%) were university graduates, and 16 (20.7%) were high school or vocational school graduates. Most participants graduated from web development (76.2%, n = 48) and computer science (12.7%, n = 8) fields. Other fields reported by the participants were tourism and management, music, and nature science.

The most common response among the participants regarding their work experience was between two and five years of experience (34.7%, n = 25), followed by participants with between ten to twenty years of experience (25%, n = 18). The least represented experience group was those with more than twenty years of experience (4.2%, n = 3). Most of the participants (59.2%, n = 42) were working in large companies (100 + employees), followed by small-sized companies (under 50 employees) (33.8%, n = 24) and medium-sized companies (50–100 employees) (7%, n = 5). The use of documentation was the most common channel (80.5%, n = 62) for acquiring new knowledge regarding practices and coding in general. Documentation was closely followed by video tutorials (74%, n = 57) and courses through work (66.2%, n = 51). Other learning channels used by the participants included learning from colleagues, courses, and conferences.

3.2   Practices

A majority (61%, n = 47) of participants reported writing reusable code "Often", while 20.8% (n = 16) reported "Always". Further, 13% (n = 10) reported doing so "Sometimes". A small minority of 2.6% (n = 2) reported that they "Rarely" write reusable code, while the same amount (2.6%, n = 2) reported that they "Never" write reusable code. These results indicate that a significant portion of the participants places a high value on writing reusable code and that it is a common practice in their development process. When excluding designers from the data, none of the relevant participants reported that they "Never" write reusable code.

On modern OLED screens, black is the most energy-efficient colour, while white is the most energy-consuming [11]. Therefore, using darker colours for the website or offering the users a dark mode is beneficial. The results revealed that only 1.3% (n = 1) of the participants "Always" offer the users a light and dark mode, while 7.8% (n = 6) reported offering it "Often". Additionally, 20.8% (n = 16) answered that they offer the feature "Sometimes", and 37.7% (n = 29) "Rarely". On the other hand, 32.5% (n = 25) of the participants reported that they "Never" offer the feature. These results indicate that most developers (around 70%) do not frequently prioritise the implementation of a dark and light mode feature.

The participants were then asked about their practices on images and videos for websites. These results are vital to establishing the current usage among the participants in reference to each format's respective level of sustainability. To verify the sustainability of each format, we conducted several tests.

Image. While the 250 × 50 px logo rasterised from an SVG ranges from 1.76 KB (AVIF) to 673KB (EPS), the differences grow when comparing a 6000 × 3376 px photo taken with a camera in different formats. The camera image ranges from 480 KB (AVIF) to 138 MB (TIFF). It should be noted that the compression of the AVIF format seems to smooth out some of the colours, yet this is only noticeable when zooming in, and in this case, it looks better when zoomed out than the grainy colours of the TIFF.

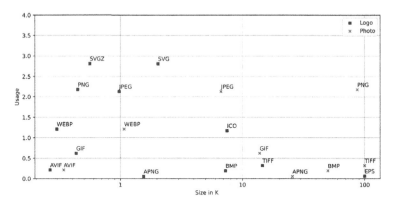

Fig. 1. Usage of image file formats.

The x-axis in Fig. 1 shows the file sizes of the different image formats in kilobytes, scaled between 0–100(K). The y-axis represents the average response from a Likert scale, where each option is given a number between 0 and 4, ranging from "Never" to "Always", and then multiplied by the number of responses.

AVIF is the smallest file format, however, using vector images has additional advantages from a design perspective. In the photo comparison, the space savings of AVIF are immense, coming in at 1/10 of WEBP, the second-best file format in size. According to the survey answers, PNG and JPEG are popular when displaying pictures, however, JPEG is 70 times larger than AVIF, while PNG is almost 100 times larger. The participants' most popular file formats were SVG, PNG and JPEG, while the least popular were EPS and APNG. The result also shows that the logo format with the smallest file size is AVIF, and the largest file size is EPS.

Video. The participants were asked if they use video, which video format they use and how often they use it. In total, 67.6% (n = 52) of participants answered that they use video in website development. Of those participants, 80.8% (n = 42) said they use the video format MP4. Figure 2 shows screenshots from a video, transcoded into different codecs and saved in the same video format (MP4), with the same video bitrate. The original video size was 64.7 MB, and after transcoding the video the size was reduced to ~1.1 MB for all codecs, showing that file size correlates with bitrate rather than file extension. To achieve the same quality as AV1, both H264 and H265 need to increase their bitrate, resulting in larger file sizes.

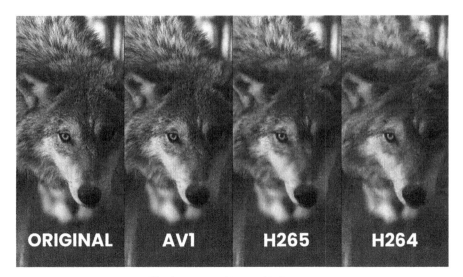

Fig. 2. Usage of image file formats.

The comparison shows that file format has a negligible effect on file size when transcoding with the same codec. Previous research by Greenwood [11] hints at the file format being the major contributor to size savings. The author explains that they reduced the video file size by saving their WEBM file as an MP4. However, our research shows it is more nuanced. It is rather the codec it is transcoded with that dictates the file size, not the file format. When transcoding with the AV1 codec, the difference between MP4 and AVI formats in file size is minimal (0.09MB) and provides the same video quality.

Font. Most participants (44.2%, n = 34) reported using external fonts "Often," while 16.9% (n = 13) indicated they "Always" use them. A total of 19.5% (n = 15) reported using them "Sometimes," while 14.3% (n = 11) said "Rarely". Only 5.2% (n = 4) answered "Never." These answers indicate widespread usage of external fonts, with most participants using them regularly. By creating a subset of a font, also called font subsetting, the font sizes can be significantly reduced by removing the unused glyphs and characters [13]. We found that most participants (83%, n = 64) were unaware of font subsetting and therefore do not optimise their external fonts. Only 16.4% (n = 12) of the participants were both familiar with and used font subsetting, while 61.5% (n = 8) who use external fonts "Always" and 91% (n = 31) who use external fonts "Often" were not familiar with font subsetting.

Compression. Participants most commonly compressed images (62.4%, n = 48), videos (46.8%, n = 36), and code (61%, n = 47). They rarely compressed sound files (58.5%, n = 45) and software (52%, n = 40). Interestingly, 61% (n = 47) of the participants stated that they regularly use external fonts and of those, 29.8% (n = 14) answered that they "Never" compress them, while 23.4% (n = 11) answered "Rarely".

3.3 Awareness

The participants were shown two pictures of the same website: one with a dark theme and one with a light theme. They were then asked to pick the option they believed was the most efficient on modern mobile phones. Almost all participants answered correctly (94%, n = 72), which is the version with a dark theme. Correct answers refer to the most sustainable option. Then, the participants were shown four pictures of websites: one with a coloured image covering the whole page, one with a monochrome image covering half of the page, one with a coloured image covering half of the page, and a website with only text. A majority (82%, n = 63) correctly identified the text-only website as the most sustainable of the four websites.

When asked which image format was believed to be the most efficient, 49% (n = 38) answered WEBP. WEBP is one of the most efficient formats for photographs, however while AVIF is less than half the size of WEBP, it ships with less compatibility [11]. As part of the practices section of the survey, 45.5% (n = 35) answered that they use JPEG. It seems therefore that the participants are aware that WEBP is a more sustainable image format yet still prefer JPEG.

Further, 90% (n = 69) of the participants answered that they think system fonts are the most energy-saving when loading web pages, which according to Greenwood [11] is the correct answer. However, a majority (44.2%, n = 34) of the participants answered they used external fonts "Often" and 16.9% (n = 13) "Always", showing a discrepancy between awareness and practices regarding fonts. Most of the participants (90%, n = 69) chose the correct answer of system fonts when asked which way of implementing fonts was believed to be the most sustainable, among the options of system fonts, external fonts, and that they are equally efficient.

Figure 3 shows the average number of correct answers to the previously mentioned questions. The data is divided into years of working experience, and the participants' highest achieved education grade within those groups. The x-axis represents the participants' years of work experience, and the y-axis represents the average correct answers within the different work experience groups. The overall average score across all groups was 69%. Those with less than one year of experience had the highest score of 79%, while students had the worst score, a score of 58%. Both the experience groups with one to five and over five years of experience hovered around the average, where the former scored 67%, and the latter scored a higher 71%.

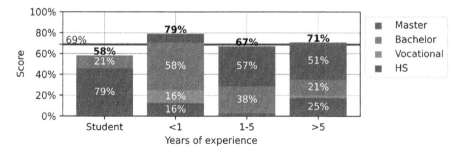

Fig. 3. Awareness test score vs. years of experience and education level.

Finally, participants were asked to give their opinion on a scale from 1 (not at all) to 5 (very much) on how much they think bot traffic affects energy consumption and how much they think websites affect the environment through CO_2 emissions. Most participants believed that websites and bot traffic have a medium to high impact on the environment. The average response was between medium and medium-high, with a score of 3.49 for websites and 3.55 for bot traffic. Combining the scores of 4 and 5, which are considered a fair amount, 56% (n = 42) of the participants answered in this range for bot traffic and 46% (n = 36) for websites.

4 Discussion

This study provides an overview of web developers' current practices and awareness regarding sustainable web design. Data from 77 web developers showed that while web developers are generally aware of the web's impact on the environment, they are not consistently using the right practices to minimise their impact.

Being the single largest source of carbon emissions on an average website [11], images are crucial to handle properly. Our comparisons of different file formats show that choosing the proper format may have a significant impact on the environment when most of the developers prefer to use less sustainable formats such as JPEG and PNG instead of AVIF or WEBP. However, picking the most sustainable format might not always be trivial. Broz [6] performed a similar comparison where they found that in certain use cases, like text images, PNG had a better quality-to-size ratio than both WEBP and AVIF. The best-performing formats for images in Broz's comparisons line up with our comparison results, with AVIF and WEBP being the most effective formats.

Data costs money, both in the form of bandwidth and storing it. One would expect developers to be using either AVIF or WEBP which are the most all-around efficient image formats for photos [6]. The businesses developers work for could save money by replacing more inefficient formats with new efficient ones. However, the data showed that developers still use the former. Edge, which has a global market share of 4.46%

[35], does not at the time of writing support AVIF [7]. In the use case where Edge is a necessity, we recommend WEBP, the second-best option. In an ideal world, AVIF would have been supported by every single client and browser. Despite the results in our comparison depicting that AVIF is better than SVG and SVGZ, it is important to note the advantages these vector formats include. Vectorised formats offer scalability, and depending on the display resolution, might be smaller in size compared to rasterised images.

All the online compression tools we tested [9, 28, 32, 33] transcoded our input video file with the H264 codec by default, which in our test was the worst codec for saving bandwidth. From this, we might assume that developers who are using online compression tools, without changing any settings, are not compressing files to an optimal degree.

Design decisions might be a factor that is a potential cause for the high usage of external fonts. Designers, companies, and product owners often have styles, policies and expectations connected to their branding and companies, that may include or exclude certain fonts that the companies use. This may be to establish a recognisable brand. Therefore, using system fonts from a designer's perspective might be less valuable, or recognisable to users reading the websites.

Almost all participants reported that dark mode of a website would be the most energy efficient. Yet only a single participant reported always implementing it, followed by a very small minority implementing it often. The small implementation rate could be related to developers finding it tedious to implement such a feature. It is, however, proven that a dark mode is easily implemented with just a few lines of code [4]. In addition to the sustainability aspect, a survey conducted by Spiceworks [34] revealed that most website users prefer to have a dark mode available and use it across their devices.

There are easily implementable methods to mitigate unnecessary data transfer, like page caching, file compression [11] and GZIP compression for websites [23]. However, there is a lot of room for improvement in efficient use of sustainable design practices and resources for websites and web-related software.

A sustainable web design approach needs to be embraced by all stakeholders in web design, from developers, designers, and DevOps to managers, companies, communities, and government. By incorporating sustainable design principles into governmental policies and regulations, the web design industry would be held accountable to these standards, much like the Norwegian government requires developers to follow WCAG [27]. We, therefore, suggest developing a guideline similar to WCAG, for all the aforementioned stakeholders. Increased focus on education would be beneficial to raise awareness and teach sustainable design methods, leading to increased awareness and practices in the industry. By introducing legal regulations at national or international levels, the industry could be regulated and evaluated based on their practices more systematically. This could accelerate the process towards a more sustainable web industry.

5 Conclusion

This research aimed to explore and analyse the awareness and practices of web developers regarding sustainable web design. In general, the survey participants were aware of the web's impact on the climate and which practices would be considered more sustainable.

However, the participants do not use the most sustainable practices related to topics such as file formats, font subsetting and colour to minimise the environmental impact. In order to standardise sustainable web design, we recommend developing a more systematic and extensive approach involving all parties in the ecosystem. Limitations of this research paper consist of the sample size of the questionnaire and the lack of qualitative data. Higher participation could have resulted in a more accurate representation of the industry. Qualitative data could have explained the reasons for the lack of usage of sustainable development and design methods. Future research should focus on finding the reasons the web design industry seems to be aware of sustainable web practices but does not fully implement them.

References

1. Adobe Illustrator. https://www.adobe.com/products/illustrator.html
2. Alim, S.: Web accessibility of the top research-intensive universities in the UK. SAGE Open **11**(4) (2021). https://doi.org/10.1177/21582440211056614
3. Alshayban, A., Ahmed, I., Malek, S.: Accessibility issues in android apps: state of affairs, sentiments, and ways forward. In: Proceedings of the ACM/IEEE 42nd International Conference on Software Engineering, pp. 1323–1334 (2020)
4. Arjun, A.: One line - dark mode using CSS. https://dev.to/akhilarjun/one-line-dark-mode-using-css-24li. Accessed 7 Feb 2023
5. Belkhir, L., Elmeligi, A.: Assessing ICT global emissions footprint: trends to 2040 & recommendations. J. Clean. Prod. **177**, 448–463 (2018). https://doi.org/10.1016/j.jclepro.2017.12.239
6. Broz, M.: Image format comparison (JPEG, PNG, WEBP, & AVIF) - 2023 statistics. https://photutorial.com/image-format-comparison-statistics/. Accessed 7 Feb 2023
7. Deveria, A.: AVIF image format. Can I use. https://caniuse.com/?search=AVIF. Accessed 7 Feb 2023
8. FFmpeg. https://ffmpeg.org/. Accessed 25 Jan 2023
9. FreeConverter.: Video compressor. https://www.freeconvert.com/video-compressor. Accessed 5 Feb 2023
10. Frick, T.: Designing for sustainability: a guide to building greener digital products and services. O'Reilly Media (2016)
11. Greenwood, He, R.: Sustainable web design, vol. 34. A book apart (2021)
12. Griffiths, S.: Why your internet habits are not as clean as you think (2020). https://www.bbc.com/future/article/20200305-why-your-internet-habits-are-not-as-clean-as-you-think. Accessed 25 Jan 2023
13. Hempenious, K., Pollard, B.: Best practices for fonts. https://web.dev/font-best-practices/. Accessed 25 Jan 2023
14. Antonelli, H.L., Rodrigues, S.S., Watanabe, W.M., de Mattos Fortes, R.P.: A survey on accessibility awareness of Brazilian web developers. In: Proceedings of the 8th International Conference on Software Development and Technologies for Enhancing Accessibility and Fighting Info-exclusion, pp. 71–79 (2018). https://doi.org/10.1145/3218585.3218598
15. Hunter, J.D.: Matplotlib: a 2D graphics environment. Comput. Sci. Eng. **9**(3), 90–95 (2007)
16. ImageMagick. https://imagemagick.org/index.php. Accessed 25 Jan 2023
17. Inal, Y., Ismailova, R.: Effect of human development level of countries on the web accessibility and quality in use of their municipality websites. J. Ambient. Intell. Humaniz. Comput. **11**(4), 1657–1667 (2019). https://doi.org/10.1007/s12652-019-01284-4

18. Inal, Y., Guribye, F., Rajanen, D., Rajanen, M., Rost, M.: Perspectives and practices of digital accessibility: a survey of user experience professionals in Nordic countries. In: Proceedings of the 11th Nordic Conference on Human-Computer Interaction: Shaping Experiences, Shaping Society, pp. 1–11 (2020). https://doi.org/10.1145/3419249.3420119
19. Inal, Y., Mishra, D., & Torkildsby, A.B.: An analysis of web content accessibility of municipality websites for people with disabilities in Norway: web accessibility of Norwegian municipality websites. In: Nordic Human-Computer Interaction Conference, pp. 1–12 (2022). https://doi.org/10.1145/3546155.3547272
20. Inal, Y., Rızvanoğlu, K., Yesilada, Y.: Web accessibility in Turkey: awareness, understanding and practices of user experience professionals. Univ. Access Inf. Soc. 1–12 (2017). https://doi.org/10.1007/s10209-017-0603-3
21. Internet Live Stats: Total number of websites. https://www.internetlivestats.com/total-number-of-websites/. Accessed 25 Jan 2023
22. Ismailova, R., Inal, Y.: Web site accessibility and quality in use: a comparative study of government Web sites in Kyrgyzstan, Azerbaijan, Kazakhstan and Turkey. Univ. Access Inf. Soc. **16**(4), 987–996 (2016). https://doi.org/10.1007/s10209-016-0490-z
23. Juviler, J.: How to Enable GZIP Compression for Faster Web Pages. https://blog.hubspot.com/website/gzip-compression. Accessed 25 Jan 2023
24. Król, K., Zdonek, D.: Local government website accessibility - evidence from Poland. Admin. Sci. **10**(2), 22 (2020). https://doi.org/10.3390/admsci10020022
25. Laufer Nir, H., Rimmerman, A.: Evaluation of Web content accessibility in an Israeli institution of higher education. Univ. Access Inf. Soc. **17**(3), 663–673 (2018). https://doi.org/10.1007/s10209-018-0615-7
26. Lazar, J., Dudley-Sponaugle, A., Greenidge, K.D.: Improving web accessibility: a study of webmaster perceptions. Comput. Hum. Behav. **20**(2), 269–288 (2004). https://doi.org/10.1016/j.chb.2003.10.018
27. Lovdata: Forskrift om universell utforming av informasjons- og kommunikasjonsteknologiske (IKT)-løsninger (FOR-2013-06-21-732). Lovdata (2013). https://lovdata.no/dokument/SF/forskrift/2013-06-21-732
28. Lunaweb GmbH.: WEBM to MP4 Converter. https://cloudconvert.com/webm-to-mp4. Accessed 5 Feb 2023
29. McFadden, C.: Internet energy usage: how the life-changing network has a hidden cost. https://interestingengineering.com/innovation/whats-the-energy-cost-internet. Accessed 25 Jan 2023
30. Mozilla.: The Internet uses more electricity than.... https://internethealthreport.org/2018/the-internet-uses-more-electricity-than/. Accessed 25 Jan 2023
31. Parajuli, P., Eika, E.: A comparative study of accessibility and usability of norwegian university websites for screen reader users based on user experience and automated assessment. In: Antona, M., Stephanidis, C. (eds.) HCII 2020. LNCS, vol. 12188, pp. 300–310. Springer, Cham (2020). https://doi.org/10.1007/978-3-030-49282-3_21
32. Smith, C.: Top 6 web video compression software: How to compress video for web easily. https://videoconverter.wondershare.com/compress/compress-video-for-web.html. Accessed 25 Jan 2023
33. Softo Ltd.: Compress Video. Clideo. https://clideo.com/compress-video. Accessed 25 Jan 2023
34. Spiceworks.: Light mode vs. dark mode. Which do you prefer? The Spiceworks Community. https://community.spiceworks.com/topic/2456118-light-mode-vs-dark-mode-which-do-you-prefer. Accessed 25 Jan 2023

35. Statcounter.: Statcounter Global stats. Browser Market Share Worldwide. https://gs.statco unter.com/. Accessed 7 Feb 2023
36. WAI Policy. Web accessibility laws & policies. https://www.w3.org/WAI/policies/. Accessed 25 Jan 2023

Experience Design Based on Values and Psychological Needs in a Corporate Context

Anne Elisabeth Krüger[1]([✉]) [iD], Maria Ivanova[2], Danica Sattink Rath[1] [iD],
and Stefan Brandenburg[3] [iD]

[1] Fraunhofer-Institute for Industrial Engineering, 70569 Stuttgart, Germany
`anne-elisabeth.krueger@iao.fraunhofer.de`
[2] Technische Universität Berlin, Berlin, Germany
`maria.ivanova@campus.tu-berlin.de`
[3] Department of Psychology, Technische Universität Chemnitz, Chemnitz, Germany
`stefan.brandenburg@psychologie.tu-chemnnitz.de`

Abstract. In Experience Design the focus is shifting from users to the technology creators. These people need to have a human-centred mindset to design for positive user experience of digital products and services. Hence, the traditional user-centred perspective of usability and user experience design expands to also include the values and psychological needs of company employees creating user-centred technology. To succeed in practice, companies need to be aware of their employees' values and psychological needs and its impact on the success of the company. In this paper we present empirical results assessed to transfer the theoretical concepts of values and psychological needs into the context of companies. The findings suggest that the employees psychological needs and values are important in a corporate context. Also, it seems to be possible to transfer methods from experience design to the domain of designing for values. However, additional results indicate that companies should facilitate a supportive company culture and the correct mindset to foster the consideration of the employees and users psychological needs and values.

Keywords: Experience Design · Psychological Needs · User Values · Corporate Context

1 Introduction

The human-centred design of interactive products and services with the goal of creating a positive user experience of interactive products has been a topic in human-computer-interaction research for a long time [17]. It has also made its way into standardized norms like the DIN EN ISO 9241–210 [10]. New developments in the field go beyond mere usability and user experience design but include psychological needs and values. Despite this successful history of experience design, the transfer of knowledge from academia to companies is often difficult. One issue is a lack of practical methods for the designers - the technology creators [33]. Furthermore, necessary preconditions in the companies like

A. Marcus et al. (Eds.): HCII 2023, LNCS 14030, pp. 146–163, 2023.
https://doi.org/10.1007/978-3-031-35699-5_12

expertise, time, etc. are not met. Finally, there are different approaches to define sets of rather abstract psychological needs [8,14,18–20] and user values [11].

To successfully address psychological needs and values of users, companies should care about the psychological needs and values of their employees. The idea is that experience design can successfully implement psychological needs and user values if needs and values of the employees are also met. Companies have to know *that* and *why* they are important (sensitisation). Furthermore, they need basic knowledge about relevant values and psychological needs and structured methods to consider them in their products and services. However, awareness, knowledge, and methods concerning psychological needs and values and how they relate to each other are not sufficiently spread in companies.

Following this line of thought, the contribution of this manuscript is to answer the following research questions:

1. What is the relevance of psychological needs and values in the corporate context and under what conditions can they be fulfilled?
2. Can methods from the design for psychological needs be transferred to the design for user values?

2   Needs and Values in Experience Design

2.1   Psychological Needs and Values

It is essential for designing positive user experiences in the context of interactive products and services that psychological needs of users are considered [16] [20]. Hassenzahl et al. [18–20] define a typology consisting of eight psychological needs. Desmet and Fokkinga [8] list thirteen different needs and Fronemann and Peissner [14] consider ten psychological needs to be relevant for product design. Fronemann and Peissner's taxonomy of needs for example includes psychological needs for security, keeping the meaningful, self-expression, relatedness, popularity, competition, physical well-being, competence, influence and stimulation. It is believed that meeting psychological needs in the context of products and services can lead to a positive user experience and well-being [16,20]. Although these compilations and related materials exist to concretise individual needs, the basic concepts of psychological needs often remain very abstract in practice or even appear esoteric to technology creators.

Some psychological needs correspond to user values, for examples autonomy or fairness. Values are deeply held, meaningful, and pervasive beliefs, attitudes, ideals, and needs that are shared indefinitely by members of a society. They essentially contribute to a person's character, identity, and culture. We understand the world around us through values and orient ourselves to them. Therefore, values can be understood as the basic perspective in which people see and judge the world. In general, academic research on values has been going on for 25 years yielding for example Friedman's [11] list of values with ethical import: human welfare, ownership and property, privacy, freedom from bias, universal usability, trust, autonomy, informed consent, accountability, courtesy, identity, calmness, and environmental sustainability. In this respect, the importance of ethical aspects in the human-centred development of digital products and services has been growing for some years [22]. Employees increasingly value fair working conditions. Customers increasingly want to recognise their values in companies and their products and take them into account when making consumption decisions [34]. Nevertheless, these aspects have so far been insufficiently taken into account in digitalization [38]. Thus, only a few companies manage to define values for themselves and to successfully communicate them internally and externally. A well-known example is the search engine Ecosia [1], which, among other things, puts the ecological sustainability of its service in the foreground [3]. For a better consideration of values in the process of creating digital products and services, there is a lack of general agreement on the definition of values as a construct [37] and of individual values in particular [12].

Thus, it seems necessary to sensitize companies, employees, and technology creators to the topic of psychological needs and values itself [28], its relevance for the company and to create the necessary conditions for integration into everyday work [21]. This also includes a human-centred attitude and ways of working in companies, where the psychological needs of the employees are met and values can be lived after.

2.2   Methods for Designing for Values

Value-Sensitive Design (VSD) can be used as a larger framework to use peoples' values for experience design [29,39]. Value sensitive design proclaims three interdependent steps: conceptual, empirical, and technical investigations [11]. During the conceptual investigation target groups, who will be using the concerning technology, are identified. Also, their values concerning their technology use will be determined. The goal of the empirical investigation is to find out how the target groups experience the technology regarding their identified values. To this end, both qualitative and quantitative methods can be used. The technical investigation aims at considering how the insights into target groups' values and their view on the technology can inspire a technology design, which supports these values.

The VSD framework has been in focus of researchers for over 20 years. The importance of user involvement in the design process and the need to transfer ethical design principles and values to design practice is widely acknowledged. Yet it is challenging to make the abstract VSD-concepts tangible and to integrate them into practical design work. Therefore, research has yielded few implementation approaches of the value-sensitive design framework.

There are some general ethical guidelines and heuristics that can be applied in the context of value-sensitive design. For example, basic guidelines on the ethical aspects in dealing with test persons in research and development context have been defined in the Ethical Principles for Psychologists and Code of Conduct [2]. Brandenburg et al. [5] formulated six simple rules of thumb for the handling of test persons in the human-centred research and development of technical systems. They refer in particular to the values of privacy and informed consent.

Furthermore, there are empirically constructed tools that enable researchers and developers to become aware of the ethical aspects in their work, for example, the questionnaire for recording the ethical position (ePOS) [4]. A more specific method example are the stakeholder cards, which were developed to identify and analyse the key stakeholders within the value-sensitive design framework [40].

In summary, there is a need for methods to practical implement value-sensitive design and sensitize technology creators for the meaning of certain values. There are few uniquely developed methods and some methods transferred from other research fields. A possible consideration would the transfer of existing experience design methods based on psychological needs, e.g., for sensitisation, to the field of designing for values.

2.3   Sensitisation Methods for Designing for Psychological Needs

There are already materials that attempt to introduce designers themselves to the topic of experience-oriented design based on the rather abstract psychological needs and to sensitise them to this. Here, the needs cards [18–20,36], the needs fan [6,13], and the well-being determinant cards [7] should be mentioned. The needs cards as well as the needs fan include a short description and respective visualizations concerning the psychological needs, among other things. Peters, Ahmadpour, and Calvo [33] concretize the psychological needs of autonomy, competence, and relatedness from self-determination theory [35] using cards and videos. For each need, the cards include a brief description of it and exemplary quotes from users. In addition, the cards contain hints on how to support or inhibit users' need fulfillment. In the video, these cards are explained and supplemented with design examples. Both formats form the basis for design workshops for well-being [31,32]. Desmet and Fokkinga [8] go a little further in the design direction in explaining and concretizing the psychological needs by showing the implications of psychological needs in the design of e.g. specific chairs [9]. However, all those materials are rather designed to get passive input about certain needs and their implications on design by reading or watching it or how to straightly implement the needs into the design process, rather than constructing the knowledge about the needs for yourself.

Here, the Needs Profiles method [28] comes into play. The method can be used to sensitise designers for and enable them to systematically access and gather explicit as well as implicit knowledge about psychological needs in the context of experience design [26]. This process starts with the knowledge a designer has about the needs (e.g., through the materials mentioned above) and expands it through a personal and shared reflection-in-action process with other designers. In the first step of the Needs Profiles method, the psychological needs are built metaphorically using Lego®bricks, ideally by a group of designers. The insights gained in this step are then used to construct a Needs Persona [24,27], a personification of the defined psychological needs or need sets in a specific application context (e.g., the corporate context). To develop the Needs Persona the Needs Empathy Map [24] is used. This is how Needs Personas such as "Carla Competence" or "Sebastian Security" are created. The process for using the Needs

Empathy Map can be found in [24]. Defining a Needs Persona, the participants of the method elaborate on how individuals inheriting those psychological needs would act and behave in a specific experience context and what their expressions, feelings, and thoughts are (Fig. 1).

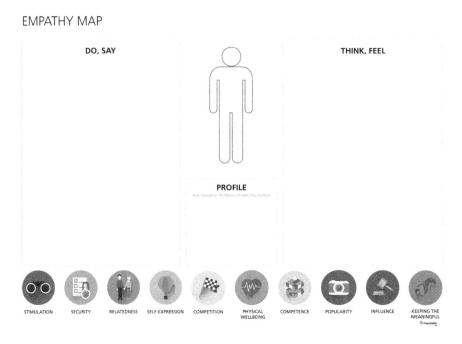

Fig. 1. Needs Empathy Map according to [25], which is used to design a Needs Persona.

3   Method

3.1   Participants

To gain first insights into the research questions, a three-hours workshop was conducted. The participants (female: 14, male: 10, average age: 32.3) had different experience levels with the topics psychological needs and values associated with work context. Six out of 14 participants had dealt with psychological needs and values, two out of 14 just with values and three out of 14 just with psychological needs related to work before. One participant had not dealt with the topics before. Five participants worked in SMEs, six in large companies, another five in academia, and one person was self-employed, although double entries were possible. Three people therefore worked in more than one type of institution.

3.2   Procedure

The workshop followed a three-step procedure (1) understanding of needs and values, (2) relevance of needs and values, and (3) materialization of needs and values in a corporate context (see Fig. 2).

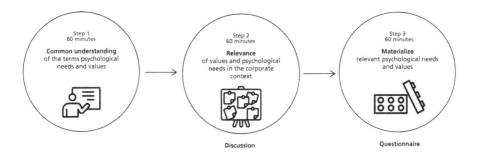

Fig. 2. Procedure of the Workshop.

1. Common Understanding of the Terms Psychological Needs and Values (60 min). In this first phase of the workshop, a warm-up [25] was conducted. Then, in the context of short impulses, the concepts of psychological needs and values in the context of human-centred design were introduced to create a common understanding among the participants. Thereby, participants were asked to listen actively by putting down on sticky notes which psychological needs and user values they considered relevant in the corporate context.

2. Relevance of Values and Psychological Needs in the Corporate Context (60 min): The participants were instructed to reflect their notes on psychological needs and user values individually. Then they were asked to come back together, to form a group and to locate their selected psychological needs and values on the predefined structure regarding the corporate context. For this purpose, a scale from the individual employee to the entire company was plotted on a brown paper. Here, the participants were asked to decide where they considered the respective values or psychological needs to be relevant (in the corporate context). Based on these results, participants were asked to spontaneously rate, using sticky dots (each participant received 2 sticky dots), which psychological need and user value they considered most relevant. Based on this evaluation result, 2 values and 3 needs were selected to be made concrete and tangible in the further course of the workshop. Another aim here was to discuss and clarify where there are differences and discrepancies between values, psychological needs and requirements considering values and psychological needs in different companies.

Table 1. Questionnaire: Items and Response Formats.

Items	Response Format
1. Demographic Details	
a. "Gender"	a. Selection ("Female", "Male", "Diverse")
b. "Age"	b. Numeric Input
c. "Employment"	c. Selection ("Self-Employment", "Science", "Small and Medium-sized Company", "Large Company", "Start-up", "Other")
2. "Prior to this workshop, have you ever considered or applied values or psychological needs in a work context?"	Selection ("Yes", "No")
3. "How do you relate the topics of value and psychological needs? Where do you see the connection?"	Free Text Answer
4. "What do you think is needed to be able to work in a psychological needs- or value-orientated way in (your) company? Why?"	Free Text Answer
5. "General feedback on the Applied Methods in the Workshop (Needs Profiles: Step 1 - Building Psychological Needs and Values; Step 2 - Creating Needs-/Value-Persona using a Needs-/Value-Empathy Map)" via "I like" and "I wish"	Free Text Answer

3. Materialization of Relevant Psychological Needs and Values in the Corporate Context (60 min): Now the previously rather abstract psychological needs and values were made tangible and concrete. The method Needs Profiles Krüger et al. [14] was used and extended to the context of values. For this purpose, the selected psychological needs and values were first metaphorically built with the help of Lego®bricks in the sense of the method Lego®Serious-Play®[23]. For this purpose, the participants were divided into small groups, each consisting of 2–4 people. In the Needs Empathy Map [24], the applied psychological needs were replaced by a typology of user values, which could then be used to create a value persona. Subsequently, the participants were guided to construct a Needs Persona (group 1) and a Value Persona (group 2), each with the aim to focus on employees of companies. Thus, the participants worked out how those Personas with the selected psychological needs and values would behave in the corporate context and how their motivations, thoughts, feelings are pronounced. In conclusion, the findings of the workshop were gathered through a questionnaire, which the participants had to fill in individually. After this last step, the participants were given a questionnaire to fill out individually via pen and paper (see Table 1).

4   Results

4.1   RQ 1: Relevance and Fulfilment of Psychological Needs and Values in the Corporate Context

In the course of the joint discussion with all participants, it was determined that the psychological needs in the corporate context tend to be oriented towards the individual, i.e., they are either located in the levels of individual employees (see Fig. 3, at the very bottom) or in the level where the company's interaction with individual potential users can take place, e.g., in the context of user experience research activities (see Fig. 3, at the very top). In the intermediate company levels, the participants tended to locate the values. The reason they gave for this was that values are also perceived as guiding principles for internal and external communication styles, especially for social groups.

Furthermore, within the framework of the survey by means of the questionnaire, additional insights regarding the research question were gained. Eight participants stated here that psychological needs pay into values or that there are (several) psychological needs behind one value. In addition, three participants had the opinion that values can create psychological needs and that values result from psychological needs. Furthermore, three participants stated that psychological needs are intrinsic and personal, whereas based on their opinion values come from external sources or are limited to interaction with others. One participant also stated that values and psychological needs have no connection at all. It was also mentioned by one participant that personal values and psychological needs could be in conflict with each other.

With regard to the conditions for a needs- and value-oriented working styles two people clearly saw the responsibility on the part of the company, which had to focus on psychological needs and values of their employees in order to make those a central topic for them. Another suggestion was to define and research contact persons, e.g., in a mentoring or coaching system, to promote a needs- and value-oriented way of working. In addition, it was mentioned that in one company

Fig. 3. Locating Psychological Needs (Green Sticky Notes) and Values (Yellow Sticky Notes) in the Company Context, starting from Individual Employees to the Company as a Whole. (Color figure online)

it is already implemented as a top-down process. However, the participant also stated that an additional bottom-up strategy would be more important in order to create strategies and insights regarding the new working styles based on values and psychological needs of the actual employees.

4.2 RQ 2: Transfer of Methods from Designing for Psychological Needs and Values

The Needs Perspectives method was successfully applied to the corporate context and transferred to the area of user values (see Figs. 4, 5, 6 and 7). Thus, 2–3 participants each metaphorically built the relevant psychological needs (Security, Relatedness and Stimulation) and values (Human Welfare and Environment) using Lego®bricks (see Figs. 4 and 6). Here, participants were asked to build what they associate with the psychological need or value in general. Participants then transferred their findings to a Needs Empathy Map and an adapted version of it - the Value Empathy Map. The participants, who had previously built the psychological needs or the values, each formed a group. Based on those Canvas' and the provided structure the participants created a Needs Persona and a Value Persona (see Fig. 5 and 7). Through the successive creation of the personas with the help of the empathy maps, the participants were guided to transfer their general insights into the respective psychological need or value into the corporate context.

Fig. 4. Representation of the Psychological Need for Relatedness using Lego®bricks.

One of the psychological needs built was relatedness. The building was subsequently described by the participants, among others, as follows - first they felt connected to the other employees as well as to the nature surrounding them (see Fig. 4, right side). They saw the users and customers rather "on the other side" (see Fig. 4, left side), but where they defined the money what needed to be achieved. They felt connected to them through the products, services as well as through the company as an external window. They wished for a direct connection to the customers and users (see Fig. 4, ladder), but this would probably not always be available in the day-to-day business of the company.

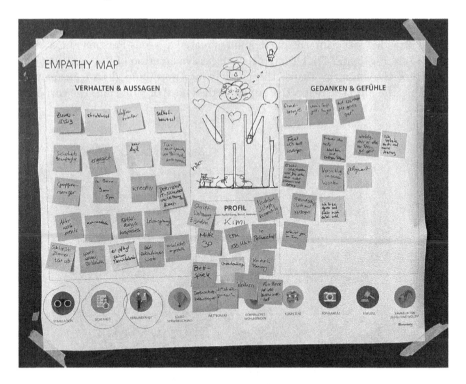

Fig. 5. Needs Persona created using the Needs Empathy Map based on the Psychological Needs Security, Relatedness, and Stimulation.

The Needs Persona Kimi (male, mid-thirties, employee in an SME) was developed, who lives out his psychological need for security in the corporate context by always locking his office door and reliably locking his computer when he leaves his workplace. In addition, he is a safety officer, insists on a permanent contract and is in favour of a regular workday (9 am-5pm). He lives out his psychological need for relatedness by always going to social events, regularly taking coffee breaks together and likes to support others by listening to them. Regular training and interaction with colleagues is important to him to satisfy his psychological need for stimulation.

One of the values built with Lego®bricks was Human Welfare (Fig. 5). The participants described their result as follows: technology is represented by a grey toothed wheel. It is developed by humans for humans, which is illustrated by the two Lego®men connected by a ladder. Technology is crucial to Human Welfare and contributes to many spheres of the society - thus the toothed wheel is connected to multiple Lego®bricks in different corners.

The Value Persona created in the course of the workshop is 27-year-old male engineer, who works in automobile industry. He lives out his value of environment in the corporate context by cycling to work and believing that climate crisis can be solved through technology and innovation. Particularly, he advocates for e-mobility in his company. Additionally, he tries to keep his footprint small by eating primarily vegetarian food and preferring second-hand items. He lives out his value of Human Welfare by seeing own responsibility as an engineer towards the society and tries to make thoughtful and considerate decisions in his work. He sees caring as a part of life and has already done a voluntary social year, besides he participates in food sharing.

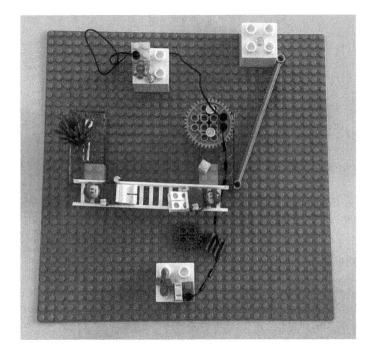

Fig. 6. Representation of the Value of Human Welfare using Lego®bricks.

Based on the responses from the questionnaire, there was feedback from seven participants that they found the use of the method Needs Perspectives to be very valuable. In particular, they also found the building of psychological needs and user values very helpful and, in their opinion, stimulated an open and appreciative discussion. In addition, the structured approach to creating the Needs or Value Persona using the Needs Empathy Map as well as the Value Empathy Map derived from it was especially highlighted by two participants.

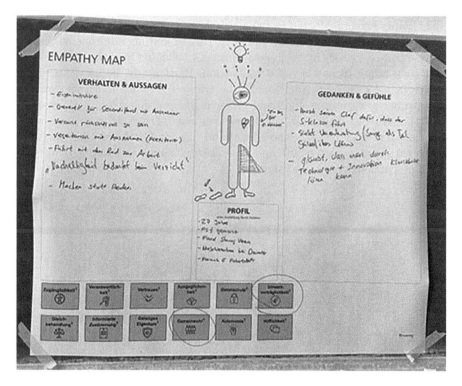

Fig. 7. Value Persona created using a modified Needs Empathy Map based on the Values Human Welfare and Environment.

5   Discussion

The present paper aimed to evaluate a) the relevance of psychological needs and values in the cooperate context and b) the possibility to transfer methods from one domain to the other.

Concerning the first research question, we were able to determine that psychological needs tend to be located close to the individual and values become more important when it comes to interaction in a group within the company. Here we should not see this as a sharp dividing line, but rather as a transition between the two concepts. However, the idea that multiple psychological needs pay into one value is interesting, and we will explore this further. Furthermore, it can be assumed that the selected psychological needs and values from the participants can only be exemplary results - as this compilation will vary depending on the participating individuals as well as different company contexts. In addition, we gained knowledge concerning the basic requirements for transferring the concept of designing for psychological needs and values in the corporate context. Here, most participants felt that a common basis of cooperation was needed to make design work possible. For example, there must be a basic awareness and openness for the topics of psychological needs and values in the respective companies. Good internal communication and respectful interaction were also mentioned by the participants. A cooperative culture is necessary so that employees can address both topics. Furthermore, a concrete discourse and exchange on specific psychological needs and values with others, in the form of discussions among individuals or also as a workshop as a team in the corporate context.

Concerning the second research question, we found that it is possible to transfer methods from one domain to the other. For example, in this paper we examined the method of Needs Profiles that is used in sensitising and designing for psychological needs. We found that we adapt it and also use it for sensitising and designing for values. This could help to address the issue of missing methods for designing for values. Additionally, we found that one can transfer the methods from the design for products and services based on needs to the corporate context and approach the design of a positive working experience. Here a reference to the first research question can be made - the elaborated constructions and Needs Personas helped the participants to get a feeling for how a psychological need or value can be expressed in the behaviour and emotional life of a potential employee in a company. In this way, the participants were able to gather information on how needs and values can be fulfilled in the company context. From this, corresponding conditions for a needs- and value-based working environment could be derived. Additionally, it is also relevant to mention that both areas - psychological needs and values - are not without overlap as mentioned above. If, for example, the work is designed according to values such as autonomy (cf. [5]), the employees' psychological need for autonomy can be addressed at the same time. In other words, by designing for values, one potentially also designs the positive experience of work. This in turn can lead to higher motivation and creativity and ultimately to well-being.

5.1   Limitations and Future Work

There are some limitations that need to be considered. First, in the present paper we report data of a single group of participants. They were very interested in the subject and had, in part, knowledge about psychological needs or values prior to the workshop. Future studies should, therefore, replicate this study using larger and more diverse samples. Second, only a selection of psychological needs and values were addressed in our workshop. Future studies could examine whether the findings of the present study could be transferred to other needs and values. Third, in the present paper we used a workshop format for sensitizing people for designing for psychological needs and values. This format has worked well for the purpose of this paper. However, it is only one of many possible formats and may not always be appropriate in a corporate context. Workshops demand resources like time and personnel with much experience in the subject. Both are scarce in small and medium sized companies. It would be good to examine further methods that need less resources in terms of time and/or that can be self-administered.

5.2   Conclusions and Outlook

The present paper addressed a contemporary topic in the design of digital systems in a corporate context, the consideration of the users' and technology creators' psychological needs and values. More specifically, it focused methodological approaches to designing for psychological needs and values, which is an important prerequisite when transferring knowledge from academia to companies. The results of the presented empirical work indicated that the attention to the psychological needs and values are important for practitioners. In addition, we found some indications that we can use the methods to shape the experience of technology creators. Also, we found evidence suggesting that sensitisation methods from experience design based on psychological needs may be utilized to also design for values. Here, it is also interesting to further investigate how the concepts of psychological needs and values are related to each other and how they might be addressed together. If one follows the idea of various participants that several psychological needs are related to one value, it can be deduced that it e.g., would make sense to design a Needs Persona with the context of a value. This could also be used to address the possible connection that psychological needs in a corporate context are more likely to be attached to the individual and values are more likely to be seen as important for communication in a group. However, the work presented is only a first step in elaborating methods for designing for psychological needs and methods. Future research should replicate and extend this work to build and promote toolboxes of methods for practitioners that want to address both concepts in their daily work. Having these toolboxes, practitioners could better focus on the requirements that contemporary digital technologies fulfil.

Technology is not value-neutral or value-free, but rather exhibits moral and political choices of its creators and users [29]. Following this line of thought, also the psychological needs of the technology creators are present in the interactive products and services. This moral aspect of technology is one of the research topics in philosophy and ethics of technology. Interdisciplinary fields such as Human Factors/Ergonomics Engineering, research have begun to develop and disseminate ethics- and values-based methods for raising awareness of social impacts of digital systems.

The design community is also increasingly publishing on ethical design principles for the design of digital products [15,30]. This growing recognition of moral, value-related, and psychological need-based aspects of technology illustrates the high importance of the field for technology design and thus also for the companies and their employees.

Acknowledgement. This paper is funded by the Mittelstand-Digital initiative funded by the German Federal Ministry for Economic Affairs and Climate Action. Furthermore, the authors would like to thank Moritz Langner from the Karlsruhe Institute of Technology for the discussions and the technical support.

References

1. Ecosia - the search engine that plants trees. https://www.ecosia.org/. Accessed 09 Feb 2023
2. American Psychological Association: Ethical principles of psychologists and code of conduct. Am. Psychol. **57**, 1060–1073 (2002)
3. Brandenburg, S., Feufel, M.: Ethik in der Softwareentwicklung: Wann, wer und wie? iX 8, 56–60 (2020)
4. Brandenburg, S., Minge, M.: Epos - an instrument for the assessment of the ethical position in software development. Theoret. Issues Ergon. Sci. **20**, 153–165 (2019). https://doi.org/10.1080/1463922X.2018.1491072
5. Brandenburg, S., Minge, M., Cymek, D., Zeidler, L.: Ethische Aspekte in der menschzentrierten Erforschung und Entwicklung technischer Geräte - Erfahrungen einer Ethikkommission. Forschung **10**, 101–106 (2017)
6. Burmester, M., et al.: Design4xperience - technologie als positives erlebnis gestalten (2016)
7. Calvo, R., Peters, D.: Positive computing: Tools for positive computing (2015)
8. Desmet, P., Fokkinga, S.: Beyond Maslow's Pyramid: introducing a typology of thirteen fundamental needs for human-centered design. Multimodal Technol. Interact. **4**(3), 38 (2020), number: 3 Publisher: Multidisciplinary Digital Publishing Institute
9. Desmet, P., Fokkinga, S.: Thirteen chairs, thirteen fundamental needs (2020). inspiratie-poster 978–94-6384-134-4
10. DIN EN ISO 9241–210: Ergonomie der Mensch-System-Interaktion - Teil 210: Prozess zur Gestaltung gebrauchstauglicher interaktiver Systeme. Beuth Verlag, Berlin (2010)
11. Friedman, B., Kahn, P.H., Borning, A., Huldtgren, A.: Value sensitive design and information systems. In: Doorn, N., Schuurbiers, D., van de Poel, I., Gorman, M.E. (eds.) Early engagement and new technologies: Opening up the laboratory. PET, vol. 16, pp. 55–95. Springer, Dordrecht (2013). https://doi.org/10.1007/978-94-007-7844-3_4
12. Friedman, B., Hendry, D.G., Borning, A.: A survey of value sensitive design methods. Found. Trends Hum.-Comput. Interact. **11**(2), 63–125 (2017)
13. Fronemann, N., Krueger, A., Burmester, M., Laib, M., Hilscher, B.: Beduerfnisfaecher (2016)
14. Fronemann, N., Peissner, M.: User experience concept exploration: user needs as a source for innovation. In: Proceedings of the 8th Nordic Conference on Human-Computer Interaction: Fun, Fast, Foundational - NordiCHI '14. pp. 727–736. ACM Press, Helsinki, Finland (2014). https://doi.org/10.1145/2639189.2641203, https://dl.acm.org/citation.cfm?doid=2639189.2641203
15. Gotterbarn, D., Wolf, M.J., Flick, C., Miller, K.: Thinking professionally. The continual evolution of interest in computing ethics. ACM Inroads **9**(2), 10–12 (2018). https://doi.org/10.1145/3204466
16. Hassenzahl, M.: The thing and I: understanding the relationship between user and product. In: Blythe, M.A., Overbeeke, K., Monk, A.F., Wright, P.C. (eds.) Funology. Human-Computer Interaction Series, vol. 3,pp. 31–42. Springer, Dordrecht (2003). https://doi.org/10.1007/1-4020-2967-5_4
17. Hassenzahl, M., Burmester, M., Koller, F.: User experience is all there is-twenty years of designing positive experiences and meaningful technology. i-com **20**(3) (2021). publisher: De Gruyter

18. Hassenzahl, M., Diefenbach, S.: Well-being, need fulfillment, and Experience Design. In: Designing Well-being Workshop, vol. 25, p. 2013 (2012)

19. Hassenzahl, M., Diefenbach, S., Göritz, A.: Needs, affect, and interactive products-Facets of user experience. Interact. Comput. **22**(5), 353–362 (2010). number: 5 Publisher: Oxford University Press

20. Hassenzahl, M., Eckoldt, K., Diefenbach, S., Laschke, M., Len, E., Kim, J.: Designing moments of meaning and pleasure. Experience design and happiness. International journal of design 7(3) (2013). publisher: Chinese Institute of Design

21. Hermosa Perrino, C., Burmester, M., Spohrer, A., Fink, V., Zeiner, K.M.: The Positive X-Warum klappt das nicht? Mensch und Computer 2021-Usability Professionals (2021), publisher: Gesellschaft für Informatik eV und German UPA eV

22. Kakar, A.K., Kakar, A.: Is the Time Ripe for Branding of Software Products (2018). https://aisel.aisnet.org/sais2018/21/

23. Kristiansen, P., Rasmussen, R.: Building a Better Business Using the Lego Serious Play Method. Wiley, Hoboken, New Jersey (2014)

24. Krueger, A.E.: Two methods for experience design based on the needs empathy map: persona with needs and needs persona. Mensch und Computer 2022-Workshopband (2022)

25. Krueger, A.E., Minet, S.: Designing positive experiences in creative workshops at work using a warm up set based on psychological needs. Multimodal Technol. Interact. **6**(10), 90 (2022)

26. Krüger, A.E., Peissner, M., Fronemann, N., Pollmann, K.: Building ideas: guided design for experience. In: Proceedings of the 9th Nordic Conference on Human-Computer Interaction, pp. 1–6 (2016)

27. Krüger, A.E., Fronemann, N., Peissner, M.: Das kreative Potential der Ingenieure-menschzentrierte Ingenieurskunst. In: Stuttgarter Symposium für Produktentwicklung, SSP 2015 Entwicklung smarter Produkte für die Zukunft, pp. 1–10 (2015)

28. Krüger, A.E., Kurowski, S., Pollmann, K., Fronemann, N., Peissner, M.: Needs profile: sensitising approach for user experience research. In: Proceedings of the 29th Australian Conference on Computer-Human Interaction - OZCHI '17. pp. 41–48. ACM Press, Brisbane, Queensland, Australia (2017). https://doi.org/10.1145/3152771.3152776, https://dl.acm.org/citation.cfm?doid=3152771.3152776

29. Manders-Huits, N.: What values in design? The challenge of incorporating moral values into design. Sci. Eng. Ethics (17), 271–287 (2011). https://doi.org/10.1007/s11948-010-9198-2

30. Mulvenna, M., Boger, J., Bond, R.: Ethical by design: a manifesto. In: Proceedings of the European Conference on Cognitive Ergonomics. ECCE 2017, New York, NY, USA, pp. 51–54, Association for Computing Machinery (2017). https://doi.org/10.1145/3121283.3121300

31. Peters, D.: Designing for psychological wellbeing Development of a research-based toolkit for wellbeing supportive technology design. Ph.D. thesis (2022)

32. Peters, D., Ahmadpour, N.: Digital wellbeing through design: evaluation of a professional development workshop on wellbeing-supportive design. In: Proceedings of the 32nd Australian Conference on Human-Computer Interaction, pp. 148–157 (2020)

33. Peters, D., Ahmadpour, N., Calvo, R.A.: Tools for wellbeing-supportive design: features, characteristics, and prototypes. Multimodal Technol. Interact. **4**(3), 40 (2020)

34. Ries, T.E., Bersoff, D.: Edelman Trust Barometer 2019 Special Report "In Brands We Trust?". Technical report, Edelman (2019). https://www.edelman.com/sites/g/files/aatuss191/files/2019-06/2019_edelman_trust_barometer_special_report_in_brands_we_trust.pdf
35. Ryan, R.M., Deci, E.L.: Self-determination theory: basic psychological needs in motivation, development, and wellness. Guilford Publications (2017)
36. Sheldon, K.M., Elliot, A.J., Kim, Y., Kasser, T.: What is satisfying about satisfying events? Testing 10 candidate psychological needs. J. Person. Soc. Psychol. **80**(2), 325 (2001). number: 2
37. Umbrello, S.: Imaginative value sensitive design: using moral imagination theory to inform responsible technology design. Sci. Eng. Ethics **26**(2), 575–595 (2019). https://doi.org/10.1007/s11948-019-00104-4
38. Whittle, J., Ferrario, M.A., Simm, W., Hussain, W.: A case for human values in software engineering. IEEE Software **38**(1), 106–113 (2021). https://doi.org/10.1109/MS.2019.2956701, conference Name: IEEE Software
39. Winkler, T., Spiekermann, S.: Twenty years of value sensitive design: a review of methodological practices in vsd projects. Ethics Inf. Technol. (23), 17–21 (2021). https://doi.org/10.1007/s10676-018-9476-2
40. Yoo, D.: Stakeholder tokens: a constructive method for value sensitive design stakeholder analysis. In: Proceedings of the 2017 ACM Conference Companion Publication on Designing Interactive Systems. DIS '17 Companion, New York, NY, USA, pp. 280–284. Association for Computing Machinery (2017). https://doi.org/10.1145/3064857.3079161

Invisible Driving Force: Design Promotion Laws in the National Design Policy Path of South Korea

Yushuai Lang[✉] [iD]

China Academy of Art, No. 218 Nanshan Road, Hangzhou, China
markyourself@sina.cn

Abstract. Through the analysis of the design promotion laws in the national design policy path of South Korea, this study aims to find a civilized model for reference and learning, to effectively strengthen public attention to and advancement of the design policy, and to promote the development of the design industry. First of all, this study judged the affiliation of the national design policy, and screened out the important "invisible driving force" —design promotion laws based on the criteria of policy issuing institutions, basic attributes, and implementation from the beginning of promulgation to the research node between December 1977 and December 2021, with a total of 17 texts screened. Secondly, it combined bibliometrics with content analysis to explore the construction and change of South Korean design promotion policy. Bibliometrics was used to analyze the distribution characteristics, quantitative relationship, policy focus and change of the design promotion laws, and changes reflected in the names of the laws and the number of clauses, etc. Content analysis mainly built an analytical framework for the content of laws and policies and compared the textual content, thus analyzing the changes, construction and configuration of the clauses of South Korean design promotion laws. Finally, by examining the temporal evolution and spatial structure related to the national design policy system of South Korea and analyzing the nature of policy subjects and so on, this study explored and summarized the successful experience of South Korean design policy system and the lessons that can be learned from.

Keywords: Design Policy · Design Promotion · Law

1 Introduction

The current fast-changing era poses great challenges to social development has led to a focus on the role of design policies in the overall development of society. The government formulates design policies to drive innovative development, changes the economic and cultural status of cities with design, and develops solutions to meet the challenges of the times. This is the role of design policies. In Asia, there are not many countries that have a clear "national design policy". Apart from Japan which has followed Europe closely, South Korea stands out. In fact, in addition to the content and methods possibly similar to the standards of Western developed countries, South Korea has added a number of country-specific methods to its design policy system. It can be said that South Korea is one of the few countries that have integrated the design strategy, planning and policy into national laws and regulations in a complete manner at present, and the basic attribute of national dominance is evident from the published texts to the implementation details.

From its origin in the early 20th century to its beginning in the 1970s and further to its achievements in the late 20th century and early 21st century, South Korea's national design policy, with explicit direction, clear path, and gradual development, has been working to achieve the ambitious goal of becoming a world design power as an emerging force in Asian design. After the outbreak of the Asian financial crisis in 1997, South Korea made design a major national policy. In 1998, President Kim Dae-jung and British Prime Minister Tony Blair jointly issued the "Design Era Declaration of the 21st Century" at their meeting. In 1999, South Korea hosted the "First Industrial Design Promotion Conference" and declaring that South Korea would become a design power within five years, and President Kim Dae-jung personally put forward the slogan "South Korea Design, Design Power". In 2001, with the International Council of Societies of Industrial Design (ICSID) as an opportunity, South Korea invested more than USD 83 million to set up the South Korea Design Center, and the Federation of Korean Industries also established a special committee for industrial design to start to support design activities (internationally known as industrial design). Since then, with the understanding and flexible application of "modern design", South Korea had quickly found the right moment and triggered off the "South Korean Trend" worldwide. With the strong support of the South Korean government, LG, Samsung and other enterprises had successfully transformed from manufacturing enterprises to design innovative enterprises. In 2010, Seoul was honored with the title of "World Design Capital". In the Global Innovation Index (GII) released by the World Intellectual Property Organization (WIPO), South Korea was ranked 11th in 2020 and 6th in 2022. The power of design policy contributes to these achievements. The 50-year history of the South Korean national design policy has witnessed the improvement of its design capability and international competitiveness, and has shown us the tremendous positive benefits that design policy can create for an industry and even a country.

The development of the South Korean design industry is also dependent on the full range of national and government policy support and guidance [1]. The study of South Korean national design policy and the understanding of the way and process of constructing its design policy system can help raise the awareness of design policy making and the adaptability of working methods in other countries, strengthen the positive interaction with the global context in the process of design policy exploration and practice, and thus further improve the comprehensive level of the design policy from formulation to application.

2 Research Methods

The methods used in this study mainly include bibliometrics and content analysis. Bibliometrics is a structural research method based on mathematical and quantitative analysis of policy literature, which is applicable to research questions such as distribution structure, quantitative relationship, and structural change [2], through which the characteristics and patterns of the applicable field are explored. Content analysis is a research method to draw conclusions by combining and comparing the "contents" of literature [3]. It aims to delve deeper from the surface of text for the hidden meaning that cannot be grasped by ordinary reading means. The above two methods have been widely used in policy research in various fields.

This study combines bibliometrics with content analysis to explore the construction and changes of South Korean design promotion laws and policies. Bibliometrics is mainly used for the distribution characteristics, quantitative relationship, policy focus and changes in the design promotion laws; content analysis mainly deals with the analysis of law contents, builds an analytical framework for the obtained policy texts and compares the contents, so as to analyze the changes, construction and configuration of the clauses of South Korean design promotion laws.

3   Policy Determination

National design policies are generally formulated under the leadership of the central government, and the framework of design policies is built through promotion strategy, talent training strategy and social education and promotion strategy in the design industry. The strengths of government, society and enterprises are gathered together to grasp the characteristics of global target markets through policy research, formulation, release and implementation. In accordance with the country-specific culture and policy mechanism, products or services with international vision and cultural characteristics are developed, and the design quality and cognition of the whole nation is improved, so as to obtain differentiated competitive advantages and influence in international competition.

The main object of this study is South Korean national design policy, and it is important to determine what kind of design policy is a national design policy. Although there are no explicit words of "national design policy" in the legal texts issued by South Korea in "Industrial Design Promotion Act", "Enforcement Order of Industrial Design Promotion Act" and "Enforcement Rules of Industrial Design Promotion Act", it is still possible to judge them by definition.

3.1   Institution for Text Preparation, Release and Implementation

The "Industrial Design Promotion Act" has different names at different times, which reflects the different focuses at different times. However, in terms of the institutions that issued the "Industrial Design Promotion Act" (Table 1), although the names are different, the departments are the same in nature (Table 2): the current Ministry of Trade, Industry and Energy. It is the central administrative organ of the Republic of Korea, and the head of the ministry is called the Minister of Trade, Industry and Energy, who is also appointed as the State Councilor and whose functions are equivalent to those of the Ministry of Economy or the Ministry of Commerce in other countries. If the issuing institution is the central administration, then the design policy issued by it is national design policy.

In order to ensure the enforcement of each "Industrial Design Promotion Act," the Enforcement Order of Industrial Design Promotion Act" and the "Enforcement Rules of

Table 1. South Korean Design Promotion Law and Legislation

Law names	Formulating and issuing institutions	Year of legislative update
"Design and Packaging Promotion Act"	Ministry of Trade and Industry	1977
"Industrial Design and Packaging Promotion Act"		1991
	Ministry of Trade, Industry and Energy	1993
		1995
"Industrial Design Promotion Act"	Ministry of Commerce, Industry and Energy	1997
		1999
		2001
		2005
		2006
	Ministry of Knowledge-based Economy	2008
		2009
	Ministry of Trade, Industry and Energy	2013
		2014.1
		2014.5
		2015.7
		2015.12
		2019

Table 2. Changes in the Ministry of Trade, Industry and Energy

Time	Name
1948	South Korea established the Ministry of Trade and Industry
1993	The Ministry of Trade and Industry was merged with the Ministry of Energy and Resources to create the Ministry of Trade, Industry and Energy
1996	The Ministry of Trade, Industry and Energy was renamed as the Ministry of Commerce, Industry and Trade
1998	The Ministry of Commerce, Industry and Trade was changed as the Ministry of Trade, Industry and Energy
2008	Parts of functions of the Ministry of Science and Technology and the Ministry of Intelligence and Communication were merged and reorganized as the Ministry of Knowledge-based Economy
2013	The trade function (foreign trade) of the former Ministry of Foreign Affairs and Trade was transferred to the Ministry, and the Ministry was renamed as the Ministry of Trade, Industry and Energy

Industrial Design Promotion Act" (Table 3) are issued specifically for each "Industrial Design Promotion Act, whose issuing institutions are all the Ministry of Trade, Industry and Energy. Such "Enforcement Order" and "Enforcement Rules" are also part of the national design policy.

3.2   Text Attributes

The most representative national design policy is the "Industrial Design Promotion Act", and South Korea is one of the few countries that have incorporated design policy into laws and regulations, and have formulated the "Enforcement Order of Industrial Design Promotion Act" and the "Enforcement Rules of Industrial Design Promotion Act" to ensure its enforcement. The "Industrial Design Promotion Act" is labeled with "Act No. x" in the released text, the "Enforcement Order of Industrial Design Promotion Act" is labeled with "Presidential Decree No. x" in the released text, and the "Enforcement Rules of Industrial Design Promotion Act" is labeled with "Ministry of Trade, Industry and Energy Decree No. x" (Table 3) in the released text. They are not local administrative regulations, but national laws (Table 4), as evidenced by their position in South Korean legal hierarchy [4], and national laws express the will of the state, and are national design policies.

Table 3. Regulatory Attributes and Institutions Corresponding to the "Industrial Design Promotion Act"

Name	No	Issuing institution
Industrial Design Promotion Act	Act No. *	Ministry of Trade, Industry and Energy
Enforcement Order of "Industrial Design Promotion Act"	Presidential Decree No. *	Ministry of Trade, Industry and Energy
Enforcement Rules of "Industrial Design Promotion Act"	Ministry of Trade, Industry and Energy Decree No. *	Ministry of Trade, Industry and Energy

In summary, the main text of South Korean national design policy: the "Industrial Design Promotion Act" and its accompanying laws only aim to promote the industrial design industry, but it plays a substantial role in the properties and essence of the national design policy, so it can be clearly determined as the national design policy of South Korea.

4   Classification Framework

Although formally defined as a law, the South Korean design promotion law is still essentially a policy tool endowed with a strong enforcement effect. Based on the classification logic and text nature, this study classifies the clauses of South Korean design promotion laws for observation, comparison and analysis, hoping to draw some conclusions on the hidden level, and the framework is divided into eight sections (Fig. 1).

Table 4. Comparison of South Korean Legal Hierarchy and Industrial Design Promotion Policy

Grade	Category	Design policy attribute
Grade 1	"The Constitution"	
Grade 2	Laws, presidential emergency orders, presidential emergency financial and economic orders, and international treaties and regulations	"Industrial Design Promotion Act", a law belonging to this grade
Grade 3	Presidential decree, rules of the National Assembly, rules of the Grand Court, rules of the Constitutional Court, and rules of the Central Election Commission	"Enforcement Order of the Industrial Design Promotion Act", a presidential decree belonging to this grade
Grade 4	Prime Minister's decree and ministerial decree	"Enforcement Rules of Industrial Design Promotion Act", a ministerial decree belonging to this grade
Grade 5	Administrative rules (including directives, regulations, notices, and guidelines) and local autonomous laws (including ordinances and rules)	

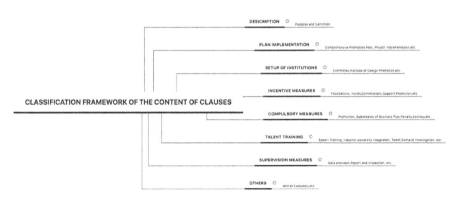

Fig. 1. Framework for Classifying the Content of South Korean Design Promotion Laws

Based on the need for content analysis and comparison, all clauses in legal texts enacted in previous years were placed in a classification framework to compare the changes in each category (Fig. 2, the numbers in the table correspond to the serial number of clauses in legal texts), which is the basis for data interpretation in this study, and classification and juxtaposition are more conducive to quantitative analysis.

	1977	1991	1993	1995	1997	1999	2001	2005	2006	2008	2009	2013	2014.1	2014.5	2015.7	2015.12	2019
Description (Purpose and definition)	1, 2	1, 2	1, 2	1, 2	1, 2	1, 2	1, 2	1, 2	1, 2	1, 2	1, 2	1, 2	1, 2	1, 2	1, 2	1, 2	1, 2
Plan implementation (comprehensive promotion plan and implementation)	3	3, 4	3, 4	3, 4	3, 4	3, 4	3, 4, 5	3, 4, 5	3, 4, 5	3, 4, 5	3, 4, 5	3, 4, 5	3, 4, 5	3, 4, 5	3, 4, 5	3, 4, 5-1, 5-2	3, 4, 5-1, 5-2
Setup of institutions	4.	5, 14.	5, 14	5, 14	5, 11	11	11	11	11.	11	11	11	11	11	11	11-1, 11-2	11-1, 11-2
Incentive measures (funds, foundations, commissions, support, protection, data provision)	5, 6, 7.	6, 9, 10, 11, 12, 13, 15, 16	6, 9, 10, 11, 12, 13, 15, 16	6, 9, 15, 16	6, 9, 10, 12, 13	6, 9, 10, 12, 13	6, 9, 10-1, 10-2, 12, 13	6, 9, 10-1, 10-2, 12, 13	6, 9, 10-1, 10-2, 12, 13	6, 9, 10-1, 10-2, 12, 13	6, 9, 10-1, 10-2, 12, 13	6, 9, 10-1, 10-2, 12, 13	6, 9, 10-1, 10-2, 12, 13	6, 9, 10-1, 10-2, 12, 13	6, 9-1, 9-2, 10-1, 10-2, 12, 13	6, 9-1, 9-2, 10-1, 10-2, 10-3, 12, 13	6, 9-1, 9-2, 10-1, 10-2, 10-3, 12, 13
Compulsory measures (prohibition, business plan, penalty, secrecy)	8, 9, 12	7, 17, 19, 20, 22, 23.	7, 17, 19, 20, 22, 23	7, 17, 19, 20, 22, 23	7, 14, 16, 17, 19, 20	7, 14, 16, 19	7, 14, 16, 19	7, 14, 16, 19	7, 14, 16, 19	7, 14, 16, 19	7, 14, 16, 19	7, 14, 16, 19	7, 14, 16, 19	7, 14, 16, 19	14, 16, 19	14, 16, 19	14, 16, 19
Talent training		8	8	8	8	8	8	8	8	8	8	8	8	8	8	8	8
Supervision mechanism (report and inspection)	10, 11	18	18	18	15	15	15	15	15	15	15	15	15	15	15	15	15
Others (writ of execution)	13	21	21	21	18												17

Fig. 2. Classification of the Clauses of South Korean Design Promotion Laws

5   Design Promotion Law Analysis

5.1   Measurement Change Characteristics

Frequency of Legal Updates.
Since the enactment of the first design promotion law in 1977, South Korea has updated 17 texts 16 times by 2022. The reasons behind the frequency of changes in the number of these laws are very complex and more difficult to analyze, but if the curve of GDP data and the frequency of changes in the number of laws (Fig. 3) are compared, the frequency of frequent and concentrated updates of laws (2004–2020) basically corresponds to the period of fast and robust GDP growth. This shows that design policy is synchronized with the development of the country and plays a very important role in promoting rapid GDP growth.

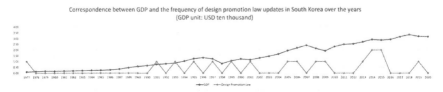

Fig. 3. Curves Corresponding to the Update of Design Promotion Laws and GDP Data in South Korea over the Years

Changes in Law Names. The design promotion laws in south korea have used three names over the past 40 years: the "design and packaging promotion act" from 1977 to 1991, the "industrial design and packaging promotion act" from 1991 to 1997, and the "industrial design promotion act" from 1997 to 2021, which are compared with the corresponding promotion institutions in the time axis (Fig. 4). The names of the design promotion laws are consistent with the changes in the names of design promotion institutions. The design promotion laws fundamentally promote the design industry, with different priorities at different times and different perceptions of the design industry. from the beginning, the focus was on packaging design policy, but later it slowly shifted to

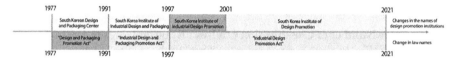

Fig. 4. Changes in the Names of South Korean Design Promotion Laws and the Corresponding Promotion Institutions

the whole industrial design system, which reflects the development of design discipline and the shift of the focus of national design policy.

Number of Clauses. The most direct part of quantitative study is the analysis of the rational data. The most obvious manifestation of the update of South Korean design promotion laws is the change in the rational data of the number of clauses, which includes the change in the deleted clauses and appendix clauses, the characteristics of the changes are obtained through the analysis of quantified data (Fig. 5):

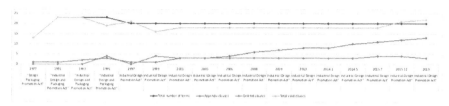

Fig. 5. Changes in Clauses of South Korean Design Promotion Laws

The total number of clauses changed from the minimum 13 to the maximum 23 in an unstable period between 1977 and 1997, and finally stabilized at 20 from 1997 to 2021, which reflected the continuous adjustment of the framework of design promotion laws and finally formed a relatively stable structural framework and number.

The changes in appendix clauses were unstable from 1977 to 1999, and showed a gradual upward trend from 1999 to 2021. The appendix is the supplementary information materials attached to the clauses in text and have the same legal effect. The number of appendixes gradually increased after 1999, reflecting the more comprehensive coverage and consideration of the design promotion laws, and they are also the result of the development of national support for design policies.

The changes in deleted clauses were unstable from 1977 to 2001, and 3 to 4 clauses were deleted every year from 2001 to 2019. The stability of deleted clauses is not only the reflection of respect for development, but also the manifestation of following the law of legislation. The design promotion laws are undoubtedly formulated to revitalize the development of design industry, regulate certain adjusted relations, and adjust and remove some legislative clauses that are unsuitable, unreasonable or hinder design promotion.

5.2   Quantitative Classification Characteristics

Changes in the Number of Classification Clauses. By quantifying the data of the content framework (Fig. 6), the largest one is in the "incentive measures" section (excluding valid clauses), which occupies the largest content clauses in all years except when it was slightly lower than mandatory clauses in 1995 and 1997. The rest of the sections following "incentive measures" are "mandatory measures" and "plan implementation", and the total number of clauses is being dynamically adjusted.

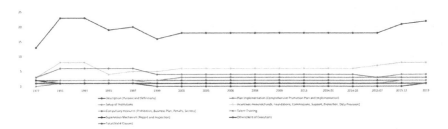

Fig. 6. Changes in the Content of South Korean Design Promotion Laws

After experiencing fluctuating changes from 1977 to 1995, "incentive measures" gradually increased from 1995 to 2020, becoming the largest step by step in terms of content and the key content and means to promoting design promotion policies.

After an upward trend from 1977 to 1997, "compulsory measures" began to show a gradual decline, i.e., less compulsory means, while more policies were internalized as a kind of responsibility to guide the will of the state.

The comparison of the changes in incentive measures and compulsory measures indicates that the industrial policies of the South Korean government had undergone fundamental changes in the late 1990s, and the most important change lied in the concept and motivation. The government realized that it harmed to replace the market mechanism by excessive use of administrative means and that the transformation of industrial structure ultimately depended on the mutual coordination and balance of various industries. After that, the government's motivation of formulating industrial policies was no longer simply to pursue economic growth, but more to promote the balanced development of all sectors.

After years of updating and iteration, stable policy clauses have been formed, which shows that the design policies played a huge role in responding to changes in the domestic and foreign environment, revitalizing the domestic industrial design cause, and strengthening industrial competitiveness, and the design policy structure has basically been formed stably.

Key Changes in the Content of Classification Clauses.
Description. The number of this clause content has not changed in each updated law and contains two items in total, namely "purpose" and "description", which indicates the meaning of the design promotion law. Although the number remains unchanged, the content has changed over time.

The content of the "purpose" clause has undergone three changes (Table 5), which is consistent with the node of the change of the law name. The main purpose of the law promulgated in 1977 is to cultivate design and packaging industries, contribute to economic development and export growth, and effectively coordinate with the national strategic transformation policy. The manufacturing industry is the leading industry of the South Korean economy, and its upgrading has promoted the transformation of the South Korean industrial structure. The period from 1972 to 1981 was the capital-intensive heavy chemical industry stage of the manufacturing industry [5], and 1977 was the export-oriented stage of the heavy chemical industry in this great stage. Therefore, the function of the promulgation of the "Design and Packaging Promotion Act" is to coordinate the export-oriented policy in the design field, thus promoting the national economic and social development. In the 1990s, the industrial policies of the South Korean government underwent a fundamental change. The new industrial policy was to "guide the upgrading of industrial structure and the effective allocation of resources through free competition". The government changed the past practice of determining key industries by itself and prevented monopoly, while advocating the enterprises should choose the "competitive industry" in the competition upon the government approval and determined it as the "leading industry". The government gave key support to guide the upgrading of industrial structure and the "effective allocation" of resources. Obviously, the government's industrial policies were increasingly reflecting the principle of efficiency and fairness. Therefore, the "Industrial Design and Packaging Promotion Act" from 1991 to 1995 aimed to promote industrial design and packaging projects, strengthening industrial competitiveness, and promoting trade and national economic development within its own attributes, rather than contribute to export growth. After the Asian financial crisis in 1997, the South Korean government officially put forward the policy of building itself into a country thrived on culture in 1998, taking culture as a strategic pillar industry for the national economy in the 21st century [6]. South Korean President Kim Dae-jung and British Prime Minister Tony Blair jointly issued the "Design Era Declaration of the 21st Century", and formulated the "Industrial Policy Direction and New Development Plan on Knowledge-based Industries for the 21st Century" in order to accelerate the industrial restructuring. The document clearly proposed to focus on the development of 28 knowledge-based industries and service industries such as computer, semiconductor, biotechnology, new materials, new energy, fine chemicals, aerospace, etc.[7]. The Korean government promoted the improvement of industrial technology level and industrial development, and created "Design Korea" and "Cultural Korea" through a large number of policies and measures mentioned above. Therefore, since 1997, the purpose of the "Industrial Design Promotion Act" has changed to "making contributions to strengthen industrial competitiveness."

Plan implementation. In terms of the overall trend, the updated clauses have been increased from one to four over time (Fig. 6).

It can be seen from the classified list that the plan implementation in 1977 is a programmatic policy: "the government should formulate policies, and departments responsible for policy review and the organization and operation of the policies should be stipulated in the Presidential Decree". The laws updated after 1977 have made many

Table 5. Description of Korean Industrial Design Promotion Laws - items with the same purpose

Name	"Design and Packaging Promotion Act"	"Industrial Design and Packaging Promotion Act"	"Industrial Design Promotion Act"
Year of promulgation	1977	1991, 1993, 1995	1997, 1999, 2001, 2005, 2006, 2008, 2009, 2013, 2014.1, 2014.5, 2015.7, 2015.12, 2019
Number of laws used	1	3	13

modifications, which can be divided into several stages according to the different content (Table 6). The macro changes can be seen through quantitative classification analysis:

Changes to department responsible for review: such department was stipulated in the Presidential Decree in 1977, and reviewed by the Industrial Design and Packaging Promotion Committee from 1991 to 1999. After 1999, it was stipulated that "when the Minister of Commerce, Industry and Energy plans to develop or change the comprehensive plan on the promotion of industrial design, it no longer requires the review and approval of the Industrial Design and Packaging Promotion Committee". The power was more delegated to the Ministry of Trade, Industry and Energy to address development challenges and create better conditions for policy decisions.

Changes to educational institutions for the implementation of research and development projects: from 1991 to 1995, the educational institutions for the implementation of research and development projects were universities or colleges specified in Article 81 of the "Act on Education"; from 1997 to1999, it was prescribed universities, colleges or technical colleges; after 1999, it was prescribed universities, industrial colleges, junior colleges and technical colleges. Obviously, the range of educational institutions participating in research and development projects is expanding, which also reveals the severe reality of the shortage in talent reserves in the design promotion amid the long-term pressure of talent construction.

The emergence of industrial design promotion and development projects: after 2001, the clauses of industrial design promotion and development projects appeared to improve the competitiveness of national industrial design: "the government implements industrial design awards, and supports excellent brands, and the Ministry of Trade, Industry and Energy undertakes and supports industrial design exhibitions, companies in the industrial design, the construction and support of industrial design information systems, and the business of industrial design transactions". In July 2015, the Ministry of Trade, Industry and Energy added the "implementation of entrepreneurship conservation plan"; in December 2015, the "formulation and promotion of standard contracts", namely the standard contracts formulating and promoting industrial design services was added. The increasing number of developments promoting projects shows that the design policy has made many attempts to promote the transformation of industrial design mode and structure, and the results show that development projects are the main support for the transformation and upgrading of industrial design.

Table 6. Content Classification of Korean Industrial Design Promotion Laws - Planned Implementation Items

Time	1977	1991, 1993, 1995	1997	1999	2001, 2003, 2005, 2006, 2008, 2009, 2013,2014.1, 2014.5	2015.7	2015.12 2019
Clauses included in classification	Article 3	Article 3	Article 3	Article 3	Article 3	Article 3	Article 3
		Article 4	Article 4	Article 4	Article 4	Article 4	Article 4
					Article 5	Article 5	Article 5–1
							Article 5–2

Setup of Institutions. There are 1–2 changes in the setup of promotion institutions, namely the design promotion institution and the promotion committee (Table 7).

Table 7. Content Classification of Korean Design Promotion Laws—Changes in Institution Name

Date	1977	1991,1993,1995	1997	1999	2001,2003,2005, 2006,2008,2009, 2013,2014.1,2014.5,2015.7	2015.12, 2019
Name of promotion institution	South Korea Design and Packaging Center	Industrial Design and Packaging Promotion Committee	Industrial Design Promotion Committee	South Korea Institute of Industrial Design Promotion	South Korea Institute of Design Promotion	South Korea Institute of Design Promotion
		Industrial Design and Packaging Development Institute	South Korea Institute of Industrial Design Promotion			Regional Design Centers

Through the comparative analysis of the content above, the following changes can be seen:

Changes to name: in 1977, the name was "Korean Design and Packaging Center; from 1991 to1995, it was changed to "Industrial Design and Packaging Promotion Committee" and "Industrial Design and Packaging Development Institute"; in 1997, it was the "Industrial Design Promotion Committee" and "South Korea Institute of Industrial Design Promotion"; in 1999, it was the "South Korea Institute of Industrial Design Promotion"; from 2001 to July 2015, it was renamed as "South Korea Institute of Design Promotion"; after December 2015, it was "South Korea Institute of Design Promotion" and "Regional Design Centers". During the period from 1991 to 1999, two institutions were set up to be in charge of different work. The committee had administrative functions, focusing on grasping the development direction, coordinating resources, linking development, etc., while the Development Institute or the Promotion Institute, like China's domestic research institutions, was responsible for specific operational work such as policy implementation, design services, education and training, and strategic research. After 1999, it was changed to set up one institution (in December 2015 and 2019, it was essentially an institution, that is, one central institution with regional branches), combining the functions of the two separate institutions into one. It is more similar to China's national industrial design and research institute, with the responsibilities of both the committee and the research institution. The unification of institutions can better clarify the boundaries of responsibilities and help grasp the current specialized trends and hot spots, which is of great significance for promoting the optimization of industrial design layout and structural adjustment, improving the efficiency of resource allocation, improving the degree of business specialization, streamlining management, and accelerating the effectiveness of policies.

Change to responsibilities of design promotion institution: in 1977, the institution's responsibility was to promote the development of the design and packaging industry and enhance the image of products made by South Korea. From 1991 to 1995, the institution's responsibility was to promote the development of design and packaging via holding activities; in 1997, the organization changed its name to South Korea Institute of Industrial Design Promotion and its function changed from development and design to industrial design promotion, focusing on product design and development of small and medium-sized enterprises; from 2001 to July 2015, the organization began to include the training of talents into its responsibilities, and set up branches at home and abroad; after December 2015, the responsibility of the organization has increased to set up branches or offices, namely, regional design centers (such as Gwangju, Busan, Daegu, Daejeon, etc.) at home and abroad, further expanding the influence of design. The expansion of responsibilities shows that the influence of the design policies is continuously extending, and the responsibilities of the design policies are gradually clarified, which helps to connect the work chain and improve the work efficiency.

Incentive Measures. Incentive clauses have always been an important content in the update of the south korean design promotion laws (Fig. 6). The incentive measures have been continuously updated (Except in 1977):

The general purpose of the selection of excellent design products is to promote the development of excellent industrial design. The products selected as excellent design products can be appropriately awarded and sold with the logo of excellent industrial product design, which is equivalent to the international IF Design and Red Dot Awards. If the products were found inconsistent with awarded ones later, they would be ordered to stop using the award logos. Although the direction of the clauses is consistent, the content is constantly being slightly tuned: From 1991 to 1997, the selection of excellent design products was divided into excellent design products and excellent packaging products. After 1997, the selection content was unified as excellent industrial design products, indicating that the definition of products has been broadened. From 1991 to 1997, the selection institution was the government; after 1997, it was the Ministry of

Trade, Industry and Energy. The delegation of selection authority brought the enthusiasm of various agencies into play, and also contributed to the construction of the legal system.

Support for professional companies: The government may provide support to enterprises specialized in research and development, investigation, analysis, consultation and other work related to industrial design and packaging. From 1991 to 1997, the scope of support was: research and development and technical guidance, expert assignation, and the joint use of expensive equipment; the scope of support since 1997: providing research results and guidance on cutting-edge development technologies, installation and operation of business incubation facilities, supporting the entrepreneurship of professional industrial design enterprises, and the joint use of expensive equipment. The change and update of research and development and technical guidance included "to provide technical guidance for cutting-edge development technologies", reflecting the sharp changes in the awareness of the South Korean government. The foresight of "cutting-edge" will bring huge development opportunities to the country, so that they have the advantage of early layout and can start ahead in the right direction.

Requirements for data provision: The state, regional governments, social organizations, government investment institutions, research institutions, educational institutions, etc. can be required to provide the necessary data for the implementation of projects. From 1991 to 1999, the Development Institute can request the above institutions to provide the necessary information for project implementation. Since 1999, it has been updated that the two institutions can request information: the promotion institution and the promotion department. The promotion institution has followed the requirements of the development institute, and the promotion department can request the regional government to cooperate in promoting regional industrial design projects. Horizontally, the number of institutions given with power is increasing from one to two; vertically, the scope of incentives given is expanding from providing information to cooperating with regional governments to jointly promote projects.

Compulsory Measures. The number of compulsory clauses has decreased generally since 1991. By the comparison of textual content, some particularities are shown:

Protection of names and logos: protection of promotion institutes. From 1977 to 1999, no one, other than the promotion institutes, shall use the name of South Korea Institute of Design Promotion or similar names. The protection of excellent industrial design spanned from 1977 to May 2014: products, other than those registered as excellent design products, shall not be attached to excellent design logos.

Submission of business plan: This clause has always existed in previous updates. In 1977, it was just required ambiguously to formulate a business plan for each fiscal year and obtain the approval of the Minister of Trade and Industry. After 1991, it was improved relatively: a business plan and budget plan shall be submitted before the start of each business year, and then the settlement statement for each business year shall be submitted usually before the end of February of the business year. The settlement shall be determined with approval before the end of March.

Talent Training. There were no regulations on talent training in 1977, but new addition and updates have been made since 1991 with mainly one clause and three points (Table 8).

Point 1: strive to train talents related to industrial design. The policy implementation entity was the government from 1991 to 2001, and changed to the country or special

Table 8. South Korean Design Promotion Laws—Classification of Talent Training Content

Date	1977	1991, 1993, 1995	1997, 1999	2001	2005, 2006, 2008, 2009, 2013, 2014.1, 2014.5, 2015.7, 2015.12, 2019
Talent training content	None	Article 8 Talent training, etc	Article 8 Talent training, etc	Article 8 Professional talent training, etc	Article 8 Professional talent training, etc

city, metropolitan cities, Jeju Metropolitan Autonomous City, provinces, and Jeju Special Autonomous Province from 2005 to 2019. The scope of the policy implementation entity was expanding, reflecting that talent training was a kind of overall responsibility at the national level as well as the development needs for all regions.

Point 2: encourage industry-school cooperation in industrial design and re-education. The policy implementation entity has always been the government, and the content changed slightly through years: it was industry-school cooperation in industrial design and packaging from 1991 to 1995, and updated to industry-school cooperation in industrial design and re-education after 1997.

Point 3: investigate the actual situation of design-related professionals according to the needs, and develop plans to improve the supply and demand of professionals. The policy implementation entity was the Design Promotion Center from 1991 to 1999, the Ministry of Trade, Industry and Energy in 2001, and the Minister of Trade, Industry and Energy or the mayor of special and metropolitan city, mayor of metropolitan cities or governors of provinces from 2005 to January 2014, and the government from May 2014 to 2019. While implementation entity of most policies changed from the centralized ones to the decentralized ones (that is, from the central government to the regional ones), the implementation entity of this policy is reversed, that is, from the regional governments to the central one. It should be said that the actual situation of design-related professionals surveyed by the central government is more objective and comprehensive than that of regional or institutional organizations.

Supervision Mechanism. The clause of supervision mechanism (except that in 1977) mainly includes report and inspection (Table 9): Order the design promotion institutes to report their business status or entrust public officials to inspect books, documents or other items in design promotion institutes; the public officials conducting the inspection shall present a certificate proving their authority to the relevant persons.

The supervision mechanism in 1977 contained two clauses: in addition to report and inspection, there was also "Article 10 Report on Implementation: the center shall report the implementation of the project plan in the first and second halves of each year to the Minister of Trade and Industry within 30 days after the end of each half year." This article was incorporated into the "Submission of Business Plan, etc." after 1991.

The report and inspection policy implementation entity of supervision mechanism is the Minister of Trade, Industry and Energy (previously named as the Ministry of

Table 9. South Korean Design Promotion Laws - Classification of Talent Training Content

Date	1977	1991, 1993, 1995	1997, 1999, 2001, 2005, 2006, 2009, 2013, 2014.1, 2014.5, 2015.7, 2015.12, 2019
Content	Article 10 Report on implementation	Article 18 Report and inspection	Article 18 Report and inspection
	Article 11 Report and supervision		

Trade and Industry, the Ministry of Commerce, Industry and Energy, and the Ministry of Knowledge-based Economy). There were no requirements for public officials conducting inspections in 1977. However, inspection officials were required to take certificates showing their authority since 1991, which indicates the rationality of continuous improvement of law enforcement and legal construction, so as to ensure the quality and assurance of design policy implementation.

Others. In this section, the "Fee Clause" appeared briefly in the updated legal documents in 1991, 1993, 1995, and 1997: fees for registration of excellent design products shall be paid in accordance with the regulations of the ministry of Trade and Industry (Ministry of Trade, Industry and Energy). The clause was deleted after 1999, that is, there has been no need to pay since then. the implementation of such policies promotes the enthusiasm for policy implementation and exerts the same expansion effect as the incentive policies, which strengthens and improves the role of national design policy, and is conducive to the establishment of national image.

6 Conclusion

South Korea's economic rise is neither a spontaneous extension of the country's 5,000-year history nor a product of the country's traditional culture, but largely depends on the government's industrial policies. In particular, the industrial design promotion policies elevated to legal level with the assistance of state power can promote, consolidate and optimize the framework of the manufacturing industry in a timely manner in response to the changes in national industry, resulting in an increase in the industrial added value. Policies promote economic development, and the improvement of the economic environment has strengthened the state's image as a strong player in design and industry. It's clear that the South Korean government takes the design policies as a national strategy capable of generating competitive advantage.

In South Korea, a relatively complete framework for industrial design promotion laws has been formed after 40 years or so, mainly including incentive measures, compulsory measures, plan implementation measures, supervision measures, and institution setting. In general, incentive measures account for the largest proportion, including the selection of excellent designs, support for professional companies, and related financial support; compulsory measures mainly protect intellectual property rights, the submission and implementation of business plans, and penalties against related violations; the content of plan implementation measures is the "design plan" issued in a planned and hierarchical manner according to the national industrial development needs and international design trends at each stage; both national centers and regional centers shall be set according to the situation; in addition, centers shall be adjusted in response to domestic and international environment changes and attention shall be paid to the suitability and systematization of the scope.

Many years of development and update of the design promotion laws have greatly boost the economy, matured the design policy system and resulted in many achievements, such as the South Korean Design Packaging Center was commended by the President on the "Export Day" in 1973; "Design in South Korea" was held in Shanghai in 2006; Seoul, South Korea, defeating Singapore and Dubai, was awarded the World Design Capital by the International Council of Societies of Industrial Design in 2007; "Design in South Korea" was also held in Guangzhou in 2008; South Korea successfully applied for the World Design Capital in 2010; South Korea Design Center (Hanoi) opened in 2018…

The accomplishments listed above fully reflect South Korea's great success in design policies in the field of design. South Korea's design industry is still expanding in size today. According to the "South Korean Design Statistics Summary Report 2020" published on the official website of the South Korea Institute of Design Promotion, there were 35.1million design workers in South Korea as of 2020. The design industry is worth 19.4 trillion won, and the number of companies using design exceeds 76.4% of the industry scale [8]. Since the 1970s, design in South Korea has taken a massive leap within just a few decades, and the country is constantly striving to become a world-class design power, all of which are owed to the national design policies.

Acknowledgements. This research was funded by Major Projects in Arts of the 2020 National Social Science Foundation of China: "Research on National Design Policy under the Background of the 'Belt and Road' Initiative", project number: 2020ZDG216.

References

1. Yi, Z., Chonghuai, N., Juhai, J.: Research on the development stage of korean industrial design industry and its policy enlightenment. Ecol. Econ. **05**, 190–195 (2014)
2. Jiang, L., Yuanhao, L., Cui, H., Jun, S.: Using bibliometric research to reshape policy text data analysis-the origin, migration and method innovation of policy bibliometrics. J. Public Manag. **02**, 138–144 (2015)
3. Wei, L.: Application of content analysis method in public management research. Chin. Administrative Manag. **06**, 93–98 (2014)
4. Jipeng, W., Mengyu, C.: Korea Import and Export Food Safety Management. China Quality Inspection Press, Beijing (2016)
5. Mingjie, R., Xiaoyun, Z.: Research on Industrial Development and Structural Transformation-Based on Value Chain Reconstruction-Shanghai Producer Service Industry and Advanced Manufacturing Dynamic Matching Research. Shanghai University of Finance and Economics Press, Shanghai (2012)

6. Yonghao, Z., Jian, G.: Economic effect analysis of Korean cultural industry and "Korean Wave" marketing. Northeast Asian J. **02**, 44–47 (2013)
7. Junhong, W.: A comparative analysis of the two financial crises at the end of the last century and the enlightenment to my country. Master's degree thesis, Southwestern University of Finance and Economics (2004)
8. Korea Design Promotion Institute homepage. Korea Design Statistical Data 2021_ summary report. https://www.designdb.com. Accessed 10 Jan 2023

Comparing VR Modeling Tool and Hand-Sketching in the Inspiration of Classic Chair Design and Modeling

Yu-Hsu Lee[✉] and Yan-Jie Peng

National Yunlin University of Science and Technology, Yunlin 64002, Taiwan, Republic of China
jameslee@yuntech.edu.tw

Abstract. The purpose of this study is to compare the differences between traditional hand sketching and VR (Virtual Reality) sketching software (Gravity Sketch) in the field of industrial design. For centuries, traditional hand sketching has been the primary method in the initial stage of design. Most designers are trained and accustomed to visualizing their ideas with 2D sketches on paper. While this is a fast, intuitive, and expressive way to generate, present, and evaluate ideas, as technology advances, the use of computers and design software has become a great alternative for those who want more convenience and flexibility. Using VR devices (headset and controllers), Virtual Reality provides stylists with an immersive virtual environment to sketch and model instantly in 3D, combining the sketching and modeling stages of the design process. The ultimate goal of design tools is to help express ideas more freely and easily. Traditional hand sketching and VR tools are all viable options and can reach their greatest potential at different stages of the design process. For example, pen and paper may be the best option for a sudden rush of ideas, 2D computer rendering is more accurate for outlining the structure, and 3D computer modeling is better for building curves, radii, and more modeling details. Every inspiration and thought starts from scratch, and yet it's easier to express ideas using VR modeling tools. The ability for designers to use their traditional hand sketching skills with VR tools creates new possibilities for design workflow and inspiration.

Keywords: Immersive Environment · Styling Ideas · VR Modeling · Hand-Sketching

1 Research Background

In this study, 6 experienced designers with more than 10 years of experience and 6 industrial design students are invited to participate in the development of a chair design. The participants are asked to present design proposals created by hand sketching and VR modeling tool. During the process, participants are videotaped and asked to think aloud (express their thoughts and verbally describe their actions) for observation purposes. Finally, the researchers collect the participants' experiences through an evaluation survey and retrospective interviews.

© The Author(s), under exclusive license to Springer Nature Switzerland AG 2023
A. Marcus et al. (Eds.): HCII 2023, LNCS 14030, pp. 182–192, 2023.
https://doi.org/10.1007/978-3-031-35699-5_14

First, the participants are presented with both paper and digital samples of design elements, which are divided into 4 main categories based on a morphological analysis chart: Curve, Geometric, Block, and Hybrid. Participants are asked to select 3 of these as their main design components. Before the design process begins, the participants are presented with instructional tutorials of the VR tool. The tutorials include a series of video demonstrations that introduce the user interface, various design tools, and how to use them. Participants are then given 30 min of practice time to familiarize themselves with the VR tool. After the design process, the researchers analyze the changes of behavior patterns between hand sketching and VR modeling tool for both groups of participants.

As a result, most novices perceive VR modeling tools between traditional hand sketching and computer 3D modeling software. VR tools provide them with an immersive environment that allows more flexibility in drawing outlines of curves and surfaces. In addition, changes and revisions to modeling ideas can be made and presented instantly, which is convenient and allows chains of ideas to flow and connect smoothly. However, VR tools have a steeper learning curve than traditional hand sketching, and it takes more effort to become proficient. On the other hand, most experienced designers suggest that VR tools are great alternatives to traditional hand sketching and computer 3D modeling software. VR tools offer the opportunity to enhance the stylist's skills and expressive creativity in an immersive environment, and allow ideas to be created directly in a three-dimensional space, without the need to draw the same object many times from different angles. It's a great step-two between traditional hand sketching and computer 3D modeling software.

1.1 Research Purposes

The rapid growth of AR and VR technologies has become a crucial aspect in enhancing people's lives. From video games, art tutorials, exhibition viewing, gallery visits, creative styling to physical and mental therapy, professionals are exploring these applications to develop more tools that support human life. In the past, designers utilized computer-aided design, such as the Sketchpad program introduced by Dr. Ivan Sutherland in 1963, which was a major breakthrough in computer graphics. As technology continues to advance, designers' efficiency in creating drawings has significantly increased. Although traditional hand-drawing is still useful for visualizing designs, VR modeling tools now offer more interactive and detailed modeling options. Technology continues to assist designers in their creative efforts by offering engineering calculations, 3D modeling and immersive VR environments. Since the release of the Oculus Rift, a leading video game console in 2012, Oculus has been a player in the VR headset market. In 2022, Facebook officially renamed Oculus Quest to Meta Quest, breaking free from the computer connection and allowing for direct wireless internet connection from the device, and claims to enable creators to freely draw curves and surfaces in an immersive 3D environment. The acceptance of new technology by transportation and product designers has received positive feedback, and immersive VR technology has reached a mature stage.

In product design, designers use various tools to thoroughly examine the form and communicate it to others (Schön 1992). Before moving forward, it's critical to narrow down ideas, finalize the shape development direction and details, and select the appropriate presentation tool to evaluate and communicate the shape with accuracy and efficiency. Hand-drawn sketches are ideal for quick shape ideation, 2D renderings are useful for outlining external contours and component composition, while 3D digital and physical models are effective for discussing shape details such as surface variations and R-angles. This study, using classic furniture shapes as case studies, refers to shape classification for conceptualization and compares the thinking patterns of expert and novice designers in the conceptualization and refinement phases, the usage patterns of design tools, and the impact of different design aids on design outcomes through VR immersive environment simulation, while preserving the freedom and feasibility of shape ideation. It not only demonstrates the feasibility of VR immersive design aids in conceptualization and refinement, but also explores the issues and principles of their application. The key points of the furniture design study include:

1. Investigating the user acceptance of VR design tools in the conceptualization and refinement stages.
2. Comparing the operation and effectiveness of VR design tools between expert and novice designers in the form development phase.
3. Investigate the role, advantages and disadvantages of traditional hand-drawn and 3D digital models and corresponding VR tools in the design process.

2 Literature Review

The product design process involves expressing and exploring different shapes using tools such as paper and pencil, computer software, foam, wood, and clay. As designers continue to refine their ideas and consider shapes from different perspectives, they may move to more advanced tools to achieve greater accuracy and precision. The use of traditional hand-drawn sketches is often sufficient for early-stage exploration, while 2D or 3D designs are required for further development. However, the need for physical prototypes to address ergonomics and usability leads to increased production costs and time. This study aims to investigate the impact of VR technology on the efficiency, depth, and quality of the design process by reviewing related literature on the design process, hand-drawn sketches, computer-aided design, furniture design, and VR applications. The goal is to establish a standard VR-based design process.

Professor Rowena Kostellow has been involved in industrial design education for nearly half a century and has dedicated her life to developing the "visual compositional relationships" approach to teaching as the basis for all types of design. She pointed out that computer-aided design and visual media can be used to explore the fourth dimension of time and motion, but still cannot replace what the human eye and hand can do. Today, the development of computer technology, from resolution and realism to immersive VR devices, has significantly narrowed the distance between the virtual world and the real world, and the simulated 3D displayed on computer screens, although the rendering of materials and environmental light and shadow, such as Keyshot software, can present extremely realistic images, but there is still a discrepancy with the real world objects, and even too much beautification of virtual objects. For design students, it is difficult to judge directly from the computer screen what the 3D object will look like when it is actually made into a real product, and they even have no sense of the 3D shape and cannot distinguish the beauty of the shape. Students will be able to view their own models from different angles and distances in an immersive environment, achieving what Professor Kostellow calls "direct thinking in three-dimensional space".

2.1 Design Process

According to Zeisel (1981), involves three phases: imagination, expression, and evaluation, forming a spiral of continuous development. Designers first imagine a solution, express the concept through sketches and models, communicate with clients, define the scope of the design, and continually refine the concept until it meets the requirements. Goel (1995) conducted a verbal analysis comparing the training of architects, engineers, and industrial designers at different stages of the design process and found that there are four phases: problem solving, initial design, revision, and detailed design. This requires a balance of both theoretical and practical aspects, taking into account factors such as human development, purpose, behavior, structure, and function. This project aims to investigate the acceptance of VR tools in the design process by experts and novices, and the need for complementary tools at different stages, including the three components proposed by Zeisel.

2.2 How Designers Think About Sketching

Lee and Yan (2016) compared the effects of novice designers when thinking about shapes before and after using computers. They used two different 3D tools with two different interfaces to perform two different design tasks. They then compared the amount of time each student spent using the two 3D tools in generating, modifying, moving, changing viewpoints, changing tools, recovering, thinking, and testing tools, and analyzed the process of using 3D tools and its impact on styling concept. The results suggest that even SketchUp, which is easy to use and suitable for beginners, can limit the development of styling ideas for novices. Prats et al. (2009) investigated the process and rules of manual styling changes. They asked architecture and product design students the same design questions and extracted about 300 hand-drawn designs for design behavior analysis. Based on the classification results, they summarized how the subjects constructed their own subshape systems using stylistic elements through rules of disassembly, rotation, and combination (parallelism, intersection, and difference).

2.3 Furniture Design Type Analysis

Feng and Chen (2019) conducted a study on the influence of Bauhaus style on furniture design in Taiwan. They extracted the five components of Bauhaus style: function, technology, form, color, and material, and transformed the theme of Bauhaus style into an evaluation tool for design development and strategic management. Meanwhile, Chuang and Hsiao (2009) used morphological analysis to examine the differences in features and control elements and stylistic elements in specific styles, and Yoo et al. (2007) used morphological analysis to decompose the composition of Mackintosh style chairs. These studies demonstrate the importance of considering style elements in furniture design and how they can be used to evaluate and analyze design styles.

The design process involves a continuous expression and search for the ideal form using a variety of tools. Zeisel (1981) identified three parts of the design process: imagination, expression, and verification, which form a spiral development process. Lee and Yan (2016) found that even easy-to-use 3D tools, such as SketchUp, can limit the development of styling ideas for novice designers. Feng and Chen (2019) used morphological analysis to extract the five components of Bauhaus style in furniture design, transforming the theme into an evaluation tool for design development and strategic management. Wei and Lu (2019) used morphological analysis and card sorting to understand consumers' introduction to product shape and visual complexity. In this project, morphological analysis and card sorting are also used to distinguish different components of furniture and to reference hand-drawn or VR furniture design.

2.4 VR Design Applications

The current application of VR equipment in industrial design, in addition to the evaluation and verification of the shape after the realistic rendering, for example, Alias software can interface with the modeling work, directly in the immersive environment, providing a highly realistic rendering effect; in recent years, there are also beginning to invest in the application of VR in the modeling stage, such as Gravity Sketch has been widely implemented in foreign transportation design and design education units. For example, Gravity Sketch has been widely implemented in overseas transportation design and design education units. AR/VR/MR opens another window for the application of creative machine interfaces Flavián et al. (2019). The immersive environment of VR removes the barrier between the screen and the user object, providing a more direct space for manipulation (Kelly and Siegel 2017) and exploring the possibilities of shape development through parameter changes in the virtual environment. This study explores the use and preferences of VR technology for styling suggestions in the design process-including curve and surface drawing-for both novice and experienced users.

The application of VR technology has evolved through the accumulation of various technologies in different industries, such as computer games, military industry, and high-tech manufacturing, as well as the promotion of movies and science fiction novels, before it became popular to today's social communication and immersive devices known to the general public (Petrov 2018). However, due to the advantages of VR, scholars have continued to study its use in front-end design concept development and digital modeling after modeling ideas have been created. Arora et al. (2017) evaluated the accuracy of VR tools by drawing curves and circles with 12 participants (8 males and 4 females) who were not trained in drawing, and their results showed that the immersive space of VR increased the freedom of drawing but affected the accuracy of drawing.

Ekströmer and Wever (2019) planned two design tasks, a toaster and a tape table, and invited 16 first-year master's students, divided into two groups (8 students each), to compare the difference between drawing with pen and paper alone and drawing with pen and paper followed by VR (Gravity Sketch). In addition, VR is superior to straight line modeling in the idea of curved surface and block modeling, and through observation of the experimental process, it is also found that because VR tools have the function of undo, users are able to repeat the drawing action until they draw a nice line, which makes the finished proposal less than the pencil drawing that cannot be undone. Ekströmer and

Wever also suggest that the subsequent VR usability study should use the sound playback method and the retrospective interview method to further understand what users really think when they use different tools to draw or think about their ideas and the process of shape change. This project draws on the research of the aforementioned scholars to illustrate the differences in the use of different computer tools and VR for different types of furniture design, and uses retrospective interviews to understand the change in the thoughts of design veterans and novices when they use different design tools for shape conception and detail correction.

2.5   Design Hand Sketching and VR

Schön (1992) argues that designers are in dialogue with themselves through sketching, while Goldschmidt (1991) observes the mental processes of designers engaged in design behavior and distinguishes the design process into "moves" and "arguments. The "moves" are the actual acts of design, a coherent process of making proposals, and he divides a series of design activities into smallest units or blocks in a verbal agreement to present design conclusions; the "arguments" are related to specific design activities. "Arguments" is related to specific move, related to the design itself or the design direction statement, and pointed out that sketch is the designer to systematically change, give graphic characteristics rational mode, is a kind of interaction between the concept and the graphic argument (Goldschmidt 1994), sketching activity consists of two kinds of "seeing as" and "seeing that", with "seeing as" directly linked to sketching. Seeing as" is directly related to sketching itself, that is, how the designer "sees" and reinterprets the graphic material, or emerges from the reinterpretation of the sketch as a new image, while "seeing that" is related to the non-image state of the design process arguments, Goldschmidt studies the designer's design behavior process, presenting the "seeing as" dialectic and the "seeing that" dialectic from verbal analysis. Goldschmidt thus points out that the design process must, on the one hand, produce valid details and coherent entities and, on the other hand, propose knowledge about the appearance of abstract concepts that do not refer to specific entities.

2.6   VR and Digital Modeling

CAD design models and hand drawing processes each has its own merits, it cannot effectively explore the possibilities of shape finding in 3D. Ron Arad used digital boards to give digital sketches a sense of uncertainty even after having a digital shape, reversing the traditional order of drawing and then rethinking the shape by blurring it with digital hand drawing, and Zaha Hadid's shape creation was partly due to a mix of working methods and hand drawing with digital design, which would not be able to complete or express the idea. The study by Stones and Cassidy (2007) found that students were accustomed to working digitally in a way that was more akin to working with off-the-shelf objects or with an indeterminate form of a digital design, rather than using tools to create ideas from scratch. The idea begins with a form of uncertainty.

Vlah et al. (2021) explored the capabilities of VR 3D modeling and compared the effectiveness of CAD and VR tools in 3D modeling by inviting seven participants (six males and one female) with engineering backgrounds and familiarity with SolidWorks or

NX software tools to form an expert group to perform modeling experiments and questionnaire interviews for a given mouse shape. The researcher also assisted in informing the participants about the functional location of VR when needed, and recorded the operation process and opinions in VR. The results of the study showed that the participants thought that the intuitive and spatial sense of VR was more suitable for concept development and 3D sketching than constructing precise 3D models on the computer, and most of them were interested in the free-form surface of VR and thought that the immersive environment of VR was helpful for spatial awareness and intuitive operation.

3   Research Methods

3.1   VR Experiment and Design Operation

This study compares the differences between design expert and novices using VR 3D drawing tools and traditional sketching hand drawing tools by proposing VR aids to support shape development. Theoretically, design expert are more comfortable with drawing and have a better sense of dimensionality, so they can perform better when entering three-dimensional space in VR. Novice designers can only draw simple curves and surfaces to build models without assistance. The ideal VR aids should be able to provide simple structural guidelines based on specific modeling directions while maintaining freedom of development. In this study, VR manipulation experiments were conducted to evaluate the effect. Based on the results of the study, three to four classically designed chair structures were set up and the participants were allowed to choose one of them for their styling suggestions. To avoid the effect of task and tool familiarity on the results, six design experts and six novices were asked to complete the three chair proposals by hand drawing and VR, and six drawing experiments were conducted for each method to improve the reliability and effectiveness of the study. Participants were asked to select one to three types of chairs from a categorized list of classic chairs and sketch them on the provided A4 paper while recording the entire process. Wearing the Meta Quest VR equipment, participants had to select three pre-constructed chair surfaces and legs (Figs. 1 and 2) and draw matching legs and seats according to their own styling ideas. Prior to the experiment, the VR images were projected onto a laptop computer and the entire interview was screen recorded and the entire content of the styling idea was retrospectively recorded (Fig. 3).

Fig. 1. Participants tried sketching in a VR environment.

Fig. 2. Six different types of chair seats design in VR modeling tool provided by this search.

Fig. 3. Six different types of chair legs design in VR modeling tool provided by this search.

3.2 Design Novice Experiment Results and Feedback

The six novice designers were all Master of Industrial Design students (3 males and 3 females, ages 25–28) with 2–4 years of education, and all six novice designers had learned how to use the Gravity Sketch software in class. In the experiment, all six novice designers completed their assigned tasks. The advantages of VR include: the ability to undo, simplifying curves or surfaces, easier to draw with references, suitable for large areas or volumes, and the ability to view shapes from different perspectives. You can see the shape from different angles, feel the actual proportions of the object, think and draw in a more consistent way, represent the imagination in your head, have a good sense of three-dimensional space, tubes and lines are more suitable for presentation in VR, be able to produce more shapes, and be able to discuss modifications or show the proposed shape remotely through the Internet and equipment (Tables 1 and 2).

Table. 1. Result of six novices' creation both VR modeling tool and hand sketching.

	Novice 1	Novice 2	Novice 3	Novice 4	Novice 5	Novice 6
Hand Sketch						
	30 Minutes	34 Minutes	30 Minutes	23 Minutes	19 Minutes	30 Minutes
VR Sketch						
	38 Minutes	66 Minutes	39 Minutes	71 Minutes	37 Minutes	38 Minutes

3.3 Design Expert Experiment Results and Feedback

The 6 design expert are university design faculty and designers. Three of the design expert focus on hand-drawn expression, while the other three focus on 3D modeling. All 6 design expert had more than 10 years of experience in hand drawing or CAID design and teaching (all were male, aged 38–47). Two of them said that they use hand drawing only for pre-modeling, not as a drawing tool, because the shape is generally thought out and they do not need the help of hand drawing. They felt that efficiency was the key to using the tool, as hand drawing would not be very helpful in thinking about the shape, and the other respondents in the retrospective interviews agreed with this view. They believe that real styling ideas don't happen during the drawing process, but rather before they pick up a pen, when they discover in their lives what they want to design, a chair with character and material, or when they suddenly have a flash of inspiration during their normal routine. The CAD experts drew the chair during the hand drawing experiment, but said it was not the final product, but a random drawing that would be constructed in 3D to confirm the details if the shape was confirmed.

Table. 2. Result of six experts' creation both VR modeling tool and hand sketching.

	Expert 1	Expert 2	Expert 3	Expert 4	Expert 5	Expert 6
Hand Sketch						
	15 Minutes	26 Minutes	13 Minutes	27 Minutes	15 Minutes	8 Minutes
VR Sketch						
	45 Minutes	33 Minutes	30 Minutes	35 Minutes	30 Minutes	22 Minutes

3.4 Observational Method and Think-Aloud Method

Without disturbing the participants, VR immersive environment is suitable for observing the participants' operation behavior from the side, but it is not easy to get the feedback of the participants' feelings at the moment. In order to analyze the hidden needs and operation difficulties of different participants, as well as the relevance of designers' thinking and drawing behaviors during design development, the participants were asked to explain the steps they performed when using the VR tool for design development, and the whole operation process of the experienced designers was recorded by video recording, so as not to interfere with the observation of the participants' thinking during design development. The researcher will help to solve the problem of tool operation only when the participant is not familiar with the function of the tool and asks questions. If the researcher observes a critical turning point or has questions about the participant's execution of the action, he or she can record the time point and then play the video clip after they completes the modeling proposal. For novice designers, in the actual implementation of VR experiments, because of the need learning the functions of VR in a short period of time, and to complete the specified tasks, the participants generally said that they could not say what they wanted to perform while operating or styling ideas, so the questionnaire and retrospective interviews were designed to analyze and understand the participants' thinking about the development of styling.

3.5 Questionnaire Survey and Retrospective Interview

The purpose of this study was to investigate the use of VR tools by experienced and novice designers during the modeling development phase and to understand their opinions on the strengths, weaknesses, and desired features of current VR tools. For the verbal analysis, time-point recordings were used to determine the participants' actions during rotation, viewing the model and constructing the main face/line, pulling the face, and placing the cylinder. Further analysis was conducted to determine if there were specific behavioral patterns between expert and novice designers in model development and retraction, or differences in model thinking, viewing angles, use of specific features, and model reinterpretation. Through repeated observations, more than three researchers obtained the behavioral patterns of stylistic thinking and virtual reality operations of designers with different design experience based on the tools used, stylistic categories, and disassembly-combination actions, which will serve as important reference data for future design thinking, stylistic research, and development of virtual reality design tools.

4   Research Results and Discussion

The structural classification results in the division of the seat into upper and lower parts. The shape of the seat is often different depending on the material, and there are different structures in the feet and seat. For example, steel tube feet with plastic or wood seat, then the classification may be tube and plate. This classification suggestion is very important for VR experiments, to provide a part of the seat shape in the VR environment so that the participant can complete another part of the shape, instead of asking the participant to draw a chair, which can reduce the difficulty of operation and make it easier to obtain the data needed for research. The participants gave feedback on the VR furniture design, saying that despite the high degree of freedom in VR, it was difficult to conceptualize the shape without a reference object and without being familiar with VR operation. Therefore, this study adapts the experimental process to divide the structure of the seat into two constructions: the legs and the cushion. In the VR environment, different shapes of legs and cushions were constructed first, so that the participants could choose the leg that inspired the shape to draw the cushion, or choose the cushion to complete the design of the legs, in order to reduce the difficulty of operation and make it easier to obtain the data that this study wanted to investigate.

4.1 Experimental Results of the Design Process

Hand-drawing is considered to be a quick way to capture the imagination of the mind and assemble and improve it, which is faster and more suitable for drawing shapes with many details and the presentation of curves can be as one wishes. However, the disadvantage is the need to draw while thinking about other perspectives, some complex shapes are not easy to express, or need to draw a number of different perspectives, but also limited by the designer's ability to three-dimensional, perspective and other concepts. Most of the respondents think that VR is a good tool for pre-development, but the final product presentation still needs to be done in computer graphics software. Because VR is more difficult to adjust than computer graphics software, such as not being able to find the center line and center point, it is impossible to make the final product shape. But because VR is so good for pre-development, it can also help designers to keep thinking. VR has many useful features, but it can focus on adjusting settings, making it relatively slow to create. VR is much faster than hand-drawn graphics, but it requires more settings than computer graphics software. Therefore, VR can be considered an integrated tool for both graphic drawing and computer graphics software. Before entering computer graphics software, if you are not sure how to convert graphic drawing to 3D, you can operate and confirm in VR first to deepen your imagination of the final result. Or, if you enter VR first and then go to computer software to create 3D, you can complete the task faster.

References

Affairs, A.S.: Running a Usability Test, 15 May 2014. Accessed 29 January 2018. https://www.usability.gov/how-to-and-tools/methods/running-usability-tests.html

Berg, L.P., Vance, J.M.: Industry use of virtual reality in product design and manufacturing: a survey. Virtual Reality **21**(1), 1–17 (2016). https://doi.org/10.1007/s10055-016-0293-9

Chuang, M., Shiau, K.: A study on the key form elements and the operation in constituting the product style of "Loop Chairs". J. Des. **1**(1), 51–66 (1996)

Flavián, C., Ibáñez-Sánchez, S., Orús, C.: The impact of virtual, augmented and mixed reality technologies on the customer experience. J. Bus. Res. **100**, 547–560 (2019)

Fong, W., Chen, T.: The influences of the bauhaus style on furniture design in Taiwan: using the furniture brand "TW.U.C.M." as an example. J. Des. **24**(4), 17–40 (2019)

Goel, V.: Sketches of Thought. MIT Press (1995)

Goldschmidt, G.: The dialectics of sketching. Creat. Res. J. **4**(2), 123–143 (1991)

Goldschmidt, G.: On visual design thinking: the vis kids of architecture. Des. Stud. **15**(2), 158–174 (1994)

Lee, S., Yan, J.: The impact of 3D CAD interfaces on user ideation: a compara-tive analysis using SketchUp and Silhouette Modeler. Des. Stud. **44**, 52–73 (2016)

Lewis, J.R., Sauro, J.: Item benchmarks for the system usability scale. J. Usability Stud. **13**(3) (2018)

Prats, M., Lim, S., Jowers, I., Garner, S.W., Chase, S.: Transforming shape in de-sign: observations from studies of sketching. Des. Stud. **30**(5), 503–520 (2009)

Schön, D.A.: Designing as reflective conversation with the materials of a design situation. Knowl.-Based Syst. **5**(1), 3–14 (1992). Zeisel (1981)

Siegel, Z.D., Kelly, J.W.: Walking through a virtual environment improves per-ceived size within and beyond the walked space. Atten. Percept. Psychophys. **79**(1), 39–44 (2017)

Wei, W., Lu, M.: Influence of product form attributes on visual complexity and consumer preferences. J. Des. **24**(2), 49–69 (2019)

You, H., Chen, K., Deng, Y.: A study on the form generation of mackintosh style chairs. J. Des. **12**(3), 17–31 (2007)

Research on Interaction Design Based on Artificial Intelligence Technology in a Metaverse Environment

Yaqi Li[✉], Zenglong Ma, and Lili Zhang

School of Art, Shandong Jianzhu University, No. 1000, Fengming Road, Licheng District, Shandong 250101, Jinan, China
1719755294@qq.com

Abstract. At the beginning of 2021, the term "metaverse" appeared in the public eye in an almost demonized manner, some people are crazy about it, some question it, and some feel disdainful, but at the root, it is an underlying desire of human beings when faced with limited choices. The New Crown epidemic has broken the threshold of people's desire for a virtualized society, and more frequent online life has made people in the global village even more eager for parallel worlds, for breaking the limits of time and space, for unlimited experiences and possibilities.

We are moving from Industry 4.0 to Industry 5.0, from a technology-driven industrial model to a human-centered value-driven industrial model, and from a touchable reality to a novel and fantastical virtual world, often thanks to the integration of multiple emerging technologies. The application of artificial intelligence technology has dramatically changed the way people interact with each other. Under the new domestic epidemic quarantine policy, the time spent online has increased dramatically across society, and a new type of "home economy" has emerged, with artificial intelligence opening up new spaces for production and life, public health, education and employment, economy and finance, national security and many other areas. As online life becomes more and more normalized, real-world life is unable to meet people's needs, and a virtual world parallel to the real world - the metaverse - is opening up the online and offline worlds.

In 2020–2022, domestic and foreign enterprises continue to promote the digital transformation of enterprises and march towards the meta-universe, with giants such as Ingame, Nvidia, Microsoft, Tencent, NetEase and Byte Jumping laying out industries related to the meta-universe concept, expanding from the state of the real economy to the meta-universe economic system, empowering the development of the real economy and feeding back to the real world through the virtual world. The spirit of the 20th National Congress of the Communist Party of China states that the development of the digital economy should be accelerated and the deep integration of the digital economy and the real economy should be promoted. The integration and development of technologies related to the metaverse continue to expand the application space, enriching the real space and reaching all things. In the future, the metaverse will become the mainstream social place in the future human world, where things in the virtual world interact with each other and form a native ecosystem. Humans will cross-connect with other people, objects and virtual environments in the metaverse with virtual images that have social attributes or social relationships, and carry out interactive activities. Social interaction, voice interaction, gesture interaction, eye interaction, eye interaction, as well as the act of touching the frames of glasses and iris recognition for identity encryption, are among the more important technologies of the future.

Based on artificial intelligence technology, this thesis will study how to design interaction in the metaverse environment from four aspects: virtual digital human, the humanoid robot, digital collection, and spatiotemporal intelligence. In order to promote the integration of natural life, virtual life and machine life, provide systematic suggestions for creating multi-sensory interaction, time and space jumping, data interconnection, immersive and interactive virtual space, and metaverse feeding back to the real industry.

Keywords: Artificial intelligence · Interaction design · Metaverse

1 Introduction

In recent years, the metaverse has become a topic of great concern. The metaverse is a virtual digital world where people can use virtual reality to interact with others, explore virtual spaces, and engage in various activities. In this digital age, the concept of the metaverse has expanded to different fields, such as gaming, education, entertainment and work. With the continuous development of the metaverse, how to provide a better user experience and more efficient interaction has become a hot issue for researchers.

In the metaverse environment, AI technology can provide users with a better interactive experience. Artificial intelligence technology is a brick to build the metaverse. Among them, technologies such as natural language processing, computer vision, and machine learning are grains of sand that can be piled up to make it easier for users to interact with virtual characters, objects, and environments in the metaverse. Through the application of artificial intelligence technology, users can use the metaverse more naturally and feel a more realistic experience.

Interaction design also plays a vital role in the metaverse. Interaction design is like painting with different colors and materials to create a different sense of atmosphere and direct experience. In the metaverse, interaction design needs to take into account the user's interaction with the virtual world, the communication between the user, and the interaction between the user and the metaverse. Therefore, a successful interaction design needs to consider user needs, technical feasibility, and the characteristics of the virtual world.

2 Virtual Digital People

2.1 Definition and Current Development of the Virtual Digital Person

A virtual digital human is a humanoid simulacrum that is modeled on the human form and realized through computer graphics, artificial intelligence, human kinematics and other technical means to achieve autonomous representation in a virtual environment. The development of the virtual digital human originated from computer graphics and computer animation technology, and after years of development and refinement, it has now become an integral part of virtual environments such as the metaverse.

The development of the virtual digital human dates back to the 1960s, when computer graphics techniques were only capable of drawing simple geometries. As computer performance improved, computer graphics technology gradually developed and attempts were made to use computers to simulate human movement and performance. The earliest virtual digital humans were hand-made by human artists, but their development was once constrained by high production costs and difficulties in reuse. It was not until the development of computer graphics technology and artificial intelligence that virtual digital humans were able to be generated and represented autonomously on computers.

With the development of artificial intelligence technology, the performance and autonomy of virtual digital humans continue to improve. Currently, the performance of virtual digital humans can be very realistic, capable of representing various human movements, expressions, and sounds, and adaptive to changes in the environment. At the same time, the autonomy of virtual digital humans is also increasing, allowing them to learn and adapt to new environments and tasks through techniques such as deep learning.

The use of virtual digital humans is also becoming increasingly widespread. In addition to being widely used in areas such as gaming and film, virtual digital humans can also be used in a variety of fields such as education, healthcare and entertainment. For example, in the education sector, virtual humans can simulate various scenarios and situations to help students better understand and grasp knowledge; in the medical sector, virtual humans can help doctors perform surgery simulations and diagnose conditions.

The development of virtual digital humans still faces several challenges and issues. For example, the performance and autonomy of virtual digital humans still need to be improved, especially in terms of performance and adaptability in complex environments; also, the data and privacy security of virtual digital humans needs to be given sufficient attention.

2.2 Application of Artificial Intelligence Technology in the Design of Virtual Digital Human Interaction

Artificial intelligence technology can improve the intelligence and autonomy of the virtual digital human, for example, through natural language processing technology to achieve dialogue interaction between the virtual digital human and the user; (Fig. 1) through machine learning technology to achieve the behavioral simulation and learning of the virtual digital human to improve the intelligence and autonomy of the virtual digital human; through emotion computing technology to achieve the emotional expression and emotion recognition of the virtual digital human to improve the interactivity and The project is designed to improve the interactivity and expressiveness of the virtual digital human through emotion computing technology.

Using AI to drive virtual digital humans, while computing the voice expression, facial expressions, and action forms of digital humans, the digital human is calculated by deep learning models, and the results are driven in real time or offline, and rendered. At present, the mainstream way is to drive digital human interaction through text-driven around natural language capabilities, the essence is to drive digital human interaction through the closed loop of perception-decision-expression through ASR-NLP-TTS and other AI technologies, digital humans can simulate the human learning process for question and answer after big data training, and need to set up relevant knowledge maps or question answering libraries in advance, etc., and connect with the dialogue system of digital humans.

Computer vision (CV) is currently relatively complete in digital vocal lip synchronization, and has been widely used in games; Other expressions and actions also need to be driven by descriptive data or tags, and have not yet been intelligently synthesized, and expression actions are also the key direction of AI-driven future development. At the same time, with the continuous development of action recognition technology, deep learning + CV technology can already identify human actions from video, combined with the learning ability of the model, can promote the virtual digital human to continue to progress to human action, intelligently synthesize human actions, and help virtual digital humans interact with humans.

The key direction of future AI technology is to realize multimodal perception input at the input end, improve multimodal interaction capabilities at the output end, comprehensively improve the expressiveness of digital humans, and transform from the current text-based interaction to semantic-based interaction, especially the need to strengthen the perception and expression of human emotions. In addition, in addition to using ASR-NLP-TTS and other technologies to drive digital human interaction, AI technology is also applied to video generation of 2D digital humans, modeling of 3D digital humans, video driving, physical simulation and other links.

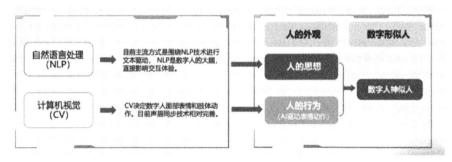

Fig. 1. Ways in which artificial intelligence technology improves the intelligence and autonomy of virtual digital humans

2.3 Practical Examples of Virtual Digital Human Interaction Design and Evaluation Methods

The interaction design of virtual digital humans needs to consider the needs and experience of users, such as improving user engagement and experience through virtual digital human expressions and voice interactions. Practical examples include virtual digital human game characters, virtual actors, virtual customer service, etc. Evaluation methods include indicators such as user satisfaction, interaction efficiency, and emotional performance.

At present, domestic service-oriented virtual digital humans are mainly used to replace real people for content generation such as broadcasting, and simple Q&A interaction, etc., and other scenarios also include virtual teachers, navigation guides (subway stations, hospitals, etc.), and exhibition introductions (guided tours "Xiaochunni") that have been planned in many countries. Foreign countries have technical advantages in CG (Computer Graphic, Computer Graphics), which can create virtual digital humans with a high sense of care, and take the lead in landing virtual companion assistants and psychological counselors in medical and other scenarios.

In China, virtual anchors (Fig. 2) are one of the application scenarios with the greatest development potential, represented by DeepWisdom Technology Company, some manufacturers have begun to provide one-stop services, including supporting services such as clients, layout solutions, hardware systems, and even traffic applications. Individual manufacturers will integrate the operational details in the live broadcast scenario into the product design to better cater to consumer psychology and the platform's traffic distribution mechanism.

Fig. 2. Virtual host

At the same time, the price threshold of virtual live streaming (Fig. 3) has dropped from tens of thousands to thousands, and the threshold for use has also been greatly reduced. Under the existing technical conditions, customer service scenarios with relatively clear business requirements and rules and processes have become an ideal way for virtual digital humans to land. In addition to replacing real people, virtual humans have unique advantages in areas where background knowledge such as customer service will change rapidly due to faster business knowledge upgrades based on knowledge graphs and data iterations. Virtual customer service can better serve customers through software and hardware integrated large screens, electronic broadcast screens, etc. at the service site, and online through apps and other forms.

198   Y. Li et al.

Fig. 3. 3D virtual live broadcast

3 Humanoid Robots

3.1 Definition and Current Development of Humanoid Robots

A humanoid robot is a robot designed to mimic human appearance and behavioral characteristics, and can play various roles in human society, such as assistant, cleaning, companionship, etc. There is no standard definition of a humanoid robot worldwide, and it is often vaguely defined as a robot that looks and behaves close to a human. From the perspective of global pioneer explorers, whether it is Honda "ASIMO", which has regrettably ended, or Tesla "Optimus", the vision of the participants in the global humanoid robot track is relatively consistent, that is, they hope to achieve human-computer interaction, enter every household, and share a social division of labor with humans. At present, humanoid robots have been widely used and studied, including robot vision, speech recognition, machine learning and other aspects. The development of humanoid robots can be divided into 3 stages: (1) 1928–1973, the initial exploration stage, led by Europe, America and Japan, the research mainly focuses on the structure and drive of humanoids, robots do not have perception and decision-making functions; (2) From 1973 to 2013, in the stage of system perception, there were great breakthroughs in "vision" and "touch"; (3) From 2013 to the present, in the decision-making stage, humanoid robots have stronger independent learning and decision-making capabilities. The figure below shows a robot designed and developed by a technology company, which has been able to autonomously imitate humans to complete running jumps, squats, and even backflips. (Fig. 4).

Fig. 4. A robot designed by a technology company does a flip like a human

3.2 Application of Artificial Intelligence Techniques in Humanoid Robot Interaction Design

Artificial intelligence technology can improve the intelligence and autonomy of humanoid robots, such as realizing the behavior simulation and learning of humanoid robots through machine learning technology; The emotional performance and emotion recognition of humanoid robots are realized through emotion computing technology, and the interactivity and expressiveness of humanoid robots are improved. AI aims to provide machines with the ability to perform logic, reasoning, planning, learning, and perception in the field of science. Artificial intelligence helps create the comprehensive controllability and intelligence of robots, which is a combination of artificial intelligence and robotics, and artificial intelligence software is embedded in the robot system. In other words, AI holds a key role in making robots intelligent. The most advanced robots are those controlled by artificial intelligence that can learn from their environment and experience and then build their capabilities based on that knowledge. Artificial neural networks (ANNs) and variants allow AI to perform tasks relative to "perception". When combined with current multicore parallel computing hardware platforms, many neural layers can be stacked, providing a higher level of perceptual abstraction when learning their own feature sets, eliminating the need for manual features, a process known as deep learning. Various algorithms for deep learning have emerged to improve the intelligent interactivity of robots: Promobot promotional robot. It is able to respond to inquiries, recognize faces, provide details about the company's services, scan and complete documents, collect payments, and display promotional materials; The robot kitchen (Fig. 5) system contains a complete set of appliances, cabinets, calculations, safety functions and robotic arms are all included in the robot kitchen system, which can accurately imitate the activities of professional chefs, make delicious dishes and clean up by themselves, as well as learn recipes, prepare dishes from all over the world, and even prepare their own dishes.

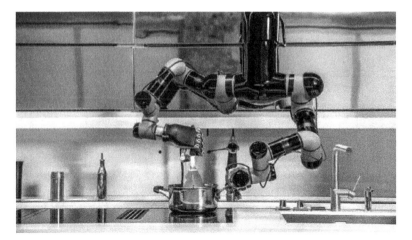

Fig. 5. Robot kitchen

The above examples are a microcosm of humanoid robots, integrating artificial intelligence algorithms, with good operating systems and intelligent interaction capabilities, and continuously bringing a sense of technology into people's lives.

3.3 Practical Examples of Humanoid Robot Interaction Design and Evaluation Methods

The interaction design of humanoid robots needs to consider human society and human-robot interaction. Practice cases include assistants, cleaning, accompaniment, etc. of humanoid robots, and evaluation methods include user satisfaction, interaction efficiency, emotional performance and other indicators. Humanoid robots should not only be adult-oriented, but also able to move forward in the direction of 'pedestrians': the popularization of technology continues to bring about the improvement of efficiency and quality of life scenes, such as sweeping robots, Xiaoai voice robots, etc. slowly integrated into our lives; at the same time, adult-type robots should have better performance improvement and scene applications, elderly care robots, bank assistant robots and other scenarios can continue to improve the quality of interaction with humans, only when consumers' feelings of use are improved, can they slowly accept and love it. In 2022, Tesla brought the world premiere of the Tesla Bot humanoid robot "Optimus" prototype. During the release session, the humanoid robot slowly walked to the front desk from behind the scenes, waved to the audience and made several simple actions (Fig. 6). The robot completes simple actions without forgetting to estimate people's feelings and walks to the front desk to pay tribute; In the future, we need more comprehensive products, speech semantic analysis is becoming more and more important, people will also pay attention to emotional support in the future, not just action assistants, we also hope to help robots have the ability to listen, speak, understand and think, has achieved better interactive performance.

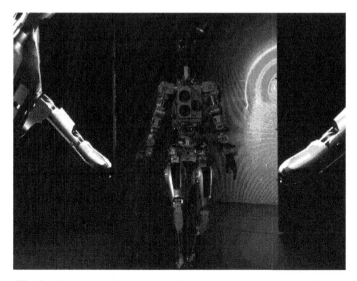

Fig. 6. The humanoid robot takes the stage and waves to the audience

4 Digital Collections

4.1 Digital Collections in the Metaverse and Their Technological Basis

Digital collectibles are a new type of collectibles that refer to virtual objects stored, exchanged and circulated in digital formats on digital platforms such as blockchains, games, social networks, etc. Its birth can be traced back to the 1990s, when, with the popularity of the internet, people began to invest and trade in digital content as collectibles. The explosion of digital collectibles happened in 2017, with the rise of cryptocurrencies and a gradual increase in interest in digital assets. Especially after 2020, interest in secure digital assets has increased due to the social restrictions and economic instability caused by COVID-19. The uniqueness, exchangeability, negotiability, digital traceability, and value of digital collections make them promising for a wide range of applications in the digital economy.

Unlike other digital collections, a digital collection in a metaverse is a digital asset that is generated in the metaverse and can be used within the metaverse. Digital collections in the metaverse usually have a higher level of interactivity, interaction and uniqueness. The stable development of digital collections in the metaverse is closely related to blockchain technology, smart contract technology, artificial intelligence technology, distributed computing technology, 3D graphics technology, digital encryption technology, etc. Digital versions of collections generated through the underlying blockchain technology, such as digital art, digital music and digital games, can be stored and managed digitally, which enables digital collections to be irreproducible, tamper-proof and indivisible, ensuring their uniqueness and authenticity. Smart contract technology enables smart contracts for digital collections and regulates the process of transactions. Distributed computing technology is used to increase the computing power of the metaverse and to support a large number of users interacting simultaneously. 3D graphics technology is an important tool for generating the virtual environment and characters of the metaverse. Artificial intelligence technology, on the other hand, can better create virtual scenarios and interaction methods to ensure that digital collections are used in different scenarios in the metaverse and often have their unique characteristics and functions. The difference between a digital collection in a metaverse and other digital collections is therefore that a digital collection in a metaverse is a digital asset that can be physically used in the metaverse, while other digital collections are digital assets that can only be collected and traded.

4.2   Artificial Intelligence Technologies to Support Digital Collections

Influenced by artificial intelligence technology, digital collections in the metaverse undergo groundbreaking changes in storage, identification and use. Digital collections are able to get rid of the inconvenience of physical storage methods and greatly improve the level of identification in terms of professionalism and accuracy, fun and display. The impact of artificial intelligence technology on digital collections is reflected in six specific areas: storage, analysis, creation, protection, trading and display of digital collections.

Storage: Digital collections, when digitized, can be stored in large databases or cloud storage systems. Artificial intelligence systems can help manage and organize these digital collections through big data analysis techniques. For example, an AI system can automatically classify digital collections for easier retrieval.

Analysis: Artificial intelligence systems can analyze digital collections to understand their content, value and possible uses. For example, an AI system can analyze an image digital collection and identify objects, scenes and events within it. Similarly, it can analyze textual digital collections to extract information such as keywords, summaries and sentiment. Artificial intelligence technology can help identify and verify the authenticity of digital collections. By analyzing the shape, color, text, and other features of digital collections, AI systems can identify genuine and fake digital collections.

Creation: Artificial intelligence can use generative models to create new digital collections. For example, an AI system can generate content such as music, images and videos. In this case, the AI can use the information and features of an existing digital collection to generate new works of art.

Protection: Artificial intelligence can help protect digital collections against infringement. For example, an AI system can monitor infringements on the web, such as unauthorized use and distribution of digital collections. It can also encrypt and digitally watermark digital collections to ensure their authenticity and ownership.

Trading: Artificial intelligence systems can assist in the trading of digital collections. For example, artificial intelligence technology can help assess the value of digital collections. By analyzing historical price trends, as well as market demand and supply, the identity of traders is verified and a secure trading environment is created. At the same time, by identifying the needs of buyers and sellers and using algorithms to match transactions, AI systems can help to trade in digital collections run more smoothly.

Display: Artificial intelligence systems can help present digital collections to the public, for example by creating virtual exhibitions and providing online previews.

Overall, digital collections are closely linked to artificial intelligence, and AI technology can provide powerful support for the management, protection, analysis and trading of digital collections. It can also help to identify, evaluate and trade digital collections, thereby increasing the efficiency and transparency of the digital collections market.

4.3 Digital Collections and Human Interaction

In the metaverse, digital collections can interact with people through virtual communication, active games, currency exchange, investment, art appreciation and more. Artificial intelligence technology has brought many innovations and changes to the way digital collections and people interact in the metaverse world. The main applications are in the generation and display of digital collections, personalized recommendations, community interaction, and intelligent management.

Artificial intelligence technology can generate high-quality digital collections, which can include 3D models, images, sounds and other forms, providing a more realistic display of digital collections, for example, through virtual reality technology that allows people to experience real-time interaction and physical properties of the collections. At the same time, artificial intelligence technology can recommend digital collections that are suitable for users based on their interests and preferences. By analyzing users' historical data and behavior, AI can better understand their needs and provide them with a more personalized service. Digital collections in the metaverse can also become a medium for community interaction. Artificial intelligence technology can provide digital collections with more social features, such as allowing users to share collections, participate in comments and interact with other users. Through these features, digital collections can become a topic for people to share and interact with, thus further enhancing the user experience and social interaction. Through artificial intelligence technology, intelligent management of digital collections in the metaverse can be achieved, such as classifying, labeling, archiving and retrieving collections in an automated manner. This improves the efficiency and accuracy of managing digital collections and makes it easier for users to find the collections they want. Decentraland, for example, is a 3D virtual world that allows users to buy and sell houses in that world (Fig. 7). Players can create and buy their own virtual houses in Decentraland and interact with other players in that world. The game or website features blockchain technology to guarantee the uniqueness of all houses and the security of transactions. A player can use the digital collection to make investments, buy other players' virtual houses and rent them to other players. Players can earn income from renting houses and also maintain the state of the houses to keep their value high. Over time, the value of the house may increase, resulting in higher returns for the investor. At the same time, the owner of the house can also use the digital collection for virtual communication and entertainment activities in the metaverse. This case illustrates the multiple uses that digital collections in the metaverse can have as an investment tool as well as an interactive entertainment tool.

As technology In social int to develop, we can expect more intelligent features and a more intelligent user experience. Virtual reality technology combined with artificial intelligence technology: As virtual reality technology continues to advance, artificial intelligence technology and virtual reality technology will become more closely integrated, bringing a more realistic and intelligent experience to the way digital collections

PROPERTY	COORDINATES	TRAITS	AREA	ACTIVE PLAYERS	LAST SOLD	ESTIMATE
NEAREST to GENE Decentraland	📍 29, -5	• 1 from Road	16m²	0	-	⬦ 2.76 $4,183.80
Prime Gallery 1 Decentraland	📍 20, -127	• 4 from Plaza • 0 from Road	16m²	0	-	⬦ 3.02 $4,577.38
Prime Gallery 2 Decentraland	📍 21, -127	• 5 from Plaza • 0 from Road	16m²	0	-	⬦ 3.00 $4,547.07

Fig. 7. Decentraland virtual property sales and purchases

and people interact with each other. For example, artificial intelligence can recognise human gestures and emotions to better understand the needs of users, and virtual reality technology can bring a more immersive experience to users. Diversification of digital collections: In the future, digital collections will become more diverse, including not only traditional collections such as artworks, collectibles and historical artifacts, but also more digital objects such as digital copyrights and digital goods. The variety of these digital collections will be even richer, providing users with a more diverse choice and experience. The intelligence of personalized recommendations: In the future, personalized recommendations will become more intelligent, with artificial intelligence technology providing more accurate recommendations for users based on their behavior, preferences, social networks and other aspects of data. At the same time, personalized recommendations will be made in a variety of ways, such as voice and image. Intelligent sharing of digital collections: In the future, digital collections will be shared and exchanged more intelligently. Artificial intelligence technology can provide more social functions for digital collections, such as allowing users to share collections, participate in comments and interact with other users. At the same time, the management and sharing of digital collections will also become more intelligent, for example by ensuring the security and authenticity of digital collections through technologies such as blockchain.

In short, the way digital collections and people interact will become more intelligent and diverse in the future, bringing a richer and better experience for users. At the same time, the intelligent sharing and management of digital collections will also become an important trend, bringing more opportunities and challenges to the development of the digital economy.

5   Time and Space Intelligence

5.1   Concept and Current Status of Spatiotemporal Intelligence

Spatiotemporal intelligence refers to a capability covering both time and space awareness, the ability to perceive, understand and process time - and space-related information to make decisions and take action. Often combined with artificial intelligence technologies and Internet of Things technologies, spatiotemporal intelligence can be applied in areas such as transportation, logistics, urban planning, environmental protection and natural disaster prediction to provide more accurate and efficient support for decision-making and management in these areas.

Specifically, spatiotemporal intelligence technology can employ various sensors and devices to collect data from spatial and temporal dimensions, such as weather, geographical location, traffic flow, crowd density, etc. These data are transmitted to the cloud via IoT technology and analyzed and processed using artificial intelligence algorithms. By analyzing this data, spatiotemporal intelligence systems can make predictions and plans for future traffic, logistics and urban planning, optimizing decisions and improving efficiency and quality.

Spatiotemporal intelligence technology can also be applied to areas such as environmental protection and natural disaster prediction. For example, by sensing meteorological and geographical information, spatiotemporal intelligence systems can predict climate change and provide support for environmental protection decisions; by sensing natural disasters such as earthquakes and floods, spatiotemporal intelligence systems can assess and predict disaster risks, and provide early warning and rescue services. Spatiotemporal intelligence is an intelligent technology capable of sensing and processing temporal and spatial information, which can be applied to a wide range of fields to provide accurate and efficient support for decision-making and action.

5.2 Metaverse and Spatiotemporal Intelligence

The development of spatiotemporal intelligence in the metaverse has made some progress, but is still at an early stage. Existing spatiotemporal intelligence technologies and applications include spatial awareness technologies, time-aware technologies, metaverse planning and management, virtual transportation and logistics management.

In the metaverse, spatial awareness technology can be implemented through virtual reality (VR) and augmented reality (AR) technologies, such as head-mounted displays, joystick controllers, panoramic cameras and other devices. These devices can sense the user's position and posture in virtual space, enabling the user to interact more naturally with the virtual environment. Time perception technology is mainly involved in virtual time flow and virtual seasons, for example in the game Animal Mori Friends, where seasonal changes and time changes can affect the objects and characters in the game. Realizing real-time synchronization, seasonal changes, cross-time zone gaming experience and real-time updates makes the game more vivid, interesting and interactive. The time and date of the game is synchronized in real-time. This means that if the gamer plays the game at night, the game world will also change tonight (Fig. 8); if it is a weekend, the characters in the game will also perform their activities accordingly. This design allows for a more realistic gaming experience. The seasons in the game are consistent with real life. In spring, the characters dig for radishes in the grass; in summer, they fish in the river; in autumn, they pick fruit; and in winter, they build snowmen and ski (Fig. 9). This design makes the game more lively and interesting. As players from all over the world are playing the game, the developers have designed a system that allows trading and interaction in different time zones through time fiddling intelligence in order to meet the needs of players in different time zones, which allows players to feel a global gaming community. In-game events and items are updated in real-time. This means that when a special event or holiday arrives, players can access the corresponding items and rewards through the game.

Fig. 8. Day and night scenes from the Animal Moroi game

Fig. 9. Scenes of the changing seasons in Animal Samurais

In addition, spatiotemporal intelligence technology can be applied to the planning and management of the metaverse. For example, through data analysis and prediction technology, problems such as population growth and resource bottlenecks in the virtual world can be predicted in advance and the planning and design of the virtual world can be adjusted in time.

Furthermore, spatiotemporal intelligence technology can be applied to virtual traffic and logistics management in the metaverse, for example by stimulating the flow of urban roads and public transport routes through virtual reality technology and predicting the demand and supply of virtual goods, thus optimizing logistics transport and traffic management.

5.3 Artificial Intelligence Technology and Spatiotemporal Intelligence

The impact of artificial intelligence technology on spatiotemporal intelligence in the metaverse is extensive and far-reaching, and it brings many new opportunities and challenges to the development and progress of the metaverse. In the digital world of the metaverse, AI technology can help process and analyze large amounts of spatiotemporal data and improve the accuracy and efficiency of data processing. At the same time, through intelligent decision-making and prediction technologies, AI can also help with decision-making and planning in the virtual world, such as predicting future traffic flow and demand for goods, thus increasing the intelligence of the metaverse.

In addition, AI technology can also improve the interaction and user experience in the metaverse, for example, by helping users to communicate more naturally with virtual characters through natural language processing technology, thus enhancing user engagement and satisfaction. At the same time, AI technology can also help the spatiotemporal intelligence system in the metaverse to perform intelligent security and risk control, identify security hazards and risks in the virtual world, and safeguard users' security and privacy.

Finally, AI technology can also bring about intelligent creation and art in the metaverse, such as the automatic generation of virtual characters, buildings and landscapes through deep learning algorithms, thus increasing the creativity and beauty of the metaverse. In summary, AI technology has great potential and impact on the application and development of spatiotemporal intelligence in the metaverse, and will help the metaverse to achieve a more intelligent, interactive and better future.

6   Conclusion

With the rapid development of artificial intelligence technology, the metaverse, as a new virtual reality environment, has attracted more and more attention. This paper discusses how to carry out interaction design in the metaverse environment from four aspects: virtual digital human, humanoid robot, digital collection, and spatiotemporal intelligence. On this basis, we believe that the metaverse can provide many opportunities and challenges for the real industry.

We need to recognize that the essence of the metaverse is a whole new virtual world with independent economic systems, social networks, cultures, and values. Therefore, when designing the interaction mode of the metaverse, it is necessary to consider the behavioral and psychological characteristics of metaverse users, as well as their behavior and values in the virtual world. At the same time, since the metaverse is a new environment, it is also necessary to constantly explore and try new interaction methods and design methods. The metaverse empowers the real economy and provides many opportunities for the real industry, such as providing a new digital display platform for cultural institutions such as museums, libraries, and art galleries to digitally present cultural heritage and attract more audiences to visit and understand.At the same time, the metaverse can also provide new development opportunities for education, entertainment, tourism and other industries, such as providing a more realistic virtual teaching environment for online education platforms and a richer virtual tourism experience for the tourism industry. Realizing the organic combination of the metaverse and the real industry requires us to continue to explore and innovate. For example, when designing digital collections in the metaverse, it is necessary to consider how to combine these digital collections with physical exhibitions to provide viewers with a richer cultural experience. When designing humanoid robots in the metaverse, it is necessary to consider how to integrate these robots with physical stores to provide customers with a more realistic shopping experience.

In short, when designing the interaction mode of the metaverse, it is necessary to consider the behavioral and psychological characteristics of metaverse users, and at the same time, it is necessary to constantly explore and try new interaction methods and design methods. Through continuous innovation and exploration, we can realize the organic combination of the metaverse and the real industry, bringing users a richer and more authentic experience. To this end, we propose the following: (1) Strengthen cross-border cooperation. The metaverse is a complex that covers multiple industries, and close cooperation between various industries is required to achieve a seamless transition between the metaverse and the physical industry. For example, cultural institutions can work with digital technology companies to digitize artifacts and combine digital collections with physical exhibitions; Merchants can partner with AI companies to design smarter, more realistic humanoid robots that provide customers with a more realistic shopping experience. (2) Strengthen technological innovation. The metaverse is a new virtual world that requires constant exploration and experimentation with new technologies and methods in order to achieve organic integration with the physical industry. For example, new virtual reality technologies can be researched to provide users with a more realistic experience; Artificial intelligence technology can be studied to provide more intelligent and personalized services for humanoid robots. (3) Strengthen user experience design. The interaction mode of the metaverse is very different from the physical world, and a new user experience design is required to bring users a smoother and more pleasant experience. For example, a more intuitive and simple user interface can be designed to facilitate user operation; More personalized user services can be designed to improve user satisfaction.

To sum up, the metaverse offers many opportunities and challenges for the real industry. Realizing the organic combination of the metaverse and the real industry requires us to continue to explore and innovate, strengthen cross-border cooperation, strengthen technological innovation, and strengthen user experience design. We believe that through continuous efforts and innovation, the metaverse will bring broader development space to the real industry and create a better future for mankind.

References

1. Lee, B.: The Metaverse: the Creation, Development and Future of Virtual Worlds. Science Press (2021)
2. Bin, L.: Artificial Intelligence and Human Society. Tsinghua University Press (2019)
3. Bing, X.: Virtual Digital Human Technology and Its Application. Publishing House of Electronics Industry (2020)
4. Honglei, W.: Humanoid Robots: Design, Modeling and Control. China Machine Press (2018)
5. Zhongmin, Y.: Protection and Utilization of Digital Cultural Heritage. Beijing Normal University Press (2019)

6. The Metaverse Roadmap: Pathways to the 3D Web. Metaverse Roadmap Overview Group (2008)
7. Russell, S., Norvig, P.: Artificial Intelligence: A Modern Approach. 3rd edition (2021)
8. Boos, C.: Digital Humans: The Past, Present, and Future of AI-Driven Avatars (2021)
9. Kagami, S., Yoshida, E., Yokoi, K.: Humanoid Robotics: A Reference. Springer (2018)
10. Moggridge, B.: Designing Interactions. The MIT Press (2007)

On the "Meaning System" of Design from Kao Gong Ji

Xiangyang Li[✉] ⓘ and Lianghua Ma ⓘ

Guangzhou Academy of Fine Arts, 168 Waihuan Xilu, Higher Education Mega Center, Pa-Nyu District, Guangzhou 510006, China
lixiangyang@gzarts.edu.cn

Abstract. As the earliest monograph recording the technological practice in China, *Kao Gong Ji* was initially used as a pithy formula for various processes and served as the earliest system of production management and construction. Thanks to the long-term practice of the traditional society, it has gradually formed the meaning system of "object-thing-belief". With the intrinsic regulations of the relationship between man and nature and society contained in the design culture, it became the earliest form of the Chinese design ideological system.

Keywords: Kao Gong Ji · Design Culture · Meaning System

1 Introduction

As the earliest Chinese monograph recording the technological practice, *Kao Gong Ji* systematically describes the construction standards in the pre-Qin period. In particular, the saying of "Only by combining the order of nature, the regional climate, the fine materials and the superb technology perfectly can we produce exquisite works." Has always been regarded as the most classic that gathering the oriental wisdom of traditional craftsmanship. Among them, "order of nature" and "regional climate" were the mandatory conditions due to the constraints of productivity development in the earliest technological practice. To date, the developing productivity has advanced us into an industrialized and information-based era. Thus, the factors of "order of nature" and "regional climate" may not pose so much impact on people's production and labor as in the past, and people can organize production activities more from their own wishes. However, this does not mean that the consideration of both factors has become void in today's activities of fabrication and production. We should perceive that our self-cognition with "heaven" and "earth" as the "meaning coordinate" has been formed as a result of the long-term relationship with nature in the past. It is also the continuous effectiveness of the cognition in this dimension that forms all aspects of Chinese design culture. In the face of the global economic and cultural transformation in particular, where will we head our life to with the tides of constant changing? Perhaps we can get a little enlightened from the wisdom of *Kao Gong Ji* (Fig. 1).

A. Marcus et al. (Eds.): HCII 2023, LNCS 14030, pp. 210–219, 2023.
https://doi.org/10.1007/978-3-031-35699-5_16

Fig. 1. Kao Gong Ji, noted by Xu Zhaoqing, reviewed by Mei Dingzuo, Huae Building Edition of Ming Dynasty

2 Practicality-Based to Meaning-Based Use

"Those people of wisdom invent and create things first, then skilled people followed the ideas of their ancestors, and then pass them on from generation to generation. Such is noted as craftsmanship. All works are achieved by people with wisdom."
-- The Ritual Works of Zhou · *Kao Gong Ji.*

In The Ritual Works of Zhou · Kao Gong Ji (hereinafter referred to as Kao Gong Ji), the character "知"(knowledge) is interchangeable to the "智" (wisdom), and "圣人"(saints) refers to people with wisdom, who are outstanding among the crowd. The "various works and crafts" are created by people with wisdom, which suggests people's affirmation and praise of creativity. Since the "various works and crafts" were signified to the range of "people with wisdom", which to some extent, indicates that Kao Gong Ji is a normative text with the effect of social identification. However, what it recognizes is not only the spark of creativity, but also its considerations of systematic design.

In the version of Annotated Translation of Kao Gong Ji by Mr. Zhang Daoyi, who repositioned and advocated the interpretation of Kao Gong Ji, and suggested that the interpretation of Kao Gong Ji should be changed from the perspective of Confucian classics to the design art, which shed more light to its scientific and humanistic brilliance. Seen from the contents, in the description of "the six duties of the country", "the national superb craftsman" and "people of wisdom" and "the fine tools", a mutually-echoing plan has been made from the material base to the superstructure. Under such a general guidance, detailed descriptions have been made to six categories of work, such as "woodwork", "metalwork", "leather craft", "dyeing and coloring", "carving and polishing", "pottery craft", and thirty types of work [1]. Therefore, this could cover most of the scenes of social production and construction at that time. Even seen from today, it is a set of specific and detailed system design governance scheme in terms of subject attributes and practical guidance. When adopted in the Warring States period, the ideology of "establishing education" is contained in "ruling the world by artifacts" of the Confucian, which applied etiquette in all aspects of life through the regulation of artifacts. It is such a close connection that serves the reason why the system is effective.

"Only by combining the order of nature, the regional climate, the fine materials and the superb technology perfectly can we produce exquisite works." The description of standard for fine tools in *Kao Gong Ji* has always been regarded as the most classic that gathering the oriental wisdom of traditional craftsmanship. Among them, "order of nature" and "regional climate" are the basis of "fine materials", which also corresponds to an old Chinese saying "God disposes". Not only food, but also production materials are bestowed by God. Hence, the production of objects has to follow the nature of God. Seen from the present, the objective reason is the low level of productivity at that time, people were highly reliant to nature, and they can master some laws of nature after a long time of coexistence. When people do things, it is half and half, both by people and by God. This is in line with the production characteristics of the agricultural era and can be interpreted as the material connection in production activities. However, after thousands of years, people have entered an industry and information based era, which shadows the dependence of "human" on "nature". For instance, now we can enjoy four seasonal fruits from all over the world at anytime and anywhere. Time and space no longer pose a challenge to people. The development of modern science and technology has broken the limits of original climate, geography, space, time and even material properties. As Giddens put in *The Consequences of Modernity*, "For most people, the calculation of time, which forms the basis of daily life, is always linked with time and place, and is usually imprecise and variable". This "embedability" makes people "virtual" and "disembeded", and the ecological connection of material in such production relationship weakens or even breaks. Another consequence of modernity is the change of people's concept from "eat from the nature" to "man will conquer nature".

In 1962, *Silent Spring* was published in the United States. It was written by Rachel Carson, an American biologist and popular science writer, with his sensitive and delicate perspective and years of investigation. The book impresses readers by revealing the changes in the relationship between man and nature with the silent spring. At that time, the United States was undergoing the third industrial revolution and vigorously developing its industrial economy, demonstrating its power to "transform the world" by transforming and consuming natural resources. In order to increase food production and timber export, a great amount of highly toxic pesticides have been used to cause the death or escape of a large number of animals that should've been in the ecological cycle chain, while chemicals entered the human body through the natural ecological chain, thus making major diseases such as cancer or fetal malformation more common in modern life. Rachel Carson also put forward the concept of "ecology", which put human beings and all things on the earth in an equal and interdependent relationship, and voiced that "human beings are part of nature, and to declare war on nature is to declare war on human beings". This is indeed a harsh declaration in the context of global economy in the 20th century. In the Western world, the development logic of the industrial revolution is to take the exploration, utilization and transformation of natural resources as the standard, and even take "if your brute force does not work, it means it's less intensified" [2] as the motto. Marx put forward "humanized nature" in the *Economic and Philosophical Manuscript of 1844*. After the long history of social production practice, humans have fundamentally changed the relationship between human and nature. Nature is controlled, conquered, transformed and utilized by human beings, thus human goals are realized in nature. The logic of large-scale industry and mechanized operation is not so much to liberate individual physical labor as to give up the "human" with individual limitations, and conquer nature more with technical logic. From the perspective of taking oneself as the subject of the world, "the 'conquest' of the uninhabited land is regarded as a cultural and even a spiritual need" [3].

Qing Nian proposed that the handicraft design and production of Kao Gong Ji was based on the basic principle of "solid and refined" at that time, and the term is from the *Classic of Rites· Proceedings of Government in the Different Months*: "In this month orders are given to the chief Director of works to prepare a memorial on the work of the artificers; setting forth especially the sacrificial vessels with the measures and capacity (of them and all others), and seeing that there be no licentious ingenuity in the workmanship which might introduce an element of dissipation into the minds of superiors; and making the suitability of the article the first consideration. Every article should have its maker's name engraved on it, for the determination of its, genuineness. When the production is not what it ought to be, the artificer should be held guilty and an end be thus put to deception." *Classic of Rites· Proceedings of Government in the Different Months* describes the norms of various activities in the traditional Chinese society under the system of "etiquette". "The 'etiquette system' is a tool for rulers to maintain and consolidate their rule; As far as its cultural significance is concerned, 'etiquette' also represents the dominant culture of that era. It is a combination of religion, philosophy, ethics, customs and so on. The cultural character of "etiquette" is also the foundation of its political character of governing and ruling the country. The obedience of the ancestors to 'etiquette' is not only deterred by the majesty of 'punishment', but also stems from certain spiritual needs, that is, the awe and worship of the gods of heaven and earth, and the reliance of the universal order, including social order [4]." It can be seen that the art of building and construction related to people's livelihood with detailed description are not only scientific in accordance with the laws of nature, but also has its political governance significance. More importantly, the spiritual connection has formed a unique regional life culture due to their coexistence for thousands of years. For example, people's perception of the "order of nature" is transformed into seasonal solar terms, and under the corresponding solar terms, the relevant culture of etiquette and customs and artifacts are formed, which constitute an important part of self-identity among Chinese. From the process of survival-identity-order, a set of "meaning system" that transcends the "need for survival" and implies the genes of oriental culture has been imperceptibly formed. It is under this set of "meaning system" that Chinese design behavior is generated.

3   Action Mechanism of the Meaning System in Kao Gong Ji

Professor Xu Ping, a design theorist, once described the process of establishing the meaning system of design from the perspective of design education: Humanistic spirit is continuously injected into the design behavior for gradually establishing definite, healthy and active design values, and based on that, other design skill educations can produce an effective and active education function [5]. It is a positive process of values influencing behaviors. From this paragraph, we can see the relevance between the meaning system of design and the design behavior. It is not a simple concept origin for design or a creation story, but a spiritual orientation that influences human life values. During the two thousand years of *Kao Gong Ji* influencing traditional creation activities, a meaning system of creation based on farming culture was gradually established. Of it, "order of nature" and "regional climate", as "meaning coordinates", are playing an important role.

> *"Oranges in the south will become trifoliated in the north. The mynah will not cross the Jishui River. The nyctereutes procyonoides will die if crossing the Wenshui River. All these are caused by regional climate. If knives of Zheng State, axes of Song State, chops of Lu State and swords of Wuyue State are not produced locally, they cannot be excellent. All these are caused by regional climate"* [6].

> *"Nature sometimes makes all things grow and sometimes makes all things wither. Trees and grass sometimes grow and sometimes wither. Stone sometimes has cracks. Water sometimes freezes and ice sometime thaws. All these are caused by the order of nature"* [7].

The above two paragraphs are direct descriptions about "regional climate" and "order of nature" in Kao Gong Ji. The so-called direct description does not mean a description about the objects themselves. "regional climate" and "order of nature" are not entity objects, but people can directly perceive them through changes of crops and the natural environment. More specifically, the "trifoliated orange" is not delicious, the mynah will not fly northward across the Jishui River, and the "nyctereutes procyonoides" will die if going southwards and crossing the Wenshui River. All these cannot be done due to the restriction of natural conditions. All things including trees and grass will grow and wither. From it, we can learn the survival principle of "preparing boats in a dry season and preparing wagons in a flood season". It can be seen that people have learned what is "order of nature" and what is "regional climate" from their own limitations in nature.

From the perspective of biology, the German philosopher and sociologist Arnold Gehlen (1904–1976) mentioned that human beings are inborn "deficient" as compared with animals in nature. Human beings do not have wing-like organs that can make them fly in the sky like birds, nor do they have gills and a streamlined body that can make them swim in an ocean like fishes. Due to lack of these special organs, the German philosophical anthropologist Michael Landmann thought that human beings "are forced to start a journey when nature completes only one half, leaving the other half to be completed by themselves [8]." Based on this biological "deficiency", when facing the restrictive conditions of nature, human life needs creative labor and cooperation to make up for its limitations in nature. Based on the deficiency, people begin to create. Based on the creation, people begin to gain wisdom. Therefore, in the early relations between man and nature, wisdom and craftsmanship live together. More importantly, during this process, "human beings" have gradually formed a self-cognition of symbiosis and mutual growth with all things in the universe.

This self-cognition of symbiosis and mutual growth also originated from a deeper thought on design. *Kao Gong Ji* describes "three timbers for a wheel" as follows: "When the craftsman makes a wheel, the three timbers for making the hub, spoke and external surface must be felled in proper seasons. When the three timbers are prepared, the skilled craftsman will process them into a wheel. The hub should facilitate the rotation of the wheel; the spoke should directly point to the external surface; and the external surface should hug the wheel tightly. Even if the wheel is damaged due to abrasive wear, the hub, spoke and external surface will not become loose or deformed. It can be called perfect [9]." The precise grasp of the "three timbers", seasons and direction of sunshine makes the products "easy to use" and "durable" so that people cannot help wondering that even the creation wisdom more than two thousand years ago cannot be attained by contemporaries. The design value is not only embodied in "craftsmanship" but also is embodied in the discovery and utilization of materials. This daily insight comes from the perception of the reality. If the creation process can be divided into two parts, then the insight in the first half embodies the perception factors between man and the world, and the "craftsmanship" in the second half embodies man's ability to solve problems in real society.

From the perception of the real world, value judgment is formed. Apart from "Craftsman Making a Wheel", *Kao Gong Ji* has recorded many products that have to be completed over a long period by considering seasons and territorial limitations. For example, "One Thing for One Year": "For making a bow, wood will be split for making the stem in winter, the cornual plate will be boiled in spring, the tendon will be treated in summer, and the stem, cornual plate and tendon will be combined into a bow in autumn. The main body will be fixed in winter and the paint pattern will be checked to see whether it has peeled off in frozen winter. The stem can be treated well if wood is split in winter, the cornual plate will become flexible if boiled in spring, the tendon will not become disorderly if treated in summer, the stem, cornual plate and tendon will become solid and compact if combined together with glue, paint and silk in autumn, the main body and string will not be deformed if fixed in severe winter, and it is easy to judge whether the circular paint pattern meets the requirements if checked in frozen winter. When the string is installed in the spring of the next year, one complete year has passed. The wood for making the stem should be split following the texture, the cornual plate should not be split in a slanted way, the knots on the wood for making the stem should be cut slowly. If the knots are not cut slowly, the tendon outside the stem will be damaged when the bow is used for a long time. Wooden knots are solid, and will cause abrasive wear to the tendon outside them. It is often for this reason that the tendon bulges instead of fitting to the stem. Therefore, the cornual plate should be boiled thrice and the stem should be boiled twice. If the crosser in the middle part of the stem is too thick, the stem will become too solid. If the crosser is too thin, the stem will become too weak. Therefore, the stem should be boiled for a long time and added with proper crosser. The stem should be twined with a cord, but not fully twined. The twining density must be even [10]." In the traditional TCM theory, spring dominates sprouting, summer dominates growth, autumn dominates harvest and winter dominates storage. The making of a bow must conform to the features of the four seasons to make the materials fit and durable. The handling of comprehensive materials in bow making is evidently more complicated than the handling of wheels, and the technology, time and mentality for creation are more synchronous with the rhythm of nature. The section of "Cover Drums on the Waking of Insects" describes the season as follows: "Drums must be covered on the Waking of Insects. The paint marks on the leather of a good drum is like an accumulated ring. If the surface is big and the body is short, the sound will be rapid and transient. If the surface is small and the body is long, the sound will be slow and durable [11]." Hibernating worms will wake up upon hearing thunders. Ancient people thought that thunders came from the thunder god's beating the heavenly drum with a hammer. Therefore, to cover drums with leather on this day is a response to the season. This is how the custom of covering drums on the Waking of Insects began. For making in modern society, it is naturally unnecessary. However, in the past, covering drums - thunder - beginning of spring corresponds to the design of action - medium - event. In this customary scene, the drum is not only a musical instrument but also a medium for mobilizing "events", and gradually it has become a ceremony or a part of cultural memory.

Jan Assmann, a German anthropologist, believes that cultural memory is the collective memory of a nation and a country, and it is a cultural identity question that answers "Who are we" and "Where are we from and where are we going [12]". The presence of cultural memory is the condition of establishing identity, and establishing identity is the basis of inheritance and development. The initial stage of our traditional China social identity is based on blood identity, and then it develops into geographical identity and ethnic identity, which is reflected in the evolvement from family training to ritual and music culture. That is Assmann's so-called two major media of cultural memory: text and ritual. Ritual is a living cultural memory, which is generally reflected in festivals, celebrations, activities and other events. Every year, important festivals are held in the form of fixed celebrations, and the "ritual association" is repeated among ethnic groups [13]. In rural life living off the land, rituals, festivals or resulting daily life such as language, clothing, utensils and handicrafts are the realistic carriers of cultural memory, that is, the material entourage ("entourage matériel") which enters cultural identity [14]. These specific matters are the embodiment of internal cultural differences, and once they are separated from the local field, they will exist in modern life in the form of cultural symbols. The design and production of "things" are related to "events", resulting in the experience of meaning. The effective mechanism of such a set of "meaning system" is based on the design methodology with " order of nature" and " regional climate" as the coordinate, which is the wisdom of creation beyond "practical and meticulous style as the standard".

4   Significance of "Meaning System" to the Construction of Current Design Ecology

In the 19th century, the British industrial revolution officially kicked off the prelude to modernization. Machinery reconstructed the cooperative system of things-events-people, and the subjective position of people was abstracted. Labor has become a means of economic development and capital proliferation. The perception of labor by people is no longer a matter of squeezing the soil and smelling the fragrance, but a series of data and norms. Mr. Fei Xiaotong talked about the past farming society in *From the Soil*, where the daily work was basically completed by individuals and there was no need for too deep division of labor. This real grasp of weighing one's own needs can effectively adjust the contingency that appears in the labor process directly. However, the division of labor in industrial mass production is driven by a flat world. The cross-regional division of labor and production supply cut off the connection between people and land, and also cut off the "human characteristics" in labor output. In the 1980s, the postmodern exploration with "Memphis Group" appeared, which formally resisted this kind of stereotyped, mechanical and cold modernism style, but in fact, postmodernism was a kind of promotion, revision and supplement of modernism. In the process of diversification of modernism style, the design based on traditional culture has also entered the international stage in recent years. In 2012, Mr. Wang Shu won the Pritzker Architecture Award, and his comments from the organizing committee were: "His architecture not only opens a new horizon for us, but also arouses the resonance between realistic scenes and historical memories. His architecture is original and can evoke the past, but it doesn't directly use historical elements… In his works, history is given new life, just like exploring the relationship between the past and the present. Nowadays, it is a key issue to discuss the proper relationship between the past and the present, because the urbanization process in China today is causing a discussion about whether architecture should be based on tradition or only face the future." In the Salone Satellite of Milan Design Week 2014, for the first time, the design team from China, PINWU, won the grand prize for its design innovation based on traditional handicraft research. The world has seen China's wisdom of creation hidden in materials, which reflects the relationship among things-events-people based on natural symbiosis, and it is just ignored in the industrialized cooperative system. Cassirer talked about the question of "what is man" in his *An Essay on Man*, pointing out that the distinctive feature of man lies not in his metaphysical or physiological nature, but in his work. Work is all kinds of human activities, which define and determine the circumference of "human nature", for example, its language, mythology, religion, art, science and history, etc. are an organic whole [15].

At the end of 2019, a Chinese contemporary handicrafts academic nomination exhibition was held in the Folk Art Museum of China Academy of Art. At the beginning of curating, the curator raised several basic questions for the exhibition: "Does today's 'handicraft art' really reach the height of elegance and classicism? Is it beyond? Why are handicrafts for daily use shrinking but arts and crafts for appreciation still flourishing? Is there a young 'modern handicraft' in China when 'inheritance' is becoming an authority? If so, what is it like?" [16]. Centering on these basic problems, the curatorial thinking of three sections was launched: Give it to loved ones who you miss day and night - the exquisiteness and elegance of tradition; Fast as boarding - back to the "craft" of pure art; Tao has no cause - craft should follow the "contemporary". These three sections just respond to the development of handicrafts in China since modern times. Since handicrafts were gradually divorced from practical significance, the relationship between handicrafts and people has also gradually shifted from the needs of life to the needs of spirit. By observing today's design practice on this account, we may also see more individual care. Mr. Lv Pintian also said in *Practical Active*: "Today's manual labor will become a practical form of public participation in artistic creation in the general sense of non-professionalism, and will become a 'folk art' activity under the new historical conditions." "This kind of ecological free labor in free time enriches the concept of 'productivity' or 'production benefit' with humanistic significance, which is a positive correction to the neglect of life time caused by the simple pursuit of material benefit in modern production." This is a turn of spiritual construction.

"The meaning system of human is manifested in two kinds of relational order: the secular order in the field of daily life and the transcendental order in the field of spiritual life [17]." "Meaning system" is a kind of value recognition based on the long-term lifestyle. When it is put forward separately and considered in the discipline of design, it is a revision and supplement to the development of modernism as a methodology. It is also the thinking based on the exploration of different economic development forms of Chinese design discipline since the founding of New China. From "pattern", "arts and crafts" to "art design", it has experienced the impact of "industrialization" and "intellectualization" and entered the era of Industry 4.0. The rapid development of science and technology subverts people's imagination of life, and the so-called "tradition" and "daily life" may be rushed to another life experience before landing. At this time, the determination of design thinking is particularly precious. The value of conviction must come from the source of life: the real existence of "man" with "heaven and earth" as coordinates.

5   Conclusion

Xunzi said: "A gentleman is served by things, while a villain serves things." From the level of design thinking, what we need to grasp is the spiritual orientation beyond the "thing" itself. The structural characteristics of design behavior itself are a kind of thought and behavior, and the establishment of its meaning system and cultural logic not only marks the characteristics of a country's design style, but also shows the wisdom of human life in this region. What *Kao Gong Ji* endows the present time should be not only the archaeology of traditional creation skills, but also the discovery of the meaning system of traditional creation, so as to reshape the design method with local characteristics based on it.

Acknowledgement. Phased achievements of the academic promotion plan for Guangzhou Academy of Fine Arts's school-level project "Research on Beijing Jade Carving Skills" (No.: 21XSC58).

References

1. Daoyi, Z.: Annotated translation of Kao Gong Ji. Shaanxi People's Fine Arts Publishing House, Xi'an, October 2004. Page 18
2. MacDonald, W., Brangatt, M.: Translated by China-US Center for Sustainable Development of the Administrative Center for China's Agenda 21, Cradle to Cradle: Remaking the way we make things. Tongji University Press (2005). Page 28
3. MacDonald, W., Brangatt, M.: Translated by China-US Center for Sustainable Development of the Administrative Center for China's Agenda 21, Cradle to Cradle: Remaking the way we make things. Tongji University Press (2005). Page 23
4. Mian, Q.: Practicality Leads to Success -- Research Notes on Kao Gong Ji. Decoration, (04) (1990). Page 42
5. Ping, X.: Indispensable Design "Concept" - On the Meaning of the Semantic System of Art Design, Art Observation, January 2004. Page 52
6. Daoyi, Z.: Notes to Kao Gong Ji. Shaanxi People's Fine Arts Publishing House, Xi'an, October 2004. Page 12
7. Daoyi, Z.: Notes to Kao Gong Ji. Shaanxi People's Fine Arts Publishing House, Xi'an, October 2004. Page 14
8. Pintian, L.: Contribution of Doing Manual Work - Viewing Handwork from a Cultural Perspective. Chongqing University Press, Chongqing, August 2014. Page 2
9. Daoyi, Z.: Notes to Kao Gong Ji. Shaanxi People's Fine Arts Publishing House, Xi'an, October 2004. Page 27
10. Daoyi, Z.: Notes to Kao Gong Ji, Shaanxi People's Fine Arts Publishing House, Xi'an, October 2004. Page 96
11. Daoyi, Z.: Notes to Kao Gong Ji. Shaanxi People's Fine Arts Publishing House, Xi'an, October 2004. Page 219
12. Xiaobing, W.: Cultural Skills, Traditional Innovation and Festival Heritage Protection. J. Renmin Univ. China (1) (2007). Pages 41–48
13. "Ritual connection" was put forward by Jan Assmann [Germany] in the book of Cultural Memory. Peking University Publishing House, May 2015. Page 7
14. Assmann, J.: [Germany], Cultural Memory. Peking University Publishing House, May 2015, Page 31
15. Rong, L.: Refer to An Essay on Man by Ernst Cassirer [Germany]. Shanghai Culture Publishing House, 1st edition, January 2020. Page 81
16. Jian, H., Guangrong, W., Kezhen, W.: "Three Paths - Academic Nominated Exhibition of China's Contemporary Craft", "Folk Art", sponsored by Chinese Folk Literature and Art Association, January 2020, total issue 13. Page 36
17. Mo, H.: Existentialism of Ideological and Political Education Based on Human Meaning System. Educ. Res. Monthly, May 2011. Page 46

Government-Promoted Design Resource Integration and Design Ecology Construction

Taking the UK Design Council as an Example

Shuang Liu[✉]

Langfang Normal University, AiminWest Road, Langfang City, Hebei Province, China
53835448@qq.com

Abstract. At the macro level of the country and the government promoting the progress of the design industry, the construction of design ecology has become an important issue with long-term significance and profound impact. The UK was the first country in the world to bring design into the policy spotlight, and the UK Design Council is also the longest running design council in the world. Since its establishment, the UK Design Council, as an entity platform between the British government, enterprises, design institutions and individual designers, education, scientific research and other fields, has effectively integrated many resources for the design field. This integration is mainly reflected in the following five aspects: establishing an industry image and cultivating a design ecology; integrating industrial resources and breaking through innovation bottlenecks; strengthening knowledge sharing and improving industrial skills; expanding social effects and creating multiple values; implementing interdisciplinary education and creating excellence center. Through more than 70 years of continuous efforts, the UK Design Council has comprehensively promoted the construction and development of the British contemporary design ecology at the national macro-industrial level, make important contributions to the creative development of the British economic system. Through the study of the most important international design promotion organization in the 20th century, we can reveal the policy, method, path, effect, significance and value of design resource cooperation and design ecological construction promoted by the government, which can provide a practical reference for the development of design industry and creative economy theory and practice in various countries.

Keywords: Design Council · Design Resource Integration · Design Ecology

1 Introduction

The output value and scale of the design industry itself may still be limited, but as long as you think about the huge profits that Apple Design has brought to the entire US consumer digital products and related Internet industries, no one should deny the huge "pull" effect unique to the design industry. This is also the reason why governments of various countries are scrambling to encourage and support the design industry. After

2000, more and more countries began to consider the relationship between design and national competitiveness. It also includes Brazil, India, China and other developing countries.

From tangible daily necessities to intangible services and network content provision, design touches all walks of life. Under the route promoted by the government, the integration and collaboration of design resources has always been the focus of national efforts. These resources include independent design companies, studios, design schools, design industry associations and organizations, as well as enterprise design and R&D departments scattered in all walks of life and broad industrial and social basic resources (such as entrepreneurs' associations, national and local standards institutions, various industry associations, and civil organizations), and of course government resources. How to effectively aggregate and optimize the allocation of design resources in such a wide range; How to build an efficient resource sharing model, and how to promote the connection and interaction between the design industry and all walks of life are the key to realize the "pull" effect of design on other industries.

The UK is the first country in the world to promote design under the policy spotlight. The UK Design Council is also the world's oldest professional design promotion organization with a government background. Its continuous work of more than 70 years is of great significance to the development of the British design industry. In terms of resource integration, it serves as an important platform between a series of individuals and public domains such as the British government, various industries and enterprises, design companies, firms, and individual designers, as well as universities, research institutes, and various social groups. It organically connecting many elements in a broad field, greatly promoted the process of industrialization of British design and the degree of resource integration. In terms of design ecology construction, its activities are quite extensive, including consulting, exhibitions, public promotion, design education, design award creation, design research, design criticism, design standards and design value construction, and the development of design thinking, design methods and design tools.Through extensive and sustained activities and the publication of numerous online and offline publications, UK Design Council has promoted the British contemporary design ecology into a virtuous circle.

After entering the year 2000, with the appearance of a "resource integrator", it has influenced the development of the British design industry in an all-round and multi-level manner. In recent years, it has been committed to the creative development of all walks of life driven by design and then extended to the entire national economic system. Through the study of this most important official design promotion organization in the contemporary world, we can see the route of design resource collaboration and design ecological construction promoted by the British government, and have a deep understanding of its policy, method, path, effect, value and significance. It can provide a practical reference for the development of design industry and creative economy theory and practice in various countries.

2 History and Background

The UK Design Council (hereinafter referred to as UKDC) was established in 1944, with the name of Council of Industry Design. It was founded by the Board of Trade under the leadership of the British wartime government with a starting fund of 55000 lb. When it was established, its goal was to "promote the design progress of British industrial products by all feasible means" [1]. It was mainly committed to "Developing strategies for the production and distribution of British industrial goods, both domestically and internationally, in the competitive economic climate of the Reconstruction Era". And its longer-term intention is to try to "advise, train and educate manufacturers, governments and the public on design issues" [2].

During the post-war reconstruction period, they focused on reforming design education and cultivating the new industrial designers needed in Britain after the war. They insisted on "Good Design" and carried out a lot of publicity and promotion for this. In 1949, their journal "Design" began to be published, which vigorously advocated "good design" and then quickly became a very representative and authoritative design magazine in the world. In 1956, their "Design Center" in Haymartet, London was completed, with the goal of displaying excellent contemporary British industrial design products to the public, manufacturers, retailers, and domestic and foreign traders.

In 1972, the Council of Industry Design changed its name to UK Design Council, and its focus range expanded from the initial daily and consumer product design to a broader design field including heavy industry, cities, and the environment. From the 1980s to the 1990s, the awareness of design in the UK was increasingly strengthened, the number of design firms continued to grow, and the British design industry ushered in a round of vigorous development. Faced with this new situation, UKDC adjusted its strategy in a timely manner and began to provide a series of specific project support plans for enterprises. This approach has achieved certain success, not only allowing enterprises to take a step towards accepting excellent design services, but also opening a path for the subsequent development of British design talents.

In July 1982, UKDC co-sponsored the International Design Policy Symposium with the Department of Design the Royal College of Art and other institutions. Margaret Thatcher delivered a foreword, and design professionals from all over the world attended the meeting. This is the first design policy conference in the world, which has had a profound impact on the successive introduction of design promotion policies by governments around the world.

The Commission underwent a series of economic cuts in the mid-80s until 1994, when it was restructured after a thorough review. They closed their London design center, shut down Design magazine, and made massive layoffs. They released a reorganization work report - "The Future Design Council", in which a comprehensive assessment of the agency's role positioning, organizational structure, work functions, etc., thus further clarifying its new position in the future development - "a small, compact and flexible collaborative think tank", it will no longer directly provide design consulting services for enterprises and designers, but will be transformed into a strategic institution that influences policies, integrates resources, promotes design, and cultivates ecology, in order to "stimulate the best use of British design in a global context, to enhance prosperity and healthy life" [3]. This reorganization marks a new transformation of the UKDC -

they began to participate clearly in the coming era as a resource integrator and ecological nurturer, and participated more widely in government decision-making on design, while focusing on stimulating the wider application of design by the society and the public in various ways.

In the mid-1990s, under the advice and promotion of the UKDC and other organizations, the UK began to fully implement the national strategy of "Creative Britain". The UKDC then focused on using the power of design to improve the international competitiveness of the UK. In 1998 they moved from Haymarket to new offices on Bow Street. When the new century comes, the "Millennium Products" international tour exhibition hosted by it set off a "British design" wave. More than 1,000 carefully selected British design products have demonstrated its design ability and innovation power to the world.

After entering the 21st century, the work of the UKDC are more extensive. They provide enterprises and governments with powerful integration of design resources, focus on design education and the improvement of the skills of the UK design industry, and jointly carry out design research with relevant institutions, provide support for the development of design methodologies and design tools, and more profoundly influence policy decision. Since 2000, they began to explore to bring design into a broader social and public sphere. They cooperated with the British government and other relevant departments to carry out a series of public projects, which pushed the development of the British design industry to a new level.

Today, the UKDC has become an important platform between the British government, various industries and enterprises, design companies, offices, individual designers, universities, research institutes and various social groups, playing a very important and positive role in the resource integration and ecological construction of the British design industry.

3   Establish an Industry Image and Cultivate a Design Ecology

What is design? What can design do? Where is the value of design? Such an important and fundamental question needs a strong answer. Compared with other industries, the design industry appears to be more decentralized. From a global perspective, the scale of independent design companies is generally small. How can we make many scattered small enterprises make a cohesive voice? A powerful design promote organization should take on this task. In the UK, the work of establishing the image of the industry and cultivating the design ecology has continued for more than 70 years. Since its establishment in 1944, the UKDC has been working hard to promote the far-reaching influence and unique value of design to all society through various ways such as exhibitions, design awards, publishing and online media.

3.1   Design Center—A Window for Continuous Publicity of the Industry Image

In 1956, the UKDC's "Design Center" in Haymartet, London was completed. Its mainly to present excellent contemporary British industrial design to the public, manufacturers, retailers, and domestic and foreign traders. Over the next forty years, it became an important and highly well-known window for the promotion of design industry in UK, and has also become the target of many countries to emulate. Opened in 1956, the center had 22,500 visitors in its first week, where they could see more than 1,000 products from 433 UK companies. The Design Center has held many influential exhibitions, such as the "Designed in Britain—Made Abroad" in 1981. Such long-term and continuous promotion have made the value of the design widely recognized by all walks of life, and also laid a solid foundation for the whole society and the public to understand design.

3.2 Annual Award - Concretization of Design Concept

The creation of design awards is crucial to the construction of design ecology. It is an important platform for the publicity and promotion of design concepts. Its main target group is the core group of the design ecosphere—manufacturers and designers. A design award with high quality and good reputation can not only attract the attention of design circles at home and abroad, but also shoulders the mission of clarifying good design values through actual works. This plays a great public guiding role in the construction of design ecology. Through it, the established standards of "good design" will affect designers, production business and consumer groups in a visible and tangible form. A successful design award can convey ideas about design, changes in ideas, and reflections on such changes.

In 1957, "The Design Center Awards Scheme" began to be awarded. For the first time, The first award selected 12 products that best represent the model of British contemporary design, mainly a series of daily consumer goods such as sofa beds, televisions, tableware, lampshades and so on. Several years after the award was established, the scope of its awards has been greatly expanded. From 1960 to 1965, the award-winning products include a series of public products such as street lampposts, pay phones, and hospital wall lamps. In 1967, the category of "means of production" was added to the award, and the award-winning products included excavators, diesel locomotives, hairpin cars and other industrial products. The expansion of the category of award-winning products can reflect the expansion of the objects of British design promotion from general consumer goods to engineering design, infrastructure, public domain and other broader fields. At that early age, its thinking about the connection between design and social effect was quite far-sighted. More than 40 years later, the UKDC's goal of "using design to solve complex social and public problems" has actually begun to appear here. The design concept advocated by the policy, the change of the concept, and the abstract thinking about this change can all be embodied through awards, so as to play a clear value-oriented role in the construction of the design ecology.

3.3 "Labelling Scheme" - The Deepening of Design Concepts in Daily Life

Two years after the launch of the Annual Award, the UKDC launched the Design Center Labeling Scheme, which allows manufacturers who have displayed products in the center to use this label. Through this scheme, the awareness of "good design" has further entered thousands of households. If the award is only a concrete manifestation of the design values advocated by the policy, then the "label" can allow thousands of households to be subtly influenced by the concept of "good design" in the continuous use of daily life, so that the general public understands, recognizes, comprehends, and appreciates the beauty of design, and finally establishes a virtuous circle of design ecology.

Internationally, how to establish a good and unique image of domestic design? This is a major work related to enhancing the competitiveness of the domestic design industry. It is of great significance to promote the sustainable development of the domestic design industry, fully "stimulate" the innovation of enterprises, improve the competitiveness of products from all walks of life, drive employment, and improve the economy. In the UK, the government's support for building the international image of the country's design industry began as early as the 1950s.

3.4 "Britain Can Make It" -Build British Design Brand Effect

The exhibition of "Britain Can Make It (BCMI)" was held at the Victoria and Albert Museum in September 1946. The purpose is to showcase the UK's industrial design capabilities to the world and promote export trade. The exhibition covers a wide range of categories, including almost all categories of British manufacturing industry, including household and gardening supplies, jewelry, fashion, personal decorations, clothing fabrics, toys, interior decoration, packaging, family entertainment, office and sports facilities, and children's furniture and facilities. The exhibition is divided into three sections: "From War to Peace", "Designers Look Ahead", and "What Industrial Design Means". Among them, the section "What industrial design means" was specially designed by the famous designer Misha Black [4].

In fact, after the end of World War II, due to the war, a large amount of American capital returned, giving American manufacturers great opportunities to invest in new equipment, new technologies, and new product development. In contrast, British manufacturers have a very conservative attitude towards innovation and development. Some British manufacturers have outdated concepts and outdated equipment, and only rely on providing a large number of products to make profits. Therefore, in the early stage of exhibition preparation, there were great differences between the manufacturer and the UKDC on the selection of products. Some representatives suggested that the exhibition should first consider the selection of foreign designs, and at the same time, handicraft products and some 17th and 18th century designs should be included in the list of exhibitors. UKDC insisted that the exhibition should be a firm break with the past, they believed that the exhibition of those things was "useless to show that the manufacturing industry was ready to provide something for the post-war market" [4]. They suggested that industrial designers should be committed to key industries and produce excellent products for new markets and new masses, so as to convince the industry that design is a worthwhile long-term investment.

Finally, the original intention of the UKDC was implemented, and BCMI became a stage to showcase the best design capabilities of the United Kingdom to all walks of life and the international community. Under the influence of the exhibition, the attention paid to design in the UK has been unprecedentedly improved. At the same time, foreign manufacturers also began to notice such a national business card as "British design". According to the official report, the total number of visitors to the exhibition reached 1,432,546, which was 3–4 times higher than its original expectation, so that the organizer twice postponed the end of the exhibition by one month. It is estimated that there were 43,000 trade visitors and 7,000 buyers from 67 countries, who signed orders worth around 25–50 million pounds [4]. The BCMI exhibition has achieved considerable influence both domestically and internationally, so that in the subsequent research on design history, the research literature on BCMI is quite rich and detailed. All these have played an inestimable role in the vigorous development of the British design industry in the future.

Establishing an industry image is a protracted task. Up to now, the UKDC is still collecting excellent cases of design and value creation across the country. The cases have been specially sorted out and disseminated to all walks of life through their website. At the same time, they publishes a large number of surveys and research reports on the value and influence of the design industry all year round. The reports often provide very detailed data to prove how companies can increase added value and sales performance through design, and enhance competitiveness. For example, "The Design Economy 2015 Report", which goes beyond the traditional definition of the design industry, uses gross value added (GVA) and statistical data related to productivity, turnover, employment and exports of goods and services to summarize the contribution of design to the British economy in that year. This is a long-term and far-reaching work that requires specialized institutions to continue to operate. Its most important role is to create a better design ecology and make the business community, government departments and the general public realize the great value of design. And then take the initiative to support the design and use the design.

4   Integrate Industrial Resources and Break Through Innovation Bottlenecks

Innovation is a high-investment, high-difficulty, and high-risk behavior. Although the investment of world-renowned brands and enterprises in innovation has increased year by year, innovation is still a difficult task for many small and medium-sized enterprises that constitute an important part of the national economy. Comparatively speaking, small and medium-sized enterprises are relatively weak in anti-risk ability, and at the same time, their innovation motivation is relatively insufficient, and compared with large companies that can fully provide research and development funds, their innovation ability needs to be improved. How to help this A large number of enterprises break through innovation bottlenecks and drive business growth? This not only reflects the level of a country's design ecological construction, but also tests its ability to integrate resources. As a pioneer in the government's promotion of design and innovation, the UK has carried out in-depth and extensive work in this area.

4.1   "Designing Demand"-SME Design Enhancement Program

In 2004, with the support of the British government, the UKDC launched a project called "Designing Demand", which is a national long-term business support plan for small and medium-sized enterprises. Its purpose is to integrate various resources to help enterprises, Universities use design to break through innovation bottlenecks, improve products and services or transform research results, and develop successful commercial products and services.

From 2007 to 2012, "Designing Demand" was officially approved to be implemented in seven regions of the UK. Local governments across the UK provide an average of £2.5 million a year in financial support for the scheme. Project participants include local governments and regional development agencies, design associations, design companies, design colleges and ordinary small and medium-sized enterprises across the UK. This is a huge design resource collaboration project supported by the government. It has a large number of participants, a wide range of influence, and a time span of more than five years.

How it works: First, the British national training institution in charge of technology transformation will provide technical transformation guidance for designers (including professionals from design associations, design institutions and design enterprises) who will be responsible for guiding design upgrading or technology transformation in the project. Then, these trained professional designers will guide the participating enterprises to carry out a series of work related to creative generation, product development, user research, sample testing, etc. In addition, the project also provides systematic design support to scientific researcher and technical workers, so that they can develop their own subjects and form commercial achievements. In terms of specific operation, the "Design for Business" project provides three levels of participation, the intensity and effect of which are gradually increased, and there are different points for enterprises to enter and exit, which will be determined according to the size, willingness and ability of the enterprise:

Level 1, Introduction: This is a set of heuristic workshops aimed at business consultants and designers in SMEs. The goal of the workshop is to introduce the specific content and focus of the program. The UKDC also specially designed a thinking tool to identify possible design opportunities in different companies, and thus formulate design strategies that are in line with the company's development goals.

Level 2, Growth service: this layer is for new companies and innovative companies, the main work is to carry out specific interventions in key areas such as product development or brand strategy, with the guidance and support of design experts to help companies implement reforms, shorten new technologies or Time-to-market for new services, strengthening business capabilities, attracting external funding, mitigating risk and getting to market quickly. Each innovative company will carry out development work for up to 12 months under the guidance of design experts.

Level 3, design investment and design innovation service: this level is for rising enterprises, and the selected enterprises will have the opportunity to develop and implement a design-led reform project. The project will provide design guidance within 12 to 18 months, and will also provide expert workshops on branding, innovative product development and user experience, and provide peer-to-peer in-depth learning opportunities for participating companies.

In addition, the UKDC has also formulated a special version of the plan for colleges and universities to help them realize the commercial transformation of scientific research results and intellectual property rights, improve investment attractiveness, reduce R&D and innovation risks, shorten time to market, make up for the lack of social links between colleges and universities (including the design majors in colleges and universities). And at the same time provide valuable training opportunities for college students. In the end, the UKDC also established a resource network for small and medium-sized enterprises to help who have completed the support plan to continuously obtain new information and new technologies and build business relationships. While, through the circle effect, the project can gain sustainable influence and reach more potential participants.

Progress and achievements: The "Designing Demand" project has been highly valued by the government. By the end of 2005, more than 150 enterprises have participated in the project, and 97% of them highly evaluated the project, 61% of them have completed the entire two-year process and indicated that their performance has improved significantly or even reached a high level of reform.

As of December 2006, more than 700 enterprises in Yorkshire alone have tried this project. At the Competitiveness Summit in December 2006, Alistair Darling, former secretary to the UK Department of Trade and Industry, said: "More than 700 businesses in Yorkshire have trialled the project and the results are impressive. The businesses involved in the project have a record of improving sales performance, and have released new products, attracting new investment."

In 2007, under the suggestion of the committee, the British Department of Trade and Industry intervened in the project to promote the full participation and implementation of local government agencies in the UK, and the project was launched on a large scale throughout the UK. As of March 2008, the project's partners have included dozens of UK regional development agencies, universities, regional development funds, non-profit associations and business development agencies.

By 2012, more than 2,000 small and medium-sized enterprises in the UK have been supported by the program, and more than 700 of them have received intensive guidance from design experts. The projects generated a total of £96.3 million in commercial revenue nationwide, with a gross value added of £66.5 million and a net value added of £43.9 million. For every £1 spent on design by businesses participating in the scheme, they generate £5 in revenue, £4 in net operating profit and £20 in turnover[5]. With the help of the project, many small and medium-sized enterprises have expanded their business scale, upgraded their brands, improved product performance, lowered prices, and expanded their potential customer base. The project has expanded the company's sales scope to overseas markets and enhanced the international competitiveness of British local products. At the same time, the project has also enabled many local small and medium-sized enterprises to find business decisions and development paths that suit their own characteristics in an increasingly competitive economic environment, and let many enterprises with potential but still in their infancy have the ability to attract external investment and develop enterprise scale.

The successful implementation of "Designing Demand" has had a major impact on British companies and the design community. The improvement in performance has allowed the industry to further recognize the value of design, and to regard design as an important part of product innovation and development, and even incorporate it into corporate culture. Most of the participating companies believe that the project has made their internal organizational culture more focused on design and innovation, the internal working atmosphere is more relaxed, and the external corporate image is more vivid and dynamic. In addition, many companies expressed after participating in the project that they will have a more positive attitude towards investing in design innovation in the future [6]. At the same time, with the help of the project, they also began to master more deeply how to use design thinking and methods to break through the original innovation bottleneck, further deepen design skills, and improve innovation capabilities. Of course, all this is due to the strong resource integration of the project.

Design is a highly innovative behavior, and it is the key factor to transform a large number of the latest scientific and technological achievements into practical products that can bring commercial profits to various industries. However, for small and medium-sized enterprises, the cost, risk and difficulty of innovation may be very large, and the resources that need to be integrated often exceed the scope of the company's capabilities. Through the "Designing Demand" program, the design industry with limited scale and output value can finally generate a huge "pull" for the entire economy. It also has a profound impact on the virtuous circle and sustainable development of design ecology. With the support of the government, a large number of resources are integrated through various channels to serve to break through innovation bottlenecks, which can help of innovation in the overall economy, accelerate the transformation of scientific and technological achievements, promote the integration of industrial chains, and enhance the overall economic competitiveness of the country.

5   Strengthen Knowledge Sharing and Enhance Industrial Skills

Design is an activity that integrates various resources for innovation. From the design of tangible products such as automobiles and furniture to the design of intangible products such as services, networks, and content provision, the knowledge involved varies in thousands of ways. No designer can master all the design knowledge and skills he will use in the future in advance, the key is to learn quickly. So, how to share knowledge in the field of design? How to promote knowledge circulation and exchange in the field of industrial practice and design education? How can potential design process participants get the knowledge resources they want when they need them? Britain has made a very far-sighted plan in this regard.

5.1   "Design Blueprint"-Future Industrial Skills Development Plan

At the end of 2007, the UK Design Skills Alliance (hereinafter referred to as the "Alliance") was jointly formed by the UKDC, the Creative & Cultural Skills Committee, the Design Skills Advisory Panel. The purpose is to break through the original barriers between the industry and education, integrate various resources, strengthen the knowledge sharing about design through a series of activities, and improve the professional level of the British design industry to meet the challenges of international design capabilities from emerging economies including China and Brazil. At the beginning of 2008, the alliance submitted an important policy document to the British government - "Design Blueprint" [7]. In fact, this is a detailed national-level design industry skills development plan, which is 58 pages long. The main activities are planned to be carried out at the two levels of industry and education at the same time, reflecting the ambition of the UK to improve the overall level of the design industry.

Industrial Level: It aims to help designers obtain a series of career tools, information and guidance, and improve the overall design skills and professional standards in the UK, including the following three aspects:

Construct the Professional Knowledge Base of Designers: The Designer's Business Knowledge Base is a professional learning framework shared by designers, design educators, corporate employers, and design students. It is an industry-oriented guide that emphasizes four skill areas including designer expertise, designer experience and insight, designer values and beliefs, and design management, methods and processes. These four fields are significantly different and have their own characteristics, and the knowledge involved is broad and rich. The alliance intends to use the existing expert resources to link the rich design research results with a large number of successful business practice cases. Knowledge, skills, abilities and key elements will be deeply described and release through the network platform, as a kind of industry-specific basic knowledge for corresponding people to learn.

Develop Professional Training Courses for Designers: The alliance intends to cooperate with design groups, organizations, institutions and business associations to develop a series of training courses for future designers. This will improve the existing curriculum and meet those needs that were not effectively met before. In particular, it advocates joint efforts of design companies and colleges across the UK to develop vocational training activities with sustainable design skills, leadership skills, and the ability to conduct business diagnosis (they will be oriented to future design leadership and management talents). In terms of sustainable design skills, it mainly focuses on long-term thinking and awareness of global and environmental issues beyond design, and cultivates the ability to transform this thinking into practical design strategies. Meanwhile technical knowledge related to the life cycle and materials, and a deep understanding of shifts in human behavior will be needed. In terms of leadership skills, develop projects to help senior designers learn leadership skills, mainly focusing on designers' corporate management capabilities and strategic skills. Finally, the alliance will develop and test a set of tools and services for diagnosing individual and business needs.

Strategy Analysis and Future Thinking: The Alliance will provide up-to-date information on the UK design industry and identify current skills needs in the industry. The alliance will establish links with external research resources such as universities, domestic and foreign design institutions, research institutions, etc., to conduct a strategic analysis and forward-looking thinking on the development of the British design industry (and share research results with them), and then form a national "Design Skills Map". On this basis, the alliance will also write policy recommendations and measures for developing UK design skills and disseminate them to practitioners in the design industry and design education.

Educational Level: It is mainly aimed at helping design students face future work challenges. Specifically, it includes the following four aspects:

Create a Visiting Student Network: In order to strengthen the connection between the design education circle and the design practice field, the alliance will cooperate with collaborators from universities and industries to carry out activities for school students to visit outstanding design practitioners. The activity will be based on a nationwide network and mobilize registered members to join.

Multidisciplinary Education Center: (See Sect. 5).

Career Guidance: Establish a user-oriented design career development network platform to provide design students with recruitment information, career development case studies, career routes and planning tools.

Work with Primary and Secondary Schools: In order to improve the creative skills of primary and secondary school students, the alliance will also cooperate with the British Creative Alliance to integrate courses containing design thinking into the existing primary and secondary school curriculum. The alliance will provide corresponding activities and training to design teachers in primary and secondary schools. The "Design Education" award will be presented to primary and secondary schools that have demonstrated excellence in teaching design-related courses.

Progress and Achievements: In 2008, due to the advent of the global financial crisis, the British financial expenditure was cut, the "design blueprint" plan was partially affected, and there was a gap in the operating funds of the Design Skills Alliance. This is helpless and quite regrettable as a result. Although the implementation of the plan itself is not as good as expected, it reflects that the UK's thinking on strengthening knowledge sharing and improving industrial skills of design industry is quite wise and insightful. It is believed that with the recovery of the European and world economies, the UK will continue to practice their ambitions in this regard. In fact, in March 2020, the UKDC has restarted the plan again and made it its strategic direction for the next four years. The restarted plan also included considerations for coping with persistent challenges such as COVID-19, automation and climate crisis [8].

In fact, in Japan, the United Kingdom, South Korea, Finland, India and other countries, the government is vigorously promoting the sharing of design knowledge, and each of them has a set of methods tailored to its own national conditions. There are various channels and approaches for knowledge sharing, the core of which is to formulate special policies and plans for this purpose, and one or two strong national design promotion organizations should undertake this responsibility. Their responsibility should be to integrate knowledge resources from all walks of life and provide a long-term, stable and open platform for design knowledge sharing.

6 Expand Social Effects and Innovate in Multiple Values

The value of design is diverse. It can not only help companies increase sales, expand profits, and help people improve their quality of life, but it can also help solve many urgent but thorny social issues such as environmental pollution and gender discrimination. So, how to promote design to solve social problems? How to promote the better use of design by the public sector? Due to the socialization of interests, this work can only be led by the government or public institutions, and cannot be expected in the enterprise or private sector.

As early as around 2004, the UKDC had put forward the concept of "applying design thinking and methods to society to promote social innovation". For this purpose, they established an interdisciplinary research team - "RED", which aims to explore innovative solutions to social and public problems through design. The "RED" team is a "think tank" that cultivates innovative thinking and social practice. It also has extensive work experience in the public service field.They have in-depth studied a series of issues including health, energy conservation, crime and sustainable life, and finally formed a research report. The report notes that these problems are increasingly complex and cannot be addressed by traditional ways. There is a need to creatively reconnect public services with the everyday problems people face. In turn, design itself should be transformed to help better address such problems, including: defining and redefining the nature and direction of the problem, interdisciplinary collaboration, employing participatory design techniques, and building rather than relying on competencies, designing beyond traditional solutions, and creating fundamental change [9, 10]. These works became the theoretical basis for the UKDC to put a lot of work into the social and public domains.

Specific to the implementation method, the UKDC decided to start with a series of projects as pilots to promote design thinking and working skills to this new field. They often organizes designers to participate in some social projects. These projects are not "design" some specific products or programs in the traditional sense, they are more like a "thinking engine". They encourage designers to go deep into some representative social issues, to exchanges, discussions, and dialogues with people in ordinary life, teach them to analyze and solve problems with design thinking and methods, and let these people who are at the core of practical problems find out answers by themselves. Then, they can improve organizations and behavior, and be able to make continuous self-management according to changing situations. These projects roughly involve the following aspects:

- Help prevent crime by design
- Help reduce energy consumption through design
- Improve care and reduce medical errors through design
- Improving national health through design
- Enhancing school sustainability through design
- Help governments improve efficiency and reduce costs through design

When engaging in these projects, the UKDC often exerts its strong resource integration and professional design capabilities. They have established cross-departmental partnerships with local governments and public institutions, and deeply cooperated with many institutions and social organizations, industry insiders and experts in related fields (such as criminologists or health care organizations). With communities as the base, they work together on how best to solve specific problems in specific settings. At the same time, they organized a professional design team to go deep into the process to develop corresponding products or improve services. Then, they tested, evaluated, improved them in the actual environment, and finally put them into use. During this whole process, the initial part of the research funding is usually jointly provided by government funds, industry organizations (such as medical and health organizations), and target units (such as a hospital). The research and development work of the design company can obtain a certain amount of remuneration. After the final successful product is developed, they can flow to the society through various channels such as government procurement, target unit procurement, agency sales, etc. This also solves the problem of project funding and income balance, making the project itself "sustainable".

6.1 Using Design to Reduce Energy Consumption and Achieve a Higher Quality of Life - Dott 07

Dott 07 is jointly organized by the UKDC and the local government of the Northeast of England. Around the theme of "sustainable living", it explores how to improve the effective use of resources through design and realize an environmentally friendly and sustainable lifestyle. It was the starting point for a larger initiative by the UKDC to bring design into the public domain - "Design of the Time". The UKDC once again launched its powerful resource integration capabilities. In addition to in-depth cooperation with the Northeast local government, the project has a wide range of participants, including the British Association for Aging and Health, Newcastle General Hospital, Newcastle University and other public departments, as well as many galleries, exhibition centers, museums, and many local farms, private homesteads, and several local environmental groups, plus more than 70 schools, numerous grassroots communities, and local village websites.

How It Works: The Dott 07 project is divided into five major sections, namely: travel, energy, school, diet and health, which include important areas closely related to daily life. The project regularly hold seminars with the participation of local citizens, designers, government planners, and experts in related fields, discussing how to achieve a more environmentally friendly lifestyle and improve the quality of life through design from different perspectives. In the second half of the meeting, a brief design training will be given to the public to deepen people's perception and understanding of design.

At the same time, the project also invites a team of designers to go deep into the local area and develop creative simulation solutions through personal experience. For example, in the activities of the travel section, the project team proposed the idea of transforming the abandoned space of New Castellegs Heide into a sustainable living space, and conducted an immersive experiment. They set up the experimental camp under the piers of the Baker Bridge, using the existing round arch structure to shelter from wind and rain while reducing energy consumption. The camp encourages socialization and interaction by providing visitors with a shared kitchen and dining room. In addition, there are buses and shared bicycles for people to travel. Later, the camp became a local visitor center during the "Dott 07 Art Festival" in October of that year.

In the diet section, the team launched a plan called "soil to table", which is in conjunction with more than 80 organizations in Middlesbrough communities, voluntary organizations, primary and secondary schools, and public health agencies. It cooperated with local farmers and surrounding villages to jointly develop planting spaces in the city and establish new connections with them, upgrade market sales models, renovate production equipment, and train farmers to master more modern production methods. At the same time, under the guidance and support of the design consulting company and the food culture editor, and with the permission of the government, in May 2007, a site was opened in the main local park for planting activities. More than 1,000 people participated in the planting with the cooperation of horticulturalists and farmers. In September 2007, the project team held a large-scale banquet for 1,500 people in the square in the center of the city, and the "modern farmers" made their own harvested ingredients into dishes to share with others. This activity shows people the possibility of planting activities in the city. In the future, they will further improve the corresponding services, markets and infrastructure through design, so that the local area can achieve true self-sufficiency[11]. There are many similar activities in Dott 07, which are promoted and launched according to their respective sectors.

Progress and Achievements: In the end, the one-year Dott 07 project ended with the "Time Design 07 Art Festival" held on the banks of the Tyne River in October of the same year. The festival lasted for 12 days. In addition to a series of cultural and art celebration activities, the whole project was also summarized, and the important research results, experiences, and follow-up development plans in the process were exhibited to the public, and the "Creative Community Award" was awarded to some of the outstanding works. The number of visitors to the festival exceeded 20,000.

Dott 07 engaged more than half a million local residents, including more than 1,000 students, with eight communities achieving notable results. The project has effectively promoted the dissemination of design thinking and design methods among the public, government agencies, local associations, and public services (compared with the industry, which communicates more closely with design, these fields have less understanding of design before), so that the whole society has a deeper understanding of the value and role of design. It prompting people to connect design with solving social problems and improving public services. The project also provides a good demonstration through practical cases. At the same time, the joint collaboration between the project and the local government, community organizations, local residents, enterprises, schools, hospitals, environmental protection agencies, as well as experts and designers in related fields also promotes the integration of local resources and the construction of information networks, many local organizations have established long-term connections as a result of this project. Due to the extensive participation of schools, it has successfully stimulated more young people's strong interest in using design to solve problems[11].

Around 2008, the UKDC began to introduce design into the functional departments of the British government to help them improve their work efficiency and gain the trust of the public. In this process, the working team formed by the UKDC creatively introduced the method of cultural anthropology (this method was used more often in the design process before, but was less understood by other departments). They visited government offices in large numbers and experienced life with local people. At the same time, they held workshops where government personnel, the public and designers participated together. While conducting collaborative dialogues, multiple parties conceived solutions. In the end, the design team submitted a clear service outline on how local government departments can better carry out their work, and formulated a ten-step action guideline. Under each category of the guidelines, some very specific and actionable action plans are listed. The work of the team has been highly appraised by the local government departments, civil servants and the public. With the help of the design, they have enhanced their understanding, established smoother communication channels, and the work content has become more clear, specific and targeted. They created some unprecedented working models, both parties have gained a better experience.

Under the influence of these achievements, local government agencies have a deeper understanding of the value that design can bring in public affairs. Since then, the UKDC has begun to introduce design into the field of public affairs and social services on a large scale. Since 2008, they has helped develop a range of products and services to address a wide range of social issues across the country. These include working with the Department of Health to develop well-designed, easy-to-clean hospital furniture, working with the NHS to develop solutions to ease the doctor-patient relationship, and working with the UK National Register of Domain Names (Nominet) to develop digital services, in order to solve the youth unemployment problem. And to respond to the British government's "City Deals" on the development of sustainable cities, they deeply involved in urban planning work across the country. They help them to creatively transform communities, improve the environment, increase green land, beautify streets, upgrade buildings, optimize transportation, plan healthy and sustainable places and living environments for the future through design, and finally, promote the local infrastructure, economic growth, and improve social and people's livelihood.

As of 2015, more than 90 local public departments in the UK have participated in similar projects, and 85% of them believe that the design method is "very relevant" to their work (compared with the previous double improvement), and they said that they would use design more in other work in the future [12]. In 2017, with funding from The National Lottery Community Fund, the UKDC embarked on a project to improve the experience of aging in the community. The project created 62 social enterprises, generating £3.7 million in economic return on investment, 197 jobs (34 full-time and 163 part-time) and 818 volunteering opportunities. The project benefited 89,000 people and significantly improved the life experience of the local elderly population in their later years.

After nearly a decade of working with local government agencies, the UKDC has developed a systematic design approach and working model that supports teams working in different districts, and rapidly generating solutions to a variety of complex problems in the public domain. In February 2018, they published a summary of its methods, experience and skills accumulated from public service work in various regions of the UK in recent years [12]. Since 2020, major cities and regions around the world have been hit by the new crown epidemic, and the UKDC has devoted itself to a new journey to help respond to the epidemic and revive cities and life through design.

Design thinking is a good tool oriented to discovering problems, stimulating creativity, and solving problems. It has the characteristics of initiative, purpose, foresight, divergence, originality, mutation, and flexibility. It is a process of efficient comprehensive application and repeated dialectical development of abstract thinking, image thinking, divergent thinking, convergent thinking, intuitive thinking, inspiration thinking, reverse thinking, associative thinking. Its core is creative thinking, which can help people see problems from a new perspective and solve them in new ways. Design thinking has a wide range of uses, even surpassing general business fields such as product design and graphic design. If it is applied to service design, it can often accurately identify the real needs of users and create attractive user experiences. If this kind of thinking is extended to the field of social and public services, it will also greatly help to look at and deal with problems that have been ignored, misunderstood, or not well solved in the past with a creative eye. Because these social problems are often very complex, involving quite a lot of different stakeholders, and their appeals are often very different or even conflicting. The introduction of design thinking and methods can help find breakthroughs and creatively solve these problems, which is also one of the future trends to maximize the value of design.

As the Design Commission said in the opening sentence of "Restarting Britain II": "Design is an integral part of the DNA of every public service." The report states that merely saying that public services should use design more is not enough and more needs to be done to ensure that local authority officials, service commissioners and policymakers have sufficient understanding, capacity, skills and willingness to design to develop cost-effective, user-led public service projects [13]. As a result, the UKDC systematically developed and launched a public sector design program in 2014 to help local authority staff review and restructure their services around user needs [14].

As mentioned above, the UKDC has used its strong resource integration capabilities to introduce design into the vast and huge field of public utilities. It has expanded the future development space for the design industry and identified a orientation with extraordinary potential. The direction has delineated a new value field for the future, and its significance and influence will be far-reaching. It is foreseeable that in the near future, more and more governments, public departments and social service organizations around the world will expect to cooperate with the design industry and take new steps towards using design to solve social problems, and achieve public service innovation. This has also opened up a huge potential space for the sustainable development of the design industry ecology.

7 Implement Interdisciplinary Education and Create a Center of Excellence

Design requires an interdisciplinary problem-solving ability. It has no fixed routine to find. Many times, it comes from the collision of different disciplines, different professions, different needs, and different goals. We often have to face this reality: designers, entrepreneurs, engineers, marketing and management personnel, technical and service personnel, artists, users, each speak their own language. When facing a common goal, the inability to communicate effectively with each other reduces the scope and depth of possible impact of the design. How to overcome this obstacle, allow design to cooperate better with other disciplines, and allow people with completely different professional backgrounds and knowledge structures to collaborate with each other to generate brand-new designs, thereby contributing to economic and social development? It's a pretty challenging thing to do. The UK has already taken new steps in this direction.

7.1 Multidisciplinary Innovation Center - Centers of Excellence

As early as 2005, the UKDC put forward the importance of interdisciplinary education. In the crucial design industry policy document "Cox Review" [15], it detailed the reasons for cross-professional design education, the objectives of education, and the course of action. The document has attracted great attention from the British government and education circles. In May 2007, under the impetus of the British government and the Ministry of Education, The Royal College of Art, Imperial College London and its affiliated Tanaka Business School joined forces created the UK's first "Centres of Excellence" - "Design-London".

How It Works: "Design-London" is an multidisciplinary innovation center whose purpose is to integrate different disciplines such as design, engineering, technology and business to meet future innovation challenges and create products and services that shock the world. The entire "Design-London" cost 5.8 million pounds, of which 380 lb were provided by the Higher Education Funding Council for England (HEFCE); the National Endowment for Science, Technology & the Arts (NESTA) £900,000 is provided for the "incubator" project; the remaining funding is provided by the Royal Academy of Arts and Imperial College London. The London Development Agency (LDA) is working with other London government agencies, including the UKDC, to integrate Design-London into a broad strategy to harness the power of design to drive innovation across the UK.

"Design-London" will form an "innovation triangle" between design (represented by the Royal College of Art), engineering and technology (represented by Imperial College London's Department of Engineering), and business (represented by Imperial College London's Tanaka Business School). In this triangle, a series of teaching activities will promote the knowledge exchange between Master of Engineering, Master of Arts, and Master of Business Administration, such as providing design-oriented innovation modules in the four MBA courses of Imperial Business School. At the same time, research activities will explore how to more efficiently integrate design into business and technology to create services and products that shock the world. Graduates from both institutions will have the opportunity to develop new ideas in the "incubator" of the center. This is a dynamic multi-disciplinary business development environment, which supports some unique and unexpected cooperation between different disciplines, institutions and places. The center will also cultivate innovative capabilities through simulation training and digital tools, such as providing design visualization tools for students and commercial enterprises through its Innovation Technology (IvT) unit, and providing local enterprises with a series of services. Interdisciplinary researchers will study the value and effectiveness of 3D stereoscopic display, multidimensional modeling, digital prototyping and manufacturing technologies in the innovation process.

Progress and Achievements: Since October 2009, "Design-London" has started to teach courses for MBA, MEng, MSc, MA and PhD of the two institutions. For example, electives such as 'Design-led Innovation' and 'New Venture Creation' are taught to the final year of the MEng at Imperial's Faculty of Engineering, with a supplementary course offered to third-year engineering students in October 2010 course. Similar short courses have also reached 160 Bioengineering MSc and PhD students. Central to this is the provision of design-led innovation modules on four MBA courses at Imperial Business School under the heading of Innovation, Entrepreneurship and Design (IED). By February 2010, Design London had taught its seventh cohort of MBA students, 366 in total. At the same time, "Design-London" also opened courses on design management and innovation for 350 managers from 250 small and medium-sized enterprises.

After 2011, as the impact of the financial crisis continued to deepen, "Design-London" did not receive the expected investment in funding, but, as the UKDC wrote in "Multi-disciplinary design education in the UK": "There is no one way to introduce multidisciplinary design education into an institution. These activities and initiatives are being driven and championed by the universities themselves and come in a wide range of forms, sizes and costs" [16]. Thus, a more embedded strategy was adopted, under the vigorous promotion and activities of the UKDC, many universities in the UK have responded to this call. A series of institutions of higher learning have begun to take multidisciplinary education into consideration, and have launched different practical measures based on their own situations and characteristics. They develop courses and research projects, and some work leads to new teaching and research centres. Some institutions have created new graduate programs or embedded design-related courses in courses in other disciplines. At present, institutions all over the UK have participated in this action, including the University of Cambridge, University of Liverpool, University of Nottingham, University of Southampton, and Saïd Business School, University of Oxford etc. (See [17] for details).

8 Summary

A benign and innovative society not only needs designers who know how to use business language, but also business managers who can understand and consciously use creativity. They should know when and how to use design experts. They should be able to manage creativity and create a good environment for creativity, so that creative talents can give full play to their potential. In such an environment, talents from management, science, engineering, technology, design, culture, art and other disciplines can work together to produce great products and services with a full understanding of design.

The design industry is not isolated. It has a broad foundation. Just like cultivating a plant, supporting the design industry should not start from the design industry itself, but from its root system. In addition, we should create a suitable soil and a suitable environment for the root system. Only in this way can the seedlings of the design grow into giant trees. The methods and means of cultivating the soil and creating the environment are diverse. As mentioned above, establishing the industry image, breaking through innovation bottlenecks, promoting knowledge sharing, promoting social effects, and enhancing interdisciplinary cooperation, are only a relatively important part of the many means. And, in any aspect of these five points, the methods of promotion are also diverse. But the most important thing is that these tasks require a strong ability to integrate resources, which can break down the original layers of barriers across departments and fields, so that the education sector, industry circles, government public departments and the general public can work together. They will spontaneously become the elements in this ecosystem that can contribute positive forces, and make greater contributions to national economic growth, national cultural prosperity and social civilization progress.

References

1. Design Council Homepage. https://www.designcouncil.org.uk/. Accessed 09 Feb 2023
2. Bayley, S., Garrner, P.: Twentieth-Century Style and Design. Translated by Luo Yunyun. Sichuan People's Publishing House, China (2000)
3. Sorrell, J.: The Future Design Council. Design Council, London(1994)
4. Maguire, P.J., Woodham, J.M.: Design and Cultural Politics in Postwar Britain: The "Britain Can Make It" Exhibition of 1946. Leicester University Press, Leicester (1997)
5. Godber, D.: The Designing Demand Review. Design Council, London (2012)
6. Partners, E.: Designing Demand: Executive Summary. Design Council, London (2012)
7. Sands, J., Worthington, D.: High-Level Skills for Higher Value: Design Blueprint. Design Council, London (2008)
8. Design Council: Design Perspectives: Design Skills. Design Council, London (2020)
9. Cottam, H., Leadbeater, C.: RED PAPER 01 Health: Co-creating Services. Design Council, London (2004)
10. Burns, C., Cottam, H., Vanstone, C., Winhall, J.: RED PAPER 02 Transformation Design. Design Council, London (2006)
11. Meng, Y.: From Policy Implementation to Resource Integration-The Functional Transformation of British Design Council. Nanjing University of the Arts, China (2020)
12. Design Council: Design in the public sector: Lessons from applying design approaches in the public sector. Design Council, London (2018)
13. Kingsmill, B., Quirk, B.: Restarting Britain II: Design and Public Services. The Design Commission, London (2013)
14. Design Council: Design in the Public Sector: An evaluation of a programme of support for local authority service transformation. Design Council, London (2015)
15. Cox, G.: Cox Review of Creativity in Business: Building on the UK's Strengths. HM Treasury, London (2005)
16. Design Council: Multi-disciplinary design education in the UK: Report and recommendations from the Multi-Disciplinary Design Network. Design Council, London (2010)
17. Design Council: Multi-disciplinary design education in the UK case studies. Design Council, London (2010)

The Effect of Series Workshops on Ownership of Societal Issues: Case Study on Designing Food for the Future

Tomomi Miyata[1]([✉]), Yuki Taoka[1], Momoko Nakatani[1], Mika Yasuoka[2], Nana Hamaguchi[3], and Shigeki Saito[1]

[1] School of Environment and Society, Tokyo Institute of Technology, 2-12-1 Ookayama, Meguro-Ku, Tokyo, Japan
{miyata.t.ae,taoka.y.aa}@m.titech.ac.jp
[2] Department of People and Technology, Roskilde University, Universitetsvej 1, 260 4000 Roskilde, Denmark
[3] NTT Social Informatics Laboratories, 1-1 Hikarinooka, Yokosuka-shi, Kanagawa, Japan

Abstract. To solve social issues, it is not enough for a single entity to act; it is necessary to recognize the issues as our affairs and to have a "sense of ownership" and act toward their solution. The concept of "sense of ownership" or "psychological ownership" is used in the fields of educational psychology and business administration to encourage each individual to make matters "personal" rather than for a company or organizational unit to achieve a non- transient solution. In this study we developed a 4 day with in consecutive five months for 17–19 people in each day, series of workshop on the food of the future, and analyzed the effects on "sense of ownership". Results showed that the proposed workshop design helps cultivate a sense of ownership of societal matters by using facts as bases of discussion and a guide for collecting more information. Results also showed that repetition of workshops helped personalize societal issues giving ideas on where they can begin and some easy actions to take through providing opportunities to reflect on the issue in and outside of workshops.

Keywords: Service Design · Co-design · Sustainable Environment · Workshop · Ownership · Design for future

1 Introduction

To solve social issues, it is not enough for a single entity to act; it is necessary to recognize the issues as our affairs and to have a "sense of ownership" and act toward their solution. The concept of "sense of ownership" or "psychological ownership" [1] is used in the fields of educational psychology and business administration to encourage each individual to make matters "personal" rather than for a company or organizational unit to achieve a non-transient solution. The long-term involvement of the parties who use the service/product in the co-creation process leads to the development of a sense of ownership of the issues which in turn leads to behavioral change as the learning progresses leading to the creation and implementation of non-transient solutions [1–3]. This is a process of deepening a sense of ownership of issues and ideas [4]. People gain a better understanding of themselves when they gain new ideas and other people's viewpoints through discussions and interactions with people of different backgrounds [5]. "Use of data" such as administrative and interview data is known to reinforce the process of learning [6].

Prospective ergonomics is an approach in ergonomics used to anticipate solutions to future issues by defining future human needs [7, 8]. It analyzes numerous factors and future scenario planning to fulfill the design of human centered artifacts that provide a positive user experience [9, 10]. The use of future scenarios encourages discussion to converge more efficiently on shared issues and explore these topics in greater depth [11]. Therefore, in this study, we will examine what elements promote a "sense of ownership" in series of workshops that focus on social issues especially focusing on the use of data to promote ideas to be explored.

2   Method and Workshop Design

2.1   Design Concept

To foster participants' sense of ownership toward future incidents and to stimulate actions, both "activities to make people aware of the future issues" and "activities to enable them to connect the actions and future as if it were their own" is necessary. In addition, participants can also be involved in the activities described above outside of the workshops as an opportunity to remind them of the theme. The concept is summarized in Fig. 1. In this workshop, we will focus on the "use of facts" as an initiative to accelerate the learning process in the workshop. The theme of the workshop (WS) was "Food for the Future. This is because food is a topic that is close to everyone and food loss and food mileage have a large impact on carbon dioxide emissions making it a theme directly related to environmental issues.

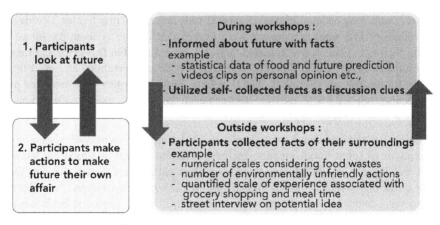

Fig. 1. Concept image of workshop design.

Growth of mini tomato, finally there is tomato.   Photos of food loss in participants' life,

May 25   **June 20**   **Too many stock.**   **Garbage.**

Fig. 2. Examples of photos donated to the workshop. (Scenes of participants' life)

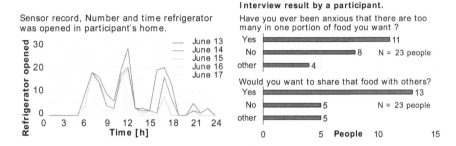

Sensor record, Number and time refrigerator was opened in participant's home.

Interview result by a participant.
Have you ever been anxious that there are too many in one portion of food you want ?

Fig. 3. Examples of data donated for the workshop. (Left: Sensor data, Right: Interview results)

2.2 Workshop Program

Each workshop started with an explanation of the purpose of the meeting, the theme of "The Future of Food in 2030" was introduced, and was explained that this activity is a place where people can work together to create a better future society. After introducing the management members and participating organizations, the team was divided into four to six members, who introduced themselves to each other. If the workshop was between the series, workshop programs and outcomes so far were introduced at the beginning. Four workshops were held within five consecutive months. Each workshop was three hours long and participants discussed and participated in activities. During the first workshop (**Day one**) participants were 1) provided with facts about the future of food through statistical information and interview recordings. On **Days two** and **three**, 2) participants brought data they had collected outside of workshops and used them as clues for discussions (Fig. 2, 3). On **Day four**, 3) table masters were provided and participants discussed by themselves. Between each day 4) participants made actions to cultivate a sense of ownership.

Day One. Two data presentation sessions were held. Eleven cards were distributed with explanations of future food statistics, including climate change and food production, world and Japan's population, and food loss. Then participants viewed six interview videos on the theme each about one minute long. While seeing the cards and immediately after viewing each video, participants wrote down their impressions and evaluated the relationship to the data. Participants shared their impressions and findings within their teams. Then, they came up with one scenario of 2030 for them and another for the whole team.

Between Days. The management team merged discussions into three main topics. 1. Tailored diets, 2. Involving citizens in the production of environmentally friendly foods, and 3. Reducing food loss without making large changes in people's lifestyles. The topics were shared, participants who reported on their choice to continue the WS.

Day Two. Participants brought three photos related to the theme in their daily lives (Fig. 2). All the pictures were printed and distributed at each table and participants chose three photos and explained their choice and evaluated the distance between them to the topic in the photo. Participants then discussed ideas to solve their topic. Then, data recording sensors (thermometer, light sensor, smartwatch, etc.) were introduced. The team discussed possible ways to collect data that would help investigate their idea. After the WS, the management team supervised participants on data collection through mail base interaction on collecting personal data.

Day Three. Participants continued with the same team. Participants shared personal data they had collected and further discussed ideas to solve their topic.

Day Four. Five tables each with a table master with varying topics were provided. Participants joined the discussions at the tables and worked on 6 sessions each for about 20 min. At the end table owners presented their ideas.

2.3 Research Variables

To measure the effectiveness of the workshop, participants were asked to answer questionnaires on satisfaction and sense of ownership on the theme before and after each workshop followed by 20 min semi-structured interview. Sense of Ownership Questions (Fig. 4) was created based on references [12, 13]. Seven relevant questions were picked and modified to suit the theme and one question was added. The low-level ownership questions Oq1, and Oq2 show a slight sense that the topic is their affairs while high-level ownership questions Oq4, and Oq5 show a strong will to act to solve the issue as their affairs. Iq01 shows an increase in the general image of the future while Iq02 and Iq03 show awareness of future issues related to the theme.

In the interviews, participants described which facts, whether facts food for the future or personal data they had collected, helped the discussions and mention any changes action and mental changed they experienced outside the workshop. Each workshop was video recorded. In this paper we will focus on analysis of sense of ownership. Questionnaires on environmental awareness were also answered however it is not our main research target so we have cut on the details [14, 15].

2.4 Participant

Participants were 39 people (23 M, 16 F) aged from the 20 s to 60 s. Ten participants were recruited based on their field of professional expertise (researchers and developers of food-related products and services and activists in the field of foodbank and

SENSE OF OWNERSHIP OF ISSUE   * invert scale
  Oq1: The theme is related to me.
  Oq2: Issues related to them are difficult to consider as my own issue.*
  Oq3: Preparing to realize an ideal future is our job.
  Oq4: We intend to actively work toward the realization of the ideal theme.
  Oq5: We must work hard towards the realization of the ideal future for the
        next generations.
Op1: low level ownership Op5 : high level ownership

IMAGE OF ISSUE AND AWARENESS   * invert scale
  Iq1: I have a realistic image of the future of the theme.
  Iq2: I can imagine the issues that will happen related to the future of the theme.
  Iq3: I believe the issues related to the theme will not become severe.*

Fig. 4. Sense of Ownership Questions (Ow-point 1 – very low, 7-ver high).

cafe owners, Experts, E). Eleven participants were native subjects who were working persons interested in workshop activities themselves (General working people, G). 18 participants were bachelor or graduate students in various fields recruited through digital poster advertisement (Student, S). At the point of recruitment, participants were advised to participate in all workshop series. Participants who participated on a single day were 17, and at least two days were 22. (two days 13, three days 4, and all four days 5).

2.5   Research Design

Research 1: To study the effect of workshop design on sense of ownership, we statistically analyzed mean point of Sense of Ownership Questions (Ow-point), before and after each workshop in Sect. 3.1. To analyze the effect of use of personal data and playing a role in the team on sense of ownership, mean Ow-point before and after statistically analyzed in Sect. 3.2 and Sect. 3.3.

Research 2: To study the effect of participation to a series of workshop, we statistically analyzed the mean Ow-point differences of each workshop to reveal effect of day on sense of ownership in Sect. 4.1. Then, to clarify the effect of participation in series, mean Ow-point at three timings were statistically analyzed in Sect. 4.2.

3   Result 1: The Effect of Workshop Activities, Use of Personal Data, and Roles in the Workshop on the Sense of Ownership

3.1   Sense of Ownership Questionnaire

T-tests were performed to compare the mean value of each questions in the Sense of Ownership Questions before and after each workshop. The mean point and standard deviation before and after the workshop for each questionnaire and the average of eight questions for each WS day are shown in Table 1.

Average Ow-Point
There was a significant effect for WS participation on all days where the mean Ow-point after the WS was higher than that of before.

DAY1: (before M = 4.74, SD = .93, after M = 5.47, SD = .63) t(18) = −4.67, p < .00,
DAY2: (before M = 5.00, SD = .76, after M = 5.33, SD = .58) t(17) = -2.63, p < .05,
DAY3: (before M = 5.02, SD = .93, after M = 5.53, SD = .80) t(16) = −3.78, p < .01,
DAY4: (before M = 5.06, SD = .95, after M = 5.54, SD = .77) t(17) = −3.00, p < .01.

Sense of Ownership on Issue

Participants in the latter days of WS, reported significant effects in questionnaire categories in a higher level of ownership (DAY3: Oq3, Oq4, and Oq5) than participants in earlier to mid-WS days (DAY1: Oq1, and Op3 and DAY 2: Oq2, Oq3, and Oq4). On DAY4 where participants discussed various issues in a world cafe style, and reported significant effects of participation in the mid-range sense of ownership questionnaires (DAY4: Oq3, and Oq4). (See Table 1).

Image of Issue and Awareness

Results indicated a significant effect of WS participation on Iq1, and Iq2 in DAY 1 and DAY 3 and on Iq1in DAY 4. On DAY 1 and 3 specificity both general and issues increased while only general image increased on issues on DAY 4.

Satisfaction.

The satisfaction of the workshop was high for each day regardless of participant attributes. Median of four days for all participants attributes were 6/7.

Table 1. Comparison of Sense of ownership before and after each workshop

	Workshop (n = number of subject)							
	DAY 1 (n=19)		DAY 2 (n=18)		DAY 3 (n=17)		DAY 4 (n=18)	
	before	after	before	after	before	after	before	after
AVERAGE Mean point (standard deviation)								
	4.74**	5.47**	5.00*	5.33*	5.02**	5.53**	5.06**	5.54**
	(.93)	(.63)	(.76)	(.58)	(.93)	(.80)	(.95)	(.77)
SENSE OF OWNERSHIP OF ISSUE Mean point (standard deviation)								
Oq1	5.53**	6.42**	5.89	5.94	5.88	6.00	5.53	5.89
	(1.68)	(.77)	(1.37)	(.94)	(1.32)	(.79)	(1.72)	(1.08)
Oq2	4.79	5.11	4.78*	5.22*	4.71	5.29	5.25	5.33
	(1.68)	(.99)	(1.63)	(1.22)	(1.72)	(1.49)	(1.35)	(1.72)
Oq3	5.21†	5.74†	5.17*	5.67*	5.47	5.88	5.28*	5.94*
	(1.26)	(1.15)	(.79)	(.69)	(1.37)	(.99)	(1.36)	(1.11)
Oq4	4.58	5.11	4.61*	5.17*	4.82*	5.29*	4.78†	5.33†
	(1.57)	(1.15)	(1.20)	(1.10)	(1.29)	(1.31)	(1.26)	(1.24)
Oq5	5.47	5.84	5.56	5.78	5.59**	6.06**	5.5	5.89
	(1.12)	(.83)	(1.10)	(.73)	(1.18)	(.90)	(.99)	(1.02)
IMAGE OF ISSUE AND AWARENESS Mean point (standard deviation)								
Iq1	3.21**	4.84**	4.28	4.44	3.71*	4.59*	4.33*	5.00*
	(1.75)	(1.08)	(1.07)	(1.04)	(1.26)	(1.18)	(.91)	(.97)
Iq2	3.58**	5.05**	4.33	4.50	4.41*	4.88*	4.50	5.00
	(1.68)	(.91)	(.84)	(.71)	(.94)	(1.17)	(1.25)	(.84)
Iq3	5.53	5.68	5.39	5.44	5.23	5.71	5.33	5.83
	(1.81)	(1.25)	(1.04)	(.98)	(1.10)	(.99)	(1.14)	(1.58)
p <.10†, p <.05 *, p <.01 **, p <.00 **								

In the interview, a majority reported that the WS helped the issues become their own as discussion topics became more specific [A01–02]. It also showed that discussing with various people increased participants' understanding and deepen the discussion [A03]. The results suggest that discussing specific topics helps participants focus on actions they can do while having various people discuss many topics may not only increase participants' understanding of the theme but also help the discussion to go deeper.

A01 From the second meeting, we started to think about what we can do, and our actions became more and more concrete, like how we can contribute to the food industry. I met various people… with a high level of awareness in this area. I also felt like I could do something myself. [Student 09.ws4].

A02 I feel that the content became more concrete from the third meeting. I feel that everyone started to think about what they could do practically, rather than just talking about the ideal future of food…. Then I would think about what I would do if it were me, and I began to think about what I could do. [Student07, ws4].

A03 (In Day four) I believe the mix of various people's ideas went in a good direction and I think my satisfaction was the highest… There were many topics and I could not see how it was connected… by seeing not only one but many tables I vaguely understand the relations to a common goal, I could think about it, get knowledge, and interact with many people, I could gain a bird's eye view and this deepened my thoughts. I think each topic was able to have a different discussion from before too and I think this was good for summarizing. [Student18, ws4].

3.2 Effect of Collecting and Use of Personal Data

Ow-Point

All participants were supervised to collect personal data. 7 participants brought data, 10 did not collect any data, and 2 donated data but did not participate in Day 3. We compared the before and after WS Ow-points of participants who collected data (n = 7) and who did not collect data but participated in the workshop (n = 10). Two-way ANOVA was performed to analyze the effect of collecting and using personal data and WS participation on the sense of ownership.

There was a significant main effect for WS participation, $F_{(1,15)} = 15.301$, p = .001, and a significant interaction, $F(1,15) = 7.167$, p < .05. The main effect of collecting personal data was not significant, $F(1,15) = 1.588$, p > .10. However simple main effects analysis showed a mean sense of ownership before WS was higher for participant who had collected personal data (M = 5.60, SD = 0.72) than for participants who did not collect any personal data (M = 4.69, SD = 0.94), $F(1,15) = 3.66$, p < .10. Therefore, we can assume that either data was collected by participant with a high sense of ownership or collecting personal data increase sense of ownership.

Using Data in Workshop

The interview report showed insights into data and a sense of ownership growth. It also showed that relevant personal data can cultivate inspiration [C01], can act as a catalyst for the discussion by revealing a common ground, and allows participants to move on to the next topic [C02]. It also suggested a possibility that data can affect the discussion without the participants knowing [C03]. We know that photos are effective tools to instantly increase, and refine image shared [C04–05]. It is important to show the connection between the data and the participant [C06].

C01 I was interested in the unexpected questionnaire answer that showed people are willing to share food with more than three people, … after discussion we came up with issues on sharing groceries, however, the questionnaire answer reinforced the merits of this idea. [student17, ws3].

C02: I rather think that sympathizing is more difficult to affect discussions. …I think sympathy is a factor that makes discussions go smoothly. … move on to the next. For example, if it was different we will discuss why that is different. [Expert01, ws3].

C03: (Did the statistical and personal data affect discussions on ideas?) Yes, with the social environmental data in mind, we could discuss based on the recognition that personal data is close to us. I think it's the part that is most difficult to realize but it affects us a lot … because things that we care about already we do not say opinion about it. (Did it affect the ideas discussed?) I think it does so strongly at a level where the speaker is not aware [Expert 01, ws3].

C04: When I saw just the picture, I honestly did not understand what it wanted to say. When it was explained, I understood deeply ….. I think having the photo explained by the one who took was strongly effective. [General working person 05, ws2].

C05: Then I saw the picture of the other team harvesting tomato, I was amazed because tomato is difficult to make. It gave inspiration that maybe there is a lack of realization of how difficult it is to make food in society [General working person 08, ws3].

C06 I think personal data will be effective in discussions. I am very interested in how one will consider and analyze the data he/she had collected in their life while discussing with one we know face to face vaguely imagining their lifestyles through two-hour discussions [Expert08.ws3].

3.3   Effect of Role on Ow-Point

Two-way ANOVA was performed to analyze the effect of being a table manager (5) or general participant (13) and WS participation on sense of ownership level in Day 4. There was a significant main effect of being a table owner, $F(1,16) = 6.19$, $p < .05$, indicating sense of ownership was higher for table owners (M = 5.96, SD = 0.31) than for participants (M = 5.05, SD = 0.19) throughout Day 4. There was also an effect of participation in WS for all regardless of participants.

Interview comment reported that table owners experienced effects of workshop surrounding activities. He felt the effect of before and after workshop questionnaires asking participants to answer their level of awareness of environmental issues.

D01 I felt that everyone naturally goes toward that way… I am not sure what it is, may be the before surveys imprint these keywords. Everyone cared about societal issues like it is common thing to do. [Expert 03, ws4, Table owner].

Therefore, we know two things. 1) participation in WS raises a sense of ownership significantly, and 2) WS activity affects the level of sense of ownership. Workshop that provided information about the present and future environment significantly increases the sense of the relation of the theme to oneself and strengthens the realistic image of the future. However, being provided information during the WS is insufficient to encourage a high-level sense of ownership where they are willing to make actions toward a realization. Discussing action plans to realize the ideal future, using personal visual and numerical data to evaluate their understanding of the issues, and reviewing their action plans help increase a high level of sense of ownership through the workshop.

4   Results 2: Effect of Attribute and Participating in Series

4.1   Workshop day on a Sense of Ownership

A one-way unpaired analysis of variance showed that the effect of which day participants came was not significant on Ow-point increase before and after the WS, $F(3,68) = 1.38$, $p = 0.258$. Therefore, participants equally experience an Ow-point increase as a result of WS participation is independent of the WS day.

4.2   Attribute and Participating in Series

A two-way unpaired analysis of variance was performed to analyze the effect of WS participation in series and participant attribute on Ow-point. We compared Ow-point of 21 participants who participated in more than two workshops at three points throughout the WS. Point 1: initial point before any workshop, Point 2: just after first workshop, and Point 3: just after participating last workshop. The participant number, means, and standard deviation for the 3×3 factorial design are presented in Table 2.

Table 2. Mean Ow-point and attribute (1 Very low, 7 Very high)

Attribute (number of participants)	Ow-point Mean (standard deviation)			
	Point 1	Point 2	Point 3	Attribute
1. Expert (5)	5.33 (.78)	5.85 (.47)	5.93 (.52)	5.70 (.26)
2. General worker (4)	5.47 (.62)	5.44 (.46)	5.56 (.41)	5.49 (.29)
3. Students (12)	4.45 (.78)	5.25 (.64)	5.53 (.86)	4.98 (.17)
Series participation	5.08 (.18)	5.51 (.14)	5.57 (.18)	

It revealed that there was not a statistically significant interaction between the effects of participation in series and attribute, $F(4,18) = 1.351$, $p = .27$. The main effect of series participation was significant, $F(2,18) = 5.48$, $p < .01$, and attribute was marginally significant, $F(2,18) = 3.21$, $p < .10$.

Attribute

Simple main effect analysis revealed that experts had a higher Ow–value than students at the .10 significance level. Also, Bonferroni's test for multiple comparisons showed that the increase of Ow-point through point1 to point 3 was significant for Students, $p < .01$. Interview results revealed that attribute had different motivation to participate hence different view on satisfaction. Experts experienced rich insights of their activity as well as connection of their activity to society [D01] and students focused more on what they could do [D03].

D01 I am strongly aware and interested in the system because it is necessary to change society in the end. Of course, as this is base, to be not too focused on logic, it is also very important that there is action. I participated with a wish to be able to enjoy with various generations in a good balance of action and system. I think we can know each other more to be close [Expert 08, ws3].

D02 I don't work hard on food issues and sped a rather lazy food style so I think there is a mental gap. Others whose daily activities are already solving issues said that they want to kaizen it, while I whom I don't work on it in daily life, talked about the minimum things that can be done.. [student 10, ws3].

Series Participation

Simple main effect analysis showed mean Ow-point at point 2 (after the first workshop) had a higher Ow-point than Point1 (before any workshop) at a .10 significance level and the mean Ow-point at point 3 (after more than one workshop) had a higher Ow-point than Point1, $p < .05$. The multiple comparisons found that the general worker had marginally significant higher Ow-point before the first workshop than students, $p < .10$.

Therefore, we can say that any single participation in the WS increase means Ow-point significantly, however, the mean increase after series participation increases even more significantly. Also, before the workshop, students had a lower Ow-point than general workers, and after the single WS participation, students' Ow-point increased at the level of general workers.

Interview results revealed that the series WS provided a sense of continuation [A01], and participants felt they understood the theme deeply and connected to the situation [A02–03]. While some felt less inspired working on the same topic. [A04].

A01 (between Days 1 to 2) I think there was a continuation of awareness of the importance of thinking about the theme that hadn't changed, maybe I thought more specifically about the ideas. … I feel more like it's continuing there, just as it was before. [Student10.ws2].

A02 I felt I could enter a little more easily when the topic is what I did before… when I joined a different group it took some time, in the beginning, to get used to it. [student 07, ws4, table owner].

A03 I think I get emotionally connected to the theme. In the second meeting, I was objectively thinking about the topic like how should it be. Eventually, I became more subjective, like eventually, the work had my mind… in the beginning, I was more objective 'how is it?' and it became more 'this seems good', more objective, connection to other members. [general working person, ws4].

A04 I think maybe at the last meeting I had more discoveries, we worked in the same group so maybe I had little to discover [student 10, ws3].

Action and Mindset Change

Participants were asked to report any new actions they took or mindset changes they had experienced related to the theme of the future of food through Days 1 to 4 periods (Table 3).

A total of 19 changes were reported and about 1/3 were related to the prevention of food loss in their households [EX1~6], and 1/3 were on the strengthening of awareness of factors related to food in general in their living [EX7~12]. Three experts reported on feed back to their work [EX15~17] and one reported on care of wellbeing [EX19].

Two third of the changes were reported in an interview after Day 4 showing the lasting effects of WS participation. Also, 1/3 were reported from students. S12 reported food loss preventive actions, and mindset change and also participated in food production showing that increased awareness leads to many related actions.

Therefore, series of workshops:

1. Participants remember past discussions and could build on top of it. This can help the discussion to become deeper,
2. Repeated participation in workshops not only helps cultivate a sense of ownership but all the other surrounding activities, including interviews, and before and after questionnaires help participants focus on the topic and encourage them to develop a sense of ownership.
3. Also, even though four WSs were not enough to make all the people perform on change of actions, it helped team members to build a connection to the theme acting as a reminder to make the ideas sink in.

Table 3. Action and mindset changes

EX1	I used to buy lots in supermarkets when food was cheap, I don't do this now and also eat what is left [student09.ws2]
EX2	I used to just throw it away that it's sad when it expires. But after I learned about food loss and other useful words, I don't make it go bad. [student12.ws3]
EX3	I try to use up the vegetables I bought, and eat what I made even if I have to do so repeatedly. I want to reduce buying convenience food when I have food I made. [tudent09, ws3]
EX4	I tend to buy food with lots and force myself to eat it all when forget about caring for environment, but I want to decrease food loss and have a plan in advance so I do not have to force myself to eat it. [student17, ws3]

(*continued*)

Table 3. (*continued*)

EX5	I care about food loss a little. I buy food in bunch because its cheap but put it where I see. It doesn't go away. [student15, ws4]
EX6	I cook more often. I remember what I have. When I shop for milk I think of what to use it for example cereal, French toast, milk tea… [student12, ws4]
EX7	I realized seasonal food is related to food loss, eating well, tastes good… I see what is seasonal food in farmer's shop. [student13, ws3]
EX8	I am aware of the very high price of expensive eggs made from chicken in good environment… When I begin earning money I may buy it. [student 16, ws4]
EX9	I realized that there was a share field close to where I live for the first time even though I was moved to the city five years ago. [student10, ws4]
EX10	I began to care more for my body hearing that everyone else care about the environment. I did not know before that soyfood which I thought used national soybean used soybean from abroad. The more times I participated the more I want to eat food that is good for my body. [expert03, ws4]
EX11	Now I feel very bad to through away food because I hear and know that we all share the same issue. [student12, ws4]
EX12	I talked about how reduced price product violate the brand of the product to students. But I just think lucky when I buy reduced price bread for my next meal on my way home. The photo student chose made me realize that I am doing something that is not good either. [expert06, ws4]
EX13	I began to be interested in oatmeal because is not expensive, high in nutrients and good for my body. I think it is inexpensive easy to buy and suit my lifestyle. [student09, ws2]
EX14	I tried cricket biscuit for the first time when the teacher told you can buy it in shops. It was good. [student 18, ws4]
EX15	My will to do something that it good for the society through my job strengthened. I say to my colleagues about what we could work on and I think they are beginning to be inspired. [expert06, ws2]
EX16	I think I have idea to do something as a company, even though my exact responsibility in not on food. [expert 01, ws4]
EX17	There was a discussion of what we could do as a company so I have a clear image on what to do. I think I can do it. [expert01, ws4]
EX18	Let's grow spice, I am aware that there is an empty land close to the station, I realized that it was used for vegetation from an early morning. [student12, ws4]
EX19	I think I am changing a little. I feel that I don't have to work too hard to take care of my family. I usually don't but I bought ready cut salad for meal. Maybe I don't have to always cook, and it makes me feel lighter. [general working people 04, ws4]

5   Discussion

Sense of ownership on the issue of experts was already high before workshop participation. There may have been a ceiling effect. They already had a high score and could not give higher points. Also, we know that Japanese participants do not give very high or very low points. An increase in sense of ownership may not have been quantitatively visible.

Through a series of participation, there may have been a qualitative change of sense of ownership that is qualitatively invisible because any new insights and change of actions, as it gradually sinks in, become part of the usual lifestyle and do not appear to be a change due to the workshop.

In workshops using social environmental statistical facts, one has to keep in mind that the provided data acts as a foundation of common awareness and the backbone of any further discussions. Discussions and ideas can be unconsciously affected by what is provided. The more common the information is to the participants, the more the effect may become invisible.

Also, from the studies, it was revealed that there is an effect of surrounding activities in the surrounding workshop have an impact.

It is not just what is provided in the workshop that affects participants, it is also questionnaires and half-structured interviews. Even though the interview questions were difficult to answer, in the end, they encouraged participants to make changes in actions.

6   Conclusion

The workshop on the theme of "Food of the Future" was held as part of the Living Lab, and the effects of statistics, video data, continuous participation, interviews, playing roles, awareness, behavior, and changes were examined.

Analysis of Ow-point before and after the workshop revealed the effect of workshop design on the cultivation of a sense of ownership. While the interview revealed the effect of workshop invisible qualitative, the results showed that participation at any point in time was effective in raising awareness of the importance of one's own life.

In addition, the results showed that participation in the WS more than once had a significant effect on the improvement of self-reliance. Research may benefit from both qualitative and quantitative approaches to understand the results.

Acknowledgement. This research was based on Future Living Labs at the Tokyo Institute of Technology. It was supported by the Laboratory for Design of Social Innovation and Global Network of the Tokyo Institute of Technology.

References

1. Pierce, J.L., O'Driscoll, M.P., Coghlan, A.M.: Work environment structure and psychological ownership: the mediating effects of control. J. Soc. Psychol. **144**(5), 507–534 (2004)
2. Hossain, M., Leminen, S., Westerlund, M.: A systematic review of living lab literature. J. Clean. Prod. **213**, 976–988 (2019)

3. Følstad, A.: Living labs for innovation and development of information and communication technology: a literature review. Electron. J. Virtual Organ. Netw. **10**, 99–131 (2008)
4. Akasaka, F., Kimura, A.: Living labs as a methodology for service design : analysis based on cases and discussion from the viewpoint of systems approach. J. Jpn. Soc. Kansei Eng. **15**(2), 87–92 (2017). (in Japanese)
5. Yasuoka, M.: Keys for CoDesign: living lab and participatory design. Serviceology **5**(3), 36–44 (2018). (in Japanese)
6. Nishio, K.: Research on the citizen participating co-creation in Japan on works in living labs. Fujitsu Research Institute Economics Research Laboratory Port 443 (2017). (in Japanese)
7. Colin, C., Martin, A., Bonneviot, F., Brangier, E: Unravelling future thinking: a valuable concept for prospective user research. Theor. Issues Ergon. Sci. (2021). https://doi.org/10.1080/1463922X.2021.1943045
8. Liem, A., Brangier, E.: Innovation and design approaches within prospective ergonomics. Work A J. Prev. Assess. Rehabil. **41**, 5243–5250 (2012)
9. Robert, J.M., Brangier, E.: Prospective ergonomics: origin, goal, and prospects. Work **2012**(41 Suppl 1), 5235–5242 (2012). https://doi.org/10.3233/WOR-2012-0012-5235. PMID: 22317531
10. Robert, J.M.., Brangier, E.: What is prospective ergonomics? A reflection and a position on the future of ergonomics. In: Karsh, BT. (ed.) EHAWC 2009. LNCS, vol. 5624, pp. 162–169. Springer, Heidelberg (2009). https://doi.org/10.1007/978-3-642-02731-4_19
11. Nelson, J., Buisine, S., Aoussat, A., Gazo, C.: Generating prospective scenarios of use in innovation projects. Le Travail Humain **77**, 21–38 (2014). https://doi.org/10.3917/th.771.0021
12. Tajima, R., Hirayama, N., Mori, T., Kawahata, T., Takata, M., Osako, M.: Effectiveness of workshop training method on development of intentions and attitudes towards disaster waste management preparedness action. J. Jpn. Soc. Nat. Disaster Sci. **34**, 99–110 (2015). (in Japanese)
13. Imoto, R., Senoo, M., Kozawa, K.: The study of awareness about global warming issues and environmentally concerned behaviors from a survey of elementary and junior high school teachers. J. Jpn. Soc. Home Econ. **52**(9), 827–837 (2001). (in Japanese)
14. Nakatani, M., Taoka, Y., Hamaguchi, N., Yasuoka, M., Miyata, T., Saito, S.: How can we achieve ownership to societal challenges?: through a workshop on food for the future. In: 191th Human Interface Society, Tokyo (2022)
15. Hayashi, Y., Stel, F.: Attitude research analysis of Students' towards SDGs in higher education. In: Proceedings of the Annual Conference of the Japan Society for Research Policy and Innovation Management 2019, Japan Society of Research Policy and Innovation Management, vol. 34, pp. 760–763. Japan Advanced Institute of Science and Technology (2019). (in Japanese)

Using Remote Workshops to Promote Collaborative Work in the Context of a UX Process Improvement

Arturo Moquillaza$^{(\boxtimes)}$ ⓘ, Fiorella Falconi ⓘ, Joel Aguirre ⓘ, Adrian Lecaros ⓘ, Alejandro Tapia ⓘ, and Freddy Paz ⓘ

Pontificia Universidad Católica del Perú, Av. Universitaria 1801, San Miguel, Lima 32, Lima, Peru

{amoquillaza,a.tapiat,fpaz}@pucp.pe, {ffalconit,aguirre.joel, adrian.lecaros}@pucp.edu.pe

Abstract. Based on the new collaborative work conditions and previous research, the need to establish a process of evaluation of the User Experience in its remote modality was evidenced. In this sense, it was considered to take an approach oriented to improving processes to elaborate a proposal. As part of the proposal, it was identified that it would be necessary to facilitate a workshop with the stakeholders involved in these processes to work collaboratively. As a case study, a virtual workshop was held with the stakeholders (UX research specialists, HCI specialists, UX designers, and Developers) to obtain feedback and pain points of the AS-IS process and proposed improvement opportunities for the TO-BE process. With the participation of 5 specialists, 19 improvements were identified for the tree testing process (8 improvements for the virtual process and 11 improvements for the face-to-face process) and 18 improvements for the face-to-face process of heuristic evaluation. Given their experience in evaluations and user experience design, the participants could prioritize the high-impact improvements for the evaluation processes analyzed. Because of the results achieved, the inputs to propose the TO-BE process, as well as the feedback received during the facilitation of the workshop, and as well at the end, the team can affirm that the whole objectives of the workshop were achieved. Besides, we can affirm that the facilitation of remote workshops allows for obtaining valuable information from key actors. Finally, we affirm as well that remote workshops allow collaboration and knowledge sharing between the participants, despite the limitations of distance, and their non-physical presence.

Keywords: Facilitation · Collaborative Work · Remote Workshop · User Experience · Process Improvement · Human-Computer Interaction

1 Introduction

The global pandemic and the government-mandated closures forced to change the performance of a lot of activities from on-site to home [1]. According to the research of Dingel and Neiman in 2020 [2], the occupations that have more activities that can be done from home are the following: Computer, education, and legal occupations, and in position number 5 we can find all the activities related to design.

With the rise of remote work and remote teams, industries are looking for ways to bring their teams together and foster collaboration in this context, remote workshops have become increasingly popular. This applies also to design workshops, where the use of digital tools such as video conferencing, and real-time collaboration platforms can help facilitate teamwork and problem-solving in a remote environment and can democratize the process [3]. Remote conduct of the workshops allows for the inclusion of participants who were previously inaccessible due to geographical limitations or inconvenience.

But there are also negative points that have to be dealt with and considered that can discourage remote workshops, such as those mentioned by Ritcher [4]: Synchronous communication, zoom fatigue, and participants having to make an additional effort to show engaged and available, because they are not in the same space.

Based on these new collaborative work conditions, the need to establish a comprehensive evaluation process of the User Experience in its remote modality was evidenced [14, 16]. In this sense, it was considered to take an approach oriented to improving processes to elaborate a new proposal in the context of a project. As part of said proposal experience, it was identified that it would be necessary to carry out a remote workshop with a variety of stakeholders involved in these processes, taking previous proposals such as AS-IS state as input and analyzing and processing their results to find insights and pain points, on which to elaborate the TO-BE state. To accomplish this goal, it is necessary for workshop participants and other relevant stakeholders to broaden their perspectives and be encouraged to explore how this can result in novel and innovative ideas that blend cultural shifts and technological advancements [5].

This paper is organized as follows: The first section presents the need to conduct a remote workshop in the context of a UX process improvement project. The second section presents a background of definitions with the main concepts developed in this research. The third section presents the proposal to carry out remote workshops, as well as the description of each proposed phase. The fourth section presents as a case study the implementation of the workshop under the previously detailed proposal, as well as the main findings of these sessions. Finally, the last section presents the conclusions reached by the work team, as well as future lines of work.

2 Background

This section defines the main concepts developed and discussed in this research.

2.1 Workshop

English dictionaries define a Workshop as a period of discussion or practical work on a particular topic in which a group compares their knowledge or experiences [6].

The workshops can be carried out on any subject, as mentioned in its definition. It is a tool used to generate new ideas in different fields, including user experience improvement.

In user experience and design activities, workshops can serve as great opportunities for engaging, learning, and democratizing processes [3].

2.2 Collaborative Work

The activities carried out by a work group that provides knowledge for the same purpose are considered collaborative work. As J. Tang [7] mentions, the needs of a work group to work collaboratively differ from the needs of a person who works alone, so for collaborative work, three moments are repeated cyclically in each of the members of a team: Observe, understand and be able to support. This can be observed in Fig. 1. With the advent of technology, many tools have been created to continue supporting this collaboration between teams working in different spaces.

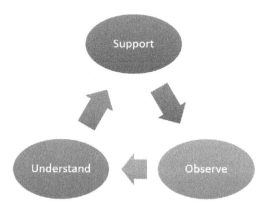

Fig. 1. Cyclical activities on collaborative work.

2.3 Remote Versus Virtual

In the industry, the term Remote is used indistinctly and interchangeably with the term Virtual. Still, defined differences make the cases in which we speak of remote more precise. Remote activities are carried out by participants from a place unrelated to their office. The most common location is the home, while virtual activities are carried out in office facilities in a controlled environment. Examples of these activities are teleconferences [8].

Following the above, in other contexts, such as education [9], "virtual" is emphasized as that which is not physical or face-to-face, and "remote" as that which is far away. In this sense, in the present research, it is considered that the challenge is to conduct remote workshops, that is, with everyone, with most of the participants in environments outside the workplace.

2.4 Facilitation

The book "The Skilled Facilitator Fieldbook" by Schwarz [10] mentions that facilitation skills can occur in any role in which a person interacts with other people, but specifically mentions that a facilitator is a neutral role that helps a group of people to have a practical and structured session.

The role of the facilitator is fundamental in the context of working sessions with different people, especially with different profiles. Facilitation has been defined as the opposite of leadership, in the sense that it is about empowering people to take control and responsibility for their own efforts [11].

2.5 Usability Evaluation Methods

Fernandez et al. define usability evaluation methods as "a procedure which is composed of a set of well-defined activities for collecting usage data related to end-user interaction with a software product and/or how the specific properties of this software product contribute to achieving a certain degree of usability" [12].

The list of usability evaluation methods is extensive; an example is heuristic evaluations, where a group of specialists judges and discuss software and if it complies with usability principles called heuristics [13, 14]. Another example is tree testing assessments, where the ability to find menu items is measured. Test results obtained from users are utilized to find usability and findability problems over the information architecture of the software under evaluation [15, 16].

3 Proposed Approach to Apply Remote Workshops

After reviewing various forms of facilitation, guidelines, and organization of workshops in the literature, especially with a remote approach [17–21], we proposed an approach of four phases: 1. Planning, 2. Execution, 3. Analysis, and finally, 4. Iteration as it could see in Fig. 2. These phases are detailed as follows.

Fig. 2. Approach for carrying out a remote workshop in four phases.

3.1 Planning

Once the need to hold a workshop to meet a specific need has been established, it is necessary to define who will conduct the workshop. In this sense, the flow starts by planning everything related to the event.

All inputs for the session or multiple sessions under consideration must be prepared in the first phase. In addition, the objectives, number of sessions, duration, identifying participants, selecting techniques, and considering all the necessary tools to carry out the following phases must be clearly established.

In this sense, each participant is selected and invited to the sessions, and they should be informed of the dates and objectives, as well as whether they should bring information to the sessions. It is also possible to have some previous sessions with certain participants to gather the information that will be presented later in the workshop sessions.

3.2 Execution

The second phase is the facilitation of the workshop, this is the actual execution. It is recommended that at least one pair of facilitators be considered to support and collaborate during all sessions.

All the resources, inputs, techniques, and tools previously prepared are used at that time. The general approach for the workshop is to present the guidelines and goals of the workshop to all the participants, and the information on the current situation (AS-IS), which is expected to be improved, and through the proposed techniques and tools, make it easier for participants to work collaboratively on said inputs and share and generate information that can be subsequently analyzed and processed. Typically, these sessions end with a self-assessment exercise on the facilitation and the work done.

3.3 Analysis

In the third phase, the team analyzes and processes the information obtained to find the most relevant insights, which serve as input to develop the desired situation (TO-BE).

The critical thing in this phase is to obtain relevant information as a product of the workshop, which should be focused on the objectives initially proposed to carry out the workshop. It is also important, if possible, to share the result of this analysis with the workshop participants as well, to make visible the results of the effort made during the working sessions in which they participated.

3.4 Iteration

In the fourth and final phase, the approach allows the iteration to improve the proposal, for example, to hold a new session to validate or obtain more feedback on the TO-BE proposal or to continue with the following stages of the process improvement being worked on.

4   Case Study

To obtain direct feedback from professionals who use heuristic evaluation and tree testing tools, we proposed to hold a virtual workshop to analyze the AS-IS process and identify improvement points to consider in a TO-BE process for the two evaluations.

4.1 Planning

The objective set for the workshop was as follows: Gather feedback, pain points, and improvement opportunities for elaborating the TO-BE process.

The stakeholders identified to participate in the session were the following:

- UX research specialists
- HCI specialists
- UX designers
- Developers

We chose tools to facilitate interaction between the participants since the workshop would be in a remote context. The chosen tools were the following:

- Google Slides, where elaborate the presentation with the workshop's content.
- Google meet, where the participants would connect to the workshop.
- Mural website, where build up the virtual boards of the session.
- Google sheets, which consolidate the results of the workshop.

The session duration would be 1.5 h, and each segment would last 10 min. The segment structure was as follows:

- Introduction
- Problem and objectives
- Presentation of the AS-IS of Tree testing.
- Improvement points for Tree Testing.
- Prioritization of improvement points for Tree testing
- Presentation of the AS-IS of Heuristic Evaluation.
- Improvement points for Heuristic evaluation.
- Prioritization of improvement points for heuristic evaluation.

The material mentioned above was created and configured before the workshop.

4.2 Execution

The workshop had the participation of 5 professionals already familiar with the Tree Testing and Heuristic Evaluation processes. We gave them access to the Mural board configured with the material for the session.

AS-IS Process

After a detailed review of each process, the participants identified improvement points and wrote them in the corresponding process section. In Fig. 3 we can see the pain points and opportunities discovered by participants in the Tree Testing process.

TO-BE Process

When the improvements proposed for each evaluation were already available, they were all consolidated on the board. A recap and deepening of each of them were carried out. After this, participants were asked to start voting based on which opportunities for improvement they considered would contribute the greatest to the TO-BE process of the evaluations. Figure 4 shows the results of the prioritization of Heuristic Evaluation improvements.

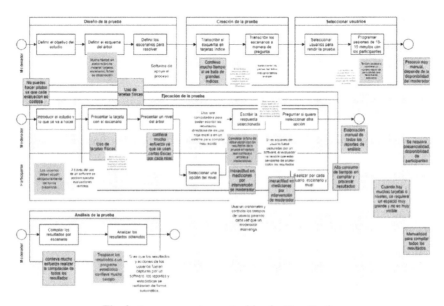

Fig. 3. Improvement opportunities for Tree Testing

4.3   Analysis

The improvement proposals ordered by priority were the following: Table 1 shows points for the Tree Testing process in a face-to-face way. Table 2 shows points for the Tree Testing process in a remote way. And Table 3 shows points for the Heuristic Evaluation process.

As feedback from those sessions, we pointed out that remote workshops can also be beneficial in promoting diversity and inclusivity. Removing geographical barriers can lead to more innovative solutions and perspectives for team members from different parts of the world.

Given their experience in evaluations and user experience design, the participants could identify and materialize high-impact improvements for the evaluation processes analyzed.

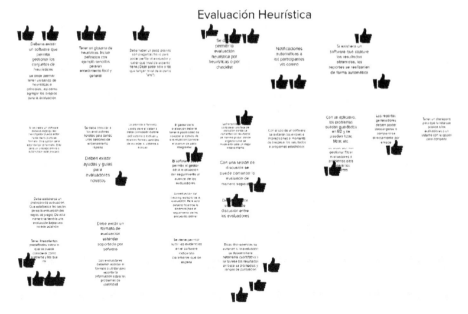

Fig. 4. Prioritization of heuristic evaluation improvements

Table 1. Improvement points for face-to-face tree testing

ID	Improvements	Votes
TTP001	There must be software to support the evaluation process remotely	3
TTP002	If the results and actions of the users were captured by software, the reports and statistics would be carried out automatically, and the evaluator would not have to be aware of recording the results	3
TTP003	The parts of the tree with the highest priority should be selected for evaluation	2
TTP004	A tablet could be taken with the cards and supported by some program or application; the user can only execute the task	0
TTP005	The face-to-face tree testing should be used according to the number of participants. That is, as long as it can be manageable. (Example max 20 cards)	0
TTP006	Use a computer to be able to write the results directly in an excel sheet or in a system to compile faster	0
TTP007	If a tablet is used with software that allows tasks to be executed, a screen recorder could be used, taking the time	0
TTP008	Use a stopwatch and control the user's times by stopping when a moderator intervenes	0

Table 2. Improvement points for remote tree testing

ID	Improvements	Votes
TTR001	The support application must allow multiple rounds of the same test	5
TTR002	The application must allow the management of questionnaires	3
TTR003	It should be allowed to modify the answers by some users "retake the test."	3
TTR004	There should be a process independent of the tool	2
TTR005	It would help to have a bank of predefined messages for reuse	2
TTR006	It must have a question bank for reuse	2
TTR007	There should be no limitation on the configuration of the end date and participants	2
TTR008	It should be possible to send reminders to participants who have not finished	2
TTR009	Other download options must be allowed	0
TTR010	The ways of access -login- to the evaluation must be simple to allow more types of user profiles	0
TTR011	The task limit should be much higher	0

Table 3. Improvement points for heuristic evaluation

ID	Improvements	Votes
EH001	An evaluation protocol should be developed. That establishes the guidelines for the evaluation (the game's rules). There should be predefined guidelines about what is considered a problem or not. In this way, there would be an evaluation under a standard view	4
EH002	Discrepancies between evaluators would be avoided if the evaluation could be carried out purely quantitatively, and the results would be based on averages and score ranges	3
EH003	Heuristic evaluation by heuristics or by checklist should be allowed	3
EH004	The tool must consider a discussion phase where the results are discussed as a group, where the manager serves as a moderator for a better understanding	3
EH005	Have a glossary of heuristics. Include definitions with simple examples for an easy and general understanding	2
EH006	Automatic notifications when a participant sees the mail	2
EH007	If there were a software that captures the results obtained, the reports would be made automatically	2

(*continued*)

Table 3. (*continued*)

ID	Improvements	Votes
EH008	There must be a previous step with filter questions to profile the evaluator and know their expertise level (Allow only those with a "high" level of expertise to pass)	1
EH009	Novice testers should be known to give them a few quick training sessions. Helps and guides novice evaluators	1
EH010	The software should allow the assessment manager to track the progress of the assessors	1
EH011	It must be allowed to manage/filter evaluators or problems to generate the reports	1
EH012	The generating reports must be able to be downloaded or shared directly by link	1
EH013	If software were to be created, it should allow the researcher to edit the format to some extent. Another option would be to standardize the format. This would be a process before automating this process	0
EH014	The software should support a standard evaluation format	0
EH015	Evidence must be allowed into the software, clearly indicating what is expected	0
EH016	The template or format used for the system must consider the details of the system to be evaluated and simple ways to access the system to be evaluated	0
EH017	Software errors and inaccuracies would be avoided when transferring the results to statistical programs	0
EH018	Have a SharePoint, so the list is public to the evaluators or a system with the option to share	0

Additionally, it is highlighted that having carried out the workshop virtually gave the possibility of working together to people who were not geographically in the same place.

4.4 Iteration

Finally, all this information was analyzed, processed, and utilized to propose the integral TO-BE User Experience Evaluation process, with an emphasis on remote attendance. That proposal continued its validation and implementation in the context of the project in progress.

5 Conclusions and Future Works

In conclusion, from previous research, we evidenced that an approach oriented to facilitate the implementation of remote design processes is necessary for this context where the COVID-19 pandemic forced us to change to remote workstations, known as home-office. During the development of the proposal, we noticed the necessity of conducting the new process in collaboration with all the stakeholders; hence, we designed, planned, and facilitated the workshop described in this paper using remote tools.

According to the literature, there were different ways of carrying out workshops; however, no detailed processes for the remote modality were reported. The definition of the 4 steps process we proposed in this paper faced different challenges (first of all, the lack of face-to-face interaction). This process was easy to understand and easy to execute for the participants, so no training was required.

From the case study where we held a remote workshop, we concluded that the face-to-face factor is not a barrier for this method to succeed. In contrast, a virtual workshop removes limitations such as different geographical locations. Virtualization of workshops may become necessary in a future where home-office becomes more adopted because carrying the sessions virtually allows the participants to collaborate effectively. However, due to the different geographical locations, setting dates and times for the sessions was the first barrier to surpass.

The virtual workshop could accomplish its objective. Despite not having face-to-face interaction, the participants could address enough pain points in both UX Evaluation processes presented as AS-IS (Tree Testing and Heuristic Evaluation). In addition, the remote workshop allows iteration, which was important in the case study where the participants found improvements to be done in the TO-BE proposal. This characteristic of being an iterative process allowed the participants to continue until satisfactory results were obtained.

The case study was an important first validation of the process, where the participants and stakeholders were satisfied with the results, the improvement points discovered, and the whole process itself. The remote approach also permitted an easy way of prioritizing the improvements found. The tools that were used were designed for remote collaborative work, supporting the process and the activities involved during the case study.

In future works, it is necessary to carry out more virtual workshops to validate the effectiveness of the Remote Workshop Approach through statistical analysis. In addition, we plan to incorporate this proposal as a tool for a bigger process or framework for designing and evaluating User Experience. Also, this process could be executed using different tools, as long as these tools support remote work (which is more common nowadays).

Acknowledgments. This work is part of the research project "Virtualización del proceso de evaluación de experiencia de usuario de productos de software para escenarios de no presencialidad" (virtualization of the user experience evaluation process of software products for non-presential scenarios), developed by HCI-DUXAIT research group. HCI-DUXAIT is a research group that belongs to the PUCP (Pontificia Universidad Católica del Perú). This work was funded by the Dirección de Fomento a la Investigación at the PUCP through grant 2021-C-0023.

References

1. Bick, A., Blandin, A., Mertens, K.: Work from home after the COVID-19 outbreak. Federal reserve bank of Dallas. Research Department. Working Paper 2017 (2020). https://doi.org/10.24149/wp2017r1

2. Dingel, J.I., Neiman, B.: How many jobs can be done at home? National Bureau of Economic Research. Working Paper 26948 (2020). https://doi.org/10.3386/w26948
3. Fesseden, T.: When Remote Workshops Fail. Nielsen Norman Group (2020). https://www.nngroup.com/articles/remote-workshop-fail/
4. Richter, A.: Locked-down digital work. Int. J. Inf. Manag. **55**, 102157 (2020). https://doi.org/10.1016/j.ijinfomgt.2020.102157
5. Quist, J., Knot, M., Young, W., Green, K., Vergragt, P.: Strategies towards sustainable households using stakeholder workshops and scenarios. Int. J. Sustain. Dev. **4**(1), 75 (2001). https://doi.org/10.1504/ijsd.2001.001547
6. Collins Dictionary: Workshop. Collins Dictionary Online (n.d.). https://www.collinsdictionary.com/us/dictionary/english/workshop
7. Tang, J.C.: Findings from observational studies of collaborative work. Int. J. Man Mach. Stud. **34**(2), 143–160 (1991). https://doi.org/10.1016/0020-7373(91)90039-a
8. Rome, J.: A Field Guide to Remote Workshops. Method (online) (n.d.). https://www.method.com/insights/field-guide-to-remote-workshops/
9. Chen, X., Song, G., Zhang, Y.: Virtual and remote laboratory development: a review. Earth Space (2010). https://doi.org/10.1061/41096(366)368
10. Schwarz, R.M.: The Skilled Facilitator Fieldbook: Tips, Tools, and Tested Methods for Consultants, Facilitators, Managers, Trainers, and Coaches, 1st edn. Jossey-Bass, San Francisco (2005). ISBN: 978-0-7879-6494-8
11. Bentley, T.: Facilitation: providing opportunities for learning. J. Eur. Ind. Train. **18**(5), 8–22 (1994). https://doi.org/10.1108/03090599410058953
12. Fernandez, A., Insfran, E., Abrahão, S.: Usability evaluation methods for the web: a systematic mapping study. Inf. Softw. Technol. **53**(8), 789–817 (2011). https://doi.org/10.1016/j.infsof.2011.02.007
13. Paz, F., Pow-Sang, J.A.: A systematic mapping review of usability evaluation methods for software development process. IJSEIA **10**, 165–178 (2016). https://doi.org/10.14257/ijseia.2016.10.1.16
14. Lecaros, A., Moquillaza, A., Falconi, F., Aguirre, J., Tapia, A., Paz, F.: Selection and modeling of a formal heuristic evaluation process through comparative analysis. In: Soares, M.M., Rosenzweig, E., Marcus, A. (eds.) HCII 2022. LNCS, vol. 13321, pp. 28–46. Springer, Cham (2022). https://doi.org/10.1007/978-3-031-05897-4_3
15. Arslan, H., Yüksek, A.G., Elyakan, M.L., Canay, Ö.: Usability and quality tests in software products to oriented of user experience. Online J. Qual. High. Educ. **5**, 79 (2018)
16. Tapia, A., Moquillaza, A., Aguirre, J., Falconi, F., Lecaros, A., Paz, F.: A process to support the remote tree testing technique for evaluating the information architecture of user interfaces in software projects. In: Soares, M.M., Rosenzweig, E., Marcus, A. (eds.) HCII 2022. LNCS, vol. 13321, pp. 75–92. Springer, Cham (2022). https://doi.org/10.1007/978-3-031-05897-4_6
17. Johnson, G., Prashantham, S., Floyd, S.W., Bourque, N.: The ritualization of strategy workshops. Organ. Stud. **31**, 1589–1618 (2010). https://doi.org/10.1177/0170840610376146
18. Bowman, C.: Strategy workshops and top-team commitment to strategic change. J. Manag. Psychol. **10**, 4–12 (1995). https://doi.org/10.1108/02683949510100732
19. Yarmand, M., Chen, C., Gasques, D., Murphy, J.D., Weibel, N.: Facilitating remote design thinking workshops in healthcare: the case of contouring in radiation oncology. In: Extended Abstracts of the 2021 CHI Conference on Human Factors in Computing Systems, Yokohama Japan, pp. 1–5. ACM (2021). https://doi.org/10.1145/3411763.3443445

20. Pham, Y.D., Fucci, D., Maalej, W.: A first implementation of a design thinking workshop during a mobile app development course project. In: Proceedings of the 2nd International Workshop on Software Engineering Education for Millennials, Gothenburg Sweden, pp. 56–63. ACM (2018). https://doi.org/10.1145/3194779.3194785
21. Martin, J., Loke, L., Grace, K.: Challenges facing movement research in the time of Covid-19: issues in redesigning workshops for remote participation and data collection. In: 32nd Australian Conference on Human-Computer Interaction, Sydney, NSW, Australia, pp. 712–716. ACM (2020). https://doi.org/10.1145/3441000.3441055

A Design Driven Approach to Innovate System Interfaces: Insights from a University-Industry Collaboration

Stefania Palmieri⬭, Mario Bisson⬭, Riccardo Palomba(✉), Alessandro Ianniello⬭, and Giuseppe Rubino

Politecnico di Milano, 20158 Milan, MI, Italy
{stefania.palmieri,mario.bisson,riccardo.palomba,
alessandro.ianniello}@polimi.it, giuseppe.rubino@polimi.t

Abstract. The user interface influences the objects and subjects on which our actions focus during the application of the artifact. The field that deals with improving the usability of digital interfaces is known as UX/UI Design (User Experience/User Interaction); many organizations or entities are focusing on this field in order to be able to "dialogue" with an increasingly broad target audience. This paper stems from a research carried out within the Interdepartmental Laboratory EDME (Environmental Design Multisensory Experience) which, in collaboration with a company in the home automation sector, sets as a goal the unprecedented design of an indoor video intercom, setting as target both the installer and the end user. The process followed involves research phases for objectivity of choices, and design development phases; as for research, it is divided into desk research, survey and testing activities in which end users are involved for direct acquisition of usage data. The objective of the paper is to demonstrate how a joint University/business research process enables innovation processes both in terms of human relations and in terms of business dimensions for the company, in line with market demands. In this context, the figure of the designer and, more generally, design-driven operations, help define a development model that overlaps and intersects with the technological one, replicable in different business and networking contexts.

Keywords: Search design · Heuristics · Design Thinking · university-industry collaboration · UX/UI Design

1 Introduction

The digital transformation that has been - and is being - experienced with the development of Industry 4.0 has brought many decisive innovations to the ever-changing everyday life, seeking practical and efficient solutions that facilitate the use of new services and/or technological devices. The digital age has encouraged the use of alternative communication platforms that are used as a means of information, but also as a means of bringing the company closer to its customers. The point of contact between any artefact (digital or

A. Marcus et al. (Eds.): HCII 2023, LNCS 14030, pp. 267–284, 2023.
https://doi.org/10.1007/978-3-031-35699-5_20

otherwise) and the user is called the 'user interface' and significantly influences the user experience of the service offered. In this sense, it is important to achieve what Thesen and Beringer refer to as 'ease of use', i.e. the combination of several factors such as software/hardware design, instruction and the user's background at the time of dialogue [1]. The subject of usability is, for the reasons stated, a highly topical issue and is understandably the subject of debates and definitions; there are also various standards that define principles, criteria, constraints, etc.: everything converges towards approaches and guidelines that design must take on board, interpret and manage in order to design effectively and on a human scale. For example, the ISO-9241-11 standard [2] defines usability as "the extent to which a product can be used by specific users to achieve specific goals with effectiveness, efficiency and satisfaction in a specific context of use", and in this sense the interface represents the point at which actions are concentrated during the use of an artefact, influencing objects and subjects in a decisive way. This is why, in recent years, the discipline of improving the usability of digital interfaces has developed more and more, this is known as UX/UI Design (User Experience/User Interaction).

Therefore, the user interface plays such a fundamental role that it can convey the very identity of a company, which, in this way, presents itself to the public. Indeed, markets and companies are attributing new value, including cultural value, to these forms of interaction in order to be able to 'dialogue' with an increasingly broader target, speaking an appropriate language that shares values and meanings that are important to the user.

Today, the digital interface is therefore an essential element in the design of a product system, as any artefact is accompanied by a service, normally delivered through digital devices or apps. Therefore, there is an increasing demand for new ways to connect products, users and their surroundings, creating meaningful experiences that bring added value to the service offered. With this in mind, it is essential that actions are simple and immediate, limiting the possibility of error and clearly showing the paths to follow when using the interface. The strategic value of correct interface design is also supported by a survey by McKinsey [3], which shows that a company that focuses on its identity and user touchpoints, implementing design and designing for the human being, will have significantly higher turnover than any other company in the sector. Therefore, it is crucial to consider the digital interface itself a product system, dealing with the complexity of a holistic design that takes into account the market, the environment and, above all, the user, and that offers a meaningful experience by bringing added value during the use of the service/product; market data states that 40% of people who experience a bad UX turn to the competition, and at the same time many products are successful because they offer excellent experiences [4].

Furthermore, the expansion of the sphere of use of information technology places a number of new requirements on the user interface, not only to solve professional problems, but also to meet a person's information, entertainment and communication needs. In addition to standard usability criteria, a modern interface should focus on aesthetic appeal, motivational appeal for the user and thus be based on the holistic, 'user-like' experience. In general, User Experience is the perception and response of a user resulting from the use of a product, system or service [5]. It is a complex process involving analysis and design phases, through loosely formalised procedures such as surveys, user work monitoring, performance testing and analysis of activity logs, focus groups, interviews [6].

2 Academic Research and Professional Approach: Co-creation and Innovation

The rapid development of technology linked to contexts involving design as a design approach has drawn attention to the cooperation between SMEs and academic institutions. Different approaches and languages open up new avenues for innovation and technology transfer, which undoubtedly increasingly represent one of the levers for competing in global markets and become accessible in a 'network' logic.

Presented here is the design process resulting from a collaboration between university and enterprise, conducted within the Interdepartmental Laboratory EDME (Environmental Design Multisensory Experience) - belonging to the Design Department of the Politecnico di Milano - with Comelit S.p.A. - a private company in the home automation sector. The research, through the design of a new intercom device, lays the foundations for the genesis of a strategic design project, aimed at the definition of guidelines for the review and design of existing and future company products. Starting from the analysis of the company's current ecosystem and catalogue products, certain invariant elements have been defined that can create a family feeling with the aim of giving strength and credibility to new products that will be placed on the market in the near future.

This can be achieved through the academic approach to pre-competitive research and the company's active participation in co-design dynamics, with the aim of creating futuristic scenarios to guide the design process.

This approach complements or follows Basic Research, which is the activity that aims to expand scientific and technical knowledge not immediately linked to industrial or commercial objectives and is usually the preserve of large organisations only. With a view to networking and value co-creation, the university-business relationship becomes a pioneer of new avenues towards innovation and development, and this allows the academic team to create awareness and co-participation on the project's progress, objectivising the choices and highlighting the strategic areas on which to operate. In this way, the company opens up to design issues, adopting innovative methodologies in product making and creating a direct dialogue with its target audience.

This collaboration mechanism allows the company to discover new themes and design cues that can improve its product system and the university to innovate by applying research and analysing the results directly in the professional field [7]: it is a novel approach to networking, which activates new relationships and creates value in a new way for all the partners involved.

The project, developed by the Politecnico team, aims at a sustainable innovation for the company that satisfies the public with the main focus precisely on usability and its meaning. The contribution of design determines from the preliminary stages a strong inclination towards the user's needs through user tests that have been designed ad hoc and carried out in the academic field.

Design, due to its multidisciplinary and transversal nature, is a candidate to play a mediating role, i.e. it becomes the possible strategic connector, the bridge between companies and academia, with the aim of activating and making research accessible also to those productive realities that would otherwise have structural limits, intrinsic to their small size, to make innovation: design, therefore, as an activator and manager of common networking actions, a driver also of the internationalisation of the local industrial system, is called upon to operate on a very high technological scale.

The project, developed by the Politecnico team, aims at a sustainable innovation for the company that satisfies the public with the main focus precisely on usability and its meaning. The contribution of design determines from the preliminary stages a strong inclination towards the user's needs through user tests that have been designed ad hoc and carried out in the academic field.

Design, due to its multidisciplinary and transversal nature, is a candidate to play a mediating role, that is, it becomes the possible strategic connector, the bridge between companies and academia, with the aim of activating and making research accessible also to those productive realities that would otherwise have structural limits, intrinsic to their small size, to make innovation: design, therefore, as an activator and manager of common networking actions, a driver also of the internationalisation of the local industrial system, is called upon to operate on a very high technological scale (Fig. 1).

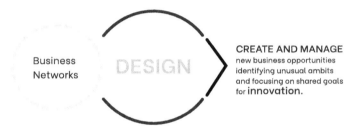

Fig. 1. Design as catalyst for innovation.

3   Design as an Activator of New Multidisciplinary Relations

The research verifies how the figure of the designer and, more generally, design-driven operations, can contribute to defining a development model based on the use of shared technological platforms. Through workshops and co-design activities, design brings innovation into business processes, involving and bringing into dialogue different disciplines, with the aim of maximising the efficiency of the design of strategies or artefacts. The construction of common visions is of paramount importance, seeking to shape innovative usage scenarios capable of significantly modifying different application domains. It is also the designer's task to try to emphasise the transversality and horizontality of his or her discipline: these characteristics make the professional figure adept at managing design complexity and the multidisciplinary integration of knowledge [8].

During design, designers followed two separate objectives that can be distinguished into a long-term and a short-term one. The first focuses on bringing innovation into the company by demonstrating new design processes and identifying new possible users who had not been considered before; in this way, more direct relationships are established in order to receive valuable feedback for the development of new products and strategies. The second - short-term - objective focuses on the design of a digital interface for one of the company's products: a next-generation video door phone. In this case, the research focused on how best to represent the functions, identifying hierarchies and a language understandable to several types of users. Starting from an analysis of the state of the art, the designers reconstructed the digital structure by reorganising the contents and activities to make the user experience fluid, immediate and comprehensible. The final objective is to synthesise the research (the canons, definitions, trends, etc.) into a graphic and functional prototype, which serves as a guide for subsequent implementation in apps by developers.

4   Design Methodology

From the perspective of designing a technological product, it is relevant to investigate the peculiarities and dynamics of the UX and UI of related and unrelated products. This analytical process makes it possible to frame and at the same time delineate the design perimeter within which to operate. The current and futuristic trends that were highlighted during the research represent a key element in the realisation of a product that responds in a simple and intuitive manner to user needs. To achieve this, it is important to adopt innovative problem-solving processes capable of providing simple and human-friendly solutions, which can be part of the approach called 'Design Thinking'. In this perspective, Design Thinking assumes a relevant role as an analytical and creative process [9] that enables innovative design responses, through a more flexible and inclusive thinking and approach to design. As reported by Gonen [10], it is a human, creative, iterative and practical approach to finding meaningful ideas and solutions with innovative activities; this approach has proven to be an effective strategy for organisational change in many companies.

The project was carried out through four project phases, during which various elements were analysed with the aim of redesigning the system to facilitate its use. At the end of each phase, an official, strategic meeting was organised with the company to discuss advancements and obtain new input and consensus to proceed in an aligned manner; the dialogue was continuous, and interaction took place during all steps, through short, operational meetings with targeted topics and attended by certain elements of the teams according to the pre-established agenda. During the general alignment meetings (at the end of each step), targeted workshops or activities were held in which the team could express their thoughts on the progress of the project, tools of fundamental importance for the success of the final product.

The project methodology mainly followed two research phases, a scenario building phase and a prototyping phase for the final proposal.

More specifically, during the preliminary phase, an internal and external analysis was carried out to understand the company's identity and vision, followed by research on competitors and opportunities in the target market; in addition, the state of the art of the existing product was analysed through a heuristic evaluation and a survey in which users could give feedback useful for the subsequent design. Subsequently, the second phase focuses on researching present and future market trends, user preferences and interests through an in-depth study of the target audience. This phase made it possible to synthesise user trends and needs into a design scenario, in which the design is hypothesised in one or more specific contexts. Each element that emerged from the previous phases allowed the creation of various design scenarios that led to the design construction phase, in which the research is synthesised and the structure that will support the entire design implementation is built: colours, icons, graphics, language and information architecture. This is followed by the prototyping of the interface and the formal proposal of the system produced (Fig. 2).

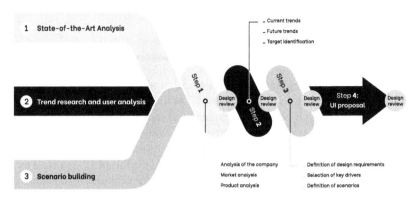

Fig. 2. Summary of research methodology.

5   Step 1: Analysis of the State of the Art

During the first phase, it was necessary for the designer to understand who his interlocutor (customer) was. With this in mind, the research aimed to define the company's brand identity, the market it covers and how it is positioned in relation to its competitors, and finally, the analysis of the product portfolio. During the brand identity analysis, the researchers' focus is on how the company addresses the market, what its values are and how it communicates them, analysing the tone of voice and proximity to the user. At this stage, it was appropriate to analyse reports or surveys previously carried out by the company itself, or to organise new ones. However, the focus is not only outward-looking, in fact an attempt is made to understand the internal hierarchical structures and the degree of employee satisfaction - starting from the dialogue with the team with which one interfaces during the project - with the aim of defining the most appropriate approach to align with the corporate image.

Once the corporate identity has been explored and mapped, we move on to the analysis of the product portfolio, starting with a division into generic clusters that group the different categories of products presented on the market by the company. On the basis of the differentiation of the offer, it is decided whether to analyse the entire company portfolio or to verticalise on a specific type of product. In this case, the focus was on video door phones, analysing their shape, the type of interaction with the user, the perceived degree of technology and the levels of feedback returned by the different interfaces. This resulted in 6 different categories of video door phones, from the simplest and cheapest to the most complex (in terms of technology) and expensive.

The research team then studied the target market based on geographical positioning, identifying the best-selling products, the areas of greatest interest and the distribution and sales channels. At this stage, the main competitors were identified and compared against objectively determined parameters.

The parameters that were identified for the research are as follows:

- Catalogue size: the number of video door phones in the catalogue;
- Morphological diversification: the aesthetic and morphological variety of the company's offer of video door phones (e.g. with or without handset, with or without buttons, …);
- Global coverage: the number of locations located globally;
- Offer differentiation: the company's variety of offerings (e.g. video door phones, security systems, home automation, …);
- Service oriented: the presence of the service side in the company's DNA;
- Training courses: the quantity of offers for training courses and certificates as a professional figure.

The purpose of the analysis is to position the company among its competitors in one or more matrices that clearly identify more saturated market segments and less explored segments, which potentially represent possible directions in which the company should turn its attention. These 'less crowded' areas are referred to as the 'Blue Ocean' [11] and denote a slice of the market where demand is created rather than fought for and there is ample opportunity for growth that is both profitable and rapid. Competition is irrelevant because the rules of the game are waiting to be established (Fig. 3).

The analysis of the brand identity, the synthesis of the product portfolio and the identification of the target market are fundamental steps in order to best direct the design process. This phase is also very important for the company, which is analysed by a group of external professionals and, depending on the feedback, can understand whether its image and market performance are in line with its declared values and mission.

5.1 Heuristic Evaluation Test

Once this first part has been defined, phase 01 continues with the in-depth analysis of the product for which the interface is to be redesigned: the video door phone. With this in mind, the information architecture is initially studied, going on to create a diagram that makes explicit, in a clear and complete manner, the levels of complexity of the flow and the groupings of the main functions. In the case presented, the information architecture was considered very complex and difficult to navigate by an end user; for this reason, a usability test (Heuristic evaluation) was organised that could - as objectively as possible - define the system's significant criticalities.

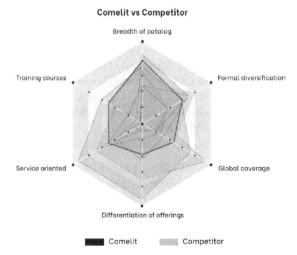

Fig. 3. Summary of the research methodology The radar graph shows the possibility of improving the offer from a service point of view, implementing a service-oriented approach and differentiating the offer by creating proposals for a family of products, different but in communication with each other.

The Heuristic evaluation is an in-depth assessment of the user interface of a product, conducted by a team of evaluators, which is based on the 10 principles of Nielsen-Molich [12].

1. Visibility of the system state;
2. Correspondence between the system and the real world;
3. User control and freedom;
4. Consistency and standards;
5. Error prevention;
6. Acknowledgement rather than recall;
7. Flexibility and efficiency of use;
8. Aesthetics and minimalist design;
9. Helping users recognise, diagnose and recover from errors;
10. Help and documentation.

Its purpose is to detect usability problems and identify ways to solve them. It is characterised by an initial process in which the expert evaluator experiences, in first person, the experience of using the product, and then subsequently detaches himself from subjective judgement in order to assimilate the experience as objectively as possible; he then compares the 10 Nielsen-Molich principles with his own experience of interaction and draws qualitative tasks from them that he will subsequently submit to the users participating in the test.

In the case presented, the Tasks generated by this process were classified into four groups:

1. Basic functionality: Task to answer the video intercom and open the door. It is the same for all, which allows more data to be obtained on the basic use of the product.

2. Keypad functionality: secondary activities to automatically manage certain every-day situations (e.g. automatic opening, sending notifications, etc.). It focuses on the recognition of icons in the keyboard in relation to their functionality.
3. Menu functionality: activities that can be performed by navigating the system at a low level.
4. Setup menu functionality: activities that can be set by navigating into deeper levels of the menu, managing different functions in the device settings. It is structured with three questions of progressive difficulty that assess the parameters of "Correspondence between the system and the real world" and "Flexibility & Efficiency".

The Tasks are, however, a part of the survey that was structured in 3 phases, in which 26 testers participated, including men and women of different ages (late Millennials and Generation Zeta) and with different qualifications (undergraduate or graduate in Product Design, Interior Design, Interaction Design, Design Engineering, Design Integrated). The profile chosen for this analysis is of young designers who are predisposed and trained in curiosity, creativity and attention to detail. This means that the activities performed by them during the test, guided by questions posed ad hoc, are extremely significant and bearers of important considerations for the possible future development of the analysed system (Fig. 4).

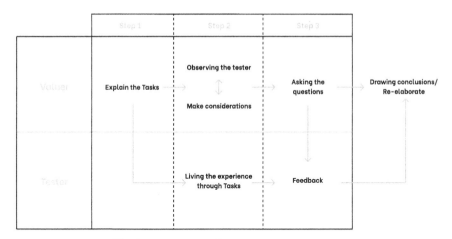

Fig. 4. Methodology followed during the survey.

Initially, the structure and timing of the subsequent phases were clarified; in the second phase, the testers were divided into 4 groups, each with 4 tasks to be carried out in a maximum of 4 min (1 min. Per task), the time taken to recognise and activate the buttons of the respective tasks was timed and any errors in use on the part of the tester were recorded; the last phase subjects the tester to a questionnaire structured in two blocks of questions: 4 closed questions assessed according to the Likert Scale [13] and 3 open-ended questions.

The results of the tasks were relatively negative, with a large percentage of users failing to complete the setup menu tasks, and many having difficulty with even the simplest tasks of the first two (Fig. 5).

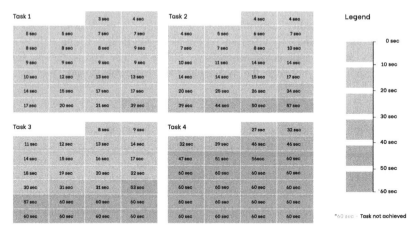

Fig. 5. Mapping the variable 'time' for task completion.

As for the results of the survey, they were summarised in a table showing the main issues in which users found difficulties. By cross-referencing the open and closed answers, a score was given relating to the number of people who mentioned one or more functions in which there were difficulties (Fig. 6).

Sample of 26 people

20	Settings
15	Scroll
14	Unintelligible icons
13	Too many commands
10	Lack of hierarchy
8	Unintelligible names
5	Distinction between menus
5	Call response
5	Feedback
4	Privacy/doctor button

Fig. 6. Summary of the main items in which the testers found difficulties during the survey (from the most complicated to the least problematic).

The survey is therefore a powerful tool for verification and exploration, supporting an applied research phase. The results must always be understood as qualitative and not quantitative and were then processed to activate a design process around the criticalities detected.

This activity led to an understanding of the current state of the digital service expressed by the video intercom, and, by defining the degree of complexity that characterises it, to identify the areas susceptible to improvement.

The following emerged from the tests (Fig. 7):

#1: Visibility of system status	The system, with regard to commands, is sufficient for the main ones (door opener and phonic), while for secondary commands the situation becomes more complicated by reducing the visibility value of system status;
#2: Match between system and the real world	The perceptual components-the words used, the icons the colors, and the feedback-are poorly correlated with the real world except with regard to the iconic components of the main commands;
#3: User control and freedom	The system does not allow much freedom to the end user since the interface is not based on an intuitive mode of paths but on a mode that must be memorized;
#4: Consistency and standards	The system is consistent with a current trend resting on similar technologies and interfaces (small and large appliances, automotive, etc.);
#5: Error prevention	There are no elements that would hint at possible error (e.g., color change in case of misspelling, which would lead to avoidance of a sense of disorientation on the part of the user);
#6: Recognition rather than recall	The level of memorization required for user operation of the interface remains high;
#7: Flexibility and efficiency of use	Some functions appear to have too many diversification options so much so as to confuse the user;
#8: Aesthetic and minimalist design	Morphologically well-structured, but excessively minimalist: consequently unrecognizable and lacking semantic identity (innovation of meaning);
#9: Help users recognize, diagnose, and recover from errors	Error indications are detected but no solutions are suggested;
#10: Help and documentation	Both digital and paper aids are good support for installers, dedicated end-user aids are basically paper-based and structured for technicians.

Fig. 7. Survey results compared with the 10 Nielsen-Molich principles.

6 Step 2: Trend Research and User Analysis

The data collected during the previous phases made it possible to better delineate which factors and processes are inherent in the use of devices with interfaces. With this in mind, a search was conducted for interfaces belonging to different product ranges on the market.

In order to best categorise the product characteristics, six polarities were defined with the aim of defining the most common elements of digital interfaces.

- Information architecture [14]: Depth and complexity of the system. A clear AI facilitates the user in the usability of the interface. A high score expresses greater complexity and depth of the system.
- Hick's Law [15]: States that if there is an overabundance of choices, the user will take longer to reach a decision. The ideal number of options for a screen is a maximum of 6 choices. A high score corresponds to a good visual organisation of the interface.

- Von Restorff effect [16]: Claims that graphically highlighting the main buttons provides immediate distinction. In an interface, hierarchy is fundamental for the user to identify the actions to be performed. A high score indicates the presence of highlighting of the main functions.
- Words - Amount of words used in the main screen of the interface. A high score indicates an overabundance of words in the interface home screen.
- Pictograms - Amount of pictograms used in the main screen of the interface. A high score indicates an overabundance of pictograms on the interface home screen.
- Feedback: Used by the system to engage or notify the user of a certain action. It can be characterised by sound, visual or tactile outputs. A high score indicates the presence and effectiveness of feedback received by the user during interaction.

Cross-referencing the various products with the analytical parameters defined above showed that most interfaces rely on the use of a well-defined, simple and intuitive graphical and structural design of the system for the user. Indeed, as described above, the system must have a high level of recognisability and clarity of use. However, in many cases this ease is only effective for certain user groups, which makes the system produced unsuitable for a wider public.

In this context, the analysis of current and future trends affecting these product categories becomes relevant. The analytical phase makes it possible to identify the factors that make the product avant-garde and at the same time usable by several categories of users.

The role of design, after all, is to allow products and services to be used by the widest possible range of subjects, promoting design for the real individual, which is inclusive and holistic, enhancing the specificities of everyone and involving human diversity in the design process. With this in mind, five user categories were analysed from different perspectives. During the analytical phase of generational profiling, the following audience groups were identified:

The Silent Generation consists of people born between 1925 and 1945. This category of users approached digital in order to stimulate social relations, not to feel lonely, and to get closer to the life habits of their children and grandchildren in order to 'speak' their language. The Silent Generation is not a representative sample among web users, yet it should be considered in communication actions and online campaigns, especially for certain markets of their interest...

The Baby Boomer Generation consists of those born between 1946 and 1964. The Boom Generation is almost completely absent from social plus, where instead the presence of Millennials is exploding. This category of users is very interested in brands and advertising messages, so it is a generation that should absolutely be considered in web marketing strategies, also because it is the one with the highest purchasing power compared to the others.

Generation X consists of people born between 1965 and 1979.

A study by Nielsen showed that Generation X people spend more time than others on social and other digital devices.

Generation Y consists of people born between 1980 and 1994.

Millennials love social media and use them to learn about current trends. They are people who are familiar with the mechanisms of communication and promotions, so they pay special attention to the message, only if it is truly appealing. More than half of Millennials use smartphones to connect online, so they pay more attention than others to short, creative communications. People of this generation are used to using more than one means of communication at a time. Therefore, it is necessary to curate communication with respect to their preferences.

Generation Z consists of people born between 1995 and 2012.

They were born among smartphones, tablets and touch screens, but unlike the 'millennials', who joined later, members of Generation Z discovered the product instructions without anyone teaching them. It is hard to imagine, then, that any daily action of these very young people does not pass through technology.

Once the characteristics and needs of the users were defined, the world and continental population density divided by user category was analysed. This step made it possible to highlight which markets can be exploited in terms of audience, opening up new project scenarios.

The previous steps provided a clear picture of the geographic areas and population density related to the five user groups. With this in mind, research was carried out with the aim of defining and graphically translating the relationship between generations and digital devices.

This process, on the one hand, delineated the user categories to which the produced system should be addressed, with the aim of identifying and categorising the target group for an inclusive and accessible design by a certain variety of users, and on the other hand, facilitated the process of generating design scenarios (Fig. 8).

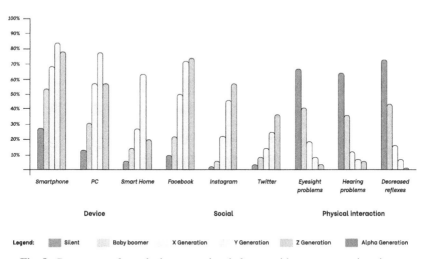

Fig. 8. Percentage of people, by generational cluster, with respect to a given input.

7 Step 3: Scenario Building and User Analysis

Scenario building is a fundamental step in the design process. It is a powerful tool for exploration, synthesis and communication, particularly useful in the phase preceding interface development and implementation.

Scenario building is used by organisations and institutions to help understand futures, expand imagination and raise awareness of changes in the business environment. The scenario planning process can help manage uncertainties in an increasingly dynamic environment, especially if they are perceived as plausible [17].

This phase therefore represents a key moment for the project: given the relevant case studies, trends and users, design requirements are defined that will constitute the project drivers and that may, depending on the situation and the different scenarios, assume different importance, falling into different hierarchies of valorisation.

In the case presented, the design requirements were categorised by semantic affinity into four drivers: identity, user, context and feedback.

- Identity: this driver refers to the analogue & digital identity that characterises the interface and indicates the recognisability of the interface with respect to a 'family' of products.
- User: this driver refers to the ease of use of the interface with respect to the user base, defining an interface adaptable to the various generations of users.
- Context: this driver refers to the context of use of the video door phone and reflects a greater adaptation to the characteristics of various contexts of use.
- Feedback: This driver refers to the feedback levels of the system (sight, touch, hearing) (Fig. 9).

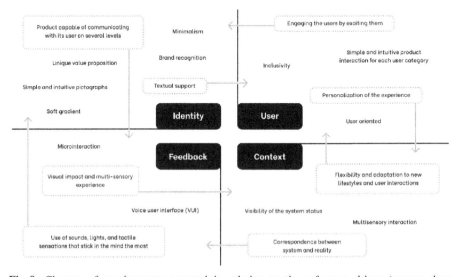

Fig. 9. Clusters of requirements grouped in relation to the reference driver (arrows show requirements common to several drivers).

These drivers represent real polarities towards which to orient the project. By taking certain requirements into consideration, rather than others, one can orient the project towards drastically different solutions, directing research towards objectives recognised by the market and in line with the values of the reference company.

With regard to the company in question, two drastically opposite scenarios were identified on which to operate: one of a disruptive nature, the other of a moderate nature, in line with the case studies on the market identified as best practice.

The first scenario has been called 'Iconic' and is based on the search for new aesthetic and functional languages that create value and relations with younger and digitally connected user segments. The scenario envisages a recognisable and iconic interface, characterised by a high degree of flexibility and adaptation to new lifestyles. The customised interaction adapts to the characteristics of the context of use, favouring a quick and easy use that reflects the user's needs.

The second scenario is called 'Smart' and aims at an interface belonging to a brand-related product family. Immediate, agile and functional solutions are sought which favour simple use and are suitable for a wide range of users. Interaction takes place through clear, multisensory feedback that, regardless of context, precisely communicates the system's state of activity.

The scenarios have been compared on a matrix in which the drivers act as polarities, the comparison sees the Iconic scenario, more disruptive, oriented towards context and identity drivers, in favour of greater personalisation and a more empathetic impact towards a user accustomed to the use of digital devices; the Smart scenario, on the other hand, leans towards the user, feedback and identity drivers, defining a simpler interface, suitable for a broad target, but which retains characteristics that stand out from the market, representing the company through several products in dialogue with each other (Fig. 10).

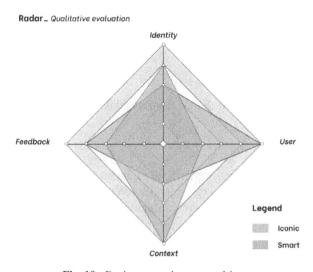

Fig. 10. Design scenarios versus drivers.

In this specific case, the company, through a workshop and dialogue with the design team, was able to choose the scenario that best represented the company's core business with respect to its positioning in the video door entry system market. The Smart scenario turned out to be best suited to the company's needs.

8 Step 4: UI Proposal

The insights that emerged from the previous phases, following a further analytical and scenario synthesis phase, guided the progressive concretisation of the UI, first theoretical and then practical.

The generation of a new interface was marked by two steps, during which the information architecture and the aesthetic-functional part of the system were defined.

The information architecture was divided into four macro-areas, each with a depth of two levels. The various levels have a number of slots following Hick's Law theory, with a maximum of six functions per subject area. This structure allows the user to be in screens that are not overloaded with information, making it easier to read and understand the system. In addition, functions have been introduced that allow the user to customise the interface in a non-invasive manner; this choice is determined by the fact that excessive customisation freedom risks distorting the functional and aesthetic design of the product, while undermining its recognisability.

With this in mind, the system's pictograms were designed, focusing on brand identity and visual familiarity. Starting from the icons of the previous interface, work was carried out to redesign new stylistic elements, based on recognised libraries. They were then reworked and characterised according to their specific function, to represent the meaning and reflect the values of the company.

Once the stylistic elements were realised, various graphic proposals were designed to communicate in a simple and intuitive way with the public. These elements pick up on the company's colours, shapes and graphic imprint so as to create a common thread between the product and brand identity.

9 Conclusions

The results obtained by Comelit S.p.A. thanks to this model of collaboration with the University are mainly two:

- The opening of a new channel to access research aimed at designing new possible business scenarios.
- The design of new products, with a level of attention to human-centred issues not yet applied in its core business (greater attention to the customer, understood as any figure dealing with the product during its entire life cycle)

The cooperation model is replicable for all SMEs, easily adaptable to individual needs, to create a common ground for growth and contamination, a strategic key to compete and innovate.

The design process, recounted here in its genesis and application, concluded with the delivery of a navigable prototype complete with all the main screens. This was built using special software that facilitates the implementation work by the programmers, defining the different components that represent the modular basis for the buttons, icons and lettering of the interface. The prototype is the result of a series of meetings (meetings, workshops) that, through shared choices, steered the project towards solutions in line with the corporate identity and market objectives.

In this context, design plays a key role, as a strategic lever and activator of relationships that bring new values and meanings.

A significant, and strategically relevant, response is to set up an in-house design centre that can play the role first and foremost of all-round technology scouting, to bring constant innovation to processes and products, creating continuity between them, capable of dialoguing with different partners to amplify knowledge.

The reported case reflects precisely on this: on the competitive advantages of an academic approach typical of the design discipline, which is research-oriented and applies a collaborative co-design process to strengthen internal and external (with users and the market) relational dynamics.

Moreover, development innovation (and not just incremental innovation) is the daily commitment of thousands of small and medium-sized enterprises, even if often in a non-continuous manner due to size or resource constraints. And it is from here that we must start if we want to promote a meeting between the productive fabric and innovation centres that is a multiplier of productive initiatives provided that companies recognise the real value for improving and expanding business. At the same time, researchers, while maintaining scientific autonomy, need to find a favourable ground favourable terrain to transform ideas into innovative industrial projects and transmit cultural and technological approaches to industry, which is often too tied to practices that come from afar (Fig. 11).

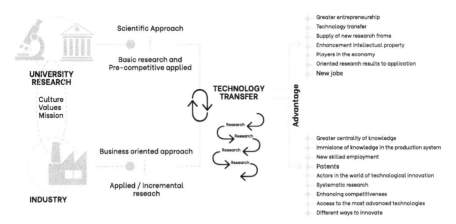

Fig. 11. University-business cooperation for innovation

References

1. Bødker, S.: Through the Interface: A Human Activity Approach to User Interface Design. CRC Press (2021). https://doi.org/10.1201/9781003063971
2. Dutsinma, F.L.I., Pal, D., Funilkul, S., Chan, J.H.: A systematic review of voice assistant usability: an ISO 9241–11 approach. SN Comput. Sci. **3**, 267 (2022)
3. Sheppard, B., Sarrazin, H., Kouyoumjian, G., Dore, F.: The business value of design. In: McKinsey, 3 July 2019
4. Yudhanto, Y., Pryhatyanto, W.M., Sulandari, W.: Designing and making UI/UX designs on the official website with the design thinking method. In: 1st International Conference on Smart Technology, Applied Informatics, and Engineering (APICS), pp. 165–170. IEEE (2022). https://doi.org/10.1109/APICS56469.2022.9918684
5. Mirnig, A.G., Meschtscherjakov, A., Wurhofer, D., Meneweger, T., Tscheligi, M.: A formal analysis of the ISO 9241–210 definition of user experience. In: Proceedings of the 33rd Annual ACM Conference Extended Abstracts on Human Factors in Computing Systems, pp. 437–450. ACM (2015). https://doi.org/10.1145/2702613.2732511
6. Kompaniets, V., Lyz, A., Kazanskaya, A.: An empirical study of goal setting in UX/UI-design. In: 2020 IEEE 14th International Conference on Application of Information and Communication Technologies (AICT), pp. 1–5. IEEE (2020). https://doi.org/10.1109/AICT50176.2020.9368570
7. Lin, J.-Y.: Balancing industry collaboration and academic innovation: the contingent role of collaboration-specific attributes. Technol. Forecast. Soc. Change **123**, 216–228 (2017)
8. Norman, D.A., Verganti, R.: Incremental and radical innovation: design research vs. technology and meaning change. Des. Issues **30**, 78–96 (2014)
9. Micheli, P., Wilner, S.J.S., Bhatti, S.H., Mura, M., Beverland, M.B.: Doing design thinking: conceptual review, synthesis, and research agenda: doing design thinking. J. Prod. Innov. Manag. **36**, 124–148 (2019)
10. Gonen, E., Brown, T.: Change by design: how design thinking transforms organizations and inspires innovation. MGDR **04** (2019)
11. Kim, W.C.: Blue ocean strategy: from theory to practice. Calif. Manag. Rev. **47**, 105–121 (2005)
12. Nielsen, J., Molich, R.: 10 Usability Heuristics for User Interface Design. https://www.nngroup.com/articles/ten-usability-heuristics/. Accessed 05 Feb 2023
13. Joshi, A., Kale, S., Chandel, S., Pal, D.: Likert scale: explored and explained. BJAST **7**, 396–403 (2015)
14. Rosenfeld, L., Morville, P.: Information Architecture for the World Wide Web: Designing Large-Scale Web Sites. O'Reilly Media, Inc. (2008)
15. Yablonski, J.: Laws of UX: Using Psychology to Design Better Products & Services. O'Reilly, Sebastopol (2020)
16. Green, R.T.: Surprise as a factor in the von Restorff effect. J. Exp. Psychol. **52**, 340–344 (1956)
17. Walton, S., O'Kane, P., Ruwhiu, D.: Developing a theory of plausibility in scenario building: designing plausible scenarios. Futures **111**, 42–56 (2019)

User-Centered Ethical Design - An Evolutionary Perspective

Oronzo Parlangeli[1]([✉]) [iD] and Paul M. Liston[2] [iD]

[1] University of Siena, Siena, Italy
`oronzo.parlangeli@unisi.it`
[2] Trinity College Dublin, Dublin, Ireland

Abstract. The way in which technology is designed requires reconsideration. Most importantly, a clearer consideration of ethics in the design process can ensure that, even in the planning phase, there is a move towards the creation of technologies that fit with, and support, human activity in a sustainable way. To this end, this paper presents some critical points which should be considered in the design phase to encourage reflection on the evolutionary aspects of user-centered design.

Keywords: Design · Guidelines · Ethics · HCI · Human-computer interaction evolution

1 Introduction

In recent years, the need to redefine the primary goals of Human-Computer Interaction (HCI) has become increasingly relevant. As suggested by Y. Rogers [1], we are witnessing a broadening of HCI perspectives which can no longer be considered merely focused on a user-centered approach. The mass diffusion of technologies, their reference to users who are both younger and older at the same time, are factors that expand the potential of the problem related to the design of usable, accessible and sustainable technologies. Not only do previously neglected aspects of interaction become relevant, such as the affective relationship with the technologies and cultures of reference, but also the reflection on the methods to be adopted in the processes of development of these technologies becomes increasingly important. For these reasons, as argued by S. Harrison et al. [2], in recent years we have witnessed the affirmation of a new paradigm in the field of HCI. Broadening the horizons, which were essentially focused primarily on the ergonomic aspects and then on the more properly cognitive ones, it has become increasingly relevant to include a greater variety of meanings, values, and direct references to the contexts in which the interaction takes place.

Various theorists have proposed new perspectives on how to modify the technology design process to better facilitate the consideration of shared, possibly universal values [3]. There are many reasons which lead us to believe these transformations are necessary, ranging from the evidence that interacting with a computer no longer means having to deal with a single interface (in many cases there may even be no interface at all), to the proliferation of new tools technologies that support and stimulate new activities. Any of these reasons bring us to the same idea that a modification of the design process is required so that explicit reference is made to the values connected to the development of a new technology [3]. In this way, ethical considerations are being afforded attention within the design process.

These efforts have led to perspectives which have different emphases. The first of these perspectives relates to efforts aimed at identifying new directions, new processes, new stages, and new design principles that ensure a way of developing technologies that can be defined as inclusive and focused on equity [4]. An example in this direction can be considered the set of works by Rubegni et al. [5–7] who, in order to mitigate the negative influence of gender stereotypes, consider an approach based on digital storytelling (DST). In their work, focused on the design of information tools that help to raise the level of awareness on gender stereotypes by children, three phases are envisaged: the first "Detection of stereotypes in children's multimedia stories", the second "Co-design of the concepts", the third "Prototyping and Evaluation".

The second perspective, on the other hand, is more sensitive to the consideration of the varying contexts of use and application, thus seeking to calibrate products according to the socio-technical ecosystem of reference [8]. More specifically, for example, the ability of artifacts to communicate with each other is recognized, through the advances of the Internet of Things (IoT), and therefore the generation of socio-technical contexts that pose new challenges, such as those relating to the level of automation [9], security [10] privacy [11], trust in technology [12]. Above all, it is clarified that the design of technologies cannot proceed by neglecting the social consequences that the introduction and use of new technologies can produce, and the proposal is also made for the determination of an ethical code that can inform and regulate the activity of the technology designer [13].

The third is aimed at developing guidelines, or principles, that can serve to support the design process [14]. Reflections in the latter perspective have necessarily argued the difficulty in establishing principles concerning such a complex subject, since it involves human beings and technologies in a contextualized and evolving interactive relationship. Despite these difficulties, theoretical efforts in this direction have not been few. For example, in the context of Human-Robot Interaction (HRI) Fronemann et al. [15] have tried to integrate the guidelines usually used to guarantee the usability of systems with other principles more focused on guaranteeing a human-robot relationship that can safeguard the affective and cognitive integrity of the user. Some of these, for example, suggest to guarantee the "predictability" - make sure the user knows what the robot is going to do next - or to consider the "psycho-motivational effects" - make an informed decision about whether the robot should show emotionality. With more reference to Artificial Intelligence (AI), other authors instead conducted reviews to verify how much the proposed guidelines were focused on the same principles. Thus Jobin et al. [16] identified 84 different guidelines which are related to 11 different principles. Referring to these principles Kieslich et al. [17] conducted a study with German participants to check the perceived relevance, and they were able to conclude that the different principles - explainability, fairness, security, accountability, accuracy, privacy, and limited machine autonomy - all appeared relevant. Different types of users, however, report a different level of priority in the principles considered.

2 Focal Points

Cognitive processes in their whole can be considered as constantly evolving [18–21]. This is happening because of natural mutations of the human neurophysiology, because of the cultural advances that increasingly sophisticated forms of sociality have made possible, because of the artifacts and technologies created by humans and that interact with humans to redefine themselves and reshape new possibilities for knowledge processing.

Ethical design must fit into this evolutionary flow, and needs to analyse the present in awareness of the past and put forward into the future. Ethical design, then, can express itself in understanding the "evolution of interaction" between humans and technologies, evolution that has been sustained over millions of years [22, 23]. It thus becomes possible to link the design of technologies to principles of sustainability, as the design process becomes aimed at favouring the lines of development that have so far proved capable of expressing a balanced relationship between humans and technologies. To this end, at the design stage it may be necessary to keep the evolution of humans in interaction with technologies as a guiding principle and to have focal points acting as reference points. These focal points should not be considered guidelines, but rather are issues on which the reflection of the design process must focus.

2.1 Evolving Interactions

The user is constantly evolving, not just performing tasks, but finalizing activities that change in an effort of self-realization [24]. It is necessary to think about interactions that open perspectives for other interactions. Several factors contribute to making the user an ever-evolving agent [25]. On the one hand, interacting with a technology, pursuing goals with it, naturally leads to an increase in experience. For this reason, many guidelines assume that the user has tools and dynamic interfaces available that support and stimulate the accumulation of experience. In this perspective it is possible to frame the research and studies that have tried to create interfaces and adaptive systems [26]. Adaptivity, in fact, has not only been understood as a tension aimed at giving each user the type of interface suitable for carrying out a certain task, but also as a necessity for those users who, accumulating experience over time, need increasingly agile and efficient tools. The better we know how to do things, the more we need tools that lead us to the immediate realization of our goals. However, all this must be understood in a double and reciprocal evolutionary line: tools more suited to the user's needs do not only suggest the need for a modification that concerns themselves. The progress of technologies leads to change and raise the needs, aspirations, goals of the user. This, for example, is clearly evident with educational technologies that push the user towards cognitive horizons concerning self-development which, inevitably, require a change in the same educational technology to accommodate and promote this need for development [27].

2.2 Social Interactions

The user is essentially a social being [28, 29]. Many times they may interact with technology together with other people, and so technologies need to be designed with the intention of enabling and facilitating these forms of social use.

For several decades, CSCW scholars have been trying to develop systems that serve to support collaborative work [30, 31]. However, in these cases, we are dealing with circumstances in which complex tasks must be allocated synchronously or asynchronously to collaborators with often diversified skills and objectives. The reality can also be much simpler and concern the execution of daily tasks for which no specific skill of the user is required, or should not be required.

Let's imagine a user who buys a ticket at an automatic ticket machine before traveling by train. This user and this simple task is probably what the designers of many of these technologies focused on: a single user with a single goal to be accomplished in a sequence of individual actions. Frequently, however, in reality we decide to stay in pairs, or in groups, and the execution of many tasks implies a relationship between two or more people and a technology. However, this type of relationship – multiple users, one task, one technology – is almost never envisioned by designers. However, this type of relationship is possible when our operating interface is another human being: several people can converse with a train ticket sales clerk.

Our "doing things together", even if simple, hardly corresponds to a design intention that supports our need. To support human relational skills, which have evolved over millennia, in interactions with technologies it is necessary to rethink users as a plurality of speaking people [32].

2.3 Subjective Interaction

The user has expressive elaborative and perceptual needs that favour some communication channels over others [33]. Therefore, technologies should facilitate adequate interaction according to personal modes of communication.

These differences can be individual, but also generational. It is now clear that technological diffusion, which usually concerns technologies that can be considered more "visual", has produced changes in different parts of the world in favour of the advancement of visual-spatial intellectual abilities. To date we can say, for example, that the level of abstraction of the vocabulary of young people is decreasing in favour of a greater processing capacity which calls into question visuo-spatial abilities [34].

Even at the individual level, however, substantial differences can be found. In balancing visual and verbal skills, several factors can be taken into consideration, from the span of visual short-term memory to reading skills, from verbal IQ to the speed of visual processing [35]. The combination of these individual dispositions produces differences in performance on tasks involving the processing of visual and/or textual information. For example, in tasks in which it is necessary to deal with visual-textual material such as that generally found in magazines, it emerges that a factor such as Visualization Literacy has effects both on the time dedicated to the task and on the level of accuracy of understanding the material [35]. When subjective characteristics are not adequately supported, various undesirable results can occur, one of which is increasingly documented - so-called mind wandering [36, 37].

Considering this focal point implies conceding to the subjective evolutionary lines that lead to preferring methods of codes, relational procedures that can be quite different from user to user.

2.4 Reflective Interactions

The user interprets technology as a reflective collaborator [38–40]. Relational possibilities should be provided that enable recursive processes of reflexivity between the user and technology [41, 42]. Technology is almost never experienced as a passive tool, capable of exhibiting only deterministic behaviour. It is more probable, considering the presence of various clues that the technology itself provides, that the user establishes interactive methods as if they were dealing with a collaborator. In these cases, therefore, one will behave as if the technology-collaborator were able to elaborate a model, a theory of one's own mind/functioning and that of its user-collaborator, natural or artificial [41]. We expect to be perceived, understood, interpreted, supported. Just as we ourselves do with the interactive system at hand. And sometimes we are perplexed when we feel abandoned to ourselves, as if our collaborator refuses to play his part. The clues that push in this direction can be the most diverse, from the external appearance of the instrument, which can sometimes recall that of a human being or an animal, to its behaviour, which in many cases appears not logically associated with the state of things and therefore self-determined [38]. Like when we think that the advertising presented in a given app refers to something we have been talking about, probably that app is able to listen to me and, if necessary, to provide me with suitable purchase suggestions.

However, this tendency to perceive technologies as reflexive agents, able to elaborate mental representations of our mental representations, does not depend only on their appearance or their behaviour. Probably, human beings are intrinsically inclined to establish relationships with the systems present in their operational contexts by assuming an "intentional stance" [43, 44]. This is probably our privileged perspective on the world and, contrary to what would seem logical, we wait until we are contradicted in this attitude before reconsidering a perspective based on the intentions of the designer (designer stance) or on the material, physical and chemical characteristics of the artifacts (physical stance). The designer can facilitate this tendency by making the user interpret technologies as reflective agents. From the establishment of this relationship, in fact, a real improvement can emerge in the experience and in the products that can be created through this experience. Indeed, it is through this type of relationship that circumstances of collaborative learning can be encouraged [41]. At the same time, however, dysfunctional relational conditions can occur, such as in cases where interactive technology can be interpreted as the bearer of its own needs and contrary to ours, and therefore appear worthy of being weakened, or even punished [45]. Or still appearing so much like us, as for example in the case of humanoid robots which, if represented with reference to different genders and used in certain operational fields, can confirm gender stereotypes as the basis of negative discrimination (males know how to fight, whereas females know how to care for people) [46].

2.5   Interactions Respectful of Changing and Evolving Cultures

The user participates in different cultural contexts, each of these can vary substantially with respect to the others, and different users can refer to contexts that do not overlap with each other. Therefore, not only can technologies be culturally localized or delocalized, but also the users themselves can be, in many cases, culturally nomadic [47].

As highlighted by Sun [48] we can consider that users actively engage to make sense of, to effectively incorporate technologies within the sphere of their values, their relational norms and their behaviours. This effort can be called user localization, and in most cases it does not coincide with developer localization which usually assumes the cultural references of its production context. The first obvious consequence of these localization thrusts produced by users is the expansion, the tension towards undeterminable times of the product life cycle. The experience of using the same technologies in different contexts must be welcomed by producers in order to project themselves towards production hypotheses that do not have an arrival point, but which evolve with use [48].

To date we can also witness a departure from the usual production methods to bring the design and implementation of technologies closer to areas that are those of the users themselves. The paradigm of open innovation, for example, brings the stakeholders of a product closer to the realization of the same, employing their creative potential in ways that are culturally related to the contexts of use [49]. At the same time, the creation of open technologies, such as for example 3D printers [50] creates the conditions for more and more users, perhaps also through events such as hackathons [51], to participate in the creation and continuous redesign of technologies.

It is necessary to think of users as project partners, rather than as bearers of needs and characteristics, and let the norms, values and cultural directives of their lives and operational contexts flow within the project.

2.6   Unambiguous Interactions

The user can make sense of disparate and/or dissonant things. As with perceptual illusions, care must be taken not to provide possibilities for interpretation of technologies that were not intended if these may be detrimental to the interaction itself.

A natural tendency of human beings is to make sense of things, make everything harmonious, interpret the stimulus configurations in a way that these can be assimilated with the already known. As far as optical illusions are concerned, local conditions of the stimulus, but also global aspects, i.e. parts of the stimulus that are distant from each other, can give rise to percepts quite different from the real physical stimulation [52]. Think of the perceptual rendering of an illusion such as that of Adelson [53] in which the gray tones of a chessboard are altered, through perceptive processes that occur after the low-level ones, to give a sense to the stimulation.

A particularly interesting aspect of our tendency to make sense of things is related to the fact that this tendency often leads us to see the presence of a human face even where it is not present. This tendency is called *paredolia* and occurs very quickly, in a time span of 250 ms, the same time needed to perceive the presence of a real face [54]. But not only do we perceive stimuli that are significant to us (the human face) even when this is not present, our evolution has led us to associate secondary characteristics usually associated with that type of stimuli with these percepts. Thus, if a user interface has a talking face, our reaction as users is very different from when we interact with a textual interface [55]. In the first case we attribute personality traits to the system as if they were human beings, and as users we tend to present ourselves more positively. The same happens in the interaction with humanoid robots: the presence of a face leads to judging the robot as more likeable and more endowed with a mind [56]. At the same time we also tend to see more suitable humanoid robots that have gender characteristics, male or female, more suitable to carry out operational roles that are stereotypically considered more suitable for one gender rather than the other [46].

If our evolutionary path has led us to be particularly efficient in referring experiences to already known cognitive schemes, the design of technologies must be focused on respecting this tendency. At the same time, however, in the design phase it is necessary to reflect on the possibility that, in the phase of interaction with technology, the reference to already possessed knowledge schemes does not lead to activating correlates of knowledge that are not adequately foreseen. These could cause interpretative ambiguities or even provide clues for the formulation of prejudices or for implementing discriminatory behaviours [57].

2.7 Self-determinant Interactions

The user must be empowered in the self-determination of their relationship with the technology. Thus, the technology must provide and stimulate space and opportunity for reflection on the interaction [58].

Human reflective capacities are probably the most recent and most relevant achievement of the cognitive development of our species. The first evidence of this cognitive advance must be sought in the production of artefacts that were created when, during their development, our ancestors realised the limitation of their cognitive systems. Humans who around 50,000 years ago felt the need to construct a lunar calendar probably had become aware, and therefore able to reflect on their own cognitive processes, on how limited their memory abilities were [59].

Today, our cognitive processes are expressed almost entirely in the interaction with artifacts and technologies that make them possible, support and amplify them. Our reflective abilities are naturally called into question in relation to cognitive processes that we can continue to call, for example, memory, attention, reasoning, meaning by these labels procedures that do not exclusively concern the human mind [60–63]. Today our memory, our attention and our reasoning skills are instantiated in interactions with artifacts and technologies. Our notebook, our smartphone, our computer, the virtual assistant on the school website, are parts of our cognitive processes and therefore the reflective skills must incorporate them into the awareness of our cognitive identity. In the expression of this reflective ability, which extends to include interactive technologies, the technologies themselves must be called into question, which must open and solicit moments of reflection in the course of interaction and on interaction. Obviously, this is very necessary in interactions for which the path in which a given activity is carried out is not established, that is, when the human-machine interactive system works to solve a problem. However, it appears even more necessary in those cases in which the modalities of occurrence of this interaction can have consequences on the development of human cognitive systems or in the sphere of the value systems of the cultures of reference. Thus, technologies that do not open spaces for reflection and that involve a consistent exercise of visual multitasking skills, as in the case of many video games, can cause their users to develop finer skills in discriminating target stimuli [65]. At the same time, however, these users may become less sensitive to detecting elements in the visual field that are not the target stimulus [62]. This can happen without the user being given the opportunity to reflect on these consequences of the interaction. The user thus loses the possibility of exercising choices to determine themselves. Technologies that open spaces for reflection on interaction, on the other hand, can be a tool of respect for the cognitive development of the human being, but they can also help create a way that has as a reference the values that we consciously decide to adopt as a guide for the future of humanity.

3   Discussion

The set of focal points illustrated is not concluded, and perhaps never can be. It seems relevant, however, to stimulate reflection on the values that bring humans and their evolutionary paths, back to the centre of reflection on User-Centered Design.

Several questions remain unanswered. The first could relate to how and when to incorporate reflections on these focal points into the design process. The answer to this question, however, can only be vague and consider that the design process should never be considered concluded or 'segmentable' into phases that can be precisely determined. On the other hand, it can be assumed that reflections on the possibilities of synergistic evolution of human-technology interactions must be part of a culturally developed sensitivity that permeates the entire design process and extends to the concrete uses of artifacts and technologies.

Other questions could refer to the exhaustiveness of these focal points and to their possible differentiated role, with greater or lesser relevance, within the specific projects. In this regard, various hypotheses can be formulated, but they all refer to an approach that should instead be guided by experience. Even design methods evolve by confronting reality, in this case with their application to real projects.

References

1. Rogers, Y.: The changing face of human-computer interaction in the age of ubiquitous computing. In: Holzinger, A., Miesenberger, K. (eds.) USAB 2009. LNCS, vol. 5889, pp. 1–19. Springer, Heidelberg (2009). https://doi.org/10.1007/978-3-642-10308-7_1
2. Harrison, S., Tatar, D., Sengers, P.: The three paradigms of HCI. In: Alt. Chi. Session at the SIGCHI Conference on Human Factors in Computing Systems San Jose, California, USA, pp. 1–18 (2007)
3. Sellen, A., Rogers, Y., Harper, R., Rodden, T.: Reflecting human values in the digital age. Commun. ACM **52**(3), 58–66 (2009). https://doi.org/10.1145/1467247.1467265
4. Mink, A.: Designing for well-being. An approach for understanding users' lives in design for development. Doctoral thesis, Delft University of Technology (2016). https://doi.org/10.4233/uuid:264107d4-30bc-414c-b1d4-34f48aeda6d8
5. Rubegni, E., Landoni, L.: Fiabot! Design and evaluation of a mobile storytelling application for schools. In: Idc 2014, pp. 165–174 (2014). https://doi.org/10.1145/2593968.2593979

6. Rubegni, E., Landoni, M., De Angeli A., Jaccheri, L.: Detecting gender stereotypes in children digital storytelling. In: Proceedings of the 18th ACM International Conference on Interaction Design and Children (IDC 2019), pp. 386–393 (2019). https://doi.org/10.1145/3311927.332 3156

7. Rubegni, E., Landoni, M., Malinverni, L., Jaccheri, L.: Raising awareness of stereotyping through collaborative digital storytelling: design for change with and for children. Int. J. Hum. Comput. Stud. **157**, 102727 (2022). https://doi.org/10.1016/j.ijhcs.2021.102727

8. Fiore, E.: Ethics of technology and design ethics in socio-technical systems: investigating the role of the designer. FormAkademisk **13**(1), 1–19 (2020). https://doi.org/10.7577/formakade misk.2201

9. Cummings, M.L.: Integrating ethics in design through the value-sensitive design approach. Sci. Eng. Ethics **12**(4), 701–715 (2006). https://doi.org/10.1007/s11948-006-0065-0

10. Cheng, B.H.C., Atlee, J.M.: Current and future research directions in requirements engineering. In: Lyytinen, K., Loucopoulos, P., Mylopoulos, J., Robinson, B. (eds.) Design Requirements Engineering: A Ten-Year Perspective. LNBIP, vol. 14, pp. 11–43. Springer, Heidelberg (2009). https://doi.org/10.1007/978-3-540-92966-6_2

11. Iaconesi, S.: Interface and data biopolitics in the age of hyperconnectivity. Implications for design. Des. J. **20**(sup1), S3935–S3944 (2017). https://doi.org/10.1080/14606925.2017.135 2896.

12. Lindley, J., Coulton, P., Cooper, R.: Why the Internet of Things needs object orientated ontology. Des. J. **20**(sup1), S2846–S2857 (2017). https://doi.org/10.1080/14606925.2017. 1352796

13. Chan, J.: From afterthought to precondition: re-engaging design ethics from technology, sustainability, and responsibility. In: Design Research Society 50th Anniversary Conference. Brighton, UK, 27–30 June 2016, pp. 3539–3552. Design Research Society, London (2016). https://doi.org/10.21606/drs.2016.208

14. Manzini, E.: Design, ethics and sustainability: guidelines for a transition phase. In: Cumulus Working Papers, vol. 16, no. 6, pp. 9–15 (2006)

15. Fronemann, N., Pollmann, K., Loh, W.: Should my robot know what's best for me? Human–robot interaction between user experience and ethical design. AI Soc. **37**, 517–533 (2022). https://doi.org/10.1007/s00146-021-01210-3

16. Jobin, A., Ienca, M., Vayena, E.: The global landscape of AI ethics guidelines. Nat. Mach. Intell. **1**(9), 389–399 (2019). https://doi.org/10.1038/s42256-019-0088-2

17. Kieslich, K., Keller, B., Starke, C.: Artificial intelligence ethics by design. Evaluating public perception on the importance of ethical design principles of artificial intelligence. Big Data Soc. **9**(1), 1–15 (2022). https://doi.org/10.1177/20539517221092956

18. Cosmides, L., Tooby, J.: Evolutionary Psychology: A Primer, vol. 13. Center for Evolutionary Psychology, Santa Barbara (1997)

19. Heyes, C.: Four routes of cognitive evolution. Psychol. Rev. **110**(4), 713–727 (2003). https://doi.org/10.1037/0033-295X.110.4.713

20. Gidley, J.M.: Globally scanning for "megatrends of the mind": potential futures of futures thinking. Futures **42**(10), 1040–1048 (2010). https://doi.org/10.1016/j.futures.2010.08.002

21. Thompson, B.: An ever-evolving mind. Science **378**(6620), 610–611 (2022). https://doi.org/ 10.1126/science.ade3128

22. Basalla, G.: The Evolution of Technology. Cambridge Univ. Press, Cambridge (1988)

23. Read, D.W.: Working memory: a cognitive limit to non-human primate recursive thinking prior to hominid evolution. Evol. Psychol. **6**(4) (2008). https://doi.org/10.1177/147470490 800600413

24. Kou, Y., Gui, X., Chen, Y., Nardi, B.: Turn to the self in human-computer interaction: care of the self in negotiating the human-technology relationship. In: Proceedings of the 2019 CHI

Conference on Human Factors in Computing Systems, pp. 1–15 (2019). https://doi.org/10.1145/3290605.3300711

25. Guzdial, M., Kafai, Y.B., Carroll, J.M., Fischer, G., Schank, R., Soloway, E.: Learner-centered system design: HCI perspective for the future. In: Proceedings of the 1st Conference on Designing Interactive Systems: Processes, Practices, Methods, & Techniques, pp. 143–147 (1995)

26. Langley, P.: User modeling in adaptive interface. In: Kay, J. (ed.) UM99 User Modeling. CICMS, vol. 407, pp. 357–370. Springer, Vienna (1999). https://doi.org/10.1007/978-3-7091-2490-1_48

27. Shipunova, O.D., Berezovskaya, I.P., Smolskaia, N.B.: The role of student's self-actualization in adapting to the e-learning environment. In: Proceedings of the Seventh International Conference on Technological Ecosystems for Enhancing Multiculturality, pp. 745–750 (2019). https://doi.org/10.1145/3362789.3362884

28. Herrmann, E., Call, J., Hernández-Lloreda, M.V., Hare, B., Tomasello, M.: Humans have evolved specialized skills of social cognition: the cultural intelligence hypothesis. Science **317**(5843), 1360–1366 (2007). https://doi.org/10.1126/science.1146282

29. Boyd, R., Richerson, P.J.: Culture and the evolution of human cooperation. Philos. Trans. R. Soc. B Biol. Sci. **364**(1533), 3281–3288 (2009). https://doi.org/10.1098/rstb.2009.0134

30. Grudin, J.: Computer-supported cooperative work: history and focus. Computer **27**(5), 19–26 (1994). https://doi.org/10.1109/2.291294

31. Soden, R., et al.: Fostering historical research in CSCW & HCI. In: Conference Companion Publication of the 2019 on Computer Supported Cooperative Work and Social Computing, pp. 517–522 (2019). https://doi.org/10.1145/3311957.3359436

32. Geeng, C., Roesner, F.: Who's in control? Interactions in multi-user smart homes. In: Proceedings of the 2019 CHI Conference on Human Factors in Computing Systems, pp. 1–13 (2019). https://doi.org/10.1145/3290605.3300498

33. Jonassen, D.H., Grabowski, B.L.: Handbook of Individual Differences, Learning, and Instruction. Routledge (2012). https://doi.org/10.4324/9780203052860

34. Greenfield, P.M.: Technology and informal education: what is taught, what is learned. Science **323**(5910), 69–71 (2009). https://doi.org/10.1126/science.1167190

35. Toker, D., Conati, C., Carenini, G.: Gaze analysis of user characteristics in magazine style narrative visualizations. User Model. User Adap. Interact. **29**(5), 977–1011 (2019). https://doi.org/10.1007/s11257-019-09244-5

36. D'Mello, S.K.: Zone out no more: mitigating mind wandering during computerized reading. In: Proceedings of the 10th International Conference on Educational Data Mining, EDM 2017, pp. 8–15 (2017)

37. Randall, J.G., Beier, M.E., Villado, A.J.: Multiple routes to mind wandering: predicting mind wandering with resource theories. Conscious. Cogn. **67**, 26–43 (2019). https://doi.org/10.1016/j.concog.2018.11.006

38. Parlangeli, O., Chiantini, T., Guidi, S.: A mind in a disk: the attribution of mental states to technological systems. Work **41**(Suppl1), 1118–1123 (2012). https://doi.org/10.3233/WOR-2012-0291-1118

39. Parlangeli, O., Guidi, S., Farina, R.F.: Overloading disks onto a mind: quantity effects in the attribution of mental states to technological systems. In: Advances in Cognitive Engineering and Neuroergonomics, vol. 43 (2012). https://doi.org/10.1201/b12313

40. Parlangeli, O., Caratozzolo, M.C., Guidi, S.: Multitasking and mentalizing machines: how the workload can have influence on the system comprehension. In: Harris, D. (ed.) EPCE 2014. LNCS (LNAI), vol. 8532, pp. 50–58. Springer, Cham (2014). https://doi.org/10.1007/978-3-319-07515-0_6

41. Tomasello, M., Kruger, A.C., Ratner, H.H.: Cultural learning. Behav. Brain Sci. **16**(3), 495–511 (1993). https://doi.org/10.1017/S0140525X0003123X

42. Tomasello, M.: The Cultural Origins of Human Cognition. Harvard University Press, Harvard (1999)
43. Dennett, D.C.: The Intentional Stance. MIT Press, Cambridge (1987)
44. Parlangeli, O., Liston, P.M.: Technologies for training and intentional stance. In: 17th International Conference on Cognition and Exploratory Learning in Digital Age, CELDA 2020, pp. 399–400 (2020)
45. Guidi, S., Marchigiani, E., Roncato, S., Parlangeli, O.: Human beings and robots: are there any differences in the attribution of punishments for the same crimes? Behav. Inf. Technol. **40**(5), 445–453 (2021). https://doi.org/10.1080/0144929X.2021.1905879
46. Parlangeli, O., Palmitesta, P., Bracci, M., Marchigiani, E., Guidi, S.: Gender role stereotypes at work in humanoid robots. Behav. Inf. Technol. (2022). https://doi.org/10.1080/0144929X.2022.2150565
47. Caratozzolo, M.C., Bagnara, S., Parlangeli, O.: Use of information and communication technology to supply health-care services to nomadic patients: an explorative survey. Behav. Inf. Technol. **27**(4), 345–350 (2008). https://doi.org/10.1080/01449290701760658
48. Sun, H.: Cross-Cultural Technology Design: Creating Culture-Sensitive Technology for Local Users. Oxford University Press, Oxford (2012)
49. West, J., Bogers, M.: Leveraging external sources of innovation: a review of research on open innovation. J. Prod. Innov. Manag. **31**(4), 814–831 (2014). https://doi.org/10.1111/jpim.12125
50. Murillo, L.F.R., Kauttu, P., Priego, L.P., Katz, A., Wareham, J.: Open Hardware Licences: Parallels and Contrasts: Open Science Monitor Case Study. European Commission, Brussels (2019)
51. Lifshitz-Assaf, H., Lebovitz, S., Zalmanson, L.: Minimal and adaptive coordination: how hackathons' projects accelerate innovation without killing it. Acad. Manag. J. **64**(3), 684–715 (2021). https://doi.org/10.5465/amj.2017.0712.
52. Parlangeli, O., Roncato, S.: Draughtsmen at work. Perception **39**(2), 255–259 (2010). https://doi.org/10.1068/p6500
53. Adelson, E.H.: Perceptual organization and the judgment of brightness. Science **262**, 2042–44 (1993)
54. Wardle, S.G., Taubert, J., Teichmann, L., et al.: Rapid and dynamic processing of face pareidolia in the human brain. Nat. Commun. **11**, 4518 (2020). https://doi.org/10.1038/s41467-020-18325-8
55. Sproull, L., Subramani, M., Kiesler, S., Walker, J.H., Waters, K.: When the interface is a face. Hum. Comput. Interact. **11**(2), 97–124 (1996). https://doi.org/10.1207/s15327051hci1102_1
56. Broadbent, E., et al.: Robots with display screens: a robot with a more humanlike face display is perceived to have more mind and a better personality. PLoS ONE **8**(8): e72589 (2013). https://doi.org/10.1371/journal.pone.0072589
57. Perugia, G., Guidi, S., Bicchi, M., Parlangeli, O.: The shape of our bias: perceived age and gender in the humanoid robots of the abot database. In: 2022 17th ACM/IEEE International Conference on Human-Robot Interaction (HRI), pp. 110–119. IEEE (2022). https://doi.org/10.1109/HRI53351.2022.9889366
58. Baumer, E P.: Reflective informatics: conceptual dimensions for designing technologies of reflection. In: Proceedings of the 33rd Annual ACM Conference on Human Factors in Computing Systems, pp. 585–594 (2015). https://doi.org/10.1145/2702123.2702234
59. Mithen, S.J.: Looking and learning: Upper Paleolithic art and information gathering. World Archaeol. **19**(3), 297–27. (1988). https://doi.org/10.1080/00438243.1988.9980043
60. Norman, D.: Things that make us smart. Addison-Wesley, Reading (2003)
61. Hutchins, E.: Cognition in the Wild. MIT Press, Cambridge (1995)
62. Clark, A.: Natural-Born Cyborgs: Minds, Technologies, and the Future of Human Intelligence Oxford University Press, Oxford (2003)

63. Dror, I.E., Harnad, S.: Offloading cognition onto cognitive technology. In: Dror, I., Harnad, S. (eds.) Cognition Distributed: How Cognitive Technology Extends Our Minds (2008). John Benjamins Publishing, Amsterdam
64. Green, C.S., Bavelier, D.: Action-video-game experience alters the spatial resolution of vision. Psychol. Sci. **18**(1), 88–94 (2007). https://doi.org/10.1111/j.1467-9280.2007.01853.x
65. Green, C., Bavelier, D.: Action video game modifies visual selective attention. Nature **423**, 534–537 (2003). https://doi.org/10.1038/nature01647

The Viability of User-Centered and Human-Centered Design Practices with Natural User Interfaces (NUIs)

Dorothy Shamonsky[✉]

Brandeis University, 415 South Street, Waltham, MA 02453, USA
dshamonsky@ics.com

Abstract. User centered Design (UCD) and Human-centered Design (HCD) are philosophies and methodologies that consider human needs first in the design of products, services, processes, and systems. They also involve users in the design process through observation, interviews, testing, workshops, and as co-designers. UCD and HCD emerged in the mid-century when computers interfaces were difficult to use and the profession of HCI was just emerging. Are UCD and HCD future-proof practices or does rapidly evolving technology require new design philosophies and methodologies? This paper examines how these practices apply to future interfaces, specifically Natural User Interfaces (NUIs). NUIs are interfaces that go beyond the desktop paradigm. NUIs by their definition use a wide variety of modalities and technologies including augmented and virtual reality, robotics, and wearables. They simply allow humans to interact with computer-enabled devices in ways that are more natural for humans. While NUIs are easier for humans to learn and use, they are more complicated and challenging to design because they have more capabilities than current interfaces and are more responsive to humans. They utilize more automatic behaviors. Technologies like robots and medical devices have safety concerns. What design philosophy or methodologies are needed to support good usability design in the future when NUIs will be much more common? Do UCD and HCD suffice?

Keywords: User-centered Design · Human-centered Design · Natural User Interface

1 Introduction

User centered Design (UCD) and Human-centered Design (HCD) are design philosophies that put humans at the center of a design process. More specifically they can be defined as methodologies that consider human goals, capabilities, emotions, and context of use in the design of products, services, processes, and systems. They also involve users actively in the design process [1–5]. It is roughly four decades since Donald A. Norman published User-Centered System Design: New Perspectives on Human-Computer Interaction [6]. It is over six decades since the Design School at Stanford University was started where an HCD philosophy was explored and gave birth to the concept of

© The Author(s), under exclusive license to Springer Nature Switzerland AG 2023
A. Marcus et al. (Eds.): HCII 2023, LNCS 14030, pp. 297–307, 2023.
https://doi.org/10.1007/978-3-031-35699-5_22

Design Thinking [4, 7]. Four to six decades could be considered a short time or a long time, depending on your point of view. In terms of human culture, it's a very short time. In terms of the speed in which technological changes, it's a long time. Are UCD and HCD future-proof practices or does rapidly evolving technology require new design philosophies and methodologies?

This paper examines how these practices apply to future interfaces, specifically Natural User Interfaces (NUIs). NUIs are interfaces that go beyond the desktop paradigm of screen, keyboard and mouse or another type of pointing device. NUIs can have a graphical user interface (GUI) with a screen, or they can possess other ways of interacting. Today they often use touch or voice and will eventually use other modalities of interacting such as gesture and eye-tracking. NUIs by their definition use a wide variety of technologies including augmented and virtual reality, robotics, and wearables. They simply allow humans to interact with computer-enabled devices in ways that are more natural for humans. While NUIs are easier for humans to learn and use, they are more complicated and challenging to design because they have more capabilities than current interfaces and are more responsive to humans [8, 9].

Do UCD and HCD provide appropriate design methodologies to use in the design of NUIs? Both philosophies emerged at a time when computer technology was still very new. UCD has been the foundation upon which the best practices of user experience (UX) design have been built. UCD has fostered a robust GUI pattern language used in most interfaces out in the world. The value of UCD processes to assist in the design of good usability cannot be underestimated. Almost all current UX designers could be said to take part in some aspect of UCD in their practice no matter how small it may be. But in contrast, technology in evolving in leaps and bounds. Although legacy technologies will remain in use for many years to come, new technologies are already redefining interactivity.

HCD and Design Thinking have enabled businesses to develop innovative, highly useable products and services with problem-solving processes that include extensive user research. They have empowered many organizations to be more innovative, more customer-focused, more efficient, and more successful.

We know that the progress of computer technology is away from general purpose devices and more toward specialty devices [10]. Or another way to say this is, computation will be embedded in, or augmented to our existing world. Rather than existing as standalone devices, computation will be in smart appliances, in the infrastructure of towns and cities, in our cars, and in our bodies. We have a habit of thinking about technologies as defining interaction. GUI screens require one kind of interaction, robots require another kind, virtual reality requires yet a third. But as a designer I would posit that UX design will have many similarities across these diverse emerging technologies. We see that now, with voice and touch GUIs combined in our smart phones. To design usability for NUIs, one can imagine there will be a need for more specialists in modalities such as gesture, and in human behavior such as instinct. Usability on NUIs is more complicated and subtle than on GUIs. They utilize more automatic behaviors. Technologies like robots and medical devices have safety concerns. What design philosophy or methodologies are needed to support good usability design in the future when NUIs will be much more common? Do UCD and HCD suffice?

2 User-Centered Design

User-centered design (UCD) emerged from the field of Human-computer Interaction (HCI) as a philosophy that put user needs as the driver of the design of computer interfaces rather than the priorities of the technology design. UCD eventually developed into a best practice methodology to design and develop highly useable computer interfaces. In its simplest form it can be described as a four-step process: 1. Observation of users, 2. Ideation of designs, 3. Prototyping of designs, 4. Testing of prototypes with users. In the early decades of HCI design it was the foundation upon which computers evolved into more useable devices. As a best practice methodology, it expanded and refined the language of graphical user interfaces patterns which populate most of our interfaces today. It has been a powerful, positive influence in improving the usability of computers and computer-enabled devices [1–3].

The first use of the expression "user-centered design" is attributed to Rob Kling in 1977 [11]. It was adopted by Don Norman and his research laboratory at University of California, San Diego. A decade later he used it in the title of a book User-Centered System Design: New Perspectives on Human-Computer Interaction in 1986 [6]. Norman went on to popularize the concept by extensively explaining the value of the philosophy in his seminal book The Design of Everyday Things originally called The Psychology of Everyday Things) [3]. Norman subsequently switched to calling it human-centered design (HCD) in his newer publications, including the 2013 revised edition of The Design of Everyday Things, after the influence of the philosophy of Design Thinking coming out of Stanford University. However, the term UCD has stuck persistently in the minds of designers and is still widely used today to refer to the methodology of iterative observation, ideation, prototyping, and testing.

Any glance at an internet search of "user-centered design" will assure you that it remains a popular philosophy and methodology of UX designers today. It is mentioned frequently by design groups on websites and in professional literature but how it is described, although consistent in philosophy – designing with user needs in the fore-front – it varies considerably in the details of the methodology. Many interpretations exist both to fit the needs of the designers and to fit the needs of the specific interface or product upon which is it applied. That is part of the power of this simple four-step philosophy – it can be applied in a wide variety of ways.

UCD is a claim to the authority of an UX professional. "I practice UCD," implies that you are well trained and knowledgeable. As such UCD is perceived to be a norm of the profession. But it is rarely practiced in its full form. Even Norman acknowledges that performing the ideal UCD process is the exception, due to budgets and schedules forcing a more economical process [3] (Fig. 1) (Fig. 2).

User-Centered Design (UCD)

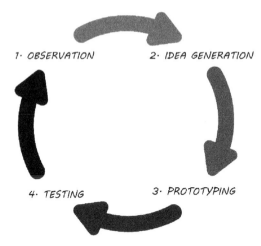

1· OBSERVATION

2· IDEA GENERATION

4· TESTING

3· PROTOTYPING

Fig. 1. User-centered design as represented by Norman and in its simple form.

Human-Centered Design (HCD)

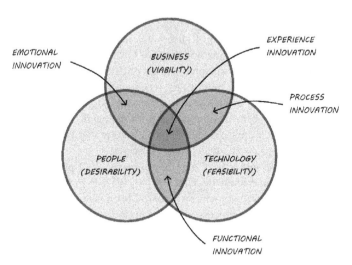

EMOTIONAL
INNOVATION

EXPERIENCE
INNOVATION

BUSINESS
(VIABILITY)

PROCESS
INNOVATION

PEOPLE
(DESIRABILITY)

TECHNOLOGY
(FEASIBILITY)

FUNCTIONAL
INNOVATION

Fig. 2. Human-centered design in its simple form.

3 Human-Centered Design

Human-centered design (HCD) is a philosophy of problem-solving that puts people's needs at the center of the process. It sounds very similar to UCD but there are distinct differences. HCD reaches beyond computer interfaces to address a wider range of applications including process, product, service, and system design. In other words, it doesn't have to apply to computers or technology but is powerful at general problem-solving in our complex, technology-rich, world. Peoples' needs and emotions are often ignored by the machinery of our current world. The goal of HCD is to maintain the human perspective in all steps of a problem-solving process; to keep users' needs, preferences, and pain points in focus. The result is expected to be efficient, intuitive, and accessible systems and products that have the potential to maintain or improve human well-being [4, 5].

There is an ISO standard for HCD: ISO 9241-210:2019(E) "Human-centered design is an approach to interactive systems development that aims to make systems usable and useful by focusing on the users, their needs and requirements, and by applying human factors/ergonomics, and usability knowledge and techniques. This approach enhances effectiveness and efficiency, improves human well-being, user satisfaction, accessibility and sustainability; and counteracts possible adverse effects of use on human health, safety and performance." [12].

To be viable, HCD stipulates a greater level of involvement of users in the problem-solving process than UCD. The goal is to get to a deeper level or dimension of understanding of human behavior, needs, and emotions. Techniques of user involvement go beyond observation and testing, to include Applied Ethnography, which requires researchers to be immersed with users in the field and to gather implicit information, actions, and unexpected details. Other activities could include design workshops with users or the inclusion users as co-designers for the duration of a project.

Design Thinking is a version of HCD promoted by Stanford University Design School. Design Thinking focuses primarily on the intersection of humans, technology, and business. It is defined as "…a human-centered approach to innovation—anchored in understanding customer's needs, rapid prototyping, and generating creative ideas—that will transform the way you develop products, services, processes, and organizations. By using design thinking, you make decisions based on what customers really want instead of relying only on historical data or making risky bets based on instinct instead of evidence." [13] The design program at Stanford was started by Professor John E. Arnold back in 1958 [14]. Arnold was a proponent of human-centered engineering as a means to promote engineering innovation. Over the years the Design School has popularized design processes for business purposes, which has made Design Thinking a hallmark of innovative technology companies.

The arguments for applying design thinking to business begin with bringing "substantial economic and social benefits for users, employers and suppliers." Other arguments state that systems and products with high usability are often more technically and commercially successful. Consumers are willing to pay more for well-designed products and systems. When users can understand and use products by themselves, training and support costs are less. And when safety and health risks are mitigated, it reduces legal exposure and customers trust your product more [4, 5].

4 Why Do We Have These Modern Design Methodologies?

Designing artifacts has been an activity practiced by humans since their earliest days. Consider the formation of primitive tools such as arrowheads, refining the shape and size to work optimally for a hunter. Usability has always been a crucial aspect of a design. Why would UCD and HCD arise in the 20th century? Did it exist before but without a label? Did design practices change then for some reason?

Obviously, computer technology plays a key role in how the world has changed; computers are complicated and were challenging to interact with in their early form. One can make the case that designing a computer interface – something that is complex, interactive, and has states – was not possible without a robust, science-based process like UCD. It is simply impossible for any designer or design team to presuppose good solutions to all the possible scenarios in any given interface, especially when there is not yet a precedent. Now we have best practice pattern languages and UI design norms that are well understood by users and allow designers to work more with pre-designed building blocks. Need a list view of items? Here are a few standard list view patterns that already handle your user needs. And it's all easy to see and understand on this high-resolution screen with sophisticated graphics. UCD solved the challenge of designing useable interfaces in the beginning of the profession when few best practices existed.

Complexity isn't the only issue with computers; speed of advancement is another. Once you developed reusable design solutions to one context of use, new hardware was available that upgraded the capabilities of devices and enabled new design challenges. Designers created good design patterns for personal computer graphical user interfaces, and then mobile devices emerge with a challenging new form factor and context of use. Now GUI patterns need to be reinvented.

Did we always have a form of UCD before computers, but it wasn't labeled or codified as such? Design is inherently iterative or involves trial and error. It takes a few or more tries to get something good enough. So, iteration in design is not something new. Also, designed products are often concerned with good usability, creating consumer demand, selling to customers, and maintaining happy customers. Testing with users or customers is not something completely new to computers, although usability did not gain such prominence, even with something as complicated and dangerous as cars.

From this perspective, UCD was a practice the evolved out of existing design practices to address the need to solve the complex problem of creating good usability for computers, in the face of fast paced technology advancement.

5 Comparing UCD and HCD

In a comparison of UCD to HCD, UCD appears to be a subset of HCD. UCD methodologies are simpler to perform than HCD methodologies, particularly the user research. HCD stipulates using more methodologies for observing and interviewing people to garner a deeper understanding of human requirements, capabilities, needs, and desires. It has a broader range of application, ranging from processes, systems, services, and products. In contrast, UCD considers the human relationship to product use and focuses mainly on the interface design. Overall, it's possible to say that HCD applies to the world, Design Thinking, although similar to HCD, is promoted for use mostly for organizations and product design, and UCD applies to computer interfaces. If HCD has a broader application and UCD has a narrower one, is UCD more tied to the needs of early computers? (Fig. 3, Table 1)

Scope of UCD Compared to HCD

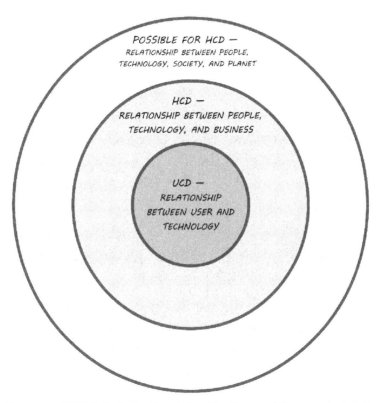

Fig. 3. The scope of UCD is limited to the relationship of user and the computer interface, while the scope of HCD is expansive although often limited to the triad of people, technology, and organizations.

Table 1. Comparison of typical UCD and HCD activities when working on products, and whether NUI would benefit from the activity; NUIs need all the activities and more.

ACTIVITY	UCD	HCD	NUI REQ.
OBSERVE SHORT TERM	X	X	X
OBSERVE LONG TERM		X	X
INTERVIEW	X	X	X
WORKSHOPS	X	X	X
CO-DESIGN		X	X
FORMATIVE TESTING	X	X	X
ITERATION	X	X	X
SUMMATIVE TESTING		X	X
ETHNOGRAPHER		X	X
ERGONOMIST			X
OTHER SPECIALISTS			X

6 Questions About the Viability of UCD Today

6.1 Do Best Practices, Component Libraries, and Design Systems Replace the Need for UCD?

As mentioned previously, UCD emerged at when HCI was a young profession. Best practices were scant because the body of knowledge about the field was so new. The less experience and knowledge there is about designing for a particular context of use, the more user research is necessary to get the design right. We can see that today with emerging technologies such as robotics, augmented reality, and VR. More user testing is necessary in those areas because the technology is newer, and the best practices are still emerging along with the technology. It means that UCD is still an effective process for emerging technologies and less crucial for longer-standing platforms like web, desktop, and mobile. But UCD is also effective just to understand user preferences. Website designers may want to test if a particular layout garners more exploration on deeper pages. So, although UCD is not a crucial for legacy platforms, it still has value.

6.2 Does UCD Maintain Status Quo?

Because UCD focuses more gathering user feedback rather than deep observation of use, and because people tend to like what they already know in interfaces and novel interfaces can confound them, does a UCD process tend to squelch innovation and favor the status quo? This is a hard question to answer or even research. The subtleties of how one does testing can influence responses. I posit that UCD can be used in a way where testing would favor the status quo as opposed to the novel. One could also argue that better design will be favored by users whether it is new or the current norm.

6.3 Will We Always Be "Users" and not just "Humans" with UCD?

As digital technology becomes more integrated with physical things, with infrastructure, and invades every aspect of our lives, it hard to image that the term "user" will stay in our vocabulary. Someday soon digital technology will be so normal and so ubiquitous that referring to "users" rather than "people" or "humans" will not be necessary. HCD does seem like the future and at least the name, "UCD" feel like it's on the cusp of being outdated.

7 Conclusion

In theory, UCD does not require application to technology, even though it is named User-centered design. It's a design process that relies on testing with "users" to evaluate the viability of a design. A designer can use UCD while designing a non-computer physical artifact, for example, a bicycle. The key is to design the testing to be appropriate to the artifact that you are testing and to garner results that answer the questions about the usability of the artifact. It is the name that dates the practice, should the term "user" fall out of favor.

UCD can be understood as a lightweight version of HCD. The terms UCD and HCD are often used interchangeably by designers who may not have clarity on the differences between them. As a result, one can assume that UCD will fade out of use as the term "user" fades out of use. What is the practice of UCD will simply be referred to as a version of HCD.

HCD by its nature, does not require application to technology. That immediately gives it a breadth of application, to not dependent on any quickly evolving technology. That also makes it have more viability as a design philosophy for NUIs, as computer technology evolves and becomes invisibly embedded in the everyday world. HCD also stipulates a more extensive involvement with user research, which makes it very appropriate for application to NUIs, since they are potentially more challenging to design than GUIs. HCD also aligns well with a greater concern for the long-term effects of technology. Extensive user research implies spending effort on more aspects of the experience of technology than simply the immediate, real-time use. HCD is poised to remain a powerful philosophy in the design process of NUIs (Fig. 4).

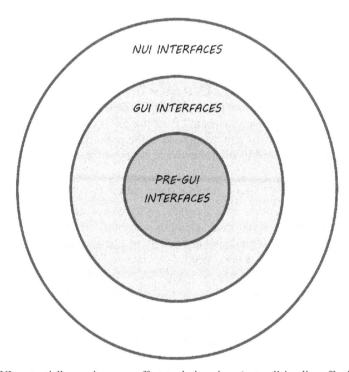

Fig. 4. NUIs potentially require more effort to design since 'natural' implies effortless to use, easy to learn, more attuned to human means of communication and interacting.

References

1. https://en.wikipedia.org/wiki/User-centered_design. Accessed 3 Feb 2023
2. https://www.usability.gov/what-and-why/user-centered-design.html. Accessed 3 Feb 2023
3. Norman, D.A.: The Design of Everyday Things. The MIT Press, Cambridge (2013)
4. https://en.wikipedia.org/wiki/Human-centered_design. Accessed 3 Feb 2023
5. Giacomin, J.: What is human centered design? Des. J. **17**(4), 606–623 (2014)
6. Norman, D.A. (ed.): User Centered System Design: New Perspectives on Human-Computer Interaction, 1st edn. CRC Press, Boca Raton (1986)
7. https://en.wikipedia.org/wiki/Design_thinking. Accessed 3 Feb 2023
8. Wigdor, D., Wixon, D.: Brave NUI World, Designing Natural User Interfaces for Touch and Gesture. Morgan Kaufman, Boston (2011)
9. Shamonsky, D.: User Experience Design Principles for a Natural User Interface (NUI). https://www.ics.com/blog/user-experience-design-principles-natural-user-interface-nui. Accessed 3 Feb 2023
10. Norman, D.A.: The Invisible Computer: Why Good Products Can Fail, the Personal Computer is so Complex, and Information Appliances are the Solution. The MIT Press, Cambridge (1998)

11. Kling, R.: The organizational context of user-centered software designs. MIS Q. **1**(4), 41–52 (1977)
12. https://www.iso.org/standard/77520.html. Accessed 3 Feb 2023
13. https://www.ideou.com/pages/design-thinking. Accessed 3 Feb 2023
14. https://en.wikipedia.org/wiki/John_E._Arnold. Accessed 3 Feb 2023

Multisensory MAYA – A Design Thinking Method to Enhance Predictability of Experience Design

Johanna Silvennoinen[(✉)] [iD] and Laura Mononen[iD]

Faculty of Information Technology, University of Jyvaskyla, 40014 Jyväskylä, Finland
`johanna.silvennoinen@jyu.fi, laura.m.mononen@ju.fi`

Abstract. The MAYA ("Most Advanced, Yet Acceptable") is a classic design principle, which aims at balancing the most advanced (novelty) with the yet acceptable (typicality) for enhancing product aesthetics and creating pleasurable experiences. The MAYA principle is established and widely examined, however, it has not been developed into a design thinking method for multisensory experience design purposes. In this paper, we present a multisensory design thinking method for MAYA, that facilitates designers' problem finding and solving during all phases of a design process. The focus is on developing the design thinking method in a manner that incorporates research knowledge on the five basic senses as well as design reasoning and the iterative nature of design thinking to enhance the predictability of multisensory experience design. The initial thought experiment questions and procedure were tested in a workshop with industrial designers. In the discussion, we elaborate on future development requirements, possibilities, and research directions.

Keywords: MAYA principle · Multisensory experience · Design thinking method · Experience design

1 Introduction

How people experience design artefacts is a complex issue. Especially from the designers' perspective concerning the possibilities of understanding and managing how design intentions transfer to users. Numerous approaches have been introduced and several research results have been presented to enhance the predictability of experience design ranging from low-level visual elements [e.g., 35, 1, 52], and higher-level design principles [6, 20, 26, 62] to, for instance, computational approaches [e.g., 36, 28, 42]. Recently, research on the role of the multiple senses in human experience has expanded. This is a natural progression in experience research focusing on humans interacting with technological artefacts as human experience is always multisensorial. We make sense of and experience artefacts through the senses in a cognitive-affective manner. Numerous studies have concentrated on elaborating the dynamics of different senses and their role in overall experience formation [e.g., 39, 59, 58, 53, 43].

Due to recent advancements, incorporating a multisensory design approach to experience design is considered an efficient strategy for controlling design communication and establishing more predictability when aiming to transfer intended experience contents from designers to users [e.g., 58, 53, 43]. Many studies report positive effects of cognitive information processing fluency on experience formation [e.g., 41, 63], which means that we tend to prefer objects that are typical, familiar and predictable. However, highly typical objects can also be experienced as uninsightful. Thus, pleasurable experiences need to balance typicality with a perceptual challenge by proving something novel allowing insights and raising interest [38]. For designers to be able to incorporate the sensory design approach in practice, methods and tools are needed to be able to manage the complex totality and underlying dynamics of experience design. Multisensory MAYA as a design thinking method aids in creating suitable outcomes and finding a solution that is in the current context the most optimal. However, creating pleasurable, awakening and intriguing designs requires the designer to sensitise and deeply understand the cognitive-emotional, socio-cultural and material environment of use.

A design thinking method called multisensory MAYA, its theoretical basis, rationale, and the possibility to increase the predictability of experience design are presented. The MAYA ("Most Advanced, Yet Acceptable") design principle indicates that in successful design the balance between novelty and typicality needs to be identified [20, 34]. The balance is context-dependent and originates from human psychological pursuits in avoiding the far ends [4]. Even though the identified balance is context-dependent, the underlying mechanisms of MAYA are more general and can thus be utilised in numerous different design contexts. Here, we focus on discussing the multisensory MAYA method from the design artefact's perspective, but the MAYA principle along with the presented method can be utilised in experience design in broader terms, such as in service design and brand design. Empirical evidence indicates that the MAYA principle operates reliably in several experience and design contexts [e.g., 7, 26, 22]. In addition, MAYA has been examined concerning simultaneous preference tendencies of prototypicality and novelty, complexity, and trendiness [26]. Overall, MAYA is recognized as an established design principle. A validated measurement has been developed (The Aesthetic Pleasure in Design Scale) which includes MAYA as one of the determinants of aesthetic pleasure [8]. However, there is no validated measurement to assess only MAYA, nor are there systematic design thinking methods to incorporate MAYA explicitly into the design processes, nor is there a MAYA-based method that would incorporate the different senses to the principle and the design process. Therefore, this paper focuses on the latter by presenting a design thinking method of multisensory MAYA.

The MAYA principle is enhanced by incorporating the multisensory nature of an experience for increased predictability of experience design and developed into a design thinking method. The method differentiates the basic five Aristotelian senses (sight, hearing, touch, taste, and smell) to be analysed based on the MAYA principle of existing artefacts, or to be utilised in designing novel artefacts. To be able to analyse the overall experience formation with the interaction of the senses, the explications of experience formation and different sensory integration mechanisms are needed. Multisensorial experiences are dynamic, as, for instance, one change in the haptic design of an artefact changes the whole experience concerning representations of the artefact pertaining to the other senses than the sense of touch. How experience occurs, sensations, perceptions, and apperceptions of multisensorial representations of properties in technological artefacts can be explicated with the cognitive-affective process through which information contents of mental representations are constructed [43, 50, 53]. Sensory properties of technological artefacts are capable of eliciting multisensorial mental contents in mental representations in which experience can be understood as the conscious part of a mental representation [50]. Sensory experiences are qualitatively attributed via apperception to non-perceptual contents, such as timelessness, uniqueness, and imaginativeness [50]. One of the main aspects of design for multiple senses is to achieve congruency and aim at avoiding incongruency (if it's not intentional) [57]. Metaphorically speaking, the whole experience should be orchestrated into a beautiful symphony. How can this be achieved as part of the design thinking process? How can we awaken designers to sensitise multisensory aspects of different designs in a new way? How can we assist the emergence of new perceptions and/or apperceptions in the designers thinking when designing for multisensory experiences? How can the design for multiple senses be integrated into the design thinking process to achieve the desired outcome? These are the questions we are aiming to answer in this article.

The paper is structured as follows. Firstly, design thinking and design thinking processes are described, including an explication of multisensory MAYA as a design thinking method within design thinking processes. Secondly, the problematisation of the predictability of experience design and how the multisensory MAYA method can be utilised in this endeavour to enhance the predictability of the desired experience outcomes is presented. Thirdly, the MAYA principle is described following with a presentation and description of the multisensory MAYA method. Lastly, discussion and conclusion are presented with future research topics.

2 Design Thinking and Design Processes

Many of the prevailing design approaches aim at understanding and emphasising human perspective in technology interaction [45]. This requires designers to profoundly understand how the human mind and the senses work, to be able to design meaningful experiences. The MAYA design principle encompasses a great and inherently human paradox, which is highly challenging to design for. Novelty and creativity are often desired attributes and are called for by designers thinking [18], however, at the same time human beings have difficulties in accepting and adapting to change, which novelty always contains. Therefore, as human beings we are living in constant conflict; on the one hand new, mysterious unknown and surprises are something we grave for, but at the same time we are comfortable in the familiar, routine and ordinary. Too much of the same bore us, but too much uncertainty scares us. Designers' understanding of these kinds of contradictions and human cognitive-emotional and sensory processing qualities are essential in creating experiences that are well received. This paper suggests that the management of complexity can be facilitated with research-based design methods based on mind sciences, such as the multisensory MAYA.

Designers' thinking is a multidimensional and complex reasoning process, especially when it aims at combining scientific knowledge with practical complex problem solving. It requires several design decisions and choices, which are both conscious and subconscious. Design methodologies have been described as falling into a line between two approaches; a) the reflective practitioner [49] which is described as an improvisational way of reasoning and reflective conversation of experts with the design situation, and b) the rational problem solver [54]. These two schools of thought have been seen in opposition to each other. However, recently Schaathun [46] has suggested that they are not necessarily exclusive, instead, similarities have been found, such as the iterativeness of the process and rationality. The design process aims to produce something (an artefact, service, experience etc.) to a particular situation, that is new and useful - in other words, a creative outcome. The nature of the process is suggested to be co-evolutive, meaning that the problem and the solution are being reformulated continuously [18, 46]. In the context of multisensory design thinking focusing on the MAYA principle, the aim is to find a balance between novelty and typicality in creating sensorial experiences conveyed with the design context at hand.

The design thinking process includes abstraction and practical rationality processes, in which reasoning takes place in problem formulation and solving evolutionarily throughout the whole design process [49, 55]. At its core are generative and evaluative phases, which are iteratively followed until a satisfactory outcome. These aspects are the foundations in several design process formulations, such as the double diamond model of design [3, 17]. These divergent and convergent phases as cognitive processes are highly studied in the research literature on creativity and underlie several process models of thinking that aims at renewal in many fields examining creativity.

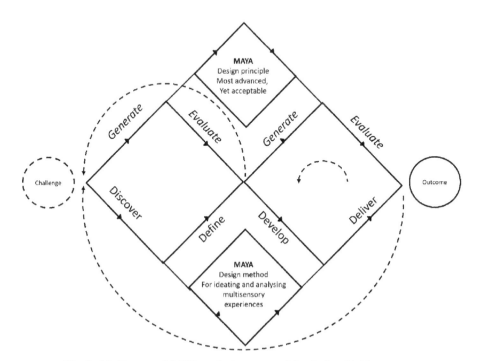

Fig. 1. Multisensory MAYA method as a part of the design thinking process.

In the design process, generative phases (i.e., moves) of discover and develop focus on producing more information (understanding, ideas, concepts, prototypes). Evaluative phases of define and deliver aim at analysing and finding the relevant knowledge for the situation at hand. Generative and evaluative phases alternate within the design process. The Multisensory MAYA method supports all phases of the design process. In Fig. 1, different phases, principles and methods of the design process are modified for the purposes of this paper and presented as part of the Design Council's framework for innovation [17] (evolved double diamond).

Here, design is seen holistically as an activity that is conducted when aiming to change the current state of affairs into something preferable [55], and design as a discipline revolves around "the conception and planning of the artificial" [9]. Within the current research goals of human-computer interaction (HCI), the aim is to integrate scientific knowledge and understanding into the design for increasing the predictability of the intended experience outcomes [e.g., 29]. Designing for targeted experiences is an interdisciplinary endeavour since it requires synthesising knowledge and balancing perspectives of different disciplines to translate obtained knowledge from abstract ideas and concepts into more concrete practical design properties. This requires an understanding of the foundational difference between the fields; sciences which are investigating the world *as it is*, and design which aims at transforming the world as *it ought to be* [13, 37]. Moreover, design is interested in artificial things, which are related to human actions, values, interests, goals, and purposes [45, 46]. Therefore, design reasoning and decision making, even when using scientific knowledge and understanding as its basis, are always propositional in the sense that they cannot be completely based on existing established laws or scientifically produced knowledge. Effective, pleasurable and ethical design requires careful argumentation and rationality, which benefits from explicating the design decisions and being based on a scientifically proven understanding of the human mind and life [45]. Facilitating this interplay of the fields is the overall goal of the multisensory MAYA method.

Despite the commonalities of the methods of Simon and Schön mentioned above, Schaathun [46] proposes that the major issue where the two paradigms of thought diverge is the way new insights are formed during the process. This is highlighted especially in wicked problems [9, 11] like multisensory design, where there are no one right formulation or solution and many interdependent factors are intermingling. In Simon's general problem solver, in the context of ill-defined problems, all the relevant information is already known, and the challenge of problem formulation is seen as the lack of computational power [54]. Instead, for Schön [49] design is essentially explorative and insights - which present themselves and are experienced as a surprise in designers' thinking - are born from the encounter with the yet unknown and unprecedented. New human behaviour, goals, and values are consciously and actively searched during the process. This way of approaching the nature of designers' thinking qualifies it as inherently creative, and the process as meaning creation. As Dorst and Cross [18] also suggest, this way of being directed towards and actively searching for surprises and insights is what assists designers to keep their thinking fresh and innovative and drives the creativity of their projects. Insight assists in thinking that transcend the existing frames of the mind. Balance their thinking between the routine way of thinking and its disruption act as the 'creative 'engine' of designers thinking. The Multisensory MAYA design thinking method is aiming to assist designers to gain insights into wicked problem solving situations by directing the focus on different aspects of the principle at a time.

Schaathun [46] proposes that Schön [49] sees expert thinkers as doing *thought experiments* when working with the design moves they have made. This is what he means by saying that design is a dialogue between the designer and the design and where the situation 'talks back' to the designer. In the multisensory MAYA method, the thought experiments can take two forms 1) generating a new, or 2) evaluating an existing artefact or experience. When creating a new concept, the designer may empathise and explore the situation as they imagine the user would, or act as the user in the situation (e.g., architect going into the building, user experience designer using the device; fashion designer using the clothes in the usage context and culture). By 'seeing' and/or 'being' with the design as the user, the designer can reframe and reinterpret problems, design properties and whole designs as well as empathise with relevant human values and goals. In the generative phase new insights and ideas are formed by experiencing and picturing the world imagined. In the evaluative phase, insights come from understanding what is relevant comes from evaluating the existing moves or parts of design and their interaction within the environment. This assists the designer in finding what is relevant to the situation at hand because there are several design decisions made in an 'ad hoc' manner and all the design decisions are not done consciously. This interplay of different cognitive processes in designers' thinking is essential for reaching rationality in design decision making because information processed with intuition and rationality are balancing and 'taming' each other [30, 46, 49]. Checking for biases in decision making and making the intuitive aspects of thinking more explicit are both supported in the multisensory MAYA method by phasing the process into focused reasoning, which concentrates on different aspects of the multisensory experience creation (experience, properties, the whole design, in Fig. 2).

According to this view, designers' reasoning progresses in an evolutive and iterative fashion: from disorder (focusing on insight) to order (focusing on relevance) and back again. The designer's own experiences assist in multisensory design experience creation by helping to generate, evaluate and integrate design moves. This suggests that designers' thinking and personal sensorial experiences as well as the outcome of the creative process and resulting user experiences are closely intermingling in designing for multisensory experiences. This interaction is supported by the multisensory MAYA design thinking method by providing research-based procedures and thought experience questions, that give boundaries and direction for the designers reasoning to evolve organically towards a desired outcome in the design situation with more predictability. In other words, it is guiding the designer towards 'where to look', but not telling 'what to see'.

3   Multisensory Design and Predictability of Experience Design

Experience research and design in different disciplines have traditionally concentrated on the sense of sight [12] as the most dominant sense in experience formation. More recently emphasis has been placed on examining the role of the other senses in how experiences occur. The multisensory design approach focuses on each sensory modality within a design process contributing to the overall experience formation in a way that the design properties convey certain experience contents [24]. At the core of understanding, experience formation is human cognitive and affective processes, especially in the context of designed artefacts to understand how experience contents are conveyed. This can be explained by the concept of apperception, i.e., 'seeing something as something' [27, 31, 44]. Apperception integrates already existing information and new information into a meaningful mental representation. Thus, apperception is different from perception as it integrates and operates as a unifying process in experience formation by incorporating existing and novel information of different sensory modalities. Understanding the contents of meaningful mental representations includes experiences conveyed via tangible design properties, but also non-perceivable contents, such as timelessness and uniqueness which are of the essence of meaning making [50]. Apperception thus can be used in shedding light on the non-perceivable experience contents and their importance. The multisensory MAYA method acknowledges in analysis and ideation phases the tangible design properties level and the semantic meaning making level by first focusing on what kind of experience contents would be targeted and then, via what kind of sensory design properties these could be conveyed.

The multisensory design approach has also been applied by some companies in developing successful multisensory design strategies [24]. However, multisensory marketing and/or design strategies are rarely created with scientific rigour, and thus, not utilising their possible full potential [25]. Multisensory design is one effective approach to enhancing the predictability of experience design. By focusing on one sense at a time and carefully analysing and designing certain experience contents via specific sensory design properties, more predictability to the overall experience formation can be obtained. As we humans are inherently multisensorial beings, all the senses play a role in the overall experience formation. If some sensory design properties are not explicated but still convey meanings to individuals, it affects the overall experience unpredictably and uncontrollably. For instance, many technological artefacts (e.g., car doors) incorporate sounds and if not deliberately designed to elicit certain experience contents, the sounds still affect the experience.

It is not simple to design specifically targeted experience contents. Understanding how human experience constructs, its underlying cognitive and affective processes, operations of the sense and their interactions, and the relationship between design properties and the elicited experience contents are in a central role. Through careful examinations of the above-mentioned central factors incorporated in design thinking and design processes, more predictability can be obtained. For example, there is more predictability of designing for cognatisation (e.g., in visual design the sense-making aspect based on the information processing fluency paradigm; an example of this in icon design, see [51]), and for touch compared to sight [53]. Stimuli evaluations focusing on sensemaking are conducted more unanimously between individuals than affective appraisals. As the ease of information processing fluency enhances the likelihood of positive affective appraisals to occur (e.g., aesthetic appeal), by focusing on the design of the sensemaking dimension more predictability can be achieved for the more unpredictable and unanimous affective dimension [51].

Key concepts in multisensory experience and design focus on sensory integration and one opposite concept with a focus on sensory incongruity. Multisensory integration combines information obtained from the different sensory modalities by harmonising sensory stimuli into one coherent experience [60]. Multisensory semantic congruency aims at designing to convey the same experience contents for the unexplicated senses based on the existing sensorial experience contents [32, 58]. Multisensory semantic congruity has been specially developed and examined in the fields of multisensory marketing and sensory branding [32, 58]. However, multisensory integration and multisensory semantic congruency do not incorporate the MAYA principle. Crossmodal correspondence focuses on spatial and temporal factors affecting sensory integration [16, 56]. Thus, crossmodal correspondencies can operate within multisensory integration to examine and explicate how integration occurs. The majority of multisensory design pursues the integration of sensory information. A contrary approach to multisensory design focuses on sensory incongruities by clashing sensory information obtained via one sensory modality to another sensory modality within a design context (Ludden et al.). This leads to incongruity in the obtained sensory information as the expectations constructed via one sensory modality are not supported by information obtained via another sense. This concept has been utilised as a design strategy for eliciting surprise via sensory incongruity and found to increase liking and elevate word of mouth [33]. However, design context plays a significant role in whether this strategy is successful or not [e.g., 19].

4   The MAYA Principle

The MAYA principle (*"Most Advanced, Yet Acceptable"*) stresses the importance of balancing the typical and the unknown or fluently cognized entities with elements disrupting the unity in designing the most pleasurable artefacts [20, 22]. The principle originates from Raymond Loewy [34]. He highlighted individual consumer thresholds for novelty. Every consumer has a certain level that novelty is wished for and if going over the threshold the novelty value transforms into a shock level. An artefact that balances the levels of typicality and novelty in the best way (highly context-dependent) reaches the MAYA level and thus, is the most successful one. The MAYA principle operates successfully based on the human tendency to avoid far ends, and therefore, the principle can be applied in a variety of domains [4].

The *"Most advanced"* part of the principle refers to novelty. Novelty is often considered in relation to typicality and stands as its counterpart [22]. Research on the effects of novelty reports positive outcomes, for example, that people prefer things that they experience as novel [6]. Artefacts appraised as novel can increase demand, accelerate the adaptation phase and redefine important aspects of personal consumption preferences [10]. In addition, novel, or atypical product designs, are also considered intriguing and are actively sought [23]. Designs appraised as novel are also apperceived as more attractive compared to highly typical designs [47].

However, in the overall experience formation influencing behaviour and interaction with artefacts, the *"Yet Acceptable"* also plays a significant role. The Yet Acceptable part of the principle refers to typicality and prototypicality. Typicality and prototypicality refer to what extent the object is a representational example of some category

[6, 22, 62]. Research also reports positive effects of typicality on artefact preferences [21]. Perceiving something as typical is a cognitive process [62]. Typical or prototypical stimulus is cognised fluently and categorised based on previous existing knowledge of an object pertaining to some category. Overall, preferences of typicality originate from human tendencies to avoid harm and danger and conduct safe choices [21]. Typical and prototypical stimulus is processed more fluently than novel stimulus [63] and the information processing fluency increases positive appraisals [40]. The fluency of the processing experience in itself has been indicated to increase aesthetic appeal [41]. Cognitive information processing fluency based on typicality or prototypicality perceptions increases the possibility of positive aesthetic appeal but involves other factors also. For instance, the design styles of different design eras question this relation, typical stimuli can be fluently processed but at the same time appraised as unappealing and old-fashioned [51]. Incorporating the MAYA principle in design practices benefits of acknowledging the effect of time and design eras on artefact evaluations.

Typicality and novelty are related in that people prefer moderated amount of typicality contrary to a high amount of typicality or novelty [5, 62]. Thus, finding the optimal balance between typicality and novelty increases preferences and aesthetic interest. The ideal balance of typicality and novelty (i.e., The MAYA level) is highly context-dependent as people assess and experience artefacts with different goals in their minds which highly influences how to design properties are aesthetically appraised [2]. Overall, novelty and typicality appraisals are separate but highly influential contextual factors, both contributing to aesthetic appeal appraisals of artefacts [7].

5   Multisensory MAYA – The Design Thinking Method

The overall rationale of the MAYA method (Fig. 2) is to analyse an existing artefact (including prototypes etc.) or ideate (design brief or challenge) separately for each sensory modality (here, the five Aristotelian senses) to find a meaningful balance within the MAYA principle for each sense. The design process is supported by the method's thought experiment questions awakening the designer(s) to investigate and ideate experience contents, design properties, and the overall experience design. The sensory design suggestions in conveying certain experience contents are ideated in terms of sensory design properties through which the experience contents could be communicated for each sense at a time focusing on a pleasurable context-dependent MAYA level. Lastly, the sensory design suggestions are analysed and further elaborated from the perspective of how the sensory design solutions interact with each other in the overall experience formation process. This phase refers to the design principle of the optimal match [20]. The principle of optimal match stresses that the information obtained via different sensory modalities is required to be internally consistent throughout the artefact to elicit meaningful experiences. Thus, optimal match functions through multisensory integration in which cross-modal correspondences operate. In addition to sensory integration, a contrary design approach can be utilised. This refers to the design strategy of deliberate sensory incongruities. In addition, experience design can take different stances concerning the intensity of the experiential goals which are incorporated in the design thinking method of multisensory MAYA.

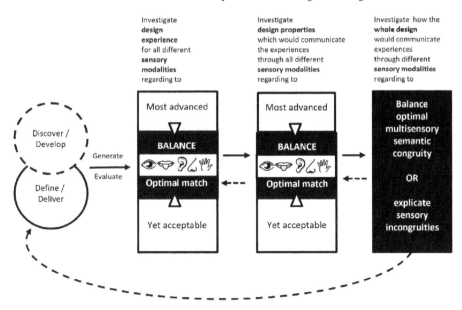

Fig. 2. Procedure for Multisensory MAYA Method.

The multisensory MAYA method was tested and utilised in a workshop involving designers of a large industrial design company and gained positive feedback on its ability to enhance design thinking for creativity and ideation providing a change in perspective. The method was also appreciated for enabling a detailed analysis of an existing artefact via different sensory design dimensions and being able to ideate novel sensory design possibilities for the different senses contributing to the overall experience formation. The results of the workshop are kept private due to the company's privacy policy and non-disclosure agreement and, thus, cannot be further reported here.

In our future research, we focus on more empirical examination of the method and development. In Fig. 3 the utilised multisensory MAYA template is presented. Firstly, (1) workshop participants were briefly introduced to the topic with an introductory lecture on the multisensory design approach, its benefits, description of the MAYA principle and its underlying dynamics in human experience, key concepts of multisensory integration and sensory incongruity and instructions on how to use the template. The next step (2) was to analyse an existing artefact to ideate ideal MAYA levels for one sense at a time regarding what kind of experience contents would be targeted. The MAYA method was conducted in pairs with printed templates in A3 size (29,7 cm × 42,0 cm). Participants carefully went through the context-dependent balancing process for each sense separately and examined carefully the balance sections of the template. The next step (3) was to ideate how MAYA balanced sensory design ideas could be conveyed to users via design properties including the context-dependent balance within the MAYA. Lastly, (4) participants wrote and drafted their novel design ideas as an entity.

The method can be used by individual designers, or it can be used by design teams. It provides a communication platform between designers in the design team, which assist in verbalising and communicating ideas. Often the language regarding sensory

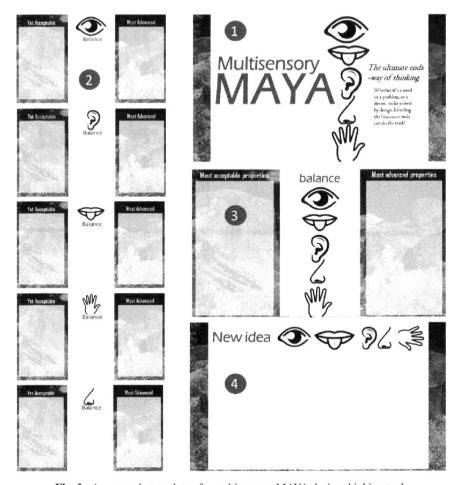

Fig. 3. An example template of a multisensory MAYA design thinking tool.

experiences is metaphorical and abstract. Therefore, multisensory MAYA is efficient when used as a collaborative design method to achieve a common understanding and shared language of design decisions related to sensory experiences.

The multisensory MAYA templates can be filled with text and/or drawings. Sketches are important design thinking tools [13, 61]. In order to accurately reason, evaluate and communicate ideas, designers need *stable forms* [46], this assists in the thought experiment to 'talk back' in Schön's terms. The sketch gives feedback to the designer on the ways the experience design is developing and advises ways to improve the design at hand. This iterative process can bring hidden and tacit expertise and knowledge about sensory experiences to light and advance design reasoning. The design process is an evolutionary system which evolves through a series of phases (moves), each phase is born from the current frame and then continues to create the next new frame [46]. By sketching the design concept is being con-figurated and re-figurated [46]. Sketches assist in the dialogue between designers' intuition and scientific information in the multisensory design, they help with design reasoning by assisting in dealing with the experiential contingencies and sensorial uniqueness of the real-world design stance.

6   Discussion and Conclusions

Designing for multisensory experiences is a complex and multifaceted process, which calls for the awakening of the designers' senses, as well as a deep understanding of human cognitive and affective processes when interacting with design artefacts. At the core of design practice is the question: How do designers' intentions transfer to users and how to manage this? And how to incorporate more predictability in designing for targeted experiences? An efficient way to approach this dilemma is to incorporate the multisensory design approach [25]. By designing for one sense at a time and analysing each sensory design solution contributing to the overall experience formation, more predictability of the experience outcomes can be obtained. The MAYA principle [22, 34] is efficient in combining human tendencies to avoid far ends [4] with the quest to find something novel and delightful. A desirable MAYA level is obtained when a balance in the design decisions is reached that balances typicality and novelty in a context-dependent manner [22, 34]. To aid in the design process incorporating the MAYA principle we developed and presented a design thinking method: The multisensory MAYA. The method development operationalises the MAYA principle into a design thinking method enhanced with the multisensory design approach to further increase the predictability of experience design.

The multisensory MAYA can be utilised in a variety of design contexts and was tested with industrial designers. Even though, the method is ready to be utilised as presented in this paper, for instance with the example template, requirements for further developments have been identified to make the multisensory MAYA method more explicit, detailed and extended with existing research on design principles. In our future research, we focus on empirical examinations of the method to get more insights into the development work and to test the method in different design phases, since in the workshop the method was only tested in an evaluative manner. It would be also interesting to examine whether the method could be digitalised enabling remote group work, co-ideation, and co-creation. The thought experiment questions are to be further elaborated to aid in the process in more detail. Also, a more structured manner to map the experience contents to be conveyed via each sensory modality with the sensory design properties would aid the design thinking process. Moreover, the multisensory MAYA method could be extended to include also other senses in addition to the five Aristotelian senses.

A continuous balancing act is required for communicating effectively to the users and customers, for example, newness can be inserted into the designs gradually like Apple does when it modifies products bit by bit [15]. On the other hand, typicality can be balanced by the conscious use of existing design conventions and common design principles, which are already familiar to users. In turn, sometimes it might be important to make a more radical sensory design to get attention or separate the design from the competition or to gain the attention of special user groups such as the young generations. This is a more risky approach since it takes time for users to accept the bigger changes made to the design. Big companies have less risk in applying newness, but for smaller companies, it might be riskier. However, they often have to find ways to bring forth originality that is lacking from the larger competitors.

Future research and MAYA method development will focus on examining and explicating which existing laws, principles, heuristics, psychological effects and design guidelines can be used in designing for typicality (e.g., conventions and standards) and what design thinking methods or ideation tools can be used for ideation for the most advanced. Future development would also include further formulation of essential thought experiment questions to guide the design thinking process. In addition, as cognitive scientific understanding of human-technology interaction can assist designers by giving vocabulary and conceptualising otherwise often implicit and intuitive aspects of interaction, such as multisensory experiences, future research focuses also to include examining the ways in which research could assist especially in the integration phase of the MAYA design process. Since the integration phase is the most challenging part of the multisensory experience design.

References

1. Altaboli, A., Lin, Y.: Investigating effects of screen layout elements on interface and screen design aesthetics. Adv. Hum. Comput. Interact. **2011**, 1–10 (2011)
2. Armstrong, T., Detweiler-Bedell, B.: Beauty as an emotion: the exhilarating prospect of mastering a challenging world. Rev. Gen. Psychol. **12**(4), 305–329 (2008)
3. Banathy, B.H.: Designing Social Systems in a Changing World. Springer, New York (1996). https://doi.org/10.1007/978-1-4757-9981-1
4. Berlyne, D.: Aesthetics and Psychobiology. Appleton-Century-Crofts, New York (1971)
5. Berlyne, D.: Studies in the new experimental aesthetics: steps toward an objective psychology of aesthetic appreciation. Hemisphere (1974)
6. Blijlevens, J., Carbon, C.C., Mugge, R., Schoormans, J.P.: Aesthetic appraisal of product designs: independent effects of typicality and arousal. Br. J. Psychol. **103**(1), 44–57 (2011)
7. Blijlevens, J., Gemser, G., Mugge, R.: The importance of being 'well- laced': the influence of context on perceived typicality and esthetic appraisal of product appearance. Acta Physiol. **139**(1), 178–186 (2012). https://doi.org/10.1016/j.actpsy.2011.11.004
8. Blijlevens, J., Thurgood, C., Hekkert, P., Chen, L.L., Leder, H., Whitfield, T.W.: The aesthetic pleasure in design scale: the development of a scale to measure aesthetic pleasure for designed artifacts. Psychol. Aesthet. Creat. Arts **11**(1), 86–98 (2017)
9. Buchanan, R.: Wicked problems in design thinking. Des. Issues **8**(2), 5–21 (1992)
10. Calantone, R.J., Kwong, C., Cui, A.S.: Decomposing product innovativeness and its effects on new product success. J. Prod. Innov. Manag. **23**(5), 408–421 (2006)
11. Churchman, C.W.: Wicked problems. Manag. Sci. **4**(14), 141–142 (1967)
12. Crilly, N., Moultrie, J., Clarkson, P.J.: Seeing things: consumer response to the visual domain in product design. Des. Stud. **25**(6), 547–577 (2004). https://doi.org/10.1016/j.destud.2004.03.001
13. Cross, N.: Designerly ways of knowing. Des. Stud. **3**, 221–227 (1982). https://doi.org/10.1016/0142-694X(82)90040-0
14. Cross, N.: Natural intelligence in design. Des. Stud. **20**(1), 25–39 (1999)
15. Dam, R.F.: The Maya principle: design for the future, but balance it with your users' present. Interact. Des. **17** (2021)
16. Deroy, O., Spence, C.: Crossmodal correspondences: four challenges. Multisens. Res. **29**(1–3), 29–48 (2016)
17. Design Council, Framework for Innovation; Design Council's evolved Double Diamond (2019). https://www.designcouncil.org.uk/. Accessed 08 Feb 2023

18. Dorst, K., Cross, N.: Creativity in the design process: co-evolution of problem–solution. Des. Stud. **22**(5), 425–437 (2001)
19. Gross, A., Silvennoinen, J.: Surprise as a design strategy in goal-oriented mobile applications. In: Rebelo, F., Soares, M. (eds.) Proceedings of the 5th International Conference on Applied Human Factors and Ergonomics, AHFE 2014, pp. 4716–4726. Advances in Human Factors and Ergonomics (2014)
20. Hekkert, P.: Design aesthetics: principles of pleasure in design. Psychol. Sci. **48**(2), 157–172 (2006)
21. Hekkert, P.: Aesthetic responses to design: a battle of impulses. In: Tinio, P., Smith, J. (eds.) The Cambridge Handbook of the Psychology of Aesthetics and the Arts, pp. 277–299. Cambridge University Press, Cambridge (2014)
22. Hekkert, P., Snelders, D., Wieringen, P.C.W.: 'Most advanced, yet acceptable': typicality and novelty as joint predictors of aesthetic preference in industrial design. Br. J. Psychol. **94**, 111–124 (2003). https://doi.org/10.1348/000712603762842147
23. Holbrook, M.B., Hirschman, E.C.: The experiential aspects of consumption: consumer fantasies, feelings and fun. J. Consum. Res. **9**, 132–140 (1982)
24. Hultén, B.: Sensory marketing: the multi-sensory brand-experience concept. Eur. Bus. Rev. **23**(3), 256–273 (2011)
25. Hultén, B., Broweus, N., van Dijk, M.: Sensory Marketing. Palgrave Macmillan, Basingstoke (2009)
26. Hung, W.-K., Chen, L.-L.: Effects of novelty and its dimensions on aesthetic preference in product design. Int. J. Des. **6**(3), 81–90 (2012)
27. Husserl, E.: The Crisis of European Sciences and Transcendental Phenomenology. Northwestern University Press, Evanston (1936)
28. Ivory, M.Y., Sinha, R.R., Hearst, M.A.: Empirically validated web page design metrics. In: Proceedings of the SIGCHI Conference on Human Factors in Computing Systems, pp. 53–60. ACM Press (2001)
29. Jokinen, J.P.P., Silvennoinen, J., Kujala, T.: Relating experience goals with visual user interface design. Interact. Comput. **30**(5), 378–395 (2018). https://doi.org/10.1093/iwc/iwy016
30. Kahneman, D.: Thinking, Fast and Slow. Farrar, Straus and Giroux, US (2011)
31. Kant, I.: Critique of Pure Reason. English Translation by Paul Guyer and Allen Wood (1998). Cambridge University Press, Cambridge (1787)
32. Krishna, A., Schwarz, N.: Sensory marketing, embodiment, and grounded cognition: a review and introduction. J. Consum. Psychol. **24**(2), 159–168 (2014)
33. Ludden, G., Schifferstein, H., Hekkert, P.: Visual–tactual incongruities in products as sources of surprise. Empir. Stud. Arts **27**(1), 61–87 (2009). https://doi.org/10.2190/EM.27.1.d
34. Loewy, R.: Never Leave Well Enough Alone. Simon and Schuster (1951)
35. Michailidou, E., Harper, S., Bechhofer, S.: Visual complexity and aesthetic perception of web pages. In: Proceedings of the 26th Annual ACM International Conference on Design of Communication, pp. 215–224. ACM Press (2008)
36. Miniukovich, A., De Angeli, A.: Computation of interface aesthetics. In: Proceedings of the SIGCHI Conference on Human Factors in Computing Systems, pp. 1163–1172. ACM Press (2015)
37. Mononen, L.: Systems thinking and its contribution to understanding future designer thinking. Des. J. **20**(Sup1), S4529–S4538 (2017)
38. Muth, C., Westphal-Fitch, G., Carbon, C.-C.: Seeking (dis)order: ordering appeals but slight disorder and complex order trigger interest. Psychol. Aesthet. Creat. Arts **15**(3), 439–457 (2021). https://doi.org/10.1037/aca0000284

39. Obrist, M., Ranasinghe, N., Spence, C.: Multisensory human–computer interaction. Int. J. Hum. Comput. Stud. **107** (2017)
40. Posner, M.I., Keele, S.W.: On the genesis of abstract ideas. J. Exp. Psychol. **77**, 353–363 (1968). https://doi.org/10.1037/h0025953
41. Reber, R., Schwarz, N., Winkielman, P.: Processing fluency and aesthetic pleasure: is beauty in the perceiver's processing experience? Pers. Soc. Psychol. Rev. **8**(4), 364–382 (2004)
42. Reinecke, K., Yeh, T., Miratrix, L., Mardiko, R., Zhao, Y., Liu, J., Gajos, K.Z.: Predicting users' first impressions of website aesthetics with a quantification of perceived visual complexity and colorfulness. In: Proceedings of the SIGCHI Conference on Huma Factors in Computing Systems, pp. 2049–2058. ACM Press (2013)
43. Rousi, R., Silvennoinen, J., Perälä, P., Jokinen, J.P.: Beyond MAYA for game-changing multisensory design. In: Proceedings of the 21st International Academic Mindtrek Conference, pp. 147–153. ACM Press (2017)
44. Saariluoma, P.: Apperception, content-based psychology and design. In: Lindemann, U. (eds.) Human Behaviour in Design, pp. 72–78. Springer, Heidelberg (2003). https://doi.org/10.1007/978-3-662-07811-2_8
45. Saariluoma, P., Cañas, J., Leikas, J.: Designing for Life: A Human Perspective on Technology Development. Palgrave Macmillan, London (2016)
46. Schaathun, H.G.: Where Schön and Simon agree: the rationality of design. Des. Stud. **79**, 101090 (2022)
47. Schoormans, J.P.L., Robben, H.S.J.: The effect of new package design on product attention, categorization and evaluation. J. Econ. Psychol. **18**, 271–387 (1997). https://doi.org/10.1016/S0167-4870(97)00008-1
48. Schön, D.A.: The Reflective Practitioner: How Professionals Think in Action. Routledge, Milton Park (2017)
49. Schön, D.A.: The reflective practioner. Ashgate Arena (1983)
50. Silvennoinen, J.: Apperceiving visual elements in human-technology interaction design. Jyväskylä Stud. Comput. **261** (2017)
51. Silvennoinen, J. Jokinen, J.P.P.: Aesthetic appeal and visual usability in four icon design eras. In: Proceedings of the 2016 SIGCHI Conference on Human Factors in Computing Systems, pp. 4390–4400. ACM Press (2016)
52. Silvennoinen, J., Jokinen, J.P.P.: Appraisals of salient visual elements in web page design. In: Advances in Human–Computer Interaction 2016 (2016)
53. Silvennoinen, J., Rousi, R., Jokinen, J.P.P., Perälä, P.: Apperception as a multisensory process in material experience. In: Proceedings of the Academic Mindtrek, pp. 144–151. ACM Press (2015). https://doi.org/10.1145/2818187.2818285
54. Simon, H.A.: The structure of ill structured problems. Artif. Intell. **4**(3–4), 181–201 (1973)
55. Simon, H.A.: The Sciences of the Artificial. 3rd edn. Cambridge (1996)
56. Spence, C.: Crossmodal correspondences: a tutorial review. Atten. Percept. Psychophys. **73**, 971–995 (2011)
57. Spence, C.: Senses of place: architectural design for the multisensory mind. Cognit. Res. Princ. Implic. **5**(1), 1–26 (2020). https://doi.org/10.1186/s41235-020-00243-4
58. Stach, J.: A conceptual framework for the assessment of brand congruent sensory modalities. J. Brand Manag. **22**(8), 673–694 (2015)
59. Stein, B.E. (ed.): The New Handbook of Multisensory Processing. MIT Press, Cambridge (2012)
60. Stein, B.E., Meredith, M.A.: The Merging of the Senses. The MIT Press, Cambridge (1993)
61. Tversky, B.: What do sketches say about thinking. In: 2002 AAAI Spring Symposium, Sketch Understanding Workshop. Stanford University, AAAI Technical Report, SS-02-08, vol. 148, p. 151 (2002)

62. Veryzer, R., Hutchinson, W.: The influence of unity and prototypicality on aesthetic responses to new product designs. J. Consum. Res. **24**(4), 374–394 (1998). https://doi.org/10.1086/209516

63. Winkielman, P., Halberstadt, J., Fazendeiro, T., Catty, S.: Prototypes are attractive because they are easy on the mind. Psychol. Sci. **17**(9), 799–806 (2006)

What is the New Future of Work for UX Research Practice? Assessing UX Research Practice During the COVID-19 Pandemic and Beyond

Lauren E. Snyder[1] , Rebecca Hazen[1], and Amanda K. Hall[1,2]

[1] University of Washington, Seattle, WA 98195, US
Amanda.Hall@microsoft.com
[2] Microsoft Research, Redmond, WA 98052, US

Abstract. The User Experience (UX) Research profession was particularly impacted by the COVID-19 pandemic shift to remote work, as their work is largely dependent on engagements with customers, stakeholders, co-workers, and colleagues. The new future of work for UX research practice is still uncertain. Therefore, our study seeks to (1) address how COVID-19-associated remote work impacted UX research practice and (2) assess changes to UX research practice considerations, including methodologies, tools, and applications. We conducted a survey of UX research professionals with 52 open- and closed-ended questions to assess demographics, application and tool use, and UX research practice factors before and during the COVID-19 pandemic. A total of 220 UX research survey respondents world-wide responded to the survey. We found an increase in use of virtual applications and tools, virtual studies, and a mix of positive and negative COVID-19 impacts on UX research practice. Respondents reported changes to how they recruit participants, what study design methods they employ, how they analyze data, and how they share findings with stakeholders as likely to persist post pandemic. This study aimed to assess the impacts of remote work on UX research practice to support the new future of work initiatives and identify best practices.

Keywords: User Experience Research · COVID-19 · Future of work

1 Introduction

The COVID-19 pandemic has impacted the way we live and, of special note for this study, the way we work. Given health concerns and uncertainty around the spread of severe acute respiratory syndrome coronavirus 2 (SARS-CoV-2), most of the world's in-person labor force activity ceased, and nonessential workers transitioned to work from home. The long-term socio-economic and socio-technical implications of a shift from traditionally in-person work cultures to completely remote work is still being realized. The COVID-19 pandemic shift was unlike pre-pandemic remote work models given the magnitude and expedience; the future of work has been significantly and permanently changed.

© The Author(s), under exclusive license to Springer Nature Switzerland AG 2023
A. Marcus et al. (Eds.): HCII 2023, LNCS 14030, pp. 324–342, 2023.
https://doi.org/10.1007/978-3-031-35699-5_24

The UX profession is rapidly growing and is anticipated to scale, from current estimates of 1 million up to 100 million professionals by 2050 (Nielsen 2017). One major subset of the UX profession is user experience (UX) research, also commonly called user research, design research, human factors engineering, and usability research, depending on the industry. UX research provides actionable, user-derived insight, with a focus on designing to improve the user experience, to a broad variety of fields ranging from oil and gas to consumer health informatics. The interaction design foundation defines UX research as:

"the systematic study of target users and their requirements, to add realistic contexts and insights to design processes through various methods to uncover problems and design opportunities." (IxDF, n.d.)

UX research is derived from the study of human-computer interaction (HCI). However, the two are inherently different when it comes to practice. The field of HCI is primarily dedicated to the academic study of human and computer interaction, whereas UX research focuses on the active process of building human-centered products. UX researchers seek to understand users' (i.e., customers') needs, challenges, and workflows (cognitive and task specific) to identify unmet user needs, opportunities, and usability issues to inform product requirements and iterative design. UX researchers empirically gather evidence (via qualitative and quantitative methodologies) by continually engaging with stakeholders and customers throughout the product design lifecycle to validate or challenge assumptions and provide evidence to unanswered questions posed by product teams. UX researchers provide insights to support product/project managers and designers to ensure teams build the right products (experiences) in the right way that addresses customers' needs. UX researchers conduct rapid discovery of customer challenges, problems, and frustrations to foster empathy for innovative solutions.

The most common UX research study methodologies, study participant recruitment strategies, analyses/sensemaking techniques, and sharing/presentation of research study findings are conducted in-person with colleagues, stakeholders, study participants, and customers (U. S. H. H. S. 2016; Klein 2013; Rohrer 2014). For instance, Vermeeren et al. conducted a multi-year study of UX evaluation methods used in academia and industry in which they found that, out of 96 methods, only 27 can be used online, with only 7 online methods available for the early phases of the product development process (Vermeeren et al. 2010). Most of the UX evaluation methods are for use in the lab and field settings (64 lab vs 66 field methods), which allows researchers the ability to collect data in the real context of use for more reliable UX data (Vermeeren et al. 2010). The COVID-19 pandemic forced most industries and people to adhere to stay-at-home-mandates, which made in-person encounters with stakeholders and customers for studies conducted in lab or field settings nearly impossible in most cases. UX researchers had to adapt to remote work life quickly.

Various international studies and reports have been conducted to monitor how the shift from in-person to remote work has affected employee work behavior: for example, the impact on productivity, collaboration, and wellbeing. Employees reported being more stressed, more siloed in their teams, more fatigued due to increased meetings and electronic communications, working longer hours, and found it more challenging to do brainstorming and creative work remotely among many other effects (Lund et al. 2021;

Teevan et al. 2022). While previous research has focused on work related impacts of the COVID-19 pandemic from a mix of occupations, there is a lack of findings on how the COVID-19 pandemic has impacted the UX researcher profession.

Two recent studies assessed the effects of COVID-19 on UX research practice. The first study analyzed 49 blog posts related to post-pandemic UX research practice experiences (Süner-Pla-Cerdà et al. 2021). The authors conducted a content analysis of the 49 UX research blog posts and found topics ranged from types of research methods used, to trustworthiness of data collected, to remote collaboration, and wellness of others as content topics being discussed online during the COVID-19 pandemic. The second study looked at the impact that COVID-19 had on UX researchers in an online survey of 57 respondents (Shah & Jain 2021). The authors of the online survey found that 67% of respondents reported challenges with working and conducting research remotely as well as with the running/execution (58%) and planning (55%) of research, and additional challenges associated with recruitment of participants and virtual collaboration as key themes. However, neither of these two studies assessed UX research practice before and during COVID-19, nor did they explore any longer-term impacts on key UX researcher practices.

Many tools that were used infrequently by UX researchers became commonplace during the pandemic. The State of User Research 2021 report conducted by User Interviews (surveyed December 2020 to January 2021, of 525 respondents who reported conducting research at least part-time) found changes in use of remote tools from 2019 to 2020. For example, Miro was used by 60% of respondents in 2020 compared to 8% the previous year and Mural was used by 22% of respondents in 2020 compared to 2% the previous year (Balboni 2021). User Interviews also found that 90% of respondents conducted their work completely remote at the end of 2020 compared to 21% the previous year. The quick adoption of remote tools, applications, and the plethora of new feature offerings to support remote work since early 2020 is astounding, and more research is needed to understand how COVID-19 has affected UX research application and tool use before and during COVID-19.

The new future of work for UX research practice is still uncertain. Therefore, our study seeks to assess UX research practice during the COVID-19 pandemic. Specifically, we aim to (1) address how COVID-19-associated remote work impacted UX research practice and (2) assess changes to UX research practice tactics, methodologies, tools, and applications that are likely to persist post-pandemic.

2   Materials and Methods

We conducted a survey with 52 open- and closed-ended questions to assess UX Researcher demographics and application/tool use, assess changes to UX Research practice before/during COVID-19, and explore any positive or negative impacts. We recruited respondents through various social media, professional networks/groups, and IM channels, leveraging a convenience sampling frame. The inclusion criteria for the study were: 1) over 18 years of age, 2) English language speaker, and 3) currently work or have worked in UX research before or during the COVID-19 pandemic. Participation was voluntary and consent was acquired at the start of the survey.

Our survey instrument included a mix of structured and unstructured question types that took approximately 15 min to complete. No questions were required, and respondents were able to skip or quit the survey at any time. Please see Supplementary File 1 for the survey instrument. We administered the survey and managed data collection through REDCap1.2, a webtool for translational research that was developed by Vanderbilt University; our instance of REDCap was hosted by the University of Washington (Harris et al. 2009, 2019). The survey was open Feb 17, 2021, to April 1, 2021. The study was reviewed and received Institutional Review Board approval.

2.1 Measures

The survey consisted of three main parts: 1) demographics and background 2) UX tool usage and 3) changes to UX practice during COVID-19. For Sect. 1, we asked respondents to report basic demographics: age, gender identity, location, race, and ethnicity. We also asked respondents for information about their professional background, including role, industry, years of experience, employment type, company size of employer, and research methods used. In section two, we asked respondents which UX tools they used before and during COVID-19 using a checkbox response for the list of preidentified tools. We asked respondents to include a list of any other tools they have used during COVID-19 and how much time they worked remotely before and during COVID-19. For the third section, we structured our questions around 4 key areas of UX research: recruitment, methods, analysis, and sharing. We asked respondents how COVID-19 has impacted each area (using a Likert response scale from "Extremely negatively" to "Extremely positively") and asked how likely they are to adopt COVID-19 related changes (using a Likert response scale from "Very unlikely" to "Very likely"). We also asked respondents open-ended questions to share additional information about how each area has been impacted.

2.2 Data Analysis

Our qualitative data analysis consisted of thematic coding with two researchers (A.H. and R. H.) with a deductive codebook and frequent checks for intercoder reliability. A third researcher (L.S.) reviewed all survey data and discussed any coding discrepancies with other researchers. Descriptive statistics were produced using R Version 1.1.419.

3   Results

Overall, we had 224 survey respondents, and four were excluded for inappropriate or offensive responses, resulting in 220 overall. All questions, including demographics, in the survey were optional. Most participants were willing to share this information, with the highest 'prefer not answer' or nonresponse rate as 12.3% for any demographic question. Respondents primarily identified as female (66.1%) and were primarily from the United States (82.1%). Participants ranged in age from 21 to 65 with an average age of 37 (SD = 9.39). The median age of respondents was 36. For ethnicity, 75.4% of respondents selected a 'Not Hispanic or Latino' response option. Respondents were allowed to provide multiple responses to our question about race, and most respondents selected their race as white (67.3%); the next highest response was 'Asian' (14.5%). Our respondents skewed towards United States participation. Approximately 12% of respondents lived outside of the United States, including respondents from Europe (n = 17), Canada (n = 5), Asia (n = 3), Africa (n = 1), and South America (n = 1).

Most respondents have been in the UX Research field for 6 years or longer and are currently salaried or full-time employees (FTE). The majority of respondents were User Experience Researchers (n = 139) and most worked at 'Big Tech' organizations (multiple responses allowed, n = 80). A number of respondents were UX Design Researchers (n = 54) and many worked at software companies (n = 45). Of note, 67 respondents noted that they work in a medical or health related organization (captured as 'medical device company', 'medical institute', 'pharmaceuticals' and 'healthcare or health sciences', multiple responses allowed). In our survey, 73 (or one third) of respondents worked on COVID-19 related. Full demographic information is available from the corresponding author.

3.1 Tools

Participants reported a drastic shift in tool use during the COVID-19 pandemic that was likely influenced by the sudden change in many other virtual work practices. Unsurprisingly, the greatest number of respondents reported using more video conferencing tools such as Zoom and Microsoft (MS) Teams (an increase of 58.2% and 46%, respectively). Survey Monkey and Maze also ranked highly for increase in percent of respondents reporting new use during the COVID-19 pandemic (an increase of 63.3% and 125%, respectively). Interestingly, some common tools, such as Adobe XD and Sketch, were noted as having less frequent tool use during the COVID-19 pandemic as they did prior (a decrease of 15.6% and 24.1%, respectively). UsabilityHub and Marvel also experienced a decrease in use from respondents, though the number of users noting a decrease in use was less noticeable than their percent change (a decrease of 40% and 44.4%, respectively).

We also asked respondents if there were any other new tools that they used frequently during the COVID-19 pandemic. Miro and Optimal Workshop (including Optimal Sort and Treejack) each received more than 20 'write in' responses (24 and 21, respectively), which accounted for approximately 10% of all respondents (n = 220). Ten or more respondents also wrote either Mural or Dovetail. We report on additional qualitative findings related to tool use in the Methods and Study Design section of the paper. A full breakdown of free text and structured tool responses are available by contacting the authors (Fig. 1).

Though we anticipated reporting on more inferential statistics, we found that regression models and Kruskal Wallis tests yielded no significant results between several variable combinations in our quantitative data analysis.

3.2 Impact on Recruitment

Of the 189 respondents who answered the question about the impact of COVID-19 on recruitment, 24.9% reported a negative impact, 21.2% reported a positive impact,

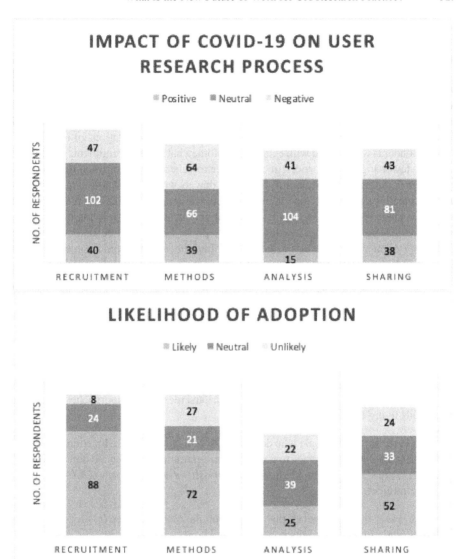

Fig. 1. Graphs of the responses to Impact of COVID-19 on UX Research Process and the likelihood that these changes would persist after the pandemic

and 54% felt there was neither a positive nor negative impact. Almost half, or 48.6%, responded that they were likely to adopt changes to recruitment resulting from COVID-19 in their future work. Few, or 4.4%, were unlikely to adopt changes. The remaining respondents reported that they were neither likely nor unlikely, 13.2%, or felt that the question did not apply to them (33.7%).

The primary job of a UX researcher is to learn from their users; whether in conducting foundational studies or small-scale usability trials, UX researchers are dependent on their ability to recruit participants to engage in research activities. Research recruitment will look different depending on factors including the type of study and the target respondent. For example, some researchers can rely on large panels made up of broad, general populations like UserTesting.com or User Interviews to connect with potential participants (e.g., people looking to buy a house, individuals who use credit unions, retail workers, individuals who have used auto loan services to purchase a car). In other cases, researchers may be forced to rely on either in-person recruitment methods like snowball sampling, or specialized services to connect to more unique populations of interest.

Respondents who replied with extremely or somewhat positive sentiments commonly reported fewer logistical barriers: it was easier to schedule participants, often due to increased flexibility and availability of times due to work-from-home situations and fewer competing activities. Respondents also noted that researchers and their participants no longer needed to travel for sessions, and that both groups were growing comfortable with participating in online activities. At some point, however, it became apparent to many respondents that there was a need to be mindful of stress, zoom fatigue (Williams 2021), and burnout associated with the pandemic and a sudden shift in many aspects of their lives due to COVID-19.

> "People are less willing to participate due to stress, limited capacity/time. However, this is balanced a bit by the lower ask for participation - it's easier to fit Zoom interviews in among other meetings and responsibilities and it requires no travel." -P84 responded 'neutral' to the impact of COVID-19 on recruitment.

Several respondents noted that it was easier to reach and recruit from populations that were previously difficult to access with traditional recruitment approaches, including individuals living in more rural areas.

> "We can recruit more people who don't live in our local area, since location doesn't matter. It also makes it easier to recruit diverse participants since we don't live in a diverse area."- P22 responded 'somewhat positive' to the impact of COVID-19 on recruitment.

There was concern, however, that certain populations would see less representation in studies, including older adults.

> "[we] recruit only online during COVID-19...I worry about not reaching older adults and less tech savvy." -P133 responded 'neutral' to the impact of COVID19 on recruitment.

There were mixed perceptions when it came to research participant quality in remote studies recruited through online panels: while many saw a benefit in terms of ability to quickly recruit research participants, some felt that the influx of "testers" due to COVID-19 had led to a decrease in the quality of available panels and a simultaneous increase in the number of "professional research participants," or individuals that were taking part in research as a full- or part-time job.

"There are more career participants now and it can be harder to get quality participants vs. people who give fake data." -P9 responded 'somewhat negative' to the impact of COVID-19 on recruitment.

In either case, researchers felt that they needed to be more aware and wary. Respondents noted that they had made adjustments to recruitment and screening activities as a result of changes experienced during the pandemic.

"I used to have a mix of both remote and in-person research sessions. Now they are all remote, so there is a lot more survey screeners for recruitment and less individual interaction to determine the right fit." -P10 responded 'neutral' to the impact of COVID-19 on recruitment.

3.3 Impact on Methods and Study Design

When it came to examining the impact of the COVID-19 pandemic and associated changes on research methods and study design, responses were more varied. Of the 169 respondents who answered the question about the impact of COVID-19 on research methods and study design, 37.9% reported a negative impact, 23.1% reported a positive impact, and 39% felt there was neither a positive nor negative impact. Almost half, or 44.2%, responded that they were likely to adopt changes to their methods resulting from COVID-19 in their future work. Much less, or 12.9%, were unlikely to adopt changes. The remaining respondents reported that they were neither likely nor unlikely, 17.2%, or felt that the question did not apply to them, 25.8%.

As the name implies, UX research is, at core, a heavily research-oriented field of work. Careful selection of methods and conceptualization of study design is imperative. Methods can vary greatly across UX research study design, from high-tech eye-tracking and biometric testing to simpler methods like card sorting and storyboarding. Various methods include a mix of data collected, spanning both qualitative and quantitative sources as well as a combination or mixed methods approach. Best practices in UX research necessitate the consideration of methods, tools, sample size or number needed for recruitment, data collection to facilitate analysis, among many other details. Study design in UX research is typically the planning of all these considerations to ensure that the overall UX research questions and/or objectives are successfully met.

Many respondents noted the need to make changes to their research methods and study design to adapt to changes occurring as a result of the COVID-19 pandemic. Some of these changes were positive and involved urging/inspiring researchers to reevaluate their approaches and expand their toolsets. Respondents noting a more positive impact of COVID-19-related effects reported that they were exploring new methods including surveys and asynchronous (unmoderated) methods for capturing feedback on concepts and designs. This was seen as a benefit as they were able to step back and had time to assess other methods and learn, rather than relying on "old habits.

"Because we do everything remotely now, I have been able to use new tools that I may not have used in-office (like Miro) to conduct workshops/activities with my team."- P143 responded 'extremely positive' to the impact of COVID19 on UX research methods.

The addition of new tools also contributed to researchers' abilities to explore new methods, including diary studies, that provided additional depth and insights that may not have been previously accessible.

"It has made me aware of more online tools/methods. Furthermore, it has made participants/users more savvy that increases feasibility for future work to use these tools." -P112 responded 'somewhat positive' to the impact of COVID-19 on UX research methods.

Other changes to research methods were not as positive as researchers struggled to adapt to new constraints and find alternative approaches for capturing insights of need. In-person or lab studies were off the table for most researchers in 2020. Respondents that primarily worked with hardware, devices, and physical experiences (n = 32) were especially hard hit because of this.

"We do a lot of device work and industrial design...remote just doesn't do this well. Our current products have target populations with real physical jobs...they lend better to ethnography, contextual inquiry, and observation. Very difficult done remotely." P13 responded 'extremely negative' to the impact of COVID-19 on UX research methods.

In addition to challenges associated with the lack of physical presence for these studies, certain studies were limited by logistical challenges. Some researchers struggled with finding tools that met compliance needs virtually, in contrast to in-person methods to ensure compliance.

"We now have collaborative and digital research tools, but they unfortunately don't allow us to share confidential information in a safe way. –P29 responded neutral to the impact of COVID-19 on UX research methods.

For those still able to run lab studies, the need to develop and implement complex protocols added additional challenges.

"We do research on hardware, so it's required that we do in-person research because people need to physically touch and use the product. We have had to develop protocols internally where the researcher and employee participant never comes into physical contact and can be in different rooms. Then there is all the cleaning/disinfecting we have to do between participants. We also have shipped product to people and then conducted online usability tests and interviews for more stable builds that are further along in the dev process." P123 responded 'extremely negative' to the impact of COVID-19 on UX research methods.

In several cases, researchers noted challenges associated with adapting methods that were commonly used during in-person research activities including ethnography, contextual inquiry, cognitive walkthrough, co-design or participatory design.

"[It is] impossible to have context of a shared real-life experience." –P77 responded 'extremely negative' to the impact of COVID-19 on UX research methods

While some respondents had been able to adjust methods and accommodate these challenges, others anticipated a need to get creative and find alternative solutions.

> "[We] have to get creative about co-design exercises so they can get done remotely." –P17 responded 'somewhat negative' to the impact of COVID-19 on UX research methods.

> "I don't spend time observing participants as much as I would like to, so I am starting to use dscout and rely on participants to provide video footage of their experiences."- P76 responded 'somewhat negative' to the impact of COVID-19 on UX research methods.

3.4 Research Data Analysis

Of the 161 respondents who answered the question about the impact of COVID-19 on data analysis, 26.1% reported a negative impact, 9.3% reported a positive impact, and 64.6% felt there was neither a positive nor negative impact. Only 16.1% of respondents reported that they were likely to adopt changes to analysis resulting from COVID-19 in their future work; conversely, 14.2% were unlikely to adopt changes. The remaining respondents reported that they were neither likely nor unlikely, 25.2%, or felt that the question did not apply to them, 44.5%.

Being able to analyze and garner insight from UX research studies is an important component of the job. Without data analysis, UX research would lose a great deal of value, as it helps meet research and project objectives and, ultimately, allow for storytelling and sensemaking. Like the great variation in methods for UX research, the corresponding data analysis is disparate. Qualitative data collected during an interview might be extensively analyzed using rigorous grounded theory methods or more abstractly coded for themes and high-level ideas. Similarly, robust quantitative data could be analyzed using sophisticated processes such as machine learning and data science, or more straightforward approaches like descriptive summaries. Historically, UX research data analysis would frequently take place in an in-person group setting where fellow researchers could discuss and synthesize findings, using tangible tools like whiteboards and sticky notes.

Respondent sentiments regarding impact on data analysis approaches were overwhelmingly neutral (n = 104), with a skew toward moderately negative. Respondents reported challenges associated with working collaboratively with teammates to analyze data, as well as dealing with the cumulative fatigue of working in front of the computer for long hours. Many participants shifted to using digital whiteboarding tools like Miro to support data analyses activities. For some, this shift provided a means for collaborative and inclusive analyses with the added benefit of forcing organization and streamlining of activities.

> "We use Miro which makes the process much more organized than when we used only post-its." -P143 responded 'extremely positive' to the impact of COVID-19 on UX research data analysis.

> "I've adopted new methods for research analysis, based on improv and using Miro. In the "before times" I sometimes did sticky note/affinity mapping analysis but that didn't always work well because I worked out of various buildings and locations."

-P39 responded 'somewhat positive' to the impact of COVID-19 on UX research data analysis.

The lack of physical spaces and materials like whiteboards and sticky notes to help support early sensemaking and storytelling presented major challenges and required adjustments for many respondents. Although it benefited some, simply replacing physical whiteboarding experiences with digital tools was not a smooth transition for all respondents. Some respondents noted struggles with the shift to these kinds of remote collaborative analysis tools.

"Prior to the pandemic, our team would take notes on physical post-its and use time after each session to debrief and affinitize observations. All note taking is now digital. We have had difficulty scaling analysis of digital notes to more than 2 or 3 people working together at a time." -P72 responded 'somewhat negative' to the impact of COVID-19 on UX research data analysis.

The sense of isolation that comes with remote work was also notable when it came to data analyses for these respondents.

"We have to be more creative when doing group analysis or workshop type activities, so I miss the face-to-face discussions, but what we have seen, is that it can still be done and now there's room to include people who might otherwise not have been able to attend those types of activities." -P109 responded 'somewhat negative' to the impact of COVID-19 on UX research data analysis.

These feelings may have been especially impactful for groups that are accustomed to doing shared analysis, and for more junior researchers.

"Inability to brainstorm with my fellow researchers - [I am] on my own to figure out how things are done." -P78 responded 'somewhat negative' to the impact of COVID-19 on UX research data analysis.

Respondents also noted zoom fatigue and burnout that interfered with their ability to properly analyze data.

"It's harder to make time to bounce ideas off my team. We all have zoom fatigue. -P10 responded 'somewhat negative' to the impact of COVID-19 on UX research data analysis.

It's harder to collaborate and share. It's harder mentally to stay engaged." P176 responded 'somewhat negative' to the impact of COVID-19 on UX research data analysis.

Some respondents also noted the need to consider how this data would compare to data captured through previous iterations of in-person studies, and whether the COVID-19 pandemic had an impact on the actual data that should somehow be accounted for. Not only should there be a shift in data analysis at large for UX research to better understand the field and temporal user populations, but also a careful consideration of data over time as the context for UX research participants has likely been affected by COVID-19.

Of the four stages of UX research, respondents noted lower impact by COVID-19 on data analysis. There were certainly some positives – such as more representation and learning of virtual tools – and some negatives – such as burnout and the loss of in person research collaboration. However, many of these themes were also expressed in other UX research stages. In the future, it appears likely that data analysis will also be impacted, but perhaps not as starkly as other areas of UX research.

3.5 Impact on Sharing Research Findings

Of the 162 respondents who answered the question about the impact of COVID-19 on sharing UX research findings, 26.5% reported a negative impact, 23.4% reported a positive impact, and 50% felt there was neither a positive nor negative impact. About a third, or 32.7%, of respondents reported that they were likely to adopt changes to sharing research findings resulting from COVID-19 in their future work; 15.1% were unlikely to adopt changes. The remaining respondents noted that they were neither likely nor unlikely or felt that the question did not apply to them, 31.4%.

Of the 162 respondents who answered the question about the impact of COVID-19 on sharing UX research findings, 26.5% reported a negative impact, 23.4% reported a positive impact, and 50% felt there was neither a positive nor negative impact. About a third, or 32.7%, of respondents reported that they were likely to adopt changes to sharing research findings resulting from COVID-19 in their future work; 15.1% were unlikely to adopt changes. The remaining respondents noted that they were neither likely nor unlikely or felt that the question did not apply to them, 31.4%.

A skilled UX researcher should hone their skills in UX research sharing. UX sharing involves translating and communicating UX research findings to many different audiences, including engineers, managers, designers, practitioners, and even the public. UX research sharing may involve artifacts like written reports, short briefs, slide decks, and designs and oral communication methods like presentations, conference talks, and discussions with senior leadership.

Shifting into a remote work environment because of the global COVID-19 pandemic fundamentally changed the way that many respondents shared their findings and engaged both their core stakeholders and broader audiences. Respondents had to make a change to primarily remote presentations with digital materials. Some were able to embrace the digital transition, while others struggled.

Although a subset of respondents noted that it was often easier to schedule share-out meetings in a remote environment, many struggled to find ways to recreate in-person experiences and engage stakeholders in ways that they were used to.

"It's hard to replicate being in a room and making things participatory. Research readouts were a lot of fun and great teambuilding thing, and now they just feel like another really long meeting, and it's difficult to keep people engaged or get excited over a video call. I've started relying less on readouts and more on video snippets and more passive sharing to limit the amount of onscreen meetings we need to have." -P9 responded 'extremely negative' to the impact of COVID-19 on sharing UX research findings.

These challenges extended beyond sharing findings with design, product, or engineering teams, impacting how we share learnings as a research community as well.

"As an academic researcher, I often disseminate my findings through publications and academic conferences. Unfortunately, most of my recent conferences have been held remotely, and the online conference presentation platforms did not allow me to engage with my audience in the way that I usually do." -P130 responded 'extremely negative' to the impact of COVID-19 on sharing UX research findings.

Several participants noted that it was easier now to reach broader audiences, as more people were in an "online first" or "remote first" mentality.

"It's easier for people to hop on research share out meetings, so I would say attendance has been better for sharing."-P9 responded 'somewhat positive' to the impact of COVID-19 on sharing UX research findings.

It was also noted that for many, this brought about a sense of equity or a "level playing field" when it came to participation from audience members.

"These days our presentations are all on Zoom, which is better than the old way where we had some people in the same conference room and others on Zoom. If every person is on Zoom there is more equality in the discussion and everyone can see/hear the same thing. However, when everyone is remote there are more distractions." -P38 responded neutral to the impact of COVID-19 on sharing UX research findings.

Finally, one theme that carried through each of these topics, from recruitment to dissemination, was zoom fatigue and the emotional drain that researchers and partners had experienced as a result of the sudden and prolonged shift to remote work during a global pandemic.

"Emotional drain + screen fatigue is harder on everyone - need to be more mindful of share outs and the time I ask from others." -P58 responded somewhat negative to the impact of COVID-19 on sharing UX research findings.

Perhaps unsurprisingly, sharing UX research was also positively and negatively impacted by COVID-19. Many themes were similar to other stages, such as the benefits of engaging with more people and easier space logistics of in-person methods. The negative impacts were also salient, such as fatigue of online meetings and lack of human engagement effecting both the quality of work as well as job satisfaction. Though respondents were more neutral on the overall impact of COVID-19 on research sharing, some did note that the impact on sharing was going to be felt beyond the pandemic. Unfortunately, respondents did not share details of how this impact would be experienced, but they were twice as likely to answer that they were likely to adopt changes than unlikely (32.7% vs. 15.1%).

4   Discussion

The COVID-19 pandemic and its concomitant changes to everyday user behavior called for a crisis-responsive UX research approach, acknowledging that the world – and thus, most user research subjects – faced similar or identical new challenges. UX researchers quickly adapted, looking to find solutions to unprecedented new challenges and shifting away from any in-person research methods and recruitment strategies to working in a remote agile product development process (Shah & Jain 2021; Kieffer & Macq 2017). The need for UX research shifted as teams were faced with a new challenge: to understand user needs related to remote work paradigms and the uncertainty of constantly evolving COVID-19 evidence. We witnessed this in various sectors, and especially in healthcare settings, where organizations and teams needed to create new protocols and find solutions to problems associated with prevention, testing, and treatment of COVID-19. For example, Filo et al. reported on the design and development process of a dashboard for the management of ICU beds in Brazil, which was developed in one week (Filho et al. 2021). The quickness of solutions needed during COVID-19 resulted in many new case studies of how UX researchers were able to more effectively collaborate to develop impactful solutions to problems. UX research sprints were leveraged to quickly assess user needs and behaviors during COVID-19; findings were then used to inform business and public health communication, products, and service needs.

The COVID-19 pandemic brought countless changes to the practice of UX research. These changes necessitate careful consideration and understanding, as the positive and negative impacts are likely to shape the ways in which UX researchers recruit participants, design studies, analyze data, and share findings in the future. One challenge of this assessment is disentangling bidirectional impact. The practice of UX research has not only been impacted by the COVID-19 pandemic, but also has shaped tools and solutions to address the pandemic. Much as the literature on COVID-19 research has grown exponentially, there are numerous papers sharing UX research experience and findings on studies related to the COVID-19 pandemic. This bidirectional impact surfaces in the literature in two ways: 1) applying UX research to understand COVID-19 impact on products and services, and 2) using UX research approaches to design solutions that address COVID-19 impacts. Further, new UX research approaches have not been confined to healthcare: they have been used to understand the context of the user experience for online education (Chen et al. 2020; Parra et al. 2011), transportation (Tuchen et al. 2020), and financial services (Abdillah 2020; Shishah & Alhelaly 2021).

In the UX research field, there are other notable surveys that captured similar structured information that can serve as a comparison for our sample of respondents. For one such survey, the State of User Research report, we referenced a comparator year of 2021. For our respondents, we found similar demographics (i.e., gender, race, ethnicity), but different segments of the workforce, including domestically focused, with an emphasis on large technology companies and the medical field. Due to our convenience sampling methodology, our respondents are likely reflective of our own professional and personal networks. The State of User Research 2021 report respondents reported 68% female participants. Our respondents skewed slightly older than The State of User Research 2021 report findings, where the majority of respondents (52%) were 25–34 years old. Our study respondent demographics were similar to The State of User Research 2021 report demographics, where 62% of respondents identified as white, 15% as 'Asian and/or Desi,' and 9% identifying as Hispanic/Latinx/Latina/o). Similarly, The State of User Research 2021 report found that 51% of their respondents lived in the United States and most of their respondents reported less than 10 years of experience (53%), a plurality work at enterprise companies (40.5%), and a plurality work in tech (30%), which are comparative to our respondent findings as well.

Our study sought to expand on previous work and add to the research literature by assessing the impacts and lasting changes that the COVID-19 pandemic is likely to have on UX research practice. Survey findings conducted by User Interviews found an increase in use of remote tools such as Miro and Zoom when comparing 2019 to 2021 survey findings, and respondents reported conducting 90% of their UX research work remotely where 87% rarely or did not work remote before (Balboni 2021). In our study, respondents reported working remotely 25% pre COVID-19 and 100% during COVID-19. Additionally, a User Interviews survey report found increases in remote tool use, such as video conferencing tools, in 2020.

Limitations. This research provides insight into major changes to the UX research profession caused by the COVID-19 pandemic, but there are limitations to our study design that can impose possible sources of bias, such as sample size and possible confounding factors. We used convenience sampling to recruit survey respondents and collect data. Our sample was certainly influenced by our own professional networks, potentially biasing our sample. Though our number of survey responses is comparable to similar studies, a larger sample size would have allowed for additional statistical analyses and/or a powered study design. Finally, our intention was to gather breadth rather than depth into impacts of COVID-19 and not to burden respondents' time. Additional qualitative data, gathered through interviews or focus groups, would provide deeper insights into causal and confounding factors regarding changes due to COVID-19.

Another limitation speaks to the field of UX research: the need to formalize and quantify the workforce, methods, and vocabulary. During conceptualization of this work, it was challenging to understand representativeness of our sample or what our denominator should be for analyses. There has been tremendous UX research growth recently as adjacent fields begin to recognize the applicability and value of UX research to their own work. This growth has not been met with professional bodies or organizational oversight that might provide systematic guidance for the field to move forward. Relatedly, we found heterogeneity in the application of methods and vocabulary among respondents to describe their own work. Common UX research language would allow for better collaboration, comparison, and analysis.

4.1 Emerging Trends in UX Research and Future Research Recommendations

The impact of the COVID-19 pandemic caused major shifts in how, when, and with whom work is done across nearly all fields and professions (Lund et al. 2021, Chung et al. 2020). The concept of the 'future of work' became a more salient theme in professional discourse as changes were realized or anticipated. The global workforce continues to explore hybrid work models, embrace new technology, and recover from the effects of COVID-19. Our survey intended to share a snapshot in time and describe a mid-pandemic picture of UX research. In the process of surveying the field, new trends emerged in how UX research practice is conducted. These trends can be grouped into three main areas: 1) remote and hybrid work considerations, 2) speed of change, and 3) the embrace of new technology.

Remote and Hybrid Work. While some industries supported UX research remote hires as well as flexible hybrid work schedules prior to COVID-19, this was not the norm for the majority of UX researchers. Not only were colleagues remote during the pandemic, but there was a need to adjust to conducting rapid customer needs assessments virtually. UX researchers were tasked with trying to replicate in-person collaboration and virtual events to allow people to participate and network remotely. For instance, Miro (an online visual collaboration platform for teamwork) grew from being used by 5% of respondents in 2019 to 33% in 2020, according to the 2020 Design Tools Survey by UXTools (Taylor & Bowman 2020). UX researchers continue to experiment with new work and remote collaboration models by enacting novel ways to collaborate across physical divides.

There was also transformation of customer recruitment and engagement. The world population was affected by COVID-19, which offered a large cohort to recruit and engage. Products that required in-person usability testing changed to adhere to COVID-19 health guidelines, including the use of contactless testing labs and remote product testing. We saw an increased demand by industries to engage with customers to address evolving customer needs and challenges during the COVID-19 pandemic. Motivation to engage with customers shifted work cultures to be more user-centered and design thinking in their approach to problems and product development. Furthermore, virtual engagement meant that UX researchers could engage a larger, more diverse, and systematically different population than prior to the pandemic, ultimately changing findings from UX research studies. Careful curation of these findings as well as thoughtful attention to population differences will benefit the field moving forward.

Speed of Change. Another continually emerging trend is the evolving scientific clarity and speed to design in a crisis. Recovering from the pandemic is a global research and development effort. Scientific publications are often reviewed and published rapidly, competitors may come together to conduct research, and contracts are signed more quickly. We saw a growing number of medical devices and diagnostic tests seeking FDA Emergency Use Authorization (EUAs), a process developed to help make medical products available as quickly as possible by allowing unapproved medical products to reach patients in need when there are no adequate FDA approved available alternatives in a crisis. We saw the collective effort and impact of the world coming together to solve a shared problem to advance medical discovery that is likely to persist. Balancing speed with rigor is a challenge, and one for which the UX research community is well positioned.

New Technology. The final trend is the widespread use of new technology, especially artificial intelligence (AI) and machine learning (ML). The proliferation of these technologies was evident prior to the COVID-19 pandemic (Howard 2019) and has increased drastically in recent years. Indeed, there is much excitement about conversational AI in

UX communities. A recent study by Zheng et. al. Found 449 papers in their initial literature search of conversational AI and UX research in ACM journals alone (Zheng et. al. 2022). We saw an increase in the use of conversational AI agents such as bots to address COVID-19 scenarios related to symptom checkers, for example, and aggregated COVID-19 data from around the world was showcased on dashboards to keep experts and the public informed about the spread and track travel behaviors for contact tracing. We saw how ML was applied in the discovery of new COVID-19 diagnostic tests to meet unmet clinical needs (Alballa & Al-Turaiki 2021). The growth and successful implementation of AI and ML technologies through the worst of the pandemic makes clear that the application of this technology can be productively used to quickly address new user scenarios and needs, even in the face of a dramatic global crisis.

These UX trends are likely to remain post pandemic and forever change how we view wellness, work, experience healthcare, and more. Future research is needed to assess these trends and re-evaluate the impacts of the COVID-19 pandemic on UX research practice in 2023 and beyond.

5   Conclusion

The practice of UX research is collaborative and dependent on engagement with customers and stakeholders throughout the product design and development process. The COVID-19 pandemic brought many changes to the way UX research is practiced. These positive and negative impacts are likely to shape the ways in which UX researchers recruit participants, design studies, analyze data, and share findings in the future. We found changes in the tools that UX researchers use with the switch to remote work. Burnout and video conferencing fatigue were salient themes across the spectrum of UX research. Some UX research practices, like whiteboarding and observations, were almost completely lost in the view of many of our respondents. Among the beneficial changes were the ability to engage with more diverse participants/users, flexibility to pivot to remote methods very quickly, and the addition of new tools and skills.

This study aimed to understand the impacts of remote work on UX research practice to support new future of work initiatives and best practices. Our study provides value to the literature by: 1) establishing a baseline that may continue to help researchers document and understand the impact of the COVID-19 pandemic, 2) addressing a gap in the UX research literature that surveys change directly tied to COVID-19, 3) providing a rigorous assessment of the current field, and, finally, 4) presenting a call to action for best practices supporting the future of UX research practice.

References

Abdillah, L.A.: FinTech E-commerce payment application user experience analysis during COVID-19 pandemic (2020). ArXiv Preprint ArXiv:2012.07750

Alballa, N., Al-Turaiki, I.: Machine learning approaches in COVID-19 diagnosis, mortality, and severity risk prediction: a review. Inform. Med. Unlocked **24**, 100564 (2021)

Balboni, K.: The State of User Research 2021 Report (2021). https://www.userinterviews.com/blog/state-of-user-research-2021-report

Chen, T., Peng, L., Yin, X., Rong, J., Yang, J., Cong, G.: Analysis of user satisfaction with online education platforms in china during the COVID-19 pandemic. Healthcare **8**(3), 200 (2020). https://doi.org/10.3390/healthcare8030200

Chung, H., Seo, H., Forbes, S., Birkett, H.: Working from home during the COVID-19 lockdown: Changing preferences and the future of work (2020). https://kar.kent.ac.uk/83896/1/Working_f rom_home_COVID-19_lockdown.pdf

Filho, I. de M.B., Sampaio, S.C., Cruz, A.P., Ramalho, V.H.F., Azevedo, J.A.R. de., Silveira, Á.C., da.: More agile than ever: the case study of the development of a dashboard for the management of ICU beds during the coronavirus outbreak. In: 2021 IEEE 34th International Symposium on Computer-Based Medical Systems (CBMS), pp. 324–329 (2021). https://doi.org/10.1109/CBMS52027.2021.00028

Harris, P.A., et al.: The REDCap consortium: building an international community of software platform partners. J. Biomed. Inform. **95**, 103208 (2019)

Harris, P.A., Taylor, R., Thielke, R., Payne, J., Gonzalez, N., Conde, J.G.: Research electronic data capture (REDCap)—a metadata-driven methodology and workflow process for providing translational research informatics support. J. Biomed. Inform. **42**(2), 377–381 (2009)

Howard, J.: Artificial intelligence: implications for the future of work. Am. J. Ind. Med. **62**(11), 917–926 (2019)

IxDF. (n.d.). What is UX Research?. https://www.interaction-design.org/literature/topics/ux-res earch. Accessed 3 Feb 2023

Kieffer, S., Ghouti, A., Macq, B.: The agile UX development lifecycle: combining formative usability and agile methods. In: Proceedings of the 50th Hawaii International Conference on System Sciences, pp. 577–586 (2017)

Klein, L.: UX for Lean Startups: Faster, Smarter User Experience Research and Design. O'Reilly Media, Inc. (2013)

Lund, S., Madgavakar, A., Manyika, J., Smit, S., Ellingrud, K., Robinson, O.: The future of work after COVID-19 McKinsey (2021)

Nielsen, J.: A 100-Year View of User Experience (2017). https://www.nngroup.com/articles/100-years-ux/

Parra, O., et al.: Early treatment of obstructive Apnoea and stroke outcome: a randomised controlled trial. Eur. Respir. J. **37**(5), 1128–1136 (2011)

Rohrer, C.: When to use which user-experience research methods. Nielsen Norman Group **12** (2014)

Shah, S., Jain, A.: Impact of the COVID-19 pandemic on user experience (UX) research. In: International Conference on Human-Computer Interaction, pp. 599–607 (2021)

Shishah, W., Alhelaly, S.: User experience of utilising contactless payment technology in Saudi Arabia during the COVID-19 pandemic. J. Decis. Syst. **30**(2–3), 282–299 (2021). https://doi.org/10.1080/12460125.2021.1890315

Süner-Pla-Cerdà, S., Töre Yargın, G., Şahin, H., Danış, S.: Examining the impact of covid-19 pandemic on UX research practice through UX blogs. In: Lecture Notes in Computer Science (Including Subseries Lecture Notes in Artificial Intelligence and Lecture Notes in Bioinformatics), vol. 12779 LNCS, pp. 579–592 (2021). https://doi.org/10.1007/978-3-030-78221-4_40/COVER

Taylor, P., Bowman, J.: 2020 Design Tools Survey | UX Tools (2020). https://uxtools.co/survey-2020?utm_source=convertkit&utm_medium=email&utm_campaign=+Take+the+2021+Design+Tools+Survey–6815131. Accessed 14 Aug 2022

Teevan, J., et al.: Microsoft new future of work report 2022. In: Jenna Butler (Senior Applied Research Scientist) (2022)

Tuchen, S., Arora, M., Blessing, L.: Airport user experience unpacked: conceptualizing its potential in the face of COVID-19. J. Air Transp. Manag. **89**, 101919 (2020)

U.S.H.H.S.: Applying human factors and usability engineering to medical devices guidance for industry and food and drug administration staff preface public comment. In: U.S. Department of Health and Human Services, Food and Drug Administration (2016)

Vermeeren, A.P.O.S., Law, E.L.-C., Roto, V., Obrist, M., Hoonhout, J., Väänänen-Vainio-Mattila, K.: User experience evaluation methods: current state and development needs. In: Proceedings of the 6th Nordic Conference on Human-Computer Interaction: Extending Boundaries, pp. 521–530 (2010)

Williams, N.: Working through COVID-19: zoom gloom and zoom fatigue. Occup. Med. **71**(3), 164 (2021). https://doi.org/10.1093/OCCMED/KQAB041

Zheng, Q., Tang, Y., Liu, Y., Liu, W., Huang, Y.: UX research on conversational human-AI interaction: a literature review of the ACM digital library. In: Proceedings of the 2022 CHI Conference on Human Factors in Computing Systems, pp. 1–24 (2022)

Gender Inclusive Design in Technology: Case Studies and Guidelines

Anna Szlavi[1]([envelope]) [ORCID] and Leandro S. Guedes[2] [ORCID]

[1] Norwegian University of Science and Technology (NTNU), Trondheim, Norway
anna.szlavi@ntnu.no
[2] Università della Svizzera Italiana (USI), Lugano, Switzerland
leandro.soares.guedes@usi.ch

Abstract. The importance of inclusivity as a value in our social contexts is increasing; thus, it is not unusual that the software industry has started to embrace it. The need for such a consideration stems from the fact that the composition of the IT sector, especially of positions responsible for decision-making and the design of tools, reflects a workforce that is not diverse enough. This can result in blind spots in the design process, leading to exclusionary user experiences. Therefore, the idea of inclusive design is gaining more prevalence; in fact, it is becoming a general expectation to create software that is useful for and used by more people. With a focus on intersectionality - the understanding that social and digital difficulties result from a complex web of overlapping factors - inclusive user experience seeks to actively and consciously integrate minority, vulnerable, and understudied user groups in the design. UX that is based on inclusive design aims to overcome social disadvantages in all of their intersectional complexities arising from gender, sexual orientation, age, education, dis/ability, socioeconomic status, and race/ethnicity, among others. At the same time, it must be acknowledged that gender-inclusive design has challenges and limitations: the idea of gender inclusion in design is not yet a reality. Our research investigates academic literature, as well as tech industry practices, like the websites of Microsoft, Apple, Google, and Meta. We aim to understand how inclusive design is theorized and implemented nowadays. Our analysis shows that intersectionality suffers even when inclusivity is intended to be taken into consideration. We also offer guidelines for factors that might be explored for a more inclusive design. Our paper's analysis leaves an opportunity for additional study; the complexity of identities and how disregarding them in software design can exacerbate inequality call for even more investigation and awareness.

Keywords: gender inclusive design · inclusive design · intersectionality · user experience · technology · human-computer interaction

1 Introduction

The demographics of the IT sector, especially of positions responsible for decision-making and the design of tools, reflect a workforce that is not diverse enough.

A. Marcus et al. (Eds.): HCII 2023, LNCS 14030, pp. 343–354, 2023.
https://doi.org/10.1007/978-3-031-35699-5_25

This homogeneity, characterized by a preponderance of Global Northern, educated, middle-class, white, heterosexual, young to middle-aged men and the tendency in Software Design to design for "self-as-user" [29] leads to inherent biases in the industry. This results in a potential for blind spots and exclusionary user experiences when it is assumed that all users are like the designers themselves.

Inclusivity as a principle is increasingly important in our social environments, so it is not surprising that even the Software Industry has started to embrace it recently. Researchers and practitioners have produced multitudes of papers, case studies, opinion articles, design examples, and even tool-kits about inclusive design [8, 14, 21, 24].

The concept of inclusive design is spreading more extensively; in fact, it is becoming a general expectation to create useful and usable software for more people [29]. Yet, inclusive design is more than just a guiding principle for creating products for a broader user base; it is also a deliberate method for addressing the needs of consumers who could encounter exclusionary situations on a regular basis [24]. Moreover, inclusive User Experience (UX) wants to actively and purposefully include and involve minorities, vulnerable, and understudied user groups in the design, with specific attention to intersectionality.

Gender equality is one of the UN Sustainability Goals [4]. As Goal 5 out of the 17, it calls to "achieve gender equality and empower all women and girls." For the sustainable development of the world, we need to overcome gender disparity, which involves not just social but also digital inclusion. Digital design, therefore, needs to consider gender inclusiveness as a priority.

However, gender-inclusive design has challenges and limitations. Overviewing hiring processes to consciously create more diverse teams, especially if team members do not perceive gender diversity to be essential [9], can put a strain on companies. Alternatively, applying tools, such as the Gender Inclusiveness Magnifier (GenderMag), to detect how the software measures up can risk cost-efficiency [14, 32]. As a consequence, the idea of gender inclusion in design is not yet a reality.

This paper has the following structure: Sect. 2 introduces the methodology we used in this research. Section 3 analyses the literature and introduces concepts related to inclusive design (Non-Binary Gender, Intersectionality, and Inclusive Imagery). Further, Sect. 4 presents case studies of big tech companies (Microsoft, Apple, Google, and Meta) and discuss their impact on the real world. Section 5 provides a discussion of gender-inclusive design in technology. Also, we introduce guidelines based on our analysis of literature and industry case studies in Sect. 6. Finally, we conclude this paper in Sect. 7, with reference to future works to be done.

2   Methodology

We conducted exploratory research in which we surveyed the literature and expanded the analysis on the strategy and role of companies in order to see how the principles of inclusive design are theorized in the literature and applied in the tech industry. We searched for procedures, repositories, papers, toolkits, and website directories in order to better understand key concepts and position the industry's most prominent players. In addition, we offered a critical analysis by compiling a list of statements and strategies, contrasting those with the data that was available.

In the course of the design process, we investigate how they think about and implement inclusivity as a guiding principle. With the help of this analysis, our goal is to map how the concept of inclusive design is theorized and implemented in the modern world. This will allow us to identify inconsistencies and brainstorm new areas of inquiry. Based on the analysis, we also offer guidelines for gender-inclusive design.

3   Background and Literature Review

In this section, we look at the main concepts in connection with inclusive design, such as Non-Binary Gender, Intersectionality, and Inclusive Imagery.

Non-Binary Gender. The analysis of the gendered aspects of web interfaces typically starts from the notion of binary gender, namely, that people are conceptualized as a binary opposition: women and men. This idea is built on the concept of biological sex, which tends to be female or male for most people, lending the belief that gender derives from this binary [16]. However, gender is not something we are born with, and not something we have, but something we do [33]. It is a series of social practices, which are not clear cut.

Yet, many of the gender research done in HCI and UX still approach the issue from a binary perspective [7,18,20]. How "gender-inclusive" a site is becomes the question of how much it considers "female" aspects, which maintains the binary notion. On the other end, it must be noted that gender inclusivity is not gender neutrality either [26]. Instead of rigid binaries or complete ignorance of the concept, gender is fluid and flexible.

The literature on non-binary gender explores the challenges and opportunities of representing non-binary gender identities and provides recommendations for designing technology that is inclusive of individuals who do not identify as belonging to either of the two gender binaries [25,28]. Recognizing the manner in which technology either sustains or undermines binary gender norms is essential [13]. The intersectional experiences of non-binary individuals in the technology industry highlight how important it is to take into consideration gender diversity while designing technology [27]. Therefore, gender-inclusive design needs to acknowledge the diversity of gender, overwriting the traditional gender binary [23,31].

Intersectionality. Another concept that is often missing from analyses of inclusive design is intersectionality, that is, the recognition that barriers are not one-dimensional.

Intersectionality is a term coined to account for the fact that challenges (or social oppression) come from a complex web of intersecting factors, rather than from one source [11]. The notion is that "race, class, gender, sexuality, ethnicity, nation, ability and age operate not as unitary, mutually exclusive entities, but as reciprocally constructing phenomena that in turn shape complex social inequalities" [10].

Even if we are far from having a fully accessible digital community, accessibility, that is, the acknowledgment of disability as a barrier to digital use has a relatively long tradition in UX and HCI [22]. Nevertheless, UX that is based on inclusive design is not only about addressing mental and physical disadvantages, that is, solely accessibility. It should also be about attempting to overcome social disadvantages. The data-driven technology that permeates our daily lives also channels social issues into the digital sphere; therefore, people can experience exclusion in their daily lives and in virtual space because of multiple other factors, such as gender, sexuality, age, education, socioeconomic status, race, and ethnicity. As a consequence, there is a need to critically examine if the software surrounding us is fair and inclusive, yet the analysis is often approached from a single identity dimension, such as disability, gender, or race [11,17,34], even if barriers are more complex.

In fact, a design that is truly inclusive must respect the complexities of identity and overcome the one-dimensional focus. More research that includes the gender and the sexuality aspect in their complex form is needed. The exclusion of Trans and Non-Binary people in Software Design is just starting to get attention [19], for reasons described above. Just like gender, sexuality also needs to be viewed as a complex and integral part of social and digital identity that inclusive design considers.

Inclusive Imagery. It is important to note that the representation of identities in computing is heavily influenced by imagery [12]. People who identify as gender non-conforming or have disabilities are frequently left out of discussions centered on Diversity, Equity, and Inclusion (DEI). These categories are frequently underrepresented in computing-related jobs, products, and even the methods used to design products.

Individuals are predisposed to believe that everyone is in some way similar to them [15], which also reflects the challenges of reflecting diversity in design when choosing images to represent consumers and people in the IT business. Images, texts, forms, and personas must be aligned for a non-binary and non-stereotypical gender portrayal [21,29]. It is crucial to avoid normalizing stereotypical gender roles and make room for gender as a spectrum, rather than as a binary choice, in portrayal as much as in analysis.

Moreover, the computing industry is responsible for promoting inclusion and appropriately representing all identities. This may be accomplished in design through the use of diverse and representative images, texts, forms, and personas. Furthermore, businesses and organizations should take proactive initiatives to enhance workforce diversity and give DEI training to their staff. This not only contributes to a more inclusive workplace but also leads to the development of more diverse and representative products. The significance of appropriately reflecting all identities in computing cannot be overstated, since it has a tremendous influence on the daily experiences and views of those who use technology. The computer industry may contribute to breaking down societal barriers and fostering a more fair and just society by supporting diversity and inclusivity.

4   Tech Industry Case Studies

In this section, we examine how some of the leading tech companies approach inclusivity in design. We decided to look at the top 10 tech companies by market capitalization in 2022 and chose to focus on the top three of the list [2] – Microsoft, Apple, and Google – and add the biggest social network company available – Meta. Some examples of screenshots from the companies' websites are available in Fig. 1.

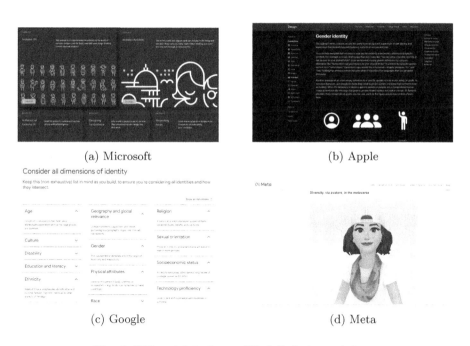

(a) Microsoft

(b) Apple

(c) Google

(d) Meta

Fig. 1. Different interfaces of Tech Industry websites.

Microsoft. It is an important fact that Microsoft, one of the top tech companies of the world, acknowledges the significance of inclusivity in design. In fact, Microsoft has a dedicated site to inclusive design. Their site [3] not merely mentions inclusive design but it also goes into both theoretical and practical details about it.

First, it explains the main principles or rather the steps to take in order to realize inclusivity: 1) "recognize exclusion", 2) "solve for one, extend to many" and 3) "learn from diversity". Each of these principles is further exemplified and elaborated on the site. Second, Microsoft even provides resources for design practitioners in the form of a manual, a video, activities, and booklets, all free of charge, in order to give practical tools for implementing the above principles in design (see Fig. 1a).

The manual does a great job explaining why there is a need for inclusivity when designing products. The info video presents a case study, which is audio-narrated, thus making it accessible to people with visual impairments as well. Not only is the material a study-like presentation of the principles but it is also an example of how to put sensitivity to difference into practice. Finally, the activity cards give specific tool-kits to practitioners so they can check whether their design is in fact inclusive, for example by applying the notion of "persona spectrums".

While the site is an excellent example to follow regarding social responsibility, we have to underline that it has shortcomings. Microsoft addresses inclusivity on the axis of (mental and physical) dis/ability only. On the one hand, the explicit examples are limited to accessibility; on the other hand, even if "social challenges" are also mentioned in the text, the imagery maintains and reproduces the gender binary, one of the main sources of social challenge [30].

Apple. Apple also has a dedicated site for design foundations, listing areas of consideration such as Accessibility, Color, Images, and Typography, among others [6]. There is also a tab for Inclusion, labelling it as an essential part of the design process. The page starts by stating that an app's communication, content, and functionality need to prioritize inclusion.

The site presents a rather detailed description of what the company thinks about inclusive design. The framework that they use for the definition of inclusivity is much broader and more comprehensive than what we saw on Microsoft's site. In fact, Apple approaches inclusion by listing a great number of factors to consider, going far beyond accessibility. Some of the elements underlined are language use, gender identity, contexts, stereotypes, and regions.

Regarding the copy of the app, it is emphasized that the tone needs to be welcoming and tailored to different perspectives. For example, it should not be taken for granted that only educated people will (manage to) read your texts. Plain language is more inclusive and considerate than technical language or colloquialism.

As far as gender identity is concerned, it is better to avoid referring to specific genders, especially through the gender binary. This means both text and images, including emojis and avatars as well (see Fig. 1b).

In close relation to this, the contexts in which we illustrate people, whether in writing or in visuals, matter a lot too. For example, a fitness app should portray its products or services with people, with different looks and backgrounds, not just, say, young white women.

It is also important to avoid gender stereotypes and biases. If an app wants to refer to a family, it should have a broader definition of the unit than the traditional woman + man + child(ren). It is also necessary to overcome the stereotypical association of women as being in charge of family duties, thus, targeting only female audiences for apps connected to family life.

In addition to the above, Apple underlines that a consideration for regional and cultural backgrounds is vital too. If the design of an app avoids stereotypes, illustrates a diversity of people, and uses plain language, it is easier to create versions localized into more languages and cultural contexts.

As opposed to Microsoft, Apple does not provide its users or designers with a lot of practical tools on how to do inclusive design. At the bottom of the page, there is a Resources section, but it only contains two – lengthy, thus not too user-friendly – videos which focus on the "practice" of inclusive design. The videos have subtitles and the people sharing their thoughts represent different genders, ethnicities, and roles, demonstrating the consideration for intersectionality.

Google. Google [1] acknowledges the continuous effort of constructing equality and inclusion on their products by prioritizing the voices of the most underrepresented groups throughout the product creation process. The company presents a list of diversity considerations for designers on its website, listing various identity segments to consider (see Fig. 1c). Google's mission was complemented with three respects: respect for the user, the opportunity, and each other.

To make information universally accessible and useful, Google focuses on providing the same experiences for everyone, as more voices at the table lead to better outcomes. The company claims to provide access and opportunities for historically underrepresented groups, even if its 2021 Diversity Annual Report still highlights the majority of its employees being Asian or White, with about two-thirds of men, and with a decreased amount of self-identified LGBTQ+, and people with disabilities.

For the technology design, the company provides examples highlighting how inclusive testing allowed for improving camera technology for all and how virtual voice assistants are designed to ensure everyone's voice. They also provide questions in different design phases to include different perspectives and center on underrepresented voices:

– First phase - Ideation, specifications, and design: focus on teams with historically marginalized representation; who benefits from your product; needs of novice users; mitigate bias on machine learning; discuss ideas with an accessibility expert and with inclusivity-focused co-creators; and centering community-based market research.
– Second phase - Prototype and evaluation: share insights from the first phase; build a testing plan; center historically marginalized groups through language, images, graphics, and avatars; make the content clearly understandable for everyone; consider cultural factors; and ensure delight for users with disabilities.

- Third phase - Build and user test: including a range of perspectives in the user testing; test the accessibility considerations; use a screen reader or other accessibility tools in your product; and test with slow internet speeds.
- Fourth phase - Market, measure and monitor: check if the audience character-istics include and reflect what you expected; check if the audience is diverse; check if language and localization features are being used as you expected; are the geographic location of the audience matching your intentions?; make sure all users have a similar and positive experience; marketing should tar-get a diverse audience; the team should keep gathering consumer product feedback.

Meta. Meta, a leader in the field of social networks, has demonstrated a com-mitment to inclusivity in design. The company is evolving to recognize the importance of developing products that are accessible and inclusive to all users, regardless of race, ethnicity, gender identity, or ability.

The company has implemented several key strategies in its design process to accomplish this. One approach is to use diverse and representative imagery, such as avatars and virtual environments (see Fig. 1d). This is also true about their product design, even if some extra customizability is still required. In addition, the company favors accessibility in its design, taking into account the needs of users with disabilities for a better overall UX.

Meta also conducts user research and testing on a regular basis with a diverse group of participants to gather feedback and identify areas for improvement. Their most recent press [5] aims to overcome cultural bias, provide diversity through avatars, and increase access through immersive learning. After years of being chastised for its lack of privacy, Facebook has publicly acknowledged the importance of this aspect to all of its customers.

5   Discussion

We observed that the traditional approach to analyzing the gender aspect of web interfaces is based on the binary opposition of women and men, which is built on the concept of biological sex. This approach, however, is limited as gender is a social construct that is fluid and flexible. It is critical to highlight the challenges and opportunities of representing non-binary gender identities and make recommendations for designing technology that is inclusive of individuals who do not identify as belonging to either of the two gender binaries.

We also introduced the concept of intersectionality, which acknowledges that barriers to digital use are caused by a complex web of intersecting factors, rather than by a single source. This paper argues that the UX based on inclusive design should aim to overcome social disadvantages, such as those caused by gender, sexuality, age, education, socioeconomic status, race, and ethnicity, rather than addressing only mental and physical disadvantages.

Our literature review concludes by emphasizing the significance of inclu-sive imagery in computing, noting that individuals who identify as gender non-conforming or have disabilities are frequently underrepresented in the products and design methods used in the technology industry.

Furthermore, our previous section, Tech Industry Case Studies, describes the approach to inclusivity in the design of leading tech companies, Microsoft, Apple, Google, and Meta. Companies have inclusive design websites that explain the principles of inclusivity and provide resources for practitioners in the form of a manual, video, activities, and/or booklets.

Throughout this paper, we argue that truly inclusive design must consider the complexities of identity and overcome a one-dimensional focus, and that more research on the exclusion of trans and non-binary people in software design is needed.

6   Guidelines

Considering the exploratory research we conducted in this paper, we are providing guidelines for designing gender-inclusive tools in technology. Our guidelines can be applied to both academia or industry.

– **Consider intersectionality:** avoid simplifying people to one-dimensional characters. Note that people have complex identities, which go beyond belonging to one specific gender, race, or sexuality group.
– **Avoid propagating stereotypes:** note that by attaching typical looks, occupations, and traits to a person based on their gender, race, or sexuality, you are contributing to social stereotypes that aggravate misogyny, racism, and homophobia.
– **Overcome the gender-binary:** avoid producing text and images that reinforce the gender binary and social stereotypes, regarding appearance, jobs, preferences, or skills.
– **Make your text, tone, and imagery consistent and inclusive:** note that it is necessary that you maintain your efforts to inclusivity throughout your copy, visuals, communication, and products.
– **Show the diversity of each community:** make a conscious effort to illustrate how multi-colored communities are, instead of simplifying them to stereotypes.
– **Involve people with that particular identity:** diversity and inclusion should be taken seriously, and there's no better person than the one with that particular identity to tell you about their concerns and challenges.
– **Avoid concentrating on a single mode of communication:** adapt your copy, images, and communication to different languages, cultures, and levels of complexity.
– **Provide training in Diversity, Equity, and Inclusion:** help your business or organization by providing constant training and mentorship.

7   Conclusions

The findings of our research highlight a significant issue within the field of software design. Regardless of efforts to promote inclusivity mainly in terms of gender, the intersectionality of identities is frequently overlooked and ignored in design. This is concerning because it has the potential to exacerbate inequality and the marginalization of certain communities. Our analysis sheds some light on the issue, but it is clear that much more work is needed to fully comprehend the complexities of identity and its impact on software development. Researchers and practitioners must continue to investigate this topic and raise awareness about the importance of considering intersectionality, when trying to achieve gender inclusivity, in software design. By doing so, we can contribute to the development of more inclusive and equitable technology that benefits everyone, regardless of identity.

Acknowledgement. We would like to thank the COST Action CA19122 - EUGAIN (European Network for Gender Balance in Informatics) for partially supporting this project.

References

1. Google - guide to product inclusion and equity. https://about.google/belonging/product-inclusion-and-equity/
2. Largest tech companies by market cap. https://companiesmarketcap.com/tech/largest-tech-companies-by-market-cap/
3. Microsoft design. https://www.microsoft.com/design/inclusive/
4. Un goal 5: Achieve gender equality and empower all women and girls. https://sdgs.un.org/goals/goal5
5. Meta - helping to build a diverse, equitable and inclusive metaverse (2022). https://www.metacareers.com/life/helping-to-build-a-diverse-equitable-inclusive-metaverse
6. Apple: Inclusion - apple developer. https://developer.apple.com/design/human-interface-guidelines/foundations/inclusion/
7. Aufderhaar, K., Schrepp, M., Thomaschewski, J.: Do women and men perceive user experience differently? IJIMAI **5**(6), 63–67 (2019)
8. Bennett, M.: Beyond the binary: 5 steps to designing gender inclusive fields in your product (Feb 2020). https://uxdesign.cc/beyond-the-binary-5-steps-to-designing-gender-inclusive-fields-in-your-product-ff9230337b4f
9. Catolino, G., Palomba, F., Tamburri, D.A., Serebrenik, A., Ferrucci, F.: Gender diversity and community smells: insights from the trenches. IEEE Softw. **37**(1), 10–16 (2019)
10. Collins, P.H.: Intersectionality's definitional dilemmas. Ann. Rev. Sociol. **41**(1), 1–20 (2015)
11. Crenshaw, K.: Demarginalizing the intersection of race and sex: a black feminist critique of antidiscrimination doctrine, feminist theory, and antiracist politics (1989). In: Feminist Legal Theory, pp. 57–80. Routledge (2018)
12. Edwards, E.J.: Putting the disability in dei through inclusive imagery. XRDS **28**(4), 26–29 (2022). https://doi.org/10.1145/3538545

13. Fiani, C.N., Han, H.J.: Navigating identity: experiences of binary and non-binary transgender and gender non-conforming (tgnc) adults. Int. J. Transgenderism **20**(2–3), 181–194 (2019)
14. Guizani, M., Letaw, L., Burnett, M., Sarma, A.: Gender inclusivity as a quality requirement: practices and pitfalls. IEEE Softw. **37**(6), 7–11 (2020). https://doi.org/10.1109/MS.2020.3019540
15. Holtz, R., Miller, N.: Assumed similarity and opinion certainty. J. Pers. Soc. Psychol. **48**(4), 890 (1985)
16. Hyde, J.S., Bigler, R.S., Joel, D., Tate, C.C., van Anders, S.M.: The future of sex and gender in psychology: five challenges to the gender binary. Am. Psychol. **74**(2), 171 (2019)
17. Johnson, B., Smith, J.: Towards ethical data-driven software: filling the gaps in ethics research & practice. In: 2021 IEEE/ACM 2nd International Workshop on Ethics in Software Engineering Research and Practice (SEthics), pp. 18–25. IEEE (2021)
18. Knoll, B.: Viele facetten-empfehlungen für eine gender-und diversity-freundliche mediengestaltung. Gender-UseIT: HCI, Usability und UX unter Gendergesichtspunkten, pp. 143–151 (2014)
19. Masure, M.: How square can be more trans and gender inclusive (Oct 2017). https://medium.com/gender-inclusivit/gender-inclusivity-in-a-daily-user-experience-89e33a217c7c
20. Metaxa-Kakavouli, D., Wang, K., Landay, J.A., Hancock, J.: Gender-inclusive design: sense of belonging and bias in web interfaces. In: Proceedings of the 2018 CHI Conference on Human Factors in Computing Systems, pp. 1–6. CHI 2018, Association for Computing Machinery, New York, NY, USA (2018). https://doi.org/10.1145/3173574.3174188
21. Palm, A.: The need for gender inclusion in UX design (Oct 2019). https://medium.com/coformaco/the-need-for-gender-inclusion-in-ux-design-700fa3dbe11e
22. Petrie, H., Bevan, N.: The evaluation of accessibility, usability, and user experience. Univ. Access Handbook **1**, 1–16 (2009)
23. Querini, V.: Vale has a background in UX design and communication. They believe in shaping a better: inclusive design: how to design for every gender (Aug 2021). https://careerfoundry.com/en/blog/ux-design/design-for-every-gender/
24. Querini, V.: Vale has a background in UX design and communication. They believe in shaping a better: What is inclusive design? a beginner's guide (Nov 2021). https://careerfoundry.com/en/blog/ux-design/beginners-guide-inclusive-design/
25. Richards, C., Bouman, W.P., Seal, L., Barker, M.J., Nieder, T.O., T'Sjoen, G.: Non-binary or genderqueer genders. Int. Rev. Psychiatry **28**(1), 95–102 (2016)
26. Smith, P.H., Bamberger, E.T.: Gender inclusivity is not gender neutrality. J. Human Lact. **37**(3), 441–443 (2021)
27. Spiel, K.: "why are they all obsessed with gender" - (non)binary navigations through technological infrastructures. In: Designing Interactive Systems Conference 2021. p. 478–494. DIS 2021, Association for Computing Machinery, New York, NY, USA (2021). https://doi.org/10.1145/3461778.3462033
28. Starks, D.L., Dillahunt, T., Haimson, O.L.: Designing technology to support safety for transgender women & non-binary people of color. In: Companion Publication of the 2019 on Designing Interactive Systems Conference 2019 Companion, pp. 289–294. DIS 2019 Companion, Association for Computing Machinery, New York, NY, USA (2019). https://doi.org/10.1145/3301019.3323898

29. Stumpf, S., et al.: Gender-inclusive HCI research and design: a conceptual review. Found. Trends® Human-Comput. Interact. **13**(1), 1–69 (2020). https://doi.org/10.1561/1100000056
30. Szlavi, A.: Barriers, role models, and diversity. Central-Eur. J. New Technol. Res. Educ. Practice **3**, 2582 (2021)
31. Szlávi, A., Landoni, M.: Human computer interaction-gender in user experience. In: Stephanidis, C., Antona, M., Ntoa, S. (eds.) HCI International 2022 Posters. HCII 2022. Communications in Computer and Information Science, vol. 1580, pp. 132–137. Springer, Cham (2022). https://doi.org/10.1007/978-3-031-06417-3_18
32. Vorvoreanu, M., Zhang, L., Huang, Y.H., Hilderbrand, C., Steine-Hanson, Z., Burnett, M.: From gender biases to gender-inclusive design: an empirical investigation. In: Proceedings of the 2019 CHI Conference on Human Factors in Computing Systems, pp. 1–14. CHI 2019, Association for Computing Machinery, New York, NY, USA (2019). https://doi.org/10.1145/3290605.3300283
33. West, C., Zimmerman, D.H.: Doing gender. Gender Soc. **1**(2), 125–151 (1987)
34. Winchester, H., Boyd, A.E., Johnson, B.: An exploration of intersectionality in software development and use. In: 2022 IEEE/ACM 3rd International Workshop on Gender Equality, Diversity and Inclusion in Software Engineering (GEICSE), pp. 67–70. IEEE (2022)

How to Involve Users in Online Co-design Workshops? A Participation Method Based on the Customer Engagement Theory

Meilin Wang, Xiong Ding$^{(\boxtimes)}$, and Shan Liu

Guangzhou Academy of Fine Arts, Guangzhou 510006, China
dingxiong@gzarts.edu.cn

Abstract. In the context of design-driven innovation and the digital era, users have more and more say in the process of enterprise product design and development, and it has become a trend for users to participate in enterprise Co-design workshops by online means. This paper discusses the possibility of holding online collaborative design workshop, and attempts to create a good online Co-design workshop experience for non-design professional users, so as to achieve sustainable value co-creation between users and enterprises. By combing the related literature of Co-design and customer engagement theory, combining their common characteristics and utilizing the key advantages of online, the basic model of user participation in online Co-design workshop under ideal condition is constructed. According to the Octalysis, dismantle and analyze the problems of different stages of online collaborative design workshop, optimize the tools involved in the process of workshop by exerting the role of driving force, and provide new ideas and solutions for users to participate in Co-design workshops. Discussing the online collaborative design workshop from the perspective of customer integration theory can fully consider and enhance the user's sense of experience and input, deepen the user's understanding of products and services, and strengthen the connection and interaction between enterprises and users.

Keywords: Customer Engagement · Co-design Workshop · Online · User Experience · Octalysis

1 Introduction

Co-design workshops have always been a key way for users to participate in design and communicate with designers. Due to the rapid development of Internet, a new way of working–online and remote working has gradually appeared, and the way of holding co-design workshops has also been reformed. Besides, users' knowledge has been greatly enhanced due to the rapid flow of information on the Internet. Users in the new era are characterized by rich knowledge, independence and positive and active [1]. Companies can create value by developing a good and continuous relationship with user [2]. At the same time, users have higher requirements for companies. The interaction experience between users and companies directly affects the impression of brand products and the following word-of-mouth spread. Based on the perspective of user participation and combined with the logic of related theories, this paper discusses the way of conducting online co-design workshops, and takes design companies as an example to design online co-design workshops with user participation by combining gamification design methods.

2 The Emergence of a New Working Pattern–Users Engage in the Design Process Online

2.1 Users Involving in the Co-design Workshops Becomes Trendy

Since the age of big machine production, design innovation took production efficiency as the key, leading to a separation between design and customer's needs in a certain period. In the mid to late 20th century, scholars began to study the relationship between design and customers, and three categories of innovation emerged (Fig. 1), technology-push, market-pull and design-driven. The key difference among these three kinds is the discourse power of customers in the process of design and development. Entities of technology-push innovation are within the company; market-pull innovation emphasizes on market demand, which gives users the opportunity to participate in the development process, but they are still the research objects [3]. Only the introduction of design-driven broke the STQ. Verganti believed that the key of design-driven is about creating product meaning [4]. Tong Huiming proposed that the design-driven innovation takes user-centric mindset and can maximize the value of design. Companies are required to put themselves at the shoes of users and dedicate themselves to gain insights on the needs and experience of users [5].

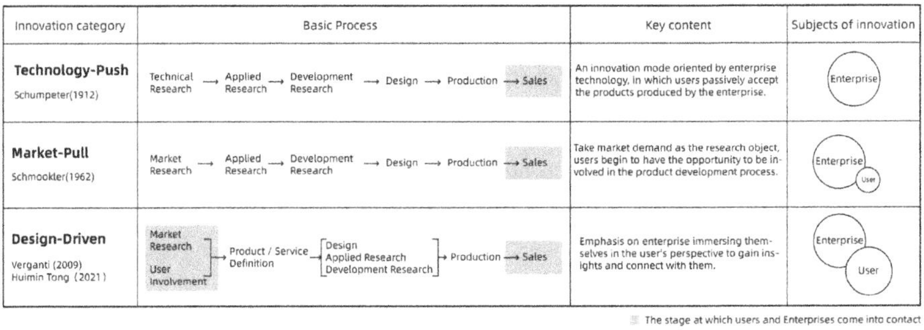

Innovation category	Basic Process		Key content	Subjects of innovation
Technology-Push Schumpeter(1912)	Technical Research → Applied Research → Development Research → Design → Production → Sales		An innovation mode oriented by enterprise technology, in which users passively accept the products produced by the enterprise.	Enterprise
Market-Pull Schmookler(1962)	Market Research → Applied Research → Development Research → Design → Production → Sales		Take market demand as the research object, users begin to have the opportunity to be involved in the product development process.	Enterprise / User
Design-Driven Verganti (2009) Huimin Tong (2021)	Market Research / User Involvement → Product / Service Definition → [Design / Applied Research / Development Research] → Production → Sales		Emphasis on enterprise immersing themselves in the user's perspective to gain insights and connect with them.	Enterprise / User

The stage at which users and Enterprises come into contact

Fig. 1. Evolving process of innovation categories

From the evolution of these three stages, it is fair to say that: a) The innovation entity has been gradually changed from a single enterprise to the co-creation between enterprises and users, in which user's initiative is valued by enterprises. Users are no longer the passive recipients of products but actively participating the development of products. b) In the past, users can only access products through sales after product development. However, nowadays, users are taken into consideration before product development. In this way, users can know enterprises and products in advance and affect the design and development of products and services timely.

2.2 Opportunities Brought by Digital Age and Covid-19

Since the outbreak of pandemic in 2020, travel restriction has become a new normal of social status. A number of online working software have emerged to overcome the difficulty coordinating among different regions. According to the 2021 online co-working industry research report by Aurora Data [6], the online platform had as much as 468 million monthly active users in early 2020 due to the pandemic, and still had 347 million monthly active users in 2021 when the pandemic eased. It is fair to say that the emergence of online co-working software has redefined the way people work. Meanwhile, there are also attempts to launch co-design online workshops which is a huge opportunity for users' participation. Compared with offline co-design workshops, the online ones enjoy obvious advantages: a) the coordination is not limited by space and time and is available when everyone is online or not at the same time.; b) the number of samples rises as groups formed; c) powerful data analysis and processing capabilities, process recording, fast traceability and enhanced utilization.

2.3 The Shortage of Online Co-design Tools Lead to Low Participation and Poor Experience

At present, the online co-design software tools on the market mainly include miro, Conference Table and Xiao Huazhuo, etc. Most of the users are designers and professionals who engage in related industries. These tools are meant to solve the communication and information presentation problems among members, and the overall using logic is centered on professionals, which has a relatively high understanding threshold and learning cost. It is quite difficult for ordinary users to understand and use, as they may have doubts on the presentation form of design tools, word choices and specific operation, which directly affect the participation willingness of customers and the quality of content output, and this is also a key factor that prevents designers from getting closer to users. Therefore, the participation method of online co-design workshops is still an area that needs to be explored constantly.

3 Related Theory

3.1 Co-design

Co-design first emerged in the business market research field, which sourced from participatory design in the late 20th century, and has further improved since the beginning of the 21st century. One of its classic case is Marc's classification of co-design and other design methods in 2007, arguing that co-design is the expression of participants' knowledge and ideas to designers, and is an exploration of future situations and opportunities [7]. In 2008, Sanders argued that users are no longer a passive study object but an active participant, and defined co-design in the first quadrant of user participation and design-oriented by sorting out the quadrant diagram of user-centered product and service design, and believed that co-design is a design and innovation process involving designers and non-designers [8]. Curedale R proposed three elements of co-design, namely participants, researchers, and tools. Participants refer to those who are not in the design profession. They will use tools to express experience and solutions under the guidance of researchers. Researchers need to design the co-design tool and guide participants. Tools are the bridge between participants and researchers, through which participants are inspired and express ideas, and these ideas and inspirations will be delivered to designers [9].

3.2 Customer Engagement

In 2010, Van Doorn defined user behavior other than purchasing as Customer Engagement, which specifically refers to the interaction and association between the company and customers, the contribution in cognitive, emotional or behavioral dimensions provided by the customer when the company develops products [10]. Yu Hongyan verified that with the increasing level of customer self-reinforcement and brand attachment, customer engagement and customer relationship obtained by the company will be greater [11]. Jiang Ting argued that customer engagement can change customers' perceptions and emotions, enabling them to gain economic benefits or non-economic benefits such as self-image building, while reducing the company's operation costs and improving its competitiveness as well as brand awareness [12].

The discussion of customer engagement could not ignore the discussion of customer participation and involvement. Zhu Yimin distinguishes between customer participation and customer engagement, arguing that customer participation is more related to purchasing, while customer engagement refers to behavior unrelated to purchasing, including recommendation and reputation which emphasizes on the association between customers and companies as well as the co-created value [13]. Customer involvement theory is used in marketing to analyze consumer behaviors. Greenwald believed that customer involvement refers to the focus of customers on certain things [14]. Celsi thought customer involvement is people's feelings about the relevance of something to him or her under specific conditions [15]. According to Zhang Yueli, customer involvement is a variable of psychological state. 'Self-relevance' refers to the degree of interest and concern of a person in something and also the level of relationship between customers and the company. Scholars classify customer involvement into two categories: low-involvement behaviors and high-involvement behaviors. Customers with high-involvement behaviors will pay more attention to things and are more loyal to the brand [16]. In summary, it is quite clear that customer participation and customer engagement can be interpreted as different level of behaviors during the interaction between customers and companies, while customer involvement is the criterion of these two states. The low involvement brings customer participation while high involvement brings customer engagement.

3.3 The Relevance Between Co-design Workshop and Customer Engagement Theory

First and foremost, these two ideas are user-centric which focus on the value co-creation between users and companies. To give full play to the initiative of users, it is expected to improve the products and services experience. The ultimate goal of these two ideas is to reach the interaction between enterprises and users and establish a much closer relationship between them. Secondly, there is a progressive relationship from theoretical guidance to concrete practice between these two ideas. The scenario advocated by customer engagement theory is an ideal goal, while co-design is rooted in concrete practice which that can be applied into different industries or fields. Thus, it is a worth-exploring perspective to take the customer engagement as the goal of co-design workshop and take the co-design workshop as the way to achieve customer engagement.

Co-design workshops are usually held before design and development, which is a way for companies to engage with users in advance. Customer engagement theory is the theory in the marketing stage, focusing on a higher participation and deeper interaction between customers and companies. To that end, co-design workshop will be combined with customer engagement theory and take the degree of customer participation into the consideration of co-design workshops, balancing the participation level while putting the interaction between companies and users ahead (Fig. 2).

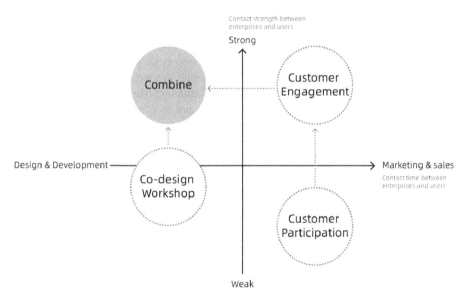

Fig. 2. The reinforcing relationship between co-design workshop and customer engagement theory

4   The Participation Model Construction of Online Co-design Workshop Based on Customer Engagement Theory

4.1   Participatory Co-creation and Engaged Co-creation

The basis of customer engagement theory sourced from value co-creation theory [17], which emphasizes that the value is generated from the interaction between producers and customers [18]. Zhu Yimin proposed that value creation is more about the interaction between companies and users which requires the building of communication platform for users and companies so that users can participate in the interaction with companies through their preferred methods, share experience, inspire their innovation and input their own value, thus affecting companies to achieve their value [13]. Based on the research of Yang Nan, optimizing the experience of users during the value co-creation can benefit the brand affinity building and enhance the brand recognition for users [19].

Value co-creation is divided into value co-creation in the service planning process and in the service delivery process. The value co-creation in the service planning process considers service as a design object, while in the service delivery process, serviced is considered as a commodity [20, 21]. This paper focuses on value co-creation in the service planning process. Based on the customer engagement theory, Ding Xiong divides the value co-creation in the service delivery process into two categories through participation time and intensity perspectives: participatory co-creation and engaged co-creation. The behavior of participatory co-creation is relatively direct and fast, with short input time and low participation intensity. In the process of engaged co-creation, users invest more time and intensity is higher, which will have an impact on their perceptions and behaviors. Users who are successfully engaged are more willing to participate in the following interactions. Companies are more likely to establish long-term relationship with users through engaged co-creation [22]. Participatory co-creation and engaged co-creation are actually descriptions of different participation conditions of users. There are also different states of participation in the service planning process of value co-creation, for example, random interviews and questionnaires are co-creation behaviors with low intensity, while design workshops and other methods are with higher intensity. Thus, the participatory and engaged co-creation are applicable during the discussion of value co-creation in the service planning process.

4.2 User Participation Model Construction of Online Co-design Workshops

According to the principles of consumer experience value co-creation theory, the interaction between companies and consumers can exist in any form related to the experience [23], and the neglect of any part that can generate value interaction should be avoided as much as possible. Therefore, the discussion of online co-design workshops should be more comprehensive and go beyond the discussion during the workshop, including actions from interviewing, distributing questionnaires, and contacting users before the workshop. The essential difference between the customer engagement perspective and other perspectives lies in the purpose. The traditional co-design workshop focuses on single project for short-term goals such as understanding of users' ideas, needs and pain points. However, the customer engagement perspective, in addition to the above short-term goals, also focuses on long-term goals, including user's participation experience, strengthening the connection and interaction between brand and users, gaining attention for the brand, and increasing user loyalty.

Thus, this paper expands the experience process of online co-design workshop discussions based on the principles of consumer value co-creation theory, and constructs a user participation model of online co-design workshops in an ideal state based on participatory and engaged co-creation with key advantages of online method combined (Fig. 3).

The Interplay of Participatory Co-creation and Engaged Co-creation. Participatory co-creation and engaged co-creation are not separated. Participatory co-creation has

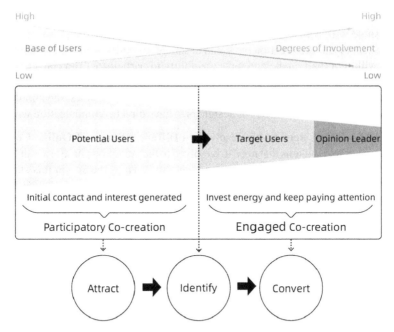

Fig. 3. User participation model of online co-design workshops

a low level of customer involvement, short participation time, low intensity and low participation cost, which can reach more customers. Engaged co-creation has a high level of user involvement, long participation time and high intensity. Thus, users who are willing to participate are only a few active ones who are willing to express themselves and have ideas and ability to participate. Participatory co-creation can be used as a quantitative basis to expand customer base and attract more potential users. Then target users can be screened out through the screening system to participate in engaged co-creation, and conversion can be achieved through engaged co-creation. In participatory co-creation, users have initial impressions and interests, but are still the onlookers. During the engaged co-creation, users enter the role of participants and they can dedicate more energy into the design, and keep their goodwill and continuous attention of the brand even after the process. This is how engaged co-creation can bring conversion. Companies and users can have continuous interaction, in which users can enhance their voicing power during the product development through participating the workshops and sharing their experience. Then companies can learn user's experience and ideas, which support further design development. User's attention and spread of reputation can also enhance brand popularity.

Key Stages and Methods During the Implementation of Online Co-design Workshops. The process of online co-design workshops covers three key stages: attract, identify and convert. The key purpose of attraction is to get more users. Having participants online not at the same time is a better way to get quantitative data, as only occupying the fragmented slots of users can bring higher flexibility and lower participation threshold with better willingness to participate. The identifying phase requires the establishment of a data collection back-end to screen user information and identify those who are willing to participate and have the ability to participate. The conversion stage is about the holding of co-design workshop during which the identified users will be invited. This stage requires a deeply interactive atmosphere. Besides, the simultaneous online channel can make it easier for designers to have direct communication with users.

Main Problems that Need to be Resolved in Different Stages of Online Co-design Workshops. The problems that need to be solved in the attraction phase is about "limited spread of content" and "user's irrelevance mentality". Thus, the key in this stage is to improve user's willingness to participate and content dissemination, which requires to dig out users' participation motivation. The content improvement should echo to users' motivation so as to attract users and improve the reach of target users. The key purpose of identifying phase is to identify target users. The key problem to be solved is to efficiently comb the collected information and accurately screen it. In this way, an online database can be established to identify target users who meet the requirements and have high willingness to participate. In addition, establishing a database can also enable the observation of target group's data changing on the basis of the continuous accumulation of data. The core of conversion stage is to build an enabling interactive atmosphere, making full use of the data processing ability and data visualization ability, quickly record and classify the data, and assist the combing before and after the workshop. The user experience issues in the process of implementation will be sorted out in details below (Fig. 4).

The Application Scope of Online Co-design Workshops. Online co-design workshops can be divided into 'online + offline' and 'pure online' modes. The former is still offline in nature, but with the help of digital devices, the efficiency and atmosphere can be enhanced. The 'purely online' form is the main research direction of this paper, where participants rely entirely on digital devices to communicate and interact. These two modes apply to different objects. The 'online + offline' approach is less likely to encounter difficulties in operating the software and is applicable to a wider range of people. The 'pure online' approach is not suitable for all users or all projects, and is applicable to people who can independently use digital devices such as computers and mobile phones, including students, young people, office workers and other projects.

5 Design Practice of User's Participation in Online Co-design Workshop

5.1 Observation Experiment, Collection and Analysis of Questionnaire

In order to better understand the problems that emerged in the process of users' participation in online co-design workshop, this paper will use the current available online coordination tools to hold an observation experiment of online co-design workshop.

The main tools involved in this workshop include Zhumu meeting software and an online collaboration tool- Conference Table. Four workshops were held and each

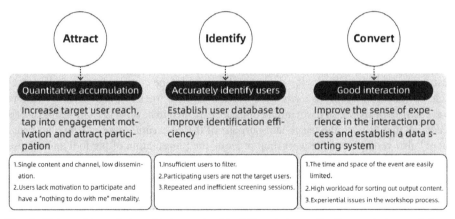

Fig. 4. Main problems that need to be resolved in different stages of online co-design workshops

session had four groups, with each consisting of three designers and two to three users, and all of whom major in industrial design, which can ensure that group members share similar knowledge backgrounds and have the ability to be inspired and to be creative. The users are mainly non-design undergraduates and young office workers, who aged between 21 and 30 and can operate computers and related software independently. Each workshop lasts for 1.5 h and each part is about 10 to 20 min. Participants joined the main meeting room through conference software. After the joining, moderators introduced the background, process and tool's rules. Then different groups entered sub-meeting rooms and discussed on the user profile that has been prepared. After reaching an initial consensus, participants completed the customer journey map at Conference Table by recalling a relevant past experience, and brainstormed based on the pain and cool points, and finally shared it in a storyboard or through sitcom (Fig. 5).

Fig. 5. Screenshot of online workshop

Finally, 66 effective questionnaires were collected, and 38 of them were from designers and 22 from users. The problems mentioned can be divided into 4 sections (Table 1): a) About inviting users, the identification and invitation of target users is a big problem for designers. b) About online software operation, multiple software were used during this online workshop, and the switching and operation between software brought poor experience to participants. c) About design tools, designers noticed that users did not know how to use design tools in a short time, had difficulty in understanding and resisted to the task of displaying design tools. d) As for the communication and interaction, designers said that the users were not active in the workshop, and the atmosphere was easily to be frozen so more interactions are expected to have. What's more, the user's feedback that "I wish the usage and purpose of the co-creation tool can be elaborated more" also verified that the workshop process, the presentation of the tool and the use of the tool which illustrated from a professional perspective is not the context that the user understands. In addition, from the user's comments such as "I hope the designer can lead the customer into the situation" and "some competition can be added to raise interest", we can see that users have higher expectations for the workshop and see it as a fun activity. They want to be better engaged into the workshop, expect more interesting and interactive parts, and want to gain a sense of accomplishment by understanding their roles in the process.

In summary, we can initially conclude the optimization objectives for improving the user experience of online co-design workshop (Fig. 6): Objective 1, weaken the 'work feeling' in the process and increase the fun elements. Users are resistant to the large 'workload' of the tool, and the communication within the group is too formal. Thus, work feeling should be weakened and more interesting interaction should be added for better interaction and more output. Objective 2, design tools should be generalized. Due to the seemingly complex rules of the tool, users are deterred and only focus on the use of the tool rather than the expression of ideas and creativity, which requires more time spent on usage explanation. At the same time, the organizational skills of the group designer have a big impact on the atmosphere and process. Thus, the tools and processes need to be expressed in a simpler way to reduce the pressure on users brought by using the tool, or to reduce the pressure on organizational members through phased task guidance. Object 3, functions of the online co-design workshop should be integrated. The frequent switching between different software can easily affect the workshop process and the fluency of expression among members. Members look forward to merging of functions between online co-design and audio and video dialogues, grouping, and the control of main meeting room.

5.2 Design Strategy

Correspondence Analysis of Online Co-design Workshop Requirements and Pain Points with Octagonal Behavior. Based on the analysis of previous sections, the same attributes exist in the optimization direction of attraction and conversion phases. Whether it is increasing the content dissemination to tap into engagement motivation, taking users in scenarios to encourage output, or generalizing the design tools, all of which can be achieved by adding fun or gamification mechanisms (Fig. 7).

Gamification is actually the application of gamified design methods and elements to non-game domains [24]. According to Lee Yuelin's research, gamification can stimulate users' interest in using the product, enhance interaction between users and the interface, thus improving the using experience and attract users to continue using it [25]. Ning

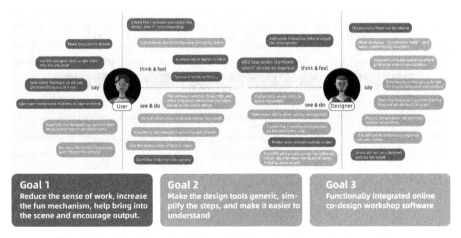

Fig. 6. Combing the optimization objectives of online co-design workshop

Lianju's study found that gamification design can improve task completion rate, enhance engagement, increase the likelihood of something happening, and users' willingness to stay engaged [26]. The key of this study is user's willingness to engage, experience and task completion efficiency of online co-design workshops. The direction of gamification design is able to match the optimization needs of online co-design workshops. The Octalysis has gained wide recognition in the industry, which is an authoritative and universal gamification theory that is well suited to solve many kinds of problems arising from the complex scenarios of online co-design workshops.

The pain points are analyzed in correspondence with the octagonal model. We can find that the reasons of many problems are caused by the same driver. In addition, some problems emerged due to multiple drivers at the same time. If we accumulate the frequency of problem corresponding to the driver, we can find that the driver with higher frequency indicates more problems can be covered. This is a way to determine the key driver that need to be focused on (Fig. 8).

Design Strategy in Attraction Stage: Interesting Quiz. The attraction phase is mainly influenced by the unpredictability, ownership and social drive (Fig. 8): First, users believe that participating in interviewing and filling out questionnaires is actually working for the company and they will not be benefited from it. Second, the regularity nature of the questionnaire leads to low dissemination. The serious title and the traditional way of asking questions, which appeared in the social platform frequently, could not arise users' interest. Thus, arising users' unpredictability and curiosity are key to enhance the dissemination. Thirdly, social drive is an important factor for interaction. When you see your friend or a group has something, you also want it so as to better integrate into the group when you share the thing. Thus, we can make full use of the herd mentality of people to create an opportunity for users to actively share, and enhance the spread of content.

Based on the above analysis, we can replace the original boring questionnaire with an interesting quiz. With interesting and revealing topics, users can be interested in the topics and content, thus willing to participate. Through methods like collection to

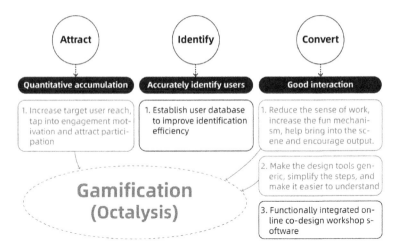

Fig. 7. Combing of optimization directions

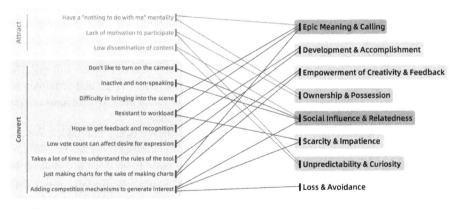

Fig. 8. Correspondence between online co-design workshop pain points and Octalysis

personalize the results, users can have a sense of ownership of the content, thus enhancing the relevance to users. Finally, driven by social and mission, we can create and share stories or take other similar ways, then add an entrance for users to "show off" as well as the social mechanism enabling forward, comment and like. Thus, users have the willing to spread content.

Design Strategy in Conversion Stage: Immersive Interaction. Analyzing the problems in the conversion stage against the Octagon model, we can find that the main drivers are sense of mission and social influence (Fig. 8): First, users focused on how to use the tool and had difficulty getting into the theme and scenario. Secondly, users are not professional designers and are prone to have bias in using tools, and are easily resistant to the work displayed in large blank diagrams. Thus, it is necessary to make full use of the mission to enhance the construction of scenarios and stories and improve users' perception of scenarios. Thirdly, users felt reluctant to switch on their cameras facing strangers and the discussion part was not active. Such performance can be related to corresponding social drivers. An enabling social atmosphere should be created to enhance users' active participation.

The secondary drivers include sense of achievement, innovation authorization and scarcity. First, users expect to receive feedback, which corresponds to the sense of achievement. Thus, we can just display participant's output and achievement so they can gain the sense of achievement. Secondly, the limitation brought by the singularity of tools and methods corresponds to innovation and feedback aspects. Thus, tools and their using methods should be re-designed and conten's innovation mechanism should be added to give more room to users to play. Besides, making full use of participant's desire for scarcity can reduce users' tiredness with some competition on the scarcity.

Based on the above analysis, the main solution in this stage is to turn the workshop into an immersive and interactive game. Firstly, by constructing stories and scenarios to help users enter the situation with tasks corresponding to their characters. Thus, users can feel interested and meaningful. Second, set up team tasks and related interaction, then they can praise and evaluate each other. The competition mechanism within the group can stimulate a more active atmosphere by leveraging the social driver. In addition, game mechanisms such as leveling rewards and rankings can enhance the sense of achievement and satisfaction of participants, and hidden treasures can enhance the interest of the game. Finally, a variety of prop can be provided for users to freely match and play.

5.3 Design Plan

Service System Design of Online Co-design Workshop. The project is based on the "New Way of Working" project of Asian Chimian Company (hereinafter referred to as Asian Chimian), a brand design company located in Haizhu District, Guangzhou, which is dedicated to creating consumption guidance for young people in the city. Asian Chimian has partnered with Service Design Research Lab of Guangzhou Academy of Fine Arts in 2022 to work on New Way of Working, which actually takes users a part of working and is a discussion on the way that users participating in design. In its essence, this theory is consistent with the goal of online co-design workshop from users' perspective. This paper will take Asia Chimian Company as the practice entity and exports a systematic solution of Asia Chimian online co-design workshop (Fig. 9). Based on the trendy and young brand culture of Asia Chimian company, a virtual world with Asia Chimian brand features– SubPlanet was built, which includes three sections: a game mini-program for personality testing in attraction stage; the data collection back-end in identification stage and immersive interaction game website in conversion stage. Quiz will take SubPlanet Accreditation Institute as the theme, laying a foundation for the workshop. Data back-end is mainly about data setting, data screening and data combing. SubPlanet Survival Institute enables designers and users to have communication and idea exchanges in an immersive situation. Designers can observe new design directions or inspirations and users can pay continuous attention on products and services. Users themselves can also experience an interesting online interactive game, getting a sense of achievement when they share their ideas and get recognition, receiving gifts and meeting like-minded friends.

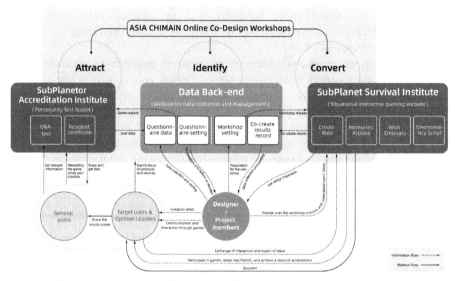

Fig. 9. Service System Map of Asia Chimian Online Co-design Workshop

User Experience Map of online co-design workshop. The participation flow shown in Fig. 10. After the setting and preparation at the back-end, the testing game of SubPlanet Accreditation Institute is released. Users are attracted by interesting topics and upload their information through personality testing. Meanwhile, the information filled by users will be uploaded to the back-end. Project members can analyze the data and apply it into the project, screening out the targeted users and send an invitation letter of SubPlanet Research Institute to attend online workshop. When users receive the invitation, they can log into the website and play games with designers and others users at a certain time. Each game section corresponds the design tools. Creating game role matches to user persona, which is the user empathy session in the workshop. Memories Archive matches to customer journey map; Wish Emissary matches to brainstorming section; Oneiromancy Script matches to storyboard. Through online platform, we can record players' speeches, deliver output, receive likes and get badges as staged rewards. In the end, the competition results and group or individual results can be generated to enhance the sense of achievement of players.

Interface Design Plan. As for the games in attraction stage, the vision interface (Fig. 11), including question box, option buttons, process bar and background VI, focuses on the theme of SubPlanet Accreditation Institute. This can emphasize the game-like atmosphere and reduce the feeling of collecting information. Compared with the words used in previous questionnaire, the words used in the game are more vivid which can enhance people's willingness to read. Besides clicking, there are also other input methods like drag, add picture and audio input. This can not only improve the interaction, but also collect more effective information. After finishing all tests, back-end system will evaluate the type of users and label them based on users' choices. Users will receive the

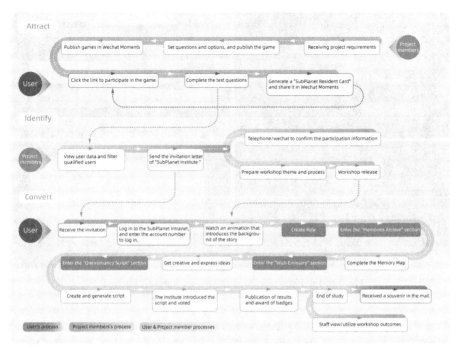

Fig. 10. User Experience Map of Asia Chimian Online Co-design Workshop

feedback in a way of 'Identification Card', including ID number, SubPlanet Address, name and group badge, which can stimulate users to acquire and share.

Fig. 11. Interface Design of SubPlanet Accreditation Institute

The theme of the game in the conversion stage is SubPlanet Survival Institute (Fig. 12). The visual style of the game echoes SubPlanet Accreditation Institute, and the design focuses on reducing the difficulty of using design tools, increasing the sense

Fig. 12. Interface Design of SubPlanet Survival Institute

of story and scenario, enhancing the sense of achievement and honor as well as social cooperation. First, players are given specific roles and tasks before the game starts, such as "Timekeeper" and "Atmosphere Controller". The story background is presented through animation to enhance the sense of story and scenario which can strengthen user's sense of mission in the game. When discuss the profile features during "Create character" section, haircut, clothing and accessories can be adjusted based on the characteristics of roles. Players can have more room to choose. The key design of other three levels of the game are: 1) Passing aids. The "Task Guide" clarifies and standardizes the tasks of each stage; "Inspiration Deck" helps members to get inspired; "Script Guide" helps members to express their designs in storyboards; 2) Increase the rewards of staged tasks, including medal rankings, group and individual honor lists, etc., to enhance users' motivation and sense of accomplishment; 3) Group cooperation and interaction mechanism. A group decision-making mechanism can be added, meaning all members agree with each other before entering the next level. Reward badges for group cooperation are given accordingly. Members can also like the approved views. Thus, group interaction can be improved through above simple procedures.

5.4 Testing and Results

Currently, only the first stage of gamified questionnaire test is produced, thus, this test is only for design in the attraction stage. The process is like inviting users to first experience the gamification questionnaire and then fill out the feedback questionnaire, with 5 points the highest, focusing on the attraction level, completion rate of content, sense of achievement and sharing willingness. Overall 42 effective questionnaires have been received (Table 2) in the end, with over 3.8 score on average. This means gamification, as the optimization direction, enhance users' experience to some extent, such as attracting users to click and enhancing users' participation motivation. The game-like images and interesting wording can arose people's interest to finish the test. The test results enable people to obtain a sense of achievement and motivate them to share. Compared with the QA format of ordinary questionnaires, users prefer this format with some game elements.

Table 1. Expectations and Ideas on Online Co-design Workshop from Designers and Users

Role	Content Type	Real Voices
Designer	Invite users	• "Hope to have more time to find users" • "Hope to invite more users" • "Should have more participants so as to dig out more ideas"
	Software operation	• "Used more than one software. The unfamiliarity to the software prevents users to deliver their ideas. Hope to have more easily-used software and offline session" • "Users found it difficulty in using the software so I need to help users on recording constantly" • "Conference Table and Zhumu should be combined"
	Usage of design tools	• "Users learned tools in a slow and hard way" • "Professional tools like Persona and Customer Journey Map are too abstract to users" • "After explaining for so many times, users still could not understand it and overwhelmed by the words which needed to be filled" • "Staring at the tool brought bad experience. Users said they felt they are like doing chart for chart" • "Fully depend on the organization and illustration of the group leader"
	Communication and interaction	• "Users are not very active, or unwilling to participate" • "About the atmosphere, sometimes it just froze" • "The process really took too many efforts from group leaders. Hope there will be more simplified process."

(*continued*)

Table 1. (*continued*)

Role	Content Type	Real Voices
User	Usage of design tools	• "Hope there are some detailed illustration on the usage and purpose of co-creation tools" • "It is better to learn the rules and purposes of these tools"
	Communication and interaction	• "The coordination among team members should be better with more thorough discussion and ideas exchanging" • "Designers are expected to take users into the scenario" • "Competition should be increased to stimulate the interest" • "We can get something from the feedback"

Table 2. Feedback on gamified questionnaire

Question (1 Strongly disagree/5 Strongly agree)	Feedback average score
Will these similar tests attract you to participate?	3.8
Will this gamified visual and wording interest you and motivate you to finish the test?	3.9
Whether the IP image or badge of test results make you receiving a sense of accomplishment?	3.8
Are you willing to share the test results and invite your friends to attend?	4.0
Compared with the question format of ordinary questionnaire, do you prefer this format?	4.2

6   Conclusion

This paper attempts to explore the level of engagement, participation methods and process of online co-design workshops while taking users as entities. Besides, a basic participation model of online co-design workshop in the ideal state is constructed. Compared with the traditional co-design workshop, the online co-design workshop guided by customer engagement theory can take the engagement level and experience of users into consideration, clarify the relationship between the low-involvement stage and the high-involvement stage, as well as the main tasks of each stage, which is a new way of thinking to establish a long-term interactive relationship between enterprises and users. The Octagonal Model for improving user experience and engagement fits well with the core purpose of this paper. Therefore, we used Octalysis to deconstruct user's pain points of the online workshop and proposed an optimization strategy to add gamification design elements to the online co-design workshop tool, and finally confirmed through testing that the optimized tool can improve user motivation, experience and sharing desire. However, since only the first half of the design has been tested, the feasibility of the second half of the design has yet to be proven by more complete testings and practices in the future. Besides, as each enterprise has its own specificity, this design may not be applicable to all types of enterprises. Thus, the characteristics of each enterprise and users should be considered.

References

1. Prahalad, C.K., Ramaswamy, V.: Co-creation experiences: the next practice in value creation. J. Interact. Mark. **18**(3), 5–14 (2004)
2. Ravald, A., Gronroos, C.: The value concept and relationship marketing. Eur. J. Mark. **30**, 19–30 (1996)
3. Di, S.: The study of Communication Methods in Co-design. Nanjing University of the Arts, Nanjing (2017)
4. Verganti, R.: Design, meanings, and radical innovation: a meta-model and a research agenda. J. Prod. Innov. Manag. **25**(5), 436–456 (2008)
5. Huiming, T.: BDD, the contemporary development goal of systemic design in China. Zhuangshi **12**, 17–24 (2021)
6. Aurora Data 2021 online co-working industry research report. Shenzhen (2022). https://www.djyanbao.com/preview/2985834?from=search_list. Accessed 5 July 2022
7. Steen, M., Kuijt-Evers, L., Klok, J.: Early user involvement in research and design projects-a review of methods and practices. In: 23rd EGOS Colloquium, vol. 5, no. 7, pp. 1−21 (2007)
8. Sanders, E.B., Stappers, P.J.: Co-creation and the new landscapes of design. CoDesign **4**(1), 5−18 (2008)
9. Curedale, R.: Service Design: 250 Essential Methods. Design Community College Inc, London (2013)
10. Van Doorn, J., et al.: Customer engagement behavior: theoretical foundations and research directions. J. Serv. Res. **13**(3), 253–266 (2010)
11. Hongyan, Y., Mingxuan, Y.: Scale development of customers integration behavior. Taxation Econ. **05**, 1–9 (2015)
12. Ting, J.: Scale Development of Customer Engagement Behaviors in Shared Travel. Chongqing University of Posts and Telecommunications, Chongqing (2021)
13. Yimin, Z., Hongyan, Y.: Literature review on customer engagement and co-creation value. Manage. Rev. **26**(05), 111–119 (2014)
14. Greenwald, A., Leavitt, C.: Audience involvement in advertising: four levels. J. Cons. Res. **11**, 581–592 (1984)
15. Celsi, R.L., Olson, J.C.: The role of involvement in attentionand comp rehension processes. J. Cons. Res. **15**(2), 210–224 (1988)
16. Yueli, Z.: The Study of Mechanism of Brand Loyalty's Formation and Development Under the Pattern of Complex Buying Behavior. Shanghai Jiao Tong University, Shanghai (2007)
17. Brodie, R.J., Hollebeek, L.D.: Advancing and consolidating knowledge about customer engagement. J. Serv. Res. (3), 283–284 (2011)
18. Wenzhen, W., Qijie, C.: Analysis on the formation path of value co-creation theory and the future research prospect. Foreign Econ. Manag. **34**(06), 66–73+81 (2012)
19. Nan, Y.: The relationship between customer participation in value co-creation and brand image building. Sci. Res. Manag. **42**(05), 87–93 (2021)
20. Xiangyang, X., Xi, W.: Co-creation and uncertainties of experiences in service design. Zhuangshi **04**, 74–76 (2018)

21. Xiong, D.: Service co-creation: co-creation in service design and its mechanism. Zhuangshi **10**, 116–119 (2019)
22. Xiong, D.: Research on the Co-creation Mechanism in Smart Tourism Service System Design. Macau University of Science and Technology, Macau (2019)
23. Prahalad, C.K., Ramaswamy, V.: Co-creation experiences: the next practice in value creation. J. Interact. Mark. **3**(1), 5–14 (2004)
24. Deterding, S., Dixon, D., Khaled, R., Lennart, N.: From game design elements to gamefulness: defining gamification. In: Proceedings of the 15th International Academic MindTrek Conference, pp. 9–15 (2011)
25. Yuelin, L., Pengfei, H.: A user study on gamified information retrieval systems: preference for game elements, attitude, and usage intention. J. Libr. Sci. China **45**(03), 62–78 (2019)
26. Lianju, N., Yuxian, X., Ran, C.: Gamification design of internet products based on Persuasion principles— taking Baicizhan, keep and ant forest as examples. J. Beijing Univ. Posts Telecomm. (Soc. Sci. Ed.) **23**(03), 67–76 (2021)

Architectural Design Landscape in the Near East in the Early 20th Century

Li Wei[(✉)]

School of Fine Arts, Beijing Institute of Fashion Technology, Beijing 100029, China
32442693@qq.com

Abstract. In the first half of the 20th century, a number of Jewish intellectual elites came to Palestine from different countries in Europe in succession. Driven by the then socialist thought, they attempted to build a new Utopian Jewish homeland in Palestine. Along with that, a number of agricultural Kibbutz and collective houses for urban workers were built continuously, and a new kind of community based on equality and labor came into being in Palestine. These new communities with strong democratic color played a critical role in the forming of the then design language, and even affected the architectural language of private homes in Tel Aviv.

Through investigating the architectural landscape of agricultural Kibbutz and collective houses for urban workers and the features of private homes in Tel Aviv, this paper studies how local Jewish architects converted European avant-garde culture into emerging Hebrew culture, and explores how the new communities shaped an organizational living environment and an orderly autonomous system. This can not only present the forming process of the local modern design system in Palestine, but also can present the unique design ecology in Palestine.

Keywords: Palestine · Tel Aviv · Utopian community · Modernist design

1 Introduction

At the end of the 19th century, against the Jew-hatred trend prevailing in European countries, the Jewish democratic thought began to emerge, and Zionist Organization (Zionism) was established in 1897, aiming at recovering the Jewish homeland in Palestine[1].

---

[1] In 1897, Herzl called the first Zionist conference in Basel, Switzerland. At this conference, World Zionist Organization (WZO) was founded, and Herzl became the first chairman. WZO aimed at building a Jewish homeland protected by the Public Law for the Jews in Palestine.

A. Marcus et al. (Eds.): HCII 2023, LNCS 14030, pp. 375–383, 2023.
https://doi.org/10.1007/978-3-031-35699-5_27

The leaders of Zionism always maintained friendly relationship with British Government. In 1917, British Government issued *Balfour Declaration* to support the Jews to establish their own country in Palestine[2].

When the First World War ended in 1918, the Ottoman Empire collapsed, and Britain controlled Palestine. Permitted by the British Government exercising administration, the Commission of Zionism entered Palestine in 1918. At the same time, the British Government exercising administration enforced "economic liberalism for the Jews" and "nonintervention of the internal life of the Jews" policies, which were beneficial to the development of the Jews, clearly supporting the Jews to recover their homeland in Palestine. Under these historical conditions, the Jews kept on coming to Palestine, and launched large-scaled construction activities, among which was the construction of collective communes, that is, agricultural Kibbutz and collective houses for urban workers.

2   Collective Communes in Palestine

With the third immigration wave (1919—1923) honored as Israeli Mayflower and the fourth immigration wave (1924—1929) with a dream, a number of avant-garde and potentially revolutionary young Jews kept on swarming into Palestine, hoping to establish an equal Utopian community, or collective communes in Palestine, which was called "Promise Land".

Agricultural Kibbutz

Agricultural Kibbutz was an agricultural collective commune established under the influence of the radical socialist revolutionary thought of Russia in the early 20th century. All members of Kibbutz must engage in collective labor and jointly assume obligations. As early as in 1909, when the Russian Jewish young immigrants established the first agricultural Kibbutz (Degania)[3], they brought the socialist thought to Palestine.

Kibbutz was a community composed of several areas, mainly including the area of public facilities in the center of the community such as restaurants, auditoriums, libraries and officers; large-area residential quarters, mainly distributed around the public facilities; and a large amount of farmland, surrounding the overall community. Different areas were harmonious in volume proportion and could coordinate with each other, thus guaranteeing the convenient labor of each household, forming an effective way of link between individuals and collectives, and having cultivated unique cultural features. It

---

[2] *Balfour Declaration* was a statement of British Government, which clearly supported Zionism. At that time, Winston Churchill and Herbert Samuel, the first High Commissioner of British Government exercising administration, were loyal supporters to Zionism. After the Commission of Zionism entered Palestine in 1918, the leaders of Zionism with Weizmann as the chief always actively maintained an alliance with British Government. For details, please see Anita Shapira, *Israel: a history*, translated from the Hebrew by Anthony Berris. BRANDEIS UNIVERSITY PRESS. 2012. p.120.

[3] Rachael Gelfman Schultz, *The Kibbutz Movement/The proud and turbulent history of Israel's experiment in communal living.* (https://www.myjewishlearning.com/article/the-kibbutz-mov ement/).

was an ideal pattern of production and life established under the drive of the then socialist thought, and with a desire for the collective way of life.

The active Jewish intellectual elites at that time participated in the construction of Kibbutz in succession. Among them were three students from Dessau Bauhaus. Shmuel Mestechkin mainly designed residential quarters of Kibbutz[4]; Arieh Sharon was responsible for the overall planning of Kibbutz; and Munio Weinraub-Gitai was responsible for the planning and construction of Kibbutz in northern Palestine all the time. After the three students returned from Germany to Palestine, they also introduced the architecture philosophy and ideology of Bauhaus into Kibbutz. Taking advantage of modern architectural technologies and design philosophy, the students of Bauhaus endowed Kibbutz with more reasonable, economic and practical living conditions, aiming at keeping on improving and developing Kibbutz serving the people.

The democracy and the principle of serving the people stressed by Bauhaus agreed with the spirit of collectivism and the socialist ideals claimed by Kibbutz. Kibbutz claimed manual labor and self-sufficiency. All members would be treated on an equal basis. The internal organizational decision-making and the execution and supervision of daily affairs of Kibbutz would involve all members. An equal and orderly internal system had been formed. At the same time, different Kibbutz maintained close ties with each other. Therefore, a new society based on equality and labor was formed in Palestine.

Kibbutz was not only a bold social experiment but also a detailed approach for the Jews to recover their homeland, making it practical to realize Zionism and socialist ideal. Kibbutz occupied a large area, thus taking an effective advantage of land and architecture resources. Moreover, through constructing Kibbutz, the Jews could gain the land ownership. Therefore, Zionism regarded it as a core assignment of the Jews building their new homeland in Palestine to vigorously develop Kibbutz. A large number of Kibbutz were built successively in northern Palestine[5]. It was a bold innovation of mankind's way of survival and production.

Kibbutz served the construction demand of the country at that time, and played an important role in agricultural development, national defense consolidation (Early Kibbutz was usually placed at national borders or in remote areas.) and political leadership (Many important military and industrial leaders came from Kibbutz.). Kibbutz was the only road to realizing the "socialist dream" on an arid land. With definite directional and demonstrative effect, Kibbutz played a critical role in the forming of the then design language, and affected the generation of urban collective communes.

Collective Houses for Urban Workers

In the early 20th century, architecture elites in Palestine such as Richard Kauffmann, Benjamin Anekstein and Dov Kutchinsky began to care about the housing problem of urban

---

[4] Chief Editor: Galia Bar Or, *Kibbutz: Architecture without Precedents,* Design and production: Michael Gordon, Pre-press and printing: Top.Print, Tel Aviv, 2010. p241.

[5] Kibbutz was built in Beit Alfa, Nahalal, Ein Gedi, Beit Ha Arava, etc.

workers. They all proposed different assumptions to solve the workers' housing problem[6]. However, what really put the assumptions into practice was Me'onot construction project in Tel Aviv.

Completed between 1931 and 1939, Me'onot construction project was funded by the then Histadrut of public institutions through financing and loan, and was designed by the team of "Hug" architecture elites composed of young architects. After the First World War, in order to alleviate the serious housing problem of urban workers, public institutions in countries such as Germany, the Netherlands and Austria organized investigation and financing for building cheap non-profit houses for low-income groups, thus generating the so-called "Cooperative Housing" project serving disadvantaged groups. The operation mode and design philosophy of Me'onot construction project were formed on the basis of the European mode. It was an important part of the modernist movement starting from building low-income residences.

Me'onot construction project included 18 residential quarters in total, and provided houses for at least 1000 worker families. Adopting large-scale connected wraparound building complexes and repeated apartments, the project greatly reduced the building cost, utilized building materials and land resources to the largest extent, and replaced the then method of dividing land into small plots. It had a strong color of socialist democracy. It was an urban collective commune established under the influence of agricultural Kibbutz. However, it was only a transitional stage for the working class. Eventually, it would become agricultural Kibbutz. In order to train the urban workers to engage in agricultural production, the school built small tillable fields in periphery so that the students could work after school. It was for cultivating their labor skills and making them realize the importance of physical labor.

The same as Kibbutz, Me'onot construction project stressed public architectures very much. For example, there was a public courtyard inside the building complex, and there were public facilities providing services for the residents such as stores, laundry rooms, clinics, reading rooms and kindergartens, which all faced the public courtyard, on the ground floor of all building complexes. The project established independent workers' communities that could satisfy the daily life of the residents, and expanded the workers' area of public activities, embodying the feature of publicity and democracy. Me'onot construction project promoted the construction of low-income residences and communities in Palestine, and a series of similar collective housing projects were built in succession in Haifa and Jerusalem.

Arieh Sharon, a student from Bauhaus, participated in the design of Hod residential quarters of Me'onot construction project from 1934 to 1935. Hod residential quarters intensively embodied the public feature of Me'onot construction project. For example, the residential quarter was composed of three groups of architectures separated by two streets (Fig. 1). In each group of architectures, residential buildings with repeated units

---

[6] For example, Richard Kouffmann (proposal for the Antiochia neighborhood, Jerusalem, 1922), Benjamin Anekstein(Tel Aviv and Jerusalem 1930s-40s), Dov Kutchinsky(Workers' Residence Bet, Jerusalem, 1934), Theodor Menkes (proposal for a workers' housing project in Haifa, 1936), Avraham and Tzipora Cherniak(Workers' Residence Aleph, Jerusalem, early 1930s). For details, please see Ada Karmi-Melamede and Don Price, *Architecture in Palestine during the British Mandate, 1917–1948*, The Israel Museum, Jerusalem. 2014. P180–185.

were arranged in a circular way. The wraparound residential buildings formed a half-open public courtyard, and guaranteed the light and ventilation of all apartments. The ground floor of the architectures along Fishman Street adopted piloti so that pedestrians could cross architecture to enter the public courtyard.

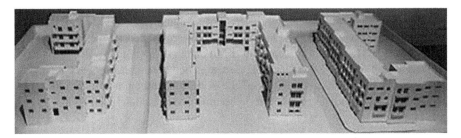

Fig. 1. Me'onot Ovdim Dalet, Heh, Vav(Hod)

Hod residential quarters comprised 154 housing units in total. Sharon boldly divided a unit house into activity area (kitchen, drawing room and balcony) and nighttime area (bedroom and bathroom). The activity area faced west, and the west balcony could provide cool sea breezes in the evening. The nighttime area faced east. The east bedroom had a small cantilever-type balcony, evidently embodying the influence of Bauhaus architectures.

The Jewish architects then active in Palestine, based on the local architecture condition, fund source and environmental factor, made an effective conversion of the European avant-garde philosophy, explored a reasonable, effective and economic design system, improved the life quality of the local residents, and created a low-cost and sustainable system of production and life.

Affected by avant-garde philosophies such as the thought of Utopian collective farm, Bauhaus design philosophy and European low-income housing project, agricultural Kibbutz and collective houses for urban workers, as collective communes, were built in large quantities in Palestine. These collective communes formed an orderly landscape layout, formed an orderly living environment and management system, and established a relation of understanding, communication and cooperation between individual effort and group construction, making Jewish immigrants from different cultural backgrounds able to establish an autonomous system within the community based on cooperation and equality in a homogeneous and organized social environment, and form social cohesion.

From 1929 on, European countries began to enforce strict immigration laws in succession. When Nazi assumed the power in Germany in 1933, Palestine became a main refuge for the Jewish immigrants. A number of Kibbutz and collective houses for urban workers were built in succession, becoming an effective way for solving the problem of mass migration. At the same time, the effective organizing force and strong cultural cohesion formed in these collective communes guaranteed that each new immigration wave could lead to a smooth cultural and mental conversion instead of destroying the original pattern. A new society with a nice Utopian vision was formed in Palestine. It was the only road to realizing the "socialist dream" on an arid land.

3 Private Homes in Tel Aviv

With the arrival of the fourth immigration wave (1924—1929) with a large quantity of private capitals, the first population and economic prosperity occurred in Palestine. However, facing the booming population and limited economic condition, effective and rapid construction and simple and practical architecture forms were required. Therefore, an architecture style with simple geometry and avoiding redundant decoration came into being in Tel Aviv. For example, the architecture designed by the architect Zaky Chelouche in 1931 was a representative of this new style (Fig. 2). The architecture form was a simple cube, the vertical staircase stretched the architecture height, and the transverse consecutive balcony extended the horizontal direction of the architecture. These architectures with a modernist style became a new fashion in Tel Aviv.

Fig. 2. Building in Art Deco style. 5 Levotin Street. Architect: Zaky Chelouche, 1931.

There were two reasons for generating this new style. One was that in Tel Aviv in the early 20th century, there were no specific architecture systems or methods for reference. Different styles coexisted. There were elements of classical architectures as well as architecture forms of local oriental features. Some architecture was integrated with traditional Jewish elements such as menorah and satellites on iron railings. In general, the architectures in this period can be called a kind of eclectic oriental architecture. The Jews were unwilling to form their own national style from so many "foreign" elements. They needed a new architecture form.

The second reason was utilization of new materials. From the 1920s on, silicate and cement bricks began to replace local soft sandstone to become popular building materials. Through prefabricated building accessories, this new material doubled the architectural efficiency and made walls easier to be handled. The utilization of new materials was also a direction of the "new architecture movement" of Europe at that time. The construction activities in Tel Aviv during that period were also an important part of the "new architecture movement".

Almost all architects then active in Tel Aviv were born or trained in Europe. They mainly studied architecture in France, Germany, Italy and Belgium[7], and introduced the modernist seeds then prevailing in Europe into Tel Aviv. For example, the stair railings and iron railings in a balcony were evidently affected by the European Art Deco movement. After the Jewish architects studying in Europe came back to Palestine successively, they boldly combined the European avant-garde culture with local actual conditions, and created a unique design adapting to the local climate condition. It was a result of converting European culture into emerging Hebrew culture.

In general, architectures in Tel Aviv in the 1930s have the following new features:

First, Unique Sun-shading Way. Due to the muggy climate and strong illumination in Tel Aviv, architects must solve the problem of strong illumination and ventilation first. Small-sized hidden windows and lengthened band-shaped balconies became an architecture feature of Tel Aviv. Shamai House designed by the architect Yehuda Lulka in 1936 was the best example to solve the local problem of strong illumination. Above a window or balcony was installed a concrete framework sun-shading board, which was about 10–12 cm thick. The vertical staircase was composed of several molded concrete laminae, which were horizontally arranged. The shadow generated by these laminae could effectively block the sun. Some architecture also adopted glass panes with an adjustable angle to replace concrete laminae. This sun-shading way of arranging several laminae in an orderly manner is still effectively adopted today.

Second, Piloti on the Bottom Floor of Architecture. The most unique landscape feature of Tel Aviv is piloti on the ground floor. Engel House designed by the architect Ze'ev Rechter in 1933 was the first architecture with piloti on the ground floor in Palestine. Through several concrete columns on the ground floor of the architecture, this structure can raise the overall architecture. The concrete columns arranged as a rectangular grid can support the architecture. It not only makes air more ventilated, but connects the ground space of architecture with streets. Actually, it connects private land with public space, effectively enhancing the coherence of public space. Later, this architecture structure became popular in both private and public architectures. Piloti on the ground floor has become a landscape feature of Tel Aviv today.

Last, Open Space. In architectures at that time, half-open public courtyards were very popular. Among them was Seminary Activity Center (already destroyed) designed by Arieh Sharon for Histadrut during 1945—1947. According to the restored model (as is shown in Fig. 1), the public courtyard is formed by arranging three groups of architectures in a circular way, with one side being open, so that pedestrians and residents can use it at any time.

Roof Terrace and Staircase. Due to low rainfall in Tel Aviv, from the 1930s, the previous slope tops were gradually replaced by flat roofs, which became a public area

---

[7] Architects studying in Belgium included Dov Karmi, Benjamin Anekstein, Genia Averbouch, Ben-Ami Shulman, Haim Kashdan, Ze'ev Berlin (son of Josef Berlin), Moshe Karassik, etc. Some architects studied in Paris or Vienna for one or two years first, and then went to Belgium for a study, for example, Ze'ev Rechter, Josef Neufeld, Genia Averbouch, Israel Dicker, Sam Barkai, Harry Lurie, etc.

used by all citizens. Some social activities and family celebrations at that time would be held on a roof terrace. The flat roof terrace could be accessed through the internal staircase, so normal work or residents' life would not be affected. The staircase often adopts large-area glass walls for people to appreciate street views. The large glass walls have also become an urban street landscape.

In summary, private architectures in Tel Aviv during this period redefined the boundary between private area and public area, and the layout inside architecture kept on being blurred or combining private space with public space. Apart from the aforementioned public courtyard, flat roof, etc., from the 1930s, the drawing room with a balcony began to face the street. It increased the social function so that residents and passersby could talk freely, thus embodying openness and democracy. Therefore, private architectures in Tel Aviv also embodied the concept of democracy, and played an active promoting role in establishing rational public order.

4 Conclusion

In the first half of the 20th century, the architecture styles of Palestine took on different forms. There were agricultural Kibbutz and collective houses for urban workers established under the influence of Russian socialist thought, Bauhaus philosophy and modernist thought as well as private homes built under the influence of new architecture movement and Art Deco movement. The architecture landscape of Palestine had the feature of multidimensional integrated development. It not only reflects that Palestine was an outpost of European avant-garde culture, but also reflects the universal low-income groups and social transformation problems in an industrial society, and Palestine's complicated political environment and the culture diversity of the Jews.

In a multiple mixed cultural pattern, Palestine always stressed the design philosophy of serving the people, took an initiative to create new architectures and communities with idealist innovation temperament, put emphasis on architecture landscape of public space and public facilities, and cultivated a social mechanism of share, symbiosis and collegiality. This mechanism infiltrated into the then social production and life structures of Palestine, forming a stable social structure and design ecology. When the General Assembly of the United Nations announced Britain's administration over Palestine to be over on Nov. 29th, 1947, the population of Jews had increased from 56,000 to 650,000 during the 30 years of Palestine being administered by Britain[8]. Through establishing their own communities and public systems, the Jews had established a complicated autonomous system to digest the Jews' influx. Palestine became a model of national construction and absorption of immigrants.

In the first half of the 20th century, the Jewish cultural elites in Palestine always planned the future practically and acutely, formed an accurate design positioning, made design involved in and serve national construction, social economy and cultural development in a deeper, more active and integrated way, created a modern design mode adapting to local survival conditions and cultural background, maintained and cultivated

---

[8] Anita Shapira, *Israel: a history*, translated from the Hebrew by Anthony Berris. BRANDEIS UNIVERSITY PRESS. 2012. P117.

unique cultural features, and formed an effective and good ecological design mechanism, which displayed good social effect and economic returns. It is still of important practical significance to reconsidering the relationship between design and modern production ways today.

References

1. Israel, S.A.: A History, Translated from the Hebrew by Anthony Berris. Brandeis University Press (2012)
2. Chief Editor: Galia Bar Or, Kibbutz: Architecture without Precedents, Design and production: Michael Gordon, Pre-press and printing: Top.Print, Tel Aviv (2010)
3. Karmi-Melamede, A., Price, D.: Architecture in Palestine during the British Mandate, 1917–1948. The Israel Museum, Jerusalem (2014)
4. Rotbard, S.: White City, Black City: Architecture and War in Tel Aviv and Jaffa. The MIT Press, Cambridge, Massachusetts (2015)
5. Metzger-Szmuk, N.: Dwelling on the Dunes/Tel Aviv/Modern Movement and Bauhaus Ideals. Kal Press Ltd, Tel Aviv, Israel (2004)

Exploration of Design Issues from an Embodied Perspective

Chenmu Xie[1], Yi Liu[2], and Hongshi Zhou[3]([⊠])

[1] Guangzhou Academy of Fine Arts, No.257 Changgang Road, Guangzhou,
People's Republic of China
[2] Province Key Lab of Innovation and Applied Research on Industry Design, No.257
Chang-gang Road, Guangzhou, People's Republic of China
[3] Guangdong Industrial Design Association, Guangzhou, People's Republic of China
151461191@qq.com

Abstract. The advancement of science and technology has shattered the dichotomy between "knowing" and "doing". The proliferation of digital technology has fragmented the view of the physical and virtual worlds as one. Thus, current design practice is challenged with the cognitive separation of the material and digital worlds, despite the integration of physical items and virtual services across international borders. Modern cognitive research is transitioning from "disembodied" to "embodied-enactive" in response to this issue. This trend demonstrates that humans are irreplaceable as cognitive subjects in both virtual and physical communities. The purpose of this article is to use the theory of embodied cognition as a research foundation and to investigate new perspectives and approaches for resolving the problem of cognitive separation in the digital world in the context of the integration of digital and reality. It inspires design practitioners to understand the object of design and related design system issues in terms of embodied experience and the overall relationship between the environment, the body, the brain, and the mind; enables people to interact with the digital world more naturally and to create and transmit meaning in the process of interaction; and assists design disciplines in focusing on "people" and investigating user behavior, perception, and "meaning" on a deeper level. Embodied design theory emphasizes the importance of the embodied connection between emotions and situations, and embodied cognition theory is essential for the study of human-intelligent interaction patterns within the context of intelligence.

Keywords: Interaction Design · Embodied Interaction · Embodied Cognition · Embodied Perception · The Digital World

1 Introduction

With the deep integration of sensation technology, artificial intelligence and digital twin into various fields, the paradigm of cognitive research based on computer metaphors has been challenged, and influenced by the theory of embodied cognition, the individual's experience in the social form of the real and the virtual has become a hot topic of research in contemporary design. Embodied cognition theory has introduced new research perspectives to the academic community and inspired the design discipline to explore the problems and solutions prevalent in design disciplines related to embodiment. The relationship between the design discipline and embodied cognition is understood in terms of embodied experience and the holistic relationship between environment, body, brain and mind, and further explores the transformation of the humanoid role of the intelligentsia and its embodied perception.

2   The Significance and Utility of Embodied Theory in Design Theory Research

2.1   The Theoretical Foundation and Significance of Embodied Cognition

The theory of embodied cognition is derived from the philosophical concept of phenomenology, which is a notion of oneness that transcends dualism. In the 1920s, the popularity of Husserl's phenomenological thought prompted an academic reevaluation of the mind-body relationship. From Husserl's notion of meaning through Heidegger's "being-in-the-world" to Merleau-Ponty's "bodily cognition", the epistemological history of phenomenology attempts to shatter the bonds of dualism and progressively construct a new world of unity. The epistemological development of phenomenology strives to remove the shackles of dualism and eventually construct a new worldview of oneness, laying the groundwork for the epistemological turn and paradigm establishment of embodied cognition theory. Thus, the psychological community began to concentrate on physical phenomena, such as the body, and their relationship with mental entities. From functionalism to behaviorism to neo-behaviorism, the field of psychology has pushed a large number of experimental research on the body, which is regarded as the foundation of embodied cognition theory.

Embodied cognition theory's epistemology and worldview are crucial to the solving of modern design issues. According to the embodied cognition theory, human perception results from the body's interaction with the objective world, which is influenced by complex environmental and physical elements and is finite and reasonable. Art design, which is emotional, and engineering design, which is rational, have gradually merged since the 1970s, and the design discipline has become more concerned with the user's experience, and more people believe that design is a search for a satisfactory solution rather than an optimal solution. The area of design no longer emphasizes efficiency, but rather the embodied core - the perceptual experience of the user.

2.2   Design Research Implications of Disembodied to Embodied Cognition

With the growth of computational research following World War II, computer metaphors emerged invisibly, and psychologists drew on computer models of information processing to comprehend models of the human mind and investigate the psychological principles behind behavior. Clearly, the premise that computer metaphors regard cognition as a symbolic processing and arithmetic process within the brain is too one-sided and has thus been contested by a number of scientists. James Jerome Gibson and F.J. Varela emphasized that physiological acts are an intrinsic aspect of the perceptual-cognitive process.

Sampson and Prilleltensky demonstrated that the development of perceptual cognition is conditioned by external variables such as environmental factors by introducing context, history, and culture as environmental factors.

With the change from disembodied to embodied cognition, the emphasis on the human body and surroundings has emerged as a trend in the design discipline, which is more concerned with user-centered interaction and experience. This emphasis on external variables has caused the design discipline to shift from a focus on the objective environment that can interact instantaneously with people to one that can have a continual impact on them. "The design object has gradually shifted from individual, material, physical products to system-oriented, virtual, experiential design" [1], which is a manifestation of the design field echoing embodied cognitive theory.

2.3   A Shift in the Cognitive Research Paradigm and an Exploration of Design Issues

Cognitive research's "embodied-enactive" paradigm arose from a mix of philosophical investigation and psychological theory. Tjeerd van de Laar and Herman de Regt synthesized the results of numerous fields and offered three fundamental premises of embodied cognition towards the end of the 20th century: the experiential of mind, the unconscious of thinking, and the metaphorical of abstract conceptions [2]. The core slogans of the second generation of cognitive science have been refined as embodied, enactive, embedded, and extended, embedded and extended can be considered as derivatives of embodied and enacted [3] (see Fig. 1).

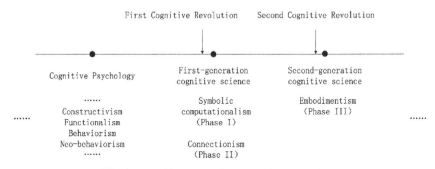

Fig. 1. Cognitive Psychology Development Chart.

The new paradigm of "embodied-enactive" cognitive research led to an emphasis on body experience and individual movement (including movement simulation) in the design field, which Donald Norman launched in the 1990s as User Experience and which eventually evolved into Experience Design [4]. The transition from user experience to experience design is an embodiment shift, in which the emphasis of design research changes from the user to the user's physical experience, individual mobility, and even the user's living surroundings.

3   Practice and Exploration in the Design Discipline

The design discipline has embraced "body and environment" as a primary design concern, and the "embodied-enactive" cognitive research paradigm is progressively being used by design practitioners to tackle design challenges.

Since the turn of the 21st century, the topic of study in the design field has shifted from items to people; the body is the base of human connection with the external world and the subject of perceptual cognition. Thomas van Rompay and Paul Hekkert originally presented "Embodied Design" [5] in 2001 and recommended that designers should consider the physiological experience of people in order to elicit their empathy. Toyo Ito, a Japanese architect, advocated "thinking about architecture with the body". This architectural theory, which is inspired by embodied cognitive theory, holds that using the body as a media, it may improve the relationship between people and architecture, elicit perceptual experiences, and communicate cognitive information. Ruoxing Li [6] criticizes the existing state of contemporary architecture without the body and offers the idea of embodied design, an architectural design method that uses the live features of the body as a starting point for the spiritual impact of people in the building. The body is a traditional subject in architecture, and the emergence of embodied cognition theory has pushed architects to re-examine space, the link between space and body, and the related psychological demands from the body's viewpoint.

First to examine the design of unconscious behavior from the standpoint of embodied metaphors were Naoto Fukasawa and Jane [7]. The conceptual metaphor hypothesis [8] states that abstract notions are mainly metaphorical and that metaphors are physical. Affordance and Signifiers on items, according to Donald Norman [9], may transmit information to consumers. Appropriate use of indicative product language can assist users in comprehending the operation and interaction behavior of the product. For instance, a short vertical handle implies that the door opens by pulling in the direction close to the body, whereas a long horizontal handle implies that the door opens by pushing in the direction away from the body. Domestically, Linxin Zheng [10] performed research within the framework of traditional culture and showed that physicals with referential features (such as traditional patterns) might build metaphorical links between items and settings (e.g., contexts and cultural experiences). Xiangyang Xin [11] believes that the brightness and darkness of buttons and colors in an interface may be utilized as metaphors to help users comprehend how to use the interface and make more accurate predictions about the result. Unconscious design figuratively translates the user's lived experience into the product design, using visual cues to rapidly and efficiently fulfill task objectives [12]. However, the "entry point" to construct metaphorical mapping is not confined to the visual level, which motivates designers to map conceptual metaphors from various dimensions of sensory experience, including bodily structure, external environment, and embodied experience.

Embodied cognitively inspired design investigates user behavior, perceptual experience, and deeper "meaning" difficulties to discover universal design methods.

4 Examining Interaction Design Issues from the Perspective of Embodiment

Important for the study of modern interaction design difficulties, embodied cognitive theory pushes scientists to consider epistemological and worldview concerns in design.

In this article, we analyzed the research dynamics and development paths of foreign literature by searching the web of science (including SSCI, SCI, and AHCI) databases (WoS) with the keywords "embody*" and "design" from 2018 to 2022. Then we used CiteSpace [13] to conduct keyword clustering analysis (see Fig. 2) and timeline analysis (see Fig. 3); the resulting knowledge graph reflects the research dynamics and development path.

Study on embodied design focuses on "virtual reality", "sustainable design", and "architectural design". The emergence of the buzzword "virtual reality" around 2016 implies that the application value and research potential of embodied design in the computer area are quite promising. The clusters "Embodied Rewriting" and "Constructing Information Models" are both theoretical and empirical investigations of digital worlds and related subjects.

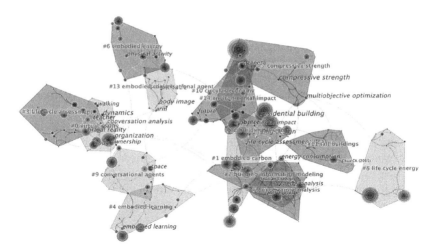

Fig. 2. Keyword Cluster Mapping (WoS).

Through a quantitative analysis of domestic and international literature, it is evident that embodied design is the result of multidisciplinary integration, with its frontier dynamics concentrated in the fields of the digital world, embodied interaction, artificial intelligence, and emotion research. This article separates the application and research trends of embodied design in the frontier areas into four categories and investigates the possibilities of addressing current design challenges from an embodied viewpoint by analyzing the hot design concerns in these four frontier domains. This paper will discuss the current state of disembodiment in the digital world and the solutions of embodiment, the intentionality and environment issues of embodied interaction, the emotions, and situations of embodiment, and the human-like role shift of intelligences and their

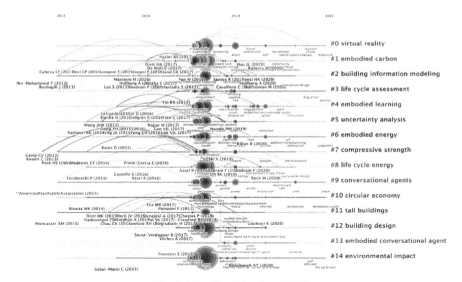

Fig. 3. Timeline Mapping (WoS).

embodiment effects, which are the concerns of artificial intelligence, in order to address these hotspots.

4.1 The Current Disembodied State of the Digital and Physical Worlds

Individuals live in an increasingly ambiguous social form in which the virtual and the reality are intermingled, and the manner in which they experience and interpret the world is inextricably linked to digital information [14]. This results in a status quo where the digital and physical worlds are divided.

Interaction design is considered as the bridge between the digital and physical worlds in the context of the Internet. Bill Moggridge [15], acutely aware of the influence of digital goods on the future of humans, started to focus on the design of interfaces and operations based on the digital world in products and dubbed it "interaction design". Dan Saffer [16] defines interaction design as the creation of human-machine-system interactions and behaviors. In the context of the Internet, the scope of interaction design has steadily grown from the original interactive screen to all "media that transmit and exchange information between people and computers", as well as the channels through which humans interpret information. People connect with the digital world through the physical world, and it is challenging for the cognitive subject to develop an identity without the mental mapping of the physical body [17]. Ishii [18] suggested the study path of Tangible Bits as a bridge between the digital and physical worlds in answer to this disembodied design challenge.

Traditional design theories have failed to handle the dematerialized state of the digital and physical worlds. Traditional design principles aim to solve the problem of individual acceptance and comprehension of the digital world by improving usability) and user experience. However, they also reveal that the design paradigm has shifted from functional design to experience-based design. Deng L.Y. [19], Song Y.Q. [20], and Sun X.X. [21] have concentrated on user behavior and perceptual cognition, but they have not investigated the link between the two and the more fundamental problem of "meaning". In investigating the transmission and interchange of information between people and computers, academics often commit the error of disembodiment, which entails neglecting the body as the subject of perceptual cognition. The disembodied approach to design research is incapable of compensating for people's sensation of absence or resolving the issue of fragmentation between the physical and digital worlds in the setting of the Internet.

The notion of embodied cognition gives a fresh approach to interface design to address the issue of fragmentation between the digital and physical worlds. Information in the digital world is flexible (intangible, dynamic, and transitory), while human-made items in the physical world are rigid (touchable, solid, and stable) [1, 22]. The notion of embodied cognition drives the design discipline to discover the awareness concealed in the body via design. The anthropomorphism of the digital world might extend the body as a cognitive process and the cognition (experience) it creates in the physical world to the digital environment, so facilitating a greater comprehension of the digital world. Through the use of digital twins or mirroring, sophisticated hybrid digital-physical worlds may be created [23], compensating for the lack of persons while engaging. Interaction design must provide design concepts and methodologies that "permit the flow and exchange of information between people and technology" and that communicate meaning.

4.2 Intentionality of Activity and Interaction Environment

The first paragraphs that follows a table, figure, equation etc. does not have an indent, either. The field of design has been motivated by embodied cognition to investigate user behavior, perception, and deeper "meaning" difficulties, as well as to develop universal design strategies. Paul Dorothy [24] argued in 2001 that Embodied Interaction involves the production, use, and transfer of meaning in the process of human participation with their environment and goods. The 2007 establishment of the TEI (Tangible Embedded and Embodied Interaction) conference by ACM signified the rise of embodied interaction as a research hotspot in HCI. The 2007 establishment of the TEI (Tangible Embedded and Embodied Interaction) conference by the Association for Computing Machinery (ACM) highlighted the emergence of embodied interaction as a focal point of HCI research. While overseas study on embodied contact has been undertaken longer and is consequently more extensive, local research on the topic of design has only increased since 2010. Tan L. [25] concludes that embodied contact consists mostly of physical and social engagement. Yao J.W. [26] and others summarize Paul Dorothy's six principles of embodied interaction with examples, highlighting "embodied interaction transforms action into meaning" as the central concept of embodied interaction, which enables human-object interaction to "construct, manipulate, and transmit meaning". This enables interaction between humans and objects to "create, modify, and transfer meaning". Xiao Y. [17] argues that embodied interaction is an interpersonal scenario in which the body is present and a cognitive condition in which the body is the major body that internalizes perceptual images into mental space.

From the previous studies, it can be summarized that:

(1) Embodied interaction is a process in which people interact with the environment (including products, etc.) in a participatory manner through a dynamic cognitive system consisting of brain-body-environment nesting, and in which meaning is created, used, and transmitted (see Fig. 4).

(2) The relevance of embodied interaction resides in the physical world's transformation as a result of interactive computing in the digital realm. Intentional consciousness precedes action, and more importantly, activity precedes intentionality [27].

(3) The focus of embodied interaction is the nature of human-environment interaction, the subjectivity of the body in the perceptual-cognitive process, and the participative and contextual character of design.

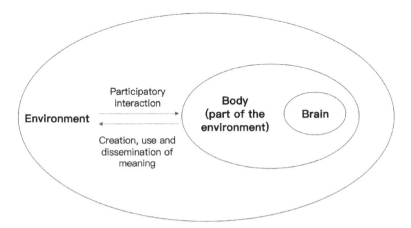

Fig. 4. The dynamic human cognitive system.

4.3   Embodied Connection of Emotions and Situations

In the realm of interface design, where metaphor bridges the gap between abstract cognition and embodied experience, embodied cognition theory introduces the notions of embodied metaphorical connections and unconscious behavior. Individuals have embodied metaphorical connections in both emotional perception cognition and physical behaviors, as shown by studies such as Barsalou [28] and Liu Y. [29]. Individuals may also comprehend others via embodied metaphorical associations. He C.Q. [12] and Susan Carey [30] sought to model the user's thinking using unconscious embodied metaphorical linkages. Li X.R. [31] used the unconscious embodied metaphorical link and the significance of the body in design in order to create behaviorally driven product metaphorical interaction prototypes. Scholars investigate the interconnections between the body and the external world through embodied metaphorical connections and unconscious behavior, as well as the interactions between the body and abstract notions such as emotional intuition produced by the human brain. The absence of brain-body-environment interconnections has hampered the creation of a comprehensive model of the user's cognition and behavior.

The emphasis of embodied interaction is on the systemic, interactive, and comprehensive aspect of the interaction system. Wang X.L. [32] suggests developing a model of embodied cognitive theory in order to show that embodied theory may assist bridge the cognitive gap between humans and machines. The interface paradigm of human-machine interaction evolves from digital product interface to spatial interface as a result of the development of digital twin and mirroring technologies. Xiao Y. [17] examines how the body and technology influence the production of "immersion" in the interaction space from three perspectives: human, technical goal, and interaction environment. He J. [33] explains the imagery schema theory based on the notion of embodiment, which is extensively employed in visual design and whose application is mostly anthropomorphic, superficial, and metaphorical. In an effort to enhance the holistic, interactive, and systematic character of human-computer interaction systems, Xiao Y.Q. [34] suggested a design process technique of imagery schema intervention in contextualized design. However, J. Hurtienne [35] acknowledges that this strategy has limitations when applied to a user community with long-term behavioral patterns. Such scholars abstract the environment as metaphorical elements, focus on the interaction relationship between the body and such elements and ignore the overall environment and the body embedded in the environment, which prevents them from considering the holistic, interactive, and systematic nature of the interactive system in a comprehensive manner.

4.4 The Transformation of Human-Like Agents' Intelligent Bodies and Their Embodied Perception

From the standpoint of embodied interaction, Human-Agent Interaction (HAI) focuses more on the intelligence created by the interaction between humans and intelligences. From an embodied standpoint, Hirotaka Osawa [36] provides a thorough evaluation of the approach to HAI. Similar to the evolution of human embodied vision, Rodney Brooks [37] hypothesized that intelligences may emerge from their own interactions with the environment.

However, the intelligent body lacks a biological body, thus the accumulated cognitive experience of the intelligent body itself paired with the embodied cognitive experience of the creator is considered the intelligent body's embodied perceptual-cognitive experience. Xu X.J. [38] demonstrates further that HAIs interact with the environment via embodied sensory-motor circuits and that intelligences learn symbols and build symbolic meanings through themselves, although with constraints. Scholars depart from the standard concept of information processing and view artificial intelligence as a humanoid entity whose information processing model is comparable to the human "embodiment-enactive" cognitive model. Ovett et al. [39–41] published a collection of papers titled The Handbook of Multimodal-Multisensor Interfaces, summarizing theoretical models of multimodal interactions and emphasizing that embodied cognitive theory can guide the models' naturalness, robustness, and adaptability. Qin J.Y. [42] proposed the development of a multimodal interaction prototype for HAI from both an embodied and disembodied standpoint. Under the premise of embodied interaction, HAI abandons the conventional interaction mode of buttons and screen taps in favor of multimodal engagement across various channels, including the five senses, limbs, information carriers, and the environment. HAI accurately simulates human-human interaction and human-intelligent body interaction.

HAI views the intelligent vehicle in the interaction process as the body of the intelligent body, which is devoid of instrumentality and possesses "behavioral logic" [43]. Through multimodal contact with embodied relations, human and intelligent body interaction behavior can be made more natural.

5   Conclusion

This paper provides a more systematic overview of contemporary design issues from an embodied perspective, inspiring the design discipline to extend the bodily cognitive mechanisms of the physical world to the digital world, thereby addressing their fragmentation. To better comprehend the connotation and meaning of embodied interaction, emphasis is placed on the intentionality of action and the context of interaction. On the basis of this, the influence of the embodied association of emotion and circumstance on the totality, interaction, and systemic nature of the interaction system is analyzed. In conclusion, HAI is used to illustrate the naturalness, robustness, and adaptability of embodied steering and multimodal interaction in intelligent bodies.

Existing research has overemphasized the role of the body in cognitive processes and ignored the crucial interaction between the body as a basis for action and a component of the environment and the world [44]. Faced with the issues that embodied design theory has not yet formed a mature theoretical system, the bias of self-comprehensive and unified understanding, and the inability to unify the definition of embodiment, the design discipline should adopt embodied cognition as its main theoretical foundation, investigate the solutions to contemporary design problems in depth, and further develop the theoretical system of embodied design.

References

1. Liu, Y.L., Song, L.W.: Towards the Embodiment: on the shift of design and its' philosophical speculation. J. Nanjing Arts Institute (Fine Arts & Design) (2), 111–116 (2021)
2. Lakoff, G., Johnson: Philosophy in the flesh: the embodied mind and its challenge to western thought, pp. 3–4. Basic Books, New York (1999)
3. Chen, W., Yin, R., Zhang, J.: Embodied Cognition in Psychology: a dialogue among Brain, Body and Mind, pp.1. Science Press, Beijing (2021)
4. Xin, X.Y.: From user experience to experience design. Packaging Eng., 60–67 (2019)
5. Van Rompay, T., Hekkert, P.: Embodied design: on the role of bodily experiences in product design. London: Asean Academic Press, 39–46 (2001)
6. Li, R.X.: On Embodied Design: an approach of architectural design from the viewpoint of body. Tsinghua University, Beijing (2014)
7. Jane, F.S.: Thoughtless Acts. Observations on Intuitive Design. Chronicle Books, USA (2005)
8. Lakoff, G., Johnson, M.: Metaphors We Live By. Chicago, IL: University of Chicago Publisher, Chicago (1980)
9. Donald, A.N.: The design of everythings, pp.11. CITIC Publishing Group, Beijing (2016)
10. Zheng, L.X., Lu, Y.Z.: Action metaphors in product design. New Arts 7, 125–127 (2016)

11. Liu, B.S., Xin, X.Y., Liu, Y.: An unconscious interaction design approach under neuropsychology. Packaging Eng. **10**, 70–74 (2016)
12. He, C.Q., Lyu, C.C.: Unconscious design from the perspective of embodied cognition. Packaging Eng. **8**, 80–86 (2020)
13. Li, J., Chen, C.M.: CiteSpace: Text Mining and Visualization in Scientific Literature, 2nd edn. Capital University of Economics and Business Press, Beijing (2017)
14. Buongiorno, F.: Embodiment, disembodiment and re-embodiment in the construction of the digital self. HUMANA. MENTE J. Philos. Stud. **12**(36), 310–330 (2019)
15. Moggridge, B.: Designing Interaction. MIT Press (MA), Massa-chusetts (2006)
16. Saffer, D.: Design for Interaction: Creating Innovative Applications and Devices. China Machine Press, Beijing (2010)
17. Xiao, Y., Wu, Y.H., Wang, Z.G.: From mapping to absorption: exploring the technical intention of "immersion" in embodied interaction. Media **17**, 87–90 (2021)
18. Ishii, H.: Tangible bits: toward seamless interfaces between people, bits and atoms. In: Proceedings of CHI, March, pp. 234–241 (1997)
19. Deng, L.Y., Jiang, X.: Research on implicit interaction design based on behavior logic. Art & Design **6**, 87–89 (2019)
20. Song, Y.Q., Yan, Y.Y., Yu, J., Wang, L.S.: Application of without thought design in app interaction and interface design. Design Res. **2**, 46–49 (2018)
21. Sun, X.X.: Decision rule of interaction design: matching logic of behaviors and information architecture. Art & Design **5**, 140–141 (2016)
22. Levy, P.: Becoming Virtual: Reality in the Digital Age. Plenum Trade, New York (1998)
23. Van Campenhout, L.D.E., Frens, J.W., Overbeeke, C.J., et al.: Physical interaction in a dematerialized world. Int. J. Des. **7**(1), 1–18 (2013)
24. Dourish, P.: Where the action is: the foundations of embodied interaction. MIT Press, Cambridge MA (2001)
25. Tan, L.: Environmental media design in context of embodied interaction: a theoretical framework and research approach. Art J. **2**, 116–122 (2019)
26. Yao, Z.W., et al.: Comparison of embodied interaction and whole body interaction. J. Comput.-Aided Design Comput. Graph. **12**, 2366–2376 (2018)
27. Liu, H.Y.: Research on multimodal wearable products design based on embodied cognition theory. Jiangnan University (2021)
28. Barsalou, L.W. : Chapter 30-Situated Conceptualization. Handbook of Categorization in Cognitive Science, 735–771 (2005)
29. Liu, Y., Wang, Z.H., Kong, F.: The view of embodied emotion: a new perspective on emotion study. Adv. Psychol. Sci. **1**, 50–59 (2011)
30. Carey, S.: Cognitive conflict science and science education. Am. Psychol. **41**(10), 1123 (1986)
31. Li, X.R.: Behaviorally oriented product metaphor interaction. Zhejiang University (2011)
32. Wang, X.L., Jiang, X., Zhao, D.L., Ma, F.J.: Interaction design of children's smart toy based on embodied cognition. Packag. Eng. **16**, 165–170 (2019)
33. He, J.: Body Image and Body Schema: a study of embodied cognition. Zhejiang University (2009)
34. Xiao, Y.Q., He, R.K.: Approach to interactive metaphor design based on image schema coding. Packag. Eng. **16**, 162–166 (2018)
35. Hurtienne, J.: How cognitive linguistics inspires HCI: image schemas and image-schematic metaphors. Int. J. Hum.-Comput. Interact. (vol. 33), 1–20 (2017)
36. Hirotaka, O., Lu, C.: Human-Agent Interaction: designing artificial intelligence system for human. Art & Design (11), 14–21 (2016)
37. Brooks, R.: Cambrian Intelligence: The Early History of the New AI. The MIT Press, Cambridge (1999)

38. Xu, X.J.: Embodied artificial intelligence and phenomenology. J. Dialectics Nat. **6**, 43–47 (2012)
39. Oviatt, S., Schuller, B., Cohen, P., et al.: The handbook of multimodal-multisensor interfaces, vol. 1: foundations, user modeling, and common modality combinations. Morgan & Claypool (2017)
40. Oviatt, S., Schuller, B., Cohen, P., et al.: The handbook of multimodal-multisensor interfaces, vol. 2: signal processing, architectures, and detection of emotion and cognition. Morgan & Claypool (2018)
41. Oviatt, S., Schuller, B, Cohen, P., et al.: The handbook of multimodal-multisensor interfaces, vol. 3: language processing, software, commercialization, and emerging directions. Morgan & Claypool (2019)
42. Qin, J.Y., An, Y.L., Lu, X.H., Wu, Z.: Interaction grammar of embodied & disembodied cognition in multi- modal interactive environment. Packag. Eng **12**, 134–139 (2019)
43. Liu, H.Y., Gong, M.S., Liang, Q.: Intentional stance of human-agent interaction from the perspective of embodied cognition. Packag. Eng. **2**, 145–151 (2022)
44. He, J.: Body Image and Body Schema: a study of embodied cognition, pp. 3. East China Normal University, Shanghai (2013)

Research on Product Interaction Design Innovation Under New Media Technology

Jun Yan[✉]

Wuhan Textile University, Wuhan, Hubei, China
yanjun@wtu.edu.cn

Abstract. New media technology is widely used and can be found everywhere in everyday life, however, artificial intelligence technology is a new subject of new media technology. It and the aesthetics applied in the process of product interaction, namely sensory beauty and technical beauty, provide new ideas and methods for product interaction design innovation. **Purpose** This article is based on new media technology as a new means of technological development and product innovation in the era, to help product interaction design to be more intelligent and humanized, so that due to the rich material culture, the cultural and artistic connotation of products should also be improved accordingly. **Methods** New media technology is used as a media intervention method, and the research is carried out from the five elements of product interaction design and interaction aesthetics. Content Demonstrate the application of artificial intelligence technology in the five elements of interaction design, namely: user, purpose, behavior, scene, media and interaction aesthetics, as well as the development trend and innovation mode of these two. **Results** The maturity of artificial intelligence technology and the progress of interaction aesthetics provide new ideas and opportunities for the innovation of product interaction design.

Keywords: New Media Technology · Artificial Intelligence Interaction · Interaction Aesthetics

1 Innovative Elements of Product Interaction Design in New Media

1.1 New Media Background Overview

Today is the era of information development, is also the era of digital media communication. The basic feature of new media is digital, and new media is relative to the traditional media, is a new media form developed after the traditional media such as newspaper, radio and television, but also to provide users with information and entertainment communication form and media form. The basic communication characteristic of new media is interactivity, and artificial intelligence technology is its new main body. This main body is applied to product interaction design and has various uses, which can change the interaction between people and products and improve the performance of products. Overall, the application of artificial intelligence technology to the design of product interaction is a major trend in product innovation and a reflection of the human-centred

© The Author(s), under exclusive license to Springer Nature Switzerland AG 2023
A. Marcus et al. (Eds.): HCII 2023, LNCS 14030, pp. 396–405, 2023.
https://doi.org/10.1007/978-3-031-35699-5_29

nature of products. It can be said that the application of new media technology to life has not only changed the lives of some people, but has also brought about a profound change in society. The new media context mentioned in this article refers to the artificial intelligence technology, and the product interaction design under the new media refers to the innovation and proliferation of product interaction design methods under the general environment of artificial intelligence technology.

Traditional media usually refers to platforms with slow information dissemination such as television, radio and newspaper, which is opposed to "new media". New media technology is a new media based on Internet technology, which provides more extensive information services for the public and is more suitable for the development of today's society. Different from traditional media technology, which only acts on one sense of the human body, such as single vision and single hearing, new media technology can jointly act on the information form and content of multiple senses of the human body at the same time in the process of information transmission, compared with traditional media. Such as text, pictures, audio, video, animation and other categories of content, which makes the new media technology has a stronger vitality and more lasting influence.

Human body receives information through its own senses: sense of balance, proprioception, heat, pain and internal sensation, which contain most of human senses. Due to the different timeliness of information reception, the most commonly used interactive senses in product interaction design are hearing, vision and touch. The original intention of product design is "people-oriented", and the purpose of product interaction is not only to meet the needs of users but also to reduce the cognitive load of users for product use. New media technology has powerful information transmission ability, which is suitable for the development of the current society and has become the mainstream trend in the application of product interaction design.

1.2 The New Body of New Media - Artificial Intelligence Technology

Artificial intelligence technology, as the new body of new media technology, has become an indispensable source of technology for new high-tech products. Nowadays, intelligent products have gradually taken over the market, and their two main features, namely intelligence and humanisation, have become the first choice of users when purchasing goods. In recent years, the number of shipments of artificially intelligent homes has been increasing year by year, reaching 3 million units in 2022 (Fig. 1). The intelligence and humanity of smart products are conveyed through interaction with users, and are loved for their convenient use, complete functionality and fast flow of information. Artificial intelligence can simulate human consciousness and thinking, and this technology is applied to the interaction between people and products in a way that is closer to their habits and lifestyles.

1.3 Aesthetics in the Interaction Process

Aesthetics, as a sub-discipline of philosophy, is a discipline that studies the aesthetic relationship between man and the world, i.e. the object of aesthetic study is aesthetic activity. Interaction aesthetics is the study of aesthetic issues in people, products and material culture, and it is centered on aesthetic experience. We divide the aesthetic

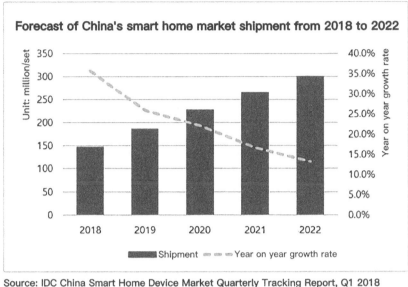

Source: IDC China Smart Home Device Market Quarterly Tracking Report, Q1 2018

Fig. 1. Forecast of China's smart home market shipment from 2018 to 2022

issues encountered during product interaction into sensory beauty and technical beauty. Sensory beauty is the process in which we interact with the product, through the external stimulation of our vision, smell, touch, hearing and some other sensory effects to make us enjoy the process. Technical beauty encompasses many things, from the beauty of technique, which is what we call the beauty of craftsmanship, to functional beauty. The aesthetics of the interaction process refers to functional beauty, i.e. the process of interacting with the product with just the right technology to help the user enjoy the process of using the product. Innovation in product interaction design under new media is highlighted through innovation in artificial intelligence technology and aesthetics in the interaction process.

2　Highlights of Innovation in Artificial Intelligence Technology

2.1　Subscribers

The user is the starting and ending point of human-computer interaction and is always present in the process. The product is the medium of HCI design. The industrial product design under interaction design should analyse the user's needs in depth, propose design solutions to meet the user's needs, and finally design industrial products that meet the user's needs and conform to the concept of human-computer interaction design. A product in the preliminary research to determine the product positioning, to understand the user, the use of the product may exist many kinds of user groups, must be based on the study of the target users. Product design has different design pain points for different age groups of users. When applying new media technology to product interaction design, different age groups will have different ways of interacting with each other. For example, in our daily lives we often use the video call function (Fig. 2), where one client communicates with another client. This mode of communication is gradually not satisfying the needs of users, and by the derivation of technology, video call has developed into something that can be used by multiple clients at the same time, and is widely used in video conferencing.

Fig. 2. Video conference

2.2 Purpose, Behaviour

The Fundamentals of Product Interaction Design suggests that in order to design a good interactive industrial product, it is necessary to meet not only the material functional requirements, but also the spiritual needs of the user. The material and the spiritual, one for simplicity and safety of use and the other for the user's pleasure in using the product. For example, to increase self-confidence, to feel happy, to enjoy the beauty of art, to stimulate a sense of creativity, etc. ◦ A simple and interesting interaction, or an immersive virtual scene interaction, would be a good way to interact. The Chinese philosophers said: "To experience with the body, to experience with the mind". The experience of body and mind is the real experience, and is an important indicator of future product design innovation.

In a product's functional transformation, users may have one purpose or multiple purposes. The purpose and behaviour of the user is to determine the requirements and to clarify how many purposes the product is intended to fulfil. Just as the interaction function of a product is comprehensive, the interaction design under AI needs to design behavioural patterns according to the different purposes of the user. For example, the design of interaction modes for smart products. Tactile interaction and voice interaction are the most used interaction methods, and these two interaction methods are the most accessible, and in everyday life touchable intelligent products and voice-activated products are the two largest types of AI.

2.3 Media and Scenes

Some people say that products are the medium of human-computer interaction, so I think artificial intelligence technology is an indispensable medium in product interaction design. Artificial intelligence technology is the new body of new media technology, the mainstream technology of product interaction today, and a means to assist human-computer interaction, which can also be called intelligent interaction methods.

Scenarios are an easily overlooked but important part of the interaction process. The functions of artificial intelligence products point to the inclusion of all aspects, so the user may use the product in any place, then the human-computer interaction scenario will occur in any place. It could be at home, at work, at school, at a restaurant, at a construction site, etc. Depending on the function of the product, it will be used in different places, and then the interaction of the product will have to be different depending on the place. For example, an AI product in a noisy public place would not be suitable for voice interaction; a crowded place would not be suitable for motion interaction. So the designer has to set the most appropriate interaction method for each scenario.

At the same time, Product design is a discipline combining art and technology. If there is only art but no technology in product design, then the product can only be called an artwork; if there is only technology but no art in the product, then the product can only be called a tool. A good product is the result of the joint action of technology and art. In product design, technology and art are closely related, and if the two can't work together, then the product can't meet the functional and psychological needs of users at the same time. The purpose of product design is to provide people with products that meet all their needs. Only when technology and art balance each other and endow the product with technical form and artistic expression, can this product be regarded as a product that meets the needs of users. For example, due to the rapid development of technologies such as computer technology and the Internet, people can transmit information, socialize, and know about the outside world through computers. For different user groups, computers are divided into desktop computers, notebook computers and handheld tablet computers. Desktop computers are suitable for people who use them in fixed places; notebook computers are suitable for people who need to work in a mobile office; handheld tablet computers are suitable for people who have no special needs and require simple office work. In these three types, products provide users with the same functional services. The features that distinguish a product from other types will bring unique user experience and emotional value to users.

2.4 Artificial Intelligence Technology Trends

Since the rapid development of Internet technology, new media technology has the dual attributes of social responsibility and cultural communication. Driven by the needs of technology and social development, new media technology has ushered in a new development period. New media technology has the excellent attributes of diversity, wide range and strong interactivity to adapt to the spread of social information, and is applied in a variety of industries, such as education, entertainment, film and television, human-computer interaction, etc. In the process of information transmission, new media technology can support the information forms and contents that jointly act on a variety of human senses at the same time, such as text, pictures, audio, video, animation and other categories of content, which makes new media technology have stronger vitality and more lasting influence. New media technology itself has very significant characteristics, mainly manifested in three aspects: wide range of dissemination, strong interaction, fast aging.

The rapid development of artificial intelligence technology is now being applied in many fields, and artificial intelligence technology is no longer a concept that has gradually entered our daily lives. For example, at the Shanghai International Import and Export Technology Fair, a programmable and controlled artificial intelligence stir-fry robot "Flavor Bar" will be unveiled (Fig. 3–4). In a 4 square metre booth, a fully functional small sample kitchen is set up, with no traditional kitchen equipment, just a few kitchen essentials and the AI stir-fry robot, which allows you to put the required ingredients and spices into the device, select the corresponding recipe and taste, and click on start stir-fry to start cooking. With a stir-fry robot, there are fixed ingredients and recipes that can be standardised for Chinese food. Even busy, overworked office workers can eat nutritious food with this stir-fry robot. The application of artificial intelligence technology to everyday life should facilitate our lifestyle and not degrade our quality of life.

In the future, artificial intelligence technology will enter the business environment of intelligent services, which is the popularity and wide application of artificial intelligence technology. Artificial intelligence technology has made innovations in the field of product interaction design to achieve an intelligent human mindset to solve problems This is not just technology, but also includes psychology and philosophy. Better study of human psychology and understanding of human behaviour. By applying convenient interaction methods to the use of products, perhaps in the future, users will only need to look at a product or a chip that can communicate their thoughts in order to convert it to a function.

3   Connotations and Innovative Points of Interaction Aesthetics

3.1 The Connotations of Technical and Sensual Beauty

In the beginning of creation, the form of products was mainly from the perspective of functional needs. With the continuous development of science and technology and the emergence of new social ideologies, people have further artistic demands for the form of products on the basis of satisfying functional needs, i.e. the demand for beauty is at an increasingly high level. A good product is a fusion of technology and art, while

Fig. 3. Programmable AI stir-fry robot 1

Fig. 4. Programmable AI stir-fry robot 2

good technology and appropriate aesthetics make a good product. If a product has no function to be used, then a product with only aesthetics is called a work of art and has an ornamental role; if a product has only technology and no aesthetics, then the product can only be called an instrument. For example, the products produced by the large machines of the industrial revolution were only functional and lacked aesthetics. In product interaction beauty is a process of enjoyment, and interaction aesthetics consists of technical beauty and sensory beauty. Technical beauty exists in the function of the product, and the process of interaction is completed between the transformation of the product's function, and technical beauty is a synthesis of the functional and structural beauty of the product. Louis Sullivan once suggested that 'form follows function', that products have a practical meaning and that function is at the heart of a product, and that the function of a product changes as people's needs change. In primitive societies our ancestors hunted for survival, so the function of the product used for hunting was to catch the prey. The pager that became popular in the late nineties, the mobile phone that emerged as a result of technological development, the touch screen mobile phone that applied new media technology to the mobile phone, people's needs are different in different times. This is the beauty of technology in interactive aesthetics. The beauty of technology is that it can better meet the growing material and cultural needs of human beings.

Technology and art are essentially two different forms. Technology is the manifestation of the material and art is the reflection of the spirit. Just like the artworks created by artists, the expression of art needs the help of technology, but the artistic aesthetic value of the artwork itself is the spiritual level that the artist conveys to the outside world through technology. Each product has its own focus. Some products are to solve the material needs of users and some products are to provide users with emotional value, but most products are the combined effect of technology and art. The combination of technology and art enables products to provide both material and spiritual services. In order to achieve a harmonious and balanced state between the applicability and aesthetics of the product, it needs to be matched according to the focus of the product. With the different focus of products, the "proportion" of technology and art is also different. If there are many artistic components in a product, then the product needs to provide users with emotional value that exceeds the needs of material functions, such as cushions. During the production process of cushions, the designer will make various styles and images according to the theme, and most consumers will be guided to buy through the external image of the cushion. Only a small part of people will buy cushions based on the material and functional form of them. The psychological value created by such products is greater than the material value. If there are more technical components in a product, then the product needs to provide more material service than psychological value, such as hair dryers. Therefore, in product design, technology is the support, and art is the auxiliary technology to improve the formal beauty of the product and enhance the added value of the product. The two are indispensable in the level of people's demand for products today [9]. The unified collaboration of technology and art in the product meets the functional and psychological needs of users and provides users with a good using experience.

The sensory beauty in interaction aesthetics exists in the effect of the interaction between human and product on the senses, i.e. the effect of the basic methods of human-computer interaction on the senses. There are visual interaction, auditory interaction, tactile interaction, olfactory interaction and virtual reality interaction, which are the most commonly used forms of interaction. Haptic interaction is one of the easiest ways to interact with the user. The touch screen mobile phones we use use this technology, where all the functions of the phone are placed in a touch screen interface and the user only needs to use their fingers to change the function of the product. Virtual reality interaction technology exists in the popular AR games, where users can interact with the virtual environment as if they were there, through an AR glasses. Auditory interaction is the most time-sensitive form of interaction today, where the user only needs to give a voice command to complete a product's function change. Sound-controlled rice cookers and stereos, such as the artificial intelligence speakers designed by Xiaomi, can be interacted with by adding artificial intelligence technology. Auditory interaction reduces the process and time of user-product interaction and facilitates the user's lifestyle. The process of interaction between people and products through the use of human senses to complete the conversion of product functions, changing the user's original way of life, bringing convenience and comfort to the user, which is the beauty of the senses of the product.

3.2 Finding a Balance Between the "Two Beauties"

Japanese minimalist design emphasises the connection with nature and the simplicity of the process of use. Japanese design evolved in the 1950s and 1960s and now occupies a place in the world of design entirely due to its minimalist and comfortable style and Zen philosophy, which exemplifies the technical and sensory beauty of the product interaction process. Contemporary society is an era of increasing scientific and technological development, and in the new media environment product interaction design has taken on a new dimension, using artificial intelligence technology to combine the way products are used with human psychological habits. Technical beauty and sensory beauty are the connotations of a good product. With new innovations and developments in product interaction design, technical beauty and sensory beauty need to reach a point of balance, where the function of the product and the way it is used is the way the user enjoys it. The aesthetics of product interaction in the future will also need to maintain a balance between technical and sensory beauty and seek new ideas for development.

4 Conclusion

The widespread use of new media technology in product interaction design is a trend in modern product design innovation. In the future, innovation in product design lies in the innovation of product interaction design, and the innovation of product interaction design lies in the advancement of humanization and intelligence in human-computer interaction; the balance of interaction aesthetics. Product interaction design is a reflection of the human-centred nature of product design, and the application of new media technology is a medium for intelligent and humane human-computer interaction. With the help of new media technology, the elements of product interaction design are interconnected and have new developments and innovations among themselves.

References

1. Zhang, C., Kong, M.: Application of interaction design in industrial design and future prospects. Packaging Eng. 68–71 (2011)
2. Li, S.: Product interaction design in harmonious vision. Packaging Eng. **137** (2009)

3. Maoqi, X., Tang, R.: Emotional product design based on interaction design. Beauty Times, 62–65(2009)
4. Sari, D.: Application of interactive aesthetics in product design in the information age . Sci. Technol. Assoc. Forum (second half), 101–102 (2012)
5. Qin, J.: Research on the influence of aesthetic consciousness on artificial intelligence and innovative design. Packaging Eng. 59–71(2019)
6. Wang, Q.: Application of technical form and artistic form in product modeling design. Packaging Eng. **39**(14), 210–214 (2008)
7. Qi, F.: Technical aesthetics and artistic aesthetics in product design. Beauty Times, 119–120 (2012)
8. Zhou, F., Deng, R., Li, S.: On fuzziness in product interaction design. Packaging Eng. 39–42 (2013)
9. Ding, M., Jin, X: New subject in new media – application of artificial intelligence. Sci. Technol. Innov. 135–138

Experience Economy and Green Economy Research in China: A 30-Year Bibliometric Analysis

Bo Yang, Kaiwen Wang, Xiaodan Zhan, Siyu Chen, and Zhen Liu[✉]

School of Design, South China University of Technology, Guangzhou 510006, People's Republic of China
liuzjames@scut.edu.cn

Abstract. With the continuous development of the global economy, coping with global climate change has become a common challenge for all mankind. As a regional power, China shoulders a major mission and plays a pivotal role. At the same time, the proportion of added value of service industry in gross domestic product in China has exceeded 50%, and reached 53.3% in year 2021. In fact, the experience economy dominated by user experience is an important part of the service industry economy. The experience and methods accumulated in the development of China's experience economy are of great significance for the development of a green economy and the realization of China's 'double carbon' goal. Analyzing the development trend of academic research in the field of China's experience economy and green economy, exploring hot issues, and understanding the current research needs will serve as a guide for building the cross-integration development system of green economy and experience economy. However, at present, few studies have conducted a comprehensive analysis of the core Chinese journals in the field of 'experience economy and green economy', having further summarized and analyzed them from the very beginning through knowledge mapping analysis. Therefore, this paper uses a bibliometric method to make a comprehensive analysis with literature visualization by using CiteSpace and SATI selecting the core journal articles indexed by Chinese National Knowledge Infrastructure (CNKI) from year 1992 which is the beginning year of Chinese "Experience economy and Green economy" research to November 2022. The results indicate that the Experience economy and Green economy in China has involved in a wide distribution of subject areas, mainly focused on economic and system reform, tourism, macro-economic and sustainable development. In recent years, China's research hotspots in the field of experience economy and green economy have mainly focused on low-carbon economy, experience design, experiential marketing, green development, and rural tourism.

Keywords: Experience Economy · Green Economy · China · Bibliometric Analysis

1 Introduction

As the world's second largest economy and the largest developing country, China's economy is constantly booming. Among them, the scale of the experience economy in the Chinese market is showing a trend of substantial growth. The term "experience" was first proposed by American futurist Alvin Toffler in 1970, and he proposed that economic development would go through three stages from "manufacturing economy" to "service economy" and then to "experience economy" [1]. In year 1992, the Central Committee of the Communist Party of China and the State Council made the "Decision on Accelerating the Development of the Tertiary Industry", vigorously improving the tertiary industry and developing the service economy [2]. The experience economy is an extension of the service economy and the fourth type of economy after the agricultural economy, industrial economy and service economy. In fact, after decades of hard work, China has achieved a world-renowned level of development in the experience economy, and accumulated a lot of valuable development experience in the process.

China general secretary Xi pointed out in the report of the 20th National Congress that high-quality development is the primary task of building a modern socialist country in an all-round way, and the meaning of high-quality development is green development. It is necessary to accelerate the green transformation of the development mode, vigorously promote green development, and promote the formation of green low-carbon production methods and lifestyles [3]. At the same time, China, as a regional power, shoulders a major mission and solemnly announced at the 75th United Nations General Assembly in 2020 that China will strive to reach the peak of carbon dioxide emissions by 2030 and strive to achieve carbon neutrality by 2060. Therefore, how to develop a green economy has become a hot spot of research and attention.

At the present, a good way is to use the advanced development experience of experience economy to develop green economy, integrate the two, promote each other and develop together. On the one hand, the green economy must be the mainstream development direction in the future, which can enable the experience economy to gain more possibilities and embrace more futures. On the other hand, the development of the green economy is a problem that the whole world needs to face. Using the experience economy professional development experience can achieve twice the result with half the effort. Hence, studying "experience economy" and "green economy" and grasping the research situation in this intersecting field as a whole can provide the necessary guarantee and foundation for latecomers to research and develop in this field.

2 Methods

2.1 Data Sources

This article uses the China National Knowledge Infrastructure (CNKI) academic journal database as the data source, and conducts a literature search with "theme = experience economy + green economy, keywords = experience economy + green economy, and the time span is all years". Considering the academic representativeness of the literature, the literature screening mainly selects SCI, EI, Peking University Core, CSSCI, and CSCD for source screening, and the retrieval time is November 7, 2022. In this paper,

1003 retrieved documents were manually screened, conference information and reports irrelevant to the "experience economy + green economy" research were eliminated, and 824 valid documents were finally selected as research samples.

2.2 Research Method

CiteSpace and SATI (Statistical Analysis Toolkit for Informometrics) are two commonly used literature analysis tools. Citespace software is a document visualization analysis tool based on JAVA platform developed by Dr. Chen Chaomei. It can realize diversified, dynamic and time-sharing visual analysis of document samples, thus helping with discovering historical research of academic research points from a large number of sample documents path and its future development trend [6]. Since its development, CiteSpace software has played an important auxiliary role in the research of various disciplines. It is the most distinctive and influential knowledge graph analysis tool among literature analysis tools in recent years. SATI (Statistical Analysis Toolkit for Informometrics) is a general statistical analysis tool for bibliographic information, which can conduct multi-dimensional analysis of bibliographic information in endnote format.

This paper uses CiteSpace 5.8.R3c software to analyze keyword co-occurrence, clustering, and emerging words, and associates with SATI online analysis tools to analyze journal publishing trends, document publishing trends, and institutional cooperation. This paper employs two analysis tools to conduct multi-dimensional comparative analysis of literature analysis samples, draws a knowledge map of "green economy" with "experience economy", grasps the research hotspots and trends in this field from a macro perspective, and lays a foundation for the further development of the field.

3   Results and Analysis

3.1   Bibliometric Analysis

Distribution Analysis of Literature Quantity Based on Time Axis. Two important indicators for exploring the research enthusiasm in the field of academic research are the number and time of publication in this field. In this paper, a rough look at the year distribution and quantity of 1003 journals obtained by searching CNKI journals with the subject and keywords as "experience economy + green economy" is shown in Fig. 1. It can be seen from the trend of publications that China's academic research in the field of "experience economy with green economy" started in 1992, but the number of publications tended to slow down until 2000 when the number of publications began to increase gradually. In 2009, the research enthusiasm increased significantly. The research peak was reached in 2010, after which the number of published papers gradually decreased, and after 2014, it showed a relatively stable trend.

In this paper, the 1003 articles were manually screened, conference information and reports irrelevant to the research of "experience economy" and "green economy" were eliminated, and finally 824 articles were selected. Through the analysis of the SATI bibliography information statistical analysis tool, the list of the publication years of the literature is obtained, and the data is graphically displayed as shown in Fig. 2. From

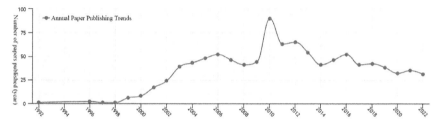

Fig. 1. Number of documents published in China on "experience economy + green economy" from 1992 to November 2022.

the publication trend, China's academic research in the field of "experience economy" associated with "green economy" started in 1992, increased significantly from 2001, and reached the first research peak in 2004. It reached 40 and entered the stage of hot research since then. Although it fell back slightly in 2006, it rebounded sharply in 2008. The annual publication volume reached 60. The research reached a climax, and in 2010 there was an explosive growth, reaching a staggering 114 articles. After the climax, it gradually entered a low ebb. The number of annual publications in this field continued to decline, and reached the lowest point in 2019, with only 4 annual publications. But it will soon usher in a rebound, and it will continue to rise in three years in 2020, 2021, and 2022, and it is expected to rise again in the future.

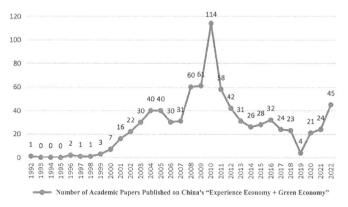

Fig. 2. The number of papers published each year on China's "experience economy + green economy" from 1992 to November 2022.

A Rough Look at the Distribution of Literature Disciplines and the Crossover of Research Topics. By analyzing the distribution of literature disciplines, the research distribution of the research topic in each discipline can be revealed. Limited to the CNKI database, only the uncensored literature data can be analyzed. Therefore, this paper takes a rough look at 1003 retrieved journal articles, and finds that the research disciplines of the theme of "experience economy + green economy" are widely distributed through graphical analysis. The subject category distribution of its main literature distribution is shown in Fig. 3. It can be found that the most published papers are economic and institutional reform, accounting for 16.89%, followed by tourism literature, which accounts for 13.06%, followed by macroeconomic and sustainable development literature, which accounts for 11.79%, environmental science and resource utilization accounted for 8.48%, and the fifth place was enterprise economic literature accounting for 6.83%.

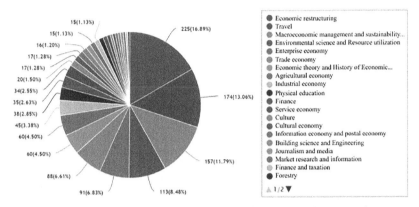

Fig. 3. Distribution of literature in subject areas involved in the research on "experience economy + green economy" (1003 articles).

In this paper, through the cross-analysis of 1003 search results of CNKI (see Fig. 4), it is found that the main cross-research fields of the research topic of user experience are sustainable development based on green economy, experiential marketing based on experience economy, and user experience-based experience economy, green economy based on green development, and green finance based on green economy. Secondly, low-carbon economy, rural tourism, circular economy, ecological economy, development model and other research fields also have relatively close cross-research.

Statistical Analysis of Literature Periodicals. By analyzing the distribution of the number of published journals, we can understand the degree to which the core journals in the research field of China's "green economy" and "experience economy" pay attention to this topic. Through the SATI platform, the 824 selected articles were analyzed, and the journals with less than 4 publications were manually merged into the "Others" item. Through graphic visualization (see Fig. 5), it can be found that publications from 1992 to 2021 are related to "green economy" and "Ecological Economy" is the journal with the most literature related to the theme of "experience economy", with a total of 46 articles published, accounting for only 5.58%. No particular focus was shown. The second most published articles are "China Business" with 32 articles, accounting for 4.12%, "Decoration" with 19 articles, accounting for 3.88%, "Business Times" with 25 articles, accounting for 3.03%, "Agricultural Economics" with 20 articles and "Business Research" 20 articles, each accounting for 2.42%. In general, the literature distribution of the research topic of "experience economy with green economy" is mainly focused on

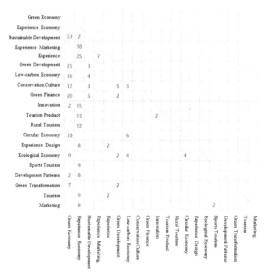

Fig. 4. Distribution of cross-subject terms involved in the research of "experience economy + green economy" (1003 articles).

several major fields such as ecology, commerce, agriculture, resources and environment, and economic management, which is consistent with the proportion of the discipline distribution field analyzed above.

Through the analysis of the SATI platform, the time series analysis of the journal publication years of 824 articles is shown in Fig. 6. The journal "Eco-Environment" with the largest number of publications has entered the research of "experience economy and green economy" since 2000. In the early stage of high-volume topics, the follow-up maintains a relatively stable number of publications. It is worth noting that "China Business", as the second largest journal in this field, ushered in a blowout growth in 2009 and 2010, reached a peak of 14 publications in 2010, and then dropped sharply in 2012. The fluctuations in the number of subject literature distribution in other journals are not significant, and the number of related articles published in the year is four or less.

3.2 Core Authors and Institutional Analysis

Core Author Visualization Map. This paper uses SATI software to analyze the authors of the 824 sample articles, and finds that the top eight authors on the topic of user experience from 1992 to November 2022 are shown in Fig. 7. It can be seen that Xiangqian Zhang, Xiaogang Zhang, and Min Liu published 12, 11, and 9 papers respectively, followed by Yuhong Ju, who published 6 papers, and Qiang Liang, Fang Fang, and Yang Yang, who each published 6 papers. 5 papers, Chunbin Liu published 4 papers. The first three researchers are the core authors in this field, and the number of papers published by the top three is 32, which is more than the total number of 25 papers published by the last five.

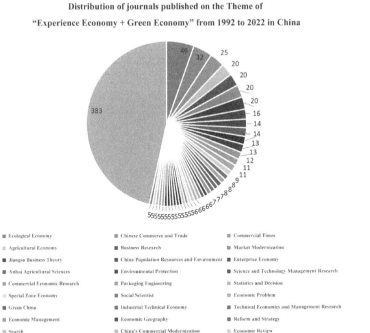

Fig. 5. Distribution of journals published on the theme of "Experience Economy + Green Economy" from 1992 to 2022 in China.

The author co-citation analysis map through CiteSpace software is shown in Fig. 8, in which the size of the nodes is proportional to the amount of papers published, the connection between the nodes represents the cooperation between the authors, and the thickness of the line represents the closeness of their cooperation.

According to the analysis, most of the researchers of "experience economy with green economy" are in a scattered state. According to the map, Zhang Xiangqian and Yu Jie, a scholar with a high number of publications, formed a two-person cooperative team. Their research mainly involves the high-quality development of green economy in provinces and cities research. Liu Min, Zhang Xin and others formed the 6-person cooperative team, whose main research field is the development of forestry in green economy. From the overall analysis, the cooperation among most researchers in this research field is relatively sparse, most of them are independent research scholars, and only a small number of them have formed a cooperative team of two or three people, and the cooperation intensity is low. At present, the overall research field a large-scale research team has not yet been formed.

Visual Map Analysis of Research Institutions. Using the SATI literature analysis tool, the co-occurrence analysis of cooperative institutions was carried out on the 824

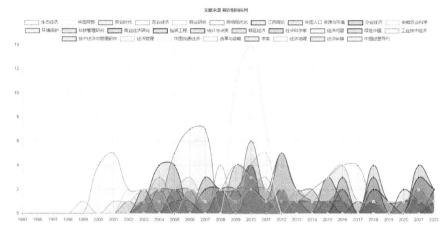

Fig. 6. Trend chart of the number of "Experience Economy + Green Economy" theme papers published by journals from 1992 to 2022 in China.

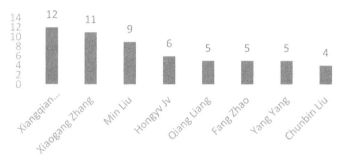

Fig. 7. Ranking chart of the number of core authors published on the theme of " Experience Economy + Green Economy" from 1992 to 2022 in China.

sample papers from 1992 to 2022, and the visualized map of research institutions on the theme of "experience economy with green economy" in China is shown in Fig. 9. Among them, the large and small nodes represent the number of academic papers published by the research institution in the field, and the thickness of the connection between nodes represents the cooperation intensity between different institutions. Analysis of the map shows that there are a large number of institutions studying this research field, but only a small number of institutions have formed cooperative relationships, and most institutions are in an independent research state.

Through map analysis, it is found that the School of Economics and Management of Beijing Forestry University, the School of Business Administration of Huaqiao University, the School of Economics of Jilin University, the School of Economics and Management of Inner Mongolia Agricultural University, and the Economic Development Research Center of the State Forestry Administration have a relatively high number of papers. Among them, the School of Economics and Management of Beijing Forestry

Fig. 8. Collaboration map of core authors of "Experience Economy + Green Economy" research in China.

University, which has published the most papers, has formed more cooperative relationships with other institutions, and has formed the most significant cooperative network with the Economic Development Research Center of the State Forestry Administration and the School of Business Administration of Zhongnan University of Economics and Law. From the map analysis, the most of the institutional partnerships in the field of "experience economy and green economy" are pair-wise cooperation. School of Business Administration of Huaqiao University and School of Computer Science and Technology of Huaqiao University, School of Economics and Management of Inner Mongolia Agricultural University and School of Science of Inner Mongolia Agricultural University, School of Economics of Jilin University and China State-owned Economic Research Center of Jilin University, School of Economics of Sichuan University and Economics of Central University for Nationalities Colleges and other institutions have formed a pairwise cooperation network.

Fig. 9. Map of "Experience Economy + Green Economy" research cooperation among institutions in China.

4   Research Hot Spots and Frontier Analysis

4.1   Analysis of Research Hotspots

Keywords Analysis

Keyword Co-occurrence Map Analysis. The keyword co-occurrence map analysis through CiteSpace is shown in Fig. 10. There are 714 nodes and 1417 connections in the research keyword contribution map of "experience economy and green economy", and the overall network density is 0.0056. Economy, green economy, experience marketing, low-carbon economy, green development, experience, rural tourism, experience design, innovation, development, sensory stimulation, consumers, ecological civilization, ecological environment, tourism products, coordinated development, single building, and large keywords such as nature and urban greening appear frequently. Each keyword shows a network connection centered on experience economy and green economy, and there are only a few isolated nodes, indicating that there is a strong correlation between the keywords; at the same time, the experience economy, green economy, and experience marketing in the figure, and experience, low-carbon economy, innovation, and consumer nodes are large, indicating that the research on China's experience economy and green economy is relatively hot in these intersecting fields.

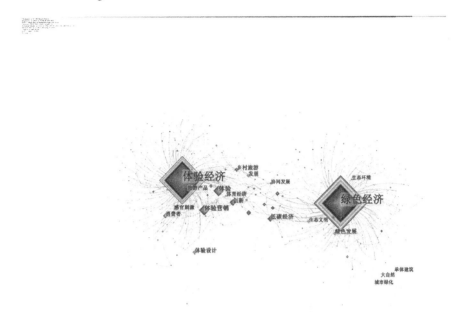

Fig. 10. Cooccurrence map of keywords in "Experience Economy + Green Economy".

Keywords Frequency and Centrality Analysis. By sorting and analyzing the word frequency and centrality of keywords in the CiteSpace keyword co-occurrence map, it can help with further understanding the development research hotspots and frontiers in "experience economy + green economy" in China. As shown in Table 1, the top ten high-frequency keywords from high to low are Green economy, Experience economy, Experience marketing, Experience, Low-carbon economy, Innovation, Tourism product, Rural tourism, Circular economy, and Development patterns. The top ten high-centrality keywords ranked from high to low are Green economy, Experience economy, Low-carbon economy, Innovation, Rural tourism, Development, Coordinated development, Value, Circular economy, and Development strategy. Therefore, it can be speculated that the research hotspots of China's "experience economy and green economy" mainly focus on several main aspects such as user experience, low-carbon environmental protection, rural tourism, coordinated development, and development strategies.

Analysis of Hot Research Topics. Using the keyword co-occurrence analysis of CiteSpace, the keyword co-occurrence network is shown in Fig. 11. These clusters can reflect that from 1992 to 2022, the top 10 issues in China's experience economy and green economy research fields focus on experience economy, green economy, low-carbon economy, experience design, experience marketing, rural tourism, green development, sports economy, path selection, ecological environment, and green tourism.

Keyword Burstness Analysis. Emerging words refer to hot research keywords that have increased sharply in a certain period of time. Obviously, the keyword emergence intensity and its emergence time can be used to a certain extent to help analyze the exploration hotspots and research trends within a certain period of time in a certain field. CiteSpace's

Table 1. Statistics of high frequency keywords, word frequency and centrality of "Experience Economy + Green Economy" research in China.

Keywords frequency			Keywords centrality		
No.	Frequency	Keyword	No.	Centrality	Keyword
1	345	Green economy	1	1.34	Green economy
2	327	Experience economy	2	1.13	Experience economy
3	33	Experience marketing	3	0.07	Low-carbon economy
4	30	Experience	4	0.07	Innovation
5	17	Low-carbon economy	5	0.07	Rural tourism
6	16	Innovation	6	0.05	Development
7	13	Tourism product	7	0.05	Coordinated development
8	10	Rural tourism	8	0.05	Value
9	9	Circular economy	9	0.04	Circular economy
10	9	Development patterns	10	0.04	Development strategy

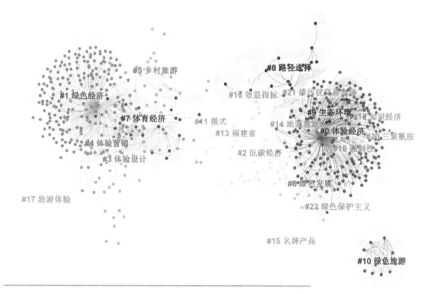

Fig. 11. Keyword clustering map of "Experience Economy + Green Economy" research via CiteSpace.

Breakout Words feature finds words that occur more frequently over a certain period of time.

This paper analyzes the emergence of 824 articles, and obtains the keyword burstness map in Fig. 12. The analysis shows that there are 12 emergence words in the research field of experience economy and green economy. The highest was 12.88. In 2003, the burst strength of experiential marketing reached 6.63, ranking second. In the same year, the strength of experience that began to emerge was 6.52, ranking third.

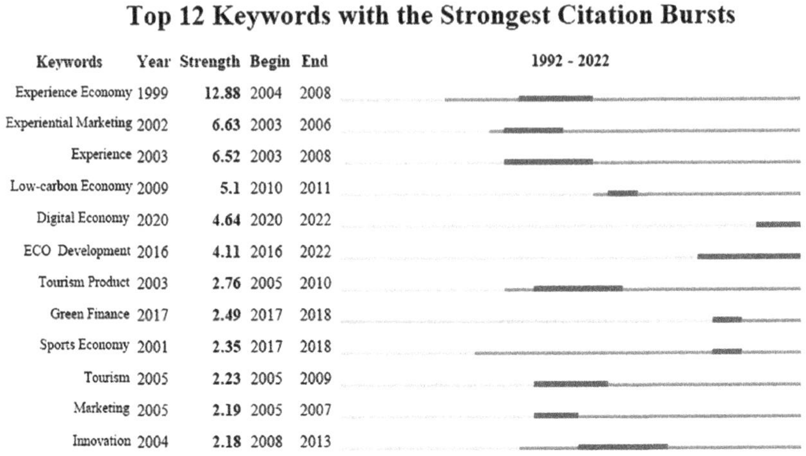

Top 12 Keywords with the Strongest Citation Bursts

Keywords	Year	Strength	Begin	End	1992 - 2022
Experience Economy	1999	12.88	2004	2008	
Experiential Marketing	2002	6.63	2003	2006	
Experience	2003	6.52	2003	2008	
Low-carbon Economy	2009	5.1	2010	2011	
Digital Economy	2020	4.64	2020	2022	
ECO Development	2016	4.11	2016	2022	
Tourism Product	2003	2.76	2005	2010	
Green Finance	2017	2.49	2017	2018	
Sports Economy	2001	2.35	2017	2018	
Tourism	2005	2.23	2005	2009	
Marketing	2005	2.19	2005	2007	
Innovation	2004	2.18	2008	2013	

Fig. 12. Keywords burstness analysis map of "Experience Economy + Green Economy" research via CiteSpace.

Judging from the year of emergence of the overall emerging words, from 2003 to 2008, the research based on the field of experience economy and green economy mainly focused on the research fields of experience marketing, experience, experience economy, marketing, and tourism, among which experience economy, experience marketing, experience emergent strength ranks in the top three, indicating that this research field has gained a high degree of attention after 2003. From 2005 to 2010, the research on tourism products, tourism and marketing in experience economy and green economy gradually heated up. Research on innovation from 2008 to 2013 gained some research enthusiasm. In 2010, the research on experience economy and green economy of China's low-carbon economy emerged very clearly, and the emergence intensity was as high as 5.1, ranking fourth. In 2017, green finance and sports economy attracted much attention. In 2016, the research on green development in terms of experience economy and green economy has attracted much attention, and has become a research hotspot that continues to grow. Starting from 2020, the research on experience economy and green economy in digital economy has also become a hot trend.

Time Zone Map Analysis of Keyword Clustering. The change of the keywords of the research topic over time can indicate the change and development trend of the hot spots of the research topic. Through cluster analysis, CiteSpace can arrange the hot spots of the same year in chronological order and gather them in the same area. Therefore, the clustered TimezoneView time zone map generated by CiteSpace is shown in Fig. 13.

From the evolution of keywords in the overall time zone map, it can be seen that research in the field of experience economy and green economy in China can be roughly divided into four stages: the first stage was from 1992 to 1996, during this period, research in this direction mainly focused on green economic theory in itself, during

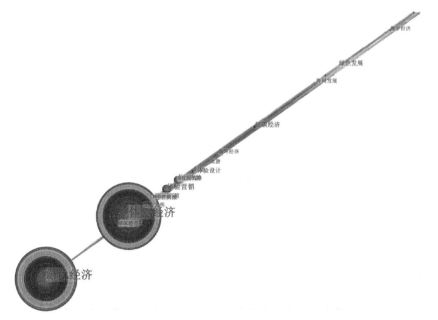

Fig. 13. Keyword clustering Timezone map of "Experience Economy + Green Economy" research via CiteSpace.

this period, there were relatively few studies on experience economy, and then, with the widespread spread of experience economy thinking in China, it entered the second stage, from 1997 to 2010, which was the stage of rapid development of experience economy, experiential marketing, experiential design, user experience, marketing and other keywords appeared quite frequently. Correspondingly, during this period, the research on green economy was relatively rare, but there were already some "experience economy and green economy" issues, such as circular economy, and rural tourism. From 2010 to 2019, it is a stage of more development of "experience economy and green economy". During this period, with the rapid development of experience economy, it also drives green economy, including low-carbon economy with related development, green development and other key words. The fourth stage, from 2020 to 2022, the stage of digital economy development. In essence, the digital economy is also a manifestation of the experience economy, so during this period, the academic circles turned their attention to the development model of digital (experience) economy with green economy. Thanks to the rapid development of computer science, the digital economy has shown a rather violent upward trend. Perhaps the next stage will be the digital economy. As a kind of experience economy, it will lead the green economy to continue to leap forward.

5   Discussion

5.1   Research Hotspots of China's Experience Economy and Green Economy

This paper sorts out the academic research papers with the theme and keywords of China's "experience economy and green economy", and associates with the keyword co-occurrence map, high-frequency keyword frequency and centrality, clustering timeline map and keyword emergence map. According to the analysis, the current hot spots of China's "experience economy and green economy" are summarized into following four aspects.

Research on Deep Integration of Digital Economy Methods.   Computer science has profoundly changed human life. In recent years, with the continuous development of algorithms such as artificial intelligence technology and deep learning, the digital economy has exploded with amazing potential. From the key word analysis map, it can be seen that since the emergence of the digital economy in 2020, it has been continuously affecting the development of this field. As Jiang from the University of Chinese Academy of Social Sciences pointed out that the high-quality integrated development of the digital economy and the green economy is an inevitable requirement for building a new development pattern in China; digitalization is an action for high-quality development; green economy transformation is the fundamental way for high-quality development; and digitization is an important path to achieve the dual carbon goals and other three aspects are discussed [4].

Research on the Method of Promoting the Development of Rural Experience Tourism.   Tourism economy, especially rural tourism, is an important part of the green economy. In fact, tourism itself is an experience economy, so tourism is an important support for the future development of "experience economy and green economy". Since 2005, China domestic scholars have done a lot of research on this, as can be seen from the key word analysis map, research in this direction is very hot. With the outbreak of the new COVID-19 epidemic in 2020, the tourism industry has come to a large-scale stagnation, which is undoubtedly a huge blow to the development of green emergency. But it is foreseeable that when the epidemic is over, the tourism industry will usher in a huge recovery, so it should be very valuable to continue in-depth research in this area. For example, Wang and Zhang pointed out that the leisure and sightseeing ranch is a new product of the integration and development of modern animal husbandry and tourism, and it is also an effective means for the transformation and upgrading of animal husbandry under the new situation such as animal husbandry work type, characteristic homestay type, and DIY experience type, which provide more solutions for China's animal husbandry industry [5].

Revitalize and Improve Local Industry Research.   In the past few decades, although China has created world-renowned economic achievements, a considerable part of them has been developed by relying on the extensive economic model, or by relying on large-scale mining, logging, and heavily polluting industries. These development methods are no longer suitable for China's current national conditions, and high-quality development must be achieved. Therefore, for some places, the green economy and the experience economy can be used to improve local industries, so as to meet the needs of transformation and development. For example, in the "Research on Industrial Transformation and Upgrading in Northeast China from the Perspective of Green Economy" published by Liu and Cui, they pointed out that traditional extensive, high-pollution and high-emission industries will not meet the actual needs of high-quality economic development in Northeast China. The energy industry should be transformed and upgraded to a new energy industry, the industrial manufacturing industry should be transformed and upgraded to a smart manufacturing industry, traditional agriculture should be transformed and upgraded to a green agriculture, and the traditional service industry should be transformed and upgraded to a green service industry, which provides a solution direction for the transformation and upgrading of Northeast China [6].

Research on the Model of Economic Evaluation Index. Any economic development model must use some evaluation index models to judge. Without a good evaluation model, it is naturally impossible to have a good economic development model. Therefore, a sound evaluation index model is an important direction of China's "experience economy and green economy" research. Jiang et al. reviewed the domestic and foreign research on the evaluation of green economic transformation, and proposed the green economic transformation evaluation theory from the three dimensions of economic inclusive development, environmental resource quality, and green transformation potential, and constructed the core indicators of the green economic transformation index System [7]. While Hu et al. based on systematically sorting out the internal mechanism of the coordinated development of the digital economy and the green economy, and constructed an index system for the coordinated development of the digital economy and the green economy, which used the Dagum Gini coefficient and decomposition, Kernel density estimation and spatial Convergence model for empirical research [8].

5.2 Research Trends of Experience Economy and Green Economy in China

From 1992 to 2022, the academic field of "experience economy and green economy" in China has a total of 30 years of development history, which fully demonstrates that this field has obvious interdisciplinary nature and is both policy-oriented and market-oriented. From the initial independent development to the later integrated development, the research in this field has experienced advanced development, and the research attention has been increasing year by year, especially in the last three years, showing a good upward trend. Associated with the analysis of China's "experience economy and green economy" research field in recent years, China's future research directions in this field may focus on the following areas.

More Combined with Artificial Intelligence Technology and Internet of Things Technology. The future world will inevitably be led and reformed by computer science. Artificial intelligence is assisting the rapid development of all walks of life. To achieve high-quality development goals, it is bound to need to be deeply integrated with computer science. However, cloud computing and the Internet of Things can effectively promote industrial development, and the era of automation may be in the not-too-distant future. Green development is the fundamental connotation of high-quality development, so the future study must think more about how to integrate computer science and technology with other industries in a greener way.

Better Achieve the Goal of "Double Carbon". The "double carbon" goal is the sacred mission and responsibility of China as a regional power. Achieve carbon peaking by 2030 and carbon neutrality by 2060. This requires people from all walks of life to provide more solutions, and scholars who are originally in the field of green economy should consider how to better achieve the "double carbon" goal.

More People-oriented to Meet the People's Expectations and Needs for a Better Life. The essence of any good development must be to meet people's expectations and needs. The original intention of the development of the green economy is to enable people to have a sustainable, beautiful, and healthy life. At the same time, the experience economy itself is based on people's senses cognition, self-awareness, and demand satisfaction, so as an intersecting field between the two, it will inevitably develop more towards meeting people's needs for a better life.

6   Conclusion

This paper uses CiteSpace 5.8.R3c and SATI bibliometric analysis software to analyze CNKI's literature on the subject and keywords of "user experience" with November 2022 as the cut-off point, and select more academic research representatives from it. Based on the multi-level analysis and visual knowledge map research of the relevant SCI, EI, Peking University core, CSSCI, and CSCD literature, the following conclusions are drawn.

China's academic research in the field of "experience economy" and "green economy" started in 1992, increased significantly from 2001, reached the first research peak in 2004, and published 40 papers annually. It began to enter the hot research stage, and then fell back slightly in 2006, but it rebounded sharply in 2008, and the annual publication volume reached 60 articles. After the climax, it gradually entered a low ebb. The number of annual publications in this field continued to decline, and reached the lowest point in 2019, with only 4 annual publications. But it will soon usher in a rebound, and it will continue to rise in three years in 2020, 2021, and 2022, and it is expected to rise again in the future.

From the perspective of subject areas and published publications, the journals with the theme of "experience economy + green economy" have obvious cross-disciplinarity, involving economic system reform, tourism, macroeconomic management and sustainable development, environmental science and resource utilization, enterprises economics, trade economics, agricultural economics, industrial economics, sports, economic theory and history of economic thought, computer science and other disciplines, among which economic system reform, tourism, macroeconomic management and sustainable development accounted for the top three, accounting for The ratio reached 41.74%. Published journals are also scattered because of their cross-disciplinary nature. "baby environment" and "China business" are the journals with the largest number of publications in this field, but compared with the number of publications of other journals There is no significant difference, which shows that China's "experience economy +

green economy" research is in the stage of a hundred flowers blooming and a hundred schools of thought contending. It can meet people's needs from more angles and is in line with the people-oriented policy direction advocated by the country.

From the perspective of the distribution of core authors and institutions, most of the researchers in China's user experience research are independent researchers, only a small number have formed research teams, most of the research institutions are universities, and there are few independent scientific research institutions. The cooperation network between them is sparse. From the geographical point of view, there are not many cross-regional and cross-unit cooperation networks, and the overall distribution of scientific research is scattered.

From the perspective of research hotspots, the current research hotspots are the deep integration of the digital economy, the research on promoting the development of rural experience tourism, the research on revitalizing and improving local industries, and the research on economic evaluation index models. Among them, with the blowout development of artificial intelligence technology in recent years, how to integrate computer technology in a more green way in all walks of life, and how to better achieve the goal of "dual carbon" and how to better meet people's yearning and needs for a better life through the green economy and experience economy may become a research hotspot and future development trend.

This paper uses CiteSpace and SATI bibliometric software as analysis tools to visually analyze the selected sample documents, and shows the relationship between a total of 824 core documents during the 30 years from 1992 to 2022. However, map interpretation is a challenging task, and problems such as omission, misreading, or selective interpretation may exist, which will affect the results of literature analysis to a certain extent. Therefore, in addition to using CiteSpace and SATI software analysis tools, this research also consulted experts in related fields of "experience economy + green economy" for guidance, and confirmed and supplemented the research results to achieve rigor.

Acknowledgements. This research was funded by the 2022 "University Student Innovation and Entrepreneurship Training Program" project, (innovation training project No. 112), 'Explore new forms of resource recovery and green economic development enabled by digital platforms' (project grant number 202210561112), South China University of Technology; and "2022 Constructing Project of Teaching Quality and Teaching Reform Project for Undergraduate Universities in Guangdong Province" Higher Education Teaching Reform Project (project No. 386), 'Innovation and practice of teaching methods for information and interaction design in the context of new liberal arts' (project grant number x2sj-C9233001).

References

1. Toffler, A.: Future Shock. Reissue. Bantam, New York (1985)
2. Zhang, J.: Reflections on accelerating the development of tertiary industry in China. J. Cent. Univ. Financ. Econ. **08**, 1–2 (1994)
3. Xi, J.: Holding high the great banner of socialism with Chinese characteristics and uniting to build a modern socialist country in an all-round Way—report at the Twentieth National congress of the communist party of China (in Chinese). Communist **918**(21), 4–26 (2022)

4. Jiang, J.: Sustainable digital era: high-quality integration of digital economy and green economy (in Chinese). Enterp. Econ. **40**(07), 23–30 (2021). https://doi.org/10.13529/j.cnki.enterprise.economy.2021.07.003
5. Wang, Z., Zhang, G.: Exploration on the development model of leisure and sightseeing ranch based on the theory of experience economy (in Chinese). Heilongjiang Anim. Husbandry Vet. Med. **554**(14), 43–46 (2018). https://doi.org/10.13881/j.cnki.hljxmsy.2017.08.0476
6. Liu, G., Cui, M.: Research on Industrial transformation and upgrading in Northeast China from the perspective of green economy (in Chinese). J. Harbin Univ. Commer. (Soc. Sci. Ed.) **182**(01), 112–118 (2022)
7. Jiang, J., Ma, L., Yu, X.: Research on the evaluation and driving factors of China's green economic transformation (in Chinese). J. Beijing Univ. Technol. (Soc. Sci. Ed.) **22**(03), 123–141 (2022)
8. Hu, S., Huang, T., Wang, K.: Coordinated development of digital economy and green economy: temporal and spatial differentiation, dynamic evolution and convergence characteristics (in Chinese). Mod. Finance Econ. (J. Tianjin Univ. Finance Econ.) **42**(09), 3–19 (2022). https://doi.org/10.19559/j.cnki.12-1387.2022.09.001

Exploring How to Improve User Experience of Enterprise Service Products through "Dual Perspective Model"

Daijun Yu, Beibei Li, Peiyi Zhao[✉], Mingyue Hu, Ruochen Fu, and Zirui Yi

Alibaba, No. 969 West Wenyi Road Yuhang District, Hangzhou, China
zhaopeiyi.zpy@alibaba-inc.com

Abstract. Technologies and software that provide a variety of services and satisfying user experiences for consumers have become ubiquitous, yet the experience of many enterprise applications is far from the former. Using the internal Alibaba enterprise as a research setting, we explore how to balance the different goals and needs of different roles in the enterprise services domain to improve the user experience of enterprise applications. Through a series of studies, this paper analyzes the users and customers of enterprise service offerings and the differences in their goals and needs.

Keywords: Enterprise Service Management · User Experience · User Role · Client Needs

1 Introduction

1.1 Research Background

Technologies and software that provide consumers with a variety of services and a satisfying user experience have become ubiquitous. In companies, employees expect similar experiences in their daily business life, for example in human resources, legal, security, sales, and finance. As a result, user experience is gaining importance in products in the area of enterprise services [1].

In the past, UX design in the consumer domain advocated finding a balance between business goals and user needs: focusing on user expectations first, while aligning these expectations with business goals, so that the business can achieve the most beneficial output. However, the complexity of enterprise service scenarios makes it difficult to use past experiences and models to solve existing problems, and it is difficult to meet the needs of existing product user experiences using past design theories from the consumer domain. Due to the hierarchical structure in organizations, the needs of management are often prioritized in the design of enterprise user experience, while the users who use the product may have different needs, which may be easily overlooked. Therefore, we need to consider how to balance the relationship between users and customers.

A. Marcus et al. (Eds.): HCII 2023, LNCS 14030, pp. 425–439, 2023.
https://doi.org/10.1007/978-3-031-35699-5_31

1.2 Research Background

Our motivation is twofold:

The external timing is such that many investments and companies are moving from the consumer market to the enterprise services market. The user experience of enterprise products is becoming more and more important and there is a trend toward the "consumerization of IT" [2].

Internally, we work for a large enterprise in China that provides services internally, and we work in an environment where we have access to the needs of our customers (managers) as well as the voices of ordinary employees (users). This has contributed to the fact that we have the ground to study the theory of in-house product design.

In addition, we have found that the problem of poor experience with corporate service products is also prevalent in many related areas of products. If design guidelines with application value can be derived from our internal research, it can provide new ideas for the design of user experience for more enterprise service products, and thus be of value to the industry as a whole.

1.3 Research Question

In this paper, we will explore how to balance the different goals or aspirations of different personas in the enterprise services space to enhance the user experience of enterprise products.

- Sub1: What are the characteristics of the different roles in the enterprise services domain? What are their goals and aspirations?
- Sub2: To explore a design process for the enterprise services domain that can be used as a guide for future product design.

The paper concludes with a series of studies that will lead to a 'dual perspective design process' model, which is presented in the result.

2 Related Research

2.1 Research of Enterprise Applications

In terms of enterprise product characteristics, Uflacker et al. illustrate that enterprise applications are characterized by having high levels of requirement complexity, functional complexity, and process complexity [3]. Newhook et al. illustrate that the characteristics of enterprise applications are described in more detail. The authors argue that enterprise applications are specifically characterized by 1) no-nonsense; 2) the ability to support very complex tasks and workflows with specificity; 3) a focus on the quantity of functionality provided rather than the quality; and 4) an interface that is clunky and complex and not intuitive, not attractive or bad to use, but gets the job done. [2]. Overall, enterprise products are complex not only in terms of underlying requirements, functionality, and processes but also in terms of visual and interface presentation.

After understanding the characteristics of enterprise application products, we further explore the reasons for the poor user experience of enterprise applications. First, the end user of a product may not have enough huge say about what the product should be like [4]. At the same time, user behavior in the enterprise systems domain is heavily task- and skill-dependent, making it difficult to understand user behavior based on user characteristics alone, which differs markedly from the consumer products domain [5].

In addition, today's more complex business processes, growing customer demands, and increasing software requirements have all added to the complexity of enterprise application development [3]. Newhook et al. [2] compare enterprise and consumer applications and argue that economic consideration is the most fundamental reason. The analysis of economic considerations and purchasers reveals the reasons why enterprise applications are difficult to have a good user experience, such as purchasers are not users, decision makers complete a purchase based on a list of product features rather than experiencing the product, and they may be more concerned about how much money is saved by internal products non-profit products [2].

2.2 Practical Examples from the Industry

We reviewed some case studies to see how different companies have reflected on and experimented with enterprise application design. Newhook et al. [2] share IBM's experience. The article points out that IBM launched an initiative called "IBM Design thinking" when identifying problems with enterprise applications, with User-Centered Design being an important part of the initiative and requiring multiple interaction designers, user researchers, and visual designers to work together on a project to generate multiple designs. Such initiatives have led to significant breakthroughs in user experience for many of IBM's more budgeted projects. However, there are limitations to this approach, as the 'IBM Design thinking' approach of investing large amounts of manpower and budget into the user experience is unrealistic for in-house products, and there is still an expectation that a more cost-effective and actionable approach will be sought.

There is a big difference between an in-house product and a consumer product. As we can see from the above examples, only the User Center Design approach is not enough to improve the user experience in an on-premise product. As mentioned by Yasu et al. [5], in the field of consumer products, it is relatively easy for UX designers and engineers to understand the actual consumers of the product and generate ideas and reach a consensus. In the enterprise application area, however, a huge gap may arise between UX designers, engineers, and the actual users of the product. To address this gap, Japanese design experts have developed UX Observation and UX Idea Mapping methods to help project participants build awareness. These methods are applied to internal projects for enterprise system development. [5].

When designers at Cisco used the UCD approach to redesign a product that had become obsolete, they found that the goals of the customer and the goals of the user were different [4]. In the literature, they give a series of pieces of advice that designers in the industry should always discuss to reach a middle ground of recommended design, but also to provide the option to modify as appropriate to avoid killing the business model [4].

In both of these cases, the limitations of UCD in enterprise application products were recognized and these were focused primarily on the stakeholders. Besides, there are some other design ideas used for products within enterprises, for example, SAP designed a complexity model to separate front-end complexity from back-end complexity, and proposed five strategies to improve user experience using the R/3 sales and distribution module in SAP software as a case study [3]. These cases show the exploration and experimentation of enterprises in the design of enterprise applications. From them, we can find that UCD has a positive effect on improving user experience, but if we simply use the UCD approach like in the design of products in the consumer field to solve the user experience problems of enterprise applications, we will face many problems, and one important of them is how to balance the stakeholders in the project.

3 Related Methods

From the literature research, we find that UCD plays a role in the research and development process of enterprise applications, but we need to balance the relationship between various stakeholders in the project, such as customers and users. In this article, we will study how to balance the relationship between customers and users in the design process for Alibaba's internal applications.

3.1 Research Environment

Our research will start from the inside Alibaba's enterprise. It should be noted that due to some factors such as rules, regulations, organizational structure, and work processes, there are certain differences between enterprises. Our research will be based on a specific environment. Alibaba's internal products can be divided into three categories according to the relationship between customers and users (see Fig. 1).

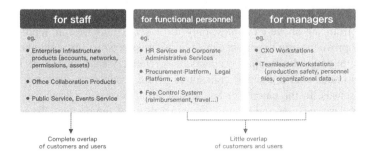

Fig. 1. Alibaba's internal products can be divided into three categories.

3.2 Research Methods

The goal of design is to meet user needs and bring enterprise and commercial value by realizing user value. In the field of enterprise services, we are faced with a particularity different from the consumer domain, that is, customers and users do not necessarily overlap. People with different perspectives have different subjective feelings and corresponding measurement standards for the value of the design scheme. Only by finding a balance point can the designer enhance the feasibility of the scheme and reduce the obstacles to implementation. Based on the previous research, we believe that in the field of enterprise services, the realization of design value is inseparable from the satisfaction of user value and customer value. Therefore, it is necessary to integrate the value appeals of users and customers and conduct value-oriented design thinking.

– User value: For users, design needs to meet user demands, bring them a better product experience, and serve users more.
– Customer value: For customers, it is more from the perspective of management to design to meet the demands of customers for enterprise management. At the same time, managers also need to serve users to achieve the purpose of management.

To explore users and customers, we organized in-depth interviews and workshops. We study from the perspective of customers and users to understand people's demands and value orientation in actual work scenarios, such as how they think about "service value" and "management value", how to make value decisions and trade-offs, and help us better understand how "service" and "management" appeals affect design in the field of enterprise services.

3.3 Conclusion

Through the research and analysis of customers of enterprise applications, we find that almost all of them say that their goals include both customer value and user value. In most cases, they believe that the relationship between the two is consistent. In special cases, conflicts may arise.

"Both management demands and user demands would be considered, and the core is to judge from the perspective of the company's commercial value."—Interviewee Jie.

"Customer goals and user goals generally have a certain degree of balance and generally would not be completely opposed." - Interviewee Chan.

"The setting of management goals is more considered from the perspective of the company's business success. Users' demands may become one of the goals, but it is not specific" - Interviewee Bei.

Through the research and analysis of product users, we find that users evaluate a product more from the perspective of service attributes. They know the existence of management goals, but they do not know the management goal. In addition, the user's personal preference for the product has nothing to do with whether the user uses the product or not.

"No understanding of these needs and the reasons why the products exist" – Interviewee Shan.

"No matter if it is good or bad, I have to use it as long as it is used in my company." –Interviewee Jin.

"There are limitations to user needs in an enterprise environment, and satisfying user needs can improve user satisfaction, but user needs do not directly affect the continued use of the product" – Interviewee Bei.

We find a major difference between the customer perspective and the user perspective. (see Fig. 2).

- From the user perspective, the population served by the product is many office workers, so the goal of the design is to meet their daily and work-related needs. The user's needs are generally efficiency and experience-oriented, and the use of the product is more purposeful and task-oriented. In addition, the user's position and function will also bring some differentiation.
- From the customer perspective, the people served by the product are bosses and managers, so the design goal is to solve the management and operation problems and focus on how to improve the operational efficiency of the enterprise. Due to the complexity of enterprise service products, standardized design is one of the key considerations for such products, which will focus on the input-output ratio of product design, involve the deployment of enterprise resources, pursue efficiency and maintain a high level of organizational vitality.

Perspective	User's perspective	Customer's perspective
Field	• to C	• to B
Target group	• Users (Consumers)	• Customers (Managers)
Product goal	• Meet user needs and win customer recognition	• Meet user needs and win customer recognition
Target group goal	• Solve life and personal problems and realize personal value	• Solve the problems of management and operation, and focus on how to improve the operation efficiency of enterprises
Factors in decision-making	• Personal preference	• Benefit
Design strategy	• Differentiated designy	• Standardized design

Fig. 2. Summary of the comparison between user perspective and customer perspective

When we combine the two, we find that for the user, the core focus is on the satisfaction of the actual needs, the object to be served, and how to help the user to complete the task well is an important goal of our product design. The customer's core requirement is inseparable from "management", and the customer needs to use product design to meet the user's needs (i.e., to serve the user) to better achieve the goal of management. (see Fig. 3).

Management and service requirements are not always halfway in real user scenarios, and different businesses are at different stages of development, so the focus of the design is also different (see Fig. 4).

- Some products are born based on customer demands, such as asset management system, which is initially designed for enterprise managers (finance) to better manage enterprise assets, achieve consistency between physical assets and financial accounts, and control the cost of enterprise operation, but as the product develops, it slowly tilts

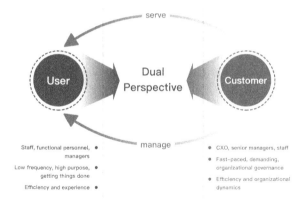

Fig. 3. Two perspectives and their relationship

toward user's perspective and considers more users' actual usage experience, such as how administrators can check in and out assets more efficiently, how to inventory assets more easily, how employees can borrow assets more conveniently, etc.

- Some products are initially for the users, for example, in Alibaba enterprise internal BBS at the beginning is to provide a service platform for staff communication and sharing, but with the expansion of product influence and the increase of user groups, the follow-up also gradually considers customer requirements, such as in the enterprise forum to reflect the organizational culture and philosophy of the enterprise publicity.

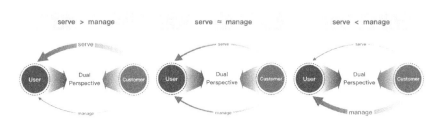

Fig. 4. The focus of the design is different.

To bridge the difference between the customer's perspective and the user's perspective, in the enterprise service scenario, designers need to consider balancing the demands of the user and the customer, to help both sides reach a consensus, finding the design opportunities where the needs of both sides are balanced, and realizing the value of both the user and the customer. When users and customers have a consensus, we could expand it; when there is no consensus, we could help users to understand customers and guide customers to think about the business more from the user's perspective.

"When customer goals (e.g., cost control) limit user goals and user goals cannot be continued through one core pathway, they can be continued through other ways of feeder pathways that both ensure manager goals and enhance user goals" – Interviewee Hui.

"When customer goals cannot be reached at a certain stage, they are assisted by extended feeder goals; or change goals" – Interviewee Jie.

4   Model in Enterprise Services

4.1   The Concept of Dual Perspective in the Field of Enterprise Services

Based on the study of the user and customer perspectives, we put forward the "dual perspective concept", which can be used as a guideline for the entire design process, which advise designers to think in two directions at the same time in the design process. The design concept has been validated in the actual scenario of Alibaba.

4.2   The Dual Perspective Design Process

To facilitate the implementation of the "dual perspective design concept", we conducted several internal analyses and discussions. Finally, we came up with a design process for Alibaba's internal products (see Fig. 5).

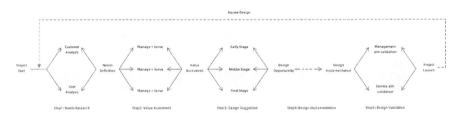

Fig. 5. The dual Perspective Design Process for Alibaba's internal products

Step 1 Needs Analysis

Through the preliminary research, we know that there is a difference between the customer perspective and the user perspective. And requirements research plays a crucial role in a project. Therefore, in the requirements study, to help designers get a more impartial insight, we give a process to analyze the requirements.

1. Obtain customer's demand
   Enterprise internal application projects are usually initiated by customers. Designers in Alibaba normally start from the customers' requirements, which include both management requirements and service requirements.
2. Identify management requirements and service requirements from customer demand
   Split the requirements into service and management, and identify the management requirements and service requirements. For example, according to the source of the requirements to split: 1) If the source of the requirements is top-down, generally for

the business perspective of the needs, such as from the business planning direction, the company's strategic objectives, etc. derived from the needs. This requirement is more likely to be a management requirement. 2) If the source of the requirement is bottom-up, for example, the user of the internal product feeds back the requirement, such as work orders, complaints, suggestions, etc. This requirement is more likely to be a service requirement.

3. Correct errors in employee requirements

After we have narrowed down the scope of requirements and identified the real needs of users, we can apply the UCD design theory to correct the deviations in user requirements from the customer's objectives. Eventually, by combining the management requirements with the service requirements, we could have a more complete and fair definition of requirements.

Step 2 Value Assessment

If the positioning of the product is not clear, it will confuse the development process, such as when the management needs and service needs conflict, whose needs are given more priority, these issues should be clearly defined in the process of a product definition to avoid subsequent confusion and repetition. As a product develops, the focus of the product may vary. If we understand the position of the product in its development cycle, we will have a clearer perception of the future direction of the product. We can discuss the value judgment of the product through three factors.

1. Product positioning is directly related to the value judgment

Product positioning plays an important role in value judgment. We can make value judgments by referring to the industry, such as

- The product is for business operation consideration, to help enterprises manage their employees, then the product has strong management attributes
- The product enables employees to enjoy certain rights and benefits, then the product has strong service attributes

We can draw some inspiration from the experience of the industry. For example, one of the functions of the financial system is to control the reimbursement of employees, so that the enterprise can operate smoothly, so the financial system has strong management attributes, while the parking app within the enterprise is to provide services for employees to commute more conveniently, and not directly to serve the business, so the product has strong service attributes.

2. The situation of the product will affect the value judgment

In addition to the category of the product, the situation of the product also affects the value judgment. When products face different environments and needs, the judgment of the value of the product is also different. Take the parking app as an example, if the parking resources are very abundant and the number far exceeds the number of employees, the management of the parking space at this time does not set up many rules for the behavior of employee parking, which has a stronger service attribute. On the contrary, if the parking resources are extremely scarce and the number of employees exceeds the parking resources, the manager will make full use of the parking spaces as much as possible by setting a series of norms to restrain the employees, such as not to park their family members' vehicles into the park, etc. At this time, the management attribute of the parking app rises.

3. The development stage of the product will affect the value judgment

The value judgment is dynamic and may change with the development of the product. Some products are set up at the beginning because of the goal of the service, and over time, when the goal of the service reaches a certain stage, the management attribute gradually rises.

Some products are set up at the beginning because of management objectives, and over time, when the management objectives are achieved, the service attributes gradually increase.

Step 3 Design Suggestions

In this step, designers can bring their expertise to bear before, during, and after the project.

4. Initially, complete the main issues

If it is a management greater than service attributes, first meet the needs of management; if it is a manager Less than service attributes, first meet the needs of service. At the same time, based on the designer's empathy and understanding of the user, help people talk equally, understand each other and reach a consensus through focus groups, co-creation, and brainstorming sessions.

5. Medium-term, close to the customer and service users

Consider both sides' demands when designing solutions, provide win-win design solutions for both sides, and keep in touch with users and customers to test the feasibility of ideas. If the management value is bigger than the service value at the beginning, designers can consider improving the service attributes to achieve the joint improvement of management attributes and service attributes in the middle term. If the management value is smaller than the service value at the beginning, consider improving the management attribute to achieve the joint improvement of the management attribute and the service attribute in the middle term.

In other words, by balancing the interests of the other party, designers can find a win-win opportunity point.

6. Late stage, reach a consensus and help to understand

At the later stage, when both customers' needs and users' needs are more fully satisfied, designers can help both sides communicate and reach a consensus. For example, designers could help users understand the product management concept, help customers understand real user use, and continue to design iterations.

Step 4 Design Implementation

Our process focuses on the pre-study and post-validation, so the specific implementation methods will not be discussed much, in fact, the design implementation has a lot of relevant materials in the literature to refer to, for example, the two-drill model and agile development, etc. Then, assuming that the design process has been completed in the process, we will enter the last step of design verification.

Step 5 Design Validation
In the previous study, we find that whether the management attributes are greater than the service attributes or the service attributes are greater than the management attributes, the validation of both perspectives would be implemented:

– Validation of management value: cost control, etc.
– Validation of service value: data analysis, usability analysis, user satisfaction research, etc.

Although both values are validated, the weight of each is different. When the management value is greater than the service value, data analysis, usability analysis, user satisfaction, and other indicators may be used only as a reference. When the service value is greater than the management value, these metrics become an important indicator of the success of the project.

5 Design Validation

Through the previous analysis, we can understand that different business products do not always have a dual perspective at different stages of development. Some products are born from the user's perspective and gradually move toward the customer's perspective; some products start by satisfying the demands of management, but as the product develops, it will move toward the user's perspective.

In this chapter, we illustrate how the 'dual perspective' model is applied to both types of corporate product design, using practical examples. The case of 5.1 shows how a product born from the user's perspective solves a current conflict by adding a management tool; The case of 5.2 describes the process of designing a product that was born from a management perspective but gradually added service attributes to meet the needs of users.

5.1 Conference Room Online Booking Upgrades

The Conference Room Online Booking system is an internal Alibaba meeting room booking product. The product was initially created to meet the needs of employees and facilitate them to choose the right time and meeting room online in advance. When our team received the request to upgrade the product, we found that employees had a poor experience in booking meeting rooms, for example, due to the tight meeting room resources, employees often could not book meeting rooms.

In this project, we used the 'dual perspective design process' model. For this product, the service attributes were more important than the management attributes. Therefore, in the mid to late stages of the project, the customer perspective was used to help improve the service through management. Therefore, to address the issue of tight meeting room resources, we have added meeting bars and open spaces to the workplace to alleviate the resource constraints. At the same time, we have implemented a series of management tools as follows (see Fig. 6).

7. Offline

An intelligent sensor system is installed in the meeting rooms, which on the one hand can achieve the energy-saving goal of lights going out when people leave and lights coming on when people come. The sensors can also identify that the reserved meeting room is currently unoccupied and remind the booker to release the room, thus reducing the idle rate of the meeting room.

8. Online

- Intelligent recommendation of nearby unoccupied meeting rooms on the user side is designed, allowing users to select unoccupied meeting rooms more quickly and conveniently, thus increasing the utilization rate;
- If a meeting ends prematurely or is canceled, the system will provide an entry point for releasing the meeting room, making it convenient for users to carry out the corresponding operation;
- Warm slogans are shown in the user interface to make people understand that meeting room resources are limited, prompting them to develop good habits of punctuality and efficiency

9. Rules

In response to the phenomenon of wasted meeting room resources, we set reasonable rules for meeting bookings. For example, we require meetings with a booking time of more than 3 h to be filled with meeting type and reason and display a countdown on the projection screen after the meeting starts to avoid delay, improve the efficiency of the meeting, and allow the room to be used rationally to the maximum extent. In addition, for users who have occupied the meeting room several times in a month but do not show up, resulting in the wastage of meeting room resources, certain restrictions on future bookings will be taken.

Through the design of the meeting room upgrade, we help staff and managers to reach a consensus on the rules so that more meeting room resources can be made available for staff meetings. From the employees' perspective, it is easier for them to find available meeting rooms quickly and book them more conveniently; from the management's perspective, the overall meeting room booking will be more orderly and achieve the maximum use of resources.

5.2 "Happy Beans" Design for Travel Fee Control

The travel system is a product under the financial management branch within the Alibaba enterprise, and its function is mainly to provide employees with booking functions for travel-related services, such as booking flights and hotels. The travel system is the most typical scenario for expense control, and it is a product born from the customer perspective of financial management. Therefore, for travel products, the product has a strong management attribute, namely the control of costs. When our team received the requirements, we communicated with the client and found that the client's request was to continue to reduce costs on top of the existing cost control.

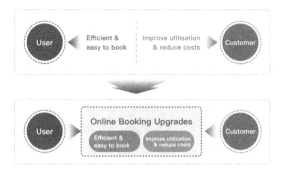

Fig. 6. The concept of Conference Room Online Booking Upgrades

In this project, we used a "dual perspective design process" to solve the problem. According to the design model, at this stage of the product's development, continued strengthening of the management attributes could result in a very poor user experience. The design suggestions indicate that at this late stage of product development, the conflict needs to be resolved more from a service perspective to achieve a balance between customer and user needs.

Therefore, in response to the current problem, instead of simply adding more usage rules and management tools to the original product, we designed a travel points system, called "Happy Beans", to achieve the integration of the customer perspective and user perspective, leading users to take the initiative to save, thereby reducing expenses and management costs. The system is a blend of customer and user perspectives. Specifically, "Happy Beans" reshapes the user's travel mindset and embeds the concept of "Happy Beans" throughout the UX chain. From the customer's point of view, employees are guided to save and travel low-carbon; from the employee's point of view, they are also more willing to save on travel costs due to the points system (see Fig. 7).

On the one hand, we provide real-time rewards and feedback to users for their saving behavior. When a user completes a low carbon saving behavior, friendly words of encouragement and interactive pop-ups will be displayed on the system, allowing users to intuitively understand the value of their good behavior and gain a sense of achievement from being motivated.

On the other hand, "Happy Beans" also provide flexibility in the choice of travel options, for example, when employees choose to travel by low-carbon modes of transport (e.g., bus, metro) or take a taxi with a colleague on the way, they will be rewarded with a certain number of "Happy Beans". These "Happy Beans" can be redeemed for airport fast track, hotel upgrades, Starbucks coffee, or converted into donations for good causes.

We expect the result to be a reduction in overall costs without reducing the employee experience, and even an increase in employee satisfaction metrics. Nearly half of all Beijing-Hangzhou travelers have used the "Happy Beans" since launched, and from the employee side, the solution has received highly positive feedback from users, while providing significant cost savings on the management side and helping to make corporate travel greener and less carbon-intensive from a social perspective.

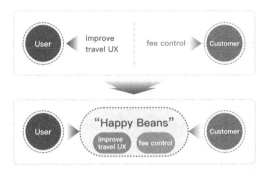

Fig. 7. The concept of "Happy Beans"

6   Conclusion and Discussion

6.1   Research Scope and Limitations

We have developed the 'dual perspective design process' through a series of studies and validated the model through two case studies. However, the research context and the research objects in this paper are still limited to the internal Alibaba enterprise, which has certain limitations:

10. Research scenario

    This paper is based on the Alibaba enterprise, which is a large Internet mega-enterprise with its scenario specificity. In the future, we can conduct further research and verification in enterprises of different sizes and types.

11. Research objects

    At present, we mainly focus on internal enterprise products for research. Additional research can be conducted in the future on products that are more mature in terms of commercialization.

Expansion in the to G (government) field. The characteristics of to G(government) products require products with very high requirements for some specific needs, such as reliability and security. Therefore, the research on management attributes and service attributes may be different.

In addition to the preliminary research scenarios and research subjects, the implementation cases shown in the validation section also come from within Alibaba, so the scope of application of this design process model is somewhat limited, and further research is needed to determine whether it can be applied more generally.

Although the "Dual Perspective Design Process" has some limitations, we believe that it can be used if the reader is in an industry environment that is very similar to the one we have described in this paper. If there are some differences in the environment, we still hope that this process model can be used as a reference to inspire designers to solve problems.

6.2   Conclusions and Future Studies

In this paper, we investigate how to balance the different goals or demands of different roles in the enterprise service sector to improve the enterprise product user experience. Finally, a "Dual Perspective Design Process" model is derived, which can be used as a reference for future enterprise product design.

There are two main directions for future research:

12. Universality

    As mentioned in the previous section, the research scenario and the target audience of the "Dual Perspective Design Process" are all from within Alibaba, therefore, in future research, we hope to expand the research scenario to more companies, to validate the model and iterate on it, making the model more widely applicable.

13. Multiple perspectives

    From the literature, we have found that existing design theories are limited by a single perspective, e.g., UCD is more user-focused and the traditional design methods for enterprise applications is more customer-focused. Our "Dual Perspective Design Process" has successfully broken down and analyzed the single perspective in more detail. In practice, however, the success of a project involves multiple stakeholders and may be more complex, so we need to take more factors into account for further refinement.

References

1. What is Enterprise Service Management? https://www.microfocus.com/en-us/what-is/enterprise-service-management. Accessed 08 Feb 2023
2. Newhook, R., Jaramillo, D., Temple, J.G., Duke, K.J.: Evolution of the mobile enterprise app: a design perspective. Procedia Manufact. **3**, 2026–2033 (2015). https://doi.org/10.1016/j.promfg.2015.07.250
3. Uflacker, M., Busse, D.: Complexity in enterprise applications vs. simplicity in user experience. In: Jacko, J.A. (ed.) HCI 2007. LNCS, vol. 4553, pp. 778–787. Springer, Heidelberg (2007). https://doi.org/10.1007/978-3-540-73111-5_87
4. Sekar, B.: Enterprise software experience design: journey and lessons. In: Bernhaupt, R., Dalvi, G., Joshi, A., Balkrishan, D.K., O'Neill, J., Winckler, M. (eds.) INTERACT 2017. LNCS, vol. 10516, pp. 356–359. Springer, Cham (2017). https://doi.org/10.1007/978-3-319-68059-0_29
5. Yasu, H., Iwata, N., Kohno, I.: Collaborative user experience design methods for enterprise system. In: Kurosu, M. (ed.) HCI 2013. LNCS, vol. 8004, pp. 146–155. Springer, Heidelberg (2013). https://doi.org/10.1007/978-3-642-39232-0_17
6. Marcus, A.: User-centered design (UCD) in the enterprise: corporations begin to focus on UCD. In: HCI and User-Experience Design. HIS, pp. 143–150. Springer, London (2015). https://doi.org/10.1007/978-1-4471-6744-0_18
7. User Centered Design. https://www.interaction-design.org/literature/topics/user-centered-design. Accessed 08 Feb 2023

From Mental Representation to Enaction

Innovation of Aesthetic Research Paradigm Under the Influence of Contemporary Cognitive Sciences

Yuefeng Ze and Xijia Fan[✉]

Shanghai Institute of Visual Art, Shanghai 202206, China
stellafxj@126.com

Abstract. This article proposes a reflection on the change of paradigme that Cognitive Sciences has provoked in the field of art and aesthetics research. Cognitive Sciences, also known as Sciences and technologies of Cognition, is a federation of new sciences dedicated to describing, explaining and simulating the main dispositions and capacities of the human mind, which has profoundly influenced the development of contemporary art both in terms of artistic practice and theoretical research. On the one hand, the technological achievements of Cognitive Sciences, namely the digital media technologies, have given rise to a new paradigm of artistic activities, known as "Human-Computer Interaction", which has gone far beyond the interpretative realm of traditional art philosophy and aesthetic, and consequently calls for a profound revolution of the art research system. On the other hand, the theorical achievements of Cognitive Sciences, including the theories and the hypotheses developed in different research branches such as Cognitivism, Connectionism and Enactionism, not only have provided art scholars with new conceptual tools and research approaches, but also have constituted a new paradigme of art research, called "cognitive aesthetics". In this paper, the author attempts to clarify the articulations between different research programs of cognitive sciences and the emergence of differents approaches of cognitive aesthetics since the mid-20th century. The author will also develop a reflection on the new conceptual inspirations brought by the theory of Enaction, and attempt to explain how this theory can become an aesthetic research approach that responds to the new art paradigm of "Human-Computer Interaction".

Keywords: Cognitive Sciences · Cognitive Aesthetics · Human-computer interaction · Enactivism · Neuroesthetic

1 Introduction

Over the past 20 years, Digital media art and related industries have experienced explosive growth worldwide. As computer science-technology has constantly reshaped human society and culture, it has also fully penetrated the field of art and design. Consequently, it

Supported by: Humanities and Social Sciences Foundation of Ministry of Education of China (18YJC760123)/中国教育部人文社会科学基金青年项目 (18YJC760123)

has brought about the rapid development of a series of cutting-edge science-technological arts that are highly innovative and advanced in the industry, which are Immersive Space, Interactive Installation, AI Art, Data-Visualization, VR/AR Art, Digital Twins, Meta-humans, Metaverse, etc. These science-technological forms of art redefine not only the methods of existence, production, expression, and dissemination of artistic works, but also the functions and values of art. Therefore, a new paradigm of artistic activities, known as "human-computer interaction", is established. The main characteristics can be summed up as four "fusion", which are the fusion of technological innovation and artistic creation, the fusion of natural intelligence and artificial intelligence, the fusion of the virtual world and the physical world, and the fusion of the creative process and the aesthetic process.

Digital media art has already caused much academic discussion and reflection in the international art research field. However, contemporary scholars have to face the dilemma that new forms of art developed on the basis of computer science-technology have gone far beyond the interpretative realm of traditional art philosophy and aesthetic. Those explanations of the nature of art proposed by traditional Western art philosophy and aesthetics, like "Imitation", "Reproduction", "Expression", "Empathy", "Form" and "Metaphor", are all unable to interpret the new paradigm of "Human-Computer Inter-action". For example, traditional theory views art as the exclusive domain of the human esprit. However, in the creation of digital art, computer calculation has partially replaced the judgement, decision, and imagination of human intelligence. In this context, is digital art still considered a form of art? Can the artificial intelligence constructed by computer also has the identity of artistic creator? Another example is that, traditional theory consid-ers artworks as the externalized expression of the artist's thoughts and emotions through some material medium. However, in the case of interactive art, the spectator is not only the viewer and receptor, but they are invited to participate directly in the creation of the work, and their actions will change the final effect of the work in real time as well. In this context, how should we define an artwork's creative process and aesthetic process? Fur-thermore, how do we define the creative subject and the aesthetic subject? In face of such questions, there is an obvious disconnection between the traditional theoretical frame-work of art research and the reality of contemporary art development. Consequently, how to modify the understanding of art ontology and to establish a new theoretical paradigm of art research that can respond to the characteristics of digital media art becomes a significant issue for contemporary scholars.

On one hand, digital media art has demanded a profound revolution of the art research systems; On the other hand, Cognitive Sciences, the foundation of the development of computer technology, has provided art theorists and aestheticians with new theoretical tools and research approaches. As an interdisciplinary research field that investigates the human mind within the perspective of natural science, Cognitive Sciences, with the theories and hypotheses of mind developed in this field, have profoundly influenced the development of contemporary philosophy and humanities since the mid-twentieth century. It has also become a critical factor in the development of contemporary art the-ory and aesthetic. In the twenty-first century, the theory of Enaction [17] has gradually developed into a new paradigm of cognitive sciences, and has shifted the epistemological foundation of humanities and social sciences once again. As a philosophy of mind, Enaction completely breaks through the opposition between Subjective Constructivism and Objective Representationalism in traditional mental research. As a conceptual model of mind, Enaction fundamentally surpasses the opposition between traditional philosophical views and the traditional scientific views of mind. And as a research framework, this theory establishes a loop of explanations between the natural sciences and the human sciences. The theory of Enaction not only inspires the creative practices of contemporary artists, but also provides more innovative theoretical tools for exploring the digital media art.

This paper proposes a reflection on the paradigmatic reformation of theoretical researches in art and aesthetics under the influence of cognitive sciences. The author will systematically clarify the intimate articulations between different research programs of cognitive sciences and the emergence of new scientific approaches of aesthetic since the mid-20th century. And then, the author will develop a reflection on the new conceptual inspirations brought by the Theory of Enaction, and attempt to explain how the Theory of Enaction become an aesthetic research approach that responds to the new art paradigm of "Human-Computer Interaction".

2   Cognitive Sciences and the Reformation of Art Research Paradigm

After the 20th century, human society has witnessed the rapid development of natural sciences. A variety of emerging sciences has fundamentally challenged the dominance of Dualism in the West, and also profoundly questioned the particularity of human beings according to traditional Western philosophy. As Michel Foucault described in his book *Les Mots et les choses*: "Since the beginning of psychoanalysis and linguistics, the humanity has been gradually dissolved in various emerging scientific theories, which constantly reveal the truth that human beings (body and mind) are not special existences, but only a subsystem that constitute the world" [8]. Under the influence of scientism, the development of Western art and aesthetic research gradually embarked on a new road of scientific development in the twentieth century. The "top-down" model of research used in traditional philosophical aesthetics is gradually transitioned to the "bottom-up" model proposed by positivist science. The exploration of the essence of art also transformed from a metaphysical conceptual logical deduction to a specific examination and scientific analysis of the process, organization, properties, functions, and values of art which is considered as a creative mental activity under different disciplinary perspectives, in combination with the phenomenological description and philosophical conceptualization for a systemic clarification. Among many of the emerging sciences that have influenced the innovation of art and aesthetic research in the twentieth century, Cognitive Sciences has played a crucial role. What are cognitive sciences? How did cognitive sciences influence the development of art and aesthetic research in the twentieth century?

2.1   The Subversion of Traditional Theories of Mind by Cognitive Sciences

Cognitive Sciences is an interdisciplinary field of research dedicated to exploring the mysteries of human minds within the scope of natural sciences. Born in the 1930s and

1940s, it has covered a range of emerging disciplines, including linguistics, psychology, biology, neurology, artificial intelligence, computer science, etc. According to Professor Daniel Andler, "Cognitive Sciences is, in fact, a scientific psychology. However, this new form of psychology goes far beyond the framework of traditional psychology in terms of its objects and methods. On the one hand, it examines the functioning of the normal adult mind as a member of the whole family of cognitive forms, the other members include the human mind during learning and growth, the incompetent mind caused by congenital physical defects or acquired injuries, the intelligence of other animal races, and so on. On the other hand, this new psychology incorporates neuroscience, linguistics, philosophy, and other social science disciplines" [1]. Among many of the disciplines covered by Cognitive Sciences, computer science occupies an extraordinary place, both as a technological achievement in the study of the human mind and as an essential simulation tool for the study of the mechanisms and functional principles of the mind. To emphasize the importance of computer science and related technological applications in the overall research system, Cognitive Sciences is also often referred to as the Sciences and Technologies of Cognition.

Strictly speaking, Cognitive Sciences is not a unified discipline in its own right but rather a loose confederation of multiple disciplines, which includes multiple research branches based on different hypotheses, with many differences and divergences, as well as extensive intersections and collaborations among them. It is generally accepted that the development of cognitive science can be divided into four stages: Cybernetic, Cognitivism, Connectionism and Enactivism [20] (pp.86–101).

The Cybernetic is generally considered the embryonic stage of Cognitive Sciences, which was developed between the 1940s and 1950s. During this period, cognition was supposed to be a computational process of information based on a system of symbolic formulas. The main object of study was the communication and automatic regulation among biological organisms, mechanical systems, and between organisms and machines. The second stage in the development of cognitive sciences was the period of "Cognitivism". Cognitivism, also known as Computationalism, is the first research program in the field which was emerged from "Symposium on Information Theory", organized by the MIT in 1956. The proposal of this research program marked the formal birth of cognitive sciences. "Cognitivism" inherits the basic concept of Cybernetic, where the computer is set up as a scientific model of mind-brain function. In this model, the animal brain is described as an information-processing device consisting of multiple local functional units; cognition is defined as the process of symbolic calculation of information performed by the brain or computer; symbols are interpreted as mental representations produced and used by human's brain to reflect the external world, similar to computer-recognizable codes. One of the most significant events in the "Cognitivism" period was the birth of artificial intelligence.

The third stage in the development of cognitive sciences was the period of "Connectionism", which began around the 1970s. Connectionism is a scientific paradigm centered on biology and neuroscience, which critiques the basic concept and research strategies of Cognitivism. Instead of computers, the model of cognition studied by Connectionist is the biological nervous system of animal brains. Instead of the computational processing of information based on abstract symbols, the focus of this study is on the principles and mechanisms by which the nervous system reorganizes its internal equilibrium in response to external stimuli and produces mental representations that reflect the external world. Connectionism proposes a series of new concept, such as "self-adaptation", "self-learning", "self-evolution", "self-organization" and "self-emergence", which have framed a scientific approach that is more closely aligned with the biological properties of cognition. Under its influence, the core objective of artificial intelligence switched to mimic the principles and processes of neural activity in the brain. Thereafter, a new generation of computer technologies, including "Artificial Neural Network", "genetic algorithm" and "machine learning", was born, accompanied by the reformation in image display technology and human-computer interaction interfaces.

The fourth stage in the development of Cognitive Sciences began around the end of the 1990s. After the 1990s, Connectionism remained in the center of the field. Meanwhile, a new research orientation was emerging. One of the most representative theories of mind is the Theory of Enaction, developed by an American neurologist Francisco Varela and his colleagues. This theory critiques the objective Representationalism shared by both Cognitivism and Connectionism. It claims that "cognition" does not depend on the representational models already exist in our brains, but on diversified life experience. The experience refers to the physical and mental experience we acquired from our interaction with the outside world by using the capacity of "sensorimotor". The mind is no longer a mirror of the world around us but an action guided par perception [17].

Cognitive Sciences is fundamentally different from traditional Western philosophy of mind or traditional psychology. As Marc Jeanerrod, a famous neuropsychologist, has pointed out: "The goal of Cognitive Sciences is to explain the human mind as a natural thing, assuming that its existence has a material basis, its operation has mechanisms and processes that can be described by science and imitated by technology technologically, and its development is in continuity with other natural things and can be logically explained. This attempt to study the human mind in the perspective of the natural sciences is unprecedented. As in the traditional theories of mind, philosophical or psychological, all spiritual phenomena, such as consciousness, intention and emotion, are regarded as irreducible entities, outside the sphere that can be explained by causality" [9] (p.9). As the tradition of Western philosophy, the spiritual world and the material world have been seen as opposite existences, and the world has consequently been studied in two unrelated parts: the material dimension, including biology and physics; and the immaterial dimension, including culture, religion, faith and art. Since the Renaissance, Dualism has dominated almost every doctrine of modern Western thoughts about humanity, mind, life and culture, it has also caused a long-standing opposition and separation of the natural sciences from the humanities. Even psychology, which developed into a independent discipline at the end of the nineteenth century, has not been able to break away from the dualism, because the mental phenomena studied in traditional psychology are detached from the biological basis and are assumed to exist in an experiential sphere parallel to the biological body. The birth of Cognitive Sciences has completely overturned this dualism, especially since the development of Connectionism, where the bio-neurology has provided for the field a new foundational hypotheses, which is "All mental states shall necessarily have a cause-and-effect influence on physical behavior, which stems from the fact that every mental state is fundamentally a brain state" [9](p.189). In this scientific hypotheses, there is a complex symbiosis between thought and brain, between mental activity and neuronal activity, which contemporary cognitive sciences attempts to reveal and understand.

2.2 The Reformation of Art Researches Guided by Cognitive Sciences

The theory of mind developed by cognitive sciences has profoundly impacted the development of philosophy and social sciences since the mid-20th century. As Varela, an American biological neurologist, indicated, "Cognitive science is the next technological and conceptual revolution after quantum physics, and it has, and will have, a lasting and profound impact on all levels of human society" [16] (p.21). Both in terms of theoretical research and technical development, Cognitive Sciences continues to reveal the fact that the "mind", once considered as a representation of humanity, is not unique to humans or some special existence outside the material world, but a biological capacity common to all animals, which can not only be explained in a natural scientific way but also artificially simulated by the machinery. These scientific discoveries have a great impact on the disciplines of philosophy, epistemology and psychology, forcing them to restart their fundamental questions, such as knowledge, subject, autonomy, will, belief, and creation in a new perspective. Ethics and anthropology also had to modify their theoretical foundations because the behavioral activities of certain animal races could already be examined in the same context as human behavior according to the findings of cognitive sciences.

The influence of Cognitive Sciences has also penetrated into the literary and artistic theory fields, becoming a critical factor in the scientific transformation of art and aesthetic research. Since the 1950s, some European and American art theorists and aestheticians began to cite the findings of cognitive sciences to reveal the fallacies of traditional theories about art and aesthetic, based on which they raised a series of new questions. Can art be studied and illuminated as a natural existence? What kind of cognitive and neurological processes drive the artistic creation and aesthetic experience? Do other animal races have the same or similar abilities or behaviors? Is the competence of aesthetic judgment a purely cultural product, or the result of phylogenesis of the human race? Is what we consider as "beauty" the common human-identifiable material structure properties, the result of individual subjective judgement, or something else? In the process of the emergence of "aesthetic joy", "aesthetic emotion", "creative impulse", "intention", and "artistic conception", how do our cognitive systems work? From these questions, art theorists, aesthetes and cognitive scientists have initiated a series of collaborations that have opened up a new direction of development for contemporary art and aesthetic theory, what the renowned French scholars Professors Jean-Marie Schaffer and Edmond Couchot call "La Naturalisation de l'art [5, 12]", which means "the study and elucidation of art as a natural object". "La Naturalisation de l'art" does not refer to an emerging discipline or school of art studies, but to an open movement of artistic theoretical innovation that includes numerous interdisciplinary research projects in the process of development. These projects are embedded in different branches of cognitive sciences, where the research ideas they propose and the theoretical results they obtain constitute a new paradigm of art research, called "cognitive aesthetics". Its innovativeness in relation to traditional Western art philosophy and aesthetic can be manifested in three ways.

The first is the reformation of epistemological foundations. From the traditional Western philosophy of mind, artistic competence (including artistic creativity and aesthetic appreciation) shall be considered as a special spiritual capacity which is innately possessed by very few geniuses and can neither be analyzed nor be acquired later through study. However, in the context of Cognitive Sciences, the artistic competence can be interpreted as cognitive capacity, not only its mechanisms and processes can be explained in terms of the perception and processing of information, but also its origins can be clarified in terms of phylogenesis and ontogenesis. The second is the reformation of the research framework. In the Western philosophical tradition, the theory of artistic creation and the aesthetic have been two separate research systems. In contrast, cognitive aesthetics examine "the process of aesthetic reception of art works (what happens in the spectator's brain and body) and the process of creation of art works (what happens in the artist's brain and body) within the same perspective simultaneously. The third is the reformation of the research approach. Edmond Couchot claimed, "Cognitive aesthetics involves cross-collaboration among many disciplines, among which brain neuroscience occupies an extraordinary place, giving birth to a new approach of aesthetic research, what we might call 'third-person', namely, Neuroesthetic. At the same time, another research approach, which we may call 'first-person', is also developed and grown. The relationship between these two research approaches is no longer opposite, but complementary and cooperative [5] (pp.8–9)". The "third-person" approach is also known as the approach of natural science, which is to rationally comprehends the world from "God's angle of view", and to objectively describe and explain the nature of world through phenomenological observations, data analysis, scientific experimentation, logical deduction, conceptual modeling, and other methods. In contrast, the "first-person" approach, also known as the empirical-phenomenological approach, is commonly used in traditional art philosophy, traditional psychology, and traditional aesthetics. The approach is to examine the inner self from the empirical connection between humans and the world, and through the introspective description and metaphysical logical deduction. These two research approaches, which were opposed to each other previously, have now become complementary and cooperative.

By the end of the 20th century, the projects related to "cognitive aesthetics" had already yielded fruitful results. In terms of scientific discoveries, relevant teams of scientists were able to make persuasive scientific explanations for various cognitive mechanisms involved in artistic activities, such as visual cognition, musical cognition, literary cognition, and aesthetic emotions based on scientific experiments. In terms of theoretical achievements, scholars have proposed a series of scientific aesthetic theories with pioneering and philosophical inspiration. Although imperfect, these research findings have proven in various ways the feasibility and rationality of studying art and aesthetics in the context of natural science, which have fundamentally contributed to the paradigmatic innovation of contemporary art theory consequently.

3   New Approaches of Cognitive Aesthetics

The emergence of scientific aesthetics can be traced back to the "Experimental Aesthetic" founded by the German psychologist Gustav Theodor Fechner in the second half of the 19th century. However, due to traditional psychology's research methods and epistemological foundation, Fechner could only make experimental measurements and generalizations on some simple aesthetic psychological responses. After the mid-twentieth century, as cognitive sciences were increasingly introduced into the field of art research, experimental aesthetics opened a new stage of development, and two approaches of cognitive aesthetics have successively formed in combination with different mental research programs, called "informational aesthetic" and "neuroesthetic". How do these two approaches go beyond the traditional experimental aesthetic in terms of methodology and epistemology? What are the relatively more innovative scientific hypotheses and theoretical perspectives on the nature of art and aesthetics that they propose? What are their positive implications for the development of contemporary art science?

3.1   Informational Aesthetics: Aesthetic Cognition as a Process of Information Communication

Informational aesthetics is generally regarded as the first cognitive aesthetic approach based on the main discipline of cognitive sciences. It follows the positivist path of Fechner's experimental aesthetics. However, its research methods and theoretical foundations are mainly derived from cybernetic science, and relevant research results are therefore embedded in the development of the cognitivist science of mind. The French sociologist Abraham Moles first applied modern theory of information directly to aesthetic research in the mid-1950s, and published in 1958 the book *Perception esthétique et théorie de l'information* [10], which systematically expounded the basic theory and the core concept of informational aesthetics, marking the birth of informational aesthetic.

The objects studied by Mols are mainly auditory arts, and his core theory can be summarized as follows. First, all works of art, or all forms of artistic expression, can be understood as a perceptual message carrying information, and the creation and reception of artworks can be understood as the process of information creation and communication. Second, the recognizability and originality of a artwork can be explained by Shannon's mathematical model of information quantification, while the measurement of information quality is originality: the higher level of originality the intellectual content and sensory effects brought by a message, the more informative and unpredictable it is for the recipient to recognize. Thirdly, the information carried by artworks can be divided into two categories: "semantic information" and "aesthetic information". Semantic information can be expressed in a symbolic logic system, which is translatable and reproducible and can trigger rational judgment and thinking, while aesthetic information mainly triggers certain emotions, which cannot be precisely expressed through written language. In general communication, these two types of information play almost the same role, but in art communication, aesthetic information has more abundant meanings than semantic information.

The theory of "informational aesthetic" proposed by Moles is not perfect but groundbreaking and forward-looking. On the one hand, Moles' informational quantification, classification and rule extraction of aesthetic experience through auditory experiments and data analysis provide an important theoretical basis for the development of artificial intelligence art. On the other hand, Moles presents a more objective scientific elucidation on many important issues involved in traditional aesthetics and experimental aesthetics from the perspective of information, such as sensory uncertainty, originality and noise, and so on. By articulating these issues, Moles defines the philosophical function of cybernetics: if the conservative scholars criticize cybernetics for the collapse of humanism, then Moles reveals in an informatics way that humans acquire images of world through individual senses with uncertainty, which are the specific way humans situated in the physical world.

Following the footstep of Professor Moles, Umberto Eco, an Italian philosopher and semiotician, proposed a similar theory of informational aesthetics four years later [7], which mainly applied to the analysis of paintings and literary works. He proposed that the value of an artwork derives mainly from the multiple dialectical relationship that the creator constructs within the following scope of work: predictability and unpredictability, chaos and order, formal stability and openness. In the following years, the theoretical achievements related to informational aesthetics were gradually enriched, among which relatively more representative ones include the semiotic aesthetics conducted by the federal German semiotician Max Bense, which incorporates mathematics, physics and computer science, and the graphical visual perception rules conducted by the French aesthetician Francois Molnar, etc.

3.2 Neuroesthetic: Aesthetic Cognition as Neuromotor Processes in the Brain

After cognitive sciences entered the stage of Connectionism, neurobiology, which has been continuously improved, began to be increasingly applied to the field of aesthetics, and formed a new research approach of Cognitive aesthetics, namely "Neuroesthetic". Neuroesthetic is an extension of the research methods and results of neurobiology, which proposes to solve aesthetic problem based on the study of brain activity mechanisms. The central goal is to understand and reveal the neurological connection between artistic activities and brain activities, especially the biological and neurological principles of the senses of beauty emerged in the process of art creation and appreciation.

Professor Semir Zeki is the founder and one of the most representative scholars of "neuroesthetic". In his early research, Zeki studied the subdivisions and functions of animal's visual brain, mainly by deconstructing the monkey brain. After the late 1980s, with the maturation of the new generation of medical vision technologies, such as functional Magnetic Resonance Imaging (FMRI), Near-Infrared Spectroscopy (NIRS), and Positron Emission Tomography (PET), Zeki began to systematically study the human visual brain, and successfully revealed the physiological functions and working mechanisms of different specialized areas of the brain visual cortex. Relevant findings were included in the scientific paper "A direct demonstration of functional specialization in the human visual cortex" [21] published in 1991 and in the scientific book *A Vision of the Brain* [22] published in 1993. Subsequently, Zeki began to adopt neurobiological research findings to solve aesthetic problems, in an attempt to understand and reveal the neurological processes involved in the appreciation of artworks, and to demonstrate the commonality between the brain and art in the context of visual cognition. In his paper

"The Neurology of Kinetic Art" [23] published in 1994, Zeki first explicitly put forward the basic idea that visual art and visual brain are compatible, indicating that both art creation and aesthetic appreciation comply with the working principles of the brain. In his book *Inner Vision* [24], published in 1999, Zeki proposed a more systematical and deep elucidation to a range of important problems, such as "autonomy of vision", "parallel aesthetic cognition of different cerebral cortical subdivisions", "eternality and ambiguity of aesthetic", and so on. *Inner Vision*, the first work on aesthetics with neurobiology as a core, marked the creation of "Neuroesthetic", which made Zeki the "Father of Neuroesthetic".

Based on the study and understanding of the physiological structure and functional mechanism of the human visual brain, Zeki proposed a scientific hypothesis that the physiological structures of the human brain are innately correlated with certain forms of the natural world, and this correlation allowed the perceived subject to acquire a certain pleasure (empathy) when seeing these forms, and enabled the perceived subject to instinctively understand certain unknown forms. Zeki demonstrated this scientific hypothesis thorough a series of scientific experimentation and proposed the Visual Initiative Theory. According to Zeki, vision is not a process of passively receiving visual information from the external world, but a process in which the brain actively explores the nature of the world thorough various visual representations which are continuously and rapidly changing over time. Firstly, the brain needs to quickly identify and extracts important information related to the fundamental properties of objective things among a large amount of visual information received and filtered out irrelevant and extra information. Secondly, the filtered information is compared, identified and classified with visual models already stored in the brain. Lastly, the brain collects the information related to the visual object but filtered out by imagination, and creates a mental image reflecting the observed objects. It is inferred that the art is similar to the brain in function, both of which are designed to acquire the knowledge about the world, which is intellectual model representing the essence hidden in the visible appearance. Taking the "pursuit of essence" as the starting point, Zeki extensively analyzed many styles of painting such as Cubism, Abstractism, Fauvism, and Kinetic Art, with a neurobiological approach, in an attempt to prove that visual art is an extension of the human visual brain function.

Another important matter in Zeki's analysis is the "uncertainty" of artistic creation and aesthetic experience. According to Zeki, if the search for essence is an instinct of the human brain, the specific way in which human cognition acquires the essence of world is "uncertainty". In the real world, no objective existence can be unchangeable or have only one characteristic expression, and the essence is hidden under these complex appearances that are continuously changing and present as different realities under different conditions, such as the fractal structure that is prevalent in nature. Therefore, "uncertainty" itself becomes a kind of eternity, which is prevalent in the sensory connection between us and the world, and is also inherent in our pursuit for the essence of the world. This dialectical relationship is not only in accordance with the objective laws of existence of the world, but also in accordance with the aesthetic cognitive mechanism of our brain. It follows that if the function of art is to provide an eternal interpretation of reality in the form of work, then this interpretation itself should contain multiple possibilities for a certain truth, which constitute the uncertainty in artworks, and uncertainty is the key to constantly activating and satisfying the brain's instinct for exploration. In other words, creating uncertainty is the concrete way in which art pursues the essence. This approach is consistent with the principle of neural activity in the brain, as it could activate the memory and imagination in different brains, engaging the brain to explore the information about the essence of the world carried by an artwork through imagination, deduction and hypothesis. Most great artists seem to consciously apply the neuroaesthetic principle of the brain since "uncertainty" is a common characteristic of most outstanding works of art.

As the founder of neuroesthetics, Zeki's innovative attempt to introduce neurobiology into the study of the visual arts has profoundly impacted the development of contemporary research of art. Many of his theoretical ideas have been developed, deepened, or modified by other neuroestheticians. The American neuroscientist Vilayanur Ramachandran, a devoted follower of Zeki, has summarized, by observing the important artistic movements in human history, ten universal aesthetic laws that enable people to get an aesthetic experience, and has tried to explain their cerebral-neural principles [11]. According to Ramachandran's research, one of the critical reasons why artworks can bring the audience an aesthetic experience is that artists can use these aesthetic laws, consciously or unconsciously, to create their work. This does not mean that the importance of cultural diversity and individual subjective differences in the creation and appreciation of art could be excluded. Jean-Pierre Changeux, a leading practitioner and promoter of neuroesthetics in the French region, does not advocate a neurobilogical study of the universal aesthetic laws, since individual subjectivity plays a more critical role in aesthetic experience. He believes that it is more reasonable to define the rules of artistic creation, which artists follow to have their works judged as art. From a neurobiological point of view, the aesthetic laws are imposed on individual by phylogenetic inheritance, while the artistic rules are epigenetic culture defined by society and his history, and acquired by individual during his cognitive ontogeny (biological and mental) in a social environment [3]. Changeux's research on artistic rules takes cultural, social, and historical factors into the analysis of the neuroaesthetic functions of the brain, and also reveals the similarities and differences between artistic and scientific creation from a neuroscientific perspective.

Another group of neuroscientists has proposed more in-depth scientific explorations specifically on emotion, sentiment, intuition and other psychological functions involved in the aesthetic process, which effectively fill in some gaps in Zeki's neuroesthetic theory. For example, biological neuroscientist Alain Berthoz's research on perceptual attention and perceptual judgment has explained how the brain can quickly judge and select a aesthetic targets in complex external environments through the sensory organs [2], thus providing a clearer and deeper scientific clarification of Zeki's theory about "Autonomy of vision". Another example is the research of American neuroscientist Antonio Damasio on the neural process of emotion and the brain's self-awareness, which explains the neurobilogical principles at different stage of aesthetic emotions such as joy, emotion, sentiment and coin the aesthetic process, as well as the complex relation between personal emotion, creative intention and behavioral will in the process of artistic creation [6].

Looking back at the entire history of art theory, neuroesthetics has undoubtedly been revolutionary, and its research findings have created a new space for exploring the nature of beauty and art. However, as with all research methods, neuroesthetics inevitably has disciplinary limitations. What is the disciplinary limitations of neuroesthestics at the levels of epistemology and methodology? Does cognitive sciences offer us more innovative theoretical tools or research approach?

4 Enactionism and New Inspiration for Aesthetic Research

The development of "cognitive aesthetics" has been accompanied by many questions and criticisms from traditional forces. Conservative scholars have expressed strong resistance to and concern about cognitive sciences and the transformation of the literary and artistic theory that it provokes. It is argued that the studies which confine art and spirituality to the realm of natural existence do not truly explain the essence of human nature. The above studies merely deny the superiority of humans in natural biological systems through reductio ad absurdum, and deprive humans of their freedom as dominants by attributing human thought and behavior to natural laws, which therefore belong to anti-humanist. Those critiques are somehow arbitrary and one-sided; however, they also reflect, to some extent, the limitations of natural science research methods in explaining the problems of art and beauty.

Both information aesthetics and neuroaesthetics are fundamentally empirical scientific research approaches from the third-person's perspective. Neuroaesthetics, in particular, is based on the observation of the brain's neural activity in response to certain sensory stimuli, which are derived from specific perceptual objects provided by scientific experiments (e.g., various paintings, Kinect art, etc.). Such aesthetic scientific experiments ensure objectivity in the understanding of beauty. However, they are not real substitutes for the real-life experience because it is impossible to simulate or reproduce all situations and all possible changes that occur in a given life experience through experimental design. Neuroaestheticians are also aware that neuroscientific research methods may not adequately explain the complexity of aesthetic experience. For example, Zeki has explicitly stated, in summarizing his personal research findings, that neuroaestheticians need to consider and take into account the variability, subjectivity, and acquired personal development of the individual aesthetic activity. The theory of Enaction, proposed by Francisco Varela (a neurophysiologist and philosopher of mind) and his colleagues, offers the possibility of breaking the disciplinary limitations of neuroaesthetics.

4.1 Enaction: Cognition as Experience Lived by Embodied Mind

While Connectionism has remained dominant since the 1990s, a new trend of research has emerged in the field of Cognitive Sciences. The famous cognitive scientist George Vignaud mentioned in the early 1990s through observation: "The recent major debates in cognitive research are no longer confined to cognitivism and connectionism, but are future-oriented, involving a series of ongoing research programs that foreshadow a new paradigm that will emerge in the future." [18] (p.330) The theory of Enaction" is the representative of this new development trend. The theory of Enaction, which was born out of the ecology of mind and combined the theories of autopoietic system and genetic evolution, has developed into a new generation of mind research program that acts as a counterweight to Connectionism. Compared with traditional cognitive science, The theory of Enaction introduces "experience", "common sense" and "culture" into the explanatory domain of cognitive sciences, and advocates exploring cognition from the infinite autopoietic properties of the living organism and setting the mind-body problem as the question of transforming a material process into a mental process.

Enaction is originally a model of embodied cognition, in which a core concept is "Autopoiesis". According to Varela and Maturana, Autopoiesis is the property of a system that reproduces itself within itself, through a closed loop between external physical processes that assail it and its own internal organisation. "An autopoietic system is organized as a network of many processes of producing components (a)which continuously regenerates the network that produced them through their transformations and interactions, (b) which constitutes the system as a concrete unit in the space where it exists, specifying the topological domain where it is realised as a network" [15] (p.45). On this basis, Varela and his colleagues proposed the concept of "Enaction", which means "being-action", to clarify the fact that the mind emerges in the continuous self-generating process of the living system. "Enaction" is a summary of the five comprehensions about cognitive system: (1) Organisms are autonomous actors that can actively generate and maintain their own identities and define their own cognitive domains. (2)The nervous system is an autopoietic system whose operations are considered as a closed sensory-motor network of neuronal interactions, thus it actively generates and maintains a coherent pattern of its own activity. (3) Cognitive structures emerge from multiple sensory-motor couplings among the body, the nervous system and the environment. The world of cognitive subject is not a preexisting independent world represented by the human brain, but a network of relations generated by a history of structural coupling between the subject and its environment. (5) Any comprehension of the mind cannot avoid the subjectivity of consciousness and experience, while phenomenology provides a concrete method to explore the experience of human life [14] (pp.13–14).

In the theory of Enaction, Varela critiques the Representationalist view of mind shared by cognitivism and connectionism, thus proposing a third approach between subjective constructivism and objective representationalism by establishing an explanatory loop between experience and scientific analysis. Varela define enaction as "the joint advent of a world and a spirit from the history of the various actions that a being performs in the world". This concept emphasizes that "sensory and motor processes, or perception and action, are fundamentally inseparable in the experience lived." [17] (p.35, 234) This means that cognition is no longer a representation of a given world by a given mind, but a continuous interaction of the embodied cognitive subject (the brain) with its surroundings based on its own "perception-reflection" capacity. In this interaction, the "self" (the cognitive capacity inherent in the individual brain) emerges. Our brain does not simply interpret the world, but influences and changes the surrounding environment in its own way, with a developmental connection between the environment and our own existence. Varela defines this developmental connection as the "cycle structural", in which the "self" (the overall cognitive capacity of the individual brain) and the external world alternately shape each other. In other words, cognition is the activity of life, the process of co-emergence, co-generation, and co-evolution of the subject and the world. The theory of Enaction is both a philosophy and a science of mind. The theory of Enaction provides a theoretical framework for exploring the mysteries of the mind that transcends dualism, through concepts such as life experience, self-emergence, autopoiesis, cycle structure, etc.

4.2 A New Inspiration for Contemporary Art

Varela does not specialize in art and aesthetics, but the theory of mind he proposed has greatly influenced the practice and theory of contemporary digital art. In the field of artistic creation, the theory of Enaction offers a series of new concepts that are highly inspirational and innovative. These concepts open up a new space for artists to think about their creative activities by prompting them to break away from their old-fashioned thinking habits, to conceive new creative themes, and to explore new modes of creation and new forms of work. For example, the "autonomous drawing robot" project conducted by Hungarian new media artist Leonel Moura, and the "virtual tightrope walking acrobat" project conducted by Michel Bret's, are both artistic experimentation which simulate the autopoiesis process based on the "cycle structure" in the context of artificial intelligence art. Another example is Anika Mignottes' project of interactive and immersive auditory environment, which focuses on the co-development and co-emergence between aesthetic subject and object while spectator's consciousness is projected in the surrounding environment.

In the field of art research, the theory of Enaction, with its closely related ecology of the mind, have inspired some innovative theoretical explorations about arts. Some of the most representative ones include Professor Edmond Couchot's theory of "second creator" [4] for interactive art and network art, Alva Noe's theoretical exploration of the dialectical unity between creative and aesthetic activities in artistic experience from the perspective of subject-object co-emergence, and Jean Vion-Dury's reflexion on history of art from the perspective of the co-evolution between the brain and the cognitive environment [19], and Professor Jean-Marie Shaeffer's theory about "transmission and evolution of aesthetic conduits [13]" which is a reflection on the nature of artistic and aesthetic activity from the perspective of the co-development of cognitive system and cognitive environment at the levels of phylogeny and ontogeny.

5 Conclusions

In conclusion, the theory of Enaction has not yet been developed into an independent approach of art research, and relevant research findings are not abundant. Nevertheless, the new paradigm of mind based on this theory has attracted more and more attention in the international art research field. Through concepts such as biological evolution, embodied cognition, and systems of autopoiesis, the theory of Enaction constructs a new epistemological basis to interpret the nature of art which has completely transcended the epistemology of the opposition between material and spirit (i.e. the dualism) through the concepts such as cycle structural, subject-object co-emergence, and so on. It provides a research approach that completely transcends opposition between subjective constructivism and objective representationalism for exploring artistic activities (i.e. creative and aesthetic activities). It further promotes the organic integration of natural sciences and humanities by introducing life experience into the scope of cognitive sciences. Thanks to the above advantages, the theory of enaction will become a new driving force for the reformation of contemporary art theory in the near future.

References

1. Daniel, A.: Introduction aux Science Cognitives. Gallimard, Paris (2004)
2. Alain, B.: La Simplexité. Odile Jacob, Paris (2009)
3. Jean-Pierre, C.: Du vrai, du beau, du bien. Une nouvelle approche neuronale. Odile Jacob, Paris (2008)
4. Edmond, C.: La nature de l'art, ce que les sciences cognitives nous révèlent sur le plaisir esthétique. Hermann, Paris (2012)
5. Edmond, C.: Des images, du temps et de machines dans les arts et la communication. Actes Sud-Chambon, Paris (2007)
6. Antonio, D.: The feeling of what happens, body and emotion in the making of con-sciousness. Brace & Compagny, New York (1999)
7. Umberto, E.: L'oeuvre ouverte. Seuil, Paris (1965)
8. Michel, F.: Les mots et les choses. Gallimard, Paris (1966)
9. Marc, J.: La nature de l'esprit. Odile Jacob, Paris (2002)
10. Abraham, M.: Perception esthétique et théorie de l'information. Flammarion, Paris (1958)
11. Ramachandran, V.: The Emerging Mind. Profile Books, USA (2003)
12. Schaeffer, J.: Comment naturaliser l'esthétique et pourquoi?. In: Grand dictionnaire de la philoshophie, Larouse, Paris (2003)
13. Schaeffer, J.: Théorie des signaux coûteux, esthétique et art. Tangence éditeur, Université du Québec (2009)
14. Thompson, E.: Mind in Life: Biology, Phenomenology, and the Sciences of Mind. The Belknap Press of Harvard University Press, Cambridge MA (2007)
15. Varela, F.: Autonomie et connaissance-Essai sur le viviant. Seuil, Paris (1989)
16. Varela, F.: Invitation aux sciences cognitives. Editions du Seuil, Paris (1996)
17. Varela, F., Thompson, E., Rosch, E.: The Embodied Mind: Science and Human Experience. The MIT Press, Cambridge (1992)
18. Vignaud, G.: Les sciences cognitives, une introduction. La Découverte, Paris, p. 330 (1992)
19. Vion-Dury, J.: Art, histoire de l'art et cognition ou l'échec du reductionnisme en neuroscience cognitives. In: Bret, J.N., Guerin, M., Jimenez, M. (eds.) Penser l'Art: histoire de l'art et esthétique. Editions Klincksieck, Paris (2009)
20. Ze, Y.: La Nouvelle Esthétique de l'Encre. Éditions Universitaires Européennes, Paris, pp. 86–101 (2016)
21. Zeki, S., Watson, J.D., Lueck, C.J.: A direct demonstration of functional specialiszation in human visual cortex. J. Neurosci. 11(3), 641–649 (1991)
22. Zeki, S.: A Vision of the Brain. Oxford University Press, New York (1993)
23. Zeki, S., Lambert, M.: The neurology of kinetic art. Revue Brain 117(3), 607–636 (1994)
24. Ziki, S.: Inner Vision: An Exploration of Art and the Brain. Oxford University Press, New York (1999)

Research on the Board-Game-Like Service Design Tools Based on SECI Knowledge Transformation Model: Take the Customer Journey Map as an Example

Ying Zhao, Xiong Ding[(✉)], and Shan Liu

Guangzhou Academy of Fine Arts, Guangzhou 510006, China
dingxiong@gzarts.edu.cn

Abstract. With the popularity of the new methodology of service design thinking, graphic service design tools, such as Customer Journey Map, Persona, Story Board, DVF Screening Map etc., began to attract the attention of non-design background participants, and gradually developed into pain point insight, inspiration bursting and concept scheme expression tools. In the co-design workshop, due to the professionalism and complexity of these tools, co-creators without design background cannot participate in the discussion efficiently. Based on SECI Knowledge Transformation Model and Game Theory, this paper explores the concept and role of graphic service design tools, as well as their core tasks and usage in different design processes. By building board game tool products and related service systems, it helps participants without design background effectively understand design tasks, quickly stimulate design inspiration, and produce creative solutions in co-design workshops. Take the Customer Journey Map as an example, redesign the representation of the tool itself and create a new ways of participation, so as to improve the process and efficiency of the workshop.

Keywords: Service Design · Graphic Service Design Tool · Customer Journey Map · Co-design Workshop · SECI Knowledge Transformation Model · Game Theory

1 Service Design Thinking

In the 1980s, service design began to receive attention from management field. G. Lynn Shostak first proposed the concept of service design at management and marketing level, and proposed the service blueprint, one of graphic tools, as a widely used service design method [1]; then Stephen J. Grove and Raymond P. Fisk proposed "service design theater model" [2], which provided a research model for service design and a visual and vivid interpretation of factors affecting service design. In the mid-1990s, IBM raised an idea of "service science", and advocated the interdisciplinary system of "service science, management and engineering" (SSME), combining service management, service marketing, and service engineering into a wider system to solve complex problems in service economy. *The Experience Economy*, published in 1999, mentioned that service design provides new ideas for economic growth's engine [3]. With the introduction of design studies, and the maturity of service design research as well as development, many related representative works have been published, such as Satu Miettinen's (2009) *Designing Services with Innovative Methods*; Sren Bechmann's (2010) *Service Design*; Mairi Macintyre (2011) et al.'s *Service Design and Delivery*; Marc Stickdorn (2012) et al.'s *This is Service Design Thinking*; Andy Polaine (2014) et al.'s *Service Design: from Insight to Implementation*, etc. Xin Xiangyang and Cao Jianzhong pointed out that service design has received greater attention in recent ten years and has been largely influenced by the service marketing concept, which distinguishes products from services [4]. The related theoretical models, concepts and methods of service design, especially the features of services like immaterial, heterogeneous, indivisible and perishable (IHIP for short) [5], are being accepted by more and more designers.

With the popularity of service design-- an emerging concept and method, graphic service design tools have gradually gained attention. In *Service Design: Definition-Language-Tools*, Chen Jiajia pointed out that consulting firms usually consider user portraits and customer journey maps as important tools in the pre-study stage and user survey stage [6]. Ding Xiong and Zhu Zhe discussed the inter-professional and cross-disciplinary application of service design tools from the perspective of psychology, revealing the importance of tools for service innovation through cases [7]. Liu Xiaowen studied service design-related tools from the perspective of visual communication and advocated cross-field thinking [8]. Jiang Ying found that service system map could not guide participants from all walks of life to engage in the related co-design activities based on the research of concept expression tools in service design. Jiang also proposed to build a 3D desktop model to display the complete service process and improve coordination efficiency [9]. The above studies show that, besides professional service designers, non-professional participants such as marketing and PD staff in the company, users in the co-design workshop, and servants, decision-makers, suppliers in the front-line, also pay attention to and use graphic service design tools.

2   Overview of Graphic Service Design Tools

Double Diamond Process can display the whole design process of the project. It can help designers visualize the whole design process in a clarified way. Thus, it is always applied in the co-design workshop for brainstorming and quick deduction. The whole process can be divided into four stages: discover, define, develop and deliver, including two diverging ad converging stages. Each stage has its corresponding graphic service design tool, shown in Fig. 1. The typical tools are Customer Journey Map, Persona, DVF Screening Map and Story Board.

Customer Journey Map takes the perspective of users and illustrates the process of using products or receiving services through a narrative and visualized way [10]. It can identify all sorts of pain points, cool points and opportunities along the journey of users through multiple perspectives, thus solving related problems in a more targeted way. A qualified Customer Journey Map should clearly reflect the following questions: What is the basic situation of users? What does the user's behavioral journey look like? How

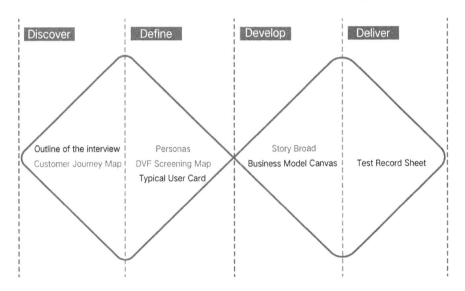

Fig. 1. The corresponding graphic service design tools in different stages of Double Diamond

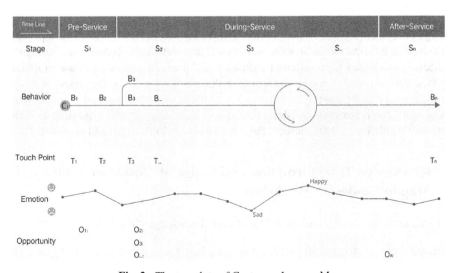

Fig. 2. The template of Customer Journey Map

users' emotions will fluctuate in certain stages? What opportunity points can be brought to service designers? In other words, it can clarify user roles, define user needs, define service touch points, describe the interaction process between users and touch points, and connecting them into an experience journey. Customer Journey Map is usually a linear process, but can also be presented as loop, etc., and can be presented in a rich variety of expressions depending on the actual project. Figure 2 shows a more commonly-used template.

Persona is a visual representation based on user's perception and is an abstract summary of user's behaviors [11]. It can reflect user's behavioral habits and characteristics [12]. There are various ways to create user profiles, such as Alen Cooper's "seven-step persona approach" and Lene Nielsen's "ten-step persona approach". Labeled and systematic persona can help teams efficiently target users and quickly capture their needs. First invented by Walt Disney in the 1830s, story boards show the detailed process of events through a series of pictures, such as service scenarios and service prototypes. With the help of specific scenario descriptions, story atmosphere can be created and emotional resonance can be triggered, leading to more specific and convincing user needs. DVF filter maps are usually used in the middle and later stages of service innovation. The main function is to discover real and suitable ideas among many concepts. The filtering dimensions are user, technology and business [13]. Among them, user agreeability is used to assess whether the product or service meets user needs and expectations. Operational or technical feasibility is used to assess whether the product or service can be implemented. Commercial feasibility is used to comprehensively assess the rationality of the business model, especially to determine the value and benefits created by the product or service for the users from the value proposition perspective.

From the above study of tool's concepts and roles, it is easy to see that a range of information and knowledge is presented within these four typical graphic service design tools. Meanwhile, these tools are not only used repeatedly in the process of service innovation, but are also favored by companies and design organizations in participatory design processes (e.g., co-design workshops). In fact, co-design workshop is a process to exchange information, achieve consensus and accumulate the knowledge. During the process, participants from different industries and professionals need to use graphical service design tools to present information that cannot be easily expressed in words or expressed clearly enough. However, due to the professionalism and complexity of these tools, co-creators without design background are often unable to participate in the discussion efficiently, which affects the achievement of knowledge and consensus.

3 Knowledge Transformation and Usage of Customer Journey Map in Co-design Workshop

3.1 Knowledge Transformation Model and Knowledge Creation

Michael Polanyi divides knowledge into "explicit knowledge" and "tacit (implicit) knowledge". He considers the former as knowledge that can be described by words, formulas, and diagrams and can be expressed in a systematic and standardized way; while, the latter one refers to knowledge that cannot be adequately expressed by language, words, or symbols [14]. Based on Polanyi's division of knowledge, Ikujiro Nonaka et al. clearly classify knowledge into explicit knowledge that "can be shared through formal language or media" and empirical and bodily tacit knowledge that "is known internally but cannot be interpreted into language". The key to knowledge creation is the mobilization and transformation of tacit knowledge. Ikujiro Nonaka and Hirotaka Takeuchi constructed SECI (Socialization, Externalization, Combination, and Internalization) model of knowledge transformation, which reveals the organizational paradigm to create new knowledge through knowledge interaction [15]. The model consists of four stages and models, a) Socialization: from implicit to implicit knowledge; b) Externalization: from implicit to explicit knowledge; c) Combination: from explicit to explicit knowledge; and d) Internalization: from explicit to implicit knowledge. The content of knowledge created at each stage varies. Socialization model refers to the process of sharing experiences and creating implicit knowledge in a public by emphasizing the observation of reality from inside and outside the organization, putting oneself in the shoes of the person and actively engaging with God at the same time, thus generating empathetic knowledge. Externalization model is a process of concept formation and a generalization of the essence and discovery. Inspired by dialogue and reflection, it is about generating conceptual knowledge by using metaphors, analogies or models to externalize tacit knowledge. Combination model is the process of connecting and systematizing various concepts and making them into a knowledge system. This involves the combination of different explicit knowledge and produces systematic knowledge. Internalization model, on the other hand, generates operational knowledge about project management, production processes, new product use, and policy implementation, which reinforce with each other in the knowledge creation spiral [16], as shown in Fig. 3.

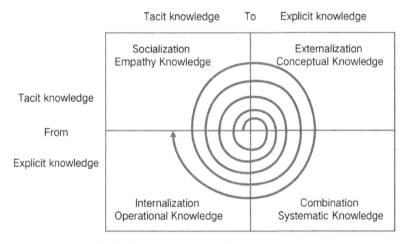

Fig. 3. The spiral process of knowledge creation

3.2 The Using Situation and Problems of Customer Journey Map in Co-design Workshop

Based on years of practice, the author believes that the evolution process of co-design workshop is basically the same as knowledge transformation. The customer journey map is the longest and most frequently-used tool in the whole co-design workshop, and it is also the most difficult tool to use among the four tools. This, to some extent, determines the smooth operation of the workshop. Therefore, the following research and design optimization will focus on the Customer Journey Map tool.

In a co-design workshop, Customer Journey Map can bring stakeholders together in a service or a service system to jointly innovate a product or service through brainstorming and discussions, and to assess the possibilities, constraints, and resources available for each touch-point. To better understand the use of Customer Journey Map, the author participated in a co-design workshop organized by Mars Wrigley and Chimian Company with the purpose in mind, and focused on observing and recording the using situations of participants, as shown in Fig. 4. 27 co-creators participated in this workshop, five of whom were students with design backgrounds and the other 22 participants were not. The workshop was conducted by two facilitators with three assistants, who will help with venue setup, material preparation, prop distribution, and timing. All four tools mentioned in the previous section were used throughout the workshop, and the most time was spent on the use of the Customer Journey Map.

Fig. 4. The site of Co-design workshop

Based on the observation and past experiences, the journey of the workshop participants using the Customer Journey Map is shown in Fig. 5 for better gaining insight into the opportunities of tools innovation. The figure clearly shows the participants' experience of using the Customer Journey Map during the workshop, including their behaviors, touch points, emotions, and pain points. In the co-design workshops, there were two types of people using Customer Journey Map: staff who provided guidance to facilitate the workshop (facilitators and assistants with service design background) and participants with non-design background, and the latter is the focus of this study. Following the order of pre-use, during the use, and after use, the behaviors of participants without design background using the Customer Journey Map are as follows: a) Learning the concept and usage of tool; b) Interview users for the first time, record user's behaviors; c) Sort out the journey stages; d) Write user needs and behaviors on sticky notes and post them at the corresponding sites on the journey map; e) Exemplifying the touch points used by users at each stage (in physical, digital, and interpersonal types) and post them at the corresponding sites on the journey map; f) Write down user's pain and cool points on sticky notes and post them at the corresponding sites on the journey map; g) Interview users for the second time, repeat steps d to f, add information to improve and optimize user journey; h) Use curves to reflect user's mood fluctuations at each stage; i) Gain insight into optimization and design opportunities. Based on the analysis of participants' journey of using Customer Journey Map and interviews, it is quite clear to see that emotion lows (helplessness, anxiety, and frustration) of participants without design background mainly appeared in the stages such as exemplifying user behavior, pain and cool points and brainstorming which required thinking. This leads to a fact of inefficient output of conceptual solutions and opportunities insight. The reasons can be concluded as follows: difficult to understand tools, do not know how to express, tools are boring and cannot trigger detailed recall and description. The emotion lows (repetitive work) of on-site staff is mainly concentrated in the tools preparation at early stage, explaining tools to co-creators repeatedly in the middle stage and gathering things in the late stage.

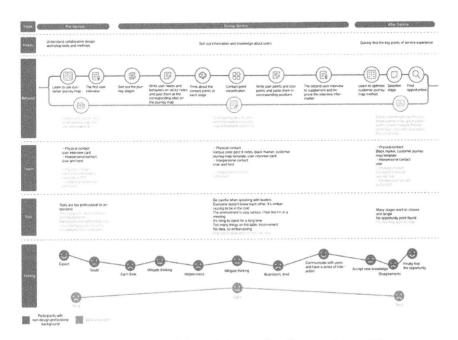

Fig. 5. Journey map of the participants using Customer Journey Map

4 Board-Game-Like Graphic Services Design Tool and Its System Design: Take the Customer Journey Map as an Example

As mentioned above, the only way to efficiently understand the design task and inspire design is to promote the understanding of tools by participants without design background in the collaboration. Therefore, the author will try to realize this goal by designing a product solution of Customer Journey Map tool based on the SECI knowledge transformation model.

4.1 Design Strategy: Board-game-like

"Gamification" was first coined by Nick Pelling in 2002, and started to attract public attention in 2010. By using game design thinking and mechanism [17], game elements and game design techniques in non-game contexts, greater commercial value can be created. Gamification involves three concepts: game elements, game design techniques, and non-game contexts. a) Game elements. Game is a comprehensive and holistic experience that consists of many small organic parts, which are game elements. b) Game design techniques. The use of game design techniques mainly addresses questions of how to decide which game elements can be used in certain places and how to make the whole gamified experience greater than the sum of the elements. Good game design techniques make the whole gamification more fun, more addictive, and more challenging. c) Non-game context. *The New Power of Gamification Thinking to Change the Future of Business* divides the use and practice of gamification in non-game contexts into three types: internal gamification, external gamification, and behavior change gamification. If players do not want to enter another virtual world though related products, the purpose of gamification is more about deeply involved in the product, business or transaction [18]. For a 2D graphic service design tool, gamification-style strategy can be used to optimize the productization which can add interesting elements to graphs. This is more user-friendly and more easy to understand for non-designer participants. The combination of gamification and productization is called as Board-game-like.

4.2 Design Thinking Based on SECI Knowledge Transformation Model

Based on Ikujiro Nonaka's SECI knowledge transformation model, the first is socialization. Co-design workshop adopts a tool in the form of board games, which makes it easier for participants to immerse in their roles, actively express and listen, then generate empathetic knowledge. The second is externalization. By writing cards, participants can externalize the knowledge and generate conceptual knowledge through classification. The third is combination, in which the knowledge is combined and formed into a system through the details of the whole journey presented by participants. The fourth is internalization, where systematic knowledge is materialized into new operational knowledge, that is, the specific conceptual solutions produced in the workshop, which are then shared through socialization and then form a starting point of new knowledge cycle. The transformation of knowledge in this way can be described as a spiral, as in Fig. 6, where each circle goes through the four transformations mentioned above.

4.3 System Building of Board-Game-Like Graphic Service Design Tool

In the era of service and experience economy, user-centered design approaches can no longer fully respond to the scale and complexity of challenges facing the design industry. In service design processes, people begin to experiment with the practice of bringing users and stakeholders together in the innovation process through co-design workshops. The co-design workshops consist of participants from design professionals, who are typically service designers, and participants who do not have design background, including service recipients, service providers, and project researchers and other stakeholders [19], as well as external suppliers of products (tools, props, materials), venues, etc.

The service system diagram provides a clear picture of multiple stakeholders in the system and the interactive behaviors and structure between each stakeholder or element. The system mainly provides board-game-like service design tools related to the themes for participants with design background (universities and companies) and those

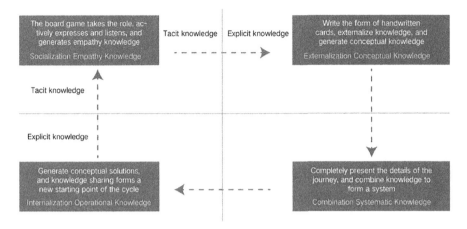

Fig. 6. Knowledge transformation process in co-design workshop

without. These tools will be used for coordination and co-creation. As for products, the system provides a series of board game products for workshops; and for services, the system provides services such as rental, accessory replacement and workshop process organization, as shown in Fig. 7.

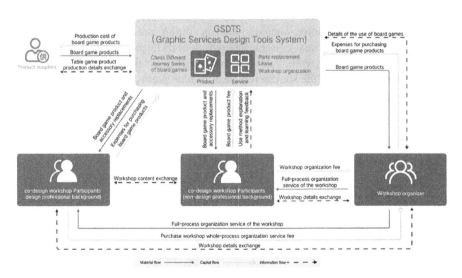

Fig. 7. System Map of GSDTS (Graphic Services Design Tools System)

4.4 Design of the Board Game "Chess Journey" and Prototype Test

The most commonly-used framework in game design is the "Mechanism-Dynamics-Experience (MDA)" framework, which are independent of each other and interconnected. Mechanism is the rule of game system, dynamics refers to the dynamic interaction between players and the game system, and experience refers to the feelings generated by players when they play the game [21]. Generally speaking, the framework of a board game can be built from two aspects, one is the game mechanism, such as inventing a component based on a certain inspiration; the other starts from game background and story perspective, and find an integrated mechanism to support each other [22]. The second approach will be adopted in the design of this board game Customer Journey Map product.

The Customer Journey Map shows a user's journey, that is, a story, and the story is set as the context of a board game, "Chess Journey". It is a board game that combines blocks and sandboxes to help participants complete the customer journey map in a fun and easy way during the co-design workshop. Different scenarios can be used to create different co-design themes, such as Hot Pot Adventure, Candy Battle, Small Town Adventure, etc. This article focuses on the Food Tycoon-themed board game design, with its overall effect shown in Fig. 8. The main body of the product is made of acrylic and consists of straight line track, corner line track, handwritten cards, scenario cards, different color bases, chess boards and other accessories. The specific guidance and steps are shown in Fig. 9: a) Connect the straight and corner tracks to create a dining story line; b) Set up scenario cards at several nodes of the story line as needed and build important scenarios in the journey, including stores, queuing, ordering, dining and paying the bill; (c) Write important pain and cool points (erasable and reusable) on the handwritten cards, such as long queuing time, slow serving, good dishes etc.; (d) Insert the handwritten cards into corresponding bases, with the shorter red base for pain points and the taller green base for pleasure points; (e) Place the pain and cool points in the corresponding scenarios on the story line, and gradually improve them to form a clear emotion line with ups and downs; f) Use sticky notes to add other information, such as secondary pain points or cool points, touch points, etc., to form a complete dining story and journey.

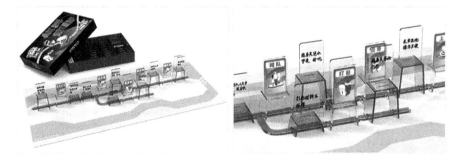

Fig. 8. Design renderings of "Chess Journey: Food Tycoon"

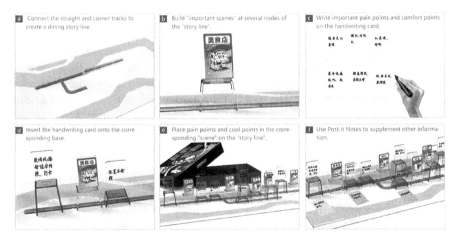

Fig. 9. Play guidance of "Chess Journey: Food Tycoon"

After completing the conceptual design, a prototype of the Chess Journey board game was created. A small co-design workshop was organized for another time, inviting participants without design background to have tests and interviews in order to test the feasibility of the product. The results of which are shown in Fig. 10, indicting that compared with the traditional customer journey map, a more vivid "Food Tycoon" board game used by participants without design background is much easier to understand, more immersive during the user behavior analysis, journey sorting, pain points digging and directions output, leading to a more specific and vivid thinking in a more efficient manner. The atmosphere of the game counteracts the boredom, tension, powerlessness and frustration of participants without design background, thus improving their workshop experience. In addition, the modular and set-based accessories and overall design make it easy for staff to organize, store and reuse products, in line with the sustainability concept.

Fig. 10. Prototype test of "Chess Journey: Food Tycoon"

5 Conclusion

This paper draws on the transformation of tacit knowledge and explicit knowledge in the SECI knowledge transformation model, and introduces gamification theory to build a board-game-like service design tool, a product and service system, including board games such as Chess Journey. The tool can replace the four commonly-used graphic service design tools in traditional workshops, namely Customer Journey Map, Persona, Story Board and DVF Screening Map. The service can be completed by product purchasing, product rental or customization in coordinated workshop, providing a brand-new, interesting and cost-effective participation way. In addition, it provides an effective, efficient and attractive organizing method for organizing owners and their staff members. Currently, the research is in the conceptual design and prototype testing stage, and positive feedback has been obtained. The final efficacy and effectiveness of the product service system still depends on the in-depth design of subsequent products, usability evaluation and full-scale design iteration.

References

1. Kimbell, L.: Designing for service as one way of designing services. Int. j. Des. **5**(2), 41–52 (2011)
2. Grove, S.J., Fisk, R.P.: The Dramaturgy of Service Exchange: An Analytical Framework for Services Marketing. American Marketing Association, Chicago (1983)
3. Pine, B.J., Gilmore, J.H.: The Experience Economy: Work is Theater & Every Business a Stage. Harvard Business School Press, Boston (1999)
4. Xiangyang, X., Jianzhong, C.: Location-based service design. J. Packaging Eng. **39**(18), 43–49 (2018)
5. Zeithaml, V.A., Parasuraman, A., Berry, L.L.: Problems and Strategies in Services Marketing. J. Mark. **49**(2), 33–46 (1985)
6. Jiajia, C.: Service Design: Definition. Language and Tools. Jiangsu Phoenix Art Press, Nanjing (2016)
7. Xiong, D., Zhe, Z.: Application analysis of service design tools from the perspective of psychology. Design **33**(13), 66–69 (2020)
8. Xiaowen, L.: On the Research of Service Design in the Field of Visual Communication. Shenyang Jianzhu University, Shenyang (2016)
9. Ying, J.: Research on Design and Application Strategy of Collaborative System Diagram Tool for Service Design. Jiangnan University, Wuxi (2018)
10. Lvting, S., Yan, L., Annan, L.: Research on service design optimization of fast fashion brand based on user journey map. Fashion Designer **12**, 116–125 (2021)
11. Cooper, A.: The Inmates are Running the Asylum: Why High-Tech Products Drive UsCrazy and How to Restore the Sanity. Sams Publishing (2004)
12. Zishu, Z.: Research on User Portrait of Virtual Tourism Community Based on Ontology. Jilin University, Jilin (2020)
13. Wei, H.: Service Design: Win Users' Following with the Ultimate Experience. Machinery Industry Press, BeiJing (2021)
14. Michael, P., Zemin, X.: Personal Knowledge Moves towards Post-Critical Philosophy. Guizhou People's Publishing House, Guiyang (2000)
15. Qinhai, W.: Yujiro Noaka's "knowledge creation." Bus. Manag. **05**, 18–21 (2017)

16. Ikujiroi, N.: By Takeuchi Honggao., Translated by Qinhai, W.: Enterprises that create knowledge. shipping broke, Beijing (2019)
17. Xiao, C.: Gamification practice of tool products. Industrial Design Research (Part III), 130–133 (2015)
18. Kevin, W., Hunt, D., Kei, Z., Xiaodan, W.: Game-Based Thinking Changes the New Power of Future Business. Zhejiang People Publishing House, Hangzhou (2014)
19. Haijing, Z.: Research on Collaborative Design Method. Guangdong University of Technology, Guangzhou (2021)
20. Tukker, A.: Eight types of product-service system: eight ways to sustainability? experiences from SusProNet. Bus. Strateg. Environ. **13**(4), 246–260 (2004)
21. Jiamin, Z., Xin, W., Yuchen, P.: Construction of scientific desktop game design framework. Sci. Educ. Museum **8**(02), 67–77 (2022)
22. Mike, S., Borui, L.: Project Team: Board Game Design Guide. Sichuan Fine Arts Publishing House, Chengdu (2017)

User Experience Design and Brand Marketing Research in China: A Bibliometric Analysis

Yuhong Zheng[1], Zhichao Liu[1(✉)], Zhiwei Zhou[1], and Zhen Liu[2]

[1] Management School, Guangzhou City University of Technology, Guangzhou 510800, China
liuzc@gcu.edu.cn
[2] School of Design, South China University of Technology, Guangzhou 510006, China

Abstract. With the continuous development of China's social and economic development, the rising production and supply capacity, and the competition between enterprises continues to intensify, corporate marketing activities pay more and more attention to the role of consumer participation. At the same time, 'how to create a strong brand' has also become one of the most hotly debated topics among enterprises today. Currently, the experience economy is on the rise globally, and the role of user experience in brand marketing is being paid more and more attention. Although China scholars have repeatedly researched in this field, yet few research have yet further sorted out the association between user experience and brand marketing, and summarized and analyzed them through knowledge mapping tools in China. Therefore, this paper selects journal articles included in China Knowledge Network (CNKI) since the starting year of user experience and brand association research from year 2006 to October 2022 as the research objects via scientific bibliometric methods, and uses CiteSpace visual literature analysis software for comprehensive analysis. The results show that: 1) domestic research on user experience and brand started in year 2006; 2) the keyword co-occurrence analysis based on knowledge graph indicates that the research mainly focuses on user experience, consumer and brand, consumer, and brand image; and 3) the knowledge maps suggest that the research on the connection between experience design and brand marketing is relatively scattered, with low cooperation density, and no large disciplinary team has been formed yet.

Keywords: User experience · Design · Brand Marketing · China · Knowledge Map · Bibliometric Analysis

1 Introduction

The futurist Toffler wrote in "The Impact of the Future" in the 1970s that the total history of human economic development for thousands of years would be expressed in three stages: the era of product economy (including the pre-product economy and the post-product economy), the era of service economy and the era of experience economy. With the development of China's economy, the era of product economy or service economy has come to an end, and the era of experience economy, which integrates the two-way degrees of product economy and service economy, has gradually emerged. Liu et al.

propose that the experience economy is a customer-centered economy, which reflects that human consumption behavior and consumption psychology are entering a new advanced form [1]. It reflects that human consumption behavior and consumer psychology are entering a new advanced form. Therefore, user experience, as the most important link in the experience economy, has become a hot spot for research and attention in various industries.

The experience economy is essentially a feeling that consumers will recall, and a strong brand is the one that brings this feeling to consumers, a feeling that will deepen and enrich the relationship between the brand and the consumer [2]. This feeling will deepen and enrich the relationship between the brand and the consumer. Establishing a theoretical system based on user experience thinking and reshaping the relationship between brands and consumers with experience thinking can provide more innovative ideas for enterprises to build strong brands [3]. This study explores the development of user experience in the field of brand marketing and grasp the research trend, which will help subsequent scholars to conduct continuous and innovative research in this field.

2 Methods

2.1 Data Source

In this paper, a literature search has been conducted using the China Knowledge Network (CNKI) academic journal database as the data source, with the theme = 'user experience' including 'brand', and the time span has been set for all years. In order to make the results of the literature sample more scientific, a literature search with "theme = 'user experience' and 'brand' and time span of all years" has been used, and all the search results in the academic journal database were selected for this study, and the search date was October 25, 2022. The data were pre-processed by CiteSpace, and 888 valid documents/articles were obtained as the research sample.

2.2 Research Methodology

This paper uses CiteSpace software to analyze annual publication volume, authors and institutions, keyword co-occurrence, clustering, and emergent words to draw a knowledge map of research on user experience in brand marketing, to explore the hotspots and development trends of experience in brand marketing research from the perspective of user experience, and to provide clearer ideas for the subsequent research of scholars in this field.

3 Results and Analysis

3.1 Bibliometric Analysis

Analysis of the Distribution of the Number of Literature. The number of articles published in the academic research field and the time of publication are the criteria to judge the research hotness of the field. The number of articles related to user experience and branding over the years reflects the theoretical level and development speed of brand marketing research in user experience. In this paper, a total of 888 articles from journals in CNKI with the subject term "user experience" and "brand" have been analyzed, in which the research on "user experience" and "brand" in China is very important. As shown in Fig. 1 the number of publications increased from year 2006 to 2010, with no more than 10 articles per year. However, the number of articles peaked at 121 in year 2017, and then decreased to 48 in year 2022. The reason could be the economic development of China. Since the 18th Party Congress, China's economic strength has made a historic leap, the service industry has accounted for half of the national economy, and consumption has become the main driver of economic growth.

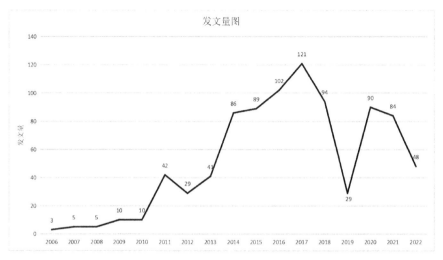

Fig. 1. The number of published articles in the China Knowledge Network (CNKI) from year 2006 to 2022.

A Rough Overview of the Distribution of Literature Subject Areas. By analyzing the distribution of literature by discipline, the distribution of research themes in each discipline can be found out. Since CNKI can only supply the uncensored literature data, this paper takes a cursory look at the retrieved documents and finds that the distribution of research disciplines on the theme of "user experience" with "branding" is mainly concentrated in economics, trade, industry, media, information and other fields through graphical representation. The distribution of research disciplines on the theme of "user experience" and "branding" is mainly concentrated in economics, which involves many fields such as enterprise, trade, industry, media, and information. The distribution of the main subject areas is shown in Fig. 2. It can be found that the top one in terms of the number of articles published is enterprise economy with 18.39% (233 articles), followed by trade economy and industrial economy with 16.73% (212 articles) each, of which the sum of the three accounts for more than 50%. The fourth is News and Media (9.23%), followed by Industrial General Technology and Equipment (5.29%).

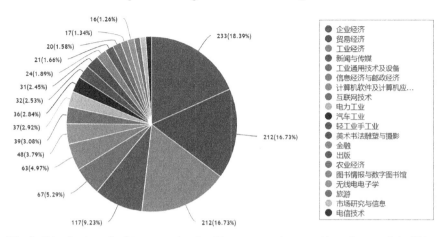

Fig. 2. Distribution of subject areas involved in user experience and brand research in China.

Statistical Analysis of Literature Journals. By analyzing the distribution of the number of published journals, the degree of attention of core journals in this field to the topics related to user experience and branding can be revealed. Through the visual analysis of CNKI, as shown in Fig. 3, the journal with the most publications on the topic of "user experience" and "branding" between year 2006 and 2022 is Design, with a total of 38 publications, which indicates that Design is the most focused in this field. The second highest is Packaging Engineering (32 articles), followed by Sound and Screen World (18 articles), Household Appliances (17 articles), and Journal of News Research (15 articles).

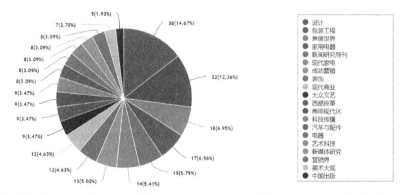

Fig. 3. Distribution of journal publications on the topic of "user experience" with "branding" from year 2006 to 2022.

3.2 Analysis of Core Authors and iInstitutions

Core Author Visualization Mapping. In this paper, authors of 888 selected papers have been analyzed by CiteSpace software. The top 10 authors in terms of the number of articles on the topic of user experience and brand association from year 2006 to October 2022 are shown in Fig. 4, which include Linghao Zhang, Zhaolong Liu, Rui Zhou, Rui Min Zhang, Chen Yang, Ting Wang, Tianping Liu, Yuan Wang, Cheng Jianxin, and Yiqi Wu.

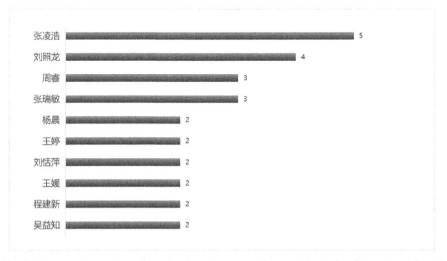

Fig. 4. Ranking the number of publications by core authors on the topic of "user experience" with "branding" from year 2006 to 2022.

Using CiteSpace visual analysis software, the author collaboration knowledge map of research in the field from year 2006 to 2022 was obtained (Fig. 5). As shown in Fig. 5, a total of 413 nodes and 97 links are formed, of which each node represents the corresponding author, and each link represents the collaboration relationship between authors, and the thicker the link, the closer the author collaboration.

The author collaboration network is relatively thin, with most of the researchers in a scattered state, and the collaboration team is dominated by two-person collaborations, including the collaboration between Linghao Zhang and Qiying Zhu, Weiting Zhou and Xie Yuan, Yiqi Wu and Gang Lin, and Zishun Su and Jianxin Cheng. In year 2022, Jiajia Zhang, Yaxin Wu, and Chunmeng Weng formed a three-person collaboration team. Therefore, there is an urgent need to accelerate the formation of a stable core group of authors in this field.

Visual Mapping of Research Institutions. CiteSpace software was used to analyze the co-occurrence of cooperative institutions on the topic of user experience and branding since year 2006, and the visualization mapping of research institutions on the topic of user experience and branding was derived as shown in Fig. 6. A total of 278 nodes and

Fig. 5. Collaboration map of core authors of user experience and branding research in China.

33 links were formed in which each node represents the corresponding institution, the node size indicates the number of articles issued by that research institution, and each link represents the cooperative relationship between institutions, and the thicker the link, the closer the institutions cooperate.

The mapping reveals that the research institutions have less mutual cooperation and less close cooperation, mostly in a scattered distribution. Sorted by the number of articles issued by institutions, as shown in Table 1 the first echelon is Jiangnan University, with the number of articles issued up to 20. The second echelon is South China University of Technology, East China University of Science and Technology, Beijing Printing Institute, and Communication University of China, with the number of articles between 7 and 9. The third echelon is Zhongshan University, Shanghai University of Engineering and Technology, Shanghai University of Technology, Zhejiang University, Nanjing University of Technology, Central University of Finance and Economics, Tsinghua University School of Fine Arts, with the number of articles between 3 and 6.

3.3 Hot Keyword Analysis

Keyword Co-occurrence Mapping Analysis. The keyword co-occurrence mapping analysis through CiteSpace is shown in Fig. 7, which shows that there are 460 nodes and 747 links in the keyword co-occurrence mapping of research related to "user experience" and "brand", with an overall network density of 0.0071. The keywords represent the core topics and research fields of the literature, and the keywords that appear frequently in the literature can be regarded as the research hotspots in this field [4]. Through the mapping, it is found that keywords such as user experience, consumer, brand image, brand, new media, interaction design, product design, experience design, service design, brand marketing, marketing strategy, packaging design, new retail, brand design, and

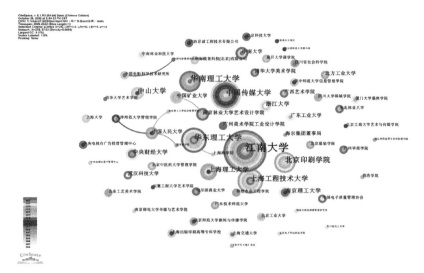

Fig. 6. Collaboration map of research institutions on the theme of "user experience" and "branding" in China.

mobile, appear more frequently; the link network between keywords is dense, which indicates a higher degree of association between keywords and stronger related research. In addition, it can be seen from the chart that the subjects involved in this theme research include smart phones, home appliance brands, smart home, ecological brands, libraries, and agricultural products.

The centrality of keywords is mainly used to measure the importance of nodes in the keyword co-occurrence network graph. Usually, the centrality of a keyword is greater than or equal to 0.1, which means that the keyword has high centrality and has significant influence in the keyword co-occurrence network graph [5]. The centrality value of the keyword is greater than or equal to 0.1. Table 2 shows that the centrality values are greater than or equal to 0.1 for user experience, consumer and interaction design.

The keyword co-occurrence chart and the frequency and centrality statistics show that user experience has the highest frequency and the highest centrality in the keyword co-occurrence, and is the most densely connected with other keywords. Second, "consumer" and "interaction design" have both high frequency and high centrality, highlighting the core research themes in the field from year 2006 to 2022.

Keyword Clustering Mapping Analysis. CiteSpace provides four label extraction algorithms for the extraction of clustering labels, and in a comprehensive view, the labels extracted by clustering using the LLR algorithm are more realistic and less repetitive. Therefore, this paper uses LLR algorithm to cluster the sample literature and filter out the top 12 clusters to obtain the keyword clustering profile as shown in Fig. 8, where the modularity clustering module value (Q value) is equal to 0.7175, and it is generally considered that Q > 0.3 means that the clustering structure is significant, and the average profile value (S value) of Silhouette clustering is equal to 0.9409, it is generally

Table 1. Core research institutions on the topic of "user experience" and "branding" in China

Serial number	Frequency	Institution	Serial number	Frequency	Institution
1	20	Jiangnan University	7	6	Shanghai University of Engineering and Technology
2	9	South China University of Technology	8	5	Shanghai University of Technology
3	8	East China University of Science and Technology	9	4	Zhejiang University
4	7	Beijing Printing Institute	10	4	Nanjing University of Science and Technology
5	7	Communication University of China	11	4	Central University of Finance and Economics
6	6	Sun Yat-sen University	12	3	Academy of Fine Arts, Tsinghua University

considered that S > 0.5 clustering is reasonable and S > 0.7 implies that the clustering is convincing.

As shown in Fig. 8, the top 12 issues of keywords for research hotspots related to user experience and branding in China from year 2006 to 2022 focus on user experience, consumers, new media, service design, branding, big data, product design, experience, Internet of Things, smartphone, brand image, and marketing strategy.

Keyword Emergent Mapping Analysis. Mutation words are mainly based on keywords, and the emergence of specialized terms in the literature published in a certain time span also reflects the research hotspots in that time period, mainly in terms of the chronological distribution of mutation words and the intensity of mutation [6]. The main aspects are the chronological distribution and the intensity of mutation. In this paper, emergent words have been analyzed for the research sample literature, set the Minimum Duration to 1 year and $\gamma = 0.7$, and conduct visual analysis to obtain the keyword emergence map (see Fig. 9).

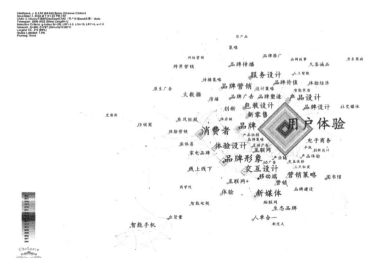

Fig. 7. Keyword co-occurrence mapping of "user experience" and "brand" themes in China.

Table 2. High-frequency keywords, word frequency and centrality statistics of "user experience" and "brand" in China.

Serial number	Keyword Frequency			Serial number	Keyword Centrality		
	Frequency	Centrality	Keywords		Centrality	Frequency	Keywords
1	198	0.72	User Experience	1	0.72	151	User Experience
2	32	0.19	Consumers	2	0.19	41	Consumers
3	27	0.06	Brand Image	3	0.11	22	Interaction Design
4	23	0.05	Brands	4	0.09	4	App Store
5	21	0.04	New Media	5	0.09	7	Smart TV
6	18	0.11	Interaction Design	6	0.07	13	Shipment volume
7	15	0.06	Product Design	7	0.07	7	Brand Marketing
8	15	0.03	Experience Design	8	0.06	24	Experience Design
9	14	0.05	Service Design	9	0.06	19	Brand Image
10	14	0.07	Brand Marketing	10	0.05	15	Service Design

(*continued*)

Table 2. (*continued*)

Serial number	Keyword Frequency			Serial number	Keyword Centrality		
	Frequency	Centrality	Keywords		Centrality	Frequency	Keywords
11	11	0.03	Marketing Strategy	11	0.05	22	Brands
12	11	0.01	Packaging Design	12	0.04	9	Smartphone
13	10	0.01	New Retail	13	0.04	10	Internet of Things
14	8	0	Brand Design	14	0.04	13	New Media
15	7	0.04	Mobile	15	0.04	7	Product positioning

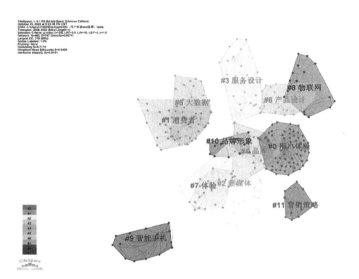

Fig. 8. Keyword clustering mapping of "user experience" and "brand" topics in China

There were 12 emergent terms for user experience in the field of brand marketing research, among which service design research emerging in year 2019 had the highest emergent intensity with a high emergent intensity of 3.94. The second is new retail research, which emerged in the same period as service design with an emergent intensity of 3.8. The third in the ranking is research on marketing strategy, which emerged in year 2016, with an intensity of 3.23.

In terms of the overall emergence years of emergent words, from year 2006 to 2016, experience, vancl, smartphone, mobile, and physical store are the main emergent words of user experience in the field of brand marketing in that period, among which the research on brand user experience in mobile is very obvious and the emergent intensity is high. The mobile internet developed rapidly during the period, and Internet + became the most hotly debated research theme during the period, with mobile devices such as smartphones continuously innovating experiences and traditional industries, since physical stores seeking new breakthroughs under the impact of the internet. A sudden increase has been taken place in the heat of research in marketing strategies in year 2016, as marketing communication accelerated in the context of the internet, enterprise competition intensified, and the marketing field developed rapidly. In year 2017, the e-commerce service industry developed strongly, and e-commerce research was hot in the academic field. On the one hand, the promulgation of the China national "Eleventh Five-Year Plan" for e-commerce development in year 2017 marked the general layout of the government's promotion of e-commerce. On the other hand, the effectiveness of e-commerce applications in enterprises and its role in promoting economic and social development have become increasingly obvious. In year 2019, new retail research and service design research became the hotspots of research in this period and up to date. An increase in the focus on packaging design has been shown in year 2020. Since the 4th International Forum on People-One-Man Model opened in Qingdao in year 2020, where the European Foundation for Management Development EFMD released the "People-One-Man Scorecard Certification System", marking a unified standard and progression system for the global replication and promotion of the People-One-Man model. Packaging design and the people-alone model also became a popular trend for post-2020 research attention.

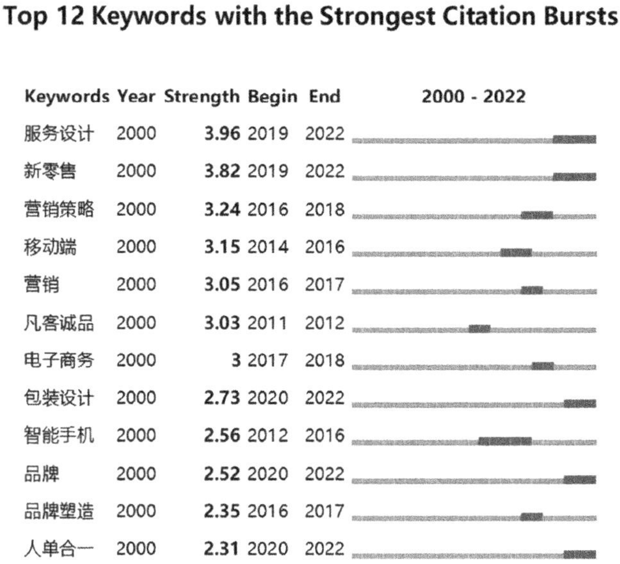

Top 12 Keywords with the Strongest Citation Bursts

Keywords	Year	Strength	Begin	End	2000 - 2022
服务设计	2000	3.96	2019	2022	
新零售	2000	3.82	2019	2022	
营销策略	2000	3.24	2016	2018	
移动端	2000	3.15	2014	2016	
营销	2000	3.05	2016	2017	
凡客诚品	2000	3.03	2011	2012	
电子商务	2000	3	2017	2018	
包装设计	2000	2.73	2020	2022	
智能手机	2000	2.56	2012	2016	
品牌	2000	2.52	2020	2022	
品牌塑造	2000	2.35	2016	2017	
人单合一	2000	2.31	2020	2022	

Fig. 9. Keyword emergence mapping of "user experience" and "branding" themes in China.

Keyword Clustering Timeline Graph Analysis. The timeline mapping of user experience and brand research was generated by CiteSpace visual analysis software based on cluster analysis (see Fig. 10). There are 12 clusters in the figure, and the labels of each cluster are keywords in the co-occurrence network, which are spread out in the clusters to which they belong according to the year in which they appear, showing the development of keywords in each cluster.

In user experience clustering, user experience and brand-related research first appeared in year 2006 and has been flourishing since then, gradually evolving from product design and web design to furniture design and other multi-dimensional development.

In consumer clustering, relevant studies based on consumer perspective have been published since year 2008, more focused on mobile experience studies before year 2015, with a sudden increase in physical stores and high-end brand studies since 2015, and new consumption patterns becoming a new trend in the context of Internet + in year 2022.

In the new media cluster, internet marketing-related research began to appear in year 2007, new media marketing emerged as a sprout, and brand communication through new media gradually became a new trend in brand marketing, culminating in new media-related research about 2013.

In the service design cluster, the first literature began to appear in year 2007 with the theme of business models, then it began to be silent and the literature was small until year 2015 when the study of service design began, and in 2019, service design began to focus on new retail, and its design strategy was mainly reflected in experiential.

In the brand clustering category, the two main areas are communication design and experience design. Year 2008 was the year of the first publication, with the keywords "wireless advertising" and "advertising placement".

In the big data clustering, the relevant literature was published in year 2011, with the keyword "innovation", and the focus ranged from advertising to column brands, and then to home appliance brands and regional brands.

In the product design cluster, product design-related literature began to be published in year 2008. This cluster mainly reflects that in the context of experience economy, in which product design is based on user experience, telling brand stories and building strong brands from three mindsets, i.e., product mindset, user mindset and brand mindset.

In the experience clustering, early scholars focused on interaction design, and the first paper was published in year 2009. The Fig. 10 shows that experience has changed from focusing on the product itself to the term "emotional" in year 2009, indicating that consumers are no longer satisfied with the functional experience of the product, but gradually focus on the emotional experience brought by the product.

In the IoT clustering, the main body of its research was mainly focused on public services, medical systems and other fields in the early stage, until year 2018 when Haier Group's people-alone model gained high attention and China domestic scholars began to focus on the research of IoT in corporate brand building.

In the smartphone clustering, the related literature is less published and mainly during year 2011 to 2014.

In the brand image cluster, brand image-related literature began to be published in year 2013, and a good brand image is created by integrating experiential and interactivity throughout all stages of integrated marketing and dynamically designing experiences to enhance consumers' experience of using them.

In the marketing strategy clustering, China domestic scholars began to focus on marketing strategy research in year 2016, and relevant studies mainly are in the period year 2016 to 2020. There is still a large gap in China domestic research on brand marketing strategies in terms of user experience.

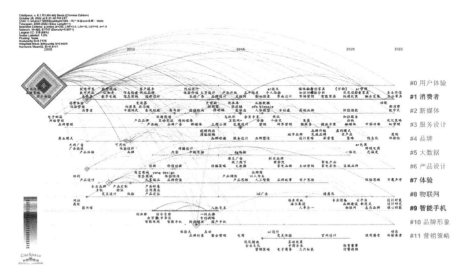

Fig. 10. Keyword timeline mapping of "user experience" and "brand" themes in China.

Keyword Clustering Time Zone Graph Analysis. On the basis of obtaining the keyword co-occurrence network mapping, in order to further reveal the evolution of the research related to user experience in the field of brand marketing in different periods, CiteSpace visual analysis software was used to obtain the keyword time zone knowledge map (see Fig. 11). Among them, the year in which the node is located indicates the time when the keyword first appeared, and the connecting line between nodes indicates that different keywords appeared in the same literature at the same time.

From the evolution of the keywords in the overall time zone diagram, the research on UX in brand marketing in China is roughly divided into four major stages: 1) The first stage is the design stage of brand marketing based on user experience, and the research keywords in this stage are service design, product design, interaction design and experience design; 2) The second stage is the mobile internet experience research stage, mainly from year 2011 to 2015, and the key words of this stage are application stores, smart phones, new media, human-computer interaction, big data, and Internet + ; 3) The third stage is the research stage of strategy research based on user experience brand marketing, mainly from year 2016 to 2018, and the research keywords in this stage are reflected in marketing strategy, branding, and design strategy; 4) The fourth stage is the research stage of new retail experience in the era of Internet of Things, since year 2019, and the key words of the research are mainly new retail, Internet of Things, digitalization, and new consumption.

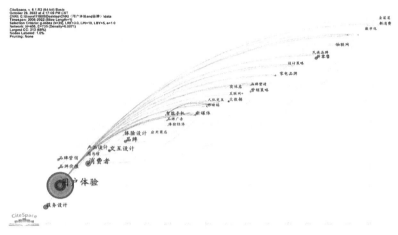

Fig. 11. Time zone mapping of keywords on the topic of "user experience" and "branding" in China.

4   Discussion

This paper composes academic research papers on the topic of user experience and branding in China, and analyzes them by visualizing keyword co-occurrence mapping, high-frequency keyword frequency and centrality, clustering timeline mapping, clustering time zone mapping and keyword emergence mapping, and summarizes the research hotspots of user experience in brand marketing in China since since year 2006 into the following three aspects.

4.1   Brand Marketing Research based on Product Experience Perspective

Through comprehensive analysis of sample literature, academic papers with keywords associated with products were screened out, totaling 369 papers, mainly including product design, product identification, and product innovation. The content mainly involves research on user experience methods in product design [7], internet product design based on product tonality [8], the design of fitness equipment oriented by user experience [9], the design of internet products, the emotional design of Internet products [10], travel APP design [11], and product packaging design [12]. User experience in product design refers to the adoption of human-centered design concept to make the whole product design more three-dimensional, so that the product presents a rich and typical image [13]. The focus of product design development should be on brand identification and product planning, as well as on target user experience and research to seek new breakthrough possibilities [14]. The product design development should focus on brand identity and product planning, as well as target user experience and research to seek new breakthroughs.

4.2 Research on Brand Marketing based on Service Experience Perspective

Through a comprehensive analysis of the sample literature, a total of 226 papers related to the keyword "service" were selected, mainly including website and APP service design, brand design, and new retail. The content mainly covers new retail business model research [15], brand upgrading research [16], FMCG product design research [17], research on mobile terminal online shopping APP [18], express terminal service system research [19], and brand promotion strategy research [20]. Interestingly, service design, as a field that uses design to develop services, is able to plan and develop the physical and non-physical elements that constitute the services in an integrated way to improve user experience and create service value [26]. Further, service design plays an important role in the construction of city branding, in which service design methodology is user-centered and human-centered, and can create city business cards in all aspects and dimensions, forming city branding effects and showing the face of city culture and tourism [27].

4.3 Brand Marketing Research based on Interactive Experience Perspective

Through a comprehensive analysis of the sample literature, a total of 88 papers related to the keyword "interaction" were selected, mainly including interaction design, human-computer interaction and interaction experience. The content mainly covers cell phone product interaction design [21], interaction design for mobile phone products, interaction design for smart city construction [22], interactive packaging design [23], intelligent home appliance interaction [24], and interactive advertising [25]. Since, the future is an era of communication and interaction, and the form of 'interaction' and 'dialogue' will become a fashion and popular. Interaction design has changed the previous tradition of industrial design, graphic design and spatial design, which directly takes human behavior as the design object. In this way, what consumers get is not just a single product, but a complete service platform with the product as the medium [28]. Further, interaction makes the product more valuable through commercial display, tells the story of the brand and the product to consumers, and makes it easier for consumers to reap the value of the experience brought by the product [29].

5 Conclusion

In this paper, all journal articles on "user experience" and "branding" on China Knowledge Network have been analyzed until October 25, 2022, using CiteSpace visual analysis software, which reveals following issues:

(1) In terms of the number of articles published and the timing, research on user experience and branding in China began to appear in year 2006 with three related articles, and then gradually developed. In terms of the growth rate of the number of publications, it entered a high growth period in year 2010 with 10 publications, and a sudden increase to 42 publications in year 2011 with 32 new publications compared with the previous year. Except for a small decline in 2012, the number of publications showed a high growth rate, reaching a peak of 121 articles in year 2017;

(2) From the viewpoint of subject areas and issuing publications, publications with the theme of user experience and branding involve a number of subject areas such as economy, finance, news media, industrial technology, computer, internet, art, publishing, and telecommunication. Interestingly, the discipline orientation is more obvious, mainly concentrated in the field of economy and news media, among which enterprise economy, trade economy, and industrial economy account for the top three, accounting for a total of 51.85%. The publications published are concentrated in the fields of design, business and media communication, among which the top three are design with 14.67%, packaging engineering with 12.36% and sound and screen world with 6.95%. It shows that China has more in-depth research on this topic in the field of design;

(3) From the distribution of core authors and institutions, the vast majority of researchers on this topic are independent, some of them are small groups of two to three people collaborating on research, and fewer form research teams of more than three people. Research institutions are mainly universities, less independent research institutions, sparse cooperative networks, few cross-unit cooperative networks, and the overall distribution of research is scattered; and

(4) From the perspective of research hotspots, the research on brand marketing based on user experience mainly focuses on the theme of product experience, service experience, and interaction experience, According to the analysis of keyword emergence, user experience based on brand new retail mode, user experience based on brand service design, user experience based on brand interaction design, and eco-brand research based on human-unit model keep emerging and developing, which may become a hot spot of research attention and development trend for a long time in the future.

Acknowledgements. This research was funded by "2022 Constructing Project of Teaching Quality and Teaching Reform Project for Undergraduate Universities in Guangdong Province" Higher Education Teaching Reform Project **(project No. 386), 'Innovation and practice of teaching methods for information and interaction design in the context of new liberal arts' (project grant number x2sj-C9233001).**

References

1. Liu, F.J., Lei, B.Y., Wang, Y.X.: Consumer demand and marketing strategy in the era of experience economy. China Ind. Econ. **08**, 81–86 (2002)
2. Lu, T.H., Zhou, Z.M.: Brand theory based on brand relationship: research model and prospect. Bus. Econ. Manag. **02**, 4–9 (2003)
3. Ma, L.L.: Experience thinking reshapes the relationship between brands and consumers. J. Jiamusi Vocational Coll. **04**, 474 (2018)
4. Lu, X.Y., Zhang, H., Wang, X.Y., Qin, Z.J.: Scientometrics-based analysis of the hotspots and frontiers of domestic corporate knowledge transfer research. Intell. Sci. **37**(03), 169–176 (2019)
5. Wu, D., Xiang, X.X., Ji, C.H.: A visual analysis of research hotspots and evolution of China's economic development. Sci. Ind. **22**(05), 15–22 (2022)

6. Chen, S.H., Wang, Y.: Scientific knowledge mapping analysis of Chinese social thought research - an integrated application based on Citespace and Vosviewer. J. Shanghai Jiaotong Univ. (Philos. Soc. Sci. Ed.) **26**(06), 22–30 (2018)

7. Ding, F., Jiang, Z.M.: Research and reflection on user experience methods in product design. Mod. Decoration (Theor.) **11**, 65–66 (2013)

8. Tang, J., Li, S.G.: Research on internet product design based on product tonality. Packaging Eng. **36**(04), 84–87 (2015)

9. Lin, X.W.: From strategy to appearance: user experience-oriented fitness equipment design. Decoration **12**, 130–132 (2021)

10. Liang, S.: An introduction to the emotional design in Internet products. Sci. Technol. Commun. **10**(20), 146–147 (2018)

11. Du, J.L.: Functional analysis and development trend of tourism APP based on user experience. J. Changsha Railway Inst. (Soc. Sci. Ed.) **15**(04), 335–336 (2014)

12. Li, Y., Wei, Y.Y.: Exploration of product packaging design based on user experience. Art Des. (Theor.) **2**(03), 42–44 (2015)

13. Jia, W.: Research on user experience and application in product design. Art Educ. Res. **16**, 40–41 (2016)

14. Li, J., Huang, D.T.: Creating the perfect user experience: the design philosophy of YANG DESIGN. Decoration **11**, 51–57 (2012)

15. She, B.R.: Exploring the new retail business model based on user experience and big data in the experience economy. E-commerce **02**, 11–12 (2018)

16. Hu, H., Hao, D.T., Bai, F.R., Zhou, J.: Research on the brand upgrading of Youzhou Miao embroidery based on service design thinking. Packaging Eng. **40**(06), 8–14 (2019)

17. Qu, J., Yu, S.L.: Research on the design of FMCG products based on user experience. Drama House **05**, 115–117 (2019)

18. Li, J.Y., Li, Y.: Research on the influencing factors of user experience of mobile terminal online shopping APP. Bus. Manag. **11**, 127–131 (2016)

19. Zhang, L.H., Zhang, Q.: Innovative strategy thinking of express terminal service system in the new context. Packaging Eng. **36**(22), 71–74 (2015)

20. Li, Z., Liu, T.Y.: Research on lifestyle brand enhancement strategy based on service design. Packaging Eng. **42**(22), 257–264 (2021)

21. Zeng, Z.H.: Interaction design and user experience of cell phone products. Art Des. (Theor.) **2**(06), 208–210 (2009)

22. Ma, H.: Application of user experience research in interaction design for smart city construction. Design **09**, 126–128 (2017)

23. Xu, C.: Exploration of interactive packaging design based on user experience. Wireless Internet Technol. **03**, 97–98 (2016)

24. Zhang, L.H., Zhang, S.F., Zhu, Q.Y.: Smart appliance interaction: a new paradigm for systematic experience design thinking. Decoration **08**, 17–23 (2021)

25. Lai, Y.: Exploring the communication value of scene interactive advertising based on media context theory. Southeast Commun. **10**, 129–131 (2018)

26. Luo, S.J., Hu, Y.: Model innovation driven by service design. Packaging Eng. **36**(12), 1–4 (2015)

27. Zhang, C., Yin, X.H.: Research on service design methodology to reconstruct the regional brand of Shenyang. Old Brand Market. **10**, 9–11 (2022)

28. Xin, X.Y.: Interaction design: from physical logic to behavioral logic. Decoration **01**, 58–62 (2015)

29. Bi, Y.Y., Huang, Z.S.: Analysis of interaction design in commercial display space. Culture Ind. **22**, 166–168 (2022)

Emotional and Persuasive Design

Behavior Design for Beverage Bottle Recycling in University Campus Towards Circular Economy

Ziheng An[(✉)] and Zhen Liu

School of Design, South China University of Technology, Guangzhou 510006,
People's Republic of China
`202120156948@mail.scut.edu.cn`

Abstract. Nowadays, circular economy has profoundly affected China's future economic development. In the process of promoting circular economy in the whole society, the implementation of waste classification is critical. With the development of education and the increase of the university campus population, the production of garbage in university campus in China is increasing. At present, the recycling of garbage in university campus is a research hotspot, and lack of applications to address problems, especially the recycling of beverage bottles. Hence, this research aims to explore the behavior of university students on resource waste on campus and propose a solution for the recycling of the beverage bottles through behavior design. This research investigates the current unsustainable behaviors of university students existing on campus through literature review, user observation, and user interviews, selects the issue of beverage bottle recycling, analyzes the pain points of users in recycling behavior, and finally proposes a Smart Vending Recycling Machine based on behavioral design theory. The results show that the Smart Vending Recycling Machine encourages university students to develop good recycling habits unconsciously, improves the participation rate of students in garbage recycling significantly, motivates students to consume beverages, and contributes to the realization of the goal of circular economy.

Keywords: Circular Economy · Garbage Recycling · Behavior Design · Vending Recycling Machine · University Campus Experience

1 Introduction

1.1 Current Status of Garbage Recycling in Chinese Campuses

With the acceleration of China's urbanization process, the urban population continues to increase, and the production of municipal solid waste also increases year by year. As of 2020, China's municipal solid waste removal volume has reached 235.12 million tons [1], and the problems of environmental pollution and resource waste caused by municipal solid waste are increasing day by day, among which campus waste has become an important part of municipal solid waste.

At present, the proportion of college students in the total population of urban residents in China is gradually increasing, especially in some cities with rich educational resources, such as Shanghai, Beijing, Xi'an and other places, the population of college students has accounted for more than 10% of the total population of urban residents, so colleges and universities The campus garbage generated cannot be ignored [2]. In 2021, the daily production of garbage on Chinese college campuses will be as high as 7.32 tons, with an average of 487 g of garbage per person per day. The current situation is not optimistic. Of the total amount of garbage produced on campus, 72.96% is recyclable garbage, 6.35% is potentially recyclable garbage, and the recycling potential is 79.31% [3]. The production of plastic waste on college campuses accounts for 11.13% of the total waste production, of which the production of PET bottles accounts for 4.04% of the total plastic waste. As the main source of recyclable plastic waste, PET bottles with a recycling grade of 1 have a high economic value in the recycling market [4, 5].

At present, the participation rate of Chinese campus students in waste sorting is still relatively low, and the convenience of waste sorting infrastructure on campuses needs to be improved. Some studies have pointed out that for campus students, incentives are more effective measures than punishments in waste sorting behavior [3]. However, care must be taken when implementing waste sorting incentives to avoid changing attitudes towards the obligatory behavior of waste sorting [6, 7].

1.2 Process and Wide Application of Behavioral Design

Behavioral design is a scientific research-based framework for intentionally and systematically changing people's behavior through persuasive modification of the physical and digital environment. There is a difference between behavioral design and user experience design. UX is about adapting a product to users without changing how they behave, while behavioral design is about persuading users to change how they behave. The three principles of behavioral design are simplicity, cues, and habits.

The design process for behavioral design is divided into five parts: The first step is to describe the situation. This includes listing all current facts about the project, identifying and summarizing target users, understanding mental models, agreeing on vision and goals, defining constraints that limit potential solutions, summarizing, and documenting. The second step is to determine the list of behaviors, including agreeing on the desired behavioral outcome, analyzing the current behavior, analyzing the context/motivation/situational variables, evaluating the current tools/sites/products/systems, and documenting the list of actions that will lead to more desirable behaviors. The third step is to design behavioral solutions, including matching action lists to tools, designing project solutions, and documenting projects and initiatives. The fourth part is prototyping, testing, and interaction. The fifth step is implementation.

The current mandatory garbage sorting policy adopted by Chinese campuses has achieved some results, but the policy lacks sustainability in the long run. Guide students correctly through behavioral design, so that students can unconsciously develop the correct habit of sorting garbage, to achieve the goal of the circular economy.

1.3 Importance of Circular Economy in CHina's Economic Development

Circular economy is a new model of economic development that advocates the harmonious development of the economy and environment, and its core is the efficient and cyclic utilization of resources. At present, there are multiple interpretations of circular economy, but there is usually a common understanding, that is, the circular closed-loop system [8]. In stark contrast to the circular economy is the linear economy, in which products are first manufactured from primary raw materials, then consumed and used by users, and finally disposed of as waste after use [9]. Therefore, circular economy models focus on optimizing end-of-life products and resources by reducing, reusing, recycling, and recovering materials during manufacturing, transportation, and consumption [10]. The circular economy is a global economic model that recycles and regenerates by design to maintain the maximum efficiency and value of products, components, and materials, and to reduce the consumption of finite resources [11].

Nowadays, the circular economy has been deeply integrated into China's mainstream economic system and has a profound impact on China's future economic development. Circular economy is a new economic growth model in line with the sustainable development strategy. In the process of promoting circular economy in the whole society, the implementation of urban waste classification is very important [12]. Garbage classification can greatly avoid various hazards caused by urban garbage to the human environment, and improve the efficiency of urban garbage recycling and efficient treatment.

2 Evaluation

2.1 Field Research

As shown in Fig. 1, through the field investigation of the Guangzhou International Campus of South China University of Technology, many "unsustainable behaviors" on the campus were recorded, including food waste in the canteen, unreasonable bus routes, vacant spaces, vacant parking spaces, Behaviors such as unsorted garbage. Although the form of resource use on campus will be relatively simple, the status quo of resource waste is still relatively serious.

As shown in Table 1, these "unsustainable behaviors" can be divided into four areas: Food, Housing, Traffic, and Learning. In terms of food, "unsustainable behaviors" include wasted food lunch box packaging, food leftovers, and empty tables. Wasted resources include plastic, food, electricity, and air-conditioning resources. In the accommodation part, "unsustainable behaviors" include daily garbage, and waste resources include recyclable items such as beverage bottles and second-hand items such as old clothes and shoes. In the transportation sector, "unsustainable behaviors" include running empty school buses, idling parking spaces, vacant campus land, and wasting resources such as fossil fuels, electricity, and land resources. In the learning part, "unsustainable behaviors" include the underuse of study rooms, old books, and second-hand learning tools, and wasted resources include electricity, air conditioning, and second-hand items including books.

Fig. 1. Resource waste on campus

Table 1. "Unsustainable Behaviors" existing on campus.

Section	Unsustainable behavior	Wasted resources
Meals	Food packing	Lunch box
	Food waste	Food
	Dining table layout	Electricity, Air Conditioning
Dormitory	Domestic waste	Beverage bottles
		Clothing
		Shoes
Traffic	School bus in vain	Fuel
	Idle parking spaces	Electricity
	Vacant land	Land resource
Study	Study room use	Electricity, Air Conditioning
	Used Book	Paper resources

The above research shows that there are still many wastes of resources on college campuses, but the problems reflected by these "unsustainable behaviors" cannot be solved in a short period. Therefore, this study selected the issue of beverage bottle recycling for more in-depth research.

There are three reasons for this:

- When recycling beverage bottles, the user's behavior is clear.
- The feasibility of beverage bottle recycling is less difficult, and there are successful business cases for reference, so the feasibility of the project is relatively high.

- The stakeholder relationship of beverage bottle recycling is relatively simple, the cooperation success is relatively high, and the project's profit is relatively considerable.

At present, there is no special beverage bottle recycling equipment on campus, and beverage bottle recycling is the same as daily garbage recycling, using sorted trash cans. As shown in Fig. 2.

Fig. 2. Current beverage bottle recycling equipment

2.2 User Research

User Observation. There are four ways to sell beverages in Guangzhou International Campus of South China University of Technology: convenience store sales (JD Convenience Store, Family Mart and canteen retail), vending machines, takeaway sales and others. Among them, convenience store sales and vending machines are the two major sources of beverage bottles. Therefore, two sales channels of convenience store and vending machine were selected, and three locations of JD Convenience Store, Family Mart Convenience Store and vending machine were selected for user observation. The results are shown in Table 2.

Questionnaire. A questionnaire survey was conducted on users in the Guangzhou International Campus of South China University of Technology, and a total of 89 people were surveyed, including 51 undergraduates, 33 masters/doctoral students, and above, and student users accounted for 94%. Boys accounted for 62% and girls accounted for 38%. The content of the questionnaire is shown in Table 3.

The results of the questionnaire show that the average score of users' consumption habits is 3.94, indicating that users are inclined to rational consumption. 67.1% of users will use vending machines at least once a week, and 82.4% of users will use vending machines for a fixed period. The main reasons for users to use vending machines are "convenient use" and "cheap price", but there are also disadvantages of "unreasonable human factors, inconvenient access" and "frequent out of stock". Only 23.3% of users will sort and recycle beverage bottles after drinking, and 68.2% of users will directly

Table 2. User Behaviors and Reasons

No	User Behavior	Reason
1	The student walked out of the Family Mart convenience store empty-handed, with a dejected expression on his face	The prices of Family Mart convenience stores are too high, and students have no desire to buy them
2	There are often groups of students buying drinks at 2 pm or in the evening	Students will purchase drinks after each day's exercise
3	Students left empty-handed when they were shopping at the vending machine	The vending machines were out of drinks
4	The students found that the JD Convenience Store was closed when they went shopping	JD Convenience Store closes earlier at night

Table 3. Questionnaire content

No	Questionnaire Topic	Questionnaire Options
1	Who are you?	a. Undergraduate students b. Master/Ph.D. students and above c. Teacher d. Staff e. Other
2	What is your gender?	a. Male b. Female
3	What are your hobbies?	Free Speech
4	What is your consumption habit?	Rational (5 points most) ----- Impulsive (1 point least)
5	How often do you use vending machines daily?	a. Use almost every day b. Use frequently every week c. Occasional monthly use d. hardly used
6	When do you usually use vending machines?	a. Exercise time b. Study and work time c. Recreation breaks d. No fixed time
7	Why do you choose vending machines to buy?	a. Easy to use b. Cheap price c. Complete range of beverages d. Use anytime, anywhere e. Other

(*continued*)

Table 3. (*continued*)

No	Questionnaire Topic	Questionnaire Options
8	What are the disadvantages of current vending machines?	a. Poor shape and low recognition b. Unreasonable human factors make it inconvenient to take c. The operation is cumbersome d. The types are not complete e. The price is higher f. Often out of stock g. There are fewer distribution points h. Other
9	What do you do with your finished beverage bottles?	a. Classified recycling b. Discard directly c. Reuse d. Other
10	What problems exist in the current beverage bottle recycling?	a. Lack of recycling facilities b. Classification rules are not clear c. The classification process is troublesome d. Other
11	What is your attitude towards "rewards for voluntary recycling of beverage bottles"?	Like (5 points most) -----Dislike (1 point least)
12	Why do you maintain the attitude in question 12?	Free Speech
13	Which incentive would you prefer to receive for voluntarily recycling beverage bottles?	a. Less cash feedback b. More coupons c. Equivalent account points

discard them. The current main problems of beverage bottle recycling are the troublesome recycling process and the lack of recycling facilities. The average score of users' attitudes towards "being rewarded when taking the initiative to recycle beverage bottles" is 4.23, indicating that users are generally optimistic about this measure, and users prefer to be rewarded with "more red envelopes for consumption".

The following conclusions can be drawn from field research and user research:

- Most of the users who use vending machines are young students, whose consumption concept tends to be rational, focusing on both product quality and price. Behavioral habits are relatively regular, and the frequency and time of using vending machines are relatively fixed.
- The use of vending machines on campus has advantages and disadvantages. Compared with convenience stores, it is easy to operate and flexible to use, but there are fewer beverage categories, often out of stock, and lack of consideration in appearance design and human factors engineering.

- At present, the main problem with plastic bottle recycling is that users feel that the recycling behavior is troublesome, and generally they will not choose to sort and recycle but directly discard it. The secondary problem is that the current garbage sorting and recycling facilities on campus are not complete enough, and sorting and recycling are not allowed.
- Most users like the suggestion of "rewards for actively recycling beverage bottles", and prefer "more coupons" rather than "a small amount of cash feedback". This provides ideas for coming up with solutions.

2.3 User Portrait

According to field research and user research, build user portraits of target users, and list user pain points and user goals. Draw a user experience map to describe the user's behavior, thoughts, pain points, etc. during the entire use process, and provide a reference for further proposals. The user portrait is shown in Fig. 3.

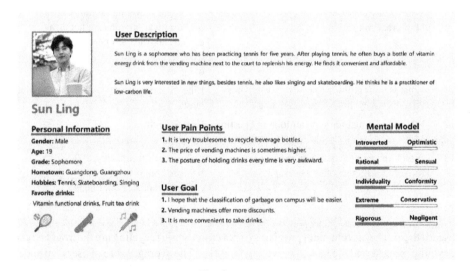

Fig. 3. Persona

The user flow chart is shown in Fig. 4. When the user is thirsty, he has the idea of buying a drink, and then anxiously finds a vending machine in the school. However, the high price and uncomfortable holding posture during the purchase process disappointed users. After drinking the drink, he feels much better, but the troublesome garbage collection process makes the user very annoyed.

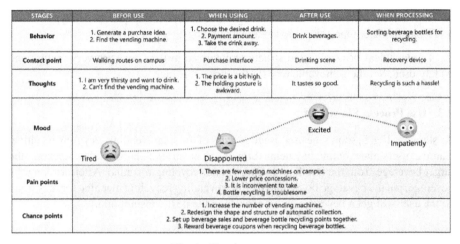

STAGES	BEFOR USE	WHEN USING	AFTER USE	WHEN PROCESSING
Behavior	1. Generate a purchase idea. 2. Find the vending machine.	1. Choose the desired drink. 2. Payment amount. 3. Take the drink away.	Drink beverages.	Sorting beverage bottles for recycling.
Contact point	Walking routes on campus	Purchase interface	Drinking scene	Recovery device
Thoughts	1. I am very thirsty and want to drink. 2. Can't find the vending machine.	1. The price is a bit high. 2. The holding posture is awkward.	It tastes so good.	Recycling is such a hassle!
Mood	Tired	Disappointed	Excited	Impatiently
Pain points	1. There are few vending machines on campus. 2. Lower price concessions. 3. It is inconvenient to take. 4. Bottle recycling is troublesome			
Chance points	1. Increase the number of vending machines. 2. Redesign the shape and structure of automatic collection. 2. Set up beverage sales and beverage bottle recycling points together. 3. Reward beverage coupons when recycling beverage bottles.			

Fig. 4. User journey map

3 Solution

3.1 Features

Based on the pain points reflected in the survey, a potential solution is proposed. This solution integrates the vending function of the vending machine and the recycling function of the beverage bottle recycling device on one device, so it is called an intelligent vending recycling machine.

The functional structure of the intelligent vending recycling machine includes:

- The function of this product is divided into two parts: the function of automatically selling beverages and the function of recycling beverage bottles.
- After the user selects the favorite drink on the product and pays through the electronic platform, the drink can be obtained.
- It will be more convenient for users to take drinks without bending over.
- When the user recycles the beverage bottle, the recycling structure will compress the volume of the beverage bottle and store it.
- The device can only recycle the same type of beverage sold in the device, and there should be no leftovers in the beverage bottle.
- After the recycling is successful, the product will issue beverage coupons to the user's electronic platform account, which can be used in the next purchase.

3.2 Technical Principle

The technical principle and structure of the intelligent vending recycling machine are as follows:

- Mechanical structure for beverage storage and removal. This structure has been widely used in existing vending machines.
- Electronic platform online payment technology. Alipay and WeChat Pay are already widely used in China.

- 3D scanning and recognition technology. Used to identify plastic bottle types.
- Plastic bottle compression and storage technology.

The technical principles and structures involved in the above are very mature and widely used. So, the achievable row for this project is high.

3.3 Use Process Flowchart

As shown in Fig. 5, shows the user usage process of the smart vending recycling machine. Campus users make online payments through the electronic platform after selecting the target beverage from the intelligent vending and recycling machine. After drinking the beverage, put the beverage bottle into the smart vending recycling machine for recycling, so the user will get a beverage coupon to use in the next consumption.

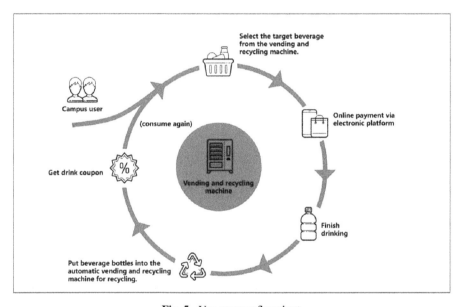

Fig. 5. Use process flowchart

3.4 Stakeholders

As shown in Fig. 6, shows the stakeholders and system map of the intelligent vending recycling machine. Stakeholders include campus users, schools, sales agents, beverage manufacturers, plastic recycling plants, and electronic payment platforms. In the system map, the intelligent vending recycling machine is located in the center, the campus users are users, the school is the setting point, and the sales agent is the operator. They are closely connected with intelligent vending recycling machine.

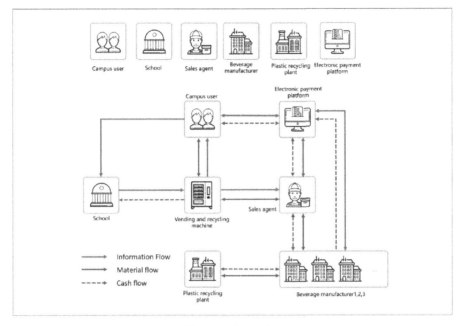

Fig. 6. Stakeholders

4 Prototype Design

4.1 Design

In terms of shape, the product follows the design principle of "Form Follows Function", and pursues the optimal solution of functional utility and beautiful appearance. The size of the product is 2000 mm*860 mm*800 mm and the basic shape is square, which conforms to the public's general perception of the appearance of public facilities and avoids users' discomfort when using the product for the first time. As shown in Fig. 7 and Fig. 8, the product shell is made of black electroplated and painted stainless steel, and a layer of turquoise and white electroplated and painted stainless steel shells are respectively wrapped on the front and both sides of the product, which not only protects the internal components but also protects the internal components. Make the product shape more beautiful.

4.2 Functional Division

The structure of the smart vending recycling machine is divided into upper, middle, and lower floors, with heights of 1100 mm, 450 mm, and 450 mm respectively.

Fig. 7. Product appearance (1)

Fig. 8. Product appearance (2)

As shown in Fig. 9, in the upper structure, the inside of the machine is a beverage storage structure for storing and refrigerating beverages; a signal receiver is installed on the top for receiving and sending signals; an OLED screen, a face recognition camera and with the fingerprint lock, users can buy drinks on the screen, and then make face recognition payment through the camera, and maintenance personnel can open the cabinet door through the fingerprint lock to replenish products.

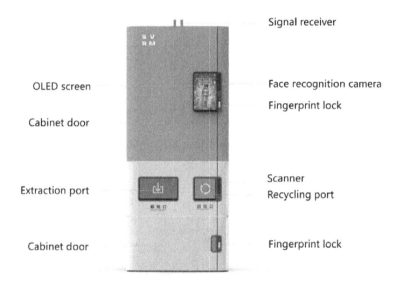

Fig. 9. Front view of smart vending recycling machine

As shown in Fig. 10, in the middle structure, the beverage outlet is on the left side of the product, and the user takes out the selected beverage from the outlet. The right side is the beverage recycling port, and a code scanner is installed next to it. Users need to scan the barcode on the beverage bottle to be recycled before putting it into the recycling port for recycling.

As shown in Fig. 11, in the lower structure, the interior of the machine is a recycling basket for beverage bottles, and a fingerprint lock is installed on the front side. The maintenance personnel open the cabinet door through the fingerprint lock and dispose of the beverage bottles in the recycling basket in time. The bottom of the product is the switch and the emergency button. At the same time, other running parts and compressors of the machine are located at the back of the middle and lower floors. After the beverage bottles are recycled, they will be compressed into a very small volume by the compressor, and then put into the recycling basket.

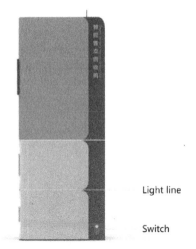

Fig. 10. Side view of smart vending recycling machine

Fig. 11. Top view of smart vending recycling machine

5 Conclusion

This article aims to explore the behavior of resource waste on campus and propose solutions for the recycling of campus beverage bottles through behavioral design. Through literature review, user observation, and user interview methods, this paper examines many "unsustainable behaviors" existing on the campus, selects the problem of beverage bottle recycling, analyzes the pain points of users in recycling behavior, and finally based on behavioral design theory Proposed an intelligent vending recycling machine. The results show that the smart vending recycling machine makes students unconsciously develop good recycling habits, significantly improves the participation rate of students in garbage recycling, motivates students to consume beverages, and contributes to the realization of the goal of circular economy.

Through the on-the-spot investigation of the campus, this study summarizes many "unsustainable behaviors" on the campus. These behaviors involve the waste of non-renewable resources such as oil and the waste of renewable resources such as food. Some of these wasted resources are completely avoidable, so this article chooses beverage bottle recycling as a practical topic for research.

Through the literature review, it is found that circular economy has profoundly affected China's future economic development, and the implementation of waste classification is very critical in the process of promoting circular economy in the whole society. The recycling of campus garbage is currently a research hotspot. Many colleges and universities have adopted mandatory measures to solve the problem of garbage classification, but this policy is not sustainable, the effect is not significant, and the participation rate of students in garbage recycling is relatively low. Low. Through behavioral design, students can be guided correctly, so that students can develop correct garbage recycling habits.

This study discovered the design opportunity of vending machines through field investigation and user observation, then drew user portraits through questionnaire surveys and analyzed the pain points and opportunity points of users in the recycling process. In the design scheme, the solution of "smart vending recycling machine" is proposed, the functional structure is summed up, the technical principle is analyzed, and the flow chart and stakeholders are drawn. In the design prototype, the design idea, size, material, and functional division of the product are introduced.

The results show that the research and analysis results of this study provide a reference for campus waste recycling. The design of the intelligent vending and recycling machine, on the one hand, stimulates students' beverage consumption and drives the development of the unmanned retail industry. On the other hand, it also makes students unconsciously good recycling habits have been developed, which has significantly increased the participation rate of students in garbage recycling. This study puts forward a new solution to solve the problem of campus garbage recycling and takes into account the campus economy, and contributes to the realization of the goal of the circular economy.

Acknowledgements. The authors wish to thank all the people who provided the time and efforts for the investigation. This research is supported by South China University and Technology, and Guangdong Provincial Department of Science and Technology 2022 Overseas Famous Teacher Project: "Behavior and Service Design Course for Sustainable Youth Development City Construction (SYCBD)".

References

1. The latest statistical briefing on the treatment of municipal solid waste in China_Gansu Public Science Network (in Chinese), http://www.gspst.com/kxsh/dtsh/ljfl1/content_120507. Accessed 21 Nov 2022
2. Li, D.: Evolutionary game analysis on the supervision mechanism of waste sorted collection in colleges and universities. Chin. J. Environ. Manag. (in Chinese). **9**, 90–94 (2017). https://doi.org/10.16868/j.cnki.1674-6252.2017.05.090

3. Hao, M.: Study on the Status Quo and Influencing Factors of College Campus Waste Sorting and Recycling (in Chinese), https://kns.cnki.net/kcms/detail/detail.aspx?dbcode=CMFD&dbname=CMFD202202&filename=1021056495.nh&uniplatform=NZKPT&v=OkBsOKMfW24KFpkkPTUx2QDjNaARCXLwGKmUQJFxUerUpY5xHqs8oWx6gUBXDxwH (2021). https://doi.org/10.27117/d.cnki.ghenu.2021.000113

4. Solid waste generation and characterization in the University of Lagos for a sustainable waste management, https://schlr.cnki.net/en/Detail/index/journal/SJES34851A3818DD83738F54D7D29EBF9EF8. Accessed 21 Nov 2022

5. Armijo de Vega, C., Ojeda Benítez, S., Ramírez Barreto, M.E.: Solid waste characterization and recycling potential for a university campus. Waste Manag. **28**, S21–S26 (2008). https://doi.org/10.1016/j.wasman.2008.03.022

6. Dahlén, L., Lagerkvist, A.: Evaluation of recycling programmes in household waste collection systems. Waste Manag. Res. **28**, 577–586 (2010). https://doi.org/10.1177/0734242X09341193

7. Berglund, C.: Burning in moral, drowning in rationality? ethical considerations in forming environmental policy. Minerals Energy - Raw Mater. Rep. **20**, 16–22 (2005). https://doi.org/10.1080/14041040510033851

8. Murray, A., Skene, K., Haynes, K.: The circular economy: an interdisciplinary exploration of the concept and application in a global context. J. Bus. Ethics **140**(3), 369–380 (2015). https://doi.org/10.1007/s10551-015-2693-2

9. Rapport_McKinsey-Towards_A_Circular_Economy.pdf, https://www.werktrends.nl/app/uploads/2015/06/Rapport_McKinsey-Towards_A_Circular_Economy.pdf

10. Kirchherr, J., Reike, D., Hekkert, M.: Conceptualizing the circular economy: an analysis of 114 definitions. Resour. Conserv. Recycl. **127**, 221–232 (2017). https://doi.org/10.1016/j.resconrec.2017.09.005

11. Liu, Z., Liu, J., Osmani, M.: Integration of digital economy and circular economy: current status and future directions. Sustainability. **13**, 7217 (2021). https://doi.org/10.3390/su13137217

12. Zhang, Z.: Research on the implementation of intelligent classification of municipal solid waste based on circular economy. Resource Recycling (in Chinese). 18–20 (2020)

Designing the User Experience to Achieve Better Engagement and Feedback on TikTok Accounts

Louna Bouillon, Dion Schouten, and Fabio Campos(✉) 🄳

BUAS - Breda University, Breda, NB, The Netherlands
ferreira.f@buas.nl, fc2005@gmail.com

Abstract. In this research, we explored how different variables influence the user experience in the TikTok social media channel. The engagement of the users in giving meaningful feedback to the posts was the main variable being observed. This is important because in several business-to-business and business-to-consumer applications the companies are interested in using meaningful feedback from the users to improve their products, be it a tangible device or a media product. So, instead of focusing on getting more followers, in situations like that, it is more important the kind of feedback received from the users. In this research, a mixed methods approach was applied. Joining the quantitative results with the insights from the qualitative part of the research, it is possible to conclude that the algorithm used by TikTok to define the content in the timelines has a bigger influence on engagement than the kind of content. To achieve the desired result of an increase in the number and quality of feedback by the viewers, it was found that being more direct can produce interesting increases. The posts where the viewers were asked to comment and reply with a certain answer have the most comments. In some instances, the increase is almost 300% more when comparing it to the average amount of comments. Most interviewees also stated that they would love to help out and would provide meaningful feedback if this was directly asked. The same goes for Q&A's and interaction-based posts.

Keywords: Social media Ux · Meaningful feeback · TikTok user experience

1 Introduction

Collecting meaningful feedback from users is becoming increasingly important in markets in which the companies must keep improving the user experience by adapting their products and solutions to a constantly changing environment.

In this research, we explored how social media channels, in particular TikTok, can be used for that. The main goal was to understand how different variables influence the engagement of the users in giving meaningful feedback.

Although the popularity (number of followers, views, "likes", etc.) is important for some strategies, in other situations, instead of focusing on getting more followers to the accounts, it is even more important the kind of feedback received from the users. Therefore, understanding how to design the content of the account to modify the user experience and promote user engagement in giving meaningful feedback is paramount.

A. Marcus et al. (Eds.): HCII 2023, LNCS 14030, pp. 503–515, 2023.
https://doi.org/10.1007/978-3-031-35699-5_36

In the specific study case of this research, the TikTok account used was from the biggest Dutch soap opera. With 33 seasons, more than 6,600 episodes and a runtime of more than 32 years, "Goede Tijden Slechte Tijden", also known as GTST, pulls more than 800.000 views every night [19].

Despite its success, competition is all around and to maintain relevancy and connection with the viewers, GTST runs social media accounts on Instagram, Facebook, and TikTok.

One of the problems of TV channels is the migration of some target groups for other entertainment platforms like TikTok.

Indeed, the new generation is more attracted to social networks than to television series. According to Statista, in 2020 18–24 year-olds watched 1h37 of tv content per day against 1h47 spent on social networks by the entire population in 2022 [14]. Thus, television and its entertainment face an attraction problem.

We can see that the time spent watching television by the entire population is 4h16, and it is strongly related to age. According to Statista in its research entitled "The Generation Gap in TV Consumption" [10] we can conclude that the older the generation, the more time they spend watching television. This is mainly due to the fact that television is no longer the only connected means of entertainment as it was 30 years ago. In the last 20 years social networks have appeared and changed the way we entertain ourselves. Platforms such as YouTube, Facebook, Instagram, and TikTok, offer, in addition to entertaining, the possibility of interacting through likes, comments, and shares.

Television channels then found themselves having to think about how to cope with the aging number of viewers and the migration of the younger generation. In this context, transmedia was born, according to Wikipedia [20], "Transmedia storytelling is the technique of telling a single story or story experience across multiple platforms and formats using current digital technologies. From a production standpoint, transmedia storytelling involves creating content that engages an audience using various techniques to permeate their daily lives. In order to achieve this engagement, a transmedia production will develop stories across multiple forms of media in order to deliver unique pieces of content in each channel. Importantly, these pieces of content are not only linked together (overtly or subtly) but are in narrative synchronization with each other."

Television channels began to create magazines related to the series that were produced, but also applications, streaming websites, video games, and active on social networks. These networks are where the young generation is very active, much more than in front of the television. Thus, GTST like other television franhcises, has created content on social networks to attract the younger generation to watch their series and also to have meaningful feedback from their viewers.

To date, GTST has nearly 490,000 followers on Facebook, 217,000 on Instagram and 80,000 followers on TikTok. Despite the fact that on Facebook the content is posted almost daily (excluding weekends) and that on Instagram and TikTok content is posted 2 to 3 times a week, it is on TikTok that we can see the most engagement, even with a much smaller number of followers than the other social channels and despite presence for only for 1 year and a half. For example, if we compare the engagement under the Facebook post of October 28 with TikTok post released on the same date we can see that the Facebook post generated 874 likes, comments, and shares and that the TikTok generated

12,360 likes and comments without counting shares ("sharing" data is inaccessible in TikTok, except for the account owner). Because of this through our example, we can see that TikTok generates more engagement than Facebook even having 6 times fewer subscribers. In addition, GTST is one of the only soap opera to have a TikTok account.

TikTok since covid has broken through and has become the leader of social networks with these 3 billion app downloads worldwide [12]. TikTok is so successful that the competitors started copying its formats with reels for Instagram or shorts for YouTube. TikTok is the perfect combination of entertainment and interaction. The platform offers billions of short videos ranging from a few seconds to 10 min. Indeed, one of the characteristics of its success is the ease and freedom of content creation; with frequent technical innovations to encourage innovative formats and trends.

Users accounts have their "timelines" populated with new content corresponding to their tastes and with ease of interaction to like, comment share, and reproduce.

In view of this enthusiasm, brands have also started to create content to this social media channel. As a result, GTST created its TikTok account to reach a younger target group but also to get feedback on its content, specificaly on its TV series.

We can see that the popularity and engagement of GTST post varies tremendously: some posts have 40 000 views and others have 1 million views. Thus, our main research question: Which factors influence engagement on GTST's TikTok?

2   Literature Review

In this section we will be exploring the topics of "profile of TikTok users", the different kinds of engagement trends on TikTok, parasocial relationship and the impacts of hash-tags use. In short, all these topics are important due to their relationship to engagment and meaningful feedback.

2.1   Profile of TikTok Users

To better understand TikTok and its commitment to this platform, it is important to know which part of the population is active there. In Table 1 it is shown the 4 sources of information we used to learn about age group and gender are the most represented on TikTok from a global and national (The Netherlands) point of view. Knowing who the users are will help us define which profile to question during our qualitative study.

Table 1. Articles focusing on age and gender of TikTok users.

	Tiktok users			
Articles	Statista, (2022) Number of TikTok users in the Netherlands from 2021 to 2022, by age group [15]	Jack Sheperd (2022), 20 Essential TikTok Statistics You Need to Know in 2022, Social Sheperd [8]	Start.io, (2022), Tiktok users in the Netherlands [13]	Daniel Ruby (2022), TikTok User Statistics (2022): How many TikTok Users Are There? [11]
Age	Of the 3 million Tiktok users in the Netherlands, 695,000 are between 20 and 24 years old and are the largest age group on the network. In second place are 15–19-year-olds, followed by 25-29-year-olds.	In the United States the most represented age group on Tik-tok, at 25% are 10–19-year-olds followed by 22.4% of 20-29-year-olds. Thus, almost half of the users of Tiktok are under 30 years old	Even though on this survey users under 18 years of age are not represented as they are very active on this platform. We can see that 18-24-year-olds represent 58.5% of Tiktok users in the Netherlands followed by 33.9% of 25-34 year-olds	Worldwide, 19-29 years-old represent 35% of Tiktok users followed by those under 18 with 28% of users. Thus, in the world 63% of users are under 30 years old.
Gender	No information	In the US, 61% of users are women and 31% are men.	In the Netherlands, 73,3% of the users of TikTok are men and 26,7% are women.	Of the billions of Tiktok users worldwide 57% are women and 43% are men

We can see that the under-30 years old are the most represented age group on TikTok representing at least from a national and global point of view half of TikTok users. It should be noted that from a global point of view, in the Netherlands, most users are between 18–24 years old followed very closely by those under 18-year-olds.

In addition, unlike TikTok users worldwide, it is not women who dominate the TikTok market in the Netherlands because nearly three-quarters of the users are men.

2.2 The Different Types of Engagement on TikTok

TikTok like other social networks creates a context allowing its users to have an engaging behavior. Through this review, we will see that they are different kinds of engagement on TikTok. These two articles, in Table 2, will allow us to understand the different levels of engagement of a TikTok user and thus allow us to define the variables that we can use for our quantitative research.

Table 2. The different levels of TikTok engagement

TikTok engagement		
Articles	Keira Shuyang Meng, Louis Leung (2021), Factors influencing TikTok engagement behaviors in China: An examination of gratifications sought, narcissism, and the Big Five personality traits; Telecommunications Policy. Volume 45, Issue 7 [7]	Social Champ, (2022) 5 Proven Ways to Boost Your TikTok Engagement in 2022 [4]
Contribution	A minimum level of engagement, in which users passively consume TikTok content: by liking, commenting, forwarding, following, and adding favorite videos into collection files	- The number of views your videos get. - People who follow you. - People who have added your videos to their favorites. - People who have shared your videos - People who like your videos or find them interesting. - People who comment your video - Total Playtime: It indicates how many people have watched your video till the end
Enhancement	Higher level of engagement, involving TikTok users proactively use different functions to enhance the video quality of TikTok contents by adding special visual effects, background music, and subtitles	- To experiment with different content formats and styles, filters, and effects.
Creation	The highest level of engagement, in which TikTok users make short-form videos, streaming live video, interacting with their favorite creators by making similar videos, sending private messages to creators	- Interaction with the followers on a regular basis. Respond to comments, run polls, put up fun quizzes, and start conversations. (Point of view of a tiktoker to increase the engagement)

In short, Engagement on TikTok can be divided into 3 categories; initially, the minimum level of engagement translates into an action directly accessible when viewing TikTok: likes, comments and shares. Then we can find the medium level of commitment which consists in resuming the video, adding filters, music and reposting it. And the highest level of engagement, with the sending of a private messages, responses to proposed content and creation of derived content taking up that of its creator.

2.3   The Different Kinds of Contents Considered as a Trend on TikTok

TikTok is known for creating content following trends. This type of TikTok content is imitated again and again and highlighted by the algorithm to create engagement. Thus, through the articles from Table 3, we can see the different types of contents that compose the trends.

Table 3. The different kinds of trends

TikTok trends			
Articles	Yingjia Hu, (2020) Research on the commercial value of Tiktok in China, Academic Journal of Business & Management [21]	Ellen Jaudon, (2022) TikTok trends: How to find them and make them your own, Bazarvoice [6]	Crystal Abidin, (2022), Music Challenge Memes on TikTok: understanding In-Group Storytelling Videos, International Journal of Communication [18]
Dancing	X	X	X
Challenges	X	X	X
Songs	X	X	X
Sounds		X	X
Features		X	X
Transformations		X	
Choose your character		X	
Mash-up		X	
Celebrities/Influencers	X	X	X

We can conclude that the most well-known trends on TikTok are essentially challenges, songs with lip-sync, dances, sounds, and features.

In addition, "something" becomes a trend after being created by a TikToker/Influencer or relayed by those who have the effect of being imitated by their subscribers.

Trends such as "TikTok transformations", "choose your character" or "mash-ups" are assimilated to very important communities on this network such as makeup, series, manga, and music passionates.

2.4 The Parasocial Relationship

GTST is a soap opera that has existed for more than 30 years. Given this scenario, many viewers can see themselves through this series and these characters. So, a high level of parasocial relationship is expected.

The articles listed on Table 4, help to better understand this relationship and its different criteria as well as the importance of social networks in this kind of relationship.

Through these articles, we can learn that the parasocial relationship is born from a character that the viewer loved or to whom he can identify. Which will create a strong bond of attachment between the two parties as evidenced by the comments under the TikTok of GTST which refers to the arrival of a child. Thus, social networks are perfect proof of this relationship with likes, comments, and fan page creations, which promote interactions and intensify the parasocial relationship.

Two of the articles express the fact that this is an imaginary relationship, or an illusion because the fan has the impression of knowing the character while they have never really talked and seen each other and that the character does not know his fan.

Table 4. The criteria of a parasocial relationship

Parasocial Relationship			
Articles	Jonathan Cohen (2004) Parasocial Break-Up from Favorite Television Characters: The Role of Attachment Styles and Relationship Intensity, Journal of social and para relationship [2]	Cynthia A.Hoffner, Bradley J.Bond, (2022), Parasocial relationships, social media, & well-being, Current Opinion in Psychology [5]	Tucker, Melissa (2020) Parasocial Relationships Among Film Consumers: Can Film Celebrities Influence Purchase Intentions? [17]
Favorite character	X	X	X
Attachment	X	X	X
Imitation / Models	X	X	
Imaginary relationships	X		X
Interaction	X	X	X

Finally, the parasocial relationship, create in the fans a desire for imitation because they see it as an example that can be translated into life choices related to the actions of the actors in the series, or the reproduction of an action from a TikTok post with their favorite character.

2.5 The Impacts of the Hashtag

Since the arrival of social networks and notably Twitter, hashtags (the famous "#") are omnipresent in messages and posts.

But what is the real impact of hashtags?

What are they used for?

Do they really have influence on engagement?

Through the articles in Table 5, we can find those answers.

Based on these articles, we can see that hashtags are accelerators that allow people with the same passions, opinions and tastes to interact more easily. Indeed, hashtags make it possible to categorize the content and allow potentially interested people to have access to it.

Some hashtags are more popular and therefore more viral and are often written when the content is a trend, a challenge. Thus, searching and finding this kind of content, thanks to the hashtags, makes it possible to gather ideas to creators for their next "potential viral" content.

Based on the literature review we established 3 hypotheses to answer our main research question: Which factors influence engagement on TikTok?

H1: The kind of content on TikTok influences the level of engagement.

H2: The number of relevant comments is influenced by the kind of content on TikTok.

H3: The number of hashtags used on TikTok influences the level of engagement.

Table 5. The impacts of hashtags

The impacts of the hashtag			
Articles	Guarda, T., Augusto, M. F., Victor, J. A., Mazón, L. M., Lopes, I., & Oliveira, P. (2021). The Impact of TikTok on Digital Marketing. SpringerLink. [3]	On Utilizing Communities Detected From Social Networks in Hashtag Recommendation. (2020, August 1). IEEE Journals & Magazine [9]	Budnik, E., Gaputina, V, & Boguslavskaya, V. (2019). Dynamic of hashtag functions development in new media. Proceedings of the XI International Scientific Conference Communicative Strategies of the Information Society. [1]
Help for creating content	X	X	X
Generate viral content	X	X	X
To capitalize on local trends	X		
Personalized recommendations	X	X	X
Hashtag Challenge	X		
Development of interactions	X	X	X

Indeed, according to the literature on trends in TikTok and the notion of parasocial relationships, we have seen their impact on interactions. However, these two types of content are not the only ones used by GTST's TikTok account so to test our first hypothesis we will consider all types of content posted and see their impact on engagement.

3 Methodology

A mixed methods approach was chosen to tackle this research problem. Both qualitative and quantitative techniques were employed to understand what content influences engagement on TikTok.

The first step was a quantitative data gathering and analysis. Some results from the quantitative phase were further explored during the qualitative step.

Both approaches will be described below.

3.1 Quantitative Step

To answer our problem and determine the influences of engagement on GTST's TikTok, we have established three hypotheses that we will seek to verify. Thus, through different tests we will test if the engagement on TikTok is related to randomness or if there is a real correlation with the chosen variables.

We collected the data that for the quantitative phase from GTST's TikTok account posts [16]. The posts were analyzed regarding the number of views, comments, likes, and hashtags. Concerning the valence of the comments, they were classified regarding their relevance, as opposed to just counting any comment. The data of all posts, 133 in total, were analysed.

The posts were labelled in six categories to see if there was a difference in engagement depending on the type of content. The categories were "trend-related content", "parasocial relationship content", a "mixed content" (trend and parasocial-relationship), "spoiler content", "promotional content" (podcasts, series, etc.), and "others".

Measures. To test the hypotheses T-tests were applied to checkif the difference between the measures/groups is statistically significant or may have happened by chance. So, independent samples t-test will be used to test the two first hypotheses. For the last hypothesis, we used the correlation test to verify the relationships between engagement and the number of hashtags.

3.2 Qualitative Step

On top of the quantitative step, semi-structured interviews with GTST fans were held, to investigate in more details the preferred content and insights leading to better engagement and feedback.

The target group for these interviews were GTST viewers who are active on not only Social Media, but also on TikTok. The interviewees were all from The Netherlands (GTST is in Dutch), aged 17 to 24 years.

After holding 11 semi-structured interviews, the saturation was reached and this qualitative data gathering finished.

The guiding questions are listed below:

- How much time do you spend on TikTok on a daily basis?
- Do you follow the GTST TikTok account?
- Have you ever interacted with a TikTok posted on the GTST account? For instance: liked a post, commented under it or shared a post?
- What content do you most enjoy on the GTST TikTok account?
- Do you follow other GTST accounts on other Social Media platforms? Why or why not?
- Is there specific content on the GTST TikTok account that influences your engagement?
- In general, do you engage a lot with content posted on TikTok? If so, what do you typically do?
- Have you ever left feedback on a GTST TikTok post before?
- Is there content you dislike on the GTST TikTok account?
- Do you have a preference when it comes to which actor or actress makes a TikTok on the GTST TikTok account?
- Have you ever looked up certain hashtags on TikTok? If so, how often do you use this function?
- What would you improve on the GTST TikTok account?

Based on what our interviewees replied, we adapted and asked further questions related to the answers given by them.

4 Findings

As a summary of the quantitative results, it was observed that the "trending" kind of content has a specific influence on engagement. It can improve the number of views (Eq. 1).

$$t(100) = 2.385, p = 0.019 \tag{1}$$

and the number of comments (Eq. 2).

$$t(82.3) = 2.042, p = 0.044 \tag{2}$$

but not the number of "likes" (Eq. 3).

$$t(131) = 0.633, p = 0.528 \tag{3}$$

"Parasocial relationship" content can influences the number of views (Eq. 4),

$$t(49.6) = -2.634, p = 0.11 \tag{4}$$

but, it doesn't influence the number of likes (Eq. 5),

$$t(131) = -0.585, p = 0.560 \tag{5}$$

and the number of comments (Eq. 6),

$$t(131) = -1.095, p = 0.276 \tag{6}$$

The "spoiler" kind of content doesn't have influence on the number of views (Eq. 7),

$$t(131) = -0.892, p = 0.374 \tag{7}$$

on the number of likes (Eq. 8),

$$t(131) = -0.22, p = 0.983 \tag{8}$$

and neither in the number of comments (Eq. 9),

$$t(131) = -0.452, p = 0.652 \tag{9}$$

The same happened with the mixed (trend and parasocial relationship) content, which hasn't influence on the number of views (Eq. 10),

$$t(131) = -0.554, p = 0.581 \tag{10}$$

on the number of likes (Eq. 11),

$$t(131) = 1.235, p = 0.219 \tag{11}$$

and the number of comments (Eq. 12),

$$t(131) = -0.258, p = 0.796 \tag{12}$$

although the sample was too small for these parts of the analysis and further research would be useful.

"Promotional" content doesn't influence the number of views (Eq. 13),

$$t(131) = -1.608, p = 0.110 \tag{13}$$

and the number of comments (Eq. 14),

$$t(131) = -1.648, p = 0.102 \tag{14}$$

however, influences the number of likes (Eq. 15),

$$t(90) = -1.922, p = < 0.001 \tag{15}$$

Regarding the valence of the comments (relevant comments), only "promotional" content showed influence on the number of relevant comments (Eq. 16),

$$t(124.9) = -3.732, p = < 0.001 \tag{16}$$

Regarding the "other" kind of content, no analysis could be done due to the limited number of posts with this kind of content.

It was also tested the correlation between the number of hashtags and the level of engagement. In all kinds of engagement, the correlation was low ($<30\%$) although statistically significant. The correlation between the number of hashtags and the number of views is (Eq. 17).

$$0.254, p = 0.003 \tag{17}$$

between the number of hashtags and the number of likes is (Eq. 18).

$$0.218, p = 0.012 \tag{18}$$

and between the number of hashtags and the number of comments is (Eq. 19).

$$0.198, p = 0.022 \tag{19}$$

5 Conclusion

The TikTok account of GTST is one of the more popular social media accounts that GTST owns. With more than 82.000 followers and 1.4 million likes and close to 140 posts in less than two years, they have built a strong audience base.

By looking at the engagement on the GTST TikTok account, and noticing that there were different outcomes per post, we asked ourselves: Which factors influence engagement on GTST's TikTok?

To help answer our research question (Which factors influence engagement on GTST's TikTok?), we established 3 hypotheses:

1. "The kind of content on TikTok influences the level of engagement."
2. "The number of relevant comments is influenced by the kind of content on TikTok."
3. "The number of hashtags used on TikTok influences the level of engagement."

We analyzed every post uploaded to the GTST TikTok account and also held semi-structured interviews with loyal viewers of GTST to see if they had additional insights.

Joining these quantitative results with the insights from the qualitative part of the research, it is possible to conclude that all our hypotheses are confirmed.

For the hypothesis "1", "The kind of content on TikTok influences the level of engagement.", we found that TikTok posts that lean into trends, has an impact on the number of views and comments.

One of the main goals from the GTST marketing team was to acquire more meaningful feedback from the viewers. With that and the second hypothesis in mind, which is "the number of relevant comments is influenced by the kind of content on TikTok", we found that promotional content, content that intrigues the viewers, and very funny content, increases the amount of relevant comments. Our interviewees stated that they do not have a habit of commenting under posts by the GTST TikTok, but they do not have this anywhere else, but they still comment when they are either intrigued or when asked for.

For the third hypothesis, "The number of hashtags used on TikTok influences the level of engagement", we found that it does influence the level of engagement, but not to a big extent. The use of hashtags allows users that like a post that has a hashtag in it, to find more TikTok's using the same hashtag. Only one of our interviewees ever used hashtags to find something on TikTok, but the data collected in the quantitative step and from the literature review, shows that it does make a difference.

After both the qualitative and the quantitative part of our research, we can conclude that the algorithm on TikTok has the biggest influence on the engagement of any TikTok account, not just GTST her account. When it comes to the wanted increase of feedback by the viewers of the show, we found that this can be increased by posting more content that:

– Has to do with the show.
– Intrigues the viewers.
– And explicitly asks viewers for feedback.

The posts where the viewers were asked to comment and reply with a certain answer have the most comments. In some instances, the increase is almost 300% more when comparing it to the average amount of comments. The interviewees also stated that they would love to help out and would comment feedback if this was directly asked. The same goes for Q&A's and interaction-based posts.

In short, focusing on the kind of content described above and explicitly ask for feedback seems to be a strategy able to increase the amount of meaningful feedback, allowing the company to use this feedback to improve the GTST episodes.

References

1. Budnik, E., Gaputina, V., Boguslavskaya, V.: Dynamic hashtag functions development in new media. In: Proceedings of the XI International Scientific Conference Communicative Strategies of the Information Society (2019).https://doi.org/10.1145/3373722.3373795

2. Cohen, J.: Parasocial break-up from favorite television characters: the role of attachment styles and relationship intensity. J. Soc. Pers. Relat. **21**(2), 187–202 (2004). https://doi.org/10.1177/0265407504041374

3. Guarda, T., Augusto, M.F., Victor, J.A., Mazón, L.M., Lopes, I., Oliveira, P.: The Impact of TikTok on Digital Marketing. SpringerLink (2021). ISBN10.1007/978–981–33–4183–8

4. Hafeez, Y.: How to increase TikTok engagement in 2022. Social Champ. https://www.social champ.io/blog/tiktok-engagement/. Accessed 29 Sep 2022

5. Hoffner, C.A., Bond, B.J.: Parasocial relationships, social media, & well-being. Curr. Opin. Psychol. **45**, 101306 (2022). https://doi.org/10.1016/j.copsyc.2022.101306

6. Jaudon, E.: TikTok trends: How to find them and make them your own. Bazaarvoice. https://www.bazaarvoice.com/blog/tiktok-trends-how-to/. Accessed 09 Sep 2022

7. Shuyang Meng, K., Leung, L.: Factors influencing TikTok engagement behaviors in China: an examination of gratifications sought, narcissism, and the Big Five personality traits. Telecommunications Policy **45**(7) (2021)

8. The Social Shepherd. 20 Essential TikTok Statistics You Need to Know in 2022. https://thesocialshepherd.com/blog/tiktok-statistics. Accessed 05 Oct 2022

9. On Utilizing Communities Detected From Social Networks in Hashtag Recommendation. IEEE Journals & Magazine I IEEE Xplore. https://ieeexplore.ieee.org/abstract/document/9086880. Accessed 01 Aug 2022

10. Richter, F.: The Generation Gap in TV Consumption. Statista Infographics. https://www.statista.com/chart/15224/daily-tv-consumption-by-us-adults/. Accessed 20 Nov 2020

11. Ruby, D.: TikTok User Statistics (2022): How many TikTok Users Are There? T https://www.demandsage.com/tiktok-user-statistics/. Accessed 19 Aug 2022

12. Sensor Tower. (n.d.). Nearly One-Third of TikTok's Installed Base Uses the App Every Day. https://sensortower.com/blog/tiktok-power-user-curve. Accessed 04 Nov 2022

13. Start.io I Tiktok Users in Netherlands Audience. (n.d.). https://www.start.io/audience/tiktok-users-in-netherlands. Accessed 05 Nov 2022

14. Statista. Average daily time spent on social media worldwide 2012–2022. https://www.statista.com/statistics/433871/daily-social-media-usage-worldwide/. Accessed 22 Aug 2022

15. Statista. TikTok users in the Netherlands 2021–2022, by age group. https://www.statista.com/statistics/1225413/tiktok-users-netherlands-by-age-group/. Accessed 08 Aug 2022

16. TikTok. (n.d.). https://www.tiktok.com/@gtstnl. Accessed 20 Dec 2022

17. Tucker, M.: Parasocial Relationships Among Film Consumers: Can Film Celebrities Influence Purchase Intentions? - ProQuest. (n.d.) from https://www.proquest.com/openview/20da77719436609c369bf7cf24c7cb7c/1?cbl=44156. Accessed 20 Nov 2022

18. Vizcaíno-Verdú, A.: Music Challenge Memes on TikTok: Understanding In-Group Storytelling Videos I Vizcaíno-Verdú I International Journal of Communication (2022)

19. Wikipedia-bijdragers. Goede tijden, slechte tijden. https://nl.wikipedia.org/wiki/Goede_tijden,_slechte_tijden. Accessed 03 Nov 2022

20. Wikipedia contributors. Transmedia storytelling. https://en.wikipedia.org/wiki/Transmedia_storytelling. Accessed 29 Oct 2022

21. Hu, Y.: Research on the commercial value of Tiktok in China I Francis Academic Press. https://francis-press.com/papers/2887. Accessed 06 Nov 2022

Research on User Experience Design Based on Affinity Diagram Assisting User Modeling – Taking Music Software as an Example

Zhengxian He and Huaming Peng[✉]

School of Design, South China University of Technology, Guangzhou 510006,
People's Republic of China
huamingpengedu@163.com

Abstract. User experience design always takes user research as the center. Designers guide the design by establishing a relatively correct user model. As a qualitative research method, user interviews are often used in user research. This paper introduces affinity graph method into how to deal with the data of consulting method, and helps to build user behavior patterns and psychological patterns in the numerous consulting data, so as to establish user models. In the specific practice, this paper takes a popular music software in China as the specific research object, and improves one module of the software by understanding the user's experience, behavior characteristics, needs, and expectations. By recruiting real users, using affinity graph to sort out interview data, and comparing users with similar line trends on the user behavior variable graph, this paper finds that the line trends of 7 interviewees can be divided into three categories, and then three typical users are discovered. Through above, this paper develops the output of design models.

Keywords: Affinity Diagram · user experience design · user modeling · behavior variables

1 Affinity Diagram

1.1 Principle of Affinity Diagram

In the early 1980s, the Japanese quality industry began to popular QC new seven techniques, they are: correlation graph method, affinity graph (KJ) method, system diagram method, matrix diagram method, matrix data analysis method, PDPC (process, decision, procedure, graph) method, sagittal graph method. The new seven QC techniques are mainly used to provide effective and scientific methods and ways for the planning stage of production. It is based on the language data, through the qualitative analysis of the information from the internal and external aspects of the enterprise, to implement the rationalization of decisions, so as to ensure the quality. The new seven techniques of

QC include the ideas of system science such as operation research, system engineering and value engineering, and they are sharp weapons for managers to make plans and coordinate and control in the new era.

Affinity diagram (KJ) method for Japan Sichuan xi tian Jiro, Affinity diagram analysis tool is type A diagram (type A diagram only applies to need time to solve the problem, does not apply to solve simple problem immediately), is the collected data and information, according to the similarity of their classification analysis method, also known as the card classification [1]. Affinity diagram is a way of thinking about questions. The human brain is divided into two parts, and the human thinking and behavior is controlled by the left part of the brain, which is rational, not creative. If the function of the left brain is suppressed and the right brain of the human brain is activated consciously, creative thinking can be conducted. Affinity diagram is based on the above principles to analyze and solve problems. In specific application, using the Affinity diagram, the first should determine the research object, then through research analysis of the problem of the object, list these problems, find the internal relationship between these problems, such as associated causal hierarchical relationship and mutual affinity classification, in the form of graphic visualization, then from the essence of the key problem, is beneficial to break through the inherent mode of thinking, finally find the best solution.

1.2 The Affinity Diagram Method and the User Modeling

In user research, qualitative research usually involves user interview, which is a method to use purposeful, planned and systematic oral conversation to understand the facts from users. User interview is a kind of research-based conversation, which is the collection and combing of the data to be consciously obtained through the oral communication between the two parties. User interviews generally have a clear time arrangement and the topic of the conversation, different from the ordinary conversation, the user interview must strive to be true in the process, cannot casually agree with or evaluate what the user said, and the recording behavior is often accompanied by the process, after the interview should be combed and summarized after the event. User interview can be divided into three types: non-structured interview, semi-structured interview and fully structured interview. Generally need to go through the following process: according to the project research purpose to build the core hypothesis, through the core hypothesis to establish interview purpose, list the interview screening criteria, the interview purpose idea related assumptions, according to the interview outline, writing interview plan (determine the interview way, time, place, etc.), recruit the interview object, interview, interview data.

Among them, the collation of the interview data is particularly critical. Whether the typical users and their characteristics can be found from the large amount of the interview data, and the construction of user portraits (user modeling) is very important for the design of the later products, which determines whether the designed products/services can be well corresponding to the real needs of the users.

In the collation of the interview data, the Affinity diagram (card sorting method) can be introduced. After clarifying the purpose of the interview, the interviewees need to be numbered first, and then for the large amount of interview data, the minimum key information needs to be extracted and written on the card, with the number of the corresponding interviewees [2]. Then to a large number of card classification, classify the card information extraction, and extract the common value information on the corresponding secondary card, after the secondary card after the same operation (see Fig. 1), and so on, generally to the third/fourth round, can find out from a large number of interview data behind the user behavior variables [3].

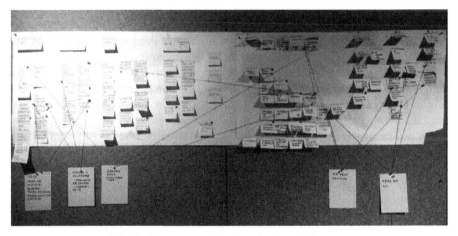

Fig. 1. The process of sorting data by affinity map

The Affinity diagram was used to sort out the interview data. After classifying the information of the secondary cards and the tertiary cards, it was observed that some significant behaviors of the interviewees could be listed as several different groups of behavioral variables. Demographic variables such as age or geographical location also seem to influence which variables can be referred to by users, but it should be noted that we cannot focus on demographics and focus on specific behavioral variables [4]. After selecting the user behavior variables, it is necessary to draw the user behavior variable map, and correspond the involved interviewees one to one on the user behavior variable map. After the connection, the trends of the behavioral variables of each interviewee were compared, and the interviewees with similar trends were classified into one category. Finally, through the above methods, the interviewees involved can be classified and facilitate for subsequent user modeling.

Below shows a learning software user behavior variable figure (see Fig. 2), the left for the Affinity diagram purification of behavior variables, such as "learning reason" "learning attitude", "learning time" "learning consumption", after each kind of behavior variables, such as "learning reason" to distinguish the "test preparation, career development, amateur interest, continuous growth" (are from affinity graph purification behavior pattern), and then each interview behavior one by one corresponding to the graph and the attachment (shown in the gray line).

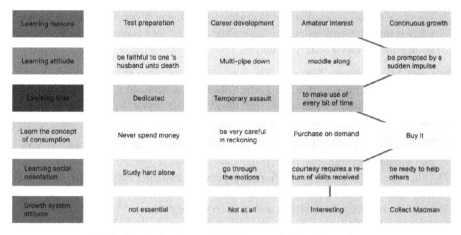

Fig. 2. User behavior variable diagram of a learning software

2 Specific Practice

2.1 Project Background

NetEase Cloud Music is an online music software launched by a Chinese Internet company named NetEase. It takes the characteristic music community as its product highlight and has received a large number of users. As the online music industry entered the stock market from the incremental market, all online music software began to focus on building their own music community to improve user activity. In 2019, Netease Cloud Music also integrated its existing social functions and launched a social segment called Yun Cun (literally translated as Cloud Village). However, according to the data, from the end of 2020 to the third quarter of 2021, the number of active users of the software has only increased by 4 million in nine months. It can be seen that the launch of Yun Cun has not brought substantial increase in the user activity of the software. I will start with the users of the Yun Cun module of the music software, conduct user research, build a user portrait of the Yun Cun, find out the shortcomings of the product, and make targeted improvements.

2.2 User Research

Purpose of User Research. Learn about Netease Cloud Music users' experience, behavior, needs, pain points and expectations in the Yun Cun module.

Desktop Research. The user group of Yun Cun is young people aged 20–29. Main characteristics of this group:

(1) The young user group is the main user group of Netease Cloud. It is more personalized. It is more willing to find users with common music interests to communicate and discuss, and use music to make friends or get topic exchanges.

(2) Users are mainly located in first-tier, second-tier and new first-tier cities; this part of users is mainly characterized by the middle class of society, moderate consumption ability and focus on quality of life.

Relevant Assumptions. Netease Cloud has such a large number of users, but the activity of the cloud village is very thin. This article wants to understand why users do not want to use the Cloud Village section. Based on the above user research purposes and desktop research, the following assumptions are proposed:

(1) The interactive activity here is low, and users can't get a certain sense of achievement and satisfaction here
(2) Other social platforms have higher quality content and can easily find the information they want to browse.
(3) Unable to interact with friends and have no desire to share.
(4) The cloud village is not closely related to the content it likes, the module is independent, and the overall use is not high.
(5) Only used to listening to music in Netease Cloud and sharing music on other platforms.
(6) Not interested in music social content.
(7) Uploading does not realize certain benefits, and the incentive mechanism is not high.
(8) The content quality is not high, the social atmosphere is weak, and there is no motivation to interact.
(9) Unable to look back at the video after interaction. The entrance is complex for users and not easy to operate.

Clearly Interview Users. Young users aged 20–30 who often use social apps and have used the Cloud Village section in the past month.

Interview Outline. This paper divides the interview into five parts in the form of structured interview. The specific interview outline is as follows.

Usage of Netease Cloud Music. The questions are as follows.

(1) Why do you choose to use Netease Cloud to listen to music?
(2) When did you first use Netease Cloud Music? How often? How long is the average time of each use?
(3) What sections and functions do you often use in Netease Cloud Music? What attracts you? Where will the interaction take place? How to interact?

Vertical analysis of user behavior. The questions are as follows.

(1) Can you briefly describe the function modules in Yun Cun?
(2) In what scenario do you usually use Yun Cun? How often? How long will it be used each time?
(3) What content do you like to browse in Yun Cun?
(4) Is the content recommended by Yun Cun what you want? Will you directly search the content you want to see in Yun Cun? How do you feel about the whole search process? Can the classification of segments meet your use needs?
(5) Do you usually interact in Yun Cun]? What are the commonly used interactive functions? Would you like someone to reply to you?

(6) How often do you use Yun Cun to publish music creation content? What type of content do you like to publish?

(7) What is your original intention of publishing videos in Yun Cun? Will you continue to follow comments and likes after the release?

(8) Can you briefly show or describe the specific operation steps of publishing music content? How do you feel during the whole operation procedure?

(9) Have you used other APP platforms to publish content?

(10) What do you think are the advantages/disadvantages of Yun Cun? Are you willing to recommend Yun Cun to the people around you? Why?

(11) Have you ever encountered any problems when using Yun Cun? Try to solve it? How to solve it?

Horizontal comparison of other products. The questions are as follows.

(1) Do you pay attention to the social sector of other platforms? What attracts you?

(2) What improvements do you hope Yun Cun can make?

Interview. Seven NetEase Cloud Music users were recruited online for interviews (see Table 1). From the perspective of user characteristics, the selected interviewees were mainly white-collar workers and students, who had used Cloud Village in the past month, and were loyal users of NetEase Cloud Music.

Table 1. Data of interviewees

Name (virtual)	Number	Gender	Occupation	Usage Frequency of Yun Cun
Qing	U1	Male	Liberal professions	Twice a week/once for 10 min
Zheng	U2	Male	Graduate student	1–2 times a week/5–10 min a time
Zhao	U3	Female	College student	Once a month/once for 10 min
He	U4	Male	Graduate student	Once a month/10 min each time
Huang	U5	Male	White collar	Twice a month/1 h each time
Chen	U6	Female	White collar	Once a week/once for 1 h
Xing	U7	Female	Graduate student	1–2 times per month/10 min per time

The interview was conducted online one-on-one (see Fig. 3).

Use Affinity Map to Organize Data. Disassemble the original interview data of seven interviewees into yellow label information (one label only shows one important information) to facilitate the construction of affinity map. More than 300 labels were finally disassembled. According to the idea of affinity map method, up to 300 yellow labels are sorted. By organizing the information, classify and group the groups with similar meanings, name the obtained groups, and repeat the process until the obtained groups can no longer be merged (see Fig. 4).

Fig. 3. Interview site

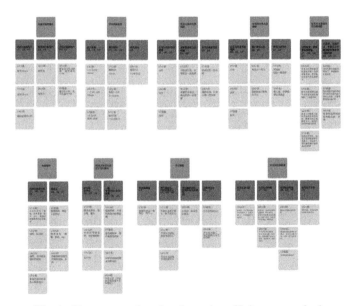

Fig. 4. The process of sorting data using affinity map method

Select the higher-level label in the affinity map as the behavior variable to facilitate drawing the user's behavior variable map. Draw the selected behavior variable into a table (see Table 2).

Table 2. Behavioral variable

Behavior	Variables of different degrees under this behavior (User number corresponding to this variable)			
Netease Cloud Usage	Frequent use (U5 U7)	Occasional use (U2 U6)	Less used (U1 U3 U4)	–
Yun Cun Usage	Frequent use (U6)	Occasional use (U1 U2 U5)	Less used (U3 U4 U7)	–
Publishing content in Cloud Village	Send videos to get attention (U2 U3)	No video has been released (U5 U6 U 7)	Send video for recording (U1 U4)	–
Frequency of publishing content in Yun Cun	Active (U1 U3)	Occasionally (U2 U4)	Almost none (U5 U6 U7)	–
Sensitivity to the musicality of cloud village content	Don't care (U3 U6 U7)	More concerned (U1 U2 U4 U5)	–	–
Content preferences	More abundant (U3 U6 U7)	Only related to music (U1 U2 U4 U5)	–	–
Social interaction of Netease Cloud except for Yun Cun	Active (U1 U3 U4)	Commonly (U5 U6 U2 U7)	–	–
Willingness to subscribe to favorite bloggers	High willingness (U3)	Moderate willingness (U1 U2 U4)	Low willingness (U6)	No subscription (U5 U7)
Interaction activity	Active (U3)	Moderate (U1 U2)	Lower (U4 U6 U7)	Almost none (U5)

Draw the above behavior variables into a graph, and connect each user's behavior variables into different color lines (see Fig. 5).

Compare users with similar line trends above to build user behavior models and refine user groups. It was found that the line trend of the seven interviewees could be divided into three categories (see Table 3), and finally three typical users of Netease Cloud Music were identified, which were: music people seeking resonance; Music lovers who record life and mood; Netease musicians eager for attention.

Design Optimization Point. Through the above user research, this paper combs out 16 design optimization points for the cloud village module.

(1) Increase the connection between Yun Cun and friends, and enhance the sense of interaction.
(2) Enhance the connection between the song listening page and the Yun Cun, and integrate resources.
(3) Rich release dynamic operability.

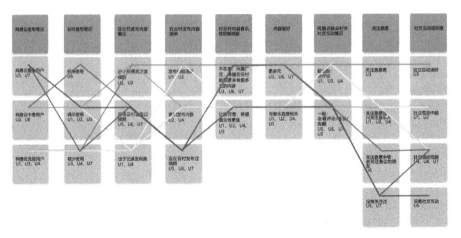

Fig. 5. Behavior variable diagram (Color figure online)

Table 3. Line trend comparison result

Name of this typical user	User characteristics	Line extracted on behavior variable graph
Music people seeking resonance	They will not actively publish content, love music, and have certain social interaction, but they are generally inactive. The few social interactions are mainly music-driven, seeking resonance in music, and have social potential	
Music lovers who record life and mood	They will upload videos. Social activities are more active than the first category of "music people". They will comment on the content they are interested in. They release videos to record life and mood	

(continued)

Table 3. (*continued*)

Name of this typical user	User characteristics	Line extracted on behavior variable graph
Netease musicians eager for attention	The videos uploaded by them are excellent and social. They pay special attention to the interactive comments of their own videos and will review back. They are a user group that can drain the cloud village and promote the sound development of the community content ecology	

(4) Rich special effects, templates and other functions.
(5) Provide users with some sources of inspiration.
(6) Provide quick access to browse and interactive records.
(7) Community content classification provides personalized services.
(8) For example, strengthen the feedback prompt of the message from visual, text and other aspects.
(9) Encourage music critics and singers to publish more, and broaden the channels of paying attention to high-quality bloggers and interaction.
(10) Summary of operation topics with obvious entrance.
(11) Introduce video guidance to improve release confidence.
(12) Enrich the differentiation between different comments.
(13) Strengthen the contact between friends and promote interaction in Yun Cun.
(14) Enhance the music attributes of Yun Cun.
(15) Provide users with a way to find resonance in Yun Cun.
(16) Help to quickly understand video content, popularity and other information.

Design Output. Through the comparison of novelty, practicability and feasibility, the following design optimization point is selected for design output: providing users with a way to find resonance in Yun Cun (see Fig. 6).

The Hi-fi Prototype

Fig. 6. Design output

3   Summary and Discussion

This paper uses the affinity graph method to sort and sort out the data of NetEase Cloud Music user interviews, sifts out the available user behavior variables from the classified higher-level card tags, and draws a behavior variable graph. The interviewees are marked and connected in the graph one by one, and the interviewees with similar line trends can be extracted into a class of user groups and subsequent user modeling. According to the analysis of user research, design optimization points are obtained and one of them is selected for design output. For qualitative research such as user interviews, affinity graph method is a good method for classifying, analyzing and sorting out data, providing a quantitative basis for the process of user modeling, enabling designers to get rid of personal subjective positions, and truly start from data, and build user models rationally and rigorously.

References

1. Takahashi, M.: Distributed interface for group affinity-diagram brainstorming. Concurr. Eng. Res. Appl. **24**(4), 344–358 (2016)
2. Yan, J., Lijuan, S., Lujun, L.: Application of KJ method in improved design. Art Des. **9**, 95–97 (2015)
3. Song, Y., Xiao, J.: Research on user potential demand mining method based on KJ method. Bus. Cult. **5**, 135 (2012)
4. Manuel, G.A., Carlos, T., Jorge, P., et al.: Effectiveness of three communication methods in a realtime KJ method creativity support groupware. Front. Artif. Intell. Appl. (2012)

A Speculative Design Perspective on the Emotional Symbiosis of Virtual Pets and People

Weixuan He, Hongyan Chen[(⊠)], and Wa An

Guangzhou Academy of Fine Arts, Guangzhou 510006, China
361959815@qq.com

Abstract. "Loneliness" has been a topic often mentioned by young people in recent years. Many studies have shown that having a companion pet can help to reduce anxiety and loneliness. However, due to living conditions and financial pressures, it is not possible to keep a virtual pet as an alternative, but the potential for virtual pets to be used as partners in life has been explored and promoted. Nevertheless, because of the restriction of the current equipment and interaction medium, we cannot genuinely build a good two-way companionship between human and virtual pets. Nowadays with the advanced smart technology, in addition to proposing the future and non-realistic aesthetics, Speculative Design is more based on the current technology and social phenomenon and issues for in-depth thinking, to go beyond people's design concept of consumption as the underlying logic, and to let themselves as the subject of driving dynamics, to make reasonable guesses about the future. The purpose of this study is to use speculative design as a baseline and teaching practice in university courses, require students to record and observe daily behaviour of animals around them. After observing and documenting the animal's instincts, behaviour and characteristics, we analyze and summarize the design strategies for speculative emotions. The design of the virtual pets is based on the interdisciplinary approach of bionics, art design, human-computer interaction, and digital media. This study aims to broaden the design thinking and vision of virtual pets to better help people generate emotional symbiosis.

Keywords: speculative design · virtual pets · emotional symbiosis

1 Introduction

In the current fast-moving social environment, the psychosocial problems caused by "loneliness" have become an important issue to be explored. Many studies have shown that keeping a companion pet can help people reduce loneliness and anxiety, according to the White Paper on China Pet Industry Trends Insights 2022, published by Jingdong, the number of local pet-owning households in China has reached 91.47 million in 2021 and is expected to exceed 100 million in 2022. However, many people are unable to keep their pets due to economic and living environment constraints. The development of virtual pets for companionship and interaction as partners in life has the potential to be explored and promoted. From the development of the world-famous game called E-Chicken by Bandai employee Aki Mamabata in 1996, to the popularity of Toei's Digital Monster anime in 1999, to the development of Sony's Aibo dogs and the popularity of Nintendo's Pokemon series, the quest for virtual pets has never stopped. As technology has developed and advanced, consumers have begun to be more than just satisfied with the functionality of virtual pets. They hope to interact with virtual pets more in a spiritual way. There are relatively few studies at home and abroad on how virtual pets can be emotionally constructed in the future, and so far there has been no clear direction on how virtual pets will be born, nurtured and emotionally symbiotic with people in the future.

2 Speculation and Design

2.1 About the Emotional Symbiosis Concept

The concept of symbiosis was developed by the German mycologist De Berry and it reflects the interdependence of organisms in their living environment, which is often referred to in social, economic and political issue [1]. This paper uses the concept of symbiosis to investigate how people and virtual pets can empathize with each other to achieve the goal of empathy. The concept of empathy comes from the field of psychology, where the psychologist Edward B. Titchener first introduced in his "Lectures on Experimental Psychology of Thought Processes". Empathy is an emotional projection, a dynamic mental process directed towards an object that is subjectively imitated by the individual [2]. Commonly interpreted as if one had experienced it by himself. Cognitive empathy is unique to human beings, also it is the act of inferring that a person can actively perceive the way of other persons' thinking and feeling, and thus make alternative feelings about the individual [3].

2.2 Virtual Pets Based on a Speculative Design Perspective

Virtual pets, also known as smart pets, are interactive toys produced through current industry and specific web-based programs developed through information technology. The first virtual pet to enter the public domain was called the "E-Chicken" developed in 1996 by Aki Manabe, an employee of Bandai Japan, who was unable to keep a pet in her flat. Soon this led to a global "chicken fever" craze. From the development of the game series called Pokemon by Nintendo in 1996, to Toei's 1999 anime Digital Monster which told the story of a world with digital pets, to the Chinese popular online pet community QQ Pet in the early 21st century, to the birth of the Aibo dog [4]. Although the popularity of virtual pets has endured, due to the limited time of development, there is relatively little research has been conducted at home and abroad on how to cultivate the emotional relationship between virtual pets and human. This study aims to provide a basic discussion of the future development of virtual pets through the means of speculative design.

The concept of speculative design is a new one introduced by Dunn and Raby in "Speculative Everything: Design, Fiction and Social Dreams" [5]. In addition to the non-realistic aesthetics of imagination and fiction, what speculative design emphasizes more is a cautious inference to a parallel world based on the technical reality of the real world. While the way of thinking can be outside of the current social situation, the inferences about the future that result from speculative thinking should be thought-provoking. Although the current technological development of virtual pets is still far from the point where they can have conscious and emotional interactions with human as subjective individuals, society and different disciplines about that have never ceased to study the relationship between virtual pets and human beings. As designers themselves, how to articulate the concept of virtual pets reasonably through speculative design? First, speculative thinking should be thought about to the fullest extent without restriction. It is not the desire to solve problems through design, but rather to stimulate human's thought through visual representation. Design is merely the medium which inspires more people to understand the development of virtual pets in the future through different means of design, offering a tangible possibility for the development of virtual pets in the future and thus catalyze the guidance of dreams [6].

3 Strategies for the Application of Speculative Design Concepts in Virtual Pet Design

A concrete idea of how to stimulate the value of the application of speculative design should be developed in the design process of virtual pets. To begin with, we learn about current researches on virtual pets then analyze and integrate systematically. Second, we expand on and understand the relevant disciplines. Moreover, the traditional virtual pet products are based on the design logic of "designer-virtual pet-human". This study combines an empathy map with the creation of virtual pet images, conducting a systematic survey to track people who are aware of and interested in virtual pets. Next, we offer related questions to develop a hypothesis about the elements of existence of virtual pet in the future through the data and images from the survey, to inspire people to think for example, in what ways can human develop emotions with their virtual pets? We create a "human-virtual pet" emotional model through data collection and cross-disciplinary knowledge analysis, lessen intervention from the designers in the emotional development process and visualized. Through design practice, the project is a real thought provoker for the audience and a catalyst for social dreams.

3.1 Exploring Virtual Pets Based on Mind-Flow Theory

In the book "Mind Flow – The Psychology of Optimal Experience", it is stated that the optimal mind flow experience is that one is completely immersed in what he is concentrating on, ignoring the influences of surroundings. Even at big cost, he can reap great joy from the process of concentration [7]. Each person's passions and what they can focus on are different, so are the opportunities for mindful flow experiences. In order to have an optimal experience of mindfulness, we must understand the various ways in which consciousness works and grasp various information, whether positive or negative, so that we can realize how subjectivity formed [7]. To foster emotional symbiosis between human and virtual pets, first we need to understand what different people actually want when they choose to keep a virtual pet, what kind of emotional feedback is desired, and what kind of activities can be used to create an emotional function with a virtual pet.

Therefore, we cannot conduct a quantitative study of big data in this data collection process, instead, we should decentralize to each individual and feedback according to each individual's real needs, enhance their experience in the process of interacting with the virtual pet, help the virtual pet to form a truly symbiotic relationship with the user in their daily lives.

3.2 Virtual Pets and Empathy Maps

In order to better achieve the goal of emotional symbiosis of virtual pets in the design process, this study conducted online user research with 61 individuals (as shown in Fig. 1). Of these, 17 people were selected for the data collection and tracking of the empathy map. Among them 34 were male and 27 were female, 14 were studying for a master's degree, and 25 were studying for a bachelor's degree, of which 10 were recent graduates, 15 were social workers aged 24–30, and the remaining seven were social workers aged 30–40. The content of the questionnaire was based on the appearance, scale and interaction patterns of virtual pets.

To better understand its design intention, the use of empathy maps in the research process allows for the translation of the user's information about the virtual pets into a pictorial language. So we can capture the user's emotional information more accurately, and convert from a one-way data collection mode to multiple ways of acquiring individual information through the mode of empathy. The empathy map provides us a lot of intuitive information. Such as "the appearance and form of the virtual pet", "how the individual interacts with their virtual pet", "in which scenes do you want to communicate emotionally", and "Can we get a better sense of the psychological activity of the research user through the images of the virtual pet's appearance?".

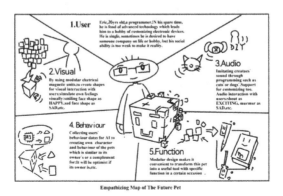

Fig. 1. Feedback from different people on virtual pets on the empathy map

3.3 Pet "Personality" and Human "Personality"

Previous research has found that pet owners are more likely to spend time with pets whose personalities are compatible with their own. In the process of selecting a pet of their choice, breeders will imperceptibly judge whether the personality of the pet they select matches their own "personality". If the pet's "personality" is incompatible with the breeder's, it is likely to be abandoned or to find a foster carer [8]. People always believe that their own pets are better, if a person is overly attached to their pets, or have an overwhelming sense of self-service, or their pets' personality is similar to their own, then they are more likely to favor their pets. From this we can also understand that people will subconsciously choose pets that have personalities similar to their own while choosing.

The same analysis of real pet's personalities and human's personalities can be applied to the matching mechanism of virtual pets. A similarity was found in Pokémon Red-Green [9], which was released on the Game Boy on 27 February 1996, in which the player starts the game by choosing one of three Pokémons – the Little Fire Dragon, the Mythical Frog Seed and the Genie Turtle as the initial companion pet. Being unaware of the strategies for passing the game and other intervening elements, players will ultimately choose their Pokémon as a partner to play with based on their preferences.

According to the psychological theory of pet's "personality", both real and virtual pets are chosen by their owners based on elements or characteristics relevant to them and their needs, rather than on their own subjective imagination (Fig. 2).

Fig. 2. Different frequency of keywords requested by people for virtual pet images

3.4 Multi-situational Interaction with Virtual Pets

The game Pokemon Go, released in 2016, became a global sensation, with the average user spending 43 min a day immersed in the thrill of collecting pokemons, according to "similar websites" [10]. The characters that once existed in the Pokemon anime series can be brought to life through augmented reality technology. Therefore, the emotions of childhood and the game can be realized in real life. With more places like museums and art galleries opening up, the combination of Pokemon Go and real space is an expecting way to access information. The Aibo dog, developed by Sony, allows children to interact with them to reduce anxiety when their parents are not around. By mimicking the interaction of a pet dog, the Aibo dog can form a relationship with the purchaser that resembles the interaction between an everyday pet and human.

In the 1999 anime Digital Monster, released by Toei Animation, eight children, led by Taichi Yagami, went on an adventure from the digital world to the real world [11], in which the virtual pets were called "digital beasts". They grew up with the children in their lives and formed an indelible emotional bond with them in various aspects of their lives. In 2021 Bandai launched the "Life Bracelet", which allowed the wearer to monitor their vital signs and behavioural patterns while wearing the bracelet in some specific conditions, enabling the users to grow up with the digital beasts. What is more, the digital beasts in the game would also evolve together through the transformation of the "Vitrl" value.

This study was based on a questionnaire survey (as shown in Fig. 3) collected in which the respondents were asked "What kind of situations and activities would you like to interact with your virtual pet in your daily life?" Among the survey respondents, "through outdoor travel and entertainment", "growing up together", "through online interaction" and "together at work" were the most frequent interaction patterns that accounted for the top four of the survey data, with 77%, 67%, 54% and 49% respectively. The low frequency interaction patterns of "not bothering each other" and "taking care of each other unilaterally" only accounted for 8% of the surveyed population. The research data showed that more people wanted to develop emotional relationships through more interaction with their virtual pets.

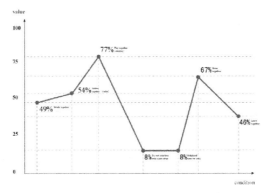

Fig. 3. What kind of activities do different groups of people want their virtual pets to develop a relationship through

4 The Design Practice of Virtual Pets Under the Concept of Speculative Design

Designers cannot just passively perceive market and social development trends, otherwise it can lead to a lag in their own development. In present environment of constant technological change, designers should be proactive in finding the gap between current technology and future development and have their own perceptions of what the world will become in the future. Speculative design, on the other hand, subverts the current single cognition of the world in the form of a fictional future with what is happening in the world at present by extrapolating the aesthetic and functional possibilities of technology [12]. Through different artistic means, speculative design uses the "imagination" to "advance" the future of a parallel world before it has even happened, to enlighten human to provoke their thought.

The following examples of design practice will explore how virtual pets can symbiotically interact with people through a variety of artistic means including digital media, installation art and programming applications, in terms of appearance, form, structure, behaviour and material respectively.

4.1 Digital Pets of the Future

Based on the characteristics of speculative design, we set our sights on a technologically refined future. By describing the personality of pets and the theory of mind-flow, we will simulate the process of choosing virtual pets as companions from a psychological perspective through installation art and digital media. As a branch of psychology, the "FPA personality colours" originated from the ancient Greek physician and theory of the four fluids by philosopher Hippocrates, which was further studied by the Chinese psychologist Le Jia. It classifies human's personalities through the four personalities "red, green, blue and yellow" [13]. The different colours are used to restore the behavioural motivations of different personalities, and the text is abstractly designed as a pet image through the different personalities (as shown in Fig. 4).

Personality Analysis	Red	Blue	Yellow	Green
Advantage	Good at socialising Highly expressive Positive and optimistic Creative	Think Deeply Steady Highly principled Good at analysis	The goal is firm Seeking efficiency Clarity of purpose Strong execution	Forgiveness Affinity optimistic good at coordination
Disadvantage	Low persistence Lack of rigour	Lack of communication Not confined	Overpowering Low inclusivity Overly strict	Too mild Low efficiency
Images	Active Explosive A short interval	Stable Quite Reflection Methodical	Strong Majestic Not easily accessible	Slow Lazy Overpowering Low efficiency
Picture				

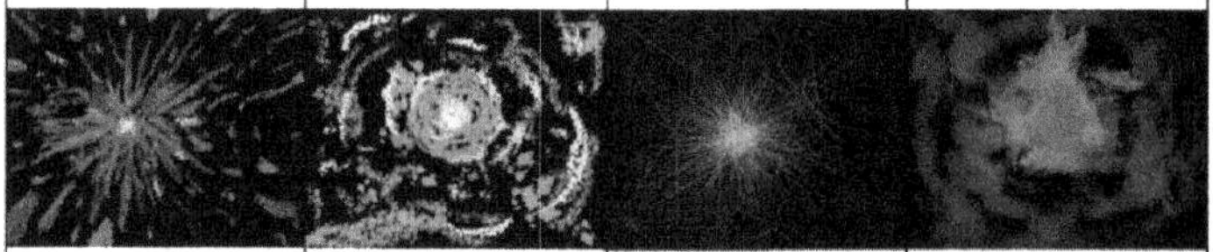

Fig. 4. Abstract pet image design under different characters (Color figure online)

The installation prop was designed with the hope of establishing a link with the pet generation by observing human behaviour, and simulating through the behavioural interaction of the audience and the virtual pet generation. Given the current imperfections in scientific and technological development, we ultimately chose to obtain behavioural data in real-time through the Kinecnt Chop node of Touchdesigner, several Chop type nodes for data processing, and judge the range of data, which was eventually summarized into four types of personality data (as shown in Fig. 5). Then we select the virtual pet form based on the data of character. When the viewer interacts with the device, it interacts with the static point cloud on the screen. In the process of interaction, the device will make a basic behavior decision by detecting the user's behavior. Moreover, static point clouds, geometry, dynamic particles and generated objects are used to take the player's Chop node data as the weight value, which can influence the behavior, appearance and sound of pets to a certain extent.

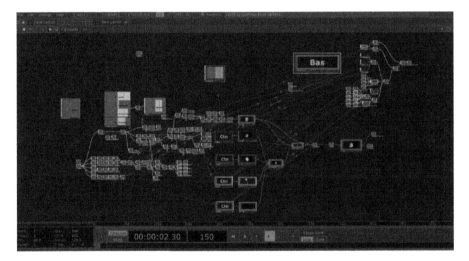

Fig. 5. Interactive interface of the Touchdesigner

The interaction process is totally divided into three parts: "Opening (personality test) – Transition animation – Pet interaction" (as shown in Fig. 6). We use TimerChop and AnimationComp to build the timeline to draw the event timeline, convert to the corresponding scene at different points in time, and activate the corresponding interactive behavioural events. Eventually when the game time is over, the whole program returns to the opening mode, thus forming a closed loop of the process (as shown in Fig. 7).

The abstract pet form is meant to be expressive, and the viewer can make a reflection on their own personality traits through the abstract image behaviour, form and sound (as shown in Fig. 8). Through the process of interacting with the abstract pet, the viewer can be given an opportunity to think about the question: "What will our future digital pet eventually look like?" "Does the personality of our pet need to match ours?" Although the work contained a thinking mode that is similar to build a utopia, it is because of this process of building a utopian future society that the imagination can be fully unleashed

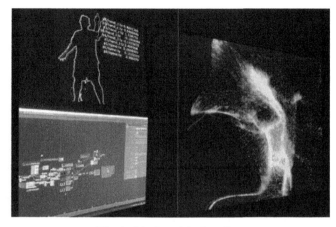

Fig. 6. Display of device effect

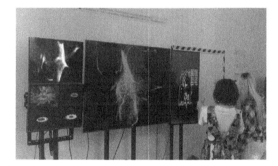

Fig. 7. Exhibition interactive effect display

and thus remain active to the poetics of the future, which re-examines how we construct an emotional symbiosis with a virtual pet.

4.2 Intelligent Guidance for Virtual Pets

In the process of emotional symbiosis between virtual pets and humans, in addition to exploring the ways in which virtual pet "personalities" are matched with human "personalities", we need to equally focus on the forms and behaviour that can build deep emotional relationships between virtual pets and humans in their daily activities.

We create a biomimetic installation design of animals' behaviour by observation, which is practiced and restored by means of programming and installation art.

Singing Mantis: By dividing into groups to observe and video record the biological characteristics, features and living environment of the mantis (as shown in Fig. 9), we analyzed the dynamics of the mantis' forelimbs as it pounces on food and discovered the process of movement of the mantis' forelimbs. We also discovered that the mantis dances when music is on, which guided us to try to combine music and the rhythmic processes of the mantis' forelimb body accordingly.

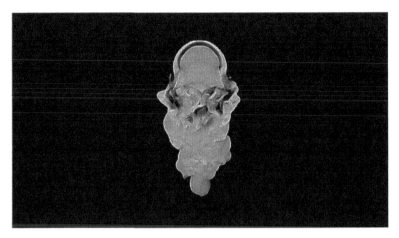

Fig. 8. A demonstration of the virtual pet form in blue (Color figure online)

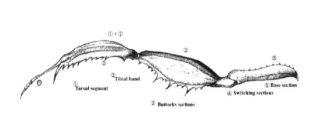

Fig. 9. Observations on the arm of a mantis

The Mantis group designed its devices with arduino program, where they tried to make a mechanical structure of movement by referring to the structure of a robotic arm. Through several selections of materials and repeated trials (as shown in Fig. 10), a stable

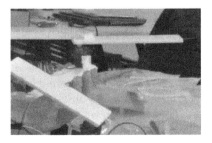

Fig. 10. Servo experimentation process

form of the robotic arm device was finally determined to represent the movement of the mantis's arm (as shown in Fig. 11).

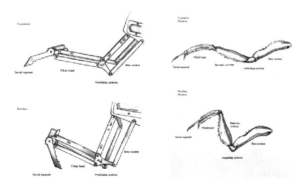

Fig. 11. Experimental process of mantis's arm transformation

By learning to manipulate the servo with Arduino, we created the device after dissecting the robotic arm structure, linking ultrasonic sensing and bionic mechanical structure by the Arduino. We also used sound sensors to receive external sound data, then converted the different sound waves into data of corresponding size, and wrote the data into the servo's angle control program in real time by processing these data with a limit input of the highest and lowest values, to enable the arduino to control the servo angle in real time through the sound sensors (as shown in Fig. 12). Besides, we added a microphone-like device to allow it to better receive sound wave data, which allowed the audience to have a more intuitive understanding of the interaction mechanism. When a person outputs sound to the microphone, the mantis's arm will oscillate in response to the frequency of the sound (as shown in Fig. 13). And the user gets feedback from the mantis's arm interacting as they are singing, making it easier to add to the human experience (as shown in Fig. 14). It is assumed that in the future without the limitations of science and technology, responsive virtual pets can help alleviate human's feelings of loneliness and anxiety through a variety of daily activities.

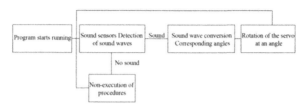

Fig. 12. Process flow chart of the Mantis unit

Shrimp Roam 2055: In contrast to the Singing Mantis installation, the other group of bionic devices captures the dynamics of shrimps through Arduino programming and device design as well. Unlike the musical interaction that fosters affection, this group

Fig. 13. Process flow chart of the mantis unit

Fig. 14. The final result of the Musical Mantis installation

aims to represent the characteristics and image of a virtual pet through the modification of its appearance.

In terms of transmission, we analyzed the anatomical muscle texture of the shrimp (shown in Fig. 15), determined the direction of the transmission based on the analysis of the muscle texture when the shrimp swims, and made a small prototype with reference to a four-rod drive. In addition, we discovered materials and finally settled on a combination of acrylic and metal drive (shown in Fig. 16). The other option was to present it as a visual decorative element by purchasing model parts (Fig. 17).

Through the design of the shrimp bionic device, we hope to provide a preliminary discussion for profile of the future virtual pets in the world. In the future, virtual pets should be more diverse in their appearance so that they can be customized according to the user's own preferences and requirements, thus making it easier for the users to develop a sense of identity with their virtual pets.

Fig. 15. Structural anatomy of the shrimp

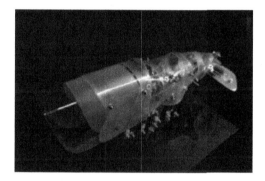

Fig. 16. Finished shrimp device1

Fig. 17. Finished shrimp device2

5 Conclusion

This paper aims to discuss how to help virtual pets and human beings develop a more intimate emotional symbiosis in the aspect of speculative design, and study by means of case studies, questionnaire research and design practice. Through the match of virtual pets, bionic device design and visual decoration and so on, we hope to stimulate the audience's vision and provoke them to think about how to build a relationship between virtual pets and themselves at the same time. Nevertheless, the present development of virtual pets is still limited by technology, the design of the props also carries a utopian conception. Therefore, the purpose of this study is to inspire more people to take part in thinking and studying through virtual pet research to help those who suffer from "loneliness" and "anxiety". Only to think about the past history and chase the dreams of the future can our present lives constantly become ever better.

References

1. Liu, F.: The Design Research of Pet Modular Furniture from the Interactive Perspective. Taiyuan University of Technology (2015)
2. Yun, C.: Design of the interactive pet products based on the concept of empathydesign, **34**(11), 22–24 (2021)
3. Li, Y.: Research on Building Symbiotic Relationship between Children and Virtual Pets with Emotional Intelligence. Harbin Institute of Technology (2011)
4. Sun, B.: Design an Realization of Building Companionship between Human and Virtual Pet Based on Emotional Design. Zhejiang University (2016)
5. Dunne, A., Raby, F.: Speculative Everything: Design, Fiction, and Social Dreaming. Trans. Zhang Li, pp. 94–145. Jiangsu Phoenix Fine Arts Publishing House, Nanjing (2017)
6. Li, Z.: From being radical to being speculative: how design catalyzes social dreams. J. Nanjing Arts Inst. **4**, 14–19 (2017)
7. Csikszentmihalyi, M.: Flow: The Psychology of Optimal Experience Trans. Zhang Ding qi, pp. 65–71. Citic Press, Beijing (2017)
8. Zhang, M.Y., Peng, X.F., Hu, C.B., Zhang, X.Y.: The nature of the bond between pets and owners: a psychological analysis. Adv. Psychol. Sci. **23**(1), 142–149 (2015)
9. Yang, Y.T.: On the application of functionality and aesthetics in animation character design – take "Pokemon" as an example. Shoes Technol. Des. **2**(5), 54–56 (2022)
10. Yao, R., Malik, O.: Experience augmented reality with Pokémon Go. World Sci. **10**, 51–52 (2016)
11. Fang, Z.: An analysis of Japanese hot-blooded anime narratives based on national culture – take the Digimon anime series as an example. Satellite TV IP Multimedia **512**(7), 169–170 (2020)
12. Li, Z.: The value of fiction: the aesthetic politics and future poetics of speculative design. Theor. Stud. Lit. Art. **39**(6), 152–160 (2019)
13. Bao, H.: Analysis of the mental health level test of university students based on personality colour science. J. Liaoning Educ. Admin. Inst. **38**(6), 107–110. https://doi.org/10.13972/(2021)j.cnki.cn21-1500/g4.2021.06.023

Exploring the Effects of Personal Impact Communicated Through Eco-Feedback Technology for Reducing Food Waste

Seonghee Lee[ID], Daniela Rodriguez-Chavez[(✉)][ID], and Jeffrey Rzeszotarski[ID]

Cornell University, Ithaca, NY 14850, USA
{sl994,dr537,jmr395}@cornell.edu

Abstract. We are surrounded by self-tracking technologies that provide us with vast amounts of personal data. Despite an abundance of information, the lack of personal impact and poor design often leads to ineffective eco-feedback technology. This paper explores how the communication of personal impact and different levels of specificity in information presentation can influence pro-environmental behavioral change. For the duration of one week, 7 participants inputted self-measured food waste data into a website that showed four data visualizations with different levels of specificity and personal impact. We found that communicating food waste data in terms of personal impact (i.e. money wasted, daily progress) better motivated participants as opposed to visualizations emphasizing altruistic values or uninterpreted data (i.e. interactive plant, aggregated waste). We identify what effects eco-feedback technologies with different levels of specificity have in user attention and satisfaction. The reported findings provide insight into elements to consider when designing eco-feedback technology.

Keywords: Eco-Feedback Technology · Data Visualization · Food Waste · Sustainability · Self-Tracking Technology

1 Introduction

Eco-feedback technology focuses on communicating feedback on individual behavior to reduce environmental impact. This field has explored various forms of eco-feedback such as ambient displays, mobile phone applications, desktop games, and interactive machines with the goal of reducing carbon footprints and electricity or thermostat usage [8]. Many eco-feedback technologies provide data on environmental impact (carbon, electricity usage, waste) to an individual in a detached form, with usually no connection to personal impact [12,13,18]. The dominant approach on eco-feedback technology has focused on highlighting the benefits to others or nature, rather than appealing to self-interest [3]. While data on carbon footprints, amount of waste, and electricity usage can create a

---

S. Lee and D. Rodriguez-Chavez—Both authors contributed equally to this research.

A. Marcus et al. (Eds.): HCII 2023, LNCS 14030, pp. 541–560, 2023.
https://doi.org/10.1007/978-3-031-35699-5_39

feeling of guilt, it is often hard for the people who are less motivated for pro-environmental impact create a direct connection from theses metrics to their personal lives to behavioral change [11]. Yet, environmental psychology research states that communicating personal impact can be effective in promoting pro-environmental behaviors for people who tend to be more self-interested [3].

While there have been studies that have used social networks and cultural context for promoting sustainable lifestyles [21], there are a lack of papers that look into using stronger personal motivators. Eco-feedback technology faces challenges in helping link feedback data to personal motivation for the individual [14,24]. Additionally, there is more to understand with how specific the information presented by eco-feedback technology should be. It is questionable whether presenting people with specific information will be effective even when there is little motivation involved [5]. While some studies suggest that information can inspire motivation, other suggest that many users "do not want to spend a lot of time reading text or interpreting graphs" [8,19]. There is also a lack of research on how different levels of specific visualizations can be used in accordance with each other [20]. For example, simple data visualizations showing total wasted cost can be effective for instigating initial interest but the lack detail in the information it provides can be troubling for users who wish to formulate specific plans to solve the issue [15].

This paper looks into how different data presentations in eco-feedback technology can motivate users to reduce food waste. We look into the outcomes of communicating food waste information through data visualizations with differing levels of personal impact and specificity for a duration of a week. The findings in this research will fill the knowledge gap for understanding what effective eco-feedback data visualizations should communicate to promote personal food waste reduction.

2   Background

2.1   The Food Waste Problem

Using 2008 metrics, it is estimated that every year in the United States, 124 kg of food is wasted per person [1]. In 2011, the total monetary waste from consumers was around 124 billion, which is 400 dollars each year per person [23]. However it is not only an economic issue, there are wider implications. In the United States, avoidable food waste accounts for about 2% of the national emissions [23]. Considering that nearly 85% of food waste occurs downstream at consumer-facing businesses and homes, addressing food waste at the personal level will help reduce overall wastage. Studies have shown that the greatest causes of personal household food waste is overbuying and negligence [22]. Therefore, deploying methods that target and reduce these behaviors is crucial to helping solve the food waste problem.

2.2   Eco-Feedback Technology for Food Waste Reduction

The advent of new types of food management technology opens up possibilities of adding more advanced technology to help people manage their food consumption. Recent explorations into technicoloring fridges, see-through fridges and smart fridges that provide you with information at the time of consumption, as well as using tangible devices to visualize the expiration dates of food have all been tested [2,7,10]. Other studies have looked into mobile applications created to target food waste reduction alongside interactive fridges that show the content of the fridge [6,16]. Despite the recent advances to different types of eco-feedback technology, challenges remain on how we can motivate people, inspire behavioral change, and find efficient methods of data collection that are sustainable on a long-term basis.

2.3   Eco-Feedback Technology Limitations and Design Questions

Many studies have focused on informing people of their environmental consumption habits through household electricity monitoring systems, intelligent thermostats, and mobile tools with the assumption that people will act pro-environmentally when presented with information on their waste [8,17,25]. However, simply presenting people with information often does not lead to long-term actionable change [17]. While environmental concerns can be strong drivers for pro-environmental behavior within those who have stronger altruistic qualities, for those who exhibit self-enhancing (egoistic) qualities, it can often not be motivating enough [3,11]. Within the field of environmental psychology, studies have shown that self-interested individuals exhibited more pro-environmental behavior when there was self-benefit involved [3]. While studies have suggested that added specificity to eco-feedback technology can help promote pro-environmental behavior, it is questionable whether presenting people with specific information will be effective even when there is little motivation involved [9].

Environmental psychology does not clarify in what ways technology should be designed to promote pro-environmental behavior. For example, would data on waste amounts by category be more effective than a visualization showing the total amount of money wasted? There is more to be understood in how information should be presented to the user to have the most effective results. Furthermore, understanding the relationship between personal motivation and the specificity of the information can provide insights into when specific information can be useful and the impact of self-interest in information communication (Fig. 1).

3   Method

We recruited participants (n = 7) by sending study recruitment messages to e-mail lists, online message boards, and word-of-mouth throughout campus. Participants were college students that owned a personal fridge. After participants

Fig. 1. Data Visualization Website. Participants input their food waste amounts after measuring it on a scale.

signed a consent form, they received digital scales and unique login usernames and passwords. The list of usernames and passwords were randomized so that all the participants would be anonymous to the researchers. The login features were implemented into the website using Django. For the duration of seven days, participants were asked to measure their food waste on the digital scale and input the data on a website. By clicking on toggle buttons in the website, participants were able to view different data visualizations. Through our website, we were able to record the food waste each user inputted, as well as when and how many times they clicked on each specific visualization. This data was recorded using SQLAlchemy. The four data visualizations were chosen on different scales of specificity and motivation. After the eight days, participants received 80 dollars in compensation and were required to fill out a post-survey that asked questions about food waste reduction and each data visualization.

3.1   Defining Specificity and Motivation

We created 4 data visualizations that would display different types of informational data to the users that would help them analyze the data in correlation with each other. The data visualizations for this experiment were created based on two measures, "specificity" and "personal impact".

Specificity (S). To study if specific information is necessary for promoting pro-environmental change, we divided our data visualizations into two groups of specificity - specific and non-specific. Specific data visualizations would provide users with multiple data points to analyze where as a non-specific data point use the data holistically to produce one final data value.

Personal Impact (P). By personal impact, we refer to whether or not the data visualization interpreted the food waste data to show directpersonal impact.

Factors such as cost, personal loss and development were considered personal impact whereas pure representation of food waste data and personification of nature was not.

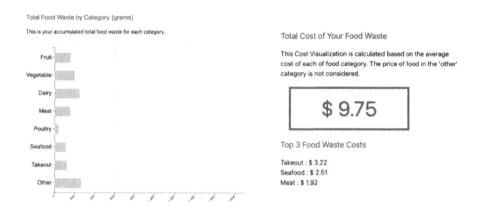

Fig. 2. Aggregated Food Waste Visualization (left) and Cost Visualization (right)

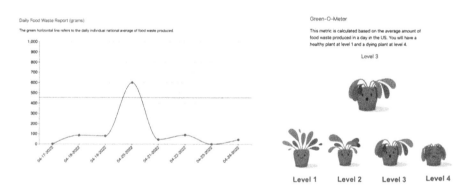

Fig. 3. Daily Food Waste Report (left) and Green-O-Meter Visualization (right) (Color figure online)

3.2   The Four Data Visualizations

After defining the metrics of "specificity" and "personal impact", four different visualization were designed with varying levels of these two metrics, as seen in

Fig. 4. The four different visualizations were named "Aggregated Food Waste" (S↑P↓), "Wasted Cost" (S↓P↑), "Abstract Plant" (S↓P↓), and "Daily Progress" (S↑P↑). The visualizations were created by the researchers using D3.js, a data visualization JavaScript library.

Aggregated Food Waste Visualization (S↑P↓). The first visualization shown in Fig. 2, displayed the amount of food waste they produced in each category (meat, poultry, vegetables, etc.) accumulated in total weight (grams). This visualization had high levels of specificity, showing more than one data points (multiple bar graph values in different food categories) as the final result. On the other hand, it had low levels of personal impact since it was simply data on the recorded aggregated amounts of food waste. As the data accumulated, users were be able to analyze what food categories were producing the most waste.

Wasted Cost Visualization (S↓P↑). The second visualization shown in Fig. 2, displayed the amount of money users had wasted in total through their food waste. This value was calculated by estimating a ruff average value of each of the food categories as listed and multiplying that with the amount of food waste the user produced in that category. This visualization had low levels of specificity since it would visualize a single numeric value of cost. On the other hand, this visualization had high levels of personal impact by showing participants their expenditures from food waste.

Abstract Plant Visualization (S↓P↓). The third visualization shown in Fig. 3, displayed 4 different levels of a plant based on the amount of food waste a person produced in a day. Like the UbiGreen Transportation Display, we used an iconic graphic to influence behavior and provide personal feedback [8]. Few prior studies have been conducted by displaying iconic nature images of feedback such as a virtual polar bear, in purpose of creating a concern for the environment and a tendency towards taking green action [9]. These studies have also highlighted the importance of emotional responses in eco-feedback technology [4]. The metric for the image change was calculated based on the average amount of food waste produced in a day in the US (1 pound) reported by the United States Department of Agriculture. If the participant performed below this level they would be shown with a level 1 plant, if they produced around average, level 2, level 3 if they were over the average, and a level 4 plant if they were twice the average. As the amount of food waste the user produced increased, they would be shown with an increasingly unhealthy plant. This visualization had low levels of specificity since it would visualize a single dying or living plant.

Daily Progress Visualization (S↑P↑). The last visualization displayed the progress of the user's food waste. This visualization records the amount of food waste a user produced each day. The rise and fall of the graph can help users reflect upon their food waste habits and motivate them towards improvement. This visualization had high levels of specificity by showing users tractable food waste data each day. It also a higher level of personal impact by showing participants a comparison of their overall food waste with that of the national average. Research on eco-feedback technology states that comparison between individuals or groups can be useful in motivating action, particularly when combined with feedback about performance [11]. To further investigate whether comparison is beneficial in bringing out pro-environmental behavioral change, we added an average line graph that shows the average amount of waste people produced.

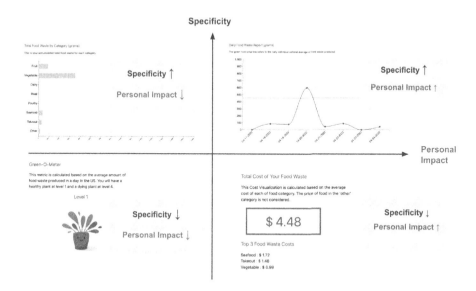

Fig. 4. Four Data Visualizations on different levels of Specificity and Personal Impact

4 Results

Before the actual study, we asked participants to fill out a pre-survey indicating their food waste habits. During the study, the participants inputted their self-tracked food waste amounts (grams). We recorded when the users clicked on each visualization throughout the week. This allowed us to compare between the amount of food waste produced against different levels of interest participants had for each visualization. After the study we conducted a qualitative and quantitative analysis on 5 participants (n=5, because 2 participants had data errors in the website recordings). The qualitative analysis was done based on the pre and post survey responses of the participants on the experiences of interacting with different data visualizations (n=7, as the participants pre and post survey data still contained valuable insights).

4.1 Pre-survey Responses

6 participants reported that they waste an average of 1 to 5 pounds of food in one week while one participant reported to wasting less than 1 pound of food waste

during one week. Participants reported that their main causes of food waste were leftover food that they forgot to eat due to lack of time, forgetting, and over purchasing. Two participants reported to eating out less than 5 times during a week and three participants reported to eating out more than 10 times in a week. 5 participants in our study reported that they eat out (takeout, dining) over 5 times in a week. 2 participants reported to cooking less than 5 times in a week. The fact that our sample of participants were all college students may have led to an overall higher amount of participants eating out. When asked about what would be the most effective method in helping them reducing their food waste, participants responded that having proper meal planning routines, reminders of expiration dates, and food items in the fridge would be most effective. "Buying only the ingredients I need to cook for the week so I don't forget about it in the fridge or having reminders food in the fridge with expiration dates would be helpful." The pre-survey revealed that a majority of food waste occurs from a lack of proper planning and forgetting to eat food items on time. Due to varying schedules and lifestyles, having methods to incorporate sustainable eating habits into their daily lives are necessary in helping people reduce food waste.

4.2 Quantitative Analysis

Participant Food Waste Statistics. The total amount of food waste that participants produced on average was 1.7 pounds (1.6 pounds for 20% trimmed mean) which is 51% lower than the national average value of 3.5 pounds in a week. We see in Fig. 5 that all of our participants produced less than the United States weekly average. Furthermore, the average cost wasted was 5.18 dollars for the users. We also found that users recorded food waste for an average of 5.8 days out of the study, and the median number of days where food was recorded by users was 6. Though users frequently recorded their daily food waste amounts, we were able to observe that food waste amount fluctuated drastically among many users (Fig. 5). This shows us that though our users were frequently throwing away food, there might be weekly or biweekly cycles where they throw away a lot of food at once, perhaps when cleaning out their fridge. A longer study might be able to more accurately analyze these cycles of food waste that happen in households.

Participant Click Data Insights. By recording the click data of the participants we were able to find that there is a varying degree of attention retention between different types of visualizations of the food waste. Of all the four visualizations, we see from Fig. 6 the Green O' Meter visualization had significantly less clicks, or attention given, than any other visualization.

Total Average Food Waste by User

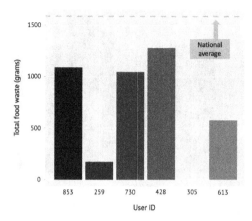

Food Waste Throughout Study by User

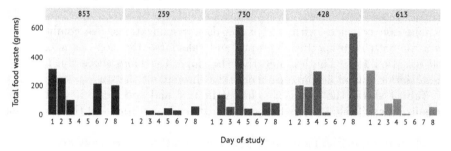

Fig. 5. Showing the total amount of food waste each user produced throughout the study overlaid with the national average in light dashed blue (left). Showing the categories of the daily food waste all users produced throughout the study (right). (Color figure online)

However from Fig. 7 it is important to note that there was both a fade in attention over the course of the study, as we see that over time the amount of clicks per data visualization decreased, as well as sporadic clicking from the users. We do not see stable retention from all the users throughout the study, but we do see a difference between each data visualization in the magnitude of the attention drop-off. We note that the Green O' Meter has the biggest drop-off besides the Accumulated Waste visualization, which is consistent with it being the least clicked data visualization. We also see that both the Cost Visualization and the Daily Progress Visualization have the least drop-off, showing that these are the visualizations that our users were the most interested in.

Though we show the individual statistics for each visualization in Fig. 8, we also explore the effects of specificity and personal impact on the clicks data. Because we have either high or low specificity and high or low motivation, each

Number of Clicks per Visualization

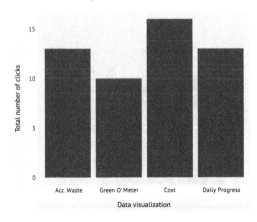

Fig. 6. Showing the total amount of clicks for each category.

combination coincides with one of the data visualizations. We combined the data for both high specificity graphs and calculated the slope as a proxy for the retention rate. The less negative the slope, the more successful the data visualization was at keeping users engaged throughout the study.

Table 1 shows the levels of personal impact and specificity in each of the visualizations. Table 2 shows the grouping for each category and their retention rates. We see that the high personal impact grouping had a significantly better retention rate (as it is more negative). This grouping corresponds to the Daily Progress and Cost visualization, and this is also represented in Fig. 8, as both of these had the least negative slopes. Interestingly, both high and low specificity groupings had the same retention rate, implying that specificity was not a strong factor. Finally, the low direct impact had the worst retention rate. Overall, direct impact plays a strong role in keeping people engaged with a data visualization.

Table 1. Showing the high (↑)/low (↓) specificity (S) and personal impact (P) category for each visualization.

Category	Visualization
S ↑ P ↑	Daily Progress
S ↑ P ↓	Accumulated Food Waste
S ↓ P ↑	Cost
S ↓ P ↓	Green O' Meter

Clicks Throughout Study by User and Visualization

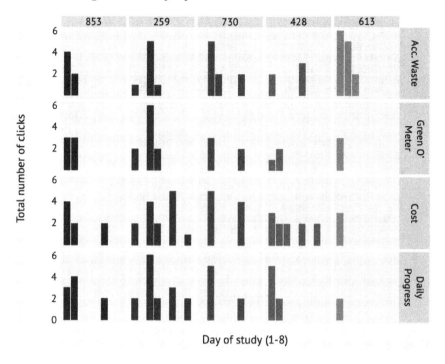

Fig. 7. Showing the daily clicks from each user for each category.

Table 2. Showing the retention rate for each grouping of high (↑)/low (↓) specificity (S)/ personal impact (P).

Grouping	Retention rate
P ↑	−0.62
S ↑	−0.81
P ↓	−0.92
S ↓	−0.81

4.3   Post Survey Results

After the study, participants were required to fill out a post-survey. The food waste reduction questionnaire consisted of two items that were about motivation and behavorial change: (1) this visualization motivated me to reduce food waste and (2) I was able to reduce food waste through this visualization. Answers were ranged in a 5-item Likert scale between (1) strongly disagree to (5) strongly agree. The user experiences questionnaire consisted of four items that were (1) I enjoyed this visualization. (2) This visualization helped me learn new information. (3) This visualization was stressful. (4) I would use this visualization

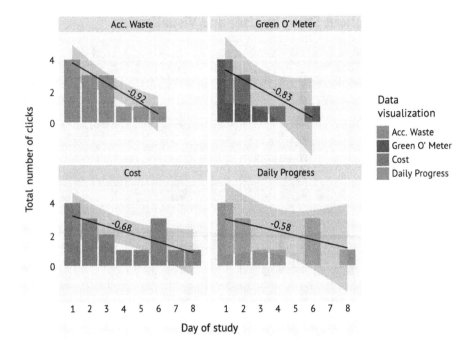

Fig. 8. Showing the daily clicks from all users for each category along with their respective slopes.

again in my daily life. Answers were ranged in a 5-item Likert scale between (1) strongly disagree to (5) strongly agree. Participants were additionally asked a series of questions on motivation levels found through the graph (Fig. 9).

Accumulated Food Waste Visualization. Participants responded that the specific information on accumulated food waste by category helped them plan strategically for food waste reduction. "Being able to observe which categories of food waste were most prevalent helped me pick and choose which types of food to consume more or less of." Participants reported using this visualization alongside the cost visualization to recognize which food categories were producing the most waste. "I could see how much money was going towards this food waste which was very interesting and something I had not considered before."

We observed mixed responses in motivation levels and behavioral change. One participant responded that while they enjoyed the graph, they did not find it motivating enough to reduce food waste. "The visualization didn't really motivate me to reduce food waste. I did like using it to see what my food waste was, though." Other participants were motivated through this graph by becoming more consciously aware of themselves. "Seeing it accumulate as well as seeing the numbers themselves (vs just throwing away my plate without thinking) made

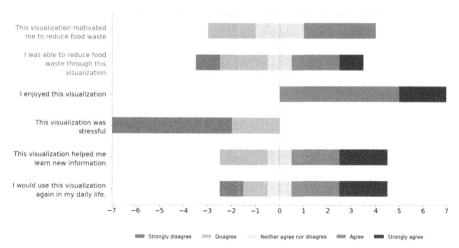

Fig. 9. Aggregated Food Waste by Category

me realize how much I was actually throwing out and I did try to throw away less food by taking less food when I go to the dining hall throughout the week."

All participants responded that they did not find this graph to be stressful. With no direct personal impact and low stress in this visualization, we found individual differences on motivation leading to behavioral change.

While we found that this graph was not a direct motivating factor for all users, the specific information offered by the accumulation graph could be used to help users plan strategically for food waste reduction goals. When used alongside direct motivating graphs like the cost graph, they were used to provide more information on how to reduce food waste (Fig. 10).

Cost Visualization. All 7 participants replied that they found themselves highly motivated by this visualization. "Knowing how much money was being wasted was really effective in helping me to reduce my waste." Participants responded that the re-framing of food waste data to show direct impact was effective in motivating them. "This visualization feels very effective as it quantified the waste in a meaningful way that has consequences on you (rather than consequences on others/the environment)" "The fact that it was looking at the implications of food waste, rather than just total food waste, made me want to waste less." Participants also responded that this visualization led to behavioral change, mentioning that they consciously made different choices in purchasing or not purchasing certain items. "I like saving money as much as the next person, so I tried to not spend money on food in the categories I was wasting food in when I went shopping for groceries." "I do feel like this application applied to my real life more in terms of actually purchasing or not purchasing certain

Cost Visualization

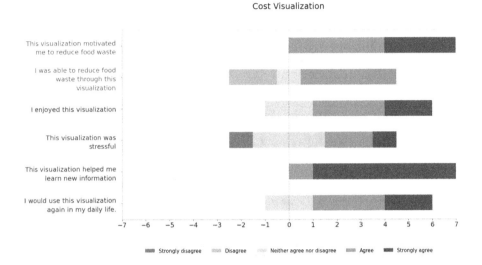

Fig. 10. Cost Visualization Likert Scale

items." "It was stressful, but eye-opening and it made me think about what I bought." We also observed that for certain participants money was not a direct impact. "Since I get most of my food from a dining hall and am required to have an unlimited meal plan, I don't think this visualization was very effective for me because I don't pay for meals/specific food, but it did make me feel a little guilty for wasting the dining hall food." Additionally, 6 participants mentioned that they felt high levels of stress in this visualization. "It was stressful, but it made me think about what I bought." While we observed high levels of stress reported from this visualization, all 7 participants also responded that they enjoyed seeing this information, learned new information from it, and would use it again in their daily life (Fig. 11).

Plant Visualization. With the plant visualization we did not give users any display of direct personal impact but showed them an image of a dying plant with increased food waste (less waste - flourishing plant, more waste - dying plant). This visualization used altruism and empathy as motivating factors. 6 participants responded that they did not find this graph to be motivating and 5 participants responded that this visualization did not lead to behavioral change. "I didn't use this visualization very much, but when the plant was sad, I knew I should waste less food." One participant who stated they felt motivated by this visualization responded to feeling high levels of empathy with the plant and high stress from this visualization. "I did not want to make the plant die, so I tried not to waste food. That stressed me out a little because I am empathetic."

In the plant visualization we found that while people did want to avoid making the plant die, the lack of information that was communicated to them led to

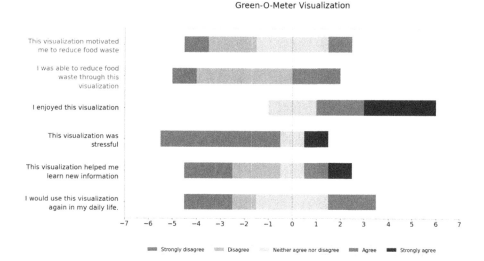

Fig. 11. Green O Meter Visualization Likert Scale (Color figure online)

frustration. "I did wonder how much food waste would make the plant die or stay healthy in general. I wish there was more of an explanation of how to keep the plant healthy through reducing food waste." The lack of information led many people to want more additional information on the plant. "I would have liked the average food waste to be displayed somewhere for comparison/understanding"

All participants responded to enjoying this visualization but showed mixed responses to stress levels and learning of new information through it. Additionally users replied that they enjoyed seeing a graphic that was non-numeric and data focused. "I liked the happy plant graphics that made the page less data driven and numeric". 4 participants also responded that they would not use this visualization in their daily life while 3 showed neutral responses (Fig. 12).

Daily Progress Visualization. With the daily progress visualization, 4 out of 7 participants responded that they felt motivated to reduce their food waste and 5 participants reported behavioral change. 4 participants responded that seeing their self-improvement progress in food waste reduction was their greatest motivating factor for this graph. Participants responded that they felt "rewarded" when they were able to observe their daily progress. "I think the daily trend was effective in encouraging/motivating me to waste less food, compared to the first visualization which accumulated the waste and didn't "reward" you for wasting less each day."

Three participants responded that comparison with the national average was their greatest motivating factor for this graph. "Knowing when I was approaching the food waste national average made me stop and think about whether I could use anything in my fridge and reduce my food waste." Unlike the cost

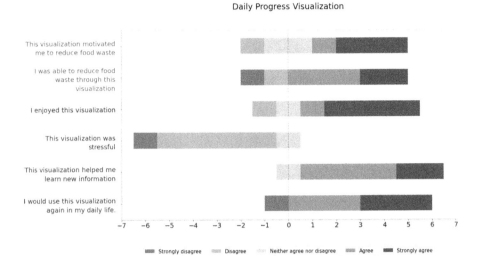

Fig. 12. Daily Progress Visualization Likert Scale

visualization, we observed low levels of stress despite having seen high levels of motivation and behavioral change. With the specific information on daily progress in the graph, we were able to find that the participants used the daily tracked total food waste amounts to compare themselves as throughout the days. Participants responded that being able to see daily logged activity and trends were enjoyable and motivating. "I enjoyed the daily comparisons and the trend lines." "I liked being able to see my data laid out over a week long period of time." "I could visualize my food waste as a whole."

5   Discussion

Our user study on eco-feedback technology for reducing food waste provides insightful findings on how information can be communicated in order to have meaningful results. However, due to the limited number of participants, the quantitative results serve as a potential baseline and should be expanded more, while the qualitative results give better insight. In addition, the short-term efficacy of the qualitative survey results may be limited compared to long-term observation of eco-feedback technology. More research is required to study what types of eco-feedback technology may be useful for long-term effective results of food waste reduction. Due to the fact that the study took place at a university campus, the study participants were college students who owned personal household fridges. There is more to understand with how different age groups respond to data visualizations in differing levels of personal impact and specificity. Further, our observations do not reveal how eco-feedback technology can combat multiple-person households or outdoor dining food waste. Further research is needed to investigate the distinct characteristics of food waste behavior when there are multiple people involved.

An essential aspect of eco-feedback design is to communicate feedback on individual behavior to help individuals gain insight on their waste habits. Through this study we found that while there is a general trend in what people find to be motivating, there were individual variations in what data visualization was motivating. For example, for more empathetic individuals, we found that using altruism (Green-O-Meter) was an effective way to reduce food waste. Future practices should look into how we can create customized motivation for participants when communicating self-tracked data. We also frequently observed participants curiosity to know more. For example, in the daily progress visualization, users wanted to see even more specific information, such as food waste categories within that certain day: "I would love if I could break down the visualization into the food categories. Seeing how much dairy, meat, poultry, and so on and so forth I have wasted over time would be very helpful." Additionally, for the plant and money visualization, participants wanted to see more information on how metrics were calculated. Future work should look into how additional data exploration and interactivity can support these needs and motivate behavioral change even on a long term.

Participants reported that the visualizations that showed personal impact motivated them more to reduce food waste compared to the ones with no personal impact involved. We found that the visualizations that had higher levels of personal impact had lower levels of drop in attention rate (M $\uparrow$: -0.62, M $\downarrow$: -0.92). For example, in the cost visualization, all 7 of the participants reported that they felt motivated to reduce food waste, while 6 people responded to feeling unmotivated or not affected by the green-o-meter visualization (which had no personal impact shown). Additionally, on the accumulated food waste visualization, which had no direct personal impact, we observed neutral responses of being motivated to reduce food waste. We also observed that different types of personal impact can be used to motivated people such as cost, comparison to others, and personal progress. While both the cost visualization and daily progress visualization proved to be very motivating, participants reported high levels of stress when interacting with the cost visualization. On the other hand, participants reported low levels of stress when interacting with the daily progress visualization.

While the cost visualization communicated negative feedback, the personal progress visualization communicated positive feedback. This may have been a factor as to why people felt different levels of stress when interacting with these visualizations. For example, one participant mentioned that they felt "rewarded" when they were able to observe a downwards trend in their food waste. This shows insights into how positive reinforcement with direct personal impact can be effective in leading to behavioral change towards sustainability.

We found that the specificity measure was not a great influencing factor in the drop in attention rate (S $\uparrow$: -0.81, S $\downarrow$: -0.81). We observed the same level of attention rate in both high and low specificity visualizations. In visualizations that had low specificity, such as the cost visualization, participants reported that they were confused and skeptical about the measures: "I was a little confused at first since I was not sure what exactly it was quantifying and the generalized/average prices were not always accurate (ex: meat from McDonald's vs a steakhouse would have been given the same price)." This confusion can give rise to skepticism and lack of trust leading to lesser impact from the visualization to the reduction of food waste.

We also observed how participants often used the specific information offered by the graphs to analyze their behavior. For example, participants would be motivated initially by the cost visualization, which led them to look at the accumulated waste visualization to analyze their behavior. One participant wrote that "[they] could see how much money was going towards this food waste which was very interesting and something [they] had not considered before." While specific information visualizations may not be direct motivating factors or effective in showing consistent attention in participants, they offer detailed information into participant's waste habits that can help analyze their behavior.

While specific data visualizations can be informative, we found that these visualizations were not the most effective in leading to behavioral change. When motivating visualizations (such as the cost visualization) were used alongside specific visualizations (such as the aggregated food waste by category), participants were able to analyze their food waste and create specific plans. In the likert scale responses, participants reported that they would like to use the Daily Progress and the Cost Visualization in the future. On the other hand, participants negatively responded to using the Green-O-Meter Visualization in the future. Contrary to how many eco-visualizations use the idea of personifying nature to promote altruistic behavior, our results show that altruistic behavior is not the most effective in motivating people to live a more sustainable lifestyle. Additionally, visualizations that participants wanted to continue using in the future were specific and often showed participants numerical values that they could further analyze.

As eco-feedback technologies are becoming more widespread, it is critical to understand how people interact with these tools and when they are most effective. This research looks into how the presentation of data on different levels of personal impact and specificity influences pro-environmental behavior. We focused on eco-feedback technology for reducing food waste in the form of data visualizations that display self-tracked food waste data. Through a week long study, 7 participants interacted with data visualizations that showed them different information on their food waste on differing levels of specificity and personal impact. We analyzed the click data of participants on each of the visualizations and computed a metric of how the attention rate was maintained throughout the week for different types of visualizations. The drop in attention rate was influenced significantly by personal impact while the specificity of the information had minimal impact. We found that participants responded to being more motivated when interacting with visualizations that showed personal impact. Additionally, specific information helped participants analyze their behavior and led them to be curious for more additional information. We suggest that future work in eco-feedback technology focus on how attention can be retained for longer terms of time through identifying personal motivation factors and allowing for more free exploration of the data.

Acknowledgments and Data Availability. The authors would like to thank the Ann S. and Robert R. Morley Student Research Fund Grant for funding the study. The full code for the website is available on Github. The code used for this analysis containing the anonymized user food waste and click data can be given upon request.

References

1. Buzby, J.C., Hyman, J.: Total and per capita value of food loss in the united states. Food Policy **37**(5), 561–570 (2012)
2. Caleca, G.: eatit!: visualizing expiry dates to raise awareness of food waste (2017)
3. De Dominicis, S., Schultz, P., Bonaiuto, M.: Protecting the environment for self-interested reasons: altruism is not the only pathway to sustainability. Front. Psychol. 1065 (2017)
4. Dillahunt, T., Becker, G., Mankoff, J., Kraut, R.: Motivating environmentally sustainable behavior changes with a virtual polar bear. In: Pervasive 2008 Workshop Proceedings, vol. 8, pp. 58–62 (2008)
5. Dove, G.: Inspired by information: combining data visualization and generative techniques in early stage design research. In: 9th ACM Conference on Creativity & Cognition (2013). https://openaccess.city.ac.uk/id/eprint/5722/, Dove, G.| ACM 2013. This is the author's version of the work. It is posted here for your personal use. Not for redistribution. The definitive Version of Record was published in Proceedings of the 9th ACM Conference on Creativity & Cognition
6. Farr-Wharton, G., Choi, J.H.J., Foth, M.: Food talks back: exploring the role of mobile applications in reducing domestic food wastage. In: Proceedings of the 26th Australian Computer-Human Interaction Conference on Designing Futures: The Future of Design, pp. 352–361 (2014)
7. Farr-Wharton, G., Choi, J.H.J., Foth, M.: Technicolouring the fridge: reducing food waste through uses of colour-coding and cameras. In: Proceedings of the 13th International Conference on Mobile and Ubiquitous Multimedia, pp. 48–57 (2014)
8. Froehlich, J., et al.: Ubigreen: investigating a mobile tool for tracking and supporting green transportation habits. In: Proceedings of the SIGCHI Conference on Human Factors in Computing Systems, pp. 1043–1052 (2009)
9. Froehlich, J., Findlater, L., Landay, J.: The design of eco-feedback technology. In: Proceedings of the SIGCHI Conference on Human Factors in Computing Systems, pp. 1999–2008 (2010)
10. Ganglbauer, E., Fitzpatrick, G., Comber, R.: Negotiating food waste: using a practice lens to inform design. ACM Trans. Comput.-Hum. Interact. (TOCHI) **20**(2), 1–25 (2013)
11. Gifford, R., Nilsson, A.: Personal and social factors that influence pro-environmental concern and behaviour: a review. Int. J. Psychol. J. Int. Psychologie **49**, 141–57 (2014). https://doi.org/10.1002/ijop.12034
12. Gustafsson, A., Gyllenswärd, M.: The power-aware cord: energy awareness through ambient information display. In: CHI 2005 Extended Abstracts on Human Factors in Computing Systems, pp. 1423–1426 (2005)

13. Ham, J., Midden, C.: Ambient persuasive technology needs little cognitive effort: the differential effects of cognitive load on lighting feedback versus factual feedback. In: Ploug, T., Hasle, P., Oinas-Kukkonen, H. (eds.) PERSUASIVE 2010. LNCS, vol. 6137, pp. 132–142. Springer, Heidelberg (2010). https://doi.org/10.1007/978-3-642-13226-1_14

14. Hancı, E., Lacroix, J., Ruijten, P.A., Haans, A., IJsselsteijn, W.: Measuring commitment to self-tracking: development of the c2st scale. Pers. Ubiquit. Comput. **24**(6), 735–746 (2020)

15. Kim, T., Hong, H., Magerko, B.: Coralog: use-aware visualization connecting human micro-activities to environmental change. In: CHI 2009 Extended Abstracts on Human Factors in Computing Systems (2009)

16. Nguyen, V.N., Nguyen, T.H., Huynh, T.T., Nguyen, V.H., Stigberg, S.K.: Interactive fridge: a solution for preventing domestic food waste. In: Geissbühler, A., Demongeot, J., Mokhtari, M., Abdulrazak, B., Aloulou, H. (eds.) ICOST 2015. LNCS, vol. 9102, pp. 361–366. Springer, Cham (2015). https://doi.org/10.1007/978-3-319-19312-0_36

17. Pereira, L., Quintal, F., Nunes, N., Barreto, M.: Understanding the limitations of eco-feedback: a one-year long-term study, July 2013

18. Petersen, D., Steele, J., Wilkerson, J.: Wattbot: a residential electricity monitoring and feedback system. In: CHI 2009 Extended Abstracts on Human Factors in Computing Systems, pp. 2847–2852 (2009)

19. Pritoni, M., Lamarche, J., Cheney, K., Roth, K., Sachs, O.: Home energy management: Products and trends, January 2012

20. Sanguinetti, A., Dombrovski, K., Sikand, S.: Information, timing, and display: a design-behavior framework for improving the effectiveness of eco-feedback. Energy Res. Soc. Sci. **39**, 55–68 (2018)

21. Senbel, M., Ngo, V.D., Blair, E.: Social mobilization of climate change: university students conserving energy through multiple pathways for peer engagement. J. Environ. Psychol. **38**, 84–93 (2014)

22. Stancu, V., Haugaard, P., Lähteenmäki, L.: Determinants of consumer food waste behaviour: two routes to food waste. Appetite **96**, 7–17 (2016)

23. Venkat, K.: The climate change and economic impacts of food waste in the united states. Int. J. Food Syst. Dyn. **2**(4), 431–446 (2011)

24. Wittkowski, K., Klein, J.F., Falk, T., Schepers, J.J., Aspara, J., Bergner, K.N.: What gets measured gets done: can self-tracking technologies enhance advice compliance? J. Serv. Res. **23**(3), 281–298 (2020)

25. Yang, R., Newman, M.W.: Living with an intelligent thermostat: Advanced control for heating and cooling systems. In: Proceedings of the 2012 ACM Conference on Ubiquitous Computing. p. 1102–1107. UbiComp 2012, Association for Computing Machinery, New York, NY, USA (2012). https://doi.org/10.1145/2370216.2370449, https://doi.org/10.1145/2370216.2370449

Exploring the Emotional Design of Digital Art Under the Multimodal Interaction Form

Xiangnuo Li[✉] and Jialu He

Beijing City University, No. 269 Bei si huan Zhong lu, Hai dian District, Beijing, China
137428167@qq.com

Abstract. Under the trend of digital age, new technologies are changing day by day. The rapid progress of science and technology has led to great progress and innovation in the forms of digital art. Digital art works under multimodality provide not only sensory experience, but also emotional value to the audience through digital technology and multi-sensory interaction, thus forming a unique artistic charm. The artistic form and characteristics show changes that distinguish it from traditional digital art, and also reflect the aesthetic paradigm of the contemporary audience. Against this backdrop, this paper analyzes the application of multimodal interaction in digital art in related cases after clarifying related concepts, and further explore how to further provide emotional value to the audience and stimulate deeper thinking in digital art works. In the meantime, from the creator's perspective, the author explores the emotional artistic features in the context of digital media from the multimodal interactive form. On the one hand, the research results can help digital art make up for the deficiency of traditional digital art in the multimodal interactive form, and realize the infinite possibilities of digital art works. On the other hand, the author puts forward that creators should pay attention to the application of emotional design expression methods in multimodal interactive form, which provides some ideas and inspiration for future artistic creation, and further improves the research system of design theory in this field.

Keywords: Emotion motivation and persuasion design · Multimodal Interaction · Digital Art

1 Overview of Emotional Design and Multimodality

Naisbitt once said: "We are moving in two directions: high technology and high emotion." We are in an era of data, mobility and intelligence. In this diversified social system, more profound emotional design has become the key word in design. Meanwhile, due to the advancement of technology, the combination of art and technology has given birth to new forms of digital media, making the development of digital art no longer limited to a single traditional medium. "McLuhan's *Understanding Media* mentioned that traditional art forms are realized by means of textual print media, which are characterized by being visual and sequential. In the digital age, art is more dependent on electronic media, and images pay more attention to function and re-conceptualization of sense in addition to inheriting symbol forms. The digital art arising from this has the features of information feedback, real-time interaction, and multi-sensory integration compared with traditional methods." [1]. In this regard, multimodal interactive design can enhance the quality of users' experience through digital and multimedia technologies and forms, bring users the physical experience of multiple sensory elements and an experience process of accepting a variety of external information, fill users with more profound spiritual satisfaction, and at the same time provide artists with new ideas and creation forms in their emotional design.

1.1 Overview of Emotional Design

Emotional design was put forward by Donald A. Norman, the author of the series *The Design of Everyday Things*. "Cognition and emotion cannot be separated. Cognitive thoughts lead to emotions: emotions drive cognitive thoughts." [2] Emotional design takes users as the center and focuses on users' inner emotional and spiritual needs. It is proposed in contrast to modernism's emphasis on the skill orientation of products and neglect of human emotional needs. The emotional design of products is to shift the material-centered design mode to the people-centered design mode. According to Donald A. Norman's statement in *The Design of Everyday Things*, emotional design can be divided into three levels: visceral level, behavioral level, and reflective level. First, the visceral level is users' visceral direct response to products' vision and first impression, and it can stimulate users' positive emotions. There are two critical points in the design of visceral level: "five senses experience" and "responding to users". The five senses experience stresses that one sense is plain, and the design that integrates multiple senses can endow users with a rich sense of experience. "Responding to users" emphasizes that users can obtain emotional feedback in anything. Second, the behavioral level refers to the interaction between users and products in behavior, and it has a certain sense of rationality and logic, so it focuses on bringing pleasure and effectiveness to users. The design purpose of behavioral level is to facilitate the positive feedback generated by users in using products and achieve pleasant user experience. Thus, the "people-oriented" design principle is the core and key of the behavioral-level stage. Third, the reflective level includes consciousness and higher levels of feelings, emotions and senses. The reflective-level design highlights the interaction with users, the subsequent service and care, the human-computer interaction in artificial intelligence, as well as the communication between products and people to make computer understand human language, improve people's work efficiency, relieve their emotions, and realize the principles of "emotional design" [3].

1.2 Overview of Multimodal Interaction

The term "modality" is a biological concept proposed by Helmholtz, a German physiologist, and it means the channel through which organisms receive information by means of their sensory organs and experiences. For example, humans can obtain external information through the five senses. "Multimodality" refers to the integration of multiple senses, including visual, auditory, tactile, olfactory and gustatory modalities. People's cognition of the world begins with "sense". What we hear, see, smell, touch and taste is the result of sense. Modality is an essential way for the human body to contact with the outside world. The perceived stimulus is transmitted to the brain through the neural transmission system, so that people can feel the information of things' attributes [4]. "Multimodal interaction" is to integrate humans' visual, auditory, tactile and other senses, employ various computer communication channels to respond to input, and fully simulate the interaction between people.

Nowadays, multimodal interaction is extensively applied in interactive works of digital art, which makes the development of digital media art not solely depend on traditional media.

1.3 Development of Multimodal Interaction

According to "A Review of Multimodal Human-Computer Interaction" Written by Tao et al., multimodal human-computer interaction is divided into five dimensions for research. The first one is the dimension of data visualization interaction, which is primarily reflected in the visualization design of big data mainly based on vision changing from the traditional two-dimensional space design to the three-dimensional interactive space design, and the supplement of visual visualization with non-visual senses including the auditory, tactile, olfactory, gustatory senses. They can improve the efficiency of users' analysis and facilitate their understanding of data. The second one is motion recognition based on sound field sense. The working principle of this dimension is to identify the audio in a specific space, locate the sound source through the sound ranging of the microphone, and recognize the specific scene and the sound emitted by human body through machine learning algorithm. The third one is the real object interaction in mixed reality, which is a combination of VR and AR. This technology builds an interactive feedback information loop between the virtual world, the real world and users by introducing real scene information into the virtual environment, so as to enhance the realism of user experience. The fourth one is wearable interaction, which includes gesture interaction, contact interaction, and electronic skin interaction. The fifth one is human-computer dialogue interaction, in which speech emotion recognition and facial expression extraction involve deep learning of algorithms.

As multimodal interaction technology develops to its current stage with diverse forms, how can artists achieve effective integration of different modalities and emotional design in the interactive system, and is it necessary to adopt a new approach and idea to guide their creation?

2 Application of Multimodal Interaction in Emotional Design

With the continuous development of multimodal interaction technology, the traditional physical experience devices have been gradually replaced by multimodal interaction devices in the creation process of interactive digital art. To focus on the brand-new experience brought by the new changes and explore the feasibility of integrating multimodal interaction and emotional design, this paper will discuss the application of multimodal interactive design in emotional design according to three levels of human emotional needs in emotional design, and analyze how designers can deepen the experience through case studies.

2.1 Application of Multimodal Interaction in the Visceral Level of Emotional Design

"Body Movies" is Rafael Lozano-Hemmer's interactive public art work, which uses a robot-controlled projector to display thousands of portrait photos previously taken on the streets of the host city on a giant screen (see Fig. 1). When pedestrians cross the square, their shadows appear on the screen, and their portraits appear randomly on the projector. The height of pedestrians' silhouette is 2 to 25 m, depending on the distance between pedestrians and the screen [5]. This work is based on a camera-based tracking system that monitors the position of shadows in real time. When the shadow matches the scale of the portrait, it will trigger the feedback sound to the computer and display the random portrait on the screen. Lozano-Hemmer seeks to evoke a sense of intimacy and empathy for the city through spectacular images. This interactive public art work captures the position of users through the computer tracking system and exhibits different portraits, thereby enhancing the richness of experience in public art. In the meantime, it also arouses the audience's initial memories of the city and triggers their empathy.

This work is a public art work in 2001. At this time, the technology was relatively backward, but the artist Lozano-Hemmer consciously avoided the traditional single presentation mode and integrated many senses into the work. Moreover, capturing the old portrait of the city can give the audience emotional feedback, so the audience will have the consciousness of actively receiving information during the digital experience. Thus, this way can boost the interest of the work, while endowing the audience with a sense of experience.

Fig. 1. Cultural Capital of Europe Festival, V2 Grounding, Rotterdam, Netherlands, 2001

2.2 Application of Multimodal Interaction in the Behavioral Level of Emotional Design

Notes & Folds (see Fig. 2) is an interactive device composed of three cylindrical sound sculptures created by artist Amor Muñoz [6]. Each cylinder is covered with pleated textiles of different textures, and various patterns on these textiles correspond to different music patterns. When viewers bring their hands close to the textiles, these sculptures will be activated, making each cylinder rotate at varying speeds and emit different sounds. The artist Amor Muñoz creates a spatial musical instrument device for the audience through stirring tactile and auditory senses. The experience brought to the audience by this device integrates multiple modalities, which are consciously combined with the device through the audience's thinking in their experience process, thus creating their own music experience. In the process, the audience integrates multimodal rational cognition with perceptual cognition, thus bringing a multidimensional and multimodal experience. Rational cognition refers to the interaction process in which users think, imagine, associate, and become curious about the device and thus intervene further in the experience. Perceptual cognition refers to the process that the device gives feedback to the audience after intervention, so that the audience can get spiritual satisfaction. The intersection of rational cognition and perceptual cognition is the key element in satisfying the behavioral level of emotional design.

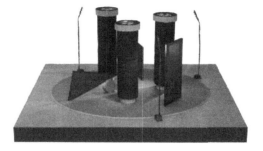

Fig. 2. Notes and Folds-Installation View, Amor Muñoz

2.3   Application of Multimodal Interaction in the Reflective Level of Emotional Design

Su Yongjian and Ba Ruiyun's work *When Breath Speaks* (see Fig. 3) creates an interactive field, trying to divest us of our existing language system [7]. The technology of the device's overhead part uses Arduino to connect the carbon dioxide sensor and employs the steering engine, so as to use breath to cause the tentacles on the top of the head to swing and produce sound. It restores the communication mode of animals to humans in an attempt to create a new way of communication with humans. This work makes people abandon the language they used to adopt, and simplifies all symbols of the existing language into signals, which tend to be barren and animal-like. The artist also raises a question: How should we redefine our connections as a member of nature? This sparks audience's thinking. In emotional design, the reflective level is the highest level, and it needs to realize the inner psychological needs and physical needs of individuals in the experience while pursuing spiritual resonance. Through the integration of multimodal interaction, the work realizes the way of guiding the audience to participate in the interaction, so as to make the audience explore the abstract emotional experience between behavior and perception, let the senses and associations be integrated, bring the audience's thinking into different time and space, and provoke audience's deeper thinking.

Fig. 3. When Breath Speaks – Installation View, Su Yongjian and Ba Ruiyun

3   Explore the Method of Integrating Emotional Design and Multimodal Interactive Design from the Creator's Perspective

The perspective of this work is the context of "mass loneliness" triggered by social media. From its formation process, it can be seen as the process of continuously constructing information cocoon. There are two main reasons: First, our dependence on social media leads to the neglect of natural and beautiful things in life when we are addicted to the screen. Second, the virtuality of social media is opposite to the authenticity of reality, and the self-presentation that people show through the Internet is different from the real self. Through investigation, it is found that the primary factor of information cocoon lies in people rather than technology. The psychology, cognition and behavior habits of individuals may be the fundamental reasons for the formation of information cocoon. Although it is difficult to transform people's psychological mechanism, changing people's behavioral patterns in some ways can mitigate people's vicious circle in a closed information environment to some extent. Therefore, the author tries to evoke the thought of using the embrace of nature in the physical world to help people acquire the need for love and belonging through a multimodal and emotional interaction device. This work is created through the following three approaches.

3.1   Construction of Narrative Environment

User research shows that constructing an immersive environment based on user sensory experience in interactive digital art creation is more conducive to improving enhancing user experience and information transmission. Moreover, people's involvement and participation is an inseparable part of interactive digital art, so "participation" and "immersion" are particularly critical. This work guides users to experience the work in a linear narrative way through two spaces. First, users enter the space of visual images, and become aware of the process of information cocoon construction through the visual impact of images and the interaction with images in this process. When watching the first interactive image, users will make their options through the prompts in the images to promote the story, and enter the second space under the guidance of the system and the images. After entering the second space, users will have a more soothing and relaxed visual experience. In this space, we will put in the projector image works and the interactive device of spatial entities, and users will feel nature by touching and embracing plants, thus helping them to gain love and belonging by embracing nature in the physical world (see Fig. 4).

3.2   Integration and Transformation of Senses

Marshall McLuhan, an original media theorist of the 20th century, pointed out in his book *Understanding Media* that all technologies are extensions of humans [8]. Multimodal interaction provides a more direct technology to extend sensory perception for emotional design, which can receive visual perception through visual devices, obtain extra-verbal speech perception of the whole scene through all-round voice components, and acquire

Fig. 4. Installation View

information through the integration of different senses and environments. The interconnection and transformation between senses constitute a comprehensive experience, thus achieving the balance of senses, space, thinking and emotion. This work realizes the integration and transformation of different senses through the switching of two scenes. In the visual style of the interactive image in the first scene, the fault-type style is constructed by using jumbled text and content stack, which produces a strong visual impact and thus forms a relatively distinct visual experience. In the process of watching interactive images, users will make interactive choices by touching, and advance the story according to the guidance and prompts of the images, so as to enter the next visual space. In the second scene, a warm and relaxed visual feeling is rendered visually through the choice of environment and lighting, while users' mood can be relieved by soothing and relaxing music in the auditory sense. In the tactile sense, users feel the growth of plants by touching and embracing them. After touching different plants, the graphic design of the corresponding plants will appear in the projector. Thus, users will feel the perception

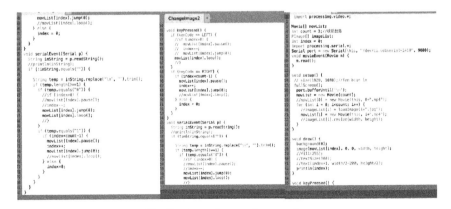

Fig. 5. The code part of processing

of nature in the physical world through the interactive projector images that are generated by embracing the plants. In the technical part of tactile sense and visual sense, Processing (see Fig. 5) is combined with Arduino. See Fig. 6 for the specific process.

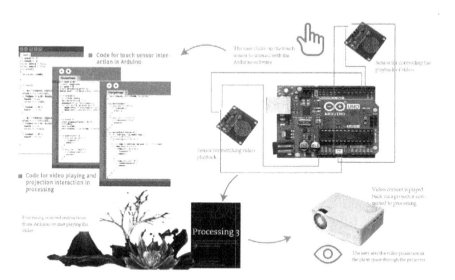

Fig. 6. The technical process in the second part of the work

3.3 Media Selection and Presentation

In the choice of media, interactive images and projector interaction are used to present, and the video is narrated in a linear way. To achieve the goal of understanding the information cocoon and causing the audience to reflect. In the video, we construct an ordinary person in daily life, and exhibit the process of being surrounded by information in various fields. By using jumbled words and content, we adopt fault-type style to bring visual impact, highlighting the characteristics of the information cocoon and arousing the audience's reflections. In the second space, the plants chosen are white orchid, jasmine and lavender, which helps to relieve stress, anxiety and depression. In the projector with touch interaction, the shape of projector adopts a relatively relaxed streamline and circle as the keynote of plants, while the shapes suitable for plant characteristics are designed according to the shapes and characteristics of different kinds of plants. Furthermore, the flow curves of different shapes are designed according to the video fluidity of the projector and the characteristics of plant growth. The visual presentation is harmonious and unified, so that the audience can have a soothing and stress-relieving feeling in this space.

4 Summary

The progress of technology undoubtedly provides an extension of the senses for the emotional design in digital art design, boosts users' sense of participation and immersion in digital experience, and also provides new possibilities for digital experience design. However, no matter how technology develops, the basic principle of creation is to take users as the center and pay attention to users' inner emotional needs and spiritual needs. In the future digital art design, technology-based multimodal interaction or user-based emotional design are bound to be integrated with each other. If we only pay attention to one side, interact for the sake of interaction, or excessively satisfy the sensory stimulation, it is against the original purpose of digital art.

References

1. Xu, J., Xi, T.: 基于多模态感官理论的交互式数字艺术研究. Journal **3**, 97–99 (2018)
2. Norman, D.A.: The Design of Everyday Things. In: The Perseus Books Group, New York, United States (2013)
3. Li, J.: 设计人工智能视野下人机交互情感化设计的应用. Journal **42**(12), 34–37 (2021)
4. Xu, W., Xu, M.T.: 多模态交互在数字体验设计中的策略探究. Journal **2**(4), 72–74 (2021)
5. Rafael, L.-H.: https://www.lozano-hemmer.com/body_movies.php. Accessed 21 Dec 2022
6. Notes & Folds-Amor Muñoz. https://artsandculture.google.com/story/notes-amp-folds-amor-mu%C3%B1oz/fQXRTO3ahVcMeA?hl=en. Accessed 10 Jan 2023
7. MANA. https://m.manamana.net/video/detail/2015371#!zh. Accessed 21 Jan 2023
8. McLuhan, M.: Understanding Media. Taylor & Francis Ltd., London, United Kingdom (2005)
9. Wei, Y.: 多模态交互电影的探索与研究. Journal **10**, 173–176 (2020)

A Survey on the Emotive Color and User Cognition for the Expression Cards

Elena Carolina Li[✉], Shih-Hsuan Lin, and Yu-Hsuan Liao

University of Taipei, Taipei City, Taiwan
elenali@utaipei.edu.tw

Abstract. Psychologists or counselors can use expression cards for counseling cases. The emotive vocabulary and colors of expression cards should align with the public's cognition or impression to help users identify, clarify, and express their situations more effectively. This study takes expression cards as the research field. It explores the differences between the colors of expression cards and the general public's cognition for providing color suggestions on expression cards. Based on the 60 basic emotive vocabularies, a total of 308 cards to be evaluated were selected from the nine sets of cards. The research team used the Pantone color chip as a survey sample. In this questionnaire, the Likert 7-point scale was used, and participants were asked to evaluate whether each color chip was in line with their cognition. A total of 62 valid questionnaires were collected, and a total of 111 color chips in this questionnaire conform to the color impressions of the participants, accounting for about 36.03% of the total chip items. Some emotive vocabularies did not any color chip cross the statistical standard by this study. This result points to a certain extent that the relationship between color and emotion is complex and diverse. However, if we spread out all the 308 swatches, it can still be seen that the colors used for positive emotions are pale, light, and bright; they tend to be warm tones. While the colors used for negative emotions prefer dark, dark, turbid, gray, and dark gray, they often use cold tones.

Keywords: Emotion · Expression Card · Color

1 Introduction

Emotions represent one of the media of interpersonal social interactions or communication [20]; the ability to identify facial expressions of fellow human beings is a key prerequisite for an in-depth understanding and formation of complex social interaction concepts [3, 36]. Emotional self-awareness and self-perception have a significant impact on mental health. Negative emotions tend to trigger mental health issues such as depression and anxiety [38]. By educating Generalized Anxiety Disorder patients on how to effectively manage their emotions, their emotional distress can be successfully alleviated [17]. Trapnell and Campbell [37] point out that psychotherapy can boost the self-awareness of patients. Positive meaning generated by such awareness experiences can help lower incidence rates and severity of depression symptoms [39].

© The Author(s), under exclusive license to Springer Nature Switzerland AG 2023
A. Marcus et al. (Eds.): HCII 2023, LNCS 14030, pp. 571–587, 2023.
https://doi.org/10.1007/978-3-031-35699-5_41

In addition, visual counseling tools such as Expression Cards are highly conducive to self-awareness and expression of emotions [23]. Research findings further indicate that colors influence people's affective judgments [6] and it is generally believed that colors affect emotions [1]. For instance, research has found that the colors of UNO cards can be utilized for psychotherapy by relying on the linkage of these colors to personal emotions [14]. In the course of their collaboration with educators with counseling expertise in the context of other research projects, the researchers of this study have realized that many counselors have numerous sets of cards. Counselors utilize different types of cards (e.g., career cards, OH cards, and expression cards) in line with the individual needs of each case. The researchers of this study also found that counselors own several sets of cards with the same functions. When the researchers questioned them, they revealed three main reasons: (1) Sometimes the visual content of cards does not resonate with patients and it is difficult to select the right cards in line with their personal context. It is therefore necessary to resort to other card types. (2) The emotive colors of each set of cards are not completely identical. Different types of cards are therefore required to bridge this gap. (3) The design of the cards reflects the life experiences of the designers who tend to prioritize aesthetic criteria over emotive theories, which does not fully conform to public perceptions.

The visual content of cards (e.g., wording, colors etc.) affects the projections or expression of emotions on the part of subjects [11, 14]. If the wording and coloring of expression cards are not consistent with the emotional awareness of the public, subjects are prone to experience neglect, confusion, or bewilderment in the course of the counseling process. This study therefore adopts expression cards as its research scope and attempts to determine whether emotional vocabulary and coloring of expression cards available on the market is consistent with public perceptions. It further aims to identify which emotions are more easily evoked by colors adopted for the cards and which emotions are more difficult to elicit. Another research objective is to ascertain relevant trends in the linkage of color hues and brightness with different emotional categories. The researchers strive to clarify the aforementioned issues with the aid of a questionnaire survey and offer recommendations for the selection of colors for these expression cards.

2 Related Works

2.1 Emotion

Goleman [19] defines emotion as a feeling and its distinctive thoughts, psychological and biological states and range of propensities to act. Ye [43], on the other hand, argues that emotion is a psychological state which is caused by a certain stimulus and encompasses physiological reactions, perceived feelings, and manifestation of behavior. Emotions influence people's cognition, feelings, learning, communication, decision making, and judgment [15]. Good emotional self-awareness enhances sensual 3 experiences and is conducive to a better understanding of one's own inner needs and taking corresponding action [20]. Higher levels of self-knowledge are associated with higher levels of mental health [37].

There are two main theories for the classification of emotions. Categorical perception, the first theory, aims to divide emotions into different categories [4, 7, 12, 16, 19, 26].

Another way to classify emotions is the Dimension Perception Method, which postulates that emotions are continuous processes with variations in intensity and represents them in 2- or 3-dimensional space [32, 34, 35, 40]. Some scholars believe that the classification of emotions involves both categorical perception and Dimension Perception rather than just a single classification method [28]. Expression cards available on the market mostly focus on the six basic emotions proposed by Ekman [6], namely happiness, anger, fear, sadness, disgust, and surprise. They provide emotive vocabulary based on the dimensions of affective valence and arousal.

With a view to gaining a better understanding of the impact of external stimuli on emotions and gaining deeper insight into emotional reactions and changes in humans, scholars have developed the International Affective Picture System (IAPS), which serves as a database of stimuli eliciting a wide range of human emotions. This system utilizes three scales to measure the three emotive dimensions (affective valence, arousal, and control) [5] triggered in the test participants. Chiang, Tam, Hua, Chen, and Chang [10] have designed 72 questions for Taiwanese college students based on the IAPS norms. Their research posits that the IAPS system can be applied to the public, patients, and the research of emotions. They further argue that affective valence and arousal dimensions can be utilized to assess the ability of human society to regulate emotive stimuli [9]. The supplied images can influence and provide a better understanding of emotional reactions and views of the test participants, which is comparable to the images on expression cards utilized to elicit responses in participants.

2.2 Expression Cards

The use of images on cards for mental projections has a history of several decades. These cards feature visual elements and are characterized by immediacy and accessibility. Subjects therefore do not view them as a threat [13]. Because the content of each card is different and they can be combined and arranged as desired, they help subjects reconstruct their personal stories by relying on their imagination. Associations made with regard to the cards can help reveal the inner world of subjects such as hidden experiences or emotions [42].

The study of Cohen et al., [13] explores the impact of therapeutic, associative cards on emotional states. It employs a set of 88 therapeutic, associative cards as its research sample. The Self-Assessment Manikin (SAM) is utilized to examine whether the card images can induce different emotional states in participants. The results of this study prove that these cards have a significant impact on the emotional states of the test participants. This study demonstrates that card images influence the emotions of participants. If the visual design of the cards does not meet the anticipated goals and expectations, the results of the counseling and guidance process will be negatively affected.

Expression cards allow the visualized, concrete representation of emotions [25]. The process of selecting expression cards can enable subjects to form self-awareness and facilitates the expression of opinions and feelings through the card images and wording. Based on their functions and usage methods, expression cards can be divided into two categories, namely clarification-type and projection-type [21, 24]. Clarification-type cards such as New Universal Expression Cards, Variety Expression Cards, and Emotional Treasure Box features wording. Subjects can scrutinize and determine the level of consistency between the wording & images on the cards and their own emotional states. Bai [2] mentions in his research that over 85% of Taiwanese junior and senior high school guidance counselors utilize clarification-type cards for their personal interviews. These cards can induce self-exploration and clarification of personal values and raise the level of self-understanding on the part of subjects. Expression cards are mostly clarification-type cards. Every emotion has its corresponding emotive image and wording on the respective card.

The researchers of this study have identified seven frequently-used types of clarification-type cards. The designation, intended users, design concept, quantity, design characteristics, and sample images of each card are shown in Table 1 and Fig. 1. The researchers have made the following observations: (1) The number of cards and emotive vocabulary of each set of expression cards is different; (2) The visual representation of emotions mostly relies on facial expression images, reinforced by colors and wording; (3) Card usage is diversified and includes identification, projection, awareness, and problem-solving methods; (4) The visual design of certain cards is incapable of generating a linkage to the originally selected emotive vocabulary. Instead, explanations by an assistant are required to clarify the meaning to the participant.

Table 1. Common clarifying expression cards in Taiwan

Title	Potential users	Concepts	Card numbers	Features
My Mood I Decide	child teenager adult	With Ekman's Discrete Theory of Emotion as the theoretical foundation	There are 25 cards with common facial expressions covering six basic emotions (happiness, anger, fear, sadness, disgust, surprise)	1. The utilized characters on the cards are both male and female 2. Five blank faces have been designed to give users a chance to express their own distinctive mood
Variety Expression Cards	child teenager adult	Emotions are divided into four dimensions (positive, negative, strong, weak)	There are a total of 56 expression cards on the strong-weak and positive-negative spectra	A fun element is added through the inclusion of a purple monkey as a character for the expression cards. Additional explanations must be provided to the children for images showing expressions that are hard to identify or rather complex images
New Universal Expression Cards	child teenager	Cognitive behavioral guidance	A total of 66 positive and negative emotion cards; 15 emotional adjustment cards; 9 event reaction analysis cards; 8 color cards	Discussion of emotions with the aid of colors An emotion thermometer has been developed to measure emotions and distinguish between different emotions through utilization of numerical values With the aid of wording

(*continued*)

Table 1. (*continued*)

Title	Potential users	Concepts	Card numbers	Features
Emotional Treasure Box	child teenager adult	On the basis of the two dimensions of basic emotion categories and intensity of emotions and feelings defined by psychologists	1. 36 emotion recognition cards 2. 30 character trait cards	1. Users learn how to recognize and express emotions in a playful manner. In the course of reading the cards, they also hone their reading skills 2. The enclosed family activity design manual enables parents to teach their children how to understand and recognize emotions through emotion cards

Resources: CardHouse [8]/Yang, Lai, and Wen [41]

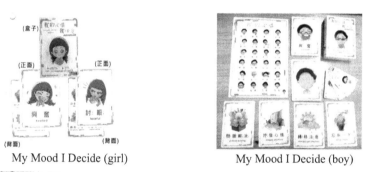

My Mood I Decide (girl)   My Mood I Decide (boy)

Variety Expression Cards   New Universal Expression Cards   Emotional Treasure Box

Fig. 1. Picture examples of common expression cards in Taiwan. Resources: CardHouse [8] / Yang, Lai, and Wen [41]

2.3 Emotion and Color

Darwin mentions in a book titled *The Expression of the Emotions in Man and Animals* published in 1872 that every emotion result in a distinctive facial expression, body language, and physiological response [31]. Shimokawa, Yatomi, Anamizu, Torii, Isono, Sugai, and Kohno [33] define emotion recognition as follows: The ability to recognize the emotions of others by relying on facial expressions or situations. Generally speaking, it is easier to recognize basic emotions (e.g., happiness, sadness) than complex emotions (e.g., surprise). Machajdik and Hanbury [27] utilize images to classify emotions with reference to four elements (color, texture, composition, and content) grounded in psychology and art theory. The source of their images is the International Affective Pictures System (IAPS) [5]. Their research findings clearly demonstrate that their adopted method improves the classification of emotive images and ensures greater proximity of image classification to emotions and feelings as perceived by the general public. This study points to the following two key conclusions: (1) Image design affects image perception by users; (2) Adequate design can ensure that images are more proximate to public perceptions.

Color is another key element affecting emotions. The research of Ou, Luo, Woodcock, and Wright [29] explores which of the following three factors is most closely related to color: color appearance (chroma, value), emotion (e.g., joy and happiness), and color attributes (warmth & coolness and weight). Their findings indicate that color and emotion have the strongest relationship. Gao and Xin [18], on the other hand, discuss the impact of color tone, saturation, and value on emotion. They utilize 12 vocabulary sets and 218 colors for their experiments. Their research findings indicate that tone affects how humans define emotions, which in turn indicates that humans probably associate certain colors with certain emotions. Phongsuphap and Kamolrat [30] propose a method for judging images and emotions. They adopt 20 colors representing different emotions as the basis of their research. Their findings reveal that emotive colors have a significant impact on image judgment. The cited studies point to the conclusion that color is a key factor affecting human feelings and recognition and judgment of emotions. They further highlight the importance of maintaining consistency between human perceptions or impressions of emotions and the colors utilized for emotion cards. Unbiased and cautious selection of colors is therefore an absolute necessity.

Kaya and Epps [22] attempt to explore the correlation between color and emotion in their experiments. Their findings can be summarized as follows: (1) Red triggers 64.3% positive and 32.7% negative emotions. It is therefore the color with the highest percentage of negative associations. Red can induce happiness, excitement, and anger. (2) Yellow triggers 93.9% positive emotions including happiness, vitality, and excitement. (3) Green triggers 95.9% positive emotions including calmness, happiness, comfort, and peace of mind. (4) Blue triggers 79.6% positive and 17.3 negative emotions including calmness, happiness, comfort, peace of mind, sadness, and depression. (5) White triggers 61.2% positive and 36.7% negative emotions including purity, calmness, peace of mind, emptiness, loneliness, and annoyance. This research proves that people associate colors with certain emotions. It is therefore of vital importance to consider emotion attributes in the color planning process and select corresponding colors with a view to ensuring greater proximity of emotion recognition and projections to public impressions when designing expression cards.

3   Research Method

Prior to initiation of the research design process, the research limitations of this study have been defined as follows: (1) Data released by the Taiwanese Ministry of Health and Welfare in 2021[1] reveals that the 15–44-year-old age group is the cohort most prone to premeditated suicide. This cohort therefore represents the intended user group of the cards designed in the context of this study. (2) This research focuses on the relationship between emotive vocabulary and colors and excludes other factors (e.g., facial expression images, image patterns, card dimensions, card materials etc.). (3) The study focuses on the visual design of expression cards and does not involve professional medical conduct.

The research process is divided into the following nine steps: (1) Selection of 11 most frequently used expression card sets available on the market as the research sample (2) Matching with the Pantone color swatches to determine and register a specific color for each card of each set (3) Listing vocabulary that appears more than five times in the aforementioned 11 sets as essential emotive vocabulary (4) Compilation of emotive vocabulary that appears in the sets, classification of emotions based on applicable theories (e.g., emotion theory), and preliminary integration of various emotive colors (5) Identification of emotive vocabulary and color swatches by users in questionnaires and utilization of the 7-point Likert scale to evaluate whether emotive vocabulary and color swatches are consistent with impressions of emotions in people's minds. (6) Adoption of paper-format questionnaires to allow the test participants to fill in the questionnaire with reference to the colors on the physical cards and utilization of the Pantone Solid Coated and Solid Uncoated swatches as color samples for the questionnaire to ensure that the colors displayed on the questionnaire are almost identical to the real colors on the cards (7) Identification of five users for a pre-test as the basis for revisions (8) Printing of the final version of the questionnaire, recruitment of test participants (a minimum of 60), distribution of informed consent forms (9) Utilization of the statistical analysis software IBM SPSS Statistics 23 for descriptive and inferential statistical analysis.

3.1   Essential Emotive Vocabulary for Expression Cards

The researchers of this study have identified vocabulary that appears more than five times in the aforementioned 11 sets for preliminary listing as Essential Emotive Vocabulary for the cards. Certain words with similar meanings (e.g., regret, guilt, and remorse) have been merged and listed as Essential Emotive Vocabulary if they appear in the sets a combined five times. The final list of 60 essential emotive words compiled by the researchers upon consolidation based on the six basic emotion categories and the Emotional Treasure Box classifications. Table 2 reveals a predominance of negative emotive words, which can be explained by the fact that inferential cards which are mostly applied to groups afflicted by

---

[1] Department of Statistics, Ministry of Health and Welfarein Taiwan: "Cause of Death Statistics - Age-specific," January 7th, 2022 from https://dep.mohw.gov.tw/DOS/lp-5069-113.html

emotion recognition problems or emotional distress feature a relatively high percentage of negative emotions for selection and projections by participants. The questionnaire design and survey methods are explained below.

Table 2. List of "Essential Emotive Vocabulary" adopted for this study.

Type	Groups	Vocabularies				
Positive (N = 22)	Comfortable	Relaxed	Comfortable	Touched	Calm	At ease
		Blessed				
	Happy	Anticipating	Satisfied	Delighted	Happy	Joyful
		Grateful	Excited	Fond		
	Others	Trusting	Self-confident	Hopeful	Shy	Envious
		Proud	Thrilled	Loving		
Negative (N = 40)	Shame	Embarrassed	Humiliated	Guilt	Regretful	
	Surprise	Surprised	Shocked			
	Sadness	Disappointed	Depressed	Exhausted	Sad	Miserable
		Aggrieved	Lonely	Solitary	Sorrowful	
	disgust	Resigned	Bored	Contemptuous	Hating	Disgusted
		Averse				
	Fear	Uneasy	Doubtful	Nervous	Worried	Anxious
		Afraid	Horrified			
	Angry	Annoyed	Irritable	Frustrated	Jealous	Angry
		Furious				
	Others	Self-abasing	Void	Perplexed	Ambivalent	

3.2 Questionnaire To Determine the Degree of Fit of Expression Card Color Impressionss

With a view to determining whether the color design of expression cards available on the market is consistent with the impressions of emotive vocabulary on the part of users, test participants were asked to evaluate the degree of fit of paper-based color swatches and emotive vocabulary provided by the research team on a 7-point Likert scale based on the "Essential Emotive Vocabulary" in Table 2. Questionnaire examples are shown in Table 3, there were 308 items finally.

Source of Evaluation Items for Emotive Vocabulary: All cards of the 11 sets featuring "Essential Emotive Vocabulary" have been listed as evaluation items with reference to the aforementioned list of "Essential Emotive Vocabulary". For instance, if the word "angry" appears in all 11 card sets, the test participants had to evaluate the card color associated with the word "angry" in all 11 sets to take account of the different color selections in

Table 3. Example of questionnaire

	Totally disagree	Disagree	Slightly disagree	Neutral	Slightly agree	Agree	Totally agree
Happy	1	2	3	4	5	6	7

each set. Nine of the eleven sets utilize colors to express emotions, while two sets solely rely on wording (the color of each card is identical). Finally, 308 evaluation items were identified in these nine sets. The original concern was that the excessive number of items would negatively affect the reliability and validity of the responses provided by the test participants. However, it was detected in a pre-test that the test participants judged the color swatches rapidly and intuitively and mostly without hesitation. The number of items was therefore left unchanged.

Selection of Emotive Colors: In view of the fact that a majority of cards feature several colors, the research team has selected the color most associated with a certain emotion as the evaluation item (usually the background color or the most prominent color covering most of the card surface). Only one color has been selected per card. For instance, the background color of Variety Expression Cards represents the respective emotion (Fig. 1). The color numbers of cards have been determined through comparison with the Solid Coated and Solid Uncoated swatches in the Pantone chips book. Color swatches with consistent colors have been identified for questionnaire evaluations. The dimensions of each color swatch are identical (2*1 cm). The paper utilized for the aforementioned nine card sets can be divided into two categories (coated and uncoated). As a rule, it was attempted to identify the color swatch most similar to the original material of the card.

Filling Out of the Questionnaire: (1) Each color swatch has been trimmed to the same size and all swatches were compiled into a questionnaire booklet to be viewed by the test participants under a fixed light source; (2) The sequence of emotive vocabulary question items has been determined randomly for each test participant to avoid color fatigue; (3) However, items for the same emotive vocabulary appear consecutively on the questionnaire for within-group comparison (e.g., "angry" must be consecutively evaluated nine times); (4) There is no time limit for filling out the questionnaire. A majority of test participants can complete the questionnaire within 40 min. The questionnaire cannot be taken out of the test venue.

3.3 Participants and Field

The 20–44 years old has been selected as the age range of test participants in consideration of the target user group of the cards (15–44 cohort) and the ability to comprehend emotive vocabulary and academic research ethics (adults aged 20 and above). Purposive sampling was conducted for the target group consisting of college students (equal number of male and female participants) and members of the workforce (currently employed; equal number of male and female participants). A specific laboratory at the home university of the research team was selected as the venue for the questionnaire survey to rule out impacts of different light sources on color swatch interpretation and recognition.

3.4 Pretest and Analysis Method

Five users were invited for a pre-test of the questionnaire. After explaining the purpose of the questionnaire to these five test participants, they were asked to fill out the questionnaire in accordance with the pre-planned procedures. The questionnaire administration contents and procedures were revised based on the feedback provided by the participants after the pretest. College students, members of the workforce, and visual art professionals aged 20–44 were selected for this pre-test. Since no significant issues pertaining to the questionnaire were detected in this pre-test and all required contents were completed, the results will be included in the statistical data of the official participants.

Upon collection of the completed questionnaires, descriptive statistics of the basic information of test participants was carried out. The subsequent T-test aimed to identify which items received strong approval from the test participants. Based on a one-sample t-test, strong approval by the participants was determined to exist if the following applied: (a) statistically significant p-value of $<.05$ and a mean above 5 points (higher than the 5th point ("slightly agree") on the 7-point Likert scale) and (b) statistically insignificant p-value after administration of one-sample T-test and a mean above 5 points.

4 Results and Discussion

4.1 Results

The 62 valid questionnaires were collected by the researchers (31 male and 31 female respondents; 30 respondents aged 20-24 and 32 aged 25–44, 31 students and 31 full-time employees). Only two had experience using expression cards.

The researchers arranged the color swatch results that met the statistical criteria in sequence from left to right based on the mean values as shown in Table 4 (mean values are listed). 111 of the 308 questionnaire items accounting for 36.03% were consistent with the color impressions with regard to the respective emotions in the minds of the test participants. This clearly indicates that around 64% of the cards available on the market do not meet the expectations of the public regarding the respective emotion in terms of the selection and application of emotive colors. None of the color swatches selected for the following eight emotions met the predefined criteria: Envious, humiliated, surprised, hurt, disgusted, doubtful, nervous, perplexed. On the other hand, most of the selected color swatches or tones for the respective emotions that met the predefined criteria were highly similar. This clearly shows that consistency with the impressions of the public regarding respective emotions can be achieved if colors are selected and applied to expression cards in an adequate manner.

Table 4. Summary of the questionnaire results

Groups	Vocabulary	Item Numbers	Survey results (Mean)				Color tone
Comfortable	Relaxed	7	5.58	5.34	5.05	5.02	Pale Light
	Comfortable	8	5.76	5.58	5.55	5.06	
	Touched	7	5.06				
	Calm	7	5.82	5.27	5.06		
	At ease	4	5.24				
	Blessed	6	6.13	6.04	5.95		
Happy	Anticipating	4	5.87				Vivid Light Bright Warm tome
	Satisfied	7	5.55	5.39	5.27		
	Delighted	9	5.66	5.65	5.45	5.06	
	Happy	3	5.23				
	Joyful	6	5.87	5.41	5.18		
	Grateful	9	5.27	5.24	5.23		
	Excited	7	5.63	5.19	5.18		
	Fond	1	5.37				
Positive others	Trusting	5	5.21	5.08			Vivid Light Bright Warm tone
	Self-confident	6	5.03				
	Hopeful	6	5.92	5.45	5.00		
	Shy	4	5.26	5.21			
	Envious	6	None				
	Proud	6	5.55	5.42	5.16		
	Thrilled	1	None				
	Loving	3	5.94	5.85	5.40		
Shame	Embarrassed	6	5.58				Dark Deep Cold tone
	Humiliated	4	None				
	Guilt	5	5.26	5.11			
	Regretful	3	5.11	5.11			
Surprise	Surprised	6	None				
	Shocked	4	5.11	5.03			
Sadness	Disappointed	8	5.95	5.73			Light Grayish Grayish DK Grayish Gray Cold tone
	Depressed	6	5.84				
	Exhausted	4	5.06				
	Sad	7	5.66	5.35			
	Aggrieved	5	5.35				

(continued)

582   E. C. Li et al.

Table 4. (*continued*)

Groups	Vocabulary	Item Numbers	Survey results (Mean)				Color tone
	Lonely	3	6.03				
	Solitary	4	6.19				
	Sorrowful	6	5.40	5.36			
	Miserable	5	5.53	5.48	5.42		
	Resigned	3	5.87	5.46			
	Bored	6	5.73	5.55	5.03		
Disgust	Contemptuous	2	5.27				
	Hating	4	5.71				
	Disgusted	2	None				
	Averse	3	5.85	5.32			
	Uneasy	3	5.31				
	Doubtful	4	None				
	Nervous	5	None				Dark
Fear	Worried	5	5.48	5.45	5.29		Grayish
	Anxious	6	5.56	5.24	5.13		Dark Grayish
	Afraid	9	5.81	5.66	5.56	5.50	
	Horrified	4	5.97	5.71			
	Annoyed	7	5.40	5.28	5.27	5.03	
	Irritable	4	5.55				Vivid
Angry	Frustrated	3	6.03				Deep
	Jealous	9	5.58	5.24			Dark
	Angry	9	5.89	5.37	5.03		Dark Grayish
	Furious	5	6.32	6.02	5.47		
	Self-abasing	5	5.76	5.23			Grayish
Negative others	Void	4	5.84				Gray
	Perplexed	2	None				Cold tone
	Ambivalent	4	5.55	5.44			

4.2 Discussion

The researchers adopted 11 expression card sets available on the market as their research sample. However, the fact that the age range of the intended users and the stated purpose vary from set to set may have resulted in different numbers of emotions in each set. For instance, because young children represent the intended user group of "Feeling & Emotion", a mere 14 emotions are featured in the set. However, it should also be pointed that the following fundamental and essential emotive vocabulary is present: Calm, grateful, joyful, angry, perplexed, exhausted, embarrassed, surprised, depressed, silly, lucky, and jealous. The 14 emotions listed above also appear several times in the other sets ("angry" appears in all 11 sets). Some card sets are mostly used by adults. They feature a wider range of vocabulary. The number of emotive words in each set available on the market also reflects the intended targets and users' groups. This factor can be taken into consideration for the design of expression cards in the future.

As for the classification of emotions, this study mainly relies on the emotion classification methods adopted by Ekman [16] and the Emotional Treasure Box (the main categories are comfortable, happy, ashamed, surprised, sad, angry, averse, and afraid). Nevertheless, it is quite difficult to determine and confirm the suitable categories for certain emotive words. Such words have therefore been preliminary classified into the "other positive" and "other negative" categories. The ranking of emotive vocabulary categories and emotional intensity will be confirmed through follow-up interviews and consultations with experts in the fields of guidance and counseling. The number and wording of "Essential Emotive Vocabulary" is also subject to adjustment and confirmation through expert consultations.

The fact that merely 36% of the color swatches conformed to the color impressions with regard to the respective emotions in the minds of the test participants indicates to a certain extent that the relationship between colors and emotions is complex and diversified. Specific color swatches may be consistent with the color impressions of certain people, but they may also deviate from the impressions in the minds of other people, which in turn may be related to differing life experiences. For instance, in the minds of people who have gotten diarrhea from eating apples, red may evoke fear or aversion. Due to differing life experiences, the selection and application of emotive colors represents a significant challenge. This could also be one of the main reasons for the aforementioned survey result (merely 36% of the color swatches conformed to the color impressions). Nevertheless, certain trends in the level of correspondence between color hues & tones and emotions can be discerned despite the fact that there is no single standard answer. These findings also provide card developers with a greater degree of flexibility and a higher number of options. However, excessive deviation from public impressions must be avoided.

Although the preset number of 60 valid questionnaires has been successfully achieved by the researchers of this study, it is evident from the organized data that the observed trends could have been even more distinct if the opinions of a greater number of citizens had been gathered. In view of the insufficient number of collected questionnaires, the researchers originally planned to create color patterns tailored to different genders, age groups, and occupational identities. The insufficient number of respondents raises concerns of lacking representativeness. The researchers therefore sincerely hope that a higher number of completed questionnaires can be collected in the future to gain a better understanding of differences in the perception of emotive colors caused by respondent characteristics such as gender, age, and identity (student/full-time employee).

5   Conclusion and Suggestion

The researchers of this study have identified 60 essential emotive words in 11 sets of expression cards available on the market. These words have been classified into the following 10 categories: comfortable, happy, ashamed, surprised, other positive, sad, averse, afraid, angry, and other negative. On the foundation of these 60 essential emotive words, the perceptions of emotive colors by citizens aged 20–44 have been collected through a questionnaire survey. 308 color swatches have been extracted from nine card sets available on the market for evaluation by test participants in the context of a questionnaire survey. The statistical results of a one-sample T-test reveal that only 36% of the emotive color swatches were approved by the test participants, which in turn indicates that there is significant room for improvement in the field of color selection and application for expression cards available on the market. However, there are certain tendencies in the application of color hues and tones to different types of emotions. Correlations between colors and emotions can be verified and potential color selections and approaches can be derived from questionnaire surveys.

This study aims to gain a better understanding of the degree of fit between colors of expression cards available on the market and public perceptions through a questionnaire survey. The results of this study can serve as a design reference. Other researchers can apply the findings of this study to similar research areas. With a view to establishing a database of visual impressions of the public with regard to emotions that encompasses emotive vocabulary and colors, a database of the emotions of groups with different age, gender, and occupational characteristics should be set up. It is recommended to collect an increasing number of valid questionnaires to ensure greater data stability and objectivity and facilitate the establishment of a Taiwanese emotional visualization platform.

Design elements of expression cards other than vocabulary and colors can also affect the perceptions of subjects. It is therefore recommended to explore the possibility of utilizing other visual elements (facial expression images, body movements, and situations). Despite the fact that color represents the main research objective of this study, quite a few card sets available on the market rely on facial expressions, body movements, situations, and auxiliary symbols to enhance the expression of emotions. The researchers further suggest that future studies discuss the impact of card dimensions and materials on subjects. The visual design of projection-type expression cards also deserves further research. Emotions and culture are closely intertwined. Commonalities and differences in visual design elements utilized to elicit emotions in different language, ethnic, and cultural contexts should therefore be further explored. The meanings and connotations of colors, in particular, vary with cultural and national conditions. Finally, visual design patterns for other types of counseling and guidance cards (e.g., career cards and OH cards, etc.) represent another suggested field of research.

Acknowledgement. This study was partially supported by the Ministry of Science and Technology, Taiwan (MOST 110-2410-H-845-018). The authors are grateful for this support.

References

1. Akers, A., Barton, J., Cossey, R., Gainsford, P., Griffin, M., Micklewright, D.: Visual color perception in green exercise: positive effects on mood and perceived exertion. Environ. Sci. Technol. **46**(16), 8661–8666 (2012). https://doi.org/10.1021/es301685g
2. Bai, Y.-F.: The Status of Card Application of Secondary School Counselors and Its Relation to Creativity (Unpublished master thesis). National Chuanghua University of Education, Chuanghua City, Taiwan (2014)

3. Baron-Cohen, S.: The extreme male brain theory of autism. Trends Cogn. Sci. **6**(6), 248–254 (2002). https://doi.org/10.1016/s1364-6613(02)01904-6

4. Biehl, M., et al.: Matsumoto and Ekman's Japanese and Caucasian facial expressions of emotion (JACFEE): reliability data and cross-national differences. J. Nonverbal Behav. **21**, 3–21 (1997). https://doi.org/10.1023/A:1024902500935

5. Bradley, M.M., Lang, P.J.: International affective picture system. In: Zeigler-Hill, V., Shackelford, T. (eds.) Encyclopedia of Personality and Individual Differences. Springer, Cham (2017). https://doi.org/10.1007/978-3-319-28099-8_42-1

6. Briki, W., Hue, O.: How red, blue, and green are affectively judged: affective judgments of colors. Appl. Cogn. Psychol. **30**(2), 301–304 (2016). https://doi.org/10.1002/acp.3206

7. Calder, A.J., Young, A.W., Perrett, D.I., Etcoff, N.L., Rowland, D.: Categorical perception of morphed facial expressions. Vis. Cogn. **3**(2), 81–118 (1996). https://doi.org/10.1080/713 756735

8. CardHouse: Aspects of Emotion Cards (2020). Retrieved May 20th, 2023, from https://www.facebook.com/1tarot2cards/posts/2833755180172502

9. Chiang, S.-K.:Mental and social function in chronic schizophrenia patients with heterogeneous clinical symptom profiles (Unpublished doctoral thesis). National Taiwan University, Taipei City, Taiwan (2009)

10. Chiang, S.-K., Tam, C.W.-C., Hua, M.-S., Chen, W.-L., Chang, C.-S.: The international affective picture system: a validation study for young adults in Taiwan. Chin. J. Psychol. **54**(4), 495–510 (2012). https://doi.org/10.6129/CJP.20120403

11. Chiang, W.-L., Chen, C.F.: An analysis of significant events and session impact in counseling with low self-esteem undergraduates by using tarot. Chin. J. Guid. Counsel. **24**, 107–145 (2008). https://doi.org/10.7082/CJGC.200809.0107

12. Cho, S.-L., Chen, H.-C., Cheng, C.-M.: Taiwan corpora of Chinese emotions and relevant psychophysiological data - a study on the norm of Chinese emotional words. Chin. J. Psychol. **55**(4), 493–523 (2013). https://doi.org/10.6129/CJP.20131026

13. Cohen, R., Leykin, D., Aviv, Y., Kukis, A., Lahad, M.: Affective dimensions of COPE cards: preliminary evidence of the affective ratings of valence, arousal and dominance of associative cards for psycho therapeutic purposes. Arts Psychother. **45**, 36–46 (2015). https://doi.org/10.1016/j.aip.2015.04.004

14. Drew, F., Bitar, G.W., Gee, R., Graff, C., Springer, P.R.: Using a creative intervention to increase self-disclosure among mandated juveniles with co-occurring disorders. J. Creat. Ment. Health **2**(2), 47–57 (2007). https://doi.org/10.1300/J456v02n02_06

15. Dubey, A.K., Sisodia, D., Khunteta, D.R., Saini, A.R., Chaturvedi, V.: Emerged computer interaction with humanity: social computing. Int. J. Comput. Sci. Appl. **4**(1), 161–169 (2014)

16. Ekman, P.: Facial expressions. In: Dalgleish, T., Power, M.J. (eds.) Handbook of Cognition and Emotion, pp. 301–320. Wiley (1999). https://doi.org/10.1002/0470013494.ch16

17. Fresco, D.M., Mennin, D.S., Heimberg, R.G., Ritter, M.: Emotion regulation therapy for generalized anxiety disorder. Cogn. Behav. Pract. **20**(3), 282–300 (2013). https://doi.org/10.1016/j.cbpra.2013.02.001

18. Gao, X.P., Xin, J.H.: Investigation of human's emotional responses on colors. Color. Res. Appl. **31**(5), 411–417 (2006). https://doi.org/10.1002/col.20246

19. Goleman, D.: Emotional Intelligence: Why It Can Matter More Than IQ. Bloomsbury, London (2009)

20. Greenberg, L.S.: Emotion-focused therapy. Clin. Psychol. Psychother. **11**(1), 3–16 (2004). https://doi.org/10.1002/cpp.388

21. Huang, T.-Y., Yan, J., Kuo, J.-F., Huang, C.-C.: The general situation of the publication of "Card" and the analysis of its application in the consultation. Counsel. Guid. **365**, 59–63 (2016)

22. Kaya, N., Epps, H.H.: Relationship between color and emotion: a study of college students. Coll. Stud. J. **38**(3), 396–405 (2004). https://link.gale.com/apps/doc/A123321897/AONE?u= googlescholar&sid=bookmark-AONE&xid=96b09980

23. Kuo, C.-T., Chang, C.-S.: Visual Counseling Skills. Liwen Cultural Group, Taipei City (2010)

24. Kuo, Y.-Y., Shen, Y.-P.: A study on using cards to counseling rejected junior high school students. Counsel. Guid. **348**, 34–37 (2014)

25. Li, C.-Y.: 11 tools for seeing emotions and self-acceptance. Educ. Parent. Family Lifestyle **78** (2016). Retrieved May 20th, 2023, from https://www.parenting.com.tw/article/5070911

26. Linnenbrink, E.A., Pintrich, P.R.: The role of motivational beliefs in conceptual change. In: Reconsidering Conceptual Change: Issues in Theory and Practice, pp. 115–135. Springer (2002)

27. Machajdik, J., Hanbury, A.: Affective image classification using features inspired by psychology and art theory. In: Proceedings of the 18th ACM International Conference on Multimedia, Firenze, Italy, pp. 83–92 (2010). https://doi.org/10.1145/1873951.1873965

28. Matsuda, Y.-T., et al.: The implicit processing of categorical and dimensional strategies: an fMRI study of facial emotion perception. Front. Hum. Neurosci. **7**, 551 (2013). https://doi. org/10.3389/fnhum.2013.00551

29. Ou, L.-C., Luo, M.R., Woodcock, A., Wright, A.B.: A study of colour emotion and colour preference. Part III: Colour preference modeling. Color Res. Appl. **29**(5), 381–389 (2004). https://doi.org/10.1002/col.20047

30. Phongsuphap, S., Kamolrat, K.: Perceptual colour features for natural scene image description and retrieval. In: 2015 IEEE International Conference on Systems Man and Cybernetics (SMC) (2015). https://doi.org/10.1109/SMC.2015.304

31. Robson, D.: A new way to look at emotions – and how to master yours (2017). Retrieved May 16th, 2023, from https://www.bbc.com/future/article/20171012-how-emotions-can-trick-your-mind-and-body

32. Russell, J.A.: A circumplex model of affect. J. Pers. Soc. Psychol. **39**(6), 1161–1178 (1980). https://doi.org/10.1037/h0077714

33. Shimokawa, A., et al.: Influence of deteriorating ability of emotional comprehension on interpersonal behavior in Alzheimer-type dementia. Brain Cogn. **47**(3), 423–433 (2001). https://doi.org/10.1006/brcg.2001.1318

34. Tarasenko, S.: Emotionally Colorful Reflexive Games. Master's thesis, Graduate School of Informatics Kyoto University (2010)

35. Thayer, R.E.: The Biopsychology of Mood and Arousal. Oxford University Press, New York (1989)

36. Thomas, S.M., Jordan, T.R.: Contributions of oral and extraoral facial movement to visual and audiovisual speech perception. J. Exp. Psychol. Hum. Percept. Perform. **30**(5), 873–888 (2004). https://doi.org/10.1037/0096-1523.30.5.873

37. Trapnell, P.D., Campbell, J.D.: Private self-consciousness and the five-factor model of personality: distinguishing rumination from reflection. J. Pers. Soc. Psychol. **76**(2), 284–304 (1999). https://doi.org/10.1037//0022-3514.76.2.284

38. Tsaousis, I., Nikolaou, I.: Exploring the relationship of emotional intelligence with physical and psychological health functioning. Stress. Health **21**(2), 77–86 (2005). https://doi.org/10. 1002/smi.1042

39. Whelton, W.J.: Emotional processes in psychotherapy: evidence across therapeutic modalities. Clin. Psychol. Psychother. **11**(1), 58–71 (2004). https://doi.org/10.1002/cpp.392

40. Wu, C.-H., Wei, W.-L., Lin, J.-C., Lee, W.-Y.: Speaking effect removal on emotion recognition from facial expressions based on eigenface conversion. IEEE Trans. Multimedia **15**(8), 1732–1744 (2013). https://doi.org/10.1109/TMM.2013.2272917

41. Yang, L.-R., Lai, C.-M., Wen, M.-Y.: Emotion Treasure Box: Emotion Recognition Card 36 x Character Trait Card 30. Education, Parenting, Family Lifestyle, Taipei City (2016)

42. Yang, S.-J., Huang, T.-J.: Art tarot: a preliminary investigation of self-growth groups with artistic cards. J. Taiwan Art Therapy **2**(2), 55–67 (2010). https://doi.org/10.29761/JTAT.201 012.0004
43. Ye, C.-X.: Psychology, 5th edn. Psychological Publishing, New Taipei City (2020)

Product Appearance Design Guide for Innovative Products Based on Kansei Engineering

Jiawen Liu[1] and Zhijuan Zhu[2($\boxtimes$)]

[1] Tongji University, Shanghai, People's Republic of China
[2] Huazhong University of Science and Technology, Wuhan, People's Republic of China
zhuzhijuan@hust.edu.cn

Abstract. Appearance can affect consumers' first impression of products. Excellent product appearance design can not only meet the functional needs of products but also enhance users' emotional experience, especially for innovative technological products. However, according to the research, there is a lack of guidance for the design of such products accurately. Therefore, this paper longs for a research framework based on Kansei Engineering and takes the appearance improvement of an intelligent mite removal robot as an example to carry out design research. Finally, the paper explores the relationship among perceptual images, users' evaluation of products, and product appearance design elements. Based on this relationship, a more detailed framework is formed. This framework can help technology companies better design the appearance of products. It can also help products enhance their design competitiveness and meet consumers' emotional needs.

Keywords: Kansei Engineering · Intelligent Robot · Product Appearance Design

1 Introduction

In the highly competitive product market, the product form will affect consumers' first impression of the product [1]. With the trend of consumption upgrading, consumers are gradually not satisfied with the consumption mode of function first but pay more attention to the emotional experience brought by consumer goods [2]. Emotion plays an important role in improving customer satisfaction and loyalty to the product and service experience [3]. Competition between products is thus extended to more dimensions. However, the existing design model lacks a scientific evaluation system for the relationship between emotion and product development. This makes the effect of the design difficult to evaluate.

To adapt to the above changes, Kansei Engineering is gradually applied to the appearance design process of intelligent products. Kansei Engineering is a product development method, which can transform users' impressions, feelings, and demands on products or existing concepts into design solutions and design parameters [4]. Kansei Engineering is a more mature approach and has been successfully applied to the development of products, such as automobiles, construction machinery, household appliances, clothing, and cosmetics [5]. At the same time, existing studies show that Kansei engineering can model perceptual services and emotions of many service departments [6]. To explore more diversified design schemes.

However, the existing framework of Kansei Engineering lacks targeted judgment on consumer groups and does not match design elements with emotion and consumer decisions. So, it is difficult to give specific guidance and suggestions on design. Under this development trend, Crilly et al. proposed a conceptual framework for product appearance, which described the design as a communication process and proposed the concept of design dimension [7]. Henderson et al. put forward design principles that can be applied to the universal design to aid design [8]. Based on previous studies, Mugge et al. proposed design guidelines applicable to consumer durables. It attempts to enhance consumers' reactions to the appearance of consumer durables by investigating which design dimensions affect perception. That can help better understand these comprehensive relationships [9]. However, the above research still has some limitations. Firstly, the existing framework does not fully consider the characteristics of intelligent products. And secondly, the existing research pays little attention to the design process, evaluation, and verification. Therefore, this paper hopes to explore the design based on the existing framework and take the intelligent mite removal robot as an example, to fully consider the actual needs of users in the whole design process, and to propose better design guidelines for scientific and technological innovation products.

2 Methods

2.1 Framework of Kansei Engineering

The essence of perceptual engineering is to quantify the problems related to human perceptual cognition and design by rational methods and means, to establish a logical relationship between humans and design objects. This method can transform ambiguous and hard-to-define emotional needs into elements that can guide design and better guide the conduct of design behavior [10]. Since the development of Kansei engineering, there has been a relatively mature theoretical framework, which can be a good guide for this research (see Fig. 1).

As an important part of Kansei Engineering research, emotional vocabulary are mainly used as modeling factors of representation, so the extraction of emotional vocabulary is the first step of Kansei engineering [11]. Then, a representative sample is selected for analysis. The experimental data were carefully processed in the form of a questionnaire through a combination of quantitative and qualitative methods [12]. Finally, the corresponding relationship between emotional vocabulary and modeling elements is explored to better guide the subsequent design. The acquisition of perception evaluation, the establishment of a mapping relationship between image and design feature, and the divergent design innovation based on this relationship are three complementary and very important links in the study of perception image.

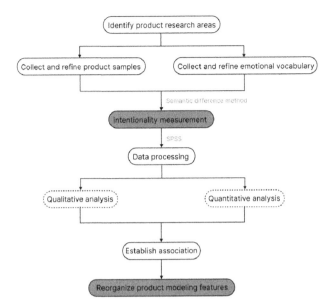

Fig. 1. The research framework of Kansei Engineering

2.2 Research Framework

The framework of the paper mainly adopts the product appearance design method based on Kansei Engineering. It is also hoped that the final design can increase the product's identification, aesthetics, emotion, and attraction. Questionnaire analysis was conducted for target users to understand their preferences, and the KANO model was introduced to sort the design dimensions. At the same time, conduct market research, analyze the existing market environment and competitive products, find the market design trend and opportunity points, and establish a product sample database. Based on the results of user research and market research, the emotional image vocabulary database is obtained, and the perceptual evaluation questionnaire is conducted to find out the relationship between design elements and emotional vocabulary.

In the design practice stage, this study guides the design based on the above research results. In the program evaluation stage, the product appearance program evaluation system is used to evaluate the design program and select the appropriate design program. At the later stage of design, on the one hand, design output and scheme verification are carried out, and on the other hand, universal design guidelines applicable to this type of product can be obtained (see Fig. 2).

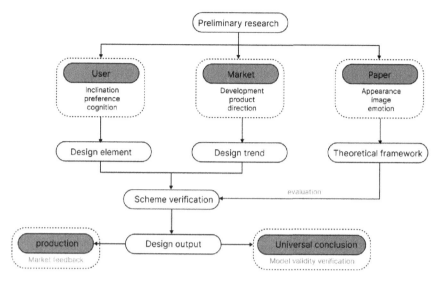

Fig. 2. The research framework of Kansei Engineering

3 Application – From the User's Perspective

3.1 Product Analysis

Product image plays an important role in consumers' preference and choice of products [13]. When consumers see the appearance of a product, they will perceive some physical characteristics that constitute the product design [14], and these physical characteristics can include form, color, material, process, etc. This topic hopes to study and discover the trend of these physical characteristics to better carry out the subsequent design. Therefore, based on the previous research, this study collected 52 products from 12 brands for the analysis of competing products.

Modeling Analysis
Product shape as a very important part of the product appearance elements has always been a very concerned aspect of designers, excellent shape design can further arouse the user's pleasant response. By classifying competing products according to two groups of emotional constraints (simple – complex, tough – soft), it can be found that existing products are mainly complex and tough, and most of the forms of products lack integrity. Research shows that products with curvy elements tend to elicit a stronger pleasure response and that more uniform product formats are more likely to affect users' positive emotions than less uniform product formats (see Fig. 3).

Color Analysis
According to existing studies, product color can affect users' attitudes toward products [15], and good color design can improve the visual appeal of products to some extent. It can be found that the existing products are mainly concentrated in the black, white, and

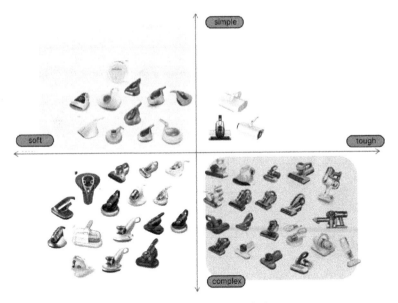

Fig. 3. Morphological analysis

gray quadrants, and such products will be embellished with local bright colors, which is a good practice to show the sense of technology and unity of the product based on preserving brand characteristics (see Fig. 4).

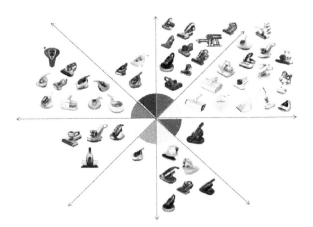

Fig. 4. Color analysis

Material Analysis

It can be found that the main material of the mite removal instruments is still plastic material, which is divided into two combinations transparent and opaque. In terms of surface texture, the more mainstream way is to use surface metal treatment and scrub treatment to increase texture and performance, which is also a more mainstream way in the small household appliances industry.

3.2 User Research and Analysis

This part is mainly used for the exploration of emotional words and the initial exploration of user preferences. At the same time, the KANO model is introduced to evaluate the importance of various design indicators to users. A total of 218 questionnaires were collected, and the reliability was 0.726. The questionnaire preliminarily explored the direction of the design and provided the following paths for the subsequent design.

Definite Perceptual Vocabulary
Ten products with different designs were selected from the competing products in the previous article for the questionnaire. The research defines the image of products in more detail: clean, friendly, innovative, technological, warm, and fresh. Then the associative design will be carried out according to these image words. And six pairs of image words (concise - fussy, innovative - retro, technological - conservative, warm - cold, fresh - heavy) were used to evaluate the sample. At the same time, the Likert scale was used to explore the emotional performance of ten products (see Table 1).

Table 1. Sample emotional questionnaire: The emotional evaluation of ten existing products in the minds of users was investigated

technological	3	2	1	0	-1	-2	-3	conservative
innovative	3	2	1	0	-1	-2	-3	retro
fresh	3	2	1	0	-1	-2	-3	thick
warm	3	2	1	0	-1	-2	-3	cold
clean	3	2	1	0	-1	-2	-3	tedious
amiable	3	2	1	0	-1	-2	-3	alienated

Enrich Design Elements
This research defines the product's modeling materials, color, and other information: in the modeling, the use of free arc shape, mainly rounded, interspersed with edges and corners; Cool colors with high intensity and low purity in color or black and white for polar design; Frosted plastic is used on the material, and frosted translucent plastic is used on the transparent material. The data in the questionnaire were processed, and the design elements were corresponding to the emotional vocabulary, eager to find the design direction for reference (see Table 2).

Table 2. Concretize the abstract image vocabulary, eager to match the detailed design elements with the image

Category	Description	Scientific	Innovation	Fresh	Warm	Clean	Friendly
Form	The lines are sharp and angular		✓			✓	
	Fewer lines, more rounded	✓		✓	✓	✓	✓
	The overall parts are few and simple	✓		✓		✓	✓
	The whole parts are many and delicate	✓	✓				
Color	Black, dark gray	✓	✓			✓	
	White, light gray	✓	✓	✓	✓	✓	✓
	Warm color		✓		✓		✓
	Cool color			✓			✓
Material	Metallic texture	✓	✓		✓		✓
	Frosted plastic	✓	✓	✓	✓	✓	✓
	Bright-film plastic			✓	✓		✓

4   Application – From the Design's Perspective

In the application part of the design, this study uses a scientific framework to compose and evaluate the design scheme, and finally explores the specific relationship among the dimensions of trust, design elements, and perceptual image in the appearance design of scientific and technological products. Form guidelines that can guide your design. The design of this part mainly focuses on the following three parts.

4.1   Combination of Design Elements

In the first round of sketches, I used the design elements corresponding to the perceptual image and combined them with the requirements of the enterprise and the results of the user survey to conduct thinking divergence and design attempts. Finally, I drew 18 sketch schemes (see Fig. 5), and initially conceived the component composition and external form of the product. The second round of sketches chose the form of modeling and drawing for presentation, combined with the internal structure, and gave more detailed consideration to the parts and forms. In the stage of effective presentation, parameters such as material, color, and presentation Angle of the scheme are unified, so that unnecessary interference can be eliminated in the second round of scheme selection purely from the perspective of form.

Fig. 5. Sketch: for subsequent analysis and evaluation

4.2 Program Evaluation

This study selects 20 dimensions that are more suitable for intelligent mite removal robots. Firstly, through consulting students majoring in design, analysis of books, guidance from mentors, and discussion from the company, the appearance of eight existing products is disassembled and the 20 dimensions are compared and selected. Then, according to the relationship between dimension and image, the corresponding radar map of the product is established to express the score of the product in five perceptual descriptions. Finally, the product scheme with the best performance is selected according to the correspondence between perceptual description and new employee evaluation (Table 3).

4.3 Relationship Summary

The designs that users prefer are described as follows: orderly, clear lines, symmetrical, stylish, angular, and delicate. Based on the cluster analysis of the six existing image words, it can be found that the six image words can be roughly divided into two categories, one is rational science and technology and innovation, and the other is sensitive to cleanliness, freshness, warmth and affinity of users' emotions. The appearance dimension and the relationship between image words are analyzed by correlation (see Table 4). We can understand the influence of appearance adjectives on each image. For example, if the product is required to have innovative features, then in the process of appearance design, it is necessary to try to use fashionable design elements, organic and delicate shapes, and avoid the use of relatively simple and traditional design methods.

Secondly, through three rounds of regression analysis, the author is eager to evaluate the relationship between the trust dimension and the perceptual image of the product at the user level. Since the company level is more inclined to improve the trust dimension, if the designer can better understand the relationship between the two, he can transform the abstract demand into an emotional experience, to make a better design (see Table 5). If users want to feel that the product is good in performance and quality, the appearance

Table 3. Physical description and emotional radar map

Scheme	appearance evaluation	image comparison
	Disordered, clear lines, unbalanced, simple, Well integrated, asymmetrical, innov tive, stylish, angular, Geometric, thin	
	Orderly, clear lines, balanced, complex, asymmetrical, innovative, unfashionable, curved, geometric, heavy, elegant	
	Orderly, unclear lines, balanced, complex, symmetrical, not innovative, not fashionable, curved, geometric, heavy, elegant	
	Disordered, unbalanced, complex, asymmetrical, innovative, stylish, curved, geometric, not heavy, not elegant, organic	
	Orderly, clear lines, balanced, simple, well integrated, symmetrical, innovative, stylish, angular, geometric, thin, simple	
	Disordered, unclear lines, unbalanced, uncomplicated, asymmetrical, innovative, fashionable, curved, natural, not heavy	

(continued)

Table 3. (*continued*)

	Order, clear lines, balance, complexity, symmetry, innovation, fashion, uncurved, geometric, thick	
	Orderly, balanced, uncomplicated, symmetrical, innovative, stylish, curved, geometric, not heavy, elegant	

Table 4. The correspondence between appearance dimension and perceptual image

	Positive	Negative
Technological	Stylish, delicate, and elegant	Traditional
Innovative	Stylish, organic, sophisticated	Simple, traditional
Fresh	Elegant molding lines	
Warm	Stylish design elements	Traditional
Amiable	Design with clear lines	
Clean	Symmetrical and delicate with clear lines	Traditional

design should try to satisfy the image of science and technology and friendliness, while avoiding the product being too warm. The same goes for ease of use and technological progress.

Table 5. The relationship between trust dimension and perceptual image

	Technological	Fresh	Innovative	Warm	Clean	Amiable
Performance quality	Positive			Negative		Positive
Ease of use					Positive	Positive
Technological progress	Positive					Positive

5 Product Design Guide

Finally, this research has formed a guide-to-guide design, which can be applied to the creative stage of product appearance design (see Fig. 6). The ability to choose design tools and elements based on desired dimensions. This guide can better meet the release and emotional needs of the product. However, the guide also has some limitations, which are mainly reflected in the limited sample base and the lack of further exploration of target users. In the follow-up research, more scientific theoretical construction is needed.

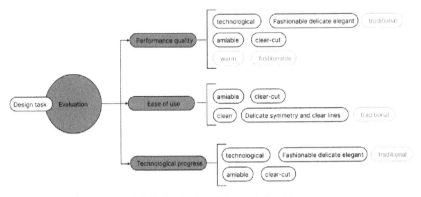

*Elements with black fonts are recommended, while elements with gray fonts are used with caution

Fig. 6. Product design guide

6 Conclusion

This study mainly uses the theory of perceptual image to guide the preliminary design and design verification and uses the product appearance evaluation system to evaluate and screen the scheme. Design practice and verification are carried out for the new product category of intelligent mite removal robot, which makes the appearance of the product increase its performance in emotional design based on satisfying aesthetics, identification and functionality. After a relatively complete design process, this design basically meets the goal mentioned above of improving the emotional experience and attractiveness of the product and tries to put forward a product appearance design guide suitable for the intelligent mite removal robot category.

In the research stage, through the analysis of corporate culture and the investigation of previous products, the perceptual vocabulary database suitable for this product is established. Then, the classification and screening of perceptual words are carried out in the form of questionnaire survey. Finally, six perceptual words are selected for the subsequent scheme design, which are respectively scientific, innovative, clean and fresh. Warm and welcoming. The product sample base is established and analyzed, and the corresponding relationship between image vocabulary and design elements is finally clarified by the semantic difference method, to guide the subsequent design process.

In the design part, use the results of user research and market research to define the design. At the same time, use the corresponding design elements applicable to the image vocabulary of this product to design the preliminary scheme. Finally, the appearance of an intelligent mite removal robot is designed. And carried out several rounds of iteration and structure coordination, to ensure the product's practical use of the possibility. After the evaluation in the late design period, the design results basically meet the expectations. It shows that this design better meets the design needs of the enterprise and provides the design direction and reference significance for future similar products.

References

1. Xiong, Y., Li, Y., Li, W.Q., et al.: Based on morphological characteristics line image quantization method of product form design. J. Sichuan Univ. Eng. Sci. **3**, 233–238 (2011). (in Chinese)
2. Su, J., Wang, P., Zhang, S., et al.: Research progress on key technologies of product image modeling design. J. Mach. Des. **30**(1) (2013) (in Chinese)
3. Hartono, M., Raharjo, H.: Exploring the mediating role of affective and cognitive satisfaction on the effect of service quality on loyalty. Total Qual. Manag. Bus. Excell. **26**(9–10), 971–985 (2015)
4. Yahaya, S.H., Sihombing, H., Yuhazri, M.Y.: The Integration Framework of Kansei Engineering (KE) and Kano Method (KM) for Product Development
5. Nagamachi, M.: Kansei engineering: the implication and applications to product development. In: IEEE International Conference on Systems. IEEE (1999)
6. Hartono, M., Chuan, T.K., Peacock, J.B.: Applying Kansei Engineering, the Kano model and QFD to services. Int. J. Serv. Econ. Manage. **5**(3), 256–274 (2013)
7. Crilly, N., Moultrie, J., Clarkson, P.J.: Seeing things: consumer response to the visual domain in product design. Des. Stud. **25**(6), 547–577 (2004)
8. Henderson, P.W., Cote, J.A.: Modifying Logos. Goodgravydesign Net
9. Mugge, R., Dahl, D.W., Schoormans, J.P.L.: "What you see, is what you get?" Guidelines for influencing consumers' perceptions of consumer durables through product appearance. J. Prod. Innov. Manage. **35**(3), 309–329 (2017). https://doi.org/10.1111/jpim.12403
10. Chen, J.L., Zhao, F., Li, Y., et al.: Product design method based on Kansei engineering. Packag. Eng. **40**(12), 162–167 (2019)
11. Li, Y.-E., Wang, Z.-Y., Xu, N.: Kansei Engineering. China Ocean Press, Beijing (2009)
12. Lin, L., Guo, Z.-E., Yang, M.-Q.: Research status and trend of shape optimization design for Perceptual image of products. Packag. Eng. **41**(2), 15 (2020). (in Chinese)
13. Kim, W.J., Ko, T., et al.: Mining affective experience for a Kansei design study on a recliner. Appl. Ergon. (2018)
14. Osgood, C.E., Suci, G.J., Tannenbaum, P.H.: The measurement of meaning. Audio-Visual Commun. Rev. **7**(3) (1971)
15. Madzík, P.: Increasing accuracy of the Kano model – a case study. Total Qual. Manage. Bus. Excel. 1–23 (2016)

Research on the Design of Office Interactive Exercise Products from an Emotional Perspective

Tianyuan Song and Hong Chen[✉]

East China University of Science and Technology, Shanghai, China
1580023957@qq.com

Abstract. The enormous job stress, high work-load style, and quick pace of life have a detrimental impact on the physical and mental health of the modern white-collar group. Many white-collar workers are in a state of subhealth and need appropriate exercise to improve. White-collar groups have a high incidence of mental illness and the number of depressed persons has been rising recently. As a result, their emotional needs should not be disregarded. Studies have shown that engaging in physical activity is beneficial for both maintaining excellent physical health and reducing stress. In order to promote users' active physical exercise and cultivate long-term habits with engaging interactive experiences, this paper starts with the psychology of the users, examines their emotional needs, and proposes a type of interactive exercise product design from the perspective of emotion. This paper solves the problem of the physical and mental health of white-collar workers while also providing a reference for comparable products.

Keywords: User emotion · Interaction design · White collar · Exercise products · Simulated planting

1 Introduction

1.1 The Exercise Needs of White-Collar Workers

Workplace stress leads to mental strain or frustration and sedentary habits lead to many white-collar workers are in a state of subhealth, facing many physical and mental health problems.

Common physiological health problems are focused on discomfort and inflammation in the shoulder and neck, lumbar spine, tendon sheath and other body parts, while sedentary habits can lead to more fat conversion and hoarding, affecting body shape, leading to obesity, and affecting cardiovascular health. Therefore white-collar groups need some physical exercise to maintain health.

Common psychological problems include depression, anxiety, irritability, etc. Excessive work pressure and lack of regular sleep are important causes of depression, and these

T. Song and H. Chen—Supported by Shanghai Summit Discipline in Design.

conditions are commonly found in the life of white-collar workers. Developing a simple and practical exercise program and developing the habit of regular exercise can enhance self-identity, which can prevent and reduce psychological disorders to a certain extent.

1.2   Concept of User Affective Experience

Jiandu Chen proposed that humans understand the world through cognition and judge things through emotion, and emotional experience is a continuous feeling that arises during the communication between humans and the environment [1].

Norman pointed out that the emotional system is not a straightforward and simple manifestation of consciousness, but consists of many layers, and the human emotional system can be divided into the instinctive layer, the action layer, and the reflection layer, which are different from each other but closely related [2]. Each of these layers contributes to the formation of different thoughts, which influence people's perceptions and feelings about the external world and together constitute the overall and emotional experience of the world [3].

Patrick proposes an alternative model of affective cognition, which describes different types of benefits that products bring to users: hedonic benefits, pragmatic benefits, and affective benefits. The hedonic benefit refers to the initial sensory pleasure brought by the product to the user, which is also at the instinctive level; the pragmatic benefit refers to the benefit of accomplishing the target task, which is also at the behavioral level; the affective benefit is the most lasting and complex relationship between the customer and the product, which is a combination of the first two benefits influenced by other factors such as cultural background and experience [4].

Desmet believes that emotion is based on the perception and evaluation of the product, and by constructing a "product emotion model", he reveals the underlying process of emotional experience. Desmet further subdivided the aspects of user attention and evaluation perspectives and classified user emotions into surprise emotions, use emotions, aesthetic emotions, social emotions, and interest emotions through their interactions (Fig. 1). The study corrects the misperception that user affective experience originates only from the aesthetic attributes of the product and reflects the limitations of contemporary user experience research that focuses only on the overall pleasantness of the user experience [5].

This paper explores emotional exercise fitness product design strategies based on Norman's three-level theory of emotional design, refers to Desmet's product emotion classification method for user experience research, analyzes the behavior and pain points of white-collar workers in the work process, focuses on the emotional level to obtain users' emotional needs, and thus proposes product design ideas.

2   Motion Product Design Strategies from an Emotional Perspective

Compared with the mid-modernist design that overlooks human emotional needs and emphasizes only the functionality of the product and the traditional mechanical line of communication, the emotional interactive design will give more emotions to the users, attract their attention, and seek a more humane solution to the problem [6].

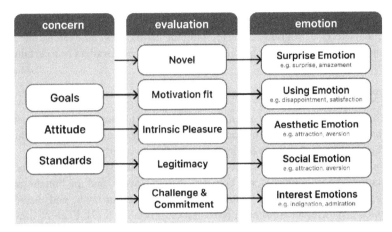

Fig. 1. Desmet's product-based sentiment classification

2.1 Design Strategy of Instinctive Level

The instinctive level of user experience originates from human nature and is at the bottom of the three levels of user emotional experience. It can bring the most direct and sensory stimulation to users, satisfy their attitudes, beliefs, and emotions, and let them respond to the emotions given by the product.

The instinctive level in the design of office sports and fitness products is mainly reflected in the form of the product design. Morphology is both a combination of points and lines and is also influenced by various factors such as environment and culture [7]. In the special space of office, the design of the form of sports and fitness products can be constructed in terms of volume, color, and form.

2.2 Design Strategy of Behavioral Level

Behavioral level is related to the function and effect of using and experiencing the product, for the pleasure and efficiency of using, focusing on how users use, how to quickly and precisely get the purpose and emotion of users, and whether new users can quickly adapt to the product. The function is the link between the product and the user, mainly influenced by the basic elements such as materials and technology. The functional design of office sports products can be developed according to the actual use of the environment and the psychological needs of users.

2.3 The Design Strategy of Reflection Level

Reflection level is the user's experience and feeling of the whole product use process, including all the content of the instinctive layer and behavior layer, only in the reflection level, can truly experience the integration of ideas and emotions, rather than mechanically for the "function" and "purposeful" The reflective level often starts from the opposite side of emotion, and makes a reasonable subjective judgment after weighing the advantages and defects of the product. Form design, function optimization and motivation mechanism that attract users to make purchase decisions can be included in the design strategy of reflection level.

3 Office Sports Exercise Product Demand Research

3.1 User Behavior Journey Map

Through observation, interviews, and big data to obtain information related to user behavior process, the user journey map of relaxation exercise process in the office is integrated as follows (Fig. 2).

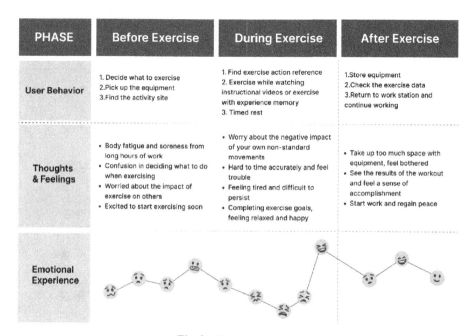

Fig. 2. User journey map

3.2 User Questionnaire Research

The following questionnaire was designed for white-collar workers' exercise needs in the work environment. The questionnaire contains 16 questions with six main samples: basic information, work situation, work fatigue, demand for exercise in the office, preference for product appearance and preference for product function.

This questionnaire was distributed among social workers nationwide, and 520 valid questionnaires were collected. The age of the sample was mainly distributed between 20 and 34 years old, accounting for 76.92%; among them, 241 were male, accounting for 46.35%; 279 were female, accounting for 53.65%.

Seven evaluation dimensions with high relevance were extracted based on three levels of user emotion: volume, color, touch, number of functions, urging strength, fun, and sociality. The questionnaire asked the user sample to rate the design of office sports products from the above dimensions in terms of preferences, and the scoring range was set from −50 to 50, with positive and negative scores representing different preferences in the same evaluation dimension (A or B), and the result data were compiled as shown in Fig. 3.

The questionnaire results reflect that users have more obvious preferences and expectations for product size, number of functions, supervision and fun in the office use scenario. In terms of product form, due to the limited space in the office, users think that the product should be small and easy to pick up and store; in terms of using experience, the product should have richer functions and stronger supervision to ensure their effective exercise; in addition, users think that the process of using the product is fun and social to make them more satisfied.

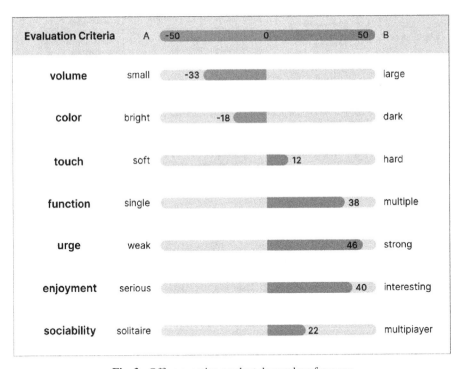

Fig. 3. Office exercise product demand preferences

4   Emotional Perspective of Office Sports Product Design Practice

4.1   Technical Support and Reference

The product design mentioned in this paper relies on holographic projection technology and Leap Motion human-computer interaction technology.

Holographic projection technology is a science and technology that uses the basic principles of interference and diffraction to record and reproduce the actual three-dimensional image of matter [8], which is divided into two parts: shooting and imaging.

The shooting process uses the interference principle to record the light wave information of an object and generate a holographic photograph; the imaging process uses the diffraction principle to reproduce the light wave information of an object and present the image in three dimensions.

Li Mang and Cai Dongna (2019) combined holographic technology and the presentation of digital plants to build an all-round interactive digital flower display system. Users can interact with the device and choose to view the growth process of a plant or a display of floral artwork about that plant (see Fig. 4). The user's view can be through either side of the quadrilateral cone and see a three-dimensional image suspended in the air through the reflection of the quadrilateral cone walls [9].

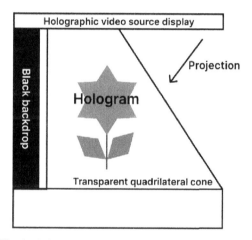

Fig. 4. Schematic diagram of holographic imaging [9]

Leap Motion Controller (Leap Motion for short) is one of the latest popular body sensing devices. It is the size of an ordinary USB flash drive and connects to a computer via a USB port [10]. It is capable of detecting 9 bones and 29 joints of the user's fingers, and is able to determine very short displacement measurements at the micron level, and is capable of detecting both the user's fingertips, palm, arm, etc., as well as finger-like physical objects (e.g., pencils, pens, etc.) [11]. Compared to Kinect, Leap Motion is more accurate in recognizing user gesture dynamics in the proximity region and has a faster data processing rate, making it a more professional, lightweight, and targeted somatosensory device.

Baoyuan Lu et al. (2018) proposed a new interactive holographic projection technology based on Leap Motion technology. This technology is based on the traditional holographic 3D projection technology and achieves the controlled display of 3D holographic images by increasing the volume of the image and adding Leap Motion sensors to reach interaction. It can be used to display both products and 3D objects, and can also control the movement and rotation of objects with gestures, and control the movement of virtual characters to simulate travel and tourism scenarios, which is a good solution to the problem of poor interaction and poor user experience of traditional projection devices. In addition, the capacity of the image is increased by adding a projector to generate holographic images using holographic projection technology, which improves the flexibility of imaging and overcomes the disadvantages of limited display devices and single generated images [12].

4.2 Product Design Idea

PLANTING is a series of exercise products designed for the busy white-collar workers in the office day and night, consisting of two parts: desktop virtual potted plant and exercise equipment. As an exercise device, it helps users relieve physical fatigue and release mental stress in the workplace with appropriate intensity of relaxation exercise; at the same time, as an intelligent interactive desktop ornament, it converts the results of exercise and gives users emotional feedback and motivation through the form of virtual plant growth.

The product design starts from three emotional experience levels to meet the user's use needs.

At the instinctive level, the product image focuses on a modern, natural and clear style. The shape of the product is extracted from the shape of plant leaves, with a vibrant decorative aesthetic. In the choice of materials, the metallic coating gives the product a modern aesthetic and a certain sense of power, and the frosted silicone shell in the holding part gives the product a comfortable feel. The color of the product is fresh green as the main color, echoing the theme of simulated planting, creating a pleasant and healing visual experience.

At the behavioral level, the products are multifunctional through serialization and consider providing users with easy-to-understand instructions for use. The product series contains three types of exercise equipment for different parts of the body, and users are free to choose according to the parts of the body they need to exercise the most. Users can set the mode and intensity through the touch screen of the device or the mobile APP to develop a personalized exercise program. In the process of use, the product will guide the user to make correct and effective exercise movements in the form of light and vibration feedback, the user does not need to be distracted during the exercise process to find other references.

In the level of reflection, the design of this product is more thinking about how to make users happy to use the product and adhere to long-term exercise. The first is to establish a feedback mechanism, all the exercise results of users will be visualized on the state of the virtual plant, and the historical data and growth level of the exercise will be recorded in the mobile APP, so that users can get a sense of achievement from it. The third is to establish a social mechanism, the social function of the mobile APP (offline friends interconnection or online community) makes the user group of the product form a social circle, users will not feel lonely in the process of achieving sports goals. In addition, transforming the exhausting and boring exercise behavior into the act of planting desktop greenery can reduce the user's psychological burden and help long-term persistence and cultivate habits (Fig. 5).

Fig. 5. Product effects (Color figure online)

4.3 Product Use Instructions

The exercise equipment of the product contains three types of aerobic pedals, elastic band ring and jump rope handle, which play different exercise purposes.

Aerobic pedals are used to perform step aerobic exercise. This is designed by the aerobic fitness trainer Kim Miller (Kim Miller) to rehab exercises recommended by his physician as a prototype of aerobic training, using the basic step pattern, step on and off the pedal, to achieve the purpose of strengthening the buttocks, exercise lower limbs, strengthen the lower body muscle groups, increase muscular endurance, and can provide sufficient exercise, fat burning is also a great help.

Elastic band ring is a left and right half of the interlocking, the middle by the elastic band connected to the long oval-shaped ring device, hands grasp the ends, you can carry out arm extension, shoulder and neck stretching relaxation and other movements, but also set in the waist for rotation, side bending and other movements.

Jump rope handle is a pair of bar handles, mainly to play the role of rope-less jump rope, suitable for the space limitations of the office environment. It also can be used as a lightweight dumbbell.

The above devices are rechargeable, touch the button on the device comes with the strength and mode adjustment (can also be in the mobile APP for more operations) (Fig. 6).

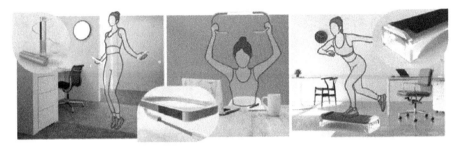

Fig. 6. Usage diagram

The essence of the desktop virtual plant ornament is a holographic projector, using 360° holographic 3D image presentation, the touch screen of the ornament itself can be operated for basic settings, exercise detailed data, achievement list, health recommendations and other more information as well as complex settings in the APP view and operation.

This product simulates the real planting behavior to set the reward mechanism: after the data record of the exercise equipment is uploaded, the virtual plant image on the desktop will produce changes such as nourishment, drying, growth and degradation. Users have the opportunity to be rewarded with random decorations such as snowflakes and ladybugs after completing the exercise goal for the day. Adhering to the punch card to complete long-term goals can unlock new plant images and also expand the capacity of the display case.

5   Conclusion and Future Work

With the rise in living standards and changes in lifestyle, indoor sports and fitness product design has advanced significantly over the past few years, giving rise to numerous new categories. Treadmills and dynamic bicycles are two examples of traditional, massive equipment that has invaded people's lives. There are also smaller items like yoga equipment. However, the majority of sports products currently on the market are primarily focused on the convenience of the user's interaction with the computer and the fundamental workout function, with little attention paid to the emotional experience of the user.

In this paper, we use white-collar workers as our target audience, study their emotional needs further in relation to their sporting requirements, investigate the design of office sports products that take into account the emotional experiences of users, and then engage in design practice to suggest an office sports product that creates engaging interactions through simulated planting.

The current product design strategy is mainly based on the qualitative evaluation of the user survey sample, which considers the user's emotional experience in terms of appearance (color, shape, volume, etc.), function (how many functions, difficulty and intensity settings, etc.), and emotional feedback mechanism. In the future work, we plan to measure the physical and physiological changes of users during the use of the product, supplement the quantitative measurement data, and make the design strategy In the future, we plan to measure the physiological changes of users' bodies during the use of the product, supplement the quantitative measurement data, and improve the design strategy.

References

1. Chen, J., Wang, N.: Analysis of factors affecting the design of old peoples walker equipment based on emotional experience. Ind. Des. **01**, 54–55 (2009)
2. Norman, D. A.: Emotional design. Publishing House of Electronics Industry (2005)
3. Zhang, B.: Emotional elements in interactive design (Master's Thesis, Jilin University) (2019)
4. Li, M., Yu, J., Wang, J., Ai, Q., Yuan, X.: Exploration of the contemporary emotional concept of product design——the example of fitness machine. China High-Tech Enterprises **28**, 16–18 (2016). https://doi.org/10.13535/j.cnki.11-4406/n.2016.28.009
5. Desmet, P.: A multilayered model of product emotions. Des. J. **6**(2), 4–13 (2003). https://doi.org/10.2752/146069203789355480
6. Yao, Z., Zhu, X.: Research on emotional design based on design level and demand level. Sci. Technol. Inf. **10**, 23–25 (2021). https://doi.org/10.16661/j.cnki.1672-3791.2011-5042-8808
7. Wu, J.: Research on the design of home projector based on user emotional experience. Ind. Des. **06**, 61–63 (2022)
8. Zhang, Z.: Holographic technology: a super wand to decorate and dazzle social and industrial space. Zhong Guan Cun **08**, 56–57 (2020)
9. Li, Z., Cai, D.: Holographic visualization and interactive system realization of digital flower plants. J. Graph. **06**, 1017–1023 (2019)
10. Huang, J., Jing, H.: Gesture control research based on leap motion. Comput. Syst. Appl. **10**, 259–263 (2015)
11. Karthick, P., Prathiba, N., Rekha, V.B., Thanalaxmi, S.: Transforming Indian sign language into text using leap motion. Int. J. Innovative Res. in Sci., Eng. Technol. **3**(4), 5 (2014)
12. Lv, B., Cai, Y., Lin, W., Cao, J., Yang, J., Cai, Z.: A method of interactive holographic projection using Leap Motion. Cyber Secur. Data Govern. **10**, 78–81 (2018). https://doi.org/10.19358/j.issn.2096-5133.2018.10.018

Motivation to Adopt Gamification in NFT

Jian Wang⍟, Hao Jiang(✉)⍟, Jiahao Sun⍟, and Luyao Deng⍟

Changsha University of Science and Technology, Changsha 410000, HN, China
`haojiang1115@163.com`

Abstract. Gamification is now widely used in many fields such as medical education, marketing campaigns and human-computer interaction, and has proven to be an effective tool to attract users and enhance user engagement. Technologies such as virtual reality, artificial intelligence, and blockchain continue to develop rapidly and receive widespread attention from society, and blockchain technology-based art Non-Fungible Token (NFT) brings innovation to the existing market model. Based on the value co-creation theory, this paper studies the motivation of adopting gamification in art NFT, analyzes its connection with user engagement, loyalty and self-brand connection, and provides a theoretical basis and future development direction for the development of gamification in art NFT. Data were collected from a sample of 100 Chinese art NFT users aged between 20 and 30 years old, and the collected data were analyzed using AMOS 25 and Process Macro for SPSS. The findings show that user achievement, social and immersion motivations all positively influence art NFT interactions, as well as all three subsets of user engagement (Pleasure, Arousal, and Dominance) also play a significant positive role in increasing loyalty. User engagement fully mediated the association between motivation and loyalty, while self-branding ties weakened the mediating relationship. The findings suggest that future gamification of art NFT needs to be further personalized and expanded to explore how different gamification features, content, and styles can more effectively satisfy users and the potential to engage users of all ages.

Keywords: Gamification · Art NFT · User Engagement · Self-Brand Connection

1 Introduction

In the fog of the COVID-19 crisis in 2021, a large-scale, complex, cryptography-based digital asset registration and verification tool rushed into the art world,refreshing it with new momentum, following the gradual landing of metaverse application scenarios, with many internationally renowned companies and artists releasing blockchain cloud-based encrypted NFT artworks, for example, Audi manufacturer released a series of NFT artworks in the form of digital art blind boxes; NFT projects such as CryptoPunks, Axie Infinity, and CryptiKitties have created a buzz, and NFT has changed how artists sell their products and how the art trading market works. Nadini argues that the phrase "NFT art" is not the most accurate phrase. NFT is not an artwork perse and it is simply a technology that increases the utility of artworks by functioning as proof of ownership

A. Marcus et al. (Eds.): HCII 2023, LNCS 14030, pp. 610–623, 2023.
https://doi.org/10.1007/978-3-031-35699-5_44

and tracking [1]. Therefore, in the rest of this paper, I will also use the phrase "art NFT" instead of "NFT art." Jinkook [2] argues that art NFT is NFT technology-augmented digital art in which NFT plays the role of a medium of exchange, emphasizing the place of crypto art in digital art when viewed through the lens of modern art development, and that its characteristics of scarcity and corroboration of rights can meet the needs of Deterding defines "gamification" as the incorporation of game design elements into non-game environments. Yee, a scholar from Stanford University, studied game elements from the perspective of players' motivation (hereinafter referred to as motivation), and concluded three categories of game elements - achievement, social, and immersion - through factor analysis, and specifically divided them into three categories. Further, not all of these elements can be applied to virtual communities. In view of this, in order to better explore the role mechanism of gamification marketing, this study will mainly focus on the three major categories of gamification elements, namely social elements, achievement elements and immersion elements, and conduct an in-depth discussion on the gamification elements of virtual communities in order to summarize the specific components of the three different categories of gamification elements in the proposed brand communities.

Given the unique nature of art NFT consumption and how users' expectations differ from those of non art NFT brands, there is little research explaining art NFT user motivations to engage in gamification. The current study contributes to this research gap by demonstrating the importance of different users motivations for adopting art NFTs' gamification (achievement, social and immersion) in engaging them with the projects. Artworks always provide a unique experience for the viewer, making art consumption a co-creative process between the consumer and the artwork and artist. In the digital era, the clustered synergy of metaverse-related technologies has facilitated the value co-creation of NFT art by multiple subjects in terms of content, theme, consumption and experience, and has formed a value co-creation mechanism specific to NFT art in the dimensions of co-creation content, co-creation subjects and co-creation paths. This view based on value co-creation theory is further amplified in the gamification of art NFT, which evokes active participation of users to create immersive experiences with the game context and art. While past research has shown a positive correlation between user engagement(hereinafter referred to as UE) and self-brand connection [3], self-brand connection (hereinafter referred to as SBC) are more complicated in the context of art NFT gamification and require special attention. Artistic NFT focuses on developing brand attachment through self-brand connection with consumers [4]. However, consumers with high SBC content and art NFTs with their own preferences may expect personalized attention and services both offline and online [5]. In this case, art NFT creators and platforms need to understand the appropriate target market for their game plan and the role of gamification in their overall user experience and relationship strategy. However, current knowledge on Art NFT gamification cannot address this issue.

Therefore, in this study, we apply value co-creation theory to understand the role of different consumer motivations to adopt gamification as an art NFT program and its impact on their interaction with it.This study aims to explore the motivations of art NFT to engage in gamification; to examine whether user engagement generated by art NFT brands through gamification can lead to loyalty(hereinafter referred to as loyalty) to users; to examine the impact of self-brand association on art NFT users' motivation to adopt gamification and the impact of the association between loyalty through user engagement.

2   Theoretical Framework and Hypothesis Development

2.1   Gamification in Art NFT and Theoretical Background

Gamification is becoming increasingly popular in the art NFT space, as NFT artwork and virtual games are centered on experience and storytelling. Gamification refers to the application of game design elements in a non-game environment to make the user buying experience more entertaining and engaging, and it attempts to replicate the same positive experience felt while playing the game and subsequently influence the user's cognitive and emotional processes [6]. NFT projects such as CryptoKitties, Cryptopunks, and Axie use gamification to increase users' motivation to interact with art. The theoretical framework of this study is built on value co-creation theory. First introduced by CK Prahalad and Ramaswamy at the beginning of the 21st century, "value co-creation" refers to the interaction and collaboration of different stakeholders to create value. The core idea is that the interaction and cooperation between enterprises and consumers and other stakeholders can create common value, which will be an important way for enterprises to compete in the future. In fact, the business development of modern enterprises, including media, is increasingly inseparable from the value co-creation activities built by enterprises and other relevant stakeholders based on interaction and cooperation, integration of resources and strong relationship networks. From the perspective of value co-creation theory, the game design function can be described as the interaction and cooperation between art NFT and users, and the game can be described as a "cooperative system". Previous studies have linked gamification to value co-creation theory [7]. Huotari [8] and Hamari [9] mentioned that gamification is a process of enhancing services that are provided to the game experience to support the overall value creation of the user ". Art NFT creators and institutions provide engaging gamification platforms that allow users to become value co-creators. These users derive value from the experiences gained through gamified interactions [10]. Thus, the theory of value co-creation sets the foundation of this study.

2.2   The Association Between Gamification and User Engagement

Lately, user engagement has attracted a great deal of attention from marketers and academics. User engagement includes experiences, interactions, and connections between users and brands [11]. Numerous researchers have clearly defined the concept of user engagement [12]. However, in this study, we used the PAD affective model based on the one proposed by Mehrabian and Russell to classify user engagement into three dimensions, namely P for Pleasure, which reflects both positive and negative aspects of the user's affective state; A for Arousal; D for Dominance, which reflects the degree of mutual dominance between the user and the external environment (positive for user dominance, negative for external dominance).

Gamification is a persuasive technique to influence consumers' beliefs, motivations, and behaviors. Previous studies confirm the impact of gamification on user engagement [13]. However, a framework of key motivational drivers of user engagement in terms of gamification is lacking, especially in the area of art NFT. Research on whether users' motivations to adopt gamification lead to user engagement and loyalty to art NFT programs is scarce. Thus, this study attempts to analyze the original reasons for this using value co-creation theory.

2.3 Impact of Motivations to Adopt Gamification on User Engagement

This study posits that it is crucial to study the motivations for user engagement in gamification in order to conceptualize user engagement in the current context. Furthermore, this study claims that motivation precedes user engagement [14], and that user engagement is driven by a series of sub-processes such as achievement, social) and immersion), which users find to be (social), and immersion) that users find satisfactory in terms of achievement, social, and immersion. Based on motivation theory [15], this study hypothesized three key motivations for art NFT users to adopt gamification--achievement, social, and immersion).

Achievement Motive. According to Atkinson's achievement motivation (hereinafter referred to as AM) model, achievement motivation belongs to stable traits in personality and is a key personality factor that describes an individual's pursuit of goals and commitment. According to Koivisto and Hamari [16], technologies such as gamification make consumers' shopping trips enjoyable and fun. They further explain gamification as a "motivational information system" in which the goal of computer technology is to "increase productivity through fun". For example, Axie Infinity, a digital pet raising game built on Ether, is a digital pet community that combines collection, training, breeding, fighting and social play, aiming to provide people with a new lifestyle that integrates work and play. Users are given the opportunity to explore, experiment and get paid accordingly in the forms of games such as pet battles and breeding pets, and to advance user engagement. Therefore, we propose the following hypothesis.

H1a.Achievement motive is positively associated with user engagement.

Social Motive. Social motivate (hereinafter referred to as SM)is a driving force for gamers to socialize their games for the purpose of sharing, interacting and showing off. Gamification encourages attribution among different consumers and gives them a sense of belonging. According to contemporary art expert Noah Davis Cryptopunks is a major component of the Cyptoart movement. Cryptopunks, one of the first NFT projects, has become so popular that celebrities such as NBA star Steph Curry, Moonbird founder, Jay Chou and others are vying to buy Cryptopunks The Bored Ape Yacht Club holds offline events for members to offer rewards and accolades and build their social identities. Game components such as team, collaboration and competition make social interactions between users exciting and stimulate engagement. Art NFT uses gamification services (representing co-created value) to leverage the motivational experience generated by user and work interactions. Therefore, the following hypothesis can be proposed.

H1b.Social motive is positively associated with user engagement.

Immersion Motive. Immersion motive (hereinafter referred to as IM)is the behavioral driver associated with personal immersion satisfaction through immersion-oriented factors (profile photo/virtual identities, narratives/themes, virtual worlds, and in-game rewards). For example, in 0xUniverse users can build spaceships and explore a vast universe, and players can build "knowledge" by searching for ancient artifacts hidden on their planet to engage in the storyline. It enhances players' sense of accomplishment, grows their expertise, and establishes their unique identity among other online peers [17].From an engagement perspective, immersion motivation plays an important role in developing users' perceived value. Therefore, the following hypothesis is proposed.

H1c.Immersion motive is positively associated with user engagement.

2.4 Impact of User Engagement on Loyalty

Loyalty reflects a psychological bond between the product and the user based on identity, devotion and association. Bendapudi and Berry state that the greater the benefits of engaging with the product in question, the greater the loyalty to it. Berger et al. [18] conclude that gamified interactions increase users' attention and emotional attachment to the content. The core reason for engagement with gamification is "the celebration of the product and the connection with other product enthusiasts" [19,22]. Furthermore, games are considered the best way to encourage engagement. As a result, art NFT products are increasingly investing in gamification to develop strong user connections. Therefore, the following hypothesis can be proposed.

H2a.Pleasure is positively associated with loyalty.

H2b.Dominance is positively associated with loyalty.

H2c.Activation is positively associated with loyalty.

2.5 Mediation Impact of User Involvement

Gamification helps users meet internal needs and create a psychological bond with the product through immersive social integration activities. For example, the NFT project Potatoz, through its latest Potatoz permission list raffle entry tickets to the Memeland ecosystem, at which on-site selfie photo booths are provided to create an exclusive MEME map. In addition to the interactive game zone in Twitter,the Music Game Experience, the AR physical game Party Fowl, and the Meta Universe AiR game are presented through gamification to increase the motivation of users. Previous research has shown that motivation is the predecessor of user engagement [20], 24 while loyalty is the result of user engagement. Therefore, we propose the following hypothesis.

In addition to the interactive game zone in Twitter, the Music Game Experience, the AR physical game Party Fowl, and the Meta Universe AiR game are presented through gamification to increase the motivation of users.

H3.User engagement mediates the association between motivation to adopt gamification and loyalty.

2.6 Moderate Impacts of Self-brand Connection

The "self" can include everything a person considers themselves to be, expressed through their objects posts, images and descriptions. Art NFT can influence the concept of "self" through its promotional strategies, creating a strong connection between the product and the user. Thus, SBC is the extent to which individuals associate the perceived meaning of a product with their self-concept. Several authors have concluded that user engagement and SBC are closely related [21]. Nadeem et al. [22] confirmed the moderating role of SBC in the association between experience value and user engagement on social networking sites. Creators can achieve higher user engagement by providing users with values (cognitive, hedonic, social, and moral) to develop emotional connections and share the meaning of their work with users.Researchers such as Berger et al. argued that highly interactive and stimulating gamified interactions enable SBC because such games promote emotional cognition and creator and platform engagement. Although SBC Is not a new study, its intervening role between user motivation and loyalty through user engagement in gamification has not been explored. The present study attempts to address this gap and therefore proposes the following hypothesis.

H4.self-brand connection positively moderates the mediating impact of user engagement on the association between motivation to adopt gamification and loyalty,Therefore the effect will be stronger with an increase in SBC.

Figure 1 presents the conceptual model and assumptions developed in the study.

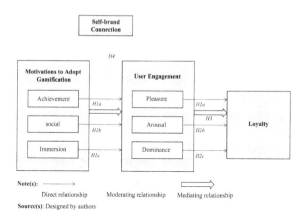

Fig. 1. Conceptual framework

3 Research Methodology

3.1 Study Background and Sampling

Data for the study were collected online. The target population was young adults between the ages of 20–30, who are typically familiar with gaming elements because of their direct and regular exposure to video games. Prior to enrolling participants in the final survey, a series of questions were called upon to check their eligibility. Thus, the final respondents included those familiar with gamification and knowledgeable about both NFT as well as art. To improve the content validity and reliability of the questionnaire, it was pre-tested with a short sample of 30 target user who had purchased NFT products in the past. The questionnaire was finalized for the main study after minor changes were made to the wording and order of the questions. The final questionnaire started with a note explaining the background of the study and a short video presentation to ensure that all participants understood the concept of gamification in NFT. The research background begins with a description of the industry overview, industry chain and application scenarios and marketing approaches of NFT, as well as an introduction to the emergence and application of the gamification concept, giving examples of gamification in the field of brand marketing. The video introduction is recorded and edited by the author. Based on the popularity of Axie Infinity game and the operation scene, an introduction will be made to illustrate the concept of gamification for the interviewees' image. The second part of the video takes Cryptopunks and Cryptokitties as examples to give an overview of their concept, gameplay and development history. The questionnaire as a whole is divided into two parts, the first part is the basic information to know about the respondents' background, the basic information columns Collect in formation such as name, gender, age, education, art major or non-art major and NFT familiarity (5 quantitative criteria from very much to not at all). In the second part, the 5-point Lister scale was used as the measurement standard, and 25 questions were set according to the conceptual map of theoretical framework and hypothesis development. 25 questions were divided into four parts, namely, motivation to adopt gamification, user engagement, loyalty and self-brand connection, among which three related to the subdivisions of gamification motivations (achievement motivation, social motivation and immersion motivation); three related to the subdivisions of user engagement (Arousal, Pleasure. Dominance); three correspond to loyalty and four related to self-brand connection.Respondents scored the questions on a scale of 1 (strongly disagree) to 5 (strongly agree) (see Fig. 2 for the flow of the questionnaire).

For data analysis, 100 responses were retained after removing incomplete, contradictory and identical responses for all items. Of the 100 respondents, 52% were male and 100 (100%) were under 30 years of age. Regarding education, 65 (65%) of the respondents had a graduate degree.

Read the Art NFT Gamification Introductory Instructions

View case studies and application scenarios Video

Fill in the questionnaire

Questionnaire Process

Fig. 2. Questionnaire process

3.2 Measures

The study focused on four parts: motivation to adopt gamification, user engagement, loyalty, and self-brand connection. All were derived from existing literature and slightly modified to fit the research context. All constructs were measured using a 5-point Lister scale, ranging from 1 (strongly disagree) to 5 (strongly agree). Items related to motivation to adopt gamification were borrowed from Claffey and Brady. The user engagement items are based on Vivek et al. [3]. The loyalty item is adapted from Hamari et al. [23], while the self-brand connection item is taken from Van der Westhuizen.

4 Data Analysis and Results

4.1 Measurement Model, Reliability and Validity

To assess the fitting degree, reliability, validity, and size of the structure of the conceptual model of gamification motivation used in Fig. 1 art NFT, a confirmatory factor analysis (CFA) was conducted using AMOS version 25. Table 1 shows the results of the CFA and shows good fits for $\chi 2/df = 2.169$ (535.712/247), CFI = 0.876, TLI = 0.96, IFI = 0.96, NFI = 0.796, RFI = 0.91, and RMSEA = 0.067. The reliability of the constructs was analyzed using the Cronbach's αcoefficient for each construct. The results in Table 1 show that the Cronbach's α measured from 25 questions including gamification motivation, user experience, loyalty and self-brand connection all ranged from 0.784 to 0.889, which is higher than the recommended value of 0.7. Fornell and Larker's recommendations were used to check the validity of the discriminant analysis. Table 2 shows the correlation values between each sub-construction and the square root of the extracted average variance (AVE), which indicates the discriminant validity. In addition, the AVE values of the construct measures and construct reliability were used to assess the convergent validity. Table 1 shows that all four constructs in the conceptual model of gamification motivation in Fig. 1 as well as all secondary AVEs exceeded 0.5 and CRs were higher than 0.7, which indicates convergent validity.

Table 1. Summary of measurement model.

Constructs and items	SFL*
Motivations to adopt gamification (M)	
Achievement motive (AM) ($\alpha = 0.84$; AVE = 0.73; CR = 0.84)	
I would like to engage in the online game for artworkNFT X because I expect to…	
-Get a sense of accomplishment from the gamification process	0.82
-Enhance my deep understanding of artists and artworks	0.81
-Improve my competitiveness as a consumer kol	0.88
Social motive (SM) ($\alpha = 0.85$; AVE = 0.77; CR = 0.86)	

(*continued*)

Table 1. (*continued*)

Constructs and items	SFL*
-Increase my interaction with other users	0.87
-Improve my image of artistic taste in the minds of others	0.83
-Enhance my sense of belonging through X artists/artworks	0.89
Immersion Motive (IM) ($\alpha = 0.80$; AVE = 0.76; CR = 0.81)	
-More likely to connect emotionally with the artwork	0.87
-Entertaining and stimulating my brain	0.89
-Getting pleasure from the gamification process	0.88
User Engagement (UE)	
Pleasure ($\alpha = 0.88$; AVE = 0.70; CR = 0.88)	
-Anything related to the gamification of nft artwork makes me feel happy	0.86
-Gamified nft artwork can brighten up my bad mood 0.89	0.89
-Buying gamified nft artwork makes me happier than buying other non-gamified nft artwork	0.88
Arousal ($\alpha = 0.90$; AVE = 0.76; CR = 0.90)	
-Gamification of nft artwork led me to other nft projects	0.88
-Gamification of nft artwork made me start buying nft artworks	0.85
-Gamification of nft artwork made me start looking at the art field	0.81
Dominance ($\alpha = 0.88$; AVE = 0.70; CR = 0.88)	
-I think the gamified nft artwork is more interesting than the non-gamified nft work	0.87
-I think gamified nft artwork is a more valuable investment than non-gamified nft work	0.87
-I think gamified nft artwork has more potential for cross-border integration than non-gamified nft work	0.88
Loyalty (L) ($\alpha = 0.90$; AVE = 0.728; CR = 0.90)	
-I am willing to keep buying gamified nft artwork by X artists	0.85
-Gamification nft artwork is very important to me	0.88
-I will introduce and recommend my favorite gamified nft artwork to my friends	0.78
self-brand connection (SBC) ($\alpha = 0.92$; AVE = 0.805; CR = 0.93)	
-Gamification nft artwork can express my personal attitude	0.83
Constructs and items	SFL*
-Gamified nft artwork (avatars/virtues) can reflect who I am	0.86
-I use X gamification nft artwork to communicate my identity to others	0.87
-I identify with platforms and artists who provide gamified nft artwork	0.87

Note(s): SFL* = Standardized factor loading
Model fit: Normed $\chi 2 = 1.74$; RMSEA = 0.07, CFI = 0.88, TLI = 0.96, IFI = 0.96, NFI = 0.80, RFI = 0.91.

4.2 Common Method Bias (CMB)

The study structure was measured through self-reported surveys using the same sources or methods used to collect data on predictors and criterion variables. This may lead to

Table 2. Discriminant validity.

	1	2	3	4	5	6	7	8
Achievement Motive	0.893							
Social Motive	0.757	0.816						
Immersion Motive	0.763	0.818	0.881					
Pleasure	0.712	0.738	0.776	0.837				
Arousal	0.535	0.681	0.670	0.773	0.871			
Dominance	0.665	0.639	0.672	0.699	0.814	0.836		
Loyalty	0.665	0.668	0.744	0.811	0.836	0.794	0.853	
Self-brand connection	0.662	0.697	0.712	0.664	0.710	0.732	0.805	0.897

Note(s): Square roots of AVEs are shown diagonally

a common method bias. This systematic error variance may lead to common method bias (CMB) and may affect the estimated relationships between the variables or measurements used in the study. Therefore, controlling for method bias is crucial. In this study, we followed a variety of methods to examine the presence of CMB in the art NFT employing a conceptual model of gamified motivation dataset. Firstly, Harman's single factor test was used. The results showed that the first factor explained 19.657% of the cumulative variance, which is below the recommended criterion of 50%. Second, we used the unmeasured latent method construct (ULMC) procedure for generic method bias assessment. We examined separately the measured model (with common latent factors) and the measured model (without common latent factors) in the conceptual model of gamification motivation using art NFT and noted their std. Path coefficient values. The difference between the std. Path coefficients varied between 0.03 and 0.16 (less than 0.2). Since the results of both models are consistent, this suggests that these relationships are not influenced by the CMB (Podsakoff et al., 2012). Both approaches suggest that the CMB is unlikely to be an issue in the conceptual model data presented here.

4.3 Structural Model and Hypothesis Testing

The eight hypotheses of this paper were tested using structural equation modeling with AMOS version 25 (for direct relationship) and Process Macro (for mediation and moderation analysis). Table 3 details the SEM results (H1aH1c, H2aH2c). We also calculated the variance inflation factor (VIF) to check for multicollinearity in the conceptual model of gamified motivation adopted by the art NFT. The VIF value were below 5.0, which indicated no multicollinearity. When examining the direct effects of AM 、 SM and IM on UE, we found that all three sub-dimensions of motivation to adopt gamification were positively associated with user engagement. Moreover, AM $\beta = 0.74$ (p $= 0.00$), for SM on UE, $\beta = 0.74$ (p $= 0.00$), and for IM, $\beta = 0.11$ (p $= 0.00$), suggesting that H1a, H1b, and H1c are all important and well supported. Furthermore, in order to investigate the association between the three sub-dimensions of UE (pleasure, Arousal, and dominance) and loyalty, it can be seen that pleasure, dominance, and arousal all have a positive and significant effect on loyalty. Therefore, we accept H2a, H2b, and H2c.

Table 3. Direct and mediation effects.

Direct effects	(β)	p-value
H1a: Achievement Motive - User Engagement	0.844	0.00
H1b: Social Motive - User Engagement	0.820	0.00
H1c: Immersion Motive - User Engagement	0.689	0.00
H2a: Pleasure - Loyalty	0.914	0.00
H2b: Activation - Loyalty	0.920	0.00
Direct effects	(β)	p-value
H2c: Dominance - Loyalty	0.889	0.00
Mediation effects	Direct (t-value)	Indirect (BootSE)
H3: Motivation for Gamification - User Engagement – Loyalty	0.07 (1.17)	0.59 (0.07)

For the mediation analysis, Model 4 Process Macro (Hayes, 2018) was used. The results showed that the direct effect was not significant, while the indirect effect of M —UE— L was significant (Direct:$\beta = 0.06$, $t = 1.20$ and indirect effect = 0.51, BootSE = 0.07, LLCI = 0.41 and ULCI = 0.78). Thus, it implies that user Engagement is fully mediated between motivation and loyalty. Therefore, we accept the mediating effects of user involvement and H3.

To check the moderate mediation impact of SBC, we used Process Macro's model7. The results of the moderated analysis are presented in Table 4, where it can be observed that the interaction term of path M—UE—L through the slowing agent SBC (-0.08, t = -2.23) is significant, which indicates the moderating influence of SBC on the mediated path. Thus, H4 is significant but not supported. SBC negatively affects the mediated path M—UE—L. The moderated mediation index = -0.08, BootSE = 0.068, BootLLCI = -0.15 and BootULCI = -0.03. In addition, examination of the conditional indirect effects of the moderator SBC at low, mean and high values of SBC showed that the effect decreases as SBC increases (β value decreases from 0.42 to 0.28). Thus, SBC would weaken the mediating relationship between M—UE—L.

Table 4. Moderation effect.

Direct effects	(β)	p-value	LLCI	ULCI
H4: Interaction effect motivations	−0.08	0.03	−0.18	−0.00
(Conditional indirect effect of Motivations to adopt gamification on Loyalty(via User Engagement) at different levels)		BootSE	LLCI	ULCI
	− 1SD(Self-Brand connection)	0.08	0.33	0.62
	Mean(Self-Brand connection)	0.07	0.26	0.53
	+ 1SD(Self-Brand connection)	0.08	0.15	0.43

5 Discussion

The purpose of this study is to understand users' motivations for adopting gamification and its impact on user engagement and loyalty to art NFT. The findings also suggest the impact of self-brand connection on the relationship between users' motivation to adopt gamification and their engagement experience at art NFT.

As hypothesized in this paper, the findings show that achievement, social, and immersion motivations all significantly influence users' interactions with art NFT programs. These findings enable users better understand while keeping in mind the user motivations for art NFT consumption. Gamified achievement motivations, from which users derive self-improvement, and gamified social and immersion motivations, from which consumers need to connect with and derive pleasure from their community, have greater synergy with art NFT consumption, which explains the significant impact of user engagement and brand self-connection.

The art NFT program strives to go beyond mere engagement to create emotional attachment, commitment, and loyalty among users. The current findings support our hypothesis that art NFT programs can increase loyalty by gamifying user engagement. We also found that all three components of user engagement, namely pleasure, arousal, and dominance, have a significant positive impact on loyalty to art NFT programs.

The current findings also suggest that SBC had a significant mediating effect on the relationship between motivation and user engagement with art NFT programs. However, contrary to our hypothesis, SBC weakened the impact of the art NFT brand on user engagement in terms of motivation to adopt the game. Users with art NFT programs have SBCs that develop from a symbiotic match between their self-concept, personality, cultural values, and brand values. The stronger the user's connection to the brand, the more important the brand becomes in terms of reflecting their self-concept, self-image and even means of social integration. With such deep and intimate SBCs often observed in the context of art NFT, consumers with such deep SBCs and art NFT brands may not find gamification to be the ideal form of engagement because they want personalized interactions and unique experiences with the brand. This may explain the negative moderation effect of SBC on the relationship between motivation and user engagement with brands.

Through the analysis of the art NFT adoption gamification motivation model, the study identifies gamification as a key motivation for engaging art NFT users, including achievement, social and immersion motivations; second, the value co-creation theory explains the importance of user engagement as a key indicator of effective user brand interactions and relationships, and this study upholds this theoretical perspective by identifying users' motivations for gaming that lead to increased user engagement; third, this study establishes that all components of user engagement, namely pleasure, arousal, and dominance, play an important role in developing loyalty to the arts NFT brand; fourth, this finding suggests that gamification may not be effective in generating user engagement among users with high SBC and preferred arts NFT products.

The findings suggest that artwork is increasingly investing in loyalty through social media, online communities and, more recently, gamification, and that art NFT programs must go beyond creating "fun" games that allow users to show and express their identity, knowledge, tastes and creativity within product categories; that advanced augmented and virtual reality technologies will enhance these gaming capabilities and enable users to experience being part of an artwork community; that a sense of belonging to a specific class, status, and community is a powerful driver of art NFT product consumption, especially in emerging markets where gamified applications can be linked to social media platforms to meet the social motivations of art NFT users; that art NFT projects can benefit from viewing gamification as a way to attract users who are relatively new to art NFT product consumption to users who are relatively new to it.

Future research could extend the findings on the relationship between different motivations for using gamification and loyalty. Since arts NFT programs have not emerged and engaged in gaming until recent years, future research could explore how different game features, formats, content, and styles can effectively meet users' achievement, social, and immersion motivations to more effectively engage users and enhance user experience. This study also demonstrates the positive impact of motivation on the loyalty of their preferred art NFT program by creating more significant user engagement. Future researchers can further extend these findings to understand whether the match between users' motivation to adopt gamification and the game plan of the art NFT program similarly improves purchase intent to spend on these platforms. The current study focuses on understanding the impact of different users' motivations to embrace the gamification created by the art NFT program on their interactions with the program. Therefore, the relationships studied here need to be validated in a non-social setting. While we believe that our findings on the moderating effects of SBC may be more important for art NFT consumption contexts, it may be important to explore whether the same results apply to non-art NFT programs. Art NFT gamification is very popular among Millennials and Generation Z. However, consumers in other age groups (especially older consumers) may have different relationships and expectations with their preferred art NFT items. With the virtual presence of art NFT itself and online gaming becoming the dominant platform for users to interact with programs, further research is needed to understand the potential of gamification to engage users of different age groups.

References

1. Nadini, M., Alessandretti, L., Giacinto, F.D., et al.: Mapping the NFT revolution: market trends, trade networks and visual features. Papers (2021)
2. Jinkook, A.H.N.: The meaning and limitation of nft in the art regime: crypto art in the dialectical movement of digital art. J. Korean Modern Contemp. Art History **43**, 395–429 (2022)
3. Harrigan, P., Evers, U., Miles, M.P., Daly, T.: Customer engagement and the relationship between involvement, engagement, self-brand connection and brand usage intent. J. Bus. Res. **88**(July), 388–396 (2018)
4. Koronaki, E., Theodoridis, P.K., Panigyrakis, G.G.: Linking luxury brand experience and brand attachment through self-brand connections: a role-theory perspective. In: Kavoura, A., Kefallonitis, E., Theodoridis, P. (eds.) Strategic Innovative Marketing and Tourism. Springer Proceedings in Business and Economics. Springer, Cham (2020). https://doi.org/10.1007/978-3-030-36126-6_86
5. Milanesi, M., Guercini S , Runfola A . Let's play! Gamification as a marketing tool to deliver a digital luxury experience. Electronic Commerce Research (2022)

6. Hassan, L., Dias, A., Hamari, J.: How motivational feedback increases user's benefits and continued use: a study on gamification, quantified-self and social networking. Int. J. Inf. Manage. **46**, 151–162 (2019)

7. Wolf, T., Weiger, W.H., Hammerschmidt, M.: Experiences that matter? The motivational experiences and business outcomes of gamified services. J. Business Res. **106**, 353–364 (2019)

8. Huotari, K., Hamari, J.: Defining gamification: a service marketing perspective. In: Proceeding of the 16th International Academic MindTrek Conference, ACM, pp. 17–22 (2012)

9. Huotari, K., Hamari, J.: A definition for gamification: anchoring gamification in the servicemarketing literature. Electron. Mark. **27**(1), 21–31 (2017)

10. Barton, J.: Luxury fashion brands turn to gaming to attract new buyers. https://www.wired.com/story/luxury-fashion-brands-video-games-shopping/. Accessed 3 Apr 2022

11. Moliner, M.A., Monferrer-Tirado, D., Estrada-Guillen, M.: Consequences of customer engagement and customer self-brand connection. J. Serv. Mark. **32**(4), 387–399 (2018)

12. Brodie, R.J., Ilic, A., Juric, B., Hollebeek, L.: Consumer engagement in a virtual brand community: an exploratory analysis. J. Bus. Res. **66**(1), 105–114 (2013)

13. Vivek, S.D., Beatty, S.E., Dalela, V., Morgan, R.M.: A generalized multidimensional scale for measuring customer engagement. J. Marketing Theory Pract. **22**(4), 401–420 (2014)

14. Gatautis, R., Banyte, J., Piligrimiene, Z., Vitkauskaite, E., Tarute, A.: The impact of gamification on consumer brand engagement. Transform. Business Econ. **15**(1), 173–191 (2016)

15. Berger, A., Schlager, T., Sprott, D.E., Herrmann, A.: Gamified interactions: whether, when, and how games facilitate self–brand connections. J. Acad. Mark. Sci. **81**(2), 1–22 (2017)

16. Claffey, E., Brady, M.: Examining consumers' motivations to engage in firm-hosted virtual communities. Psychol. Mark. **34**(4), 356–375 (2017)

17. Westbrook, R.A., Black, W.C.: A motivation-based shopper typology. J. Retail. **61**, 78–103 (1985)

18. Koivisto J , Hamari J.: The rise of motivational information systems: a review of gamification research. Int. J. Inf. Manage. 45, 191–210 (2019)

19. Meng, X., Webster, S.A., Butler, B.S.: Motivational effects of badge systems on participation in stack exchange social Q&A online community. Americas Conference on Information Systems (2013)

20. Wiertz, C., De Ruyter, K.: Beyond the call of duty: why customers contribute to firm-hosted commercial online communities. Organ. Stud. **28**(3), 347–376 (2007)

21. Hamari, J., Keronen, L.: Why do people play games? A meta-analysis[J]. Int. J. Inf. Manage. **37**(3), 125–141 (2017)

22. Claffey, E., Brady, M.: Examining consumers motivations to engage in firm-hosted virtual communities. Psychol. Mark. **34**(4), 356–375 (2017)

23. Nadeem, W., Tan, T.M., Tajvidi, M., Hajli, N.: How do experiences enhance brand relationship performance and value co-creation in social commerce? The role of consumer engagement and self brand-connection. Technol. Forecast. Soc. Chang. **171**, 120952 (2021)

Research on the Application of Regional Cultural Emotional Guide Design in Subway Space Based on Passengers' Cognitive Needs

Zhipeng Zhang⬤, Wenyi Xu⬤, and Xing Fang(⊠)⬤

Wuhan University of Technology, Wuhan 430070, Hubei, China
428037@qq.com

Abstract. From the perspective of passengers' cognitive needs, this paper discusses the impact of changes in subway space on passengers' cognitive activities in the current development of subway. Based on the theory of emotional design, it focuses on the application of emotional factors brought by regional culture in subway sign design. It can provide theoretical basis and practical model for the healthy development of metro spatial information dissemination and regional culture. The purpose of this study is to explore the new needs of passengers under the condition of subway station expansion and complex development through investigation, and to explore the application of regional culture based on emotional design in subway space identification from the perspective of cognitive needs. Based on the grounded theory, this paper constructs the theoretical framework of emotional regional culture in Wuhan Jiedaokou subway Station. According to this theoretical framework, the location sign of escalator on the riding floor of subway Station No. 8 is designed. The results show that the design of subway space signs based on the affective region theory can help to lower the threshold of cognitive active behavior and improve the cognitive needs of subway passengers for signs.

Keywords: Subway space guide · Cognitive need · Emotional design

1 Introduction

Urban rail transit, with its outstanding features of safety, speed, punctuality, large transport capacity and environmental protection, has played a huge role in promoting urban modernization, improving transport environment, guiding and optimizing urban spatial layout, and driving urban economic innovation and development, and has been accepted by governments at all levels and citizens. It has been nearly 50 years since Beijing Metro Line 1 was opened to traffic on October 1, 1969. By the end of 2020, the number of urban rail transit lines in operation is expected to exceed 7,000 km, exceed 10,000 km by the end of 2025, and approach 15,000 km by the end of 2030. At present, China ranks first in the world in terms of line scale in operation, line scale under construction and passenger flow scale. China has become a veritable "urban rail country".

According to the Ministry of Transport, 21 new urban rail transit lines will be in operation nationwide in 2022, with an additional 847 km in operation. By the end of

2022, 51 cities had opened urban rail transit. Currently, there are seven cities in China with more than 500 km of subway, namely Shanghai, Beijing, Guangzhou, Shenzhen, Chengdu, Hangzhou and Wuhan. It was followed by Nanjing and Chongqing, with more than 400 km of subway. Qingdao has more than 300 km of subway, and Tianjin, Xi 'an, Suzhou, Zhengzhou, Shenyang, Dalian, Changsha and other cities have more than 200 km of subway.

Subway space is a place for passengers to gather, disperse and ride. Therefore, the design of subway space should not only reflect the characteristics of traffic functions, but also be people-oriented, reasonably attract and organize passenger flow, meet the requirements of traffic organization, operation management and equipment, and facilitate the gathering, distribution, boarding and transfer of passengers.

According to the Code for Subway Design [1], the public areas of stations are divided into the public areas of the station hall floor and the public areas of the platform floor. The public area of the station floor is the area where passengers arrive at and exit the station after completing ticket sale and check-in. The common area on the platform floor is for passengers to get on and off the train [2].

The movement tracks of passengers in subway space are different, and the purposes of passengers in different Spaces are also different [3]. Therefore, the behavior patterns of passengers in different subway Spaces are different [4]. Passenger behavior is complex and influenced by numerous factors [5].

With the increase of the volume of subway traffic, subway lines become more complex. On the one hand, the number of transfer stations and hubs increases, and the space of subway stations increases and the degree of spatial complexity increases. On the other hand, in order to ease the traffic pressure and improve the service quality during the rush hour, the number of new subway cars tends to increase, the length of the subway ride floor increases, the number of escalators between the ride floor and the security check floor increases, and the form is complicated. These changes have resulted in more complicated routes for passengers entering and exiting the station. In this case, the complexity of passengers' cognitive activities in subway space increases, and their cognitive needs also change.

Take Subdistrict Subway Station in Wuhan as an example. By the end of 2020, Line 8 will be opened and subdistrict station will be set up. Wuhan Rail Transit Line 8 is the seventh subway line completed and operated in Wuhan City, Hubei Province, China, and the third subway line crossing the Yangtze River in Wuhan City. The construction started on October 26, 2014, and its logo color is chimes' green. The entire line runs north-south, and as of January 2, 2021, its total length of 39 km is underground, as in Fig. 1.

The subdistrict subway station has become a large transfer station, resulting in great changes in the space of the station, and these changes have an impact on the activities of passengers in the station (see the detailed content in Sect. 3). This paper takes "new demands arising from passengers getting off the train and going upstairs and leaving the station" as the entry point to study.

Fig. 1. Wuhan Metro Line 8 map.

2   Related Theories

2.1   Cognitive Needs Theory

Need for Cognition refers to an individual's tendency to engage in and enjoy cognitively challenging activities [6]. Cohen and his colleagues first proposed this concept in the 1950s and described it as "meaningful and integrated needs" to highlight the pressure on individuals when they do not get sufficient needs. Organize situations in a positive way to improve comprehension. It usually means people's needs and motivations. It is generally the intrinsic motivation of individual pursuit, cognition and understanding, such as intellectual curiosity and curiosity.

American psychologist Abraham Maslow (1953) [7] elaborated Maslow's hierarchy of needs theory in Motivation and Personality. In 1970, Maslow expanded it into seven levels, dividing human needs from low to high into physiological needs, safety needs, belonging and love needs, self-esteem needs, cognitive needs, aesthetic needs and self-actualization needs.

In contrast to Cohen et al. 's definition of "cognitive need," This definition is closer to Fiske's concept of "need of inquiring intellect" or Murray's concept of "need for understanding". [8] Although Cacioppo and Petty use this term, they literally reflect the cognitive differences of individuals, and their essence is the differences in individual cognitive motivation.

At present, scholars who study cognitive needs generally prefer Cacioppo's definition of the connotation of cognitive needs: cognitive needs are the tendency to devote to and enjoy cognitive activities that require effort. [9] People with strong cognitive needs are willing to think actively and are good at finding and enjoying complex tasks. People with low cognitive needs were thought to be less reflective. As an individual difference, cognitive need can explain the preference and motivation of individuals to choose complex information processing. This preference makes individuals willing to take the initiative to spend time and experience in dealing with these strict mental tasks [10]. The cognitive need concept of Cacioppo is also adopted in this paper. Cognitive needs reflect the differences in individual cognitive motivation [11]. Measuring cognitive needs can deeply understand the relationship between individual internal characteristics and external behavior, which can help us optimize the design and make it more suitable for users' psychology.

In 1982, Cacioppo and Petty released the first epistemological need table including four topics in four reports [9], which was revised in 1984 from 34 questions to 18 questions [12]. From the development epistemological need scale to the subsequent revision, the research was conducted using Likert 9 scoring method. On a scale of + 4 to -4; + 4 = very strong agreement; + 3 = strong agreement; + 2 = moderate agreement; + 1 = slight agreement; 0 = neither agreement nor disagreement; -1 = slight disagreement; -2 = moderate disagreement;-3 = strong disagreement;-4 = very strong disagreement.

2.2 Perceptual Cognitive Need

Cognitive need is a kind of need produced by human beings in the process of living and understanding and transforming the objective world. It can be for survival or for purely cognitive purposes. Cognitive needs are divided into perceptual cognitive needs, intellectual cognitive needs and rational cognitive needs. From the perspective of the strength of needs, perceptual cognitive needs rank first. Perceptual cognitive need is the driving force of perceptual cognitive activities. It is instinctive, perceptual and intuitive, sensory synthesis, and also pre-linguistic and pre-logical. In the subway space, a public area with a lot of information, it is very necessary to have an insight into users' perceptual cognitive needs in order to deliver information to users efficiently and with high quality, optimize users' sense of experience in the process of using subway services and improve their satisfaction [13].

2.3 Emotional Design Theory

In Emotional Design, Donald Arthur Norman proposed a three-layer theoretical model of emotional design, namely instinct, behavior and reflection [14]. Figure 6. Emotional design is a kind of art created through the form of symbols [15]. Its purpose is to find the bond and combination point between individuals and society, and explore the theoretical approach to arouse personal emotions [16, 17].

2.4 Grounded Theory

Grounded theory research method is a research method developed by two scholars of Columbia University, Ansel Strauss and Barney Glaser. It is a qualitative research method that uses systematic procedures to develop and inductively guide rooted theories for a certain phenomenon.

Researchers generally do not have theoretical assumptions before the start of research, but directly start from practical observation, summarize experience from the original data, and then rise to the systematic theory. This is a method to build a substantive theory from the bottom up, that is, to find the core concepts that reflect the phenomenal nature of things on the basis of systematic collection of data, and then to construct a relevant social theory through the connections between these concepts. Grounded theory must be supported by empirical evidence, but its main characteristic is not that it is empirical, but that it abstracts new concepts and thoughts from empirical facts. In philosophy, the grounded theory approach is based on the post-positivism paradigm, which emphasizes the falsification of constructed theories. This paper constructs the core model through grounded theory.

3   Problem Discovery

The Subdistrict station becomes a large transfer station, and the riding space of Line 8 and Line 2 is connected underground. As Line 8 bears a great passenger load, Subdistrict station is a densely populated location in the city, so a longer riding floor design scheme was adopted when Subdistrict Station was established. In this design, the number of escalators between the boarding floor and the departure floor is increased to 4, as shown in Fig. 2.

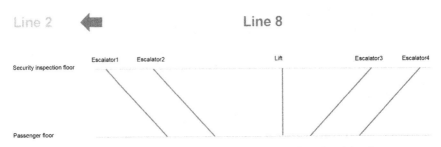

Fig. 2. The elevator distribution of ride floor of Jiedaokou Line 8.

As a result, there are more routes for passengers to go upstairs from the riding floor after getting off the train. The distance in the direction of the subway becomes longer, while the distance in the normal direction of the subway remains unchanged, which greatly weakens the observability of passengers to the setting of distant escalators, as in Fig. 3. To make better use of the underground space and prevent interference with other underground facilities, the new line is nearly twice as deep underground as Line 2. As a result, the length of escalators is longer. Under a certain slope, passengers can travel a longer lateral distance and spend more time on escalators.

Fig. 3. Vision of ride floor of Jiedaokou Line 8.

Outbound passengers may have a bad upstairs experience under the following conditions.

Situation 1: The passenger at c is going to exit F\N or Line 2 and is going up one of the two escalators on the right. When the passenger is at c, it is highly likely that he will take the nearby escalator directly. When the passenger takes the right escalator to the departure floor, the deep depth of the escalator will lead to a long ride time and a long horizontal distance, which makes the passenger feel anxious. The empty departure floor makes passengers realize that they are far away from the departure gate. Passengers who see the guide sign will find that they have to go in the opposite direction, resulting in a bad experience.

Situation 2: The passenger at Exit a is going to Exit N and goes up the leftmost escalator. Passengers at gate a did not know the position of gate N relative to the left two escalators, so they directly got on the leftmost escalator. When they arrived at the departure floor, they found that N was much closer to the exit of the second-to-last escalator on the left, and from the present position to gate N, they would pass the exit of the second-to-last escalator on the left. Passengers who realized that they chose the wrong escalator would have a bad sense of experience.

Situation 3: The passenger at b is going to exit L\J and gets on one of the two escalators on the left without knowing where he is. Passengers at b are located in the middle and have almost the same probability of choosing both sides of the elevator, which leads to the anxiety caused by the difficulty of choice. If they are elected, they will take the left escalator to the departure floor and find that the destination is in the opposite direction, resulting in a bad experience.

Situation 4: The passenger at c wants to go to exit L\J, and the right-most escalator is congested. He knows that the exit is on the right, so he continues to walk to the right and finds only stairs when he is not sure whether there is another escalator ahead. The passenger at place c was not clear about the situation of the escalator in front of him because his sight was blocked. He was unwilling to walk in the opposite direction and chose to move forward. When he found that there was no escalator in front of him, he realized that he had done a lot of wrong things and thus felt anxious and regretful. The positions of a, b and c are respectively shown in Fig. 4.

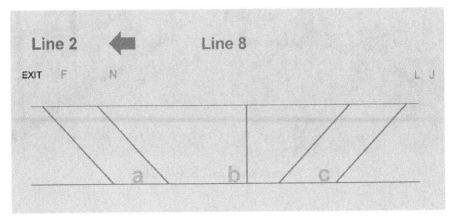

Fig. 4. Passenger position map.

It can be seen that it is not enough to indicate the direction of the transfer line at the escalator entrance, as shown in Fig. 5.

Fig. 5. Elevator entrance sign of ride floor of Jiedaokou Line 8.

We need to let the passenger know the location of the escalator he is in, the distribution of all escalators, the location of the exit and the location of the ground facilities, as shown in Fig. 6.

Fig. 6. Escalator position indication diagram.

4   Problem Analysis

When passengers get off the bus, their cognitive needs for signs will be reduced for the following reasons: 1. More passengers get off the bus, causing congestion and distracting the attention for cognitive signs. 2. Passengers are in the workflow of outbound behavior and are reluctant to interrupt work easily. 3. Not aware of the importance of signs, I choose routes with a game mentality.

Passengers' own cognitive needs are limited and cognitive load will be generated during the cognitive process. Cognitive load consists of multiple dimensions, which refers to the load imposed on individual cognition during the execution of a specific task [18]. As the amount of information required to be processed increases, cognitive load will also increase [19]. Therefore, passengers will suffer more cognitive load due to the external environment and their own working state, distracting their attention and reducing the possibility of active cognition.

How to stimulate passengers' active cognition? Introduce the concept of perceptual cognition here. Cognitive needs are divided into perceptual cognitive needs, intellectual cognitive needs and rational cognitive needs. From the perspective of the strength of needs, perceptual cognitive needs rank first. Perceptual cognitive needs are the driving force of perceptual cognitive activities. The factors affecting perceptual cognitive needs include not only physiological stimuli, but also emotional arousal. In the subway space, a public area with a lot of information, it is very necessary to have an insight into users' perceptual cognitive needs in order to deliver information to users efficiently and with high quality, optimize users' sense of experience in the process of using subway services and improve their satisfaction.

According to Norman's three levels of emotional design, we find that the reflective level contains items of "experience sharing" and "cultural value". The true meaning of "experience sharing" is; By passing on stories that are the same or similar to the experience of the user, it inspires emotional resonance among the user. The meaning of "cultural value" lies in: through the output of culture, users can have a sense of cultural belonging and cultural confidence, so as to arouse emotional resonance.

The Jiedaokou is a transportation hub, a large business district and a gathering place of colleges and universities, which has formed a unique regional culture over the years. We need to integrate and export this culture, so that people with "stories" at Jiedaokou can have cultural belonging and emotional resonance. By infusing this regional emotional culture into subway sign design, passengers' perceptual cognitive needs can be driven and active cognition can be promoted.

There are many excellent design practices in Wuhan subway, which perfectly demonstrate the excellent culture. Lotus sculptures are set up in Optical Valley Fifth Road Station. The five sculptures show the five stages of lotus growth, reflecting the lotus culture in Hubei Province, as shown in Fig. 7. Hanzheng Street subway Station displays and designs the local culture of Hanzheng Street, as well as the cultural features of old Wuhan and Old Hankou, as shown in Fig. 8. Jianghan Road Subway Station, as one of the most prosperous areas in Wuhan, combines traditional ink painting with modern technology and interprets traditional aesthetics with popular new media art. This large-screen interactive device of ink painting has been widely praised by passengers of Jianghan Road Subway Station as shown in Fig. 9.

Fig. 7. Lotus sculpture in Optical Valley Fifth Road Station.

Fig. 8. The old Wuhan style decoration of Hanzheng Street subway station.

Fig. 9. Ink interactive large screen in digital community of Jianghan Road Metro Station.

5 Experimental Process and Model Construction

Before the specific design, we need to grasp the connotation of regional emotional culture of JIedaokou more accurately. Next, I study and construct the theoretical model of the cultural connotation of regional emotion at Jiedaokou through grounded theory.

This study takes subway riders in some Jiedaokou subway stations in Wuhan as the research object, and investigates their activities, experiences, emotions and memories in the Jiedaokou area. Grounded theory method requires in-depth analysis of the original data, and summarizes the hidden internal rules and connections. The interviewees were required to be representative and undisturbed [20]. The researchers randomly selected 18 subway passengers who had been at the street entrance for more than one year to conduct semi-structured interviews and each interview lasted about 60 min. The whole interview was recorded in accordance with the principle of knowing the interviewee, voluntary and confidential, and all interview information was anonymized. The information of interviewees is shown in Fig. 10.

Number	Pseudonym	Age (years)	Gender (Male/Female)	Occupation	Years of subway ride (years)	Main activity at Jiedaokou	Whether it is a local (Yes/No)
T1	[illegible]	35	M	[illegible] Graduate	7	Dining/entertainment/shopping/learning	N
T2	Xiao Yang	23	F	[illegible] Graduate	8	Dining/entertainment/shopping/learning	Y
T3	Xiao Wen	23	M	Undergraduate student of [illegible] College	5	Dining/entertainment/shopping/learning	N
T4	[illegible]	40	M	[illegible] Staff	8	Dining/work	Y
T5	Uncle He	50	M	Mall [illegible]	[illegible]	Dining/entertainment/work	Y
T6	Aunt Zhang	52	F	Office cleaner	5	Dining/work	N
T7	[illegible]	21	M	Wuhan University undergraduate	2	Dining/entertainment/shopping/learning	N
T8	[illegible]	17	F	Senior high school students	3	Dining/entertainment/shopping/[illegible]	Y
T9	[illegible]	30	M	Restaurant waiter	2	Dining/entertainment/shopping/work	N
T10	[illegible]	23	F	Postgraduate student of HUST	6	Dining/entertainment/shopping/learning	Y
T11	[illegible]	27	M	Company [illegible]	8	Dining/entertainment/work	N
T12	[illegible]	[illegible]	F	Company HR	6	Dining/entertainment/shopping	N
T13	[illegible]	19	F	Wuhan University undergraduate	1	Dining/entertainment/shopping/learning	N
T14	[illegible]	45	M	[illegible]	7	Dining/entertainment/work	Y
T15	[illegible]	[illegible]	M	[illegible]	[illegible]	Dining/entertainment/shopping/work/learning	N
T16	[illegible]	40	F	Training organization owner	8	Dining/entertainment/shopping/work	Y
T17	[illegible]	[illegible]	M	Teachers of training institutions	3	Dining/entertainment/shopping/work	N
T18	[illegible]	38	M	Graduate of [illegible]	4	Dining/entertainment/shopping	N

Fig. 10. The information of interviewees.

5.1 Open Coding

Open coding labels each statement, compares and organizes it repeatedly, finally selects and combines important concepts, and then recombines elements similar in nature and content to produce the initial category. The researchers first randomly selected 12 of the 18 interview materials for open coding, analyzed the original sentences of the interviews, integrated the same or similar concepts, abandoned the invalid concepts that appeared less than 2 times, and focused on the concepts according to the connotation relationship between the concepts. Finally, 23 categories are formed, including food, Chicony Square, Intime Creative City, large flow of people, all kinds of bars, friendship and love, and struggle experience (sub-categories are marked as Ai).

5.2 Spindle Coding

Spindle coding can discover and establish the relationship between conceptual categories and categories, and find out the main category from the sub-categories, so as to show the relationship between various parts of the interview data. In this study, 23 subcategories obtained in the open coding stage are analyzed and summarized. Finally, four main categories (labeled as AAi) of regional features, activity content, represented things, and memory of the emotion and experience that carried are formed, shown in Fig. 11.

Fig. 11. The results of spindle coding.

5.3 Selective Coding

Through in-depth analysis of the main category, selective coding understands the relationship between each main category, extracts the core category that can coordinate other categories, and explains the logical relationship between the core category and other categories. In this paper, the core category is determined to be the Jiedaokou regional emotion culture, and finally the theoretical framework of the cultural connotation of Jiedaokou regional emotion is formed, as shown in Fig. 12.

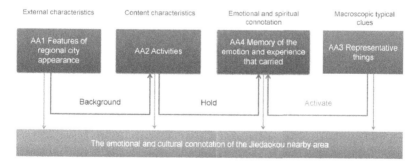

Fig. 12. Result of selective coding.

5.4 Saturation Test

The number of samples in this study was determined in accordance with the criterion of theoretical saturation. Two thirds of the interview data (12) were randomly selected for coding analysis and model construction, and another third of the interview data (6) for theoretical saturation test. A new round of open coding, spindle coding and selective coding was conducted for the remaining 5 interview data in accordance with the coding process of grounded theory. It was found that there were no new concepts and categories, and the original logical relationship was in line with each category. Therefore, the theoretical framework constituted by the cultural connotation of regional emotion at Jiedaokou passed the saturation test.

5.5 The Constitution of Cultural Connotation of Regional Emotion at Jiedaokou

When it comes to street entrance, we tend to associate it with bustling, large number of people, especially students, traffic jam, Chicony, Intime, Wuhan University, University of Science and Technology and other labels. However, through the study of grounded theory, we conclude the emotional cultural connotation of the street area from the outside to the inside: from the external and macro urban features to specific activities and then to the internal experience, emotion and spirit. We pay attention not only to the universal characteristics of the whole, but also to the existence of individual, deep, hidden emotions. Similar to the three layers of emotional design theory, AA1, AA2 and AA4 of this model respectively correspond to the instinct layer, the behavior layer and the reflection layer [21], while AA3 is the new "arousal layer", which represents the specific cultural carrier for arousing emotions.

According to the theoretical framework of output, we can roughly summarize some key words. Here, we also summarize in the order from the outside to the inside and according to the main category, as shown in Fig. 13:

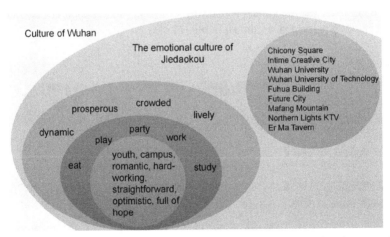

Fig. 13. Element relationship based on the framework of cultural emotional connotation of Jiedaokou region.

AA1: Prosperous, crowded and lively.
AA2: Food, entertainment, parties, work, study.

AA3: Chicony Square, Intime Creative City, Wuhan University, Wuhan University of Technology, Fuhua Building, Future City, Mafang Mountain, Northern Lights KTV, Two Ma Tavern.

AA4: Youth, campus, romantic, hard-working, straightforward, optimistic, full of hope.

6 Design

According to the output theoretical model, we carried out the design of the location sign of the exit escalator of the No.8 subway station, as in Figs. 14 and 15.

1. Convey "cultural sense" through writing;

2. Enhance richness through different fonts to deliver an active and dynamic atmosphere;

3, through the key elements to express the orientation;

4. Use Wuhan dialect to reflect the cultural background of Wuhan and convey the charm of Wuhan people's warm and straightforward character;

5. Use key elements as clues to arouse passengers' cultural affiliation and emotional resonance.

Fig. 14. Position prompt leftmost escalator.

Fig. 15. Position prompts of each escalator.

7 Summary and Outlook

7.1 Conclusion

Starting from the problems arising from the trend of large and complicated subway space, this paper studies the internal factors that promote passengers' active cognition from the perspective of passengers' cognitive needs, and combines the emotional design theory to put forward the solution of using regional emotional culture for design. To grasp the cultural connotation of regional emotion at street entrance, this paper uses grounded theory to construct its model, and takes the obtained model as guidance for design output.

7.2 Limitations

In this paper, the research process through grounded theory is rigorous, but the sample size is not large enough, and the comprehensiveness of the obtained results is doubtful. The design has not yet been tested and iterated. The richness of design needs to be improved.

7.3 Design Outlook

As metro stations become larger and more complex, the function of metro stations is not only functional, but also emotional and cultural. It is the right way to develop metro space and an effective way to inherit regional culture by refining and integrating regional culture into the design of metro stations, and making emotional culture and function promote each other by centering on people. At present, with the rapid development of technology, the cognitive field of subway space may undergo great changes. With the arrival of metaverse, the application of MR Will comprehensively update the way of subway space interaction, but emotion and culture should always be applied and inherited.

References

1. Code for subway design: GB 50157–2013
2. Jin, L., Liu, H., Jiang, L., Shan, G., Lei, W., Zheng, X.: Contact behavior oriented epidemic spread risk model of subway space research. J. Saf. Environ. **21**(6), 2694–2702 (2021). https://doi.org/10.13637/j.iSSN.1009-6094.2020.0948
3. Lai, Y., Zhang, X., Chen, J., et al.: Simulation of subway large passenger flow based on multi-level pedestrian behavior model. J. Dalian Jiaotong Univ. **40**(3), 16 (2019)
4. Li, B., Yang, X., Wang, Y.: Simulation and optimization of the passenger distribution system anylogic in rail transit stations. CAAI Trans. Intell. Syst. **15**(6), 10491057 (2020)
5. Wei, Y., Zeng, L., Lin, J., et al.: Research of virtual passenger behavior simulation on subway station and its implementation. Comput. Appl. Softw. **34**(11), 81–85, 96 (2017)
6. Peng, J., Lu, H., Zhang, J., et al.: Need for cognition moderates the impairment of decision making caused by night shift work in nurses. Sci. Rep. **12**(1), 1756 (2022)
7. Abraham, M.: Motivation and Personality. China Renmin University Press (2007)
8. Cacioppo, J., Petty, R., Feinstein, J., Jarvis, B.: Dispositional differences in cognitive motivation: the life and times of individuals varying in need for cognition. Psychol. Bullet. **119**(2), 197–253 (1996)
9. Cacioppo, J., Petty, R.: The need for cognition. J. Personality Soc. Psychol. **42**(1), 116–131 (1982)
10. He, S., et al.: The relationship between self-management ability and cognitive need and independent learning ability and leadership ability in nursing students. Chin. Health Quality Manage. **29**(12), 61–65 (2022). https://doi.org/10.13912/j.cnki.chqm.2022.29.12.14
11. Cacioppo, J., Petty, R., Kao, C., Rodriguez, R.: Central and peripheral routes to persuasion: an individual difference perspective. J. Personal. Soc. Psychol. **51**, 1032–1043 (1986)
12. Cacioppo, J., Petty, R., Kao, C.: The efficient assessment of need for cognition. J. Personal. Assess. **48**(3), 306–307 (1984)
13. Mi, J., Shang, R., Zhang, B.: Emotional cognitive effects of mobile e-government users continue to use research. J. Manage. **38**(05), 45–58+125–126 (2022). https://doi.org/10.15944/j.cnki.33-1010/d.2022.05.009
14. Niu, Q., Yan, J., Xia, Y.: Overview of quantitative analysis methods of urban design. Int. City Urban Plann. **32**(6), 61–68 (2017)
15. Norman, D.: Emotional design: why we love (or hate) everyday things. Interactions **11**(5), 81–83 (2004)
16. Lange, S.K.: Emotion and Form. In: Liu, D., Fu, Z. (eds.) Translated. Beijing: China Social Sciences Press (1986)
17. Jonathan, H.: Human emotion: a sociological theory. In: Sun, J., Wen, J. (eds.) Translated. Beijing: Oriental Press (2009)
18. Paas, F., van Merriënboer, J.: The efficiency of instructional conditions: an approach to combine mental effort and performance measures. Hum. Factors J. Hum. Factors Ergonomics Soc. **35**(4), 737–743 (1993)
19. Xin, Z., Lin, C.: The relationship between cognitive load and cognitive skills and schema acquisition and its teaching significance. J. East Chin. Normal Univ. (Educ. Sci. Ed.) **20**(4), 55–60, 77 (2002)

20. Kathy, K.: Constructing grounded theory. In: Bian, G. (ed.) Translated. Chongqing: Chongqing University Press (2009)
21. Cao, G., et al.: Emotional hierarchy theory aided regional culture experience service elements design process. J. Pack. Eng. **42**(10), 108–114+123 (2021). https://doi.org/10.19554/j.cnki.1001-3563.2021.10.015

An Emotion Driven Intelligent Product Design Method from a Quantitative Perspective

Jing Zhao[1], Zhilu Cheng[2(✉)], Xiaoyou Liu[1], and Junshuo Li[1]

[1] Beijing University of Technology, Beijing 100124, China
[2] Beijing Institute of Fashion Technology, Beijing 100029, China
zhilucheng@qq.com

Abstract. Emotional design is becoming more and more important nowadays to improve user experience in product design. Based on the research of theoretical literature, it is found that there is a gap between quantified data that embodies emotion and product design. This paper explores to propose a systematic framework and specific guideline to lead designers to use human body's quantitative data for emotional design from a quantitative perspective. Also, specific steps of this method are established. The method is applied in a master course and several design practice cases are produced. Validation is sought both from designers who use the method to design practice and also experts who evaluate the course in general by using questionnaires. The results are quite positive, with designers' reporting great acquirement and experts supporting that the method is promising and the route is applicable. It can be used as a parallel way to traditional emotional design methods, which is supplement for product design from a totally different vision. Also, by bridging the two areas of emotion measurement and product design, it can stimulate more creative design practices and further theoretical explorations for designers.

Keywords: Emotional Design · Emotional Engineering · Intelligent Product Design · Psychophysiological Measurement

1 Introduction

With the progress of society and the constant change of consumer demand, in addition to function and form, emotional needs of users are being paid more and more attention to in the design. Emotional design has gradually become a key aspect to improving user satisfaction and product competitiveness. Currently, the main research on emotional design includes the measurement, analysis, and modeling of consumer emotional factors, and the transformation from emotional factors to product design parameters, etc. Many kinds of literature have studied the relationship between product design elements such as color [1], shape [2] and material [3] and people's perceptual cognition. Traditional emotional design methods tend to make a qualitative analysis of user emotions and adopt subjective measurement methods such as questionnaire surveys to obtain users' perceptual cognitive data, which is easily affected by subjective emotions. At this time, it

A. Marcus et al. (Eds.): HCII 2023, LNCS 14030, pp. 641–660, 2023.
https://doi.org/10.1007/978-3-031-35699-5_46

is necessary to quantify user emotion data through affective computing and other ways, to capture user emotion changes keenly, and to collect users' emotional feedback and implicit emotional needs more accurately. A large number of current studies in the field of emotional quantification focus on how to accurately identify user emotions. Many types of research related to emotional design apply cluster analysis and other theories to refine consumer emotions and get emotional design parameters. However, there is no systematical method in which these emotional parameters can be used in design.

This paper attempts to establish a general and structured emotional design theory and method, linking human emotions with design elements such as product modeling, color, and material, and driving product design with quantitative emotional characteristics, so that the subjective process of product design tends to be rational and controllable.

1.1 Theoretical Foundations of Psychology

In previous studies of psychology, sociology and neuroscience, some theories have explained the influencing factors and physiological manifestations of emotion formation, which provides a theoretical basis for emotion measurement. Paul Ekman's theory of emotion pointed out that human beings have basic emotions independent of regional culture, namely happiness, sadness, anger, surprise, disgust and fear. These basic emotions have a genetic basis and are innate human expressions. In addition, Ekman suggested that emotions hidden deep inside the heart can be identified by recognizing individual facial expression and body posture [4]. This theory has become a vital basis for traditional emotion recognition.

1.2 Traditional Emotional Design Methods

Based on the Ekman individual emotion recognition theory [4], traditional emotion design methods are more inclined to assess individual subjective emotion and conduct a qualitative analysis of user emotion. Among the theories of emotional design, only the three levels of design proposed by Professor Donald Arthur Norman and Kansei engineering in Japan [5] are widely recognized. Norman and Draper first proposed "user-centered design" in 1986 [6, 7], which divided emotional design into instinctive design, behavioral design and reflective design, focusing on appearance, humanization and humanistic care. For example, the "Chill" chair designed by Frog Design uses plastic materials and rotatable structures that are completely different from traditional outdoor furniture, which jointly stimulate users' emotional experience from emotional behavior level and reflection level [8]. Wang [9] pointed out that the commonly used quantitative method of perceptual engineering is psychological measurement. Bradley et al. [10] proposed SAM emotional detection and evaluation scale, which has become one of the main methods to test the effect of emotional design. For example, Jiang et al. [11] used SAM tool to guide users to subjectively describe coping behaviors of emotional changes to verify the human-computer interaction results in the design experiment of the intelligent shawl. Based on the VTs analysis method, Wang [9] proposed the widely used emotion quantification method "perceptual information hierarchy scale method", which includes three steps: determining the evaluation object and evaluation index, developing the product evaluation index hierarchy and determining the psychological scale, establishing the perceptual image vocabulary and making questionnaires to collect data. Li [12] summarized the methods to improve the emotional experience of intelligent products as demand analysis, establishment of the design framework, establishment of correlation between emotional intention and product attributes, which explained the product iteration process comprehensively. In addition, Song et al. [13] proposed a design mythology called future-tool-scenario-body-technology. The use of canvas tools is emphasized for deductive imagination of future scenario instead of the quantification of user measurement of emotional data in the early stage of design, so there are still limitations in the quantification of emotional design.

Emotion design methods show a trend of refinement in research content, focusing more on the identification and expression of personalized and differentiated emotions to create a better user experience [6]. The scientific acquisition and emotion recognition is still the focus of future research, and the combination of quantitative emotional physiological signals and design products is the future development trend.

1.3 Quantified Emotional Design Methodology

Currently, in the exploration of how emotion quantification can be organically integrated with design, most design and research focus on how to accurately obtain multimodal emotion signals, lacking macro guidelines and specific guidance on the overall design thinking and process. For example, James Lange theory of peripheral emotion suggests that certain emotional states can be identified by using physiological data to infer the current emotional state of an individual [4]. Explicit and implicit multimodal emotion signals can be used to analyze human emotions. The explicit multimodal focuses on the physical changes of facial expression, eye movement, voice, and EEG, while the implicit multimodal focuses more on user information obtained from multimedia platforms [14]. In terms of integration with design, multimodal emotional signals are mainly used in two areas: product feedback collection and interactive product design. Among them, product feedback collection has formed a relatively perfect design method, while the design method of interactive product design is still lacking. Lin et al. [15] proposed an eye-movement empowerment and EEG imagery cognition-based perceptual-engineering model for product morphology, which includes: Determine the target perceptual imagery words and product objects; Reconstruct products to form new appearance samples; Implement imagery evaluation and eye-brain cognitive experiments to calculate the perceptual weight of morphological features; Establish kansei engineering model. The model can objectively and accurately predict the image of product form, thus more effectively assisting designers in perceptual innovation design. Liu&Wang [16] combined multimodal emotional signals, used eye tracking experiment to obtain subjects' eye-movement data when observing car styling, and combined with online comments from car users to derive users' real affective design needs regarding car styling. This research has made a new breakthrough in providing the connection between the most concerned product design elements and emotional needs of users at the large semantic granularity level.

In the literature survey, some scholars combined multimodal emotional signals in the design process for human-computer interaction. Li & Qi [17] used the "perception-cognition-action" emotional interaction agent model to create an emotionally interactive robot, which first used sensors and image acquisition devices to perform apparent physiological recognition for users, and based on this, user emotion analysis is conducted, and the robot gave voice feedback. Kim et al. [18] proposed the use of specific adhesive sensors in the design process of conformal multimodal sensory mask (cMaSK) to detect air pressure and humidity data in real time and transmit them to the user's cell phone using Bluetooth and wifi, thus providing valuable feedback on the quality of the mask for the user. Further, they conducted performance tests under different physical use environments at the end of design to ensure that different weather will not affect the effectiveness of the product. Their design process is relatively well developed and has reference significance in terms of design methodology generalization. Rosello [19] used heart rate recognition in the HeartBit design project to synchronize the user's heart rate with the hand-held heart beat frequency, which visualized the user's physiological signal visualization. At the same time, light color changes are added to give different feedback under different emotional states of users. The project realizes human-computer emotional interaction in tactile and visual aspects, assists users to relax physically and mentally and enhance self-consciousness. Kao et al. [20] proposed the "form-movement-interaction" design principle, and explored multiple forms in the process of combining jewelry and robotics. Kosmyna&Maes [21] used AttentivU device to perceive brain activity through electroencephalogram (EEG), and actively or passively intervene user's state through audio or tactile feedback to realize human-computer interaction.

In the field of emotional design, quantified method is still in lack while existing studies are mainly focused on the accurate measurement and recognition of emotions. Kansei engineering is established with models to study the relationship between design elements such as color, form, and material of a specific product and people's perceptual cognition. However, there is still no general and structured emotional design method for how to connect quantified emotion with product design. This paper tries to establish a systematic emotion quantification design theory and method to assist designers to design. By using this method, designers can connect human emotion with design elements such as product shape, color, and material, drive product design with quantified emotional characteristics, improve the efficiency and success rate of emotional design, and make the subjective product design process tend to be rational and controllable.

1.4 The Main Content of This Paper

By analyzing the existing emotional design methods and techniques, this paper summarizes and refines the general and structured theory of quantitative emotional interaction design method to assist product designers in emotional interactive product design. The main content of this paper includes five parts: introduction, method framework creation, method application practice, evaluation of theoretical achievements, summary and prospect. Firstly, the industry background of this research field is introduced, and the difficulties faced by traditional emotional quantitative design methods are analyzed. Secondly, by searching relevant literature and design practice, the current research degree in this field and the shortcomings of theoretical methods in application are summarized. In the process of creating the framework of emotional quantification design method, firstly, the current general emotional quantification interactive design ideas are summarized, combining multiple design practices and traditional design methods, then further refine the framework and steps of design method. Subsequently, several interactive product design practices are carried out according to the method. In order to further verify the design methods and practical results, they were evaluated by questionnaires for designers and experts. Finally, the main research results are summarized. The paper also analyzes the advantages and development space of the research, and makes further prospects for the subject.

2 The Design Method

2.1 The Framework of the Method

According to the current research results in the field of emotion quantification and the design process and method used by people in daily life (The Double Diamond) [22, 23], this paper proposes an emotion-driven intelligent product design method based on the quantitative perspective (see Fig. 1). As a thinking mode used by designers in emotional design, it can assist designers to complete the design centered on user emotion. This structured method divides the whole design process into three stages. Firstly, the user's emotion is taken as the starting point to study the user's emotion. Secondly, establishing the mapping relationship model between user emotion and product state is to realize the emotion-based human-computer interaction function. Finally, the mapping relationship model between user emotion and product state is placed in the whole system, combined with function and form, to complete the final design.

Designing the Right Thing—User Emotion Research. This stage is specifically divided into two parts. The first part is divergent exploration and research, through an extensive collection of users' emotional information and divergent thinking, to explore and study the nature of the problem. Through an in-depth study of the current situation through primary and secondary data, designers can understand user characteristics, the current situation of the product, how users use the product, and their attitude towards the product, analyze the emotional needs of users, and define the target emotion to be studied. In the second part, more in-depth and specific research is carried out to realize the quantification of emotion. Objective and subjective measurement methods are used to measure the target users' emotions in both physical and psychological aspects, to obtain the perceptual cognitive data and digital signals of the user's emotions, and carry out emotional recognition to obtain the users' emotional characteristics.

How to Design—Emotional Feature-Product State Model Construction. In this stage, the emotional characteristics of users are taken as the starting point, and the Emotional Feature-Product state model is sought to realize the corresponding transformation from emotional characteristics to product status, and to guide designers to design thinking. This mapping model is based on Donald Norman's three-level theory of emotional design [24], and proposes a rough correspondence between emotional features and product states: The instinctive layer is the immediate emotional effect, realized through sensory stimulation, and related to product design elements such as shape, color, and material. The behavior layer is the feeling of using the product. Whether the product is easy to use and understand is closely related to the function, performance, and usability of the product. The reflection layer is the feeling of the meaning of the product, including

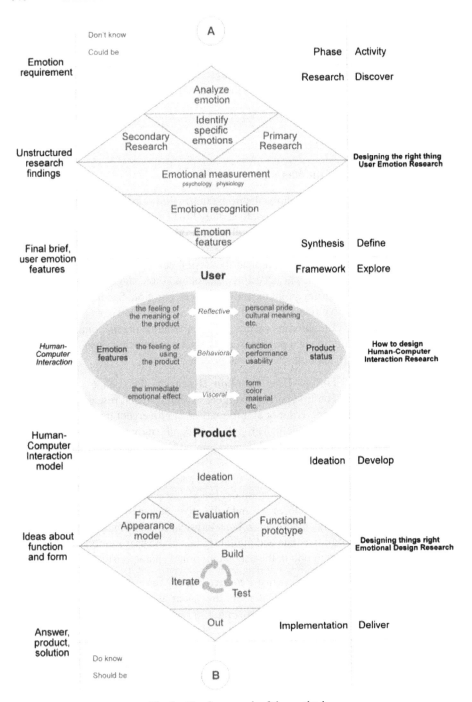

Fig. 1. The framework of the method

self-image, social status, etc. Whether users can get the care and social identity from the product is closely related to the product's culture, information, and utility.

Designers can make bottom-up thinking and deduction through this model, and deduce the corresponding product state according to the user's emotional characteristics obtained in stage one.

Designing Things Right—Emotional Design Research. This stage is the real design stage, which is also divided into two parts. The first part looks for potential solutions based on previous results. This part is the divergence phase of the solution, focusing on generating a large number of ideas, and then trying to make the initial assessment of feasibility in terms of both functions (mainly referring to the model derived in Stage two) and form (the appearance of the product). The second part is to determine the final solution and the final implementation of the product. Analyze and verify all the previous potential solutions one by one, select the most suitable one or more, make product prototype, test, iterate, constantly improve and optimize, eliminate unreasonable ideas, and finally output the most appropriate design.

2.2 Guideline of the Specific Steps

The emotional design methodology summarized in this article is shown in Fig. 2. This method can systematically guide designers to design interactive products using emotional quantification techniques. The design process consists of five main parts that designers can fine-tune with their design goals.

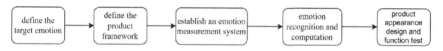

Fig. 2. Step flow

Define the Target Sentiment. In the early stages of design, designers need to define clear design goals based on user analysis to ensure that interactive products can meet user needs or provide human care.

User Profile. Firstly, user background research is conducted by means of user interviews, questionnaires, behavioral observations, etc., focusing on users' behavioral characteristics and psychological arousal in specific social scenarios. Then the target emotion of the product is determined. The target emotion can be selected from the six basic emotions in Ekman's emotion theory, including happiness, sadness, anger, fear, disgust, and surprise. In addition, the user's ability boundaries, such as cognitive ability and coordination ability should be investigated, which is conducive to analyzing the potential needs of users, such as obtaining care, social recognition, experiencing happiness, etc., and can also help the design of product interaction patterns [25].

Canvas of the Future. Future canvas refers to the imagination of new scenarios in the future based on the current social development trend, which will help further explore the possible application value of interactive products in the future [13]. Designers can use the future canvas to further adjust the scope of the target emotion, and through creative thinking patterns, structural analysis methods, perception and inspiration methods to diverge thinking and innovate product interaction patterns [25].

Target Emotion. The target emotion of the product is finally established, combined with the results of the preliminary research on users and thought dispersion [26]. Designers should ensure that the target is close to the user's needs and has application significance.

Define the Framework of Interactive Products. Product interaction design framework establishes the overall architecture of product behavior, including the underlying organizational principles, workflow, product interaction, and information transmission based on product semantics.

Interaction Flow. Sketch the product experience and conceptualizing the interaction between the product, environment, and user behavior [25]. In the process of sketching, attention should be paid to exploring possible product interaction forms and designing user experiences. Current forms of product interaction can be divided into two categories: graphical interaction and non-graphical interaction. Among them, graphical interactions emphasize changes in appearance of products such as color, material, and contours, which are easily recognized by the naked eye and can prompt users with different emotional states; non-graphical interactions emphasize the use of touch, smell, voice, etc. to give feedback to users [20]. Appropriate application of interactive feedback can actively or passively intervene in the user's state and help the user to alleviate emotional problems [21].

Product Design. Combined with the product experience sketch, further refine the interactive form of the product, and preliminarily draw the product appearance design. At this stage, designers should appropriately reserve space for circuit components to reduce the possibility of frequent changes in appearance later. The product appearance design should contain the basic form of the product and all possible interaction forms.

System Functions. Build a wireframe flowchart of the product's function behavior [25]. In the flowchart, designers should clearly describe how the product is used and how it works. When describing the product workflow, it should include all operations and product feedback from the time the user starts using the product until the interactive feedback is completed. In addition to product interaction feedback design, designers should also pay attention to the semantic design of product button feedback, indicator color feedback, etc., so as to improve product information transfer and guide users to understand the emotional feedback given by the product.

Establish an Emotion Detection System. Convert physiological signals into digital signals that can be recognized by machines with the help of specific sensors. At present, the emotion measurement technology based on psychology and physiology mainly includes instrumental measurement, behavior and expression observation, comprehensive measurement and software measurement, which can qualitatively measure basic emotions such as happiness, sadness and anger (Table 1).

Table 1. Emotion measurement methods

Classification	Main methods		Characteristic
Measures of emotion based on physiological signals	ECG	EOG	The measurement results are reliable as a variety of sensors are used. They can detect emotional changes that are hard to detect
	EMG	EEG	
	EDA	PSP	
	FSTBF	SCL	
Psychology-based emotional assessment	SAM		They can quickly assess the emotion type and intensity of the participant. Those methods are particularly suitable for the measurement of a given emotion
	PrEmo		
	Emocards		
	PAD		

Determine How Emotions Are Measured. Firstly, according to the design goals, determine the multimodal physiological signals that need to be acquired to achieve the interactive function. One or more physiological signals such as eye movement, heart rate, skin conductivity (SC), finger temperature, EMG activity, and RSP velocity can be selected [28]. Next, identify the relevant sensor elements, such as electromyographic sensors (EMG), electrocardiographic sensors (ECG), temperature sensors, and various other sensing devices. The size of the sensors used in the product should be as small as possible to ensure a clean and aesthetic appearance of the product model.

Build Hardware Platform. Connect sensors to data terminals such as a computer to complete the physical circuit. The hardware platform can be built using programming components such as Arduino or using other circuits with integrated sensors. Test the circuit by connecting it to a power supply to ensure that all sensors can be supplied with power smoothly and that the computer can recognize the connected sensors.

Emotion Measurement. Pilot run the built hardware platform and test the participants with multiple physiological data measurements. Check the test results to ensure that the sensor functions properly, and the physiological signals can be converted into digital signals through the sensor and output at the device terminal. This hardware platform will become an emotion measurement system for interactive products.

Emotion Recognition. Analyze user's physiological state data based on mathematical algorithms to identify the user's emotional state, which will provide the basis for product interaction.

Data Filter. Data were compared using computer programming combined with existing numerical algorithm theories such as one-way analysis of variance (ANOA), ant colony algorithm, genetic algorithm, and particle swarm algorithm to filter out valid data [4]. Giving specific weights to different data and prioritizing them as a way to improve the availability of physiological data helps to improve the accuracy of emotion recognition.

Emotion Recognition Computing. Extract digital features of valid physiological data, such as elevated blood pressure, increased heart rate, muscle tension and other physiological changes. Then write computer programming algorithms to compare the data with the relevant features in the theory of emotional physiological effects. Then construct a user emotional model to identify their emotional states and changes [17].

Validate Experiment. Conduct emotion measurement experiments on multiple participants using existing emotion measurement systems, triggering as many of their target emotions as possible during the test. Use sensors to detect multiple physiological signals from the participants, and the computer to analyze and build a model of the user's emotions in real time based on the feedback data, then outputs digital feedback when it recognizes the user's emotional changes. Designers should record the digital feedback output by the computer throughout the process. Next, the participants are asked to complete one or more relevant subjective emotion assessment scales, such as SAM emotion assessment, Emocards measure, PrEmo measure [10, 26]. After the measurement, compare the user's self-perception and computer feedback data after the measurement to evaluate the accuracy of the emotion measurement platform.

Product Assembly and Testing. Create physical models based on product design drawings and conduct functional tests. After the test, conduct a feedback survey on user experience.

Circuit Assembly. Identify all the components needed for the product to implement interactive functions, such as robots, LED strip lights, speakers, etc. Connect all components to the circuit of the emotion measurement system to complete all circuit connections of the product.

Software Implementation. Write computer programming algorithms so that the digital signals output by the sensor can be conveyed by the computer algorithm to the corresponding product interaction instructions, and control the interactive elements to complete the emotional interaction feedback.

Product Detail Design. Further improve the internal structure design drawing of the product [25], considering the current circuit volume, wiring mode, power supply and other factors. Focus on considering the combination of circuit and product scheme, without directly exposing sensors or components as much as possible while not affecting the function of the circuit [20]. Then combine with ergonomics and other theories, further optimize the product appearance in terms of size, contour, material and other details to make the product beautiful and easy to use.

Product Assembly. Create a physical model of the product. Computer-aided modeling can be performed to create the product shell using 3D printing, or the product shell can be made by hand using available materials. Then, according to the product internal structure design drawing, assemble all the circuits in a specific way to make the product achieve the expected effect.

Functional Testing. Enable multiple participants to experience the physical model of the product, observe and record the interactive feedback of the product under participants' different emotional states. After the test, the participants should be asked to evaluate the product experience again using the affective assessment scale. Next, compare the correlation between product interaction feedback and participants' emotional changes. In addition, multiple functional tests can be conducted considering different environmental factors, such as different places of use, climate, or time of use [25].

3 Applied Cases

3.1 LUMiA—Hand Training Toys Based on Emotional States

As shown in Fig. 3, this case is an interaction design for patients with mouse hands. It can detect the emotional state of users and remind them to do hand exercises in an appealing interactive way. LUMiA has two operating modes: one is to quantify users' emotions and give real-time feedback of their emotions using the light cube and the other is to detect the pressure users put on GSR sensors during hand relaxation training, then the light cube presents the corresponding pattern. Five different dynamic patterns of light cube including rotating heart, small hexagon, big hexagon, breathing and wave rolling can be triggered as pressure varied, with the intention of guiding the user to better hand relaxation. This product realizes the interactive function of "detection - feedback" through the arduino circuit equipped with LED and GSR sensor. The product achieves the goal of arousing users' interest and alleviating their hand fatigue, which is an innovative exploration of using emotional interaction products to solve social problems.

3.2 Aroma Diffuser Design for Alleviating Anxiety

As shown in Fig. 4, the design goal of this case is to help reduce the mental anxiety prevalent in modern life with an aroma diffuser. This design takes the incense burning culture, one of China's intangible cultural heritages as the carrier to provide users with visual, olfactory and other multi-sensory interactive experiences, which would help divert user's attention and change the mental state of anxiety. The aroma diffuser is connected with GSR sensors, which can detect the users' emotional state. After the recognition, the smoke shape in the aroma diffuser will change accordingly. This product is mainly realized through Arduino programming and circuit. GSR sensors are used to identify the anxiety state of users and LED strip lights are applied to give visual feedback in the form of colors. Besides, the steering arm of the steering gear is used to squeeze the rubber conduit to form a pressure difference, which changes the sinking smoke shape of the backflow incense and produces a graceful and smooth shape change. This emotional interaction products use smoke that jumps with emotions, with dim lighting and elegant aroma, which can shift users' attention, and at the same time, it can help users stay away from anxiety temporarily and produce benign feedback on mental health.

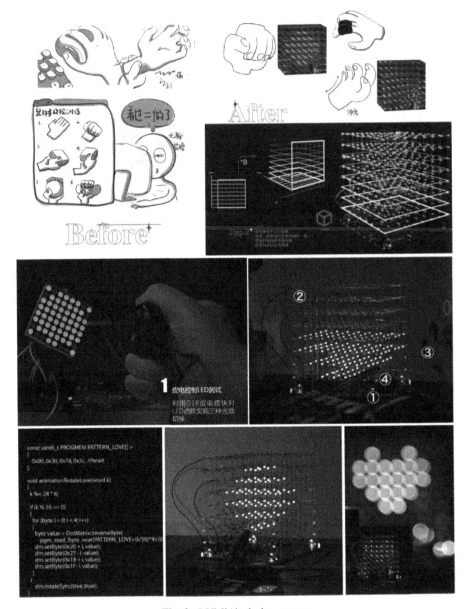

Fig. 3. LUMiA's design process

Fig. 4. Aroma diffuser's design process

3.3 Heart Rate Sensing Interactive Device

As shown in Fig. 5, this case focuses on loneliness. It shows people's different emotional states through dissimilar lighting and color forms of the heart-shaped lamp in the device, aiming at alleviating people's loneliness through interaction with the product. At the same time, the device also has social properties, can be touched by different users to form an emotional interaction between the two ends. The interaction between the two users can jointly affect the state of the product, through this emotional interaction to close the emotional distance between people. This product uses Arduino circuit which carries two heart rate sensors (named sensor 1 and sensor 2) and a LED strip as interactive components. The heart rate sensors by monitoring the user's heart rate and connecting the strip and other components can achieve the effect of flashing lights with the user's heart rate. When sensor 1 detects alone, that is, when a single user touches the sensor, the light beads are bright yellow, while when sensor 2 detects alone, the light bulb is bright blue. When both sensors are detected at the same time, the light bead is bright red. This emotional interaction product visualizes the change of the user's heart rate, transforms the user's emotion into light, and realizes emotional interaction with the user, which helps stimulate more possibilities for people to express their emotions. This product has rich application scenarios, especially in interactive public facilities, public welfare exhibitions and other scenarios that need to shorten the social distance between people in a short period of time.

Fig. 5. Design process of heart rate sensing interactive device (Color figure online)

4 Verification and Results

After innovatively proposing the design method, framework and implementation steps of emotion quantification, we further verified the effectiveness of the design methodology through questionnaire surveys and expert evaluation. The validation work includes two parts: a questionnaire survey on the methodological framework and implementation steps themselves, and an expert assessment of the design practice outputs of applying the methodology. The results of both work are positive and encouraging, demonstrating that our approach not only innovatively proposes new ways to address the quantitative emotional design, but also has high credibility and effectiveness. Specifically, this design methodology is implemented for graduate students in the course of teaching the graduate course Quantitative Design Methods for Emotion. Through the training and practice of the method for junior designers, mainly graduate students, the designers mastered the method and then carried out specific design practice, which is the method application process. Thereafter, four experts (associate professors and professors) were invited to evaluate the design practice works of all graduate students to further verify the innovative guiding effect of the method on design practice.

4.1 Survey on the Methodology

In the course named Quantitative Design of Emotion, the framework and steps of this method ran through the teaching process of the whole course. After postgraduate students learned and mastered this method, they did emotional design which is different from the traditional way. Lots of interesting pieces were designed, and prototypes were made and tested. To verify the effectiveness of this method for users and the innovation of the works designed following this method, we conducted a questionnaire survey among these postgraduate students. The questionnaire questions are mainly aimed at the practicability and effectiveness of the method as well as the usability and innovation of the output results, which are scored and evaluated by the course participants according to their subjective judgment. According to the results of the questionnaire, most of them said that using this method to design can get more inspiration, practice programming and prototyping skills, and the design of the work is more innovative.

This questionnaire adopts a seven-point scale to evaluate the course harvest and the appearance, user emotional experience, innovation, and stability of the products designed by themselves (see Fig. 6). The average scores of 15 people are 6.47, 5.47, 5.87, 5.67, and 5, respectively. The mean values of prototype usability related ease-of-use, feeling confident, and quickly learning to use are 5.4, 5.67, and 5.93, respectively (see Fig. 7). It shows that the practice of this method can significantly improve the emotional experience attribute of the product, and method users are satisfied with the appearance and usability of the prototype designed according to this method. In terms of whether the method is inspirational and innovative, and whether it will be used and referred to in the future, 100% of the respondents hold a positive attitude (see Table 2), indicating that the method is feasible and innovative, and has a good guiding significance for designers.

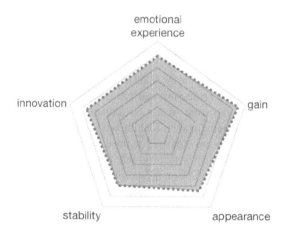

Fig. 6. The respondents' evaluation of different aspects of the product and personal gain

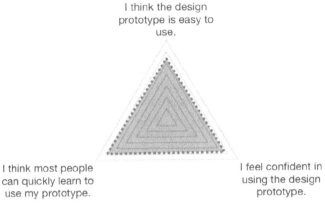

Fig. 7. The respondents' evaluation of prototype usability

Table 2. The respondents' attitude towards the problems

QUESTION	YES	NO
Do you think product design based on emotional quantification is more innovative than traditional design methods?	100%	0
Do you think the methods taught in this course are enlightening to your design?	100%	0
Are you willing to refer to the methods taught in this course in your future designs?	100%	0
Do you think intelligent product design driven by emotional quantification is one of the future trends?	100%	0

4.2 Expert Assessment of the Design Practice Outputs

To verify that the design methodology is instructive in terms of design practice, we asked four experts (associate professors and professors) to evaluate the results of our guided design practice in the form of a questionnaire to verify whether the method can guide designers to design forward-looking and innovative emotional interaction products. The questionnaire mainly focused on the experience and impact of the product, scoring the product in terms of practicality, intelligence, humanization and foresight. All evaluation questions were based on a 7-point scale, and the reliability and validity of the questionnaire data were relatively high. According to the analysis of the valid questionnaire results, the design practice provided in the paper is recognized by experts in the matter of emotional interaction intelligence and humanization, and the design practice has social value. The verification proves that the design method of emotional measurement proposed in this paper is innovative, forward-looking and replicable, and has a strong guiding effect on designers' quantitative emotion design.

This questionnaire uses a seven-point scale to evaluate the design practice. Four experts scored from the three dimensions of product appearance, emotional experience, and innovation. The survey results are shown in Fig. 8. All experts affirmed the appearance design and innovation of interactive products to varying degrees, and three experts approved the user experience of products. This indicates that this method is effective in helping intelligent product design to improve product appearance, innovation and user experience. In the question related to product emotional symbolism, all experts affirmed the cultural value of the interactive products guided by this methodology (see Table 3). In addition, three experts recognized that the design practice can promote the application of emotion quantification techniques and the method itself is enlightening, indicating that the method has social promotion value and its output can have a positive impact on emotion design.

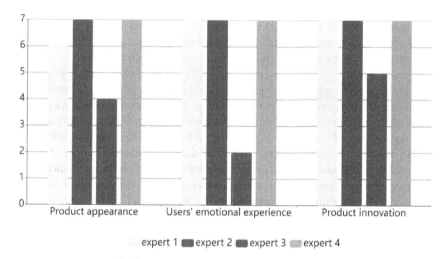

expert 1 ▇ expert 2 ▇ expert 3 ▨ expert 4

Fig. 8. Grouped column chart of expert scoring

Table 3. Expert evaluation form

QUESTION	YES	NO
Whether the product is innovative in content and human-computer interaction?	3	1
Whether the product has certain emotional symbolic significance and cultural value?	4	0
Whether the practical application can promote the application of emotion quantification technology?	3	1
Do you think the emotional quantitative design method is enlightening for your future product design?	3	1
Overall, whether the method has social promotion and practical application value?	3	1

5 Conclusion

This paper proposes a systematic and structured emotion quantization design method, including both conceptual model and concrete implementation steps. By applying this method, designers can start from the definition of target emotion, go through product conceptual design and interaction design, emotion measurement, product design, and prototype testing, and finally achieve the goal of guiding designers to carry out emotional design from a quantitative perspective. This study creatively proposed a whole set of systematic emotional quantization product design methods that built a bridge between the field of emotional measurement research and the field of product design, made up for the deficiency of quantitative methods in previous research on emotional design, and promoted the intersection and organic integration between fields. More importantly, by linking human emotion with design elements such as product shape, color, and material, and driving product design with quantified emotional characteristics, the quality of emotional product design can be effectively improved, which has been proved by the applied cases. The application shows that this method is applicable and promising, also making the previously relatively subjective process of product design gradually become objective and rational, and the output results more humanized and intelligent.

This paper provides a general method framework for quantified emotional design, further exploration and research are still in need in the future. Next step, we will conduct research from the following aspects: First, with the continuous deepening of research in related technical fields, we will improve the method model and steps, to more deeply depict the mapping relationship between product elements and perceptual terms, and further clarify the relationship between emotional features and product state in human-computer interaction for designers. Secondly, we will make a deeper exploration of the application level of this method and put it into practice in the real design process to enrich its application scenarios, so as to inspire designers to complete more innovative and surprising designs.

References

1. Quan, H., Li, S., Hu, J.: Product innovation design based on deep learning and Kansei engineering. Appl. Sci. **8**(12), 2397 (2018). https://doi.org/10.3390/app8122397
2. Lv, Z.: Application of kansei engineering in product form design. Adv. Mater. Res. **2526**(753–755), 1515–1518 (2013). https://doi.org/10.4028/www.scientific.net/AMR.753-755.1515
3. Vieira, J., Osório, J.M.A., Mouta, S., et al.: Kansei engineering as a tool for the design of in-vehicle rubber keypads. Appl. Ergon. **61**, 1–11 (2017). https://doi.org/10.1016/j.apergo.2016.12.019
4. Cheng, J., Liu, G.: Research progress of affect detection in interdisciplinary perspective (学科交叉视角下的情感识别研究进展). Comput. Sci. **39**(5), 19–24 (2012). https://doi.org/10.3969/j.issn.1002-137X.2012.05.004
5. Ding, J., Yang, D., Cao, Y., Wang, L.: Theory, method, and trend of emotional design (情感化设计的主要理论、方法及研究趋势). J. Eng. Des. **17**(1), 12–18 (2010). https://doi.org/10.3785/j.issn.1006-754X.2010.01.002
6. Chen, Y., Jiang, Y., He, R., Wu, X.: Emotional design trends and research progress: a scientometric analysis-based study (基于文献计量学的情感化设计研究进展、热点与趋势分析). Pack. Eng. **06**, 32–40 (2022). https://doi.org/10.19554/j.cnki.1001-3563.2022.06.004

7. Norman, D.: Design Psychology 3: Emotional Design. HE Xiao-me, OU Qiu-xing, Translate. Beijing: CITIC Press (2015)

8. Yin, J., Wu, Z.: Methods and trends of product emotional design (产品情感化设计的方法与趋势探析). J. Hun. Univ. Sci. Technol. (Soc. Sci. Ed.) **16**(1), 161–163 (2013). CNKI:SUN:XTGS.0.2013-01-037

9. Wang, S.: Research on the emotional quantification process of product design scheme evaluation (产品设计方案评价的情感量化流程研究). Mark. Modern. **02**, 67–68 (2011). https://doi.org/10.3969/j.issn.1006-3102.2011.02.046

10. Bradley, M.M., Lang, P.J.: Measuring emotion: the self-assessment manikin and the semantic differential. J. Behav. Ther. Exp. Psychiatry **25**(1), 49–59 (1994). https://doi.org/10.1016/0005-7916(94)90063-9

11. Jiang, M., Bhömer, M.T., Liang, H.-N.: Exploring the design of interactive smart textiles for emotion regulation. In: Stephanidis, C., Duffy, V.G., Streitz, N., Konomi, S., Krömker, H. (eds.) HCII 2020. LNCS, vol. 12429, pp. 298–315. Springer, Cham (2020). https://doi.org/10.1007/978-3-030-59987-4_22

12. Li, X., Cai, S.: Emotional design for intelligent products using artificial intelligence technology. In: 2021 2nd International Conference on Intelligent Design (ICID), pp. 260–263 (2021). https://doi.org/10.1109/ICID54526.2021.00059

13. Song, Y., Cheng, Z., Zhang, C.: Possibilities of the wearables: teaching method for digital jewelry design of the future. In: Soares, M.M., Rosenzweig, E., Marcus, A. (eds) Design, User Experience, and Usability: Design Thinking and Practice in Contemporary and Emerging Technologies. HCII 2022. LNCS, vol. 13323, pp. 100–413. Springer, Cham (2022). https://doi.org/10.1007/978-3-031-05906-3_30

14. Yao, H., et al.: An overview of research development of affective computing and understanding (情感计算与理解研究发展概述). J. Image Graph. **06**, 2008–2035 (2022). https://doi.org/10.11834/jig.220085

15. Lin, L., Yin, X., Guo, Z., Deng, Y., Yang, P.: KE model of product form based on eye-tracking weighting and image cognition by EEG (基于眼动赋权及脑电意象认知的产品形态感性工学模型研究). Pack. Eng. **43**(14), 37–44 (2022). https://doi.org/10.19554/j.cnki.1001-3563.2022.14.004

16. Liu, C., Wang, Z.: A method of requirement acquisition for emotional design of automobile styling based on kansei engineering and online comments — taking the design of automobile front face as an example (基于感性工学和在线评论的汽车造型情感设计需求获取方法——以汽车前脸的设计为例). J. Anhui Polytechnic Univ. **37**(1), 62–70 (2022). https://doi.org/10.3969/j.issn.2095-0977.2022.01.009

17. Li, J., Qi, N.: Research on design of robots accompanying empty nesters based on emotional computation (基于情感计算的空巢老人陪伴机器人设计研究). Ind. Des. **11**, 26–28 (2021). https://doi.org/10.3969/j.issn.1672-7053.2021.11.014

18. Kim, J., et al.: A conformable sensory face mask for decoding biological and environmental signals. Nat Electron. **5**, 794–807 (2022). https://doi.org/10.1038/s41928-022-00851-6

19. Rosello, O.: HeartBit. MIT Media Lab. https://www.media.mit.edu/projects/heartbit/overview/

20. Kao, H., et al.: Exploring interactions and perceptions of kinetic wearables. In: Proceedings of the 2017 Conference on Designing Interactive Systems, pp. 391–396 (2017). https://doi.org/10.1145/3064663.3064686

21. Kosmyna, N., Maes, P.: AttentivU: an EEG-based closed-loop biofeedback system for real-time monitoring and improvement of engagement for personalized learning. Sensors. **19**(23), 5200 (2019). https://doi.org/10.3390/s19235200

22. Council, D.: Eleven Lessons: Managing Design in Eleven Global Companies, Desk Research Report. Engineering (2007)

23. Best, K.: Design Management: Managing Design Strategy. Process and Implementation. AVA publishing, Los Angeles (2006)
24. Norman, D. A.: Design Psychology 3: Emotional Design. He, X., Translate. China Citic Press, Beijing (2010)
25. Gu, Z.: Principles & Processes of Interaction Design (交互设计—原理与方法). Tsinghua University Publishing House, Beijing (2016)
26. Lin, L., Yang, M., Zhang, C., Liu, L.: The product emotion and key technologies for emotional measurement. J. Graphics. **34**(1), 122–127 (2013). https://doi.org/10.3969/j.issn.2095-302X.2013.01.023

The Influence of User Emotion on Design Preference Based on Personality Type

Shiyuan Zhu🆔, Meixian Li^(✉) 🆔, and Jiahao Sun🆔

School of Design Art, Changsha University of Science and Technology, Changsha, China
lmx990312@163.com, sunjiahao@csust.edu.cn

Abstract. Personality is one of the important psychological characteristics that affect people's emotions. Individuals with different personalities have different emotions, and emotions, as an unconscious element, always affect people's subjective choices and preferences. In this study, the personality type of users is understood through the Myers-Briggs Type Indicator (MBTI), and based on the user type, the Mannheim Dream Questionnaire (MADRE) is adopted as a method to obtain the emotional fluctuations and types of users, and then the painting elements in the House-Tree-Person Technique (HTP) are extracted as the criteria for the consideration of users' design preferences. Finally, emotions and design preferences as variables were combined with the four dimensions of the Myers-Briggs personality type to conclude. Studies show that different personalities have significant differences in emotional Perception and have different design preferences and aesthetic uniqueness. Introversion personality has higher emotional fluctuations and negative emotions than Extraversion, and the perception type likes a circle shape more than Judgment. The Sensing Judgment type likes a quadrangular shape (square, trapezoid, etc.). The Sensing type prefers design which is like the shape of a vase (thick at both ends and thin in the middle) to the Intuition type, while the Intuition Thinking type prefers vertical oval and triangle elements. These findings will be helpful to effectively evaluate users' emotions towards design from the aspect of personality and provide new ideas for future research on differentiated design.

Keywords: Personality types · Emotion · Design preferences · Subconscious · Projective drawing test

1 Introduction

Personality is one of the important psychological characteristics that affect people's emotions. Personality types may have the greatest impact on how we prefer to interact with others, how we collect and understand data, and how we tend to deal with a given problem [1]. The influence of individual differences on personality types is very important, and individuals with different personalities also have different emotions and behavioral motivations [2]. If the personality types and psychological functions of human target groups are considered first, their emotions can be more effectively understood and they can be persuaded to achieve the desired behaviors [3]. Personality traits continue to influence our lives, from our behaviors to our career decisions. With the help of personality traits, we can design more accurate products and develop more effective design strategies [4]. For the design industry, the influence of personality type on users' emotional perception and aesthetic preference should not be underestimated, but the research on design preference of personality type has not received due attention.

Personality types have been proven to have a direct driving effect on human behavior and have been widely used to assist social workers in all walks of life. There are also precedents for assisting the development of design schemes with personality types. It has been proved that product design specifications for individual users' personality types are fruitful, and this approach has been used as a new design rule in some product design fields [5]. Based on personality attributes and design applications, appropriate creative tools can also be selected for designers [6], and targeted design professional training models can be provided for them [7]. Although the research on personality types has played an important role in promoting the development of various industries, it is important to note that the limitations of the research on personality types are that the results may vary by gender and age group, and the results may vary in different countries [8].

Emotion is one of the factors that lead to individual differentiation. Emotions can affect human behavior and decision-making, and different personality types have different emotions, so different individuals have different preferences [9]. To find design strategies for users with different personality types, methods based on mental function and various disciplinary techniques have been studied and applied. In 2001, Kostov V et al. investigated the relationship between personality types (Myers-Briggs or Kersey Temperament sorter) and user preferences for the construction of a graphical user interface (GUI) and proposed a method to standardize general rules for human-machine interface synthesis and design. It also proves the feasibility of developing GUIs based on users' innate personality tendencies [10]. In addition, in a study on user satisfaction, Subaramaniam et al. used Myers-Briggs Type Indicator (MBTI) to classify students' personality types and then linked these types to specific user interface functions. Found that a user interface tailored to their mental functional preferences effectively improved learning efficiency [11]. Although the research methods and level have improved to a certain extent over time, there is still no complete paradigm to advance the research of user emotions and behaviors (personality type as a measure).

Most previous studies have applied the personality theory and its derivative methods as the data analysis standard but failed to conduct an in-depth and systematic analysis of the behaviors of users with different personality types from the perspective of psychology. However, this study will utilize the projection of the subconscious to analyze and explain the differences in users' emotions and behaviors from the perspective of personality types. It is convenient to give different strategies for different users to improve the design level. The study is divided into five steps: 1. Identify the link between personality type theory and the unconscious mind. 2. Select appropriate personality type indicators as measurement criteria. 3. Sorted out the research logic, designed the experimental questionnaire and carried out the investigation. 4. Analyze the relationship between the emotional and design element preference data produced in the experiment and personality types and conclude. 5. Put forward design suggestions and differentiated design strategies for users with different personality types according to the conclusions obtained from the experiment.

2   Research Method

MBTI types refer to types of consciousness [12]. The subconscious mind is the basis and source of consciousness, and human consciousness and the subconscious mind can affect the decision-making process [13], the subconscious mind is directly and indirectly involved in human daily activities all the time, and this causal relationship is decisive for the decision and development of any human activities [14]. Known as the X-ray of the unconscious mind, dreams always produce more acceptable symbolic pieces of information for us to see or perceive while using and releasing the unacknowledged emotional energy within us since yesterday's events [15], information not noticed by the individual, information noticed but not understood, Memory information retained from real events and fictional memory information are the main ways for the subconscious to influence human decision-making [16]. Awake visual experience may also be affected by individual psychological factors. Personality and emotional factors also have a non-negligible impact on the recall of medium images [17]. Emotion, especially the change of emotion, has a great correlation with the choice of visual images [18]. In other words, the subjective experience of dreams can reflect not only waking emotional experience [19], but also relevant issues and strategies related to aesthetic choices and preferences. The projection test is one of the personality measurement methods, which is used to explore the activities deep in individual psychology and involves the subconscious content of the individual personality of the tested person [20]. As this paper studies design preferences, design is derived from art, and the inspiration and source of artistic creation mainly come from the expression and symbol of the subconscious mind [21], so the drawing test is chosen as one of the experimental methods. Drawing test, as a form of projection test, is based on mental projection in psychology [22]. House-Tree-Person Technique (HTP) is a projection test with a simple method and clear analysis criteria. Thus, both dream and drawing tests are unconscious expressions of psychological problems, belonging to a kind of psychological projection.

To sum up, this study takes the personality type theory as the core, combines the Mannheim Dream Questionnaire (MADRE) and House-Tree-Person Technique (HTP) to study and analyze the emotional characteristics of users with different personality types, and summarizes their design preferences. Give some specific design suggestions. To analyze the relationship between users' emotional characteristics and their personality types, questionnaires were used to collect relevant data such as emotion fluctuation and personality types. Firstly, an appropriate personality tester is selected. On this basis, combining personality testing, Mannheim Dream Questionnaire (MADRE) and House-Tree-Person Technique (HTP), experimental questionnaires are designed. Finally, the method of data analysis is determined, especially the analysis method of emotional atmosphere and intensity.

This study first surveyed the personality types of user groups and then calculated the emotion fluctuation and types of users by taking the Mannheim Dream Questionnaire

(MADRE) on dream atmosphere and intensity. Finally, according to the clinical experience of the House-Tree-Person Technique (HTP) summarized by predecessors, painting elements such as tree crowns and tree trunks are extracted to analyze and organize the psychological expression of users in the creation process, to obtain the relationship among users' personality types, emotions, and aesthetic preferences. The logical framework of the research is shown in Fig. 1.

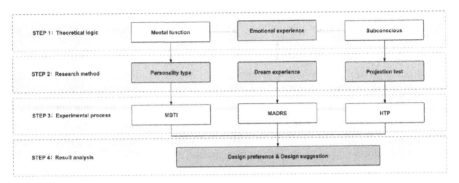

Fig. 1. Research work frame

2.1 Personality Test Method

Myers-Briggs Type Indicator (MBTI), Big Five Personality, Enneagram Personality Test, Eysenck Personality Questionnaire (EPQ), Sixteen Personality Factor Questionnaire (16PF), DISC Personality Test, Four-colors Personality Analysis (FPA) is several commonly used personality analysis tests, which define the basic dimensions of personality from different perspectives based on the trait theory of analytical psychology. The MBTI scale based on the Jungian theory of mental type has advantages in the following aspects, so it can judge the personality type of the tested person more clearly in this study. It is not only used for career assessment but is widely used to interpret personality test results for individuals [23, 24]. It not only divides personality into 16 types, but its core lies in the fact that individual differences are reasonable results based on specific facts and are external manifestations of differences in psychological functions within individuals. MBTI based on Jungian psychological type theory is superior to other psychological tests in the above aspects, so it can judge the user's personality type more clearly in this study and is more conducive to the analysis of design preferences.

2.2 Experimental Method

There are three main methods to investigate personality-related information: questionnaire, projection, and operation. The questionnaire method is mainly used for personality assessment. The projection method can stimulate the subconscious motives and thoughts of the subjects. The operation method is to make individuals participate in some activities. According to the individual's operation and reaction make a comprehensive judgment.

The questionnaire method has a low threshold and is easy to operate. The projection method requires subjects to have high language expression ability or drawing ability, while the operation method requires subjects to have mathematical operation ability. It is not suitable for the implementation of group tests. As The experimental group is large and difficult to operate, the questionnaire method combined with the projection method is adopted in this study to collect the user's personality type and related information. The limitations of the method (including, for example, the subjectivity and authenticity of the subjects' answers) have been fully recognized, and the difficulties encountered in the distribution and collection of questionnaires and test kits have been solved accordingly.

2.3 Questionnaire Design

The experimental questionnaires in this study are divided into three parts: basic information (including personality test), Mannheim Dream Questionnaire (MADRE) and House-Tree-Person Technique (HTP). After completing the basic personal information, the subjects will complete the questionnaire.

Personality Test Lite. Based on Jung's theory of mental types, the Myers-Briggs Personality Type Test, developed by the Myers-Briggs mother and daughter, systematically explains the differences in people's aptitude and describes four dominant mental functions: Extraversion and Introversion, Sensing and Intuition. Combined with four auxiliary mental functions, such as Thinking, Feeling, Judgment and Perception, the characteristics of sixteen personality types are formed. These basic differences in mental function are the way that different individuals prefer to use their brains and specifically, the way that we use to perceive and judge things. "Perception" is our perception of things, people, circumstances or ideas, and "judgment" is our judgment of the information we perceive. Perception and judgment constitute the main body of our mental activities and control most of our behavior. From the definition of these two mental functions, we can see that perception determines how we perceive our environment, while judgment determines how we will react to it. Therefore, different ways of perception or judgment will naturally lead to different behaviors and thus lead to differences between people [9]. To save time and make the subjects more patient to complete the follow-up test, this study summarized and sorted out the theoretical prototype of MBTI and adopted the refined version of the MBTI test to investigate the personality type of users.

Mannheim Dream Questionnaire (MADRE). Several studies have demonstrated that dreams tend to reflect emotional experiences in waking life, which indicates that the emotions of waking life are often included in dreams, so the investigation of dreams is adopted in the research to explore the emotions of users [25–27]. The Mannheim Dream Questionnaire (MADRE) adopted in this study is a comprehensive questionnaire designed to measure different aspects of dreams [28], including frequency of dream recall, emotional aspects of dreams, different dream types, attitudes towards dreams, and questionnaires. How dreamers record and recount their dreams, including creative dreams, problem-solving dreams, Deja vu experiences, and other influences on waking life. Mannheim Dream Questionnaire (MADRE) consists of 28 questions, most of which have high retest reliability and are suitable for psychometric measurement [29]. In this study, the emotional intensity and emotional atmosphere of dreams will be analyzed in detail. The English version of the Mannheim Dream Questionnaire (MADRE) was translated into Chinese by two graduate students and was directly used to measure the emotional experience of users' dreams.

House-Tree-Person Technique (HTP). House-Tree-Person Technique (HTP) is a well-known painting projection experiment. By analyzing the subjects' painting works on the theme of the House-Tree-Person Technique (HTP), we can understand the emotional characteristics projected by it. A technique for measuring personality traits and levels of intellectual development. It is now widely used to measure intelligence and personality. House-Tree-Person Technique (HTP) can project the user's mental intention under the influence of the subconscious on paper, which makes it possible for the researcher to fully and truly understand the psychology of the tested person, especially their mental characteristics. Several studies have shown that the House-Tree-Person Technique (HTP) has good reliability [30-32]. What the painter shows in his painting is stable painting characteristics, and the analyst can also rely on objective criteria to identify these characteristics stably. In addition, some researchers also conduct comprehensive studies by combining the House-Tree-Person Technique (HTP) with other scales [33-36].

To sum up, the study first used the Myers-Briggs Type Indicator (MBTI) to distinguish user personality types and then used the Mannheim Dream Questionnaire (MADRE) to summarize users' emotional tonality and intensity based on user types. Then, the user carries out the House-Tree-Person Technique (HTP), in which the painting elements are extracted as the criteria to evaluate the user's design preference. Finally, the user's emotion and design preference are taken as variables and combined with the four dimensions of the Myers-Briggs personality type to conclude.

2.4   Quantitative Analysis

To effectively analyze the data related to users' emotional characteristics and design preferences, such as the value of emotion fluctuation and the choice of geometric shapes, this study determined an appropriate quantitative method.

Quantification of Emotional Traits. Emotional fluctuation refers to the fluctuation of a person's mental state due to some big or small factors, which can also be understood as the behavior state generated by people's irrational emotions. According to the views discussed above, this study adopts hierarchical counting to quantify the degree of emotional fluctuation and adopts low, medium, and high grading to quantitatively describe the degree of fluctuation of emotional fluctuation. The minimum score for the included questions is 3 points and the maximum score is 15 points. The scoring system for questions 2 and 5 is 1 point for choosing the minimum value and 2 points for choosing the next minimum value. 3 points are scored for choosing the middle value, 4 points for choosing the next highest value, and 5 points for choosing the highest value. The scoring system for question 3 is 1 point if you choose neutral, 2 points if you choose positive, 3 points if you choose slightly negative, 4 points if you choose very positive and 5 points if you choose very negative. Assuming that the emotion fluctuation value is m ($3 \leq m \leq 15$), the statistics are divided into three levels. $3 \leq m \leq 6$ is low emotion fluctuation, $7 \leq m \leq 10$ is moderate emotion fluctuation, $11 \leq m \leq 15$ is high emotion fluctuation.

There are five choices for the question, which are very negative, slightly negative, neutral, relatively positive, and very positive. In the specific analysis, the very negative and slightly negative are classified as negative emotions, and the relatively positive and very positive are classified as positive emotions. The result is neutral without unnecessary explanation.

Quantification of Design Choices. The quantitative aspect of design selection is to extract and analyze design elements according to the classification of the House-Tree-Person Technique (HTP) in objective experience. House-Tree-Person Technique (HTP), as a form of mental projection test, imperceptibly projects individual psychological needs, personality, emotion, motivation, and other internal states. House-Tree-Person Technique (HTP) consists of portraits of houses, trees, and people, among which tree elements play a very important role in painting tests, and it usually reveals the deep unconscious personality of an individual without the painter's awareness. The crown of the tree represents the interaction between the individual and the overall environment, the object of satisfaction and the scope of interest. The trunk of a tree not only reflects the current energy of an individual but also has a clear internal correlation with people's emotional skills [22]. In addition, the changes in tree painting were minimal in the process of repeated tests, so this study extracted the crown and trunk features of tree painting in the House-Tree-Person Technique (HTP) of subjects to analyze the preferences of design elements such as lines and shapes.

3   Data Collection and Analysis

3.1   Distribution and Collection of Questionnaires

The Questionnaire consisted of personal information, the MBTI personality test, Mannheim Dream Questionnaire (MADRE) and House-Tree-Person Technique (HTP). In the early stage of the experiment, the research carried out three preliminary tests, including two individual tests and one group test. After each preliminary experiment, the subjects were interviewed, and the difficulties encountered in the completion of the questionnaire were recorded and adjusted accordingly. After modification and improvement, the third preliminary experiment was carried out smoothly without any problems and good feedback from users, which confirmed that the questionnaire has good universality and usability.

The questionnaire was anonymous and voluntary, and all the subjects had a good cultural level. Due to many subjects, to ensure the accuracy and rigor of the experiment, the experiment was conducted in three batches on December 5, 2022, and the following steps were taken: 1. The subjects were tested in the professional course classroom of colleges and universities. With the help of the teacher, each subject was able to answer independently and patiently. 2. Before the test, pencil, A4 paper, eraser and other experimental tools were given out, and the purpose, composition, content, and answer requirements of the questionnaire were introduced (House-Tree-Person Technique (HTP) pre-emphasis guidance). If the subjects don't understand, explain to them. All the above measures are helpful to improve the rigor and effectiveness of the survey, but the influence of subjects' subjective interpretation and understanding ability on the final answer of the questionnaire cannot be ignored. A total of 108 questionnaires were sent out in the experiment, and 106 were collected. Due to the implementation of the above measures and the requirement of the educational level of the subjects, the number of effective questionnaires accounted for 94.4% of the total number of questionnaires. Invalid questionnaires included 3 blank questionnaires and 1 questionnaire with non-standard answers. A total of 102 valid questionnaires (for specific analysis) were finally collected. The overall process of the experiment was shown in Fig. 2.

Fig. 2. Questionnaire distribution and collection

3.2 Data Analysis of Personality Types

As mentioned above, MBTI consists of four dimensions and eight directions: two life attitudes: E-Extraversion and I-Introversion, based on two modes of perception: S-Sensing and N-Intuition, and two modes of judgment: T-Thinking and F-Feeling, two lifestyles: P-Perception and J-Judgment. There are sixteen personality types: ENFP, ENFJ, INFP, INFJ, ENTP, ENTJ, INTP, INTJ, ESFP, ESTP, ISFP, ISTP, ESFJ, ESTJ, ISFJ, ISTJ. According to the four dimensions of the personality type theory, the personality types of 102 subjects were obtained. Among the 16 personality types of MBTI, the three most common personality types in this survey are ISFJ (11.7%), ISFP (9.8%), ESTJ (9.8%), and ENTP (1.9%), ENTJ (2.9%), ESTP (2.9%) with the least number of people.

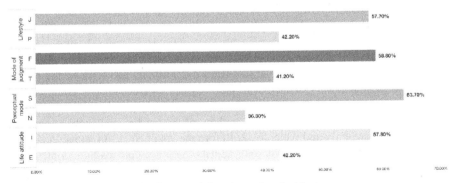

Fig. 3. Mental function ratio of subjects

Subjects (undergraduates majoring in design) had higher preferences for Introversion, Sensing, Feeling and Judgment than Extraversion, Intuition, Thinking and Perception: 57.8% of the subjects represented Introversion (I), 63.7% as Sensing (S), 58.8% as Feeling (F), 57.7% as Judgment (J) and 42.2% as Extraversion (E). Intuition (N) represented 36.3%, Thinking (T) represented 41.2%, and Perception (P) represented 42.2% (see Fig. 3).

3.3 Statistical Analysis of Key Experimental Data

The experimental data were collected from 102 valid questionnaires, from which key information was extracted for calculation, classification, and analysis. Emotion fluctuation and types were analyzed using Mannheim Dream Questionnaire (MADRE). Information related to design preferences (shape preference) is based on the results presented by the House-Tree-Person Technique (HTP). Firstly, SPSS 26.0 software was used to analyze the reliability, validity, and difference of the questionnaire. In terms of reliability, the reliability coefficient (Klonbach coefficient) was 0.768, which was within the acceptable range, and the questionnaire results were credible. In terms of validity, the value of Kaiser-Meyer-Olkin (KMO) was 0.554, indicating that the questionnaire data were suitable for factor analysis. In the aspect of difference, the difference (p) under univariate ANOVA analysis based on personality type variables was 0.03 ($p < 0.05$). The above data prove that the questionnaire has good reliability and validity, and the relevant survey results have significant differences. Key data details are as follows.

Emotion Fluctuation and Types. In the questions related to emotional experience, the statistical analysis of all personalities is as follows: the mean value of emotional fluctuation (m) of 102 subjects is 6.79, and most of the subjects' emotional fluctuation is relatively gentle, with low emotional fluctuation ($3 \leq m \leq 6$) and moderate emotion fluctuation ($7 \leq m \leq 10$), with low emotion fluctuation accounting for 50% of the total, and only 5.8% of the subjects classified as high emotion fluctuation ($11 \leq m \leq 15$). The maximum emotion fluctuation value was 12, with 2 people, accounting for 1.9% of the total; the minimum emotion fluctuation value was 3, with 3 people, accounting for 2.9% of the total. The following Table 1 gives average, maximum, and minimum scores for all the personality options on the emotional experience question.

Table 1. The emotional state of the subject

Variable	Fluctuation (m)	Intensity (ma)	Tone (mb)	Painful (mc)
Average	6.79	2.32	1.69	2.78
Maximum (Number, percentage)	12 (2, 1.9%)	5 (4, 3.9%)	5 (2, 1.5%)	5 (4, 3.9%)
Minimum (Number, percentage)	3 (3, 2.9%)	1 (17, 16.6%)	1 (65, 63.7%)	1 (7, 6.8%)

Design Shape Preference. Regarding the tree shapes drawn in the House-Tree-Person Technique (HTP), several important indicators were extracted and analyzed. The results showed that most of the subjects preferred round and full shapes, and 84.3% of the subjects gave similar circular patterns (circle, vertical oval, horizontal oval, multi-oval). Only one subject drew a quadrangular crown, indicating that the subject may have a conservative tendency, some stubbornness and lack of flexibility, which is contrary to the characteristics of most young people and is also the reason for the extremely low incidence of this type of crown. 8.8% of participants gave a tree crown more in line with triangular geometry, and these users were likely to be aggressive, poor at controlling emotions, and more rational. In terms of trunk shape, about a third of the subjects preferred a vase shape (thick at both ends and thin in the middle). In addition, 23.5% of the users had the tree crown stretched out within the tree trunk, which proved that their emotions were relatively stable, and sensibility and rationality coexisted. 3.9% of the subjects were likely to be emotionally confused (the tree trunk was a twin tree trunk of two different trees), and 5.8% of the subjects were not easy to accept or express their emotions (the junction between the tree trunk and the tree crown was closed). Typical cases in the questionnaire are shown in Fig. 4.

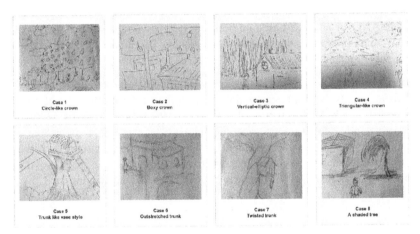

Fig. 4. Typical case

4   Results and Discussion

4.1   Emotion and Design Preference Based on Personality Type

Based on the above survey data, the study analyzed the relationship between user personality type, emotion, and design preference in detail, including emotion fluctuation, emotion type and design shape preference.

Personality and Emotion. According to the description given in the quantitative analysis section above, this study uses hierarchical counting to quantify the degree of emotion fluctuation. From the perspective of psychological function, in the investigation of emotional experience (intensity/atmosphere), personalities with different life preferences, perception modes, judgment modes and lifestyles present different levels of emotional perception: The number of Introversion with high emotion fluctuation accounted for 8.4% of the total Introversion, which was significantly higher than the number of Extraversion with high emotion fluctuation. The mean value of Intuition (m) was higher than that of Sensing (m). The proportion of the Thinking type with low emotion fluctuation and high emotion fluctuation was higher than that of the Feeling type. However, the average emotion fluctuation of the Feeling type reached 6.92, slightly higher than that of the Thinking type (6.62). The proportion of the Thinking type with moderate emotion fluctuation was significantly lower than that of the Feeling type. Judgment type (average emotion fluctuation = 7.00, 8.4% of people with high emotion fluctuation) has stronger emotion fluctuation than Perception type (average emotion fluctuation = 6.51, 2.3% of people with high emotion fluctuation). The following Table 2 gives the average scores of different life attitude preferences, different ways of perceiving, different ways of judging, and different lifestyle personalities in the questions related to emotional experience.

Table 2. The average of different items in the emotional hierarchy

Variable	E	I	N	S	F	T	P	J
Fluctuation (m)	2.21	2.41	2.54	2.20	2.47	2.12	2.28	2.36
Intensity (ma)	1.44	1.86	1.95	1.54	1.55	1.88	1.63	1.73
Tone (mb)	2.81	2.76	2.89	2.72	2.90	2.62	2.60	2.92
Painful (mc)	6.47	7.03	7.38	6.46	6.92	6.62	6.51	7.00

In terms of personality type, different MBTI personalities show different emotional perceptions in the survey of emotional experience (emotional intensity and emotional atmosphere). Personality types associated with high emotions include INFJ, INTJ, ISFJ, ESTJ, and ISTJ, and most of these personalities are introverted. Except for ENTJ, all personality types had moderate emotion fluctuation, while all personality types had mild emotion fluctuations. INFJ had the lowest emotion fluctuations among all personality types. Among the 16 personality types, INFJ and INTJ had the strongest emotion fluctuation, with average emotion fluctuation (m) reaching 8.63 and 8.50, respectively. ENTJ, ISFP, ISTJ, ESFJ, and ENTP were the personality types with the least emotion fluctuations (see Fig. 5).

In the survey on the atmosphere of emotional experience, different MBTI personalities present different emotional tones. According to the description given in the quantitative analysis section above, those who are very negative (mb = 5) and slightly negative (mb = 3) are classified as negative emotions, and those who are relatively positive (mb = 2) and very positive (mb = 4) are classified as positive emotions. According to the investigation, most of the subjects showed negative emotions, only ENFJ, ENTJ, ENTP and ESFJ personality types did not show negative emotions. In positive emotion, INFP, ENTJ, INTJ, ENTP, INTP, ESFJ, ISTP and ISFP did not present positive emotion,

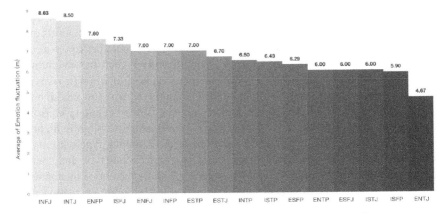

Fig. 5. The mean value of emotion fluctuation (m) of each personality type

excluding the three personality types with 100% neutral emotional tone: ENTJ, ENTP and ESFJ, it can be found that INFJ is the most obvious personality type presenting negative emotions, followed by ISTJ, and the most positive personality type may be ESTP, ESTJ, ENFJ, ENFP. The following Table 3 gives the number of people with different levels of emotional fluctuation presented by different MBTI personalities and their proportion to the total number of people with this personality in the emotional experience (intensity/atmosphere) survey.

Table 3. The emotional tone of dreams in each personality type

Emotion type MBTI	Positive		Neutral ($m_b = 1$)	Negative	
	Quite ($m_b = 4$)	Some ($m_b = 2$)		Some ($m_b = 3$)	Quite ($m_b = 5$)
ENFJ (4, 100%)	0, 0%	1, 25%	3, 75%	0, 0%	0, 0%
INFJ (8, 100%)	0, 0%	1, 12.5%	3, 37.5%	4, 50%	0, 0%
ENFP (5, 100%)	0, 0%	1, 20%	2, 40%	2, 40%	0, 0%
INFP (5, 100%)	0, 0%	0, 0%	3, 60%	2, 40%	0, 0%
ENTJ (3, 100%)	0, 0%	0, 0%	3, 100%	0, 0%	0, 0%
INTJ (6, 100%)	0, 0%	0, 0%	1, 16.6%	3, 50%	2, 33.3%
ENTP (3, 100%)	0, 0%	0, 0%	2, 100%	0, 0%	0, 0%
INTP (4, 100%)	0, 0%	0, 0%	3, 75%	1, 25%	0, 0%
ESFJ (9, 100%)	0, 0%	0, 0%	9, 100%	0, 0%	0, 0%
ISFJ (12, 100%)	0, 0%	1, 8.3%	8, 66.6%	3, 25%	0, 0%
ESTJ (10, 100%)	0, 0%	3, 30%	6, 60%	1, 10%	0, 0%
ISTJ (7, 100%)	0, 0%	1, 14.2%	3, 42.8%	3, 42.8%	0, 0%

(continued)

Table 3. (*continued*)

Emotion type MBTI	Positive		Neutral ($m_b = 1$)	Negative	
	Quite ($m_b = 4$)	Some ($m_b = 2$)		Some ($m_b = 3$)	Quite ($m_b = 5$)
ESTP (3, 100%)	1, 33.3%	0, 0%	1, 33.3%	1, 33.3%	0, 0%
ISTP (7, 100%)	0, 0%	0, 0%	5, 71.4%	2, 28.5%	0, 0%
ESFP (7, 100%)	0, 0%	1, 14.2%	5, 71.4%	1, 14.2%	0, 0%
ISFP (10, 100%)	0, 0%	0, 0%	8, 80%	2, 20%	0, 0%

Design Preference. 1. In the objective experience of the House-Tree-Person Technique (HTP), the circle-shaped tree crown indicates that subjects may lack decision-making ability and tend to be hesitant [22], which is like the strong curiosity of Perception personality (P). Lack of decisiveness and difficulty in making efficient choices [9] are consistent with the characteristics. By extracting the subjects who tended to the circle tree crown in the House-Tree-Person Technique (HTP), it was found that the proportion of people with Perception (66.7%) was larger than that of people with Judgment personality (33.3%), and among all the subjects, The proportion of Perception type is higher than Judgment type. Thus, compared with J-Judgment, P-Perception prefers the circle shape. 2. In the objective experience of the House-Tree-Person Technique (HTP), if the projection result of the subject tends to the four-corner tree crown, it indicates that the subject may have a conservative tendency, some stubbornness and lack of flexibility, and may also want to have a strong sense of social responsibility [22]. On the other hand, the Sensing Judgment personality type is pragmatic and strictly disciplined, preferring to collaborate within a clear set of rules and expecting others to accept the same requirements of Tao. However, they may also very stick to their guns and be unwilling to accept different views [9]. From the extraction of the House-Tree-Person Technique (HTP), it is found that all the subjects who prefer the quadrangular canopy are all the Sensing Judgment type. Thus, the SJ-Sensing Judgment type prefers a quadrangular shape (square, trapezoid, etc.). 3. Vase design (thick at both ends and thin in the middle) symbolizes practicality in the objective experience of the House-Tree-Person Technique (HTP), and a doer with a firm attitude to face reality [22]. This is highly consistent with the characteristics of the Sensing personality. Therefore, S-Sensing prefers a vase design (thick at both ends and thin in the middle) over N-Intuition. 4. In the objective experience of the House-Tree-Person Technique (HTP), the tree crown that tends to be vertical and elliptical indicates that the subject is likely to be more confident, ambitious, and rational. The triangular crown of the tree indicates that the subject may be aggressive, not good at controlling emotions, confident, ambitious, and rational [22]. This is in line with Intuition and Thinking personality traits: rationality and impartiality, independence, strong willpower, and confidence in problem-solving ability [9]. However, both the vertical oval shape and the triangle symbolize rationality, the dominant position of thinking, self-confidence, and ambition. However, the difference is that the crown of the triangle also projects strong aggression and is not good at controlling emotions

[22]. First, after excluding the subjects without canopy elements, the subjects who prefer to use vertical oval elements and triangular elements in the House-Tree-Person Technique (HTP) were extracted. It is found that 33.3% of Intuition Thinking types prefer vertical oval elements and triangle elements, while 27.3% of the other three personality types (Intuition Feeling type) and 25.9% (Sensing Judgment type) respectively. 23.7% (Sensing Perception), among the four personality types of NT-Intuition Thinking (ENTJ, ENTP, INTJ, INTP), ENTJ is the personality type with the highest preference for vertical oval and triangular elements, reaching 66.7%. Personality types with high levels of emotion fluctuation have also been shown to prefer triangles, with INFJ, who has the highest average emotion fluctuation, having the highest percentage of triangle lovers at 25 per cent. In the selection of a vertical oval element and triangle element, INTJ, which ranks second in emotion fluctuation, and INFP, which ranks fifth in emotion fluctuation, also have a special preference for the triangle. In conclusion, the NT-Intuition Thinking type preferred the vertical oval element and triangle element, and personality types who prefer triangles tend to have higher emotion fluctuation.

4.2 Suggestions

The following suggestions are given based on the above survey results and discussion.

Design Content. Introversion personality has more negative emotions and more intense emotion fluctuation than Extraversion personality, so a different design strategy should be adopted. For Introversion personalities, when dealing with negative themes such as blood, violence, depression, etc., the design method should be more subtle and euphemistic, to protect the psychological health of the Introversion users and prevent severe psychological impact on them.

Design Technique. When designing for Extraversion users, you can use exaggerated design techniques. In terms of design atmosphere, we can also tend to create a lively and positive atmosphere, enlarged local features or gorgeous effects of the design may be more interesting to Extraversion users.

Design Shape. The following steps can be taken when it comes to shaping elements. When designing for the Perception personality type, a circle shape can be selected to enhance its sense of identity to the design works. Sensing personality is more likely to be attracted by the design of a vase shape(both ends are thick and thin in the middle), so when designing for the Sensing personality type user, the pattern and shape of the vase style can be used as far as possible, this move may make them more interested in design. When most users are Intuition Thinking personalities, vertical ovals and triangles can be used as much as possible in design creation, which will bring more psychological security and comfort to the users. When more users belong to the Sensing Judgment, a quadrangular shape (square, trapezoid) can be used for design. This move may enable the pragmatic and conservative personality of the Sensing Judgment type to feel a sense of belonging, thus improving the effectiveness and altruism of the design. Design and care based on personality type can effectively improve design efficiency and user feedback attitude, to achieve better design results. In future studies, more extensive data are needed to further explore the information related to design preferences such as themes, and inclusiveness, d to find specific targeted strategies based on this information combined with the ersonality type theory to optimize the design scheme.

5   Conclusion

For the design industry, the influence of the user's personality and emotional perception on aesthetic preference is very important. At present, there is not enough research on the influence of user personality type and emotion on design preference, especially in the in-depth analysis of psychological characteristics from multiple perspectives. As personality is one of the important psychological characteristics affecting people's emotions and decision-making, this study analyzed the relationship between users' personalities, emotions, and design preferences from the perspective of personality type. Using MBTI as a tool to measure personality, Mannheim Dream Questionnaire (MADRE) as a tool to measure emotion and House-Tree-Person Technique (HTP) as an objective experience reference for design preference, and a questionnaire survey was conducted in a design major of a university in China.

According to the survey results: Introversion has higher emotion fluctuation and negative emotions than the Extraversion personality, especially in INFJ and INTJ groups. ENTJ has extremely low emotion fluctuation and is the personality type with the least emotional ups and downs. ENFP is also characterized by positive emotion and high emotion fluctuation. The perception type prefers a circle shape to the Judgment type, the Sensing Judgment type prefers a quadrangular shape (square, trapezoid, etc.), the Sensing type prefers a vase shape (thick at both ends and thin in the middle) to the Intuition type. Compared with the Intuition Feeling type, Sensing Judgment type and Sensing Perception type, the Intuition Thinking type prefers the vertical oval element and triangle element, and ENTJ is the personality type with the highest preference at this latitude. In addition, INFJ, INTJ and INFP are probably the most triangle-loving personality types.

Although the data are from China, the findings in the study are to some extent applicable to other countries, as the distribution of MBTI personality types in the subject group is consistent with that in the general population. Therefore, the above research results will contribute to the knowledge system of personalized design and help to propose effective design strategies and schemes in different situations. In addition, the research can also establish a set of design suggestions in line with psychological care, to improve the friendliness and universality of design works. This can not only make the adhesion between the design and users become stronger, but also effectively reduce the possibility of psychological injury to users.

This study is an exploratory study, with limitations such as a small sample size, single project, and medium reliability. In addition, personality types may not fully reflect the actual psychological causes of different emotional factors and differentiated aesthetic preferences. Future research will increase the coverage of valid samples as far as possible, involving different types of user groups of different age groups and cultural backgrounds, to improve the reliability of the research. Moreover, it will comprehensively analyze the psychological and physiological characteristics of users and expand and further discuss the design preference projects.

In conclusion, the results of this research not only help to predict the emotion characteristics of a specific user and its differences from other users but also point out practical and effective design methods to establish emotional resonance with the user, providing new ideas for future research on personalized design and humanized design. In addition, other categorical problems for human emotions and subconscious projection, such as the dream Structure and projective drawing test, may also benefit from this approach.

Funding Information. The Funding Agency is CHINA VIDEO INDUSTRY ASSOCIATION (CVIA), and the grant number is ZSXKT2023002.

References

1. Bernhard, W.: Personality-type based simulation education. Personality-Type Based Simulation Education, 394–398 (1996)
2. Valle-Cruz, D., et al.: Emotion-aware explainable artificial intelligence for personality, emotion, and mood simulation. Computación y Sistemas **26**(1), 45–57 (2022)
3. Adnan, M., Mukhtar, H., Naveed, M.: Persuading students for behaviour change by determining their personality type. In: 2012 15th International Multitopic Conference (INMIC). IEEE (2012)
4. Djatna, K., Uğur, Ö., Diri, B.: MBTI personality prediction with machine learning. In: 2020 28th Signal Processing and Communications Applications Conference (SIU), pp. 1–4. IEEE (2020)
5. Djatna, T., Wrasiati, L.P., Santosa, I.B.D.Y.: Balinese aromatherapy product development based on Kansei Engineering and customer personality type. Procedia Manuf. **4**, 176–183 (2015)
6. Yanliuxing, P.C., Hall, A.: An assessment of personality traits and their implication for creativity amongst Innovation Design Engineering masters' students using the MBTI and KTS instruments.DS 75–7. In: Proceedings of the 19th International Conference on Engineering Design (ICED13), Design for Harmonies, Vol. 7: Human Behavior in Design, Seoul, Korea, 19–22 August 2013 (2013)
7. Wu, H.: Study on the Occupational Personality of Designer and the Training Mode of Design Specialty in the Context of Diversity (2017)
8. Mishra, O., Ayatham, P.: Online retailers connecting to the youth segment through Facebook (A study on the influence of gender and personality type). J. Asia Bus. Stud. **11**(4), 387–412 (2017)
9. Myers, I.B., Myers, P.B.: Gifts Differing: Understanding Personality Type. 1st edn., pp. 23–32. Posts and Telecommunications Press, Beijing (2016)
10. Kostov, V., Fukuda, S.: Development of man-machine interfaces based on user preferences. In: Proceedings of the 2001 IEEE International Conference on Control Applications (CCA'01) (Cat. No. 01CH37204). IEEE (2001)
11. Subaramaniam, K., Palaniappan, S.: Users' satisfaction of personality types integration in HCI. In: Salvendy, G., Wei, J. (eds.) Design, Operation and Evaluation of Mobile Communications. HCII 2022, vol. 13337, pp. 191–202. Springer, Cham (2022). https://doi.org/10.1007/978-3-031-05014-5_15
12. Fang, X., Ma, Y., Cheng, C.: Development and connotation of MBTI.Psychol. Tech. Appl. **25**(9), 18–23 (2015)
13. Man, C.Y.: On the influence of the unconscious on rational andirrational decisions. Technol. Devel. Enterp. **33**(30), 137–138 (2014)

14. Gomez Torres, Roberto. The Graphics pointing to the consumer subconscious. Ciencia Unemi **5**(7), 20–31 (2012)
15. Totlis, A.: The dream as space, time, and emotion. N. Am. J. Med. Sci. **3**(6), 302 (2011)
16. Chen, J.W., Guo, Y.Y.: A study of unconsciousness in personality psychology. J. Educ. Sci. Human Normal Univ. **3**(1), 121–125 (2004)
17. Hoss, R. J. A CONTENT ANALYSIS OF COLOR IN DREAMS. In Perchance to dream the frontiers of dream psychology / (pp. 193–208). Nova Science Publishers. (2009)
18. Sutton, J.P., et al.: Emotion and visual imagery in dream reports: A narrative graphing approach. Consciousness Cognit. **3**(1), 89–99 (1994)
19. Wong, S.-S., Yu, C.K.-C.: Direct and indirect effects of dispositional emotion regulation on dream experiences. Dreaming (2022)
20. Bao Miqing, M.: A Paintings (HTP) study on personality character of financially disadvantaged students in Suzhou. In: A Paintings (HTP) Study on Personality Character of Financially Disadvantaged Students in Suzhou, pp. 376–381 (2011)
21. Zhang, B.: Discussion on the subconscious and its visual expression. In: 1st International Conference on Arts, Design and Contemporary Education (ICADCE 2015). Atlantis Press (2015)
22. Hu, Y., Chen, J.; Handbook of Painting Analysis and Psychotherapy. The Second Volume, Application: Painting Psychological Counselling and Therapy. 2nd Ed., pp. 373–794. Central South University Press, Changsha (2016)
23. McCrae, R.R., Costa, P.T.: Reinterpreting the Myers-briggs type indicator from the perspective of the five-factor model of personality. J. Personality **57**(1), 17–40 (1989)
24. Furnham, A.: The big five versus the big four: The relationship between the Myers-Briggs type indicator (MBTI) and NEO-PI five-factor model of personality. Person. Individ. Differ. **21**(2), 303–307 (1996)
25. Schredl, M.: Factors affecting the continuity between waking and dreaming emotional intensity and emotional tone of the waking-life event. Sleep Hypnosis **8**, 1–6 (2006)
26. Horton, C.L.: Memory consolidation in sleep: implications from dream science. Int. J. Dream Res. **5**, S46–S47 (2012)
27. Malinowski, J.E., Horton, C.L.: Evidence for the preferential incorporation of emotional waking-life experiences into dreams. Dreaming **24**, 18–31 (2014)
28. Schredl, M., Berres, S., Klingauf, A., Schellhaas, S., Göritz, A.S.: The Mannheim Dream Questionnaire (Madre): retest reliability, age and gender effects. Int. J. Dream Res. **7**, 141–147 (2014)
29. Zhao, C., et al.: Relationship between personality types in MBTI and dream structure variables. Front. Psychol. **11**, 1589 (2020)
30. Lehner, G.F.J., Gunderson, E.K.: Reliability of graphic indices in a projective test (the Draw-A-Person). J. Clin. Psychol. (1952)
31. Yamaguchi, M.: The stability of House Drawing in HTP test. Japan. J. Psychol. (1983)
32. Vass, Z.: The inner formal structure of the H-T-P drawings: an exploratory study. J. Clin. Psychol. **54**(5), 611–619 (1998)
33. Abell, S.C., Horkheimer, R., Nguyen, S.E.: Intellectual evaluations of adolescents via Human Figure Drawings: an empirical comparison of two methods. J. Clin. Psychol. **54**(6), 811–815 (1998)
34. Yu, Y.Z., et al.: House–Tree–Person drawing therapy as an intervention for prisoners' prerelease anxiety. Soc. Beh. Pers. Int. J. **44**(6), 987–1004 (2016)
35. Qiu, H., Wu, D.: Study on the correlation between Minnesota multiple personality Tests and Fangshu people's drawing characteristics in patients with depression. Chin. J. Health Psychol. **11**, 1341–1344 (2010)
36. Lee, E.J.: Correlations among depressive symptoms, personality, and Synthetic House-Tree-Person Drawings in South Korean adults. Psychologia **61**(4), 211–220 (2019)

Author Index

Printed in the United States
by Baker & Taylor Publisher Services